EX LIBRIS

NARRATIVE TECHNIQUE

A Practical Course in Literary Psychology

BY

THOMAS H. UZZELL, 1884

FORMERLY FICTION EDITOR *COLLIER'S WEEKLY*
EDITOR "SHORT STORY HITS"
EDITOR "THE BLUE PENCIL"

In Collaboration With

CAMELIA WAITE UZZELL

Third Edition

HARCOURT, BRACE AND COMPANY

NEW YORK

PREFACE

The purpose of this book is to outline a method of literary training. It aims to provide systematic discipline in the handling of narrative materials. It is, as the title page says, a practical course in literary psychology.

The work is planned for college students of English composition, particularly for those who are ready for special training. What the dissecting room and laboratory are to young doctors-to-be, what the modern case-book is to the beginning student of law, this book is intended to be for the future writer of narrative. Students who have finished two years of rhetoric or have had at least an elementary course in psychology and who wish to take the next step in the direction of professional writing will find this book useful. It is designed to serve also as a general manual for classes in fiction writing in departments and schools for journalism.

The independent, free lance fiction writer working out his artistic salvation alone will find in these chapters a possible solution for his major technical problems. The text and assignments in manuscript form have been used successfully by student writers at all stages of development. Beginners especially have found them helpful. They are recommended to professional writers with the reservations made on page nineteen of the introduction.

I believe that teachers of rhetoric, composition, and even of literature will find here suggestions for planning stimulating variety in writing exercises. A clearer insight into the potencies of the written word comes inevitably from the closer inspection of the ideas behind the written word, an inspection demanded by this course of study. The instructor, by seeing processes of mental manipulation of literary material more clearly, will find it easy to invent better methods to fulfill his own purposes. Chapters One and Two and Suggestions to Teachers in the Appendix contain many hints for early training in natural literary expression.

For the underlying psychological theories upon which this book and method are based, I am indebted to Professor Walter B. Pitkin of the School of Journalism, Columbia University. Ten years ago Professor Pitkin, by treating narrative writing as a laboratory problem in esthetics and psychology, which subjects he was then teaching, elaborated for his classes in fiction writing a body of doctrine on fictional technique which in 1913 he set forth in his work, *The Art and Business of Story Writing*.

During these ten years the influence of Professor Pitkin's theories has filtered into the actual writings of scores of authors whom he has trained, into the work of many teachers who have used his book, and into numerous textbooks themselves, many of which have adopted distinctions and explanations set forth in his original work. The use of his book, because of its brevity and its theoretical nature, has, however, been confined for the most part to advanced and professional writers. The present volume aims to present a simpler, more practical course, based on the same principles. Its sub-title might well be " Pitkin Applied."

The distinctive offering in this course of instruction is *not* the critical theories; most of these lie at the surface of elementary psychology and are presented in very readable form in the book mentioned above and in Professor Pitkin's new volume, *How to Write Stories. Narrative Technique* presents preëminently a *method* of study. This is its greatest novelty; in this I believe lies its greatest value. As a graduate student under Professor Pitkin, as a teacher later of his own university class, as a newspaper writer, as a fiction writer, as magazine editor and publicity director, I have used these theories and worked out the pedagogical method presented. For several years I have used it in the private coaching of writers.

The way to learn to write is — to write. This axiom is the inspiration for the large number of exercises used. I assume that little if anything can be learned by the usual method of absorption. Learning is doing, the cultivating of new reflexes — which is habit. And the habit most worth cultivating is that of thinking clearly even though inspired.

The only books or collateral reading suggested are the two books by Professor Pitkin mentioned above, and these need be used only by the more advanced students. I have rigidly limited my references to collections of " famous short stories," because one of the most stubborn habits to break in beginning writers is the imitation, conscious or unconscious, of the style of authors they have read and admired. I have tried to put into the book itself most of the material needed for analysis, and have not hesitated to use the same material as often as possible — this, I find, begets familiarity with processes and reduces the amount of necessary reading.

Save to a few exceptional students — mature persons who are pure self-expressionists — I recommend the study of the short story form as a preparation for later writing of novels, motion pictures, or stage plays. There are many reasons for this. The chief one is that this form, being the most clearly defined, provides excellent preliminary discipline for any form of dramatic writing.

Although I have made no effort to strew flowers of entertainment by the way in this drill-book, I believe that those who come to it for a deeper insight into their work will find sufficient adventure in each discovery of better ways to get their effects. My concern is precisely that expressed by Jadassohn in his famous drill-book for musicians: " Nor should the pupil be contented to treat the exercises for practice as dry school exercises and to work them out merely from this point of view; for even in them a talented student will find opportunity to display the qualities of the artist."

I am aware that the method outlined in this book will be severely criticized by certain experienced writers, book reviewers, and teachers of literature. Harsh will be their condemnation of it because (they will say) of its " attempt to reduce creative writing to a formula." " Great writing," they will say, " is inspiration whose cube root cannot be discovered by any juggling of psychology or anything else." They will say this in spite of the fact that there is not a line in this book about " creative processes," not a line which deals with the problems of writing as such, not a line which attempts to do aught but help the student of writing understand given literary *materials*. In face of the easily discoverable fact that every successful performer *has* ordered habits of handling and organizing his material, they will urge the old sentimental dogma that fiction is produced by a sort of emotional spontaneous combustion. Such strictures will do no harm except as they deny young writers help in early cultivating sound habits of thinking. Their cause I plead in my Introduction.

PREFACE TO SECOND EDITION

The six years since this textbook first appeared have seen its use extend to all the leading schools and colleges where the subject of fiction writing is taught.

A new edition is now offered. The only changes made are typographical corrections and rephrasing of directions for some of the assignments which several years of teaching by the author and others have found useful. Otherwise the content and organization of the original edition stand unchanged.

I take this opportunity to thank all those who have been kind enough to suggest improvements in the text.

T. H. U.

New York City
April, 1929.

PREFACE TO THIRD EDITION

This third edition of " Narrative Technique " was undertaken to modernize the illustrative and assignment material, to add new material which much experience in teaching with the book has suggested, and in general to harmonize the volume with today's literary standards and requirements. To both the teacher and the student the pedagogical purpose of my alterations will, I think, be apparent.

The wholly new additions to the text in this edition are a new introduction in which I plead yet again for a better understanding of the meaning of technique and its possibilities, a chapter on point of view, and, in the Appendix, sections devoted to the problems of writing (as distinct from plotting), to practical advice to writers seeking early publication, to analysis of a notably successful short story, and to the technique of the modern psychoanalytic narrative. The chief purpose of this last section is to demonstrate once for all that the basic principles of narrative technique set forth by me eleven years ago in this book, and by Professor Walter B. Pitkin ten years before that, have not been in any sense superseded or invalidated by the modern writer's revolutionary break with the past.

The usefulness of this new edition will, I feel sure, be increased by an innovation which has been premeditated for several years. Any handbook on the technique of an art should be used in conjunction with the study of contemporary worthy models of that art. To include an adequate array of stories in a literary handbook itself is impractical on the score of space alone. Heretofore stories in current magazines and established anthologies have been referred to and are still referred to throughout this text, but for many students these magazines and books are not easily available.

This has created the need of a volume of stories chosen particularly with these students in mind — a collection of excellent models annotated in harmony with " Narrative Technique." Such a volume I put forth in 1933 under the title
" Short Story Hits, 1932," and a second, compiled from the
stories of 1933, has appeared this present year. References
to these two volumes appear throughout this third edition.
For the convenience of users of *Narrative Technique,* I plan
also to include in the monthly issues of my magazine, *The
Blue Pencil,* critical analyses of current short stories and
novels.

I take this opportunity to thank the many teachers and
writers throughout the country who have kindly offered
suggestions, and, in some cases, been willing to cooperate
with me in testing their value. From Professor M. G.
Frampton of Pomona College I have received especially
valuable advice which I now acknowledge. To my wife,
Camelia Waite Uzzell, I am greatly indebted for her wide
reading, penetrating critical judgment, and her patient assistance in compiling this revision. I am especially grateful
to her for writing the chapter in the Appendix on The Technique of the Stream of Consciousness Narrative.

The steadily increasing use found for " Narrative Technique " is due, I believe, to the soundness of its method, to
its not presuming to do more than a book on technique can
do, and to its clarity. Among the thousands who have now
used it are motion picture writers and directors, the authors
of literary and popular best sellers, Broadway playwrights,
and the authors of stories and serials appearing constantly
in the entire range of American magazine fiction. That
this usefulness may continue is my hope in offering this re-
vised third edition.

                                                    T. H. U.

*New York City
August, 1934.*

CONTENTS

INTRODUCTION

NARRATIVE TECHNIQUE AND ITS USES

To the Teacher and Advanced Student

Marble, paint and language, the pen, the needle and the brush, all have their ineffable impotences, their hours, if I may so express myself, of insubordination. It is the work, and it is a great part of the delight of any artist to contend with these unruly tools, and now by brute energy, now by witty expedient, to drive and coax them to effect his will. — STEVENSON.

What do we mean by fictional technique? It is necessary that we get a clear understanding on this point. Unfortunately, there is hopeless confusion in the editorial and literary world as to the exact meaning of this word, technique. The teachers and followers of other crafts, such as painting, music and sculpture, have a fairly definite understanding of what their technique is, its importance, and how to attain it. There is no such agreement in authors' studios, editorial offices, or college classrooms about the technique of the art of writing.

I know editors who say that the mastery of technique "kills a writer's inspiration." I know of college professors who, believing they are teaching technique, do kill youthful inspirations by having the student slavishly imitate short story classics. There are text books without number on this subject, and none of the many I have seen reach the heart of the matter. Even critics who have gained considerable prestige go sadly astray. They speak cryptically of "imaginative persuasion" as "substance"; establish as a criterion a "beautiful and satisfying form" without giving any hint as to what is either "beautiful" or "satisfying." Good short stories, they say, begin in the author's brain with "visualized characters" for which a "series of situations is imagined"; if the character is seen accurately, they argue, neither the nature of the events nor the style is of much consequence. Here is a common practice arbitrarily exalted to a fixed rule for all — which, if literally applied, would exclude some of the finest stories ever written.

Rules and "recipes" of this sort compose the bulk of all the current commercial handbooks on the subject; many suggest fascinating possibilities and the struggling writer tries them all until he finds one set of rules contradicting another! What shall he do then? He has but one way out: he must learn that *a sound technique has no formulas, that it has only principles and ideals.* He must dig deeper; he must master these principles and ideals; then he can make his own rules.

In order to clarify our ideas on this subject let us, first of all, take a look at the writer's task as a whole. We can thus see what technique does *not* mean.

We may say that creative writing roughly involves three factors:

1. *A message:* Something to say, the thing the author wants to write about, the content of his narrative.
2. *Technique:* His ways and means of organizing and manipulating his material; this factor is commonly called the structure of his narrative.
3. *Style:* The writer's manner of using words in the final expression of his message.

The meaning of the first of these factors, the writer's message, is surely clear. Very little help, really, can be given on this point by any teacher. If the writer has nothing to write about, no one can give it to him. You cannot make a splash by pouring from an empty pitcher.

There is much confusion regarding the meaning of style, the third point. The essence of wisdom on this point was given many years ago by the French critic, Buffon, who said, "*Le style est l'homme même*" — "Style is the man himself." No one can give a writer style any more than he can give him something to say. The mechanical aids to style, such as grammar, rhetoric, and diction, can of course be learned in school; much help also can be given the writer by training him to use his eyes and ears, but beyond that no more can be done for him. In a larger sense, the qualities of vivacity, humor and sympathy which differentiate one writer's manuscript from another's cannot be taught any more than personality in the larger sense can be made a product of the school room. Here again the writer faces a problem of natural endowment.

The second factor mentioned above is the only one to which we shall give concentrated attention. It is the only phase of creative writing which can, or, in my opinion, should be taught. The mastery of it depends on the intellect almost altogether, as does mathematics or geology, and it can be learned in the same way these other sciences can be learned. It is not the most important asset of a writer; it is not so important as having something to say. Mastery of it alone would not make a writer, but what it *will* do we shall now learn.

I have said that the writer's technique is his manner of organizing and manipulating his material. This is, in fact, the primitive meaning of the word, its significance from the beginning.

The Greek word τεχνή means " craftsmanship." The classical meaning is more fully expressed in a phrase to be found in the Platonic Dialogues, "*ta pragmata technica,*" or, "the affairs of craftsmanship." Plato explained that technique is the craftsmanship imposed by the presence of two things — specific material and a purpose of the performer. *Technique, therefore, simply cannot be removed from any act of creation involving material and a purpose. It is actively present, whether you are aware of it or not.* You have a story idea; you wish to do something with it: technique inevitably enters at once. *The problem is im-*

posed upon you; your only choice in the matter is whether you will follow one method of technique or another, a good method or a bad one.

Scarcely anyone will, I think, refuse to accept this interpretation. Many people, however, while agreeing that there *is* such a thing as technique, insist that it cannot be taught simply because it cannot be understood. Creative writing, they declare, involves such elusive, fantastic materials and bewildering processes of mind and spirit that no one could hope to grasp and chart, much less control, them. It is a fair objection, but there is an answer, and it has been neatly expressed by Professor Pitkin. " The laws of story construction," he writes, " elude their many searchers with a persistence most exasperating. The long-discouraged investigator naturally falls into the thought that pure anarchy reigns in the domain of fantasy, and he disguises the absurdity of his thought under the hypothesis that a story is the free creation of mind, spontaneous in origin and in manner of outworking. Unfortunately for the development of fictional technique, the half-truth of the hypothesis helps to conceal the flaw in his argument.

" There is no doubt that, in some sense, a story is a free, spontaneous creation; and freedom seems to connote a certain emancipation from law: hence the plausibility of saying that the fiction writer works without rule or principle, following only the caprice of his imagination. The inference, however, is only plausible. There is no soundness in it; and, were we here discussing ethics or metaphysics, we might demonstrate this assertion by pointing out that free creation and spontaneity do not involve unpatterned behavior nor blind, impulsive fashioning. If chaos lurks anywhere in the whole performance, it lurks only in the primitive uprush of fleeting, disjointed imageries which precede, suggest, and inspire the work of art."

Here we have the word of a psychologist, writer and teacher, who has given fifteen years to a study of the creative writer's processes, that these processes can, in part at least, be understood. The acts of plotting and writing do, in Professor Pitkin's words, involve a certain patterned behavior. The issue with those who deny this is not one of literary or pedagogical opinion: it is a question of fact.

Let us therefore appeal to another noted psychologist. In his recent volume, *Human Nature and Conduct,* Professor John Dewey of Columbia University shows how mechanisms making possible a definite technique are present not only in all works of art but in the vital processes of life itself. "All life as well as art," he says, "involves a mechanism. The great mistake in either life or art is to extol one of these elements at the expense of the other. Those who base everything on mechanism reduce life to unintelligent automatism; those who preach ' truth to life ' often achieve only an aimless splurge.

"Mechanism is indispensable. . . . The artist is a masterful technician. The technique or mechanism is fused with thought and feeling. The ' mechanical ' performer permits the mechanism to dictate the performance. It is absurd to say that the mechanical performer exhibits habit and that the artistic performance doesn't. We are confronted with two kinds of habit, intelligent and routine. . . . Art and the habits of the artist are acquired by previous mechanical exercises of repetition in which skill apart from thought is the aim, until suddenly, magically, this soulless mechanism is taken possession of by sentiment and imagination until it becomes a flexible instrument of the mind.

"We do not as yet fully understand the physiological factors concerned in mechanical routine on one hand and artistic skill on the other, but we do know that the latter is just as much habit as is the former. Whether it concerns the cook, musician, carpenter, citizen, or statesman, the intelligent or artistic habit is the desirable thing, and the routine the undesirable thing."

"Temperament and vision are the first requisites, but they are not enough," writes the French philosopher,

Bergson, in discussing the psychology of creative writers. " Unless the visionary has at his command an appropriate technique, the attempt at expression will merely break up and spoil his vision without leading to the production of any work of value. . . . Inspiration does not provide a poet with his rhymes and vowels; his problem is to find the rhymes and vowels without losing the inspiration. If he has the necessary technical power he will be sufficiently free, sufficiently unhampered by the need of readjustment to exert his personality and to perpetuate his inspiration."

An all-too-common conception of technique is that it is something arbitrary or formulistic which is superimposed on material, distorting and crystalizing it into lifeless patterns. Rather, as Bergson says, it is a mental equipment that frees the spirit to achieve its purposes with the utmost naturalness and spontaneity.

There are many critics and teachers who have no quarrel with my thesis that in creative writing there are what Professor Dewey calls " desirable and undesirable habits." They believe this and they write handbooks and organize classes to provide the good habits; yet they fail to achieve the results they are after; their readers and students are appreciative but puzzled, confused, and often complain of " mechanical instruction," " vague criticism," " advice that keeps them from doing the thing they most want to do." In such instances a technique is obviously being employed, and it is equally obvious that it is a bad technique. What is the trouble?

The trouble in nearly every case is that the critic or teacher makes the fundamental error of teaching the technique of the writer's *tools* instead of the technique of the *material* with which he works. In every art there are two techniques — a technique of material, and a technique of the tools used. The significance of this fact as it bears upon our problem can be seen more clearly if we compare the techniques of painting and music with that of narrative. This can be done by a glance at the following table:

COMPARATIVE TECHNIQUES OF THREE ARTS

Art	Material (stuff)	Tools (instrument)	Technique	
			Material	Tools
Painting	Colors Visible forms	Brushes Pigments Canvas, etc.	Light (optical laws) Perspective (measurements) Anatomy Chemistry of colors.	Use of brush, etc. Preparing of canvas. Mixing oils, varnishes, etc.
Music	Sounds Tones Rhythms	Piano Violin, etc.	Harmony Counter point Mathematics Laws of Acoustics Vibrations.	Fingering Pedaling
Narrative	Life Conduct Complications	Words Sentences Paragraphs Punctuation marks.	Knowledge of the human mind and human conduct; of social relations; of places and events, etc.	Grammar Rhetoric Spelling Typing, etc.

Here we see that the technique of the *materials* of narrative is a recent discovery. Since narrative, in its primitive oral forms at any rate, is at least as old as music and painting, there would seem to be no reason why it should not have developed a technique of its material — if it had one! Its want of such a technique, it may be, is proof that none is discoverable. But consider:

The knowledge which has made possible an understanding of the materials of painting has come from the sciences of anatomy, physics and chemistry; while musical harmony is but a special application of the sciences of physics and mathematics. All these sciences were born before Greek civilization. Psychology, the science which helps us understand the writer and his materials, is less than a half century old, and is only just beginning to assume a formulated and usable shape. Man unfortunately began his study of his world by first observing the stars; after two thousand or so years he has at last begun the study of himself. Among other things, the formulation of the technique of fiction has suffered from the delay.

Other reasons there are for the slow development of this particular technique, reasons which we need here only mention. The materials of both music and painting are far simpler than those of narrative: the basis of the most elaborate symphonies and operas is a few elementary ratios; the basis of painting is the comparatively simple mathematical laws of perspective and the few fundamental relations controlling the mingling of colors. The materials of these other arts — space, forms, colors and sounds — differ among themselves far less than do the materials of narrative — instincts, impulses, dreams, passions, pathological inhibitions, and the innumerable individual traits acquired by every mature individual. The materials of music and painting, in short, can be seen, handled, measured in a way impossible with the materials of narrative.

The task of literary technique is difficult, but it is not impossible. The method of procedure must be precisely the same as that followed by all serious students of the other fine arts. The latter have their apprenticeships in anatomy, fugue writing, and colors; we must now postulate the same thing for the serious student of letters. His youthful preoccupations, however, will be the workings of the mind, the mechanics of emotion, growth, all human senses and sensibilities.

Neither rhetoric nor a study of literary style provides a knowledge of these all-important subjects. Rhetoric is the science of presenting effectively *given materials;* narrative is the art of *selecting* the materials themselves and presenting them with the object of impressing the sensibilities in a preconceived manner. Style is, as I have already said, " the man "; it is a function of personality. Teachers, like parents, *can* affect the personality of their pupils, but in so doing they are engaged in a moral rather than an artistic enterprise.

Is it possible, you may now be wondering, that you, a young writer with dreams and inspirations, yearning to express yourself, must become a hard-driven student of the " deadly " mental sciences before you can hope to write fiction? Must you be a scientist in order to be an artist? Your fear is less than the truth: all writers of narrative *are* good scientists in exactly the degree they give accurate and effective portrayals of human nature. " The novelist and dramatist " — I quote Professor Dewey again — " are much more illuminating as well as more interesting commentators on conduct than the schematizing psychologist." Good narrative is ninety per cent psychology; all great writers are great psychologists; and the fact that they may have made no *conscious* or *systematic* study of human conduct as a special body of learning lessens not a whit the truth of the statement. The fiction writer is a psychologist with an artistic purpose.

While this does not mean that you should necessarily enroll for a laboratory course in psychology, it does mean that your interest in the facts of human conduct should be as profound and enduring as is that of the laboratory worker. You will have your own way of getting at the facts. Though the data handled by the scientist and the artist are the same, their purposes are utterly different. The purpose of the scientist is to discern general tendencies and principles; the purpose of the artist is to create impressive pictures. It is inevitable therefore that when it comes to methods of application each must largely go his way alone.

What way must you go? This book has been prepared to help you answer this question. No book, no teacher, can answer it for you altogether. If you are a " genius," the one in fifty thousand writers who has not only something to say but an appropriate way of saying it, you need no assistance at all; you have only to write while the editor sits on your door-step and the world gapes at your performance. If you are a seasoned writer with well-defined habits of planning and writing, I would counsel you also against any such drill as this or any other book provides until your case has been taken under skilled personal advisement. If you are a beginner, or if you are discouraged with the technical methods you *have* been following, you may take up this book with confidence.

I should be presumptuous to claim that the method presented here is the only method possible. I simply know that it is a method which has been worked out after long experiment and which satisfies the only test that can be put to anything — results. In truth, the method of study is not of prime importance; the underlying principles alone will give you the power you seek: grasp them and you have everything technique can bestow. No technique is worth much to its possessor until it has been mastered and forgotten, until it has become an unconscious part of his mental equipment.

The one thing that saved Brahms, the most universal figure in music since Beethoven, from becoming a whimsical and subjective composer of limited powers, states Daniel Gregory Mason in his *From Grieg to Brahms*, is that he subjected himself in his formative years to severe technical drill. At the age of twenty-one, after his first precociously brilliant compositions, he devoted himself for four or five years to studies which would teach him the largest possible appeal in his music and enable him to conquer unruly eccentricities. From this time, says Mr. Mason, Brahms, until the end of his life, continued the practice of writing each day a contrapuntal exercise. " Whether my music is beautiful," he declared, " is an entirely different matter; but perfect it must be."

" Technic," writes Mr. Mason, " is in the musician what character is in the man. It is the power to stamp matter with spirit. Brahms's long apprenticeship was therefore needed in the first place to make him master of his materials; in the second place to teach him the deeper lesson that the part must be subordinated to the whole, or, in musical language, expression to beauty. This he achieved not by the negative process of suppression but by conquest and co-ordination. Emotion is not excluded, it is regulated; his work is not a reversion to an earlier and simpler type, it is the gathering and fusing together of fragmentary new elements, resulting in a more complex organism."

A study of technique in this sense is urged upon you by every thoughtful writer and critic. "As the art of fiction is an art," writes Professor Brander Matthews, "its processes have to be painfully acquired, like the processes of any other art, painting or sculpture or architecture. As these processes have to be learned, they may be taught." "The art of fiction," states Walter Prichard Eaton, "is expression rigidly restricted, bound in by a thousand rules of custom and law of its own medium. No artist of whom I am aware has ever broken these rules and laws even to the slight extent which we timidly call revolutionary, without first understanding them and acquiring the skill to work within them. Even after fracturing them a trifle, he has but imposed new ones of his own which shackle his imitators. In other words, the success of a work of art depends to a great extent upon its employment of the weapon of form, and any student-artist who is not made aware of this, who is not made familiar with form, not taught to move easily and with assurance in its bonds, is not taught the first essential of his trade."

Young writers, like young painters and musicians, should be taught the value of an intensive study, at least for a time, of technique for its own sake. Birge Harrison, that most inimitable of inspired teachers, urged all young painters "at some time to worship at the shrine of technique." Students of sculpture are admonished by the author of a popular and standard text-book on anatomy "to study form for its own sake." Why should not the same advice be given writers?

That idol of college literary students, Robert Louis Stevenson, himself wrote, after watching painters at work at

Barbizon: "To work grossly at the trade, to forget sentiment, to think of his material and nothing else, is for a
while at least, the king's highway to progress." And in
our own day we have the author of the most moving, if
not the most beautiful, poem produced during the war,
"Flanders Fields," confessing that he "wrote the poem
partly to pass away the time between the arrival of batches
of wounded, and partly as an experiment with several
varieties of poetic metre."

The truth about literary technique has been neatly expressed by a recent editorial in *The Christian Science
Monitor*. This editorial said:

Amateurs in the writing game, still absorbed in the mastery
of technique, are sometimes ridiculed by those who have
"arrived." "What's the good of studying rhetoric?" say their
tormentors. "Why take lessons in English composition?
That's not what counts. Have something to write about, and
you will find no difficulty in expressing it." This may sound
superficially convincing; but the beginner is confounded at the
discovery that, nine times out of ten, the successful writer himself has been through this same mill. If pushed to the wall in
an argument, he will admit it somewhat peevishly. For he has
reached a position from which the intermediate steps are lost
to view. Once he has achieved his little eminence, he is likely
to forget the rocky road which led thereto.

There are, as well, writers who never have considered the
matter of technique. Whatever they accomplish is done by
instinct and an inherent sense of form and language. And it
is often astonishing what excellent work they do. They are
probably not conscious that they are groping; they strongly
feel the urge to write, and perforce are impelled to give it utterance. If they contrive a moderate success, thus inadequately
equipped, it seldom occurs to them how much further they
could go if they had mastered the A B C's of their profession.
It is, then, a delight to come upon one writer who has paused
to take account of stock. She has subscribed to a correspondence course in English composition; and she recently explained
that her last lesson had dealt with the three methods of developing the essay. Her audience laughed, knowing that she had
often employed, and effectively, these three forms in her published work. "Of course," she retorted, "but I didn't quite
know why or how I was doing it. I expect after this to be

able to write with greater facility and skill because of the clearer grasp I shall have of form and its logical progression."

Nowadays there are too many who have broken into the ranks of authors, by virtue of some literary *tour de force*, being shamefully unfamiliar with the tools of their trade. So they blunder along, now and again arresting attention by the very crudeness and boldness of their efforts. No one will dispute that, on the other hand, there do spring up men of genius who have something so vital to say that it practically says itself, in spite of them. But the general run of authors, who are not geniuses, but plodding, conscientious students of their art, do well to pause now and then and realize that there is such a thing as "the infinite capacity for taking pains." Instinct is not to be disparaged; but instinct, subject to a genuine understanding of form and of the nice use of language, is immeasurably more valuable to the writer.

I have ventured thus at length into the nature of our task because I wish to engage your enthusiasm for it. I want you to feel with me that the problems we face are so deep and so real, so vitally a part of your work as an artist, that you will grapple with them eagerly. Remember that you are following in your art exactly the same path the young students of drawing and sculpture follow in theirs. They have their "life classes"; you are having yours. In a sense they study the anatomy of the exterior man, you, of the interior. They display what man looks like, you, what he is and does. In one of their text-books, *Anatomy for Artists,* by Vanderpoel, I read words which could have been addressed to you as well as to them:

"The artist stands in need of skill in the use of his knowledge of structure, his understanding of action, and his insight into character. These things require a period of profound academic study. Form should be studied for its own sake. Every stroke of the artist's brush should prove his understanding of the form of the subject to be depicted. This includes insight into the character of the model and understanding of its action."

In another volume on the technique of the materials of the artist with pen and brush, *A Theory of Pure Design,* by Ross, we find adjurations which again apply with neat appropriateness to our own tasks: "The purpose of what is called art-teaching should be the production, not of objects, but of faculties — the faculties which being exercised will produce objects of art, naturally, inevitably. Instead of trying to teach people to produce art, which is absurd and impossible, we must give them a training which will induce visual sensitiveness with aesthetic discrimination, an interest in the tones, measure, and shape of things, the perception and appreciation of order, the sense of beauty. Inducing these causes, art will follow as a matter of course. In exercising and developing the faculties I have named, we are doing all that can be done by teaching."

My purpose is to try to explain, not the artist, but the mode of expression the artist uses. To state it in scientific language, I want to help the student define, classify and interpret the phenomena of human conduct. In this sense this book is a contribution to science rather than to art.

All the processes I describe are of course known as processes to successful writers. My contribution is to isolate these processes and give them names by which they may be known and used by others. Often it has been difficult to know just what names to use. In the main I have used the terminology which Professor Pitkin adopted in his earlier studies. I have tried further to define these terms and make clear their meanings. Those who use this book will be ready to allow my terms the meanings I give them; otherwise they will scarcely be able to follow me to my conclusions.

A PLEA FOR LITERARY TECHNIQUE

A New Introduction

It seems strange that in an age of techniques, an age revolutionized by the discovery of new technique, an age given to the elaboration of methods for acquiring skill in every human activity, including creative writing, it should be necessary to plead with students in writing to believe that there is a technique to their art and that it will profit them highly to master it, but such is the case. They know that it must be learned; they hope and expect some day to learn it; but for a curriculum of systematic study and apprenticeship they have a profound indifference. That they can thus learn most easily and thoroughly — this fact, too, they casually ignore. They suffer from a common prejudice — a prejudice which I attacked eleven years ago in the original Introduction to this book which precedes this one. With the deep conviction that an understanding of the purpose of a study of technique and an enthusiasm for it is more important to the literary student than any other issue, save having something to say, I offer these additional words of explanation and encouragement.

In a recent issue of my monthly magazine for learning writers, *The Blue Pencil,* I asked my readers this question: Why is it that writers ambitious for large success show so little interest in mastering the technique of their art? Their answers were immensely interesting. One candid letter, from a physician, said that writers refuse to submit to discipline because they are afraid. "All men are frightened — about something." Most writers fear, said the doctor, that if their ideas and plans about their art are too closely examined they will discover that they have foolish plans and doubtful ideas! " The modern writer," confided a news-paper man, " is imbued with a spirit of disregard for every-thing. He casts aside technique with conventions. He in-sists on experimenting, but, I judge, his literary, like his personal, experiments are a search for sensation, not for con-trol of sensations in the interest of harmony and beauty."

Fiction writers in general disregard training in their art mainly, I think, because the learning processes as well as the materials and tools of narrative are much less obvious to them than are the materials of such fine arts as music, painting and sculpture. How much easier for the painter and musician to know when they are " getting off the track " than for the writer! If the former is slapping an orange on canvas and it begins to be a baseball, he doesn't need to study a book to tell him what to do. A composer striving for serene and lovely harmonies instantly is aware of a discord when he plays it. Not so the beginning creative writer: he has no optic or auditory nerve to tell him when he goes astray; he may wander miles from the effect he set out to produce and keep it up for days; if his artistic conscience whispers to him, he probably replies with irritation: " I know, I know, Conscience, my dear fellow, but at the mo-ment I'm inspired." Much thought and experiment are needed to avoid such errors. The unifying principles of narrative must be learned. The writer, even more than per-formers in the other arts, needs a book.

While little or nothing can be done for the writer who be-lieves there is something original about ignorance of tech-nique, who fears to expose his ignorance or who is sure he is born a genius fully equipped for fame, much can be done for the student who is wholesomely or even skeptically curious, and blessed with an open mind. With the hope of helping such writers I wish to set down categorically a few current misconceptions of technique and to try to correct them. I present these problems in the order of their fre-quency, beginning with the most common:

1. *I have not the time, the energy, or the money to de-*

*vote to a systematic mastery of technique; I must get along
without it as well as I can.*

The very many writers who express this opinion do not
question the value of technique. They merely have feeble
ambitions. I know no remedy except to be born again with
more energy or to acquire a sympathetic rich uncle. How
do thousands of students acquire college educations without
money? People seem to do what really interests them; the
mastery of fiction is no exception.

2. *I hesitate to study technique because I am not sure I
have enough talent to become a writer. If I were sure I had
talent, I'd study very hard. If only I could write and sell
two or three stories, or a novel, I think I'd be reassured and
would go ahead and learn!*

Doubt this utterance, if you must, but I have heard it in
various forms many times. Somehow or other it reminds
me of the man who earned his passage on the canal boat by
towing it. "Talent" *is* precisely the ability to learn.
Writers are made, not born. It is no easier to begin at the
top of our profession than of any other.

3. *The study of technique is a deadening influence because it ignores the personality and equipment of the writer;
it sets before the writer external standards of performance
which he must follow, and to the extent he does this, he is not
true to himself and falls short of his highest and most original utterance.*

What is meant by "personality and equipment of the
writer"? By this phrase is commonly meant the thoughts,
ideas, and feelings, which are his own individual response to
life and which most sharply differentiate him from his fellows. What a blighting ordeal it would be to undergo any
course of study which might ignore these all-important impulses to expression! The proper study of technique, as explained in my original Introduction, is concerned always
with solving problems which arise in the presence of literary
materials and a purpose. "Purpose" here means, and can
only mean, the thing the writer wants to do, and what he

wants to do is inevitably an urge compounded of his response to life, his experience, everything that makes him unique as an individual. That urge to expression, which writers who suffer from this particular misconception feel is ignored in the study of technique, is in fact the very beginning of any sound study of technique. For this reason the first chapter of this book is devoted, as its title indicates, to " the emotional purpose."

The difference between the precious, intimate, given elements of the literary personality and those that are added by effort and discipline is clearly indicated in these lines from Stevenson written half a century ago: " Passion, wisdom, creative force, the power of mystery or color, are allotted in the hour of birth, and can be neither learned nor simulated. But the just and dexterous use of what qualities we have, the proportion of one part to another and to the whole, the elision of the useless, the accentuation of the important, and the preservation of a uniform character from end to end — these, which taken together constitute technical perfection, are to some degree within the reach of industry and intellectual courage."

This is by no means a complete account of the problem of technical instruction and literary personality. I have dealt with it elsewhere [1] and shall deal with it again,[2] but to reassure those who, in spite of what I say here, may feel that the honesty, the naturalness, the genius of their message for the world will be sacrificed if they set about systematically learning how best to express that message, I must add one further word.

For some types of writers, learning technical mastery in any systematic manner is all but impossible. This seems true, for example, of all students too weak mentally or too wanting in education to be able to grasp any abstractions, and of those pronounced introverts burdened with an infe-

[1] " The Literary Learning Process," Chapter V, in *The Psychology of Writing Success*, The Business Bourse.

[2] *Writing as a Career*, in preparation.

riority or persecution neurosis which construes criticism as blame for a moral delinquency. Almost invariably such types, sensing their handicaps, on being faced with an opportunity to learn what they don't know, will rationalize their weaknesses into this false theory that study of technique blights the flower of inspiration. I'll go further and say that all theories erected against learning systematically what a writer needs to know, are products of weak egos and unconscious fears of failure. These are days of self-revealment. Modern knowledge has lighted many secret places of the heart, and this revelation about writers must be faced, for it is the truth. It is not so easy for doctors, lawyers, painters, chemists, to rationalize aside the disagreeable tasks of learning their professions. They know that they must tackle their difficulties for both the difficulties and the method of learning are fully understood, but the " temperamental " (i.e., lazy), evasive writer, because of the romantic sentimental illusions in which his art is swathed, " gets by " easily with his stubborn attitudinizing.

Some people, it is true, will never be able to master literary technique; neither will they, possibly, be able to master high-jumping or the arts of the contortionist. That they find these skills difficult does not make them unlearnable. Writers who literally cannot be taught to think will never write anything thoughtful no matter how their careers are conducted. The converse is equally true! Writers of pronounced natural ability, no matter what its sensitiveness or rareness, will lose nothing in the long-run by systematic discipline in the most effective ways to say what they have to say.

4. *The study of technique will kill spontaneity, and result in self-consciousness, stiffness in style and a mechanical product generally.*

The alarm expressed here is related to the one just treated and shows the same confusion; for surely when I say that the proper study of literary technique will not stifle personality because its entire problem is to find the best ways to express that personality, certain qualifications must be obvious. If there is no personality to begin with, no study of technique will produce one. If, on the other hand, a rich writing personality, with a natural ease and flow of style, begins to master technique and very soon loses this same ease and flow, there is no need to toss textbook and instructor out the window and call the marines. Students in all arts experience a temporary loss of dexterity when learning new ways. The juggler who can keep three balls in the air with one hand will, on trying for the first time to keep four balls in the air, lose temporarily his ability to manage three! The reason for this is manifestly the necessity of breaking up an old habit before a newer and more complicated one can take its place.

All writers ignorant of the principles of design, of ways and means of securing emphasis, most of which have been used by effective writers since the beginning of literature, are like pianists who play by ear. Often they play well, sometimes even brilliantly, but no one questions the limitation of their art. Great pianists take the trouble to learn the laws of harmony and counterpoint and to play by note. The fiction writers who begin a story without knowing how it is going to end, who can't tell whether a given " idea " is good for a novel or a story, who, baffled by the problem of how best to open a given story, pore over the pages of classical authors seeking a model — such writers are playing by ear. Writers who have taught themselves to plan before they write, to understand clearly the technical differences between stories and novels, the basic principles involved in all types of story beginnings — such writers play by note and immeasurable is their advantage over the ear-performers.

No writer, no artist, I might say, advances far in his strivings for fame unless at some time in his career he discovers in himself a passion for technique, for learning the tricks of his craft. " The best kind of originality is that which comes after a sound apprenticeship; that which shall

prove to be the blending of a firm conception of all useful precedent and the progressive tendencies of an able mind." These quaintly flavored words I find in a catalogue of printers' type! "For, let a man be as able and original as he may, he cannot afford to discard knowledge of what has gone before or what is now going on in his own trade and profession." Wisdom — for writers as well as printers! Can printers' apprentices alone understand it?

5. *The manner of telling a story is more important than the story itself. Most stories, all popular stories, use hackneyed plots but they still are interesting for the freshness and individuality of the style. Why worry, then, about plots at all?*

It is true that style is very important in all grades of fiction and that many a story and novel has, because of some rare quality in its style, survived a deplorable plot. Remember, however, that the greatest works are always triumphs of both plot and style. Remember, also, that even if you concentrate on your style alone, depending upon it to carry you along, giving little heed to your plots, you will, if you keep on, unconsciously and inevitably improve your plots. You can't avoid learning how to perfect a design of action if you are to go far with narrative. If, on the other hand, you aim only to please popular editors, seek money, not art or fame, and are willing cheerfully to imitate the plots of other successful writers, go ahead and do so; this is the way to success with most of them. One word of warning, however: imitation is also an art to be learned. You will often discover that some of these popular plots you call "hackneyed" are not hackneyed at all or, at least, are freshened by a twist which escaped you. You will also soon discover that though trite, sentimental plots are "bad" in the literary sense, it does not follow that any bad plot can be turned into a five hundred dollar story for the *Saturday Evening Post*. The trick is to know the right kind of badness. This again must be learned and learning it is a fairly complicated problem of literary technique.

6. *All really great artists break, they do not observe, rules; any writer who has something to say will find a way to say it without help from any book or teacher and the right way for him will be the way he works out for himself. Every writer is a law unto himself.*

Here are truth and error. While it is true that many a writer has by years of patient experiment forged for himself methods eminently successful, and without the systematic help of either book or teacher, it is not true that every writer is a law unto himself if by this you mean that there is nothing in common between the principles he employs and those found of use by other successful writers. Shakespeare did not go to school in his art — he worked out his plays in the theatre, testing them on his audiences directly; but does this mean that in the construction of his plays there are laws peculiar to him alone? Can no one else recognize and use the principles which served him? This seems to be the absurdity into which the " law unto himself " theorists are forced! Clearly, the principles of an art are universal in that art, and can be learned like any other universal principles; how any individual writer will apply those principles in carrying out the effects that interest him is his own unique affair.

People who claim that artists break rather than observe rules generally confuse two things. The basic facts of human nature which account for the appeal of all art every artist understands and uses when at work and always will use as long as human nature remains what it is; the innovations pointed to by the partisans of " freedom " for genius result generally from the use of new materials and from the writer's defiance, not of art principles, but of social and moral customs observed theretofore by other writers. Genius, in other words, is original in his message not his art principles.

Strictly speaking, moreover, literary technique is not concerned with " rules " at all but with principles and ideals. A rule takes the form of a command: " Thou shalt open thy

story with action or be a flop." A principle of any art is a statement of the laws of appeal based on known psychological truths. Such a principle is: Readers are stirred by action involving conflict. Rules imply external restraints; ideals, internal. The former control games, the latter liberate the art process. An artist may not take his ideals from another, but he may take from another much wisdom as to effective ways of carrying out these ideals.[1]

7. *Modern realism with its revolt against all formulism and artificiality in plotting has dispensed with the need of "inventions" and therefore of the need for any study of technique whose entire concern is inventions. To learn how to "make up things" is to drop back into an age from which modern art has graduated.*

This, our final heresy, is our best; it is the best because it springs from an observant and curious mind. I need a volume to answer it. I intend, indeed, to take considerable space in my annual anthology, " Short Story Hits," to indicate year by year just how the new writers with new materials exploit the old principles of invention to obtain ever greater realism and seeming closeness to life itself. That modern realism has, however, made fiction wholly photographic is neither true nor desirable.

So spirited has been the revolt in radical quarters against all Victorian literary conventions that older writers (who might not like to admit that they are Victorian) are found anxiously examining themselves and their art. Not all writers have the critical acumen to detect the beginning obsolescence of their own work or the courage and generosity to admit it, but those of large attainments find it possible. Joseph Hergesheimer, Edna Ferber and W. Somerset Maugham, for example, have recently reported their awareness of the changes in the temper of modern fiction and their doubts of their ability to evaluate them. Fifteen years ago Mr. Hergesheimer said to me: " Who are the younger

[1] The difference between rules and ideals is further explained on pages xv through xviii.

writers coming along and what are they up to?" Mr. Maugham finds himself "damned" with the faint praise of "competence" and stoutly, in face of the seeming lawlessness in writing going on about him, insists that his "predispositions in the arts are on the side of law and order." The issue manifestly between the old and the new in literary design is not chaos versus order, but an old type of order versus a new.

Narrative without selection, adaptation, invention, is impossible; it is impossible even to the historian who aims to record what actually happened. I suppose that the nearest approach to an absolute transcript from life is James Joyce's effort to give in *Ulysses* in some third of a million words the complete history of one man's life during twenty-four hours. Yet selection, invention are evident on every page. *Ulysses* is a classic of narrative art but not because it is a literal transcript from life.

Modern realism, it is true, has gone far in exposing the cheapness and absurdity of happy endings, of theatrical climaxes and of hero and villain characters, but what will take the place of the sappy endings, "big scenes" and stuffed characters? This itself is a problem of technique and it is a more difficult, because more subtle, problem than fiction writers have ever faced before.

T. H. U.

PART ONE

THE NARRATIVE PURPOSE
A Study of What the Writer Wants to Do

NARRATIVE TECHNIQUE

CHAPTER ONE

THE EMOTIONAL PURPOSE

It is fine to have passions.
— GUY DE MAUPASSANT.

We have learned from the preceding Introduction that technique is involved wherever we find materials and a purpose. The narrative writer has certain facts about life; these are his materials. He wants to do something with these facts; this is his purpose. This purpose, this result he wishes to attain, will be the first object of our study. Let me begin by asking you for your own testimony on this point: Why do *you* wish to write fiction?

If you expect to secure the utmost benefit from this study, I wish you to pause right here in your reading and answer this question seriously. Write it out as completely as you can. *Exactly* why are you interested in writing narrative? Why do you prefer this form of writing to other forms? What do you hope to accomplish by your writing? What is the greatest success you can think of for yourself in this field? How did you " get this way? "

The answers to these questions will not come off-hand. You'll have to do some thinking; but this is a course in thinking. Be honest with yourself; get it straight; tell the truth; and write it out. It will be an interesting document for you to keep, and we shall refer to it later.

Now examine what you have written. Have you indicated how you hope to succeed? Perhaps you have only stated what success would mean to you *if* it came. Have you expressed any interest in your future reader? Have you stated *how* you propose to reach him? Did you comment upon the peculiar effect narrative writing makes upon the reader and how it differs from the effects of other forms of writing? Did you think of your reader at all?

If you can answer these questions in the affirmative, you may well congratulate yourself; you have shown at the very beginning that your thoughts are already focused upon the most fundamental of all the principles we shall study. If your answers are negative, your case is not yet hopeless; it is simply more problematical; you have everything yet to learn; and I urge that you read this first chapter with special care. It explains the purpose of narrative writing.

1. Fictional Purpose Defined

" Purpose " as we are using the word here means, of course, the writer's literary purpose, the result he hopes to bring about by each piece of writing as a whole. In every episode, every sentence, every word, in fact, of each story there arises a particular and narrow question of purpose; I am, however, not using the word in this sense. I have in mind the general technical objective which is common to every act in producing a story. What is it? What is the purpose that most distinguishes narrative from all other forms of prose?

The purpose of fiction is to affect rather than to convince the reader. Its object is to reach him through his senses rather than through his mind. The purpose of argumentation is to convince; the purpose of description is to present a picture; the purpose of exposition is to impart knowledge, ideas, facts: but the characteristic purpose of narrative in the fictional sense in which we are taking it here is to make the reader *feel*.

What is a Story?

There is, of course, no sharp line dividing these forms of prose writing from each other. In narrative-description a picture is presented by use of the narrative form. In both argumentation and exposition abstract ideas are often presented by didactic forms of narrative. Even fiction itself presents *some* facts, clarifies others, and often strongly affects convictions; but if it *is* fictional narrative, these effects are always incidental; the main effect is registered not by the reader's mind but by his senses, his feelings, his emotions.

I use the word " feelings " as well as " emotions " because the effect of some forms of non-dramatic narrative is not strong enough to be termed an emotion. All emotions are feelings but not all feelings are emotions. I use the term " emotions " to characterize narrative purpose in general simply because the most powerful, if not most beautiful, narratives produce genuine emotion in the reader.

Professor Pitkin uses the term " definite impression " to characterize the effect of the short story. The nature of emotion as a " feeling state " is touched upon in Chapter Four.

This fact is of immense importance in understanding our two technical factors of " materials " and " a purpose." The problem of your having the right purpose in wanting to write fiction is more important than your possession of materials; if you have no materials, being young with as yet nothing to write about, you need only live and grow older and wiser to remedy the defect; or you can go out and find materials; indeed, materials even for a time may be given you by your instructor or another person; but if you have no purpose, if you don't know why you wish to write, no one can help you.

An amazingly large number of students begin a serious study of the art of fiction without an interest in the main object of this type of writing. They think of a " story "

as a string of episodes joined together in some peculiar
way more or less like life, never for a moment realizing
that the thing the editor pays for and the reader cries for
is an emotional effect. They are shocked to learn that the
average professional writer's main object is to produce
these emotional effects and that he cares not the least what
he does to life or truth or anything else so long as he gets
them; but such is the case.

Consider: What is your favorite short story or novel?
Why do you like it? Try to recall the moment when you
finished your first reading of it. Analyze that moment.
Do you remember when you finished the last page of *Robinson Crusoe* or *David Copperfield* or *Ivanhoe?* What
made it a great moment? Certainly you were impressed,
not by the facts you learned, the convictions you discovered or the pictures you saw, but rather by the thrill of
adventure, by glowing admiration for a hero, or by a
romantic desire to emulate the chivalrous deeds of some
armor-plated knight. You were detached as by some
magic from your immediate surroundings; your body was
relaxed, suffused with emotions; you wondered, were
amazed, terrified, enthralled, uplifted, inspired, — you
were, in a word, more or less hypnotized by the emotional
effect of the story.

Writer a Hypnotist

Hypnosis! There we have it. The passive state of concentration on one point only which we call hypnosis is the
spell which the artist in narrative writing should try to
cast over his audience. It is not impossible. I have seen it
done in the case of children listening to kindergarten tales
told by a vivacious and skillful teacher. The child rises
from its seat, mouth and eyes open wide, and walks toward
the narrator utterly oblivious to all else. In real life
under powerful emotional stress we are oblivious to everything except those " stimuli " which are concerned with

the crisis we are passing through. If your reader is powerfully moved by imaginatively sharing the experiences of your characters, he will be similarly subdued to something like the hypnotic state. This is an ideal towards which you should strive.

Testimony of Authors

Reading affects your emotions, you may have thought, only because you are especially " fond " of stories; you love them. True; but don't forget that the presence of these excitement-producing elements in these books is not accidental. The very greatest masters of fiction organize their whole thinking processes around this specific purpose — to thrill you. Guy de Maupassant, believed by many to be the greatest master of the short story, in writing of his idea of his audience, said: " The public is composed of numerous groups who cry to us: ' Console me, amuse me, make me sad; make me sympathetic; make me dream; make me laugh; make me shudder; make me weep; make me think.' " And when you visit Parc Monceau in Paris, you will see a memorial to de Maupassant, a marble bust of the author, beneath which sits a sculptured woman, a book open in her hand, a far-away look in her eyes, and her whole body surrendered to the emotional effect of one of the master's stories.

Such a direct attack on the emotional susceptibilities of the public is, of course, the chief objective of all forms of dramatic writing. The wisdom of de Maupassant's countryman and predecessor, Molière, greatest of French dramatists, is of value to the student of narrative. Molière went so far as to say boldly that his art was directed to the " entrails " (*entrailles*) rather than to the heads of his audience. He said: " It's not for the dramatist to object to or criticize the taste of the public. Instead of trying to analyze the effect of our work, let us pin our faith in those plays which grip our *vitals* and let it go at that. There's no use trying to penetrate this mystery any further. The greatest of all rules is to create pleasure. Any play which does this is a good play. If your rules cause you to produce any other kind of play, your rules are no good."

In our own day we find Conrad, sitting down in an introspective mood, after completing *The Nigger of the Narcissus,* and writing the following statement of the purpose of his art:

Impressed by the aspect of the world the thinker plunges into ideas, the scientist into facts — whence, presently emerging they make their appeal to those qualities of our being that fit us best for the hazardous enterprise of living. They speak authoritatively to our common sense, to our intelligence. . . . It is otherwise with the artist. . . . His appeal is less loud, more profound, less distinct, more stirring — and sooner forgotten. Yet its effect endures forever. . . .

Such an appeal to be effective must be an impression conveyed through the senses, and, in fact, it cannot be made in any other way, because temperament, whether individual or collective, is not amenable to persuasion. All art, therefore, appeals primarily to the senses, and the artistic aim, when expressing itself in written words, must also make its appeal through the senses if its high desire is to reach the secret spring of responsive emotions. . . .

Among the few American story writers who have had true insight into the processes of their work is Booth Tarkington. He writes to an aspiring young author:

"Forget, when you work, about any result but the art result to you. Pick your reader; the best reader you have inside you; then make him a person who doesn't know your artist-self's intentions. Make him see them. Realize that he is in your hands and play with his imagination. Startle him, amuse him, make him see what you see — make him feel your words — flush him with colors."

2. Examples That Show Purpose

It is the writer's business to stir the emotions of his readers.

Pick up any volume by any writer who has made a striking success on any literary level, and test the truth of this assertion.

Here, for example, is the opening of a story by Ring Lardner: [1]

The engagement was broken off before it was announced. So only a thousand or so of the intimate friends and relatives of the party knew about it. What they knew was that there had been an engagement and that there was one no longer. The cause of the break they merely guessed, and most of the guesses were, in most particulars, wrong.

Forgetting for a moment Ring Lardner's genius for laughter, consider the material he chooses, and the directness with which he makes his appeal in his first paragraph to the reader's primitive, biological response to the adventure of love.

Or take this from William March: [2]

All the men in our ward were gas patients, and all of us were going to die. The nurses knew there was nothing that could be done for us, and most of the men realized it too. . . . Three cots away a man lay straining and trying to breathe. Sweat rolled from his face, and he caught his breath with a high sucking sound. After each spell had passed he would lie back exhausted, and make a bubbling noise with his lips, as if apologizing for disturbing the ward; because each time the man strained for breath the other men unconsciously struggled with him; and when he lay back exhausted we unclenched our fists and relaxed a little ourselves.

Again a direct attack upon a primitive, biological conditioning, the universal fear of death and horror of physical agony.

[1] Reprinted by permission from *How to Write Short Stories,* by Ring Lardner, published by Charles Scribner's Sons.
[2] Reprinted by permission from *Company K* by William March, published by Smith & Haas.

Examine this passage from Conrad Aiken: [1]

A couple of years ago I saw in the " agony column " of *The Times* a very curious advertisement. There are always curious things in that column — I have always been fascinated by that odd little company of forlorn people who so desperately and publicly wear their hearts on their sleeves for daws to peck at. Some of them appear there over and over again — the person who signs himself, or herself, " C." for example: who regularly every three months or so inserts the message " *Tout passe, l'amitie reste*." What singular and heart-breaking devotion does that brief legend convey? Does it ever reach the adored being for whom it is intended, I wonder? Does he ever see it, does he ever reply? Has he simply abandoned her? Were they sundered by some devastating tragedy which can never be healed? And will she go on till she dies, loosing these lovely flame-colored arrows into an utterly unresponsive void? . . .

I never tire of reflecting on these things; but the advertisement of which I have just spoken was of a different sort altogether. This was signed " Journalist," and merely said: " Your obituary? Well written, reviewed by yourself, and satisfaction thus insured."

Now consider not the opening, but the climax scenes of a group of stories. The first is by Joseph Conrad: [2]

. . . And then these three men in the engine-room had the intimate sensation of a check upon the ship, of a strange shrinking, as if she had gathered herself for a desperate leap.

"Stop her! " bellowed Mr. Rout.

Nobody — not even Captain MacWhirr, who alone on deck had caught sight of a white line of foam coming on at such a height that he couldn't believe his eyes — nobody was to know the steepness of that sea and the awful depth of the hollow the hurricane had scooped out behind the running wall of water.

It raced to meet the ship, and with a pause, as of girding the loins, the *Nan-Shan* lifted her bows and leaped. The flames in all the lamps sank, darkening the engine-room. One went out. With a tearing crash and a swirling, raving tumult, tons of water fell upon the deck, as though the ship had darted under the foot of a cataract.

[1] Reprinted by permission from *Costumes by Eros,* published by Charles Scribner's Sons.

[2] Reprinted by permission from *Typhoon,* by Joseph Conrad, published by Doubleday, Doran & Co.

Down there they looked at each other, stunned.

"Swept from end to end, by God! " bawled Jukes.

She dipped into the hollow straight down, as if going over the edge of the world. The engine-room toppled forward menacingly, like the inside of a tower nodding in an earthquake. An awful racket, of iron things falling, came from the stokehold. She hung on this appalling slant long enough for Beale to drop on his hands and knees and begin to crawl as if he meant to fly on all fours out of the engine-room, and for Mr. Rout to turn his head slowly, rigid, cavernous, with the lower jaw dropping. Jukes had shut his eyes, and his face in a moment became hopelessly blank and gentle, like the face of a blind man.

At last she rose slowly, staggering, as if she had to lift a mountain with her bows.

Consider this from George Milburn's famous story: *The Fight At Hendryx's:* [1]

"Luther," Old Man Hendryx says to me, "what am I going to do with that there Merryweather fellow that got his throat cut over here at my dance last week."

"God A'mighty! " I says. "Is he still here? "

"Still here! — how was he going to git away? " Old Man Hendryx says. " I got him setting up out there in the mule shed, and he's froze stiffer 'n a poker. Now what do you reckon I'd ort to do with him? He ain't even got no friends nor acquaintances nor nothing. And I'm aiming to git shut of him."

"Well," I says, "why don't you just take him out and bury him? "

"Bury him! " Old Man Hendryx said, "bury him in ground froze harder than a marble slab? Talk sense, Luther. You know that a man cain't stick a spade in the ground with it froze like it is now. Anyway, I ain't going to try it. And I sure as hell ain't going to keep him out there in that mule shed until the thaw comes."

"No, that's not right," I says, "you hadn't ort to keep him out there in the mule shed, Hendryx. That ain't Christian."

Let me offer a last example from one of Dorothy Parker's best known stories, *A Telephone Call.* [2]

[1] Reprinted by permission from *No More Trumpets,* by George Milburn, published by Harcourt, Brace & Co.

[2] Reprinted by permission from *Laments for the Living,* by Dorothy Parker, published by The Viking Press.

I won't telephone him. I'll never telephone him again so long as I live. He'll rot in hell, before I'll call him up. You don't have to give me strength, God; I have it myself. If he wanted me, he could get me. He knows where I am. He knows I'm waiting here. He's so sure of me, so sure. I wonder why they hate you, as soon as they are sure of you. I should think it would be so sweet to be sure.

Why? Why do these writers, humorous, grim, ironic, adventurous, or whatever they may be, why do these writers choose such materials? The need of love, the fear of death — why are these found at the core of so much of the greatest fiction? Simply because these problems are related to the strongest human instincts and writers have found that by arrangements of such materials, they can most surely impress the reader. The whole meaning of technique to the writer is the mastery of ways by which to stir his audience.

3. Examples Without Purpose

Let us now look at a bit of writing produced by a student who had no desire whatever to produce emotional effects. I quote the end of a story, the idea of which had possibilities. A young girl, Rita Rodney, the last descendant in an old family, was forced by financial difficulties to sell the old homestead to a Mrs. Jameson. She made a fine struggle to secure money to buy the home back, and succeeded finally through the indirect aid of Lee Howe with whom she fell madly in love. The scene below was intended as a picture of their romantic passion:

Rita was interrupted by Lee Howe himself. He had come and Uncle John was not with him. For the moment all resentment left her in seeing him but she was formal in receiving him.

It was Lee Howe in his frank, open manner that went right to the point: " I wasn't sure if you wanted to see me or not! "

Rita was taken so unaware that she could hardly manage to be just natural. " Of course," she smiled.

" You've changed your mind? "

" About what? " she asked to gain ground for she would not be too eager.

Too straight-forward to cover his feeling by mincing words he asked, " I'm not a burglar. I'm not taking advantage of old ladies."

" I believe you did it through friendship for Uncle John and myself? "

" I would do anything for John Rodney, but I didn't do that for him." His words were significant.

" My ingratitude hurt and drove you away."

" Yes, but that littleness passed away after hours of thought."

" I not only forgave you long ago, but I believe you did Sarah Jameson a kindness by sending her back to the city where she longed to be, for her spite was making her unhappy, yet through force of habit she could not give up."

" And yourself? "

" I wanted the place more than I can tell."

" I may come every day? "

" But you are going West this week? "

Since the whole miserable thing had been settled she could be her own self again. She felt that this would be indefinitely.

The garden was once again in bloom for it was summer, but the Rodney home was closed for John Rodney had gone West months ago, and Rita and Lee Howe were on their honeymoon on their way East.

Now this piece of writing is weak in about every department of fiction writing except spelling, and the spelling happens to be correct because the author is a young school teacher! The main reason for all the faults is that the writer neither understood, nor was interested in, the problems of producing an emotion on the reader. She was a writer with a defective purpose.

Undynamic Ambitions

An examination of the purposes announced by many beginners in the art of fiction discloses the fact that most of them are preoccupied with the thought of *why* they would like to be literary artists rather than the thought of *what they are going to do* to get there. They want to " win fame "; they want to " earn some money," to " be independent," to " live wherever they choose," to " make the family proud of them," to "fulfill an ambition nourished since I was a child"; and, alas, all too many, having failed at nearly everything else, turn to fiction as the one thing within their slender powers! Writing appeals to them apparently because — the pen weighs so little!

Pathetic illusions! Such aspirations accompanying real artistic gifts are, of course, all possible, but very often they are symptoms of a misdirected enthusiasm. The genuine creative instinct creates; it doesn't "nourish" the idea from childhood up; it doesn't want to create another personality; it craves to express the one it has. Desires for money and fame are not at all inconsistent with a genuine literary purpose; they are generally incentives to energetic action: but if a strong desire to produce emotional effects is not prominent among these ambitions, the ambitions will never be realized. Witness the poet Keats' own expression of his immortal creative energy:

> When I have fears that I may cease to be
>   Before my pen has glean'd my teeming brain,
> Before high-piled books, in charact'ry,
>   Hold like full garners the full ripen'd grain.

4. Defective Purposes Examined

Let me illustrate now by a few actual cases. Out of a large number of people who applied for instruction in fiction writing I have selected, first, four whose diagnoses display a typical lack of the fundamental emotional purpose. I shall report the answers given by these people to just one question, the one asked you at the beginning of this chapter: "Why do you want to write fiction?"

Case One: This young lady gave her reasons for wanting to write as follows: "First: I feel impelled to write fiction; have always felt that the writing I have done up to date has been a valuable preliminary training. Second: I believe that the discipline acquired in writing will teach

me to think better and express myself more accurately.
Third: I wish to apply what I acquire to some outside
work."

Her first statement of purpose, to graduate from newspaper and publicity writing to fiction writing, promised
well: many newswriters do this; but the trouble in her
case was that it was not the truth. The real motive, it
developed, behind this statement was to satisfy a streak of
vanity. A girl friend had sold a little story. She wished
to pose as an author too.

In her second view of writing as being a helpful mental
discipline she was again on the right track. A conscientious
study of the technique of writing would, like the study of
Latin or astronomy, have developed her mind; there was
room for much improvement; and persistent application
might indeed have given her enough skill in producing
emotion to enable her to "put one over" on her friend;
but the trouble again was that Case One had an unfortunate habit of always avoiding anything that looked like
regular discipline. Fiction writing is not recommended as
a cure for a lame will. As soon as the young lady saw
that short stories do not write themselves, she unconsciously
classed the art among the many things in her life to be done
"some other day," and as soon as this was discovered she
was told where she stood and her experiment with literature came to an abrupt end.

Vanity not Inspiration

As for the third motive of wishing to apply her fiction
to some outside work — this, upon examination, proved to
be a desire to write a big fiction story, have it published
and get a coveted job by "knocking the eye out of" a
certain employer through this display of her abilities. If
the employer had been her audience, all might yet have
been well; but he wasn't. He cared nothing at all about
fiction, but he *did* care apparently for youth, feminine

grace, and a handsome coiffure, for when the young lady walked in and asked for her job she got it!

Case Two: This student gave her purpose in wanting to write as follows: " I believe there is a story inside me I could write if I knew how."

Here, on the surface, was the real promise. She saw a " story," something, that is, emotional; it moved her to think of it; it would, if told properly, move others! She visualized others being thrilled as she had been; this too excited her — the prospects here were excellent. But, alas, when the young lady was asked to prepare a rough outline of her story, she delivered the unconsciously trite and insipid plot of a love story. It was so flat it could have thrilled no one, not even the author. Obviously she was not writing what was on her mind. She was holding something back. Cross-questioned, she finally admitted: " I wanted to do this writing for one purpose, to write beautifully an experience I have had. I now know that I cannot bear to express that experience as I felt it. Count me as a failure."

A Hopeless Inhibition

She had been unexpectedly and cruelly jilted by her lover. Unable to accept the situation philosophically, she cast about for ways to recover what she had lost. She brooded endlessly over the romance of their wooing; it seemed to her like things she had read; if she could only write it out beautifully, she would make it immortal! So far, all is well; the neurotic origin of the desire did not at all invalidate it as a literary purpose; few great love stories in fact are without such an origin.

The trouble was in her *audience.* She wished to capture the passion of her experience forever for — herself! Frustrated love can be either strongly egoistic or strongly altruistic; in this case it was the former. She could not share her experience with another, not even an instructor! Unlike Case One she had an emotional message; like her she had no interest in reaching a reading audience; and like her she failed.

Case Three: The purpose for wanting to write was, in this case, announced to be " a desire to satisfy a longing."

Now what was this longing? The student explained that he had had it for fifteen years. He was certain that it was a desire to *write.* On being asked what he wanted to write *about,* he replied: " I cannot tell, but I can tell what I am interested in. I like to read about people of importance, such as actors, authors, travelers and explorers. I like to read how they advanced to their positions of importance. I like also to learn their ideas on important subjects."

The Book Lover Complex

Here are indications of a passive, brooding mind. The few writing tests given demonstrated this. The young man shrank from handling even the slightest emotional scenes. In his case, though he was twenty-seven years old, he had never *had* any genuine emotional experience! He was that kind. He had no " personality." His most moving experience, he declared, was coming from Iowa to live near New York! Here was a pure case of a " writer " with nothing to write about. He was minus a " message." He might have mastered technique, but what was the use? It would be learning to sight the target with an empty rifle.

But why, then, did he ever discover a wish to learn to write narrative? His was a typical case of confusing reading with writing. It was his opinion that people read fiction mainly " on account of curiosity and interest to know how other people live." This notion was just wrong enough to twist his whole conception of creative literature. " People who write what I like *do* know other people and interesting things," he reasoned; " if I write, *I'll* know them too." Fatuous deception! He omitted just one little link in his logic: before writing things he must master them. He was not the mastering kind.

The young man's purpose was to *get* thrills, not to pro-duce them. He was a good reader, the worst possible kind of writer. He was sent back to his mother and his books.

Case Four: This student announced her purpose thus: " I generally find it easier to write things than to say them. I should like in my writing to reveal the deep things hidden in a quiet nature."

This purpose, while not promising, was not necessarily hopeless. There have been shy natures who, often with the use of a pen name, have written effectively of life. If there were in fact " deep things " in her nature it would not have been at all impossible to bring them out in spite of mere shyness.

The Unconscious Purpose

Difficulties appeared, however, as soon as a search was started for these " deep things." Her confidence was se-cured, some uncontrolled writing was done, and every op-portunity given to show if she had anything " deep " to say about life. She hadn't. Her shyness was not a mere mannerism; it resulted from the young woman's discovery that she really knew less, thought less deeply, and, in gen-eral, reacted to her environment more passively and col-orlessly than any of her companions. This filled her with a deep sense of incapacity. She had what psycho-analysts call an " inferiority complex." She wished to defend her-self by deprecating other people in her writing and arguing that " still water runs deep," which is by no means always true. This aspirant was a victim of loneliness. She was advised to get married at the earliest possible moment.

5. Sound Purposes Examined

So much for would-be writers whose purposes were so defective that there was no possibility of their ever suc-ceeding. Now let me tell you about the announced purposes and beginning efforts of two rather typical successful students. Both sold stories written during the first six months of training in technique. I will call them Case A and Case B.

Case A expressed his purpose in wanting to write fiction in the one word, " fun." He was an advertisement writer, and, it later developed, he also had as a motive a desire to publish stories in reputable magazines which would enhance his prestige and so enable him to demand higher prices for his more purely commercial writing. The fact that he failed for some time in nearly every task set him without growing discouraged and that he evinced a keen interest in knowing *exactly what* he had done wrong indicated that the " fun " and fascination of the art were indeed his chief incentives. The secondary commercial purpose served to energize his efforts.

Fascinated by Technique

Let me tell you where the fun came in. He had worked out rather consciously a definite theory for his advertisement writing. This theory comprehended who and what his audience was, how its attention is secured, what kind of material he needed, how to organize and present it. In most cases the theory worked. It brought its possessor considerable fame in his field. He was naturally enthusiastic over it. One day in reading some fiction he was suddenly struck with the difference between the *quality* of the story and that of his own advertisements. How was it procured? *If* he could get control of it also — there was a bigger and more difficult thing to do! If he could " hit " fiction readers as he hit his newspaper readers — there was the fun!

His very first question therefore on beginning his instructions was: " How do you do it? " This indicated a correct purpose. Mastery of technique was obviously only a question of time. But had he anything to say, a message?

As an experiment he was asked to sit down and write a story, the best he knew how, without thought of technique.

I want you to read part of the story he turned off. It recounts the jealousy of a hot-headed young Spaniard who has just discovered that his wife is unfaithful to him. The Spaniard suspects that his wife's lover is with her at home while he is at his office. He leaves his office early and goes home to surprise them. Here is the account of what happened:

About nine o'clock he stole home, crept up on the porch, opened the front door stealthily, and taking off his shoes, carried them in his hand, while he padded down the hall in his stocking feet. Everything was very quiet. He listened outside the door of their rooms. His heart was beating in his throat, just below the Adam's apple. Thump — thump — long, slow, pounding beats. Two red hot needles were drilling into his temples. Was the proof on the other side?

How he wanted proof! Every muscle in his body ached for that leap to kill! The intensity of it caused him to fling open the door, suddenly, with a quick silent jerk. And there on the couch, the red plush couch he had been so proud of! — the man — "*puerco! animal!*" He flung his shoes at the man's head "Cristo!" he screamed. He threw himself on him! It was not enough that he was to have no little son, no little *bebe!* He was also to wear the "horns."

"*Condenado!*" He ripped, scratched, tore the clothes from the villain's carcass. He banged him on the floor. He dragged him to the door and cast him — with both hands and one foot — into the street — without his clothes — into the snow — naked — freezing!

Then, the man out of the way, he turned to the woman, his wife, with his fingers hooked, twitching, his shoulders raised — and he laughed! It must have been a blood-curdling laugh! He laughed at the fright which he saw in her eyes! He would take a step toward her and laugh again, to see her cower away. He flung a chair out of his path, and he roared with mirth as he saw her raise her arm to shield her head. "What a vile thing she is, and how she deserves to die," he thought. "But death? It that enough? One is dead — one suffers no more. Who knows? To kill her, is it justice enough?"

This, of course, is mere melodrama. There is also an underdevelopment of action which confuses the total effect.

The point of view is handled clumsily. *But,* the central purpose was absolutely right: the writer decided that to create emotion he had to handle emotional material. He did not see his effect clearly, but he was *trying* for one; he failed in his means to his ends, but this was a failure in technique, and technique can be learned.

Let me speak a word here in defence of melodrama. Experience inclines me to favor the student who begins with melodrama. Show me the student who has never written or imagined melodrama and I'll show you a person probably doomed to failure in writing stories other people like to read. If with the melodramatic streak runs intelligence, the case is not at all serious. Melodramatic imaginings imply energy; and creative writing demands the dynamic attack. " I should like to be able to write a story," declares Thackeray in his confessions, " in which there would be no reflections, but an incident in every other page, a villain, a battle, a mystery in every chapter. I should like to be able to feed a reader so spicily as to leave him hungering and thirsting for more at the end of each installment." Great writers may be dreamers, but, if so, they are dreamers with a " kick "!

Frank Desire for Expression

Case B is a young woman in her early thirties. She is divorced, a " society woman," has much time, and states her purpose as follows: " I have had many emotional experiences and I want to make some use of them. I do not know anything about writing and I have always been awed by the difficulties that must be involved in learning it. I am game to try, however, because I have 'lived' and I want to settle down now and write."

Inquiry disclosed that the lady had amused herself by much philandering. The problem of having something to write about was thus settled instantly; she would do love stories. The question of purpose that arose was this: Did she really want to tell what she had learned about passion or was she, like Case Two above, merely neurotic, trying to hide something, to defend her conduct, or to satisfy some jealous impulse? To get at this matter she was asked to submit some notes on a young girl's first real passion. I want to give you an idea of the nature of the data turned in. Here is some of it, a frank confession of her own experience;

Then Jack lifted my face and kissed me, my first kiss of passion.

That night riotous and colorful dreams invaded my prim white bed. I dreamed I was again at the dance, but this time Jack instead of holding me decorously at a distance, held me close, so close that I could scarcely move. I could smell the scent of cigarettes on his breath as we danced to the throbbing music. I hungered with a new and strangely intense desire; and yet I could not have said what this desire was.

I woke in the middle of the night, tired, and a bit shocked at the uncontrolled visions of the night. I did not want to sleep again. I slipped into a dressing gown and sat by the open window. The yard was a mist of silver lawn, a phantasy of moonlight. "Night *is* made for love," I said half aloud, and I thought of Jack and wished I could see him coming across the lawn, a white plume in his hat. . . .

The author of this autobiographical data, though she has wasted ten of the best years of her life in the relentless pursuit of pleasure, was not unintelligent. Now she wanted to "settle down." Settling down for her meant accomplishing something. Quite calmly she decided that she must sell the things she knows, the facts about passionate love, and the best way to do this was by writing. Cool intelligence gave her a right purpose: she would give other people her own emotional experiences. And once having decided to write them, she proceeded — *to write them!*

6. The Peril of the Proprieties

In this respect this young woman was literally one in a thousand. Very few women, young or old, can be induced, no matter how ardent their literary ambitions, to tell what they know about emotions. The conventionalities, propriety, false modesty compete with their artistic urgings; and nearly always the conventionalities win out. They will read the sonnets of Mrs. Browning, the novels of George Sand, or the short stories of Mrs. Gerould, revel in their beauties, defend their truth, envy their power, and yet, when they themselves sit down to pen their own masterpieces, they whisk into the Land of Forbidden Facts all the subjects which these women handled so effectively! They ignore their best material.

I am not adjuring women writers to espouse the " sex story " to achieve success. I am merely reminding them that since one of the very strongest instincts of life is sex, most human activity — the Freudian psychologists say *all* human activity — finds here its chief motive force and direction. Passionate love is intellectualized sex hunger. Sex need not be written about with no relation to the rest of life; but no other single thing will help *explain* the rest of life better than a knowledge of sex. Nor is it to the point to argue the absence of a realistic interpretation of passion in the classics of the past. Puritanical morality, which inspired writers in the past, is giving away to a more liberal and courageous interest in the truth. The older writers, moreover, simply didn't know the full truth; since their day revolutionary discoveries — the most far-reaching single scientific advance of our time — have been made in the realm of psychology; the discoveries here give us a new idea of the " truth," and our more intelligent readers are consequently demanding more convincing pictures of life.

Again and again I hear students, when faced with the aridity, the banality of their writings, say: " Oh, I know something a lot worse than that, but it isn't printable." Perhaps it isn't printable, but that is no reason why it should not be used. The very fact that they guard these " unprintable scandals " with such jealous terror is fairly certain proof that more emotional associations are gathered about them than about anything else in their lives. As soon as they make up their minds to use these " terrible secrets " their work invariably improves.

If an author like Conrad can coolly in one and the same story carry hunger for food to such a pitch of agony that his hero kills and devours several human beings, and then give the same hero sex hunger so intense that he chews the cushions in his room — if Conrad can do this and remain respectable, you have no need to shrink from facing the emotional facts of life.

Can you write emotionally? There is no need to wait longer for an opportunity to find out. You don't have to postpone your emotional writing until you have learned what this book can teach you about building strong plots. Everyone has had some emotional experience. Decide what your most exciting moment has been, then sit down and write it out. Write exactly what happened in your own language and in your own way. Call this your first writing assignment. Show the finished piece to someone and see how it affects him — or her. That you may realize how effective such experiments may be, I am going to quote one, an actual experience related by a beginning student — her very first attempt at emotional writing.

AN EMOTIONAL EXPERIENCE

When I was just turned nineteen my mother died. To dwell upon it even now that several healing years have passed quickens my heart with the same poignant anguish as then and again I am bereft. We had never separated even for a night. My two brothers were good to her and to me, but they were not to her what I was. All that was dear and lovely in the world lay in the circle of my mother's arms. We had the same tastes, the same sense of the ridiculous, the same idea of the beautiful, the same distrust of the merely sentimental.

The last two years of mother's life were spent in bed. She did not seem to suffer — just faded away before my eyes. The neighbors were kind and helpful, but I resented a hand that was laid upon her, or a service I did not render.

We had a little two family house and our apartment was reached by an outside staircase, an ugly fashion I never saw elsewhere. The village we lived in was small, narrow, isolated in the extreme, but my brothers earned a good living there and with my mother's small income we were not badly off.

Mother and I often talked of her "going away" and I used often to visualize the actual parting, but no preparation fitted me for the moment. To dwell on the night my mother left me is beyond me. There was no outbreak of grief, no tears even. But life itself seemed to stop.

The day after we laid her in that desolate grave a cousin came and insisted on my returning to the city with her. It would "distract" me, she said. I honestly tried to be "distracted," but by the end of the second week my cousin gave up her well meant torture and let me return to the place that breathed of my mother. I did not send word to the boys that I was coming, nor did I let Mrs. M. — the kind neighbor who lived downstairs — know. I just walked up from the station as night fell, the leaden heart in my breast making my feet drag like weights.

As I turned in at the gate, Mrs. M. saw me and came running down the path. I hated the feel of her tears on my cheek as she took me in her arms. I wanted to stiffen my body against her embrace, but could not do else but yield to the warmth of heart that prompted it. She took me into her rooms and petted me and "poored" me till I could have screamed. But at last she let me go and I mounted her stairs and opened my kitchen door, snapped on the light, and looked about me, chilled, astonished that all was just as it used to be and only I was changed.

I stood there a few moments wondering what had brought me back, looking around with sick eyes at the familiar place. In a moment the 6:35 whistle blew and I hurriedly took off my coat and hat and resolutely determined to get dinner ready for the boys and surprise them upon their return. How selfish I had been not to think of them before! They too were hers and from this moment were to be mine. I wondered if Ed had anything in the refrigerator. It stood in the dark on the top landing of the outside stairs, and as I put my hand on the door knob I heard in the same old gentle tone: "Nellie!"

Immediately, instinctively obedient to that call as I had been so many hundred times, I cried out: "Yes, mother!" and ran into the adjoining room.

The white silence of the bed hit me like a blow. I clapped my hand over my mouth and stifled the scream that rose in my throat. I stood there for a moment paralyzed. Not from fear. Even if it were my mother's voice it should not frighten me

Living, she had never hurt me; dead, she could not. But it was with a thickly beating heart that I staggered out into the kitchen.

I stood for a moment trying to pull myself together. Suddenly, what mother called my sub-stratum of common sense came to my aid and I shook off the uncanny feeling. The dinner had to be gotten ready and again I rushed to the door to get at the refrigerator. Again, this time with the little half-querulous note I knew so well, I heard her voice: "Nellie!"

How I got into the room I do not know, but instantly that call was obeyed, and I stood for a second staring at the terribly empty bed. I threw myself on my knees and called to her: "Mother! Mother!" and God sent me tears.

In my stormy passion of crying I did not know nor care that Mrs. M. came running up to me calling me all the endearing names her Irish tongue could muster: "Och, Ellen asthore! 'Twas forgetting I was to be telling you that Ed had the outside stairs taken away entirely. They were rickerty this long time back, and he has been keeping his things in my ice-box for the past few days." I realized then that if my effort to reach the refrigerator had not been checked I should have fallen to the cement pavement below!

Mrs. M. put down to nervousness the wild look I gave her, but she could not know that it was not into her eyes I looked, but into the dear eyes closed forever.

I have no explanation to give. I do not believe the dead can come back, nor have I been stirred by the wave of the occult that has swept over us since the war — but . . .

Notwithstanding the attitude of the literary sentimentalist, a curiosity as to "what the public wants" and expects is bound to be a constant preoccupation with the writer who has resolved to win success in his art. There are many kinds of audiences who can be and have been classified on the basis of their intelligence and their interests, all of whom are anxious to pay and praise you in the measure of your appeal to them. A study of this subject, however, is aside from our purpose here. What we must do now is to remember that the audience is a most vital part of your technical literary purpose.

Now, how are we to get hold of this audience and understand it? The question of determining *what* audience you wish to reach is a personal, not a technical, problem, and presents no very great difficulties. Most students can determine it simply by examining a number of the current magazines. When you know to whom you wish to appeal and what effect you wish to make, the more difficult problem is how to produce that effect. This brings us to our first task, namely, learning how to identify and name these effects.

This is not as easy as it seems. You read a story; you enjoy it; you say, " Yes, I got quite a thrill out of it; there's no mystery about that." As a *reader* that is all that is expected of you; but as a *writer* you must do more: you must analyze that effect and be able to state precisely what it was. Your purpose is to " put across " an emotional effect. What effect? You must be able to answer this question. Innumerable are the writers trying to put across all sorts of things without knowing precisely what these things are. They fail in the first step of their technique.

7. How to Identify Effects

Please turn back now to the selections used as illustrations in the passage beginning on page 7. Isolated, these bits of narrative necessarily lose much, but you will find, I think, that each makes an appreciable effect on you. Can you name this effect? We must not expect to agree absolutely on this question, since no two people respond alike to the same stimuli, but I think we will react with sufficient unanimity in each case to establish the principle.

I find that the first passage quoted stirs in me an amused curiosity as to the reasons for the broken engagement. The selection from William March stirs me to horrified pity — pity for the suffering men, horror that their agony should be treated with such indifference. The paragraph from Conrad Aiken rouses a contemplative pity for loneliness and a mild curiosity as to the situation hinted at. The scene from Conrad communicates a thrill of excitement. In the Milburn passage there is grim amusement at the shocking treatment of a dead body. The paragraph from Dorothy Parker conveys a feeling of ironic pity for the girl's efforts to forget.

Please observe that in stating the effect *you do not give a title to the piece in question, nor do you outline the plot.* You do not say that the effect of the Milburn piece is: A murdered man's body is kept in the woodshed because the ground is frozen too hard for burial. Such a statement would be a brief of the plot, and an *effect* is not a plot. THIS DISTINCTION MUST BE FIRMLY ESTABLISHED. When we state the effect of a story as written, or of a story to be written, we think of the impression on the reader which the plot or story action (plus appropriate writing) will make.

(Note: If you take your literary career seriously, I ask you, in your own interest, to give heed to the statements I have tried to emphasize in the preceding paragraph. I am anxious to spare you the puzzlements and despair most students of creative writing sooner or later experience. They do not grasp this distinction between effect and material; later they complain that they "simply can't finish their plots," not realizing that in most cases the basic cause of the difficulty is their failure to see that material is *what you work with* and effect *what you do with* the material.)

Three Examples Analyzed

Now here is a passage from *The Ordeal of Richard Feverel,* by George Meredith. It is the climax of the episode which Stevenson declared was the most dramatic scene in English prose. Richard, the hero, you remember, had deserted Lucy, his wife; had become involved in a quarrel affecting his " honor," and had accepted a challenge to fight a duel in France. Before proceeding to the combat, he comes home to see his wife and the baby son born in his absence.

"Darling! come and see him. He is here." She spoke more clearly, though no louder.

Richard had released her, and she took his hand, and he suffered himself to be led to the other side of the bed. His heart began rapidly throbbing at the sight of a little rose-curtained cot covered with lace like a milky summer cloud.

It seemed to him he would lose his manhood if he looked at that child's face.

"Stop!" he cried suddenly. . . .

O God! what an ordeal was this! that tomorrow he must face death, perhaps die and be torn from his darling — his wife and child; and that ere he went forth, ere he could dare to see his child and lean his head reproachfully on his young wife's breast — for the last time, it might be — he must stab her to the heart, shatter the image she held of him.

"Lucy!" She saw him wrenched with agony, and her own face took the whiteness of his — she bending forward to him, all her faculties strung to hearing. He held her two hands that she might look on him and not spare the horrible wound he was going to lay open to her eyes.

"Lucy. Do you know why I came to you tonight?"

She moved her lips repeating his words.

"Lucy. Have you guessed why I did not come before?"

Her head shook widened eyes.

"Lucy. I did not come because I was not worthy of my wife! Do you understand?"

"Darling," she faltered plaintively, and hung crouching under him, "what have I done to make you angry with me?"

"O beloved!" cried he, the tears bursting out of his eyes. "O beloved!" was all he could say, kissing her hands passionately.

She waited, reassured, but in terror. . . .

And he wavered. He had not reckoned on her terrible suffering. She came to him, quiet. "I knew you would remain." The words quavered as she spoke them.

He was almost vanquished by the loveliness of her womanhood. She drew his hand to her heart, and strained it there under one breast. "Come; lie on my heart," she murmured with a smile of holy sweetness.

He wavered more, and dropped to her, but summoning the powers of hell, kissed her suddenly, cried the words of parting, and hurried to the door. It was over in an instant. She cried out his name, clinging to him wildly, and was adjured to be brave, for he would be dishonored if he did not go. Then she was shaken off. Later Mrs. Berry found her sitting on the floor senseless, the child in her lap. She had taken the child from its sleep and tried to follow her husband with it as her strongest appeal to him, and had fainted.*

What is the effect of this? Saying that it is "highly dramatic" doesn't give us our answer. Saying this merely gives an idea of the *form* of the passage. The spectacle of a wife's losing her passionately loved husband under these circumstances is tragic, of course. What kind of tragedy? Do you sympathize with the characters? With the wife, certainly, and, with the husband too, as brutal as this particular action is, when you know the whole story — the author's point is that his hero's misfortunes were due to his father's methods of bringing him up. The reader therefore pities him. The effect of this scene alone, then, is tragic pathos. When the spectacle of the father's hopes and disappointments as developed in the novel is included in the picture, the effect is also ironic.

Now let me give you another example which produces an effect differing widely from the quotation from Meredith above. Level, a French writer who specializes in effects of horror, ends a story of a jealous husband who killed both his wife and the guilty lover in the following fashion.

He had slowed down. The sweep of the scythe was almost noiseless. The wheat fell to the earth without a sound. When he was almost under the tree he heard the sound of kisses. Pulling himself up to his fullest height, with a furious movement he lifted the scythe. The blade leapt up, gleaming white in the sun, came down and plunged. . . . Two horrible shrieks rang out, and two frightful things, two heads, bounded up and fell again, bespattering the stalks that broke with a grating sound. . . . The scythe flew up out of the corn waves, all red. . . .

What effect did you get from this? I think you will agree that it was pure horror. We'll let it go at that this time — unadulterated horror. Now the very great difference between this effect and that produced by the lyric

* From *The Ordeal of Richard Feverel*, by George Meredith Charles Scribner's Sons.

love scene above is not a difference in size or amount or numbers of people, or things, but a difference in *quality*, and expertness in detecting such differences in quality of feelings and emotions must become a part of your equipment.

Your first practice in naming effects will probably be more difficult than you expected and you may wonder why this is. The difficulty is explained by the fact that many effects shade into each other imperceptibly. Qualities generally, in fact, are harder to determine than quantities. Another thing: While there are an infinite number of varieties in emotional effect, as we shall learn later, the range of these effects is not very great. You have heard it said that " love is not far removed from hate." " The sadness of beauty " is also familiar. A large number of differences within a small range means inevitably that some of the differences involve very nice and subtle distinctions. You should become sensitive to these subtleties.

Here is one more example. It will probably produce an effect upon you which off-hand you may say is much like that of the first lyric example above, but really it is quite different. Billy Baxter, aged seventeen, in Booth Tarkington's classic on young love, has just been asked a question by his adored, and he is " stumped."

William, seated upon a stool at her feet, gazed up at the amber head, divinely splashed by the rain of moonlight. The fire with which she spoke stirred him as few things had ever stirred him. He knew she had just revealed a side of herself which she reserved for only the chosen few who were capable of understanding her, and he fell into hushed rapture. It seemed to him that there was a sacredness about this moment, and he sought vaguely for something to say that would live up to it and not be out of keeping. Then, like an inspiration, there came into his head some words he had read that day and thought beautiful. He had found them beneath an illustration in a magazine, and he spoke them almost instinctively. . . .

" Don't you think love is sacred? " he said in the deepest tone of which his vocal cords were capable.

" Ess," said Miss Pratt.

"I do!" William was emphatic. "I think love is the most sacred thing there is. I don't mean *some* kinds of love. I mean *real* love. You take some people, I don't believe they ever know what real love means. They *talk* about it maybe, but they don't understand it. Love is something nobody can understand unless they feel it and — and if they don't understand it they don't feel it. Don't *you* think so?"

"Ess."

"Love," William continued, his voice lifting and thrilling to the great theme — "love is something nobody can ever have but one time in their lives, and if they don't have it then, why probably they never will. Now, if a man *really* loves a girl, why, he'd do anything in the world she wanted him to. Don't *you* think so?"

"Ess, 'deedums!" said the silvery voice.

"But if he didn't, then he wouldn't," said William vehemently. "But when a man really loves a girl, he will. Now, you take a man like that and he can generally do just about anything the girl he loves wants him to. Say, f'rinstance, she wants him to love her even more than he does already — or almost anything like that — and sup'posin' she asks him to. Well, he would go ahead and do it. If they really loved each other he would!"

He paused a moment, then in a lowered tone he said: "I think *real* love is sacred, don't you?"

"Ess."

"Don't you think love is the most sacred thing there is — that is, if it's *real* love?"

"Ess."

"*I* do," said William, warmly. "I — I'm glad you feel like that, because I think real love is the kind nobody could have but just once in their lives, but if it isn't *real* love, why — why most people never have it at all, because — " He paused seeming to seek for the exact phrase which would express his meaning " — because the real love a man feels for a girl and a girl for a man, if they *really* love each other, and, you look at a case like that, of course they would *both* love each other, or it wouldn't be real love — well, what *I* say is, if it's *real* love, well, it's sacred, because I think that kind of love is always sacred. Don't you think love is sacred if it's the real thing?"

"Ess," said Miss Pratt.*

Distinctly, here, we have "young romance" again, and this time there is introduced a comic shading. The effect

* From *Seventeen*, by Booth Tarkington, Harper and Brothers.

is a variety, a sub-species, if you will, of young love. For myself I should name it thus: Tender amusement at the floundering ardors of calf love.

This is enough, I think, to make clear the first principle of narrative technique. It is this: *Have a right purpose, namely, to produce an emotional effect; understand it; name it.* Many troubles in building plots, like most disputes which get nowhere, arise from the fact that the minds involved don't know exactly what they are trying to do. They haven't defined terms. Our first aim therefore is to see distinctly how our purpose differs from that of other forms of writing. From first to last we shall be thinking and talking of emotional effects. Specific names for them will serve as mental handles by which we can grasp and control them.

Following this chapter are assignments whose purpose is to help you make these first principles your own. Technical prowess means skill *in action.* Merely understanding an *idea* is not enough. All students, except those who have had considerable experience in professional writing, are urged to do all the assignments following this and succeeding chapters. If they will devise others similar to those given and perform them also, the additional practice will put them that much further on their way.

ASSIGNMENTS: CHAPTER ONE

ASSIGNMENT A

Please read the following exercises and on a sheet of paper, numbered according to the exercise, write down as exactly as possible the effect or impression which they make on you. A word of caution: If some of these sketches produce no effect on you, say so. For those that *do* affect you, however, *let your answer indicate the precise feeling or emotion aroused* no matter how slightly. Don't repeat in your answer any part of the sketches; don't try to tell what they mean; simply give your emotional responses.

Asterisks are placed at the end of those exercises answers to which are given in the Appendix. The answers to a few of the questions are given for these and for all the later assignments of the book in order that those students who work without instructors may have some guidance in doing this part of the work. These answers are not intended to be infallible for everyone. Personal susceptibilities are bound to cause variations in the responses of different people to given narrative arrangements. I have tried, in each case, however, to suggest the answer which an average student skilled in literary technique would make.

1. The little Dauphin is dying. In all the churches of the kingdom the Holy Sacrament remains exposed night and day, and great tapers burn, for the recovery of the royal child. The streets of the old capital are sad and silent, the bells ring no more, the carriages slacken their pace. Over there, in the direction of the stables, is heard a long and plaintive neighing; it is the little Dauphin's pony, forgotten by the hostlers, and calling sadly before his empty manger.*

2. Miss Larrabee was the society editor. Her professional pride in her work was as much a part of her life as her pride in her pompadour which at that time was so high that she had to tiptoe to reach it. However she managed to keep it up was the wonder of the office. We all agreed that she must use chicken fence, but she denied this. Nothing ruffled her spirits. No other girl in town came within a quarter of an inch of Miss Larrabee's dare. When straight-fronts became stylish, Miss Larrabee was a vertical marvel, and when she rolled up her sleeves and organized a country club, she referred to her shoes as boots and took the longest steps in town. But with it all she was no mere clothes-horse. She did her work well.*

3. Today, the schooner, *Abbie Rose,* dropped anchor in the

upper river, manned only by a crew of one. The out-bound freighter *Mercury* sighted the *Abbie Rose* off Block Island on Thursday last, acting in a suspicious manner. A boat-party sent aboard, found the schooner in perfect order and condition, sailing under four lower sails, the top-sails being pursed up to the mastheads but not stowed. With the exception of a yellow cat, the vessel was found to be utterly deserted, though her small boat still hung in the davits. No evidences of disorder were visible in any part of the craft. The dishes were washed up, the stove in the galley was still slightly warm to the touch, everything in its proper place with the exception of the vessel's papers which were not to be found.*

4. In the parapet of the fine staircase in Oxford Examination Hall there is a piece of Labradorite with a bewitching blue color that recalls the tail of a peacock and the wing of a Morpho butterfly. It is interesting to notice how it rivets the attention of visitors — this little bit of color amid the stateliness and beauty of architectural form. Why is it that this changeful splash warms so many hearts, even more than the poetic tower of Magdalen? What is the magic of color? [1] *

5. There was a snort from the steers, a quick clap of horns and hoofs from far within the herd, a tremor of the plain, a roar, a surging mass — and Wade was riding the flank of a wild stampede.

And he was riding for his life. He knew it. His horse knew it. He was riding to turn the herd, too, back from the rim, as the horse also knew. The cattle were after water — water-mad — ready to go over the precipice to get it, carrying horse and rider with them. It was black as death. He could see nothing in the sage, could scarcely discern the pounding, panting shadows at his side; but he knew by the swish of the brush and the plunging of the horse that the ground was growing stonier, that they were nearing the rocks.

6. The laws pertaining to proportions that are gratifying, to balance that satisfies, are natural laws quite like those that govern equilibrium and gravity. Whatever is pleasing in music, poetry, in architecture, painting and sculpture, is so because of its appeal to our emotions. A sensing of rhythm is instinctive with us. The cadence of sounds, the contour of forms, the interesting variety of related things, all make their appeal to us through rhythm. A study similar to that required for composing in music or verse is necessary to appreciate and understand the rhythms that make a picture pleasing. In this study we must be patient with our emotional apparatus. The faculties by which we appreciate harmonies are also those by which we create them. Emotion furnishes the impulse to create. Though art has emotional rather than intellectual appeal, an intellectual study of it induces a desire to create.[2]

[1] Reprinted by permission from *Riddles of Science,* by Sir J. Arthur Thompson, published by Liveright Publishing Corporation.
[2] Reprinted by permission from *Composition and Rendering,* by A. Thornton Bishop, published by John Wiley & Sons, Inc.

7. There is nothing more disenchanting to man than to be shown the springs and mechanism of any art. All our arts and occupations lie wholly on the surface; it is on the surface that we perceive their beauty, fitness, and significance; and to pry below is to be appalled by their emptiness and shocked by the coarseness of the strings and pulleys. In a similar way, psychology itself, when pushed to any nicety, discovers an abhorrent baldness, but rather from the fault of our analysis than from any poverty native to the mind. And perhaps in aesthetics the reason is the same; those disclosures which seem fatal to the dignity of art seem so perhaps only in the proportion of our ignorance; and those conscious and unconscious artifices which it seems unworthy of the serious artist to employ were yet, if we had the power to trace them to their springs, indications of a delicacy of the sense finer than we conceive, and hints of ancient harmonies in nature.

8. Forty-nine widows of soldiers who fought in the War of 1812 are still drawing pensions. Reckoning by the age of the eldest of these ladies, it would seem that a grateful nation continues to be bled for 100 years after the actual participators in a war have stopped bleeding. In the light of its contribution to the world's joy and wisdom, the importance of the War of 1812 diminishes as time goes on and if, as is probable, a centenarian pensioner may still live in 1964, her presence alone may mean more to the world than the killing-match which she serves to recall.*

9. An Indian native tells how he saw a young girl belonging to his tribe killed by a tiger, his tale ending, in substance, as follows:

The tiger played with and tortured the girl, precisely as we have all seen a cat treat a maimed mouse. Again and again Minah crawled laboriously away, only to be drawn back by her tormentor when he seemed at last to have exhausted his interest in her. At times she lay still in a paralysis of inertia, only to be goaded into agonized motion once more by a touch of the tiger's claws. Yet, so cunningly did he manipulate his victim, that — as Mat afterward described it — "a time sufficient to enable a pot of rice to be cooked," elapsed ere the girl was finally put out of her misery.

10. Veritably he did stand in the presence of death. The place looked dead and smelled dead and was dead. The air was heavy-laden with bone-yard scents — rot and corrosion and rust and dust. With the taints of moulded leather and gangrened metal, of worm-gnawed woodwork and moth-eaten fabrics, arose also from beneath their feet that other stench which inevitably is begotten of neglect and lonesomeness within any spot inclosed by walls and a roof, provided sun and wind and human usage are excluded from it long enough. Offcutt sniffed, and, over Verba's shoulder, looked about him.

Close at hand Offcutt was aware of crawling things which might be spiders, and a long grey rat which scuffled across the floor almost beneath his feet, dragging its scaled tail over the boards with a nasty, rasping sound. He heard other rats squealing and gnawing in the wainscoting behind him. He was aware, also, of the dirt, which scabbed and crusted everything. And he felt as though he had invaded the vault of an ancient tomb. Sure enough, in a manner of speaking, he had done just that.

11. The myth is that the automobile as we know it has dropped the horse, but the fact is the opposite. Much as they bragged about the "horseless age," the pioneers missed Dobbin out in front. Without him the front seemed empty. The curved dash was too abstract a substitute and too insubstantial. They hit on the sheet-iron bonnet. Sometimes this bonnet concealed a motor, but in the beginning quite as often it did not. The fact only gradually followed the effect. Had the men of 1900 to 1910 been acquainted with modern abstract art they would have understood better what it was that they were doing. The "bonnet," now our familiar hood, was simply the horse rendered abstract, the horse stylized. And that is why Professor Klemin, already quoted, can wryly remark, "That the early automobiles were like carriages is no more remarkable than the fact that they still are like them." [1]

12. The Hon. Galahad Threepwood, in his fifty-seventh year, was a dapper little gentleman on whose gray but still thickly covered head the weight of a consistently misspent life rested lightly.

His flannel suit sat jauntily upon his wiry frame, a black-rimmed monocle gleamed jauntily in his eye. Everything about this Musketeer of the 90's was jaunty. It was a standing mystery to all who knew him that one who had had such an extraordinarily good time all his life should, in the evening of that life, be so superbly robust. Wan contemporaries who had once painted a gas-lit London red in his company, and were now doomed to an existence of dry toast, Vichy water and German cure resorts, felt very strongly on this point. A man of his antecedents, they considered, ought by rights to be rounding off his career in a bath chair instead of flitting about the place, still chaffing head waiters as of old and calling for the wine list without a tremor. [2]

13. After federal secret-service men had arrested Frank Agnello because they saw him making an unlawful sale of cocaine, went to his house and searched it for the source of supply, which they found. That evidence helped to convict Agnello; but the Supreme Court upset the conviction because the search of his house without a warrant was "unreasonable." The fact that delay between arrest and search, while a warrant was procured, might have permitted confederates to destroy the evidence made no impression on the Court. The law was laid down flatly, for murder, burglary, bootlegging, or any other crime, that "the search of a private dwelling without a warrant is, in itself, unreasonable and abhorrent to our laws." [3]

[1] Reprinted by permission from "From Automobile to Roadplane," by Douglas Haskell, published in *Harper's*, July, 1934.

[2] Reprinted by permission from *Heavy Weather*, by P. G. Wodehouse, published by Little, Brown & Co.

[3] Reprinted by permission from "If Judges Wrote Detective Stories," by John Barker Waite, published in *Scribner's*, April, 1934.

14. Under the shade of the awning, stretched out to his full length, the negro lay quiet. He lay face down against the sidewalk, his nose flattened against the gray cement. Wiping the blade neatly and thoroughly against the fallen man's back, the trucker who had done the stabbing cleaned the blade, darted next door, placed the knife on the counter, and then came back.

Both truckers started whistling a quick tune, flatly.

On the wagon-seat the small boy, his eyes popping from his head, was breathing hoarsely. He was conscious that the argument up the street was still going strong, but his eyes were glued on the negro's broad, quiet back, on a blotch of red which was spreading slowly, staining the center of the man's shirt.[1] *

ASSIGNMENT B

This assignment provides a beginning in narrative writing controlled by a single effect. To make this first experiment simple and yet illustrate quite sharply the relation between *substance* and *effect,* I offer below, for your revision, some sentences in which the substance is quite clear but the effect confused. In each sentence you will find words or phrases which differ so widely in the *effects* they create that the *total effect* of the sentence is absurd. Each sentence, as it now stands, actually makes one effect, but it is the humor of incongruity. The exercise is to test your ability to analyze these simple cases of " unintentional humor," and then to rewrite each sentence so that the incongruity vanishes, and only a single impression is produced. If this impression is to be humorous, let it be deliberate, and not inadvertent.

In the first example the incongruity of effects is produced by the juxtaposition of the casual, wholly ordinary thought of a man in a blue suit, with the shocking, overwhelming thought of his also being a corpse. These two thoughts cannot be brought so closely together without disharmony. One way to revise, then, would be to leave out the less important detail, thus: " The body was found in the bathroom."

A more difficult rearrangement would use all of the given material, modifying it in such a way as to make it all produce a single impression. Thus: " There was no clue to the victim's identity, except that he was found in the bathroom, that he was wearing a blue suit, and that he had the well-cared-for hands and soft body of a man of leisure."

In the second example, if you revise by merely cutting the irrelevant, your sentence will read: " Mrs. J. has given birth to twins."

[1] Reprinted by permission from " Going to Market," by Albert Halper, published in *Harper's*, October, 1932.

The second type would be: " Mrs. J. who speaks five languages is having hysterics in all five; she has just become the mother of twins."

Try rewriting these sentences. In each case, first, eliminate enough to unify; second, revise to produce the effect named in the brackets, *without* eliminating any of the substance given. The trick, as I have shown by my illustration, is simply to be careful that widely contrasting effects are not brought too closely together.

1. A gentleman in a blue suit is lying dead in the bath room.
   [Relate the suit and the idea in *gentleman* to the death, for an effect of mystery.]
2. A woman who speaks five languages has just given birth to twins.
   [Relate by means of the numbers, for an effect of amusement at the predicament.]
3. He has a large nose and a fine reputation as an actor.
   [Relate the first detail as a cause for the second, to make an impression of amused admiration.]
4. The scenery around his home is very beautiful and he has an excellent cook.
   [Relate both details to character, for an effect of contempt.]
5. He suffered horribly in the war and he writes good poetry.
   [Relate both details to war, for any single impression.]
6. Sarah's tea room is famous. She is making money. Her cocoanut tea cakes are especially delicious. Her husband deserted her five years ago.
   [Connect to impress the reader with an amusing comment on life.]
7. The groom is state tennis champion. He has been engaged to four other girls. He doesn't want a large, formal wedding.
   [Connect as cause and effect, for single impression of character.]
8. Jane likes good food. She is the daughter of Jonas Brown who committed suicide.
   [Combine for a single ironic impression of character.]
9. The cars crashed near the bridge. One girl was killed; the other seriously injured. Jim caught three bass that afternoon.
   [Combine for an ironic comment on character.]
10. He has large feet. His father was a clown in a circus.
   [Combine as cause and effect, for an impression of farcical amusement.]

ASSIGNMENT C

Turn back to Assignment A of this chapter and write little sketches of your own, reproducing, as nearly as you can, exactly the same emotional effect as that produced by each one of them. Do not hesitate to imitate these same sketches somewhat, if you wish. Naturally, if you can use different and original material, so much the better. In studying the models, observe not merely the vocabulary, but the sensuous details which the author has chosen.

ASSIGNMENT D

In the following sketch three sorts of materials are combined. Some details clearly suggest a love interest, others seem related to the crime situation, others build a general picture of a boy's character. The first task is to recognize in each detail its emotional relationship to one or another of these interests.

1. Read the sketch through and with pencil underline in your book the details related to the love interest. Next, copy out, literally, these details, unchanged. Now re-write to make the reader sympathize with this love situation, using any other details which will help that love interest.

2. Again go through the sketch, this time underlining the crime interest. Use blue pencil or in some other way distinguish this work from your analysis in number 1. Again copy out, literally, these details. Finally, re-write, to produce an effect of suspense as to the young criminals' activities.

3. This time, mark out the material that sharply suggests character, and again copy, literally. Re-write, to produce an effect of sympathetic understanding of the boy's character.

Pete was on his way to Clark's waterfront warehouse where Buddy Ames had telephoned him to come at midnight.

Pete was wearing a shabby blue serge suit. When he passed a street light, his yellow hair shone almost white. On his large feet he wore brown sneakers. He was very fond of flowers.

As he walked down Elm Street he passed Sam's diner. He went in and ordered a hamburger sandwich. Boy, he was hungry. He ate fast, crowding his mouth. Sam's place was next to a print shop. The presses were running — a rush job for somebody. He paid, and went on down toward the pier. His feet hurt. He'd been peddling books all day, and he wasn't any nearer a college education than he had been that morning.

He walked with his hand in his coat pocket, fingering three paper clips, two small nickel bolts and a pencil stub. The pencil stub he'd picked up on the golf links, where he sometimes caddied. They'd found the body of a man behind the caddy house, day before yesterday. Well dressed. No one knew him.

Pete stumbled over something as he crossed the lane to the warehouse door. He lighted a match and stooped. It was a dead puppy, a cute little wire, about half grown. Hit by a car, of course. Pete could remember the mutt he'd owned years ago — a blend of all the kinds of dog there are, but with just one kind of devotion. He'd died of old age one Christmas night.

Pete went on. The warehouse was dark. He moved quietly along the wall to the old door that he and Buddy had learned how to open — their first job with a jimmie. Inside he moved forward a slow step at a time, and up the stairs. The place smelled of tar, and rotten sea weed, and old wood, and dead fish.

The stairs in the courthouse were white marble. Pete's mother was a scrubwoman in the courthouse. The stairs at home were steel, with slate treads. The halls at home smelled of filth and old beer. The runway out at the beach club was polished smooth and white by sand.

At the top of the stairs, in the darkness, he waited. He didn't hear a sound except the water slopping against the piles, and an engine hooting somewhere far off. His wrist watch glowed. It was eleven thirty. Buddy was late.

Pete and Buddy had gone to public school. Buddy had been pretty good at arithmetic — for a time he'd planned to take a course in accounting. That was before he found out how easy it was to collect spending money with a black jack. Pete hadn't liked arithmetic. He liked reading and compositions. In sixth grade he'd written a piece about a vacation that had been published in the school paper.

The school had been named for Pete's great grandfather, one of the founders of the town, whose fine old house had been made into a museum. Pete looked a lot like a portrait of the old man that hung in one of the rooms, with a memorial tablet under it, but no one ever thought of Pete in connection with the town's most noted citizen. Black sheep are conveniently forgotten.

The warehouse was dark. Pete's match flared. He walked slowly to the small window. In the dark again, he took out the handkerchief that his girl had given him for his birthday. She'd embroidered on it his initial — pale blue. With it he wiped cobwebs from the dirt-crusted window.

He could see below the dark mass of the pier. It roused happy memories. An eight-year-old, he'd fished off it with his father, and he'd learned to dive from the highest pile. He'd made love to Louise in its shadows. In the bay the little catboats of the infant class were pulling at their moorings. Far at the right, two of the houseboats were lighted brilliantly. One of them belonged to a woman who had been Pete's music teacher before she married money. She'd tried to make him play Paderewski's Minuet, and he'd learned enough to recognize it when he heard it.

The other houseboat belonged to a rough crowd that spent so much money in the town that the constable never got up the nerve to object to their noise on weekends.

At twelve thirty Pete decided Buddy wasn't coming. He went down the stairs, carefully, and home. On the corner of Market Street in front of a drug store, he picked up a dime. That bought him a pack of cigarettes. Boy, a nail was what he'd needed.

At eight next morning Clark opened his warehouse. At the foot of the stairs to the loft lay a man, unconscious — blackjacked. At the hospital, the victim was identified as Buddy Ames.

ASSIGNMENT E

The five quotations below, four from stories published in two of our most distinguished literary magazines, are examples of extreme effects. Two of them illustrate the so-called " hard-boiled " style of realism which has marked much of the writing of the post-Victorian revolt, and all picture death. The commonest of all fictional effects is the romantic (see Chapter Two, Assignment C); and the strongest effects are those produced by death. If you are determined to attempt the most powerful effects in fiction, you will be repaid by this exercise; if on the other hand, you can summon no interest in the gruesome and terrible, you will be excused for passing on to more engaging lessons.

1. These five excerpts produce among them the following effects: tragic pathos, revulsion, horrified amazement, suspense, and horror. This list does not follow the order in which the passages appear. The assignment is to decide to which of the quotations each of the listed " effects " belongs. This is a simple test of analysis which should be performed by every conscientious student.

2. Having determined the precise flavor of tragedy or horror in each of these selections, write studies duplicating these effects, using other materials. This exercise is more difficult — and more valuable — than the first.

3. The effect of horror is part of the impression of three of these five quotations. Re-write these three, keeping to the material and action of the original as closely as possible, but altering each enough to eliminate entirely the flavor of horror. This is difficult. It not only requires careful analysis of these effects, but tests your ingenuity in invention. If you can't solve this third " brain teaser," omit it; return to it, after finishing with the next four chapters, and you will find it easy.

1. But inside the house was the terrible part. You could hear Duke screaming, and in between Duke was the tiger. And both of them was screams of fear, but I think the tiger was worse. It is a awful thing to hear an animal letting out a sound like that. It kept up about five minutes after I got there, and then all of a sudden you couldn't hear nothing but the tiger. And then in a minute that stopped.

There wasn't nothing to do about the fire. In a half hour the whole place was gone, and they was combing the ruins for Duke. Well, they found him. And in his head was four holes, two on each side, deep. We measured them fangs of the tiger. They just fit.[1] *

[1] Reprinted by permission from " Baby in the Icebox," by James M. Cain, published in *The American Mercury,* January, 1933.

2. He was shocked. He confessed it to himself. Shocked. The dim electric bulb, through its dirty, white-glass shade, cast a frightening light. It was only because he was familiar with his patient's features, had been so for the past ten years, that he recognized her at all. A gaunt and bony creature lay under the comforter. Its long arms, brown and stiff, were stretched over the sides of the coverlet, the hands lying tensed and open. On the white of the pillow the long, narrow head lay, a cadaverous thing, topped with a coarse wig. The skin of the forehead and chin was cross-hatched with lines.

Looks as though she had been soaking in formaline, thought the doctor, and a sensation of disgust rose in his nostrils as he saw the long, ugly hairs that sprouted from the corners of her lips and the knob of her chin. Her cheeks were furrowed, too, and led innumerable radii toward her eyes. Her eyebrows had grown wildly till they were a dark, bushy bar over the deep black, fireless coals of her eyes, but the lashes had disappeared almost entirely. Longevity also has its disappointments, he mused, as he detected about the bed the revolting odor of the unburied dead.[1]

3. " She wants to see you," he said briefly. " It'll be over in a few minutes. It isn't even worth while taking off her clothes. She's hacked to a fare-you-well."

We stepped into the tiny hospital ward. On the bed nearest the door was a huddled mound of dirty, bloody clothes — slim gray kid boots with silk laces and tassels at the top, a mauve skirt slashed into ribbons, a blood-stiffened lace blouse — and above, a head so swathed in bandages that nothing showed but a tiny circle of face with long brown lashes lying on the waxen, yellow skin. At the foot of the bed crouched Cazador, dyed scarlet with blood — scarlet like the sins of his mistress. He whined when he saw me, and sidled closer to an edge of skirt that hung to the floor.

The Doctor and I stood on either side of the bed, watching the still form, listening to the quick, painful breathing.

" God! " said the Doctor softly. " The pity of it — the waste of it. But it was inevitable. She was headed for this from the minute she was born, with her Indian mind and her Gringo soul and her beautiful body. She never had a ghost of a chance."

As he finished speaking, the long lashes lifted. Encarnación was looking at me, and in her brown-velvet eyes was neither fright nor pain — only a sort of numbed puzzlement.[2] *

4. Now that the murder was a thing accomplished, Eric felt suddenly relieved and surfeited. Miss Prung, the governess, hung from a rope in the nursery where Eric had hanged her; and no one, he felt sure, was as yet aware of the killing except Miss Prung and himself. The lady had been fully cognizant of his proceedings for a good half hour, or, to be exact, from the instant when Eric had slipped the rope over her head and encompassed the thin neck in its noose, until that

[1] Reprinted by permission from " Travail," by Louis Zara Rösenfeld, published in *The American Mercury*, December, 1932.

[2] Reprinted by permission from " Encarnación," by Alicia O'Reardon Overbeck, published in *Harper's*, April, 1930.

later and even more ecstatic moment, when, with a shiver of pain and ultimate horror, her bulging eyes had opened upon eternity. Perhaps it was more than thirty minutes, but it seemed less, his interest had so intensified the time; he had just stood there, thrillingly near her kicking feet, wringing his fingers with a nervous delight, and watched the contortions of her changing face: the expression of surprise, and anger; the screw of pain; the grimace of twitching terror, and the final mask of death. It seemed that he had hanged five Miss Prungs, not one; and he was glad, terribly glad, that he had chosen her to be his — yes, he must qualify the word — his *first* victim.

His idea, his great idea, had dawned very suddenly upon him, so late as yesterday, when, in the company of some friends, he had attended a matinee performance of marionettes.[1]

5. A gun *bammed.* "The hell you say," cried an hysterical voice, and Cormaney felt the jar as a bullet planted itself in the body of his prisoner and shield. He fired twice through the crack of the door. Someone hooted — a body tumbled, and there was the crash of heavy steel. "That's the Tom-gun," thought Cormaney, "on the floor — " He fired again. Something clipped his ear; a heavy timber seemed to slam against his left arm. He dropped the reeling Figgis and fell back beside the staircase.

The woman had gone out of the front door, screeching, crazy and dangerous, but unarmed. Olson met her on the steps and thoughtfully tripped her over on the turf below as he plunged upon the porch. Teed, with his mighty weight, caved in the flimsy kitchen door. Someone bawled, "Okay," and through the rank haze they could see two men with their hands up. The other two were on the floor. One was dead, killed by Cormaney's first shot, and the other was a young red-head with green eyes and an evil mouth, who lay there gasping for breath. The dead Figgis lay in the doorway, and the blood from Cormaney's forearm splashed down upon him.

"God," breathed Cormaney, grinning painfully, "you Newark cops — are — fast on your feet."[2]

[1] Reprinted by permission from "Introduction To Eric," by Ellis St. Joseph, published in *Harper's*, June, 1933.
[2] Reprinted by permission from "Something Like Salmon," by MacKinlay Kantor, in *Detective Fiction Weekly*, August 19, 1933, and reprinted in *Short Story Hits, 1933*, Harcourt, Brace and Co.

CHAPTER TWO

THE UNIFIED EFFECT

If you wish your audience to get a thing, you have to tell them that you are going to do it, and while it is being done you must tell them that you are doing it, and after it is done you must tell them that it is done — and then they won't understand it.

— Quoted by BRANDER MATTHEWS.

In the previous chapter we learned that the narrator's main task is to produce emotion in the reader; we studied, in other words, the principles governing the *quality* of the effect to be produced. In this chapter we shall concern ourselves with the principles controlling the *number* of such effects. Our topic is now the general problem of unity in narrative. This brings us face to face with the most important single problem in our whole study of fictional technique — the single emotional effect. It is important because, so far as the short story is concerned, it is an absolute principle; superlative narrative without drama, for instance, is often produced, but in the briefer forms of narrative high excellence, without a dominant impression, cannot be achieved. More students and writers come to grief in their short story writing because of a violation of this principle of the dominant effect, than for any other reason.

This problem of the single effect of short fiction was stated and partly explained in philosophical terms seventy-five years ago by Poe; it has been restated and re-explained by text book writers ever since until a few years ago the psychology of the matter was briefly set forth for the first time by Professor Pitkin. The issue is kept alive not because it tickles the disputatious intellect of " high

43

brow " critics or concerns some purely abstract principle, right to the discovery of which is jealously claimed by different " schools " of academic thought. No: the principle of the single effect is inherent in nature itself; it can be understood by grasping a few fairly simple facts about the human mind: and in this chapter we will take a very close look at these facts.

1. Three Important Principles

For our practical purposes in managing the art of narrative all that we need to know about emotional effects can be set forth in three brief statements of principles, as follows:

1. A short story can have only one emotional effect and this effect provides its unity.
2. The limit of length of the short story is determined by the length of time a reader can follow this single effect without fatigue.
3. A novelette or novel may have any number of emotional effects, unity being determined by subject matter.

Now let us examine these statements one at a time. May I ask you, please, to try to discard, at least for the moment, whatever ideas you may have as to the nature of unity in the different forms of narrative? I well recall that my own struggle with this subject was protracted mainly because I brought to my study my own devoutly held heresies. Again and again I see my own students grimly endeavoring to reconcile new ideas to their old ones, elaborating fancied relevancies and connections rather than relinquish their cherished theories. I shall assume as little as possible. Please have patience with every step of the development.

2. Unity of the Short Story

Let us begin with what we learned in Chapter One. We there discovered that narrative differs from other forms

of writing mainly in the nature of the *effect* it makes on
the reader: the other forms of writing, description, exposition, and argumentation, appeal mainly to the reader's
intellect, while narrative appeals mainly to the reader's
feelings or emotions. Narrative, as we learned, makes
some appeal to the intellect too: the reader has some objective interest in the thing written about; he is often
interested in the workmanship; he generally takes an active
part in the solution of any problem being worked out in
the plot; such activities are indeed mental, but they are
incidental. The reader's chief interest in narrative is in
being *moved, impressed, thrilled.*

Concrete Effects Analyzed

This afternoon I heard a Wagner program at a symphony
concert. The plaintive, poignant Prelude to *Lohengrin*
brought tears to my eyes. The " Love-Death " passage
in *Tristan and Isolde* produced a saddened and peacefully
meditative mood. The " Ride of the Valkyrie " sent cold
shivers of delight up and down my spine. During the
winter at an exhibition of paintings I saw a canvas depicting an apple orchard snowy with blossoms, with sunlight dappling the grass, and a spacious warmth and glad-
ness over all that stirred in me hatred of the winter chill,
made me restless over my plight in being unable to get
outdoors in weather I most enjoy, and brought a flash
of yearning for a hoped-for vacation. I remember also
my first view of Milan Cathedral, a never-to-be-forgotten
moment of awe and wonder. All these reactions were distinctly feelings. They are characteristic of the response
produced by all great art, and they are especially characteristic of the art of narrative.

I mention these reactions thus specifically in order that
you may have a very definite idea of what we are talking
about when we speak of narrative effects. The writer in
producing a story thinks more than he feels — to him the

process is work; the reader feels more than he thinks — to him the process is play. Our problem of unity in narrative is, as you shall see, a problem of what happens to the reader.

We can agree now, I think, that narrative writing differs from all other types of writing mainly in its deliberate appeal to the feelings and emotions. Our purpose here, however, is more narrow, namely: to determine how the *special type* of narrative called the short story differs from *all other types* of narrative. The difference here is a difference in the way the emotional effects are handled. *The short story can produce only one dominant emotional effect; longer types can produce more than one effect.*

I am going to assume, for the moment, that you do not agree to this, or perhaps do not yet see the necessity for it. To restrict a short narrative in this manner, you may be thinking, is to make it artificial and untrue to life; thus restricted, a multitude of things that happen in real life involving multiple effects are forbidden to short story treatment; and you resent any such " formalistic standards." You may even protest that if one effect is good, more effects should be still better — the more the merrier! Let us take a concrete case and see.

A Terrible Example

Our first illustration of multiple effects I will make quite extreme in order that you may see as sharply as possible the principles involved. We will revert to the close of the previous chapter and fuse together in a more or less connected narrative the last three selections of emotional writings which we analyzed: young Richard Feverel's parting with his wife, the vengeance of the husband in the French " triangle " story, and the amours of Tarkington's Billy Baxter. Here is the composite story:

THE EPIC OF THE SCYTHE

OR

PAPA'S REVENGE

Silas mopped his sunburnt brow with his bandanna, seized his scythe, and started for the hay meadow, when his wife ran after him, crying out: "Darling! don't leave me; stay with me, O Silas —"

"O beloved!" cried he, the tears bursting out of his eyes. "O beloved!" was all he could say, kissing her hands passionately.

She waited, reassured, but in terror. She came to him, quiet. "I knew you would remain." The words quavered as she spoke them.

He was almost vanquished by her womanly charm. She drew his hand to her heart. "Come, let me kiss you," she murmured.

"Stop!" he replied, "let me alone, wife. Can't you see that the hay is ripe and must be cut? Why do you suppose I have been sharpening my scythe all morning? Let me go!"

"Darling," she pleaded, holding to his arm; "come and see him. He is here — there in the kitchen, in his little cradle — yours, Silas, your son. Oh, do not leave us!"

She took his hand and led him inside again. His heart began rapidly throbbing at the sight of the little cot, with its fluffy blankets. "Stop!" he cried again, pulling out his bandanna and, in his agony, beginning to try to sharpen his scythe with it. O God, what an ordeal was this — that in a few minutes he must commit murder, kill the grass that had grown so tenderly all summer — now it must die. How could he stab his young wife's heart, shatter the image she held of him.

"O beloved!" cried he, his voice breaking. He reached for his wife's trembling hands, as a suspender button burst, and kissed them lingeringly.

She waited, somewhat reassured, but in terror. "I knew you would remain," she muttered, as she picked up the button. "I knew you would not leave me." The words quavered, for she saw him tremble, heard his sudden words of parting, watched him leap for the door, flourishing his scythe as though it were a summer parasol.

Dodging a cow and leaping over a dog that yelped with terror, he sprang upon the ripened grain beyond the pig pen and began laying it low with all the energy of a parent innocently employed. "Swish, swish," sang the keen blade, and "I'll get the young devil yet," he muttered as he labored under the summer sun. Stopping to moisten the palms of his hands, he pricked up his ears. A faint lisping rose from the depths of the grain in front of him.

Still clutching his weapon, he got down on all fours and began to creep forward. Soon among the grain he caught sight of his son, William, and that abhorred object in a flowered dimity dress and a motion picture hat covered with baby sunflowers. "Devil!" he groaned, and perched himself on a clod of dirt to listen.

"Don't you think love is sacred?" It was William's voice. He could tell it a mile away; it was changing and he could hear the squeak.

"Ess." It was the siren's voice. "French, I'll bet," thought the parent; "she's afraid to talk English, afraid I'll understand her."

"*I* do!" The concert proceeded. "I think love is the most sacred thing there is. I mean *real* [squeak] love. Some people, I don't believe they ever know what real love means. Love is something nobody can understand unless they feel it. Don't *you* [squeak] think so?"

"Ess." Silas fell off the clump of dirt. He tried to think, but he couldn't. He clutched his scythe.

"Love," continued his son, his voice lifting and thrilling to the great theme, " — love is something nobody can ever have but one time in their lives, and if they don't have it then, why prob'ly they never will. Now if a man *really* [squeak] loves a girl, why he'd do anything in the world she wanted him to. Don't you think so?"

"Ess, 'deedum!" said the silvery voice, causing the audience to swallow its tobacco and begin to slink backwards like a scotched snake. "But if he didn't, then he wouldn't — " the squeak followed the retreating figure with fateful mockery, causing him, as he regained his former station to moisten again his palms and mutter, "I'll deedum a dinger — O boy!" Whereat he set to work with the scythe.

"Swish, swish," sang the keen blade like the mellow, hearty song of harvest. The tall grain fell to the earth without a sound. "Swish, swish," whistled the sturdy tool as it drew nearer and nearer to the young philosopher and his mate. "If only she don't say 'ess' again before I arrive!" groaned the laboring parent. "I'll teach them a thing or two. They ought to be feeding the pigs, both of them, this minute!"

When he had almost reached the lovely young couple, fair and perspiring under the magic of the August sun, he heard the sound of kisses. " Good Lord," he gasped, " I didn't think he had it in him! "

Pulling himself up to his fullest height, with a furious move-ment he lifted the scythe. The blade leapt up, gleaming white in the sun, came down and plunged. Two horrible shrieks rang out, and two frightful things, two heads, bounded up and fell again, bespattering the stalks that broke with a grating sound. The scythe flew up out of the corn waves, all red.

This is probably the world's worst piece of narrative. It is bad because of its utter lack of any consistency in character, any logic of action, or unity in emotional effect. It is possible, however, that in spite of these defects, you were amused by the tale. The very incongruity of the episodes produces the humor of burlesque; and humor, you will now say, is itself an effect, the single effect, really, of the piece; and — you perhaps now argue — thus the tale *has* a single effect, after all, a single effect produced by the mingling of other effects. I admit the point; but please consider:

Real Effects were Lost

First: Our original bargain was to produce a narrative *with multiple* effects, not with a single effect secured by a horrible mixture of several others. We considered the belief, often entertained, but quite false, that since life itself produces many effects, so should a short story which reproduces life. The more effects the merrier — we were to experiment with this idea and see what there was in it. Well, here we have passionate love, humorous calf love, sheer horror, and burlesque character comedy, and yet we find that the whole makes a rather definite effect of burlesque comedy. We have therefore failed with our *intended* effects. We tried for three and got one!

Second: The effects of the original passages, those quoted from the previous chapter, were, moreover, emo-tional, or would be emotional if written out; the effect we secure by our phantasmagoria is not emotional — it is a purely intellectual response to incongruities. The artist's purpose, we learned in the previous chapter, is to produce *maximum* effects with given material. Can we say that we have done this with our burlesque action? It is *an* effect but it isn't the biggest effect. We can be sure of this in view of our knowledge of what Meredith in *The Ordeal of Richard Feverel* did with our first episode alone. The effect we have secured is really maximum *ridicule* for having failed so completely either to fuse or present intact and side by side different emotional effects.

A Triple Effect Plot

I have said above that my literary fandango was a failure because of weaknesses in character, action and effects. You may have felt that its weakness was in character and action only; you may wonder, in other words, whether it might not be possible to eliminate the distortion of character, thus removing the burlesque note, rationalize the action, and so keep our original three emotional effects. This is a fair bargain. Let us try it. I will briefly outline my story again, this time keeping as strictly as possible to the original effects, and making the action as serious and as consistent as possible.

A. Silas, a stern father and hard-working farmer, has long disputed with his wife about the proper method to control his son, William. William is being vamped by the scheming daughter of Jones, whom Silas knows to be his enemy. The girl is ten years older than William and is interested only in inheriting Silas's farm. Silas, maddened with rage, tells his wife that he knows William is love-making in the grain field with the treacherous Sally and that he is going forth to kill one or the other of them. His wife, seeing his hysterical condition and physically unable to detain him, takes the only course left to her — she pleads her own love for him and urges him to look upon the face of their month-old baby, knowing that if he does, his heart will be softened.

B. Silas, having shaken off his wife, repairs to the wheat field and becomes an irate auditor of a love antiphony between his adolescent son and the latter's mature sweetheart. Here

Silas witnesses the climax of a long-protracted campaign on the part of Sally to capture the youth's heart. The conversation between the two is deep and real and extremely pathetic because of the complete ingenuousness of the youthful victim. The latter philosophizes soulfully and ungrammatically on his love, while Sally estimates the crops which his father's farm could be made to produce.

C. The final episode is much as in the former version. The father, seeing the cunning of his ancient enemy in the daughter's face, realizing that in her questions she is seeking information as to when he, Silas, will probably die, and his hatred for the clan of Jones suddenly maddening him, picks up his scythe and cuts off both their heads.

All the above action, I think you will admit, is at least possible. The burlesque note is entirely absent. The events are logically connected, mainly by Silas's connection with them all. Big drama, deep human passions are involved: tragic pity in *A*, tragi-comic pathos in *B*, and stark horror in *C*. Why will not this outline, written out in about eight or ten thousand words, make a good short story?

Answer: No emotional unity, no single effect.

Again our emotional effects neutralize each other. Even if they didn't neutralize each other, if they were simply different, we should have this situation: The artist's purpose, by definition (Chapter One), is to produce with given materials a one hundred per cent emotional response. The above story written out might, let us say, run to nine thousand words. Each of the three parts would take three thousand words. A reading of the story would produce the following results:

A.	Tragic pity	$33\frac{1}{3}\%$
B.	Tragi-comic pathos	$33\frac{1}{3}\%$
C.	Horror	$33\frac{1}{3}\%$

Please note that I have not added up these figures and set down the total. Why not? Simply because these particular things can no more be added to produce a homogeneous sum than can apples, elephants, and old shoes. If this seems incredible to you, try to think of one emotion into which all the above emotions would blend, thus becoming a summation of them all. None exists. If we can't blend these effects, the effects stand alone; and if they stand alone, all that you can say of carrying out your artistic purpose is that you have produced narrative with given materials which has an emotional result of one-third the power it should have. In trying to grasp all the effects possible, we have really grasped none.

The only way to secure a hundred per cent emotional result is obviously to select one or the other of the three dominant effects and use only such of the materials as will develop, emphasize, and glorify this one preconceived effect. How this is done we shall discover in the later portions of this book. Just now we are seeking to understand a principle, the law governing the unity of the short story. Let us repeat it: *the short story can have one and only one emotional effect.* One thing at a time is the rule here as in most efficient performances, and the " thing " in this case is a feeling or an emotion.

A noted French painter possessed a gallery of paintings all of which he hung with their faces turned to the wall. In displaying his pictures to visitors he turned them over one at a time. In this way the full effect of each painting was neither obscured nor neutralized by competition with the unharmonious effects of its neighbors. Here was a mechanical means of ensuring the full power of the single artistic effect.

Edgar Allan Poe's Historic Analysis

All of which prepares us, I think, to read and appreciate the most famous passage in all of Edgar Allan Poe's critical writings. This historic passage roughly summarizes what we have learned so far in our talk on narrative unity.

A skillful literary artist has constructed a tale. If wise, he has not fashioned his thoughts to accommodate his incidents; but having conceived, with deliberate care, a certain unique or single effect to be wrought out, he then invents such incidents — he then combines such events as may best aid him in establishing this preconceived effect. If his very initial sentence tends not to the outbringing of this effect, then he has failed in his first step. In the whole composition there should be no word written of which the tendency, direct or indirect, is not to the one pre-established design. As by such means, with such care and skill, a picture is at length painted which leaves in the mind of him who contemplates it with a kindred art a *sense of the fullest satisfaction*.

This pronouncement, we must remember, was written *after* a single effect deliberately striven for had appeared in both American and French short stories and *not before*. Poe was the first formulator of the theory of the single effect, not its father. He does not say, you observe, that everyone who writes brief narrative should strive for this ideal; he merely says he will do it if he is "wise." He will strive for it, that is, if he wishes to insure results with his readers; and that is all that can be said for it today. As long as the *average reader* prefers a hundred per cent emotional result in his fiction reading to a ten or thirty or eighty per cent result, just so long will the single effect ideal remain fixed for story tellers who wish their writings to be read and appreciated.

The most interesting thing about Poe's critical discovery is that he for the first time saw that the unifying principle of the short story concerned something that affected not the mind so much as the senses. Note that he compares the story with a picture which " leaves in the mind . . . a *sense* of the fullest *satisfaction*." This phrase indicates that while he fully appreciated the value of the principle in practice, he did not, naturally could not, fully understand the psychology of the matter. He evidently thought of sense impressions as being purely a functioning of the mind; later in the same essay, indeed, he refers to his

" undisturbed " effect as an " idea." We now know, how-ever, that sense impressions and thinking are two quite different processes.

Effects as Sense Impressions

It will not profit us to plunge into the mysteries of this question here. It is enough for us to know that while thought is involved both in grasping ideas and in recording sense impressions, the recording of sense impressions, the supreme purpose of the artist, involves parts of the body other than the mind. Psychologists tell us today that genuine emotion is roused by a conflict of impulses which are transmitted from the nerves to the muscles and that it is the friction of various sets of muscles pulling against each other in our bodies that produces what we know as " emotional states." We may therefore say that the fiction writer in striving for emotional effects, makes an attack on the reader's muscles!

We may state the matter more briefly by saying that the ideas of a story, the logic of the plot, appeal to the reader's mind, while its effects appeal to his body. The problem of the single effect of the short story is to appeal to but one muscle combination and to keep up that particular appeal until its response is as strong as possible!

Just why it is that the body responds to certain stimuli in certain ways — why, for instance, tears come into the eyes at beholding things lovely as well as sad — we do not know; nor would the knowledge greatly profit us. It is enough if we fully realize when we are dealing with ideas only and when with ideas that bring an emotional response.

Why do we more easily detect and identify thoughts than emotions? The reason is not hard to discover. Thought, reasoning, is essential to our work, our getting ahead in the world; our feelings and emotions, being associated almost entirely with our pleasures and recreations, are of less practical importance to us, and get less attention. Here we discover where the education of the artist differs most sharply from the education of the man of more practical affairs. The artist must be schooled to think too; he has need of all the intellect possible to him: but he must also school and train his feelings and emotional susceptibilities.

A Double Effect Landscape

A simple illustration will perhaps serve us well here. The biggest emotions of narrative are, of course, produced only by dramatic conflicts, as we shall learn in Chapter Four, but very definite feelings can be aroused by mere pictures suggesting places which have at some time actually affected us in reality or in imagination. Let us take a word picture of this sort which presents two definite " feeling tones " and see if we can identify them. I have taken two of the most contrasting, well-written bits of landscape I can find in modern fiction and rearranged them so that one blends off gradually into the other. This test of your sensitivity to effects will be nothing like as easy as was that offered by my own account of the unfortunate Silas, above, but with attention you can accomplish it.

THE ENCHANTED ISLE

Every summer when my longing for fresh air and solitude became no longer supportable, I repaired to my enchanted isle. A twenty-minute walk over the rolling moors and I found myself at the bit of picturesque shore line where I did my dreaming. Sinking into the warm sand between two rocks on the water's edge, I lit my pipe and gazed idly at the creaming-waves, the deliciously deep blue of the horizon, at the gulls, blackbirds, and swallows wheeling and darting through the illimitable bright air. All day I remained there in that sort of stupor and delicious prostration which are born of gazing at the sea.

You know, do you not, that pleasant intoxication of the mind? You do not think; nor do you dream. Your whole being escapes you, flies away, is scattered about. You are the gull that plunges into the sea, the spray that floats in the sunlight between two waves — the white smoke of yonder steamer rapidly disappearing, that little coral lightship with the banner of white smoke, that tang of salty vegetation, that warm caress of the sun — you are all this, you are anything except yourself. Oh, how many such hours of half-slumber and of mental dispersion have I passed on my island!

Later in the season I was accustomed to make at least one trip of exploration to the other end of the isle. Upon this other shore what a difference — rolling hills, shaggy with fern and heather, great rocks tumbling down to a precipitous beach with eternally thundering surf. Here also was to be found that bit of forbidding water called Shipwreck Bay. This name came to it from the number of ships which have been destroyed on the reefs just beyond its entry into the ocean. Each time I have stood, exhausted by my climb over the pathless dunes in the chill company of the rocks at the base of this bay, I have shivered as at a threat in the weather. On the last occasion, the air was listless and thundery and over the purple head of Storm Cape there hung half a dozen small and ragged clouds. In the misty solitude I thought I could hear a long sigh which seemed to rise like the voice of a dead soul lost among the silent depths of the bay. That day I found the graves of three shipwrecked sailors by this northern shore. Tradition among the few inhabitants of the island goes that a pirate ship laden with rich booty had been drawn into the bay by the strong undertow and sunk at this point. I determined to investigate. Removing my clothes I stepped to the edge of a weedy rock overlooking a grove of sea-tangles and summoning resolution, dove in. All that met my touch was cold, soft and gluey, until suddenly my fingers closed on something hard and cold. I held to it and kicked myself to the surface. There I discovered in my grasp the bone of a man's leg.

The first two paragraphs, adapted from Daudet's *The Lighthouse of the Sanguinaires,* present the lazy restfulness of an iridescent summer's day; the remaining part, a revision of passages in Stevenson's *The Merry Men,* pictures a gloomy and tragic landscape. The first of these moods is delicately yet effectively expressed in the sketch by the French stylist, and the second is powerfully presented in the longer tragedy by the British master of atmosphere.

Detecting plural effects in real stories where all three factors of setting, characters, and action are involved is a complicated and subtle business; but it is not essentially different from the process of discrimination employed above. If at this point you can see exactly what is meant by a single and double effect, you have already made considerable progress. All the rest will come by practice in handling more complicated materials.

3. Practical Importance of Single Effect

Are you impatient now to know what all this psychology and these subleties have to do with your learning how to write good stories which some day you may sell, have published, and so earn fame and two motor cars? I will tell you. If you are still in college you will, let us say, be asked to write up an exciting adventure on a vacation camping trip. You remember a really exciting experience — an all-but-disastrous upset of your canoe, a shot at a bull moose, or perhaps an unwelcome encounter with bootleggers — and you are ambitious to display your artistic powers to their utmost. You write your piece. You thrill with the adventure all over again. You can hardly wait until you get the verdict of the instructor or the class to which it is read. The response is disappointing. Your story " contains some good writing but something is the matter with it; it doesn't get over." Then you are told that if you had only omitted that bit at the end about the stomach-ache from eating too many flapjacks, everything would have gone well.

You are discouraged. That stomach-ache belonged, you argue; it happened; it is the truth, why should you not tell the truth? You will then be told that not truth to life, but a single, definite appeal to the emotions is the highest ideal of short story art, and even then you will not understand unless you grasp the psychology and the " subleties " of this chapter. Had you understood these matters from the start, you would have found it in you to omit the digestive disturbance; you would have had greater joy in your performance, and firmer assurance of its success.

What practical use the single effect? A struggling young writer of my acquaintance recently sold his first big story, a beautiful narrative about a wonderful dog. When he first sent it to the editor it contained a sub-plot about a love affair with a young girl. This romantic episode had absolutely nothing to do with the *effect* of the dog story; it ruined it, in fact. Luckily for the writer, the editor was a personal friend and called him to his office. " Why this love business in *this* story? " asked the editor.

" Oh," replied the ambitious author, " I thought every story to succeed had to have a heroine in it, and I stuck her in."

" Take her out," said the editor, " and I'll buy the story."

And he did. He explained later that for a writer to do a thing like that was exactly as if a man trying to sell a beautiful piece of woodland should try to add to its appeal by setting up side shows or monuments along the path which wound through the woods. The error, in other words, was in not achieving a single effect.

The gods were with this fortunate writer in this particular instance — the editor happened to be a friend; but hundreds, yes, thousands of hard-working young writers the country over, I give you my word, are constantly blundering in exactly the same way, and there is no editor friend to point severely to their error. I have myself, as an editor, seen and rejected scores and scores of such manuscripts. The yearning owners often lack neither skill in writing nor knowledge of life; they do not want sympathy, emotion — they have if anything too many sympathies, too many emotions, too many at once anyway; they cannot control them; they simply cannot do one thing at a time; they fail here mainly because they do not see the rigid necessity for it. This necessity is the burden of this chapter.

Mastery Means Self-Discipline

Oh, the things we want to do, are determined to do, come what may, when we are young! Everything is possible to us. Today we are writing about the dastardly intrigue of a rival football team and the vengeance of fate on that team. We happen to be particularly nifty at describing moonlight scenes. We once visited a most delectable co-ed — well, anyway, we understand moonlight! We can do it as well as Poe or anyone else, and — a chunk of moonlight, in our best manner, goes into our otherwise respectable football story. Just wait until the teacher reads it! He'll realize what a genius — well, the sordid fact is that the moonlight scene gets a fat blue pencil through it, and our temple of literary dreams collapses!

If tragedy has met you in this form — and you will be unlike me or any other of the squadrons of pilgrims trying to spiral up the windy slopes of Parnassus if it hasn't — your need, Oh, believe me, will be, not inspiration, not a more appreciative audience, not an instructor who knows his job, but — self-discipline. "He that ruleth his spirit" is better "than he that taketh a city," and writers of stories that succeed are no exception to the precept. Mark Twain once confessed that he long wrestled in vain with a story until he saw that he was really trying to do two stories at once; by simply dropping one of them all went well. It will be given you to do all things in this field only by being content to do one thing at a time.

You will not be alone among artists in your struggle to master this important principle of technique. All artists wrestle with this refractory, elusive issue of effects. Behold the list of their victories. Macdowell's lovely "To a Wild Rose" — what would you feel if he had introduced into the middle of it a "peppy" strain of "jazz"? What would Paderewski's "Minuet" be with "Onward Christian Soldiers!" marching through it as an obligato! Corot's silver-gray dawns among April-budded trees —

can you imagine the effect if they were filled with red-jacketed hunters or Fra Angelico saints? Suppose Whistler's " Mother " were enlivened with a table in one corner spread with a convivial collection of wine bottles, or the Greek " Laocoön " in his struggle with the serpents of fate were confronted with the marble effigy of a goat, head down, coming full-tilt for the hapless parent? Such freaks of art would be extreme violations of the law of unity of effect.

Kipling would have been equally at fault had he ended his swift and magnificent tragedy, *Without Benefit of Clergy*, with Holden at the end walking from the scene of his unsupportable grief on his hands instead of on his feet; and Poe in *The Fall of the House of Usher*, would have dispelled the magic of this tale's sepulchral gloom if, on departing from the doomed house, the narrator, instead of walking decorously away, had thumbed his nose at it. Errors as egregious as these I hope you will not make, but errors of this *type* you are sure to make in your early work.

4. Technique of Fusing Effects

In my effort to isolate the single effect of the short story so that you may understand exactly what it is I have possibly made the problem of producing it seem simpler than it is. It is not simple. The remaining chapters of this book are devoted to an exposition of ways and means to secure it with widely different materials. We will reserve these problems for later detailed study.

We have seen how two different moods in one and the same setting produced a double effect, and you have perhaps resolved that always hereafter your settings will be kept strictly to a single mood. If so, you are precipitate. You have forgotten the possibilities that lie in the other two important elements of narrative, character and action. Complete short stories always involve a close integration and focusing of all three factors of setting, character, and action. By their use it is even possible to produce a single effect with two settings as dissimilar as those of "The Enchanted Isle." Let me give you a very simple illustration. I will use the same material in three different forms. In the first version I have simply set down together, without connecting them, an adapted passage from a sketch by Bertrand, a French writer, and part of a story by O. Henry.

A NOCTURNE

(First Version)

At the hour that separates one day from another, when the city sleeps in silence, I woke with a start upon a summer's night. My room was half dark; the moon, clad in a vaporous robe, like a white fairy, was gazing upon my sleep and smiling at me through the windows. A nocturnal patrol was passing in the street; a homeless dog howled in the distance and the cricket sang in my hearth. Soon the voices grew fainter; the patrol departed, and the cricket, weary of singing, had fallen asleep; and to me, barely rid of a tender dream, with eyes yet dazzled by the sweet marvels of another world, all that surrounded me seemed a dream. Ah, how sweet it is to awaken in the middle of the night, when the moon, that glides mysteriously to your couch, awakens you with a melancholy kiss!

It was a busy day in Maxwell's office. The ticker began to reel out jerkily its fitful coils of tape; the desk telephone had a chronic attack of buzzing. Men began to throng into the office and call at him over the railing, jovially, sharply, viciously, excitedly. Messenger boys ran in and out with messages and telegrams. The clerks in the office jumped about like sailors during a storm. Even the door-tender's stolid face relaxed into something like animation. On the Exchange there were hurricanes and landslides and snowstorms and glaciers and volcanoes, and those elemental disturbances were reproduced in miniature in the broker's office. Maxwell shoved his chair against the wall and transacted business after the manner of a toe dancer. He jumped from ticker to 'phone, from desk to door, with the trained agility of a harlequin.

The feelings produced by these brief bits are not so pronounced as those produced by the previous description,

but they are sufficient for the purpose. The first paragraph presents the mood of moonlight; the second gives the
impression of a busy office. The whole piece thus makes
a distinct double effect. The first half is told in the first
person and the second is told objectively. Now let us
present the two scenes again, this time writing both in the
first person, making the actor the same in both cases:

(Second Version)

I awoke with a start out of a disturbing dream. The room
was half dark, and the moon, which I could see through the
filmy curtains, poured its silvery streams across my couch. A
nocturnal policeman was passing in the street, whistling a lilting
air and thumping his stick against the fence posts. A homeless
dog howled in the distance, and a cricket chirped with drowsy
insistence from the hearth. Soon the noises grew fainter; the
policeman departed; the dog ceased its wails; and the cricket
fell asleep. Then, in the midst of the tender mysteries of the
night, while the moon kissed me with a melancholy kiss, I found
my memory once more living through the busy events of the
preceding day.

I could hear the ticker reeling out its fitful coils of tape, and
the desk telephone continuing its chronic fits of buzzing. Once
more I saw men thronging the office, calling me over the railing,
speaking now jovially, sharply, now viciously, excitedly. I saw
messenger boys running in and out. I saw the clerks jumping
about like sailors in a storm. I remembered how even the face
of old Jim, the door-porter, relaxed into something like animation.
The elemental disturbances taking place on Exchange I saw reflected in my own office, until at last I saw myself jumping
and dancing about again with the trained agility of a harlequin.

Now we have united the two scenes as they were not
united before. Both are the experiences of one and the
same person. We now have unity of character which before was wanting. How about the total effect on you,
the reader? Is it now single or is it still double? This is
a nice question in technique, but to answer it correctly you
do not need to resort to any technical subtleties; you need
only keep clearly separated in your mind the difference

between the effects themselves (which are determined by an honest report on your own feelings) and the means used to produce those effects (which are determined by an analysis of the material itself).

The answer surely is that the double effect is still present. The mere fact that the same person now records the two scenes does not unify the *effect* of the two scenes. One person may conceivably take part in a thousand different scenes or actions and a record of all his activities might produce a thousand different effects. Let us now fuse both these scenes so that they produce a single effect:

(Third Version)

I woke with a start out of a nightmare of horrors: I had been dreaming of the feverish events of the previous day spent in the office. I sat up in bed, my hands still trembling, my breath coming in gasps, and instantly felt the soothing effect of the moonlight pouring across my couch. Looking about the now spectral beauty of the room, my distracted eyes fell upon the envelope, sealed and stamped, that I had left on my table before lying down — my resignation from any further connection with the nerve-racking business of being a broker. I had written it but could not summon resolution enough to post it. It was difficult to give up my business career with its opportunity for an easy living, possibly wealth, luxury, abandon it for poverty and art; and yet if I did not quit business how was I ever to fulfill my life-long dream of painting beauty as I saw it and loved it? The struggle was too much for me and I lay down, exhausted, and slept.

But what a nightmare! Once more I sat in the mephitic air of the office, my pulse keeping time to the ticker reeling out its fitful coils of tape, the telephone continuing its chronic fits of bunning. As I sat up in bed, bathed in the moonlight, I heard a nocturnal policeman passing in the street, whistling a lilting air and thumping his stick against the fence posts. A simple but happy man, I thought with envy; why have not I the courage also to be simple and happy? In the back of my mind clicked the ticker — the policeman's stick on the fence must have started the ticker going in my head. I lay down again and tried to sleep.

Immediately beneath my closed eyelids I saw hysterical men thronging the office, calling me over the railing, speaking sharply, viciously, excitedly. I saw messenger boys running in and out. I saw the clerks jumping about like sailors in a storm; I myself was once more giving orders, dancing about among the desks with the trained agility of a harlequin. My body twitched; a nausea of hatred seized me; I could not sleep; I jumped out of bed and stood, irresolute, in the middle of the floor. What should I do? I could not go on living like this. I would be a nervous wreck in another year.

A homeless dog howled in the distance; a cricket chirped with drowsy insistence on the hearth. Through the curtains I saw the garden bathed in the silver radiance of the moon, the melancholy beauty of the night inundated me, soothed my distracted soul, inspired me, filled me with longing — Oh, what was life for if not to cultivate such moments as these, to record them for the pleasure and delight of others! As I stood there, transfigured, I held out my arms, I felt the moonlight bathe my face, kiss my lips tenderly, suffuse me with a new peace, a clearer understanding. Hurriedly and without further thought I dressed, picked up the letter on the table, went out of the house and dropped it in the mail box on the corner.

Now what is the effect here? We still have the same materials, the same two settings, the same character; but we have brought the setting and the character into some dynamic relation to each other now, by adding the account of the character's struggle with his problem. Because of the brevity of the sketch the effect produced is, of course, slight, but I think you will agree that it makes a definite dominant impression, namely, that of an artist's soul struggling for expression. In the first two versions the interest was in the settings only; now it is in character. Here the settings are integrated with and definitely subordinated to the action; they are used to represent and emphasize the two desires struggling with each other in the character's soul. But interest in, possibly sympathy for, that soul's struggle is the single dominant effect of the sketch.

5. "Single" Further Defined

Please have patience now while we examine one more distinction about the single effect, failure to understand which causes many students of narrative writing to go wrong. They misinterpret the meaning of the word "single." It comprehends a relative and not absolute singularity. It means that the reader must be affected in a distinct and single manner. The word "single" here does not mean that a story should produce one and only one emotion in the reader, but it does mean that it should produce one and only one *dominant* impression or emotion. By analyzing your emotions on reading a story, you are able of course to detect several emotions. This may confuse you. In reading Kipling's *Without Benefit of Clergy,* for instance, you may feel affection for the baby, pity for the mother, scorn for the rash father, and curiosity about many things only hinted at in the story; and yet the *dominant* effect of this powerful story of a misalliance in India is unquestionably tragic pity.

"Single" does not Mean Pure

"Single Effect" does not mean that you should be able to sense one single pure emotion. Some emotions are themselves complex. Complex emotions are combinations of simpler ones. Pity, for instance, is an emotion compounded of sympathy and despair. Irony is a combination of tragedy and amusement. Jealousy is a compound of love and anger or hatred. In a story of romantic love, told with a true single effect, you may feel sympathy for the hero, hatred for the villain trying to do him in, and experience a glow of satisfaction at the final peal of the wedding bells. With these feelings you might fuse some sad or happy romantic memories out of your own past. And yet the story would have produced on you a genuine single effect of happily terminated romance.

In analyzing stories for their effects, therefore, and in singling out the effects for your own stories, you should be careful to hit upon the single, dominating effect and not the component parts of that effect. This is often as difficult as it is important. It is a matter which can be learned only by much practice.

An Analysis of Russian Gloom

We are now ready, I think, to examine some condensed outlines of successful stories to see if they affect our feelings and if so whether or not the impression made on us is " single " and " dominant." I have selected two rather short stories by two acknowledged masters of the art. The first is by the Russian writer, Chekhov.

GRIEF *

It is twilight. A thick wet snow is slowly twirling around the newly lighted street-lamps, and lying in soft, thin layers on the roofs, the horses' backs, people's shoulders and hats. The cab driver, Iona Potapov, is quite white, and looks like a phantom; he is bent double as far as a human body can bend double; he is seated on his box and never makes a move. If a whole snowdrift fell on him, it seems as if he would not find it necessary to shake it off. His little horse is also quite white, and remains motionless; its immobility, its angularity, and its straight wooden-looking legs, even close by give it the appearance of a ginger-bread horse worth a kopeck. It is, no doubt, plunged in deep thought. If you were snatched from the plough, from your usual grey surroundings, and were thrown into this slough full of monstrous lights, unceasing noise and hurrying people, you too would find it difficult not to think.

All the afternoon the old cab-driver and his little horse have waited in the snow without a " fare." Suddenly an officer hails them, and demands to be taken Viborg way. Iona, stupefied by the cold, starts his horse off into the traffic clumsily, and is berated by other drivers and the officer. At last they are off, and Iona, encouraged by a friendly remark from the officer, looks around as if he wants to say something, but the only sound that issues is a snuffle.

" What? " asks the officer.

Iona twists his mouth into a smile, and with an effort says hoarsely:

" My son, *barin*, died this week."

* Complete version in *The Steppe and Other Stories*, by Anton Tchekov, Frederick A. Stokes Company.

" Hm! What did he die of? "

Iona turns with his whole body towards his fare, and says:
" And who knows? They say high fever. He was three days
in hospital, and then died. . . . God's will be done."

" Turn around! The devil! " sounded from the darkness.
" Have you popped off old doggie, eh? Use your eyes! "

" Go on, go on," said the officer, " otherwise we shall not get
there by tomorrow. Hurry up a bit! "

Off they go again, and Iona turning once more to go on with
his story, finds the officer apparently asleep. Having dropped
him at his destination, Iona and his little horse have another
long wait in the snow, until at last he is hailed by three young
men, who climb in, quarreling as to places in the sleigh. Their
talk to one another is insolent, and they jeer at Iona for his
shabbiness and his slow pace.

Iona feels at his back the little man wriggling, and the tremble
in his voice. He listens to the insults hurled at him, sees the
people, and little by little the feeling of loneliness leaves him.
The hump-back goes on swearing until he gets mixed up in
some elaborate six-foot oath, or chokes with coughing. The
lankies begin to talk about a certain Nadejda Petrovna. Iona
looks round at them several times; he waits for a temporary
silence, then, turning round again, he murmurs:

" My son . . . died this week."

" We must all die," sighed the hump-back, wiping his lips
after an attack of coughing. " Now, hurry up, hurry up!
Gentlemen, I really cannot go any farther like this! When will
he get us there? "

Iona tries to go on and tell them about his boy, but the
young men shout that at last they have reached their destination, and scramble out. He is again alone. There is no one in
the passing throng who will listen to him. His grief is deep
enough to flood the earth, but no one notices it in one so in-
significant. He can bear it no longer, and finally heads the
little horse toward the stables.

In the inn where the cab-drivers sleep around a dirty stove,
he settles down. One of the sleepers rouses and reaches toward
the water bucket for a drink. Iona fills the cup for him and
as he drinks, begins to tell him the story of his son. The man
does not listen, and Iona soon sees that he is fast asleep again.

It is nearly a week since his son's death, and he has been
able to talk of it to no one. He will go to the stable to look
after his little horse.

He puts on his coat, and goes to the stables to his horse;
he thinks of the corn, the hay, the weather. When he is alone,

he dare not think of his son; he could speak about him to any-one, but to think of him, and picture him to himself, is unbearably painful.

"Are you tucking in?" Iona asks his horse, looking at his bright eyes; "go on, tuck in, though we've not earned our corn, we can eat hay. Yes! I am too old to drive — my son could have, not I. He was a first-rate cab-driver. If only he had lived!"

Iona is silent for a moment, then continues: "That's how it is, my old horse. There's no more Kuzma Ionitch. He left us, and he went off pop. Now let's say you had a foal, you were that foal's mother, and suddenly, let's say, that foal went and left you to live after him. It would be sad, wouldn't it?"

The little horse munches, listens and breathes over his master's hand. . . .

Iona's feelings are too much for him, and he tells the little horse the whole story.

Now, what effect has the story made on you? It has certainly affected your emotions. How? The author has given the name of an emotion, grief, as his title. Is this precisely the effect it has made on you? Or is grief merely the emotion felt by the main actor in the story? Grief over the death of a son is a profound emotion. Have you felt it? You may say yes, and yet I do not believe that grief will be the true dominant effect received by the average reader.

The reader, to approximate the depth of emotion felt by the old Russian cabman, would require a much fuller knowledge of his life than this short chronicle gives us. Furthermore the author concludes with the striking picture of the cabby's talking to his forlorn little horse. What is the effect of this picture? It makes the reader sympathize with the cabman, doesn't it? We have then a heart interest in a tragic figure — pathos. A feeling of pathos is, then, the single dominant effect of the story.

An Analysis of American Humor

Let us now read another story of an entirely different type as regards the effect produced on the reader. This time the author is O. Henry. Below is a brief outline of the action of this ingenious little narrative.

THE ROMANCE OF A BUSY BROKER *

Harvey Maxwell, broker, surprises his office force one morning, by coming in at nine-thirty in the company of his stenographer, Miss Leslie. With a brisk good-morning to his confidential clerk, he plunges into the pile of work on his desk. Miss Leslie asks the clerk if a new stenographer has been engaged for her place, and on a negative answer, settles down at her accustomed desk.

This day is Maxwell's busy day. On the Exchange there were hurricanes and landslides and snowstorms and glaciers and volcanoes, and those elemental disturbances were represented in miniature in the broker's office. An applicant for the position of stenographer appeared and he dismissed her abruptly. There was no place vacant, and he did not want another interruption of that kind, he announced. On the floor they were pounding half a dozen stocks in which Maxwell's customers were heavy investors. Orders to buy and sell were coming and going as swift as the flight of swallows. Some of his own holdings were imperilled, and the man was working like some high-geared, delicate, strong machine — strung to full tension, going at full speed, accurate, never hesitating, with the proper word and decision and act ready and prompt as clockwork.

Just before luncheon there is a lull. Maxwell standing by his desk, suddenly becomes aware of the soft spring air from his open window and catches at the same time another fragrance, the odor of lilac, which belonged to Miss Leslie and to her alone.

The world of finance disappears. He dashes into the inner office to her desk. She looks up with a smile and a blush.

"Miss Leslie," he began hurriedly, "I have but a moment to spare. I want to say something in that moment. Will you be my wife? I haven't had time to make love to you in the ordinary way, but I really do love you. Talk quick, please — those fellows are clubbing the stuffing out of Union Pacific."

"Oh, what are you talking about?" exclaimed the young lady. She rose to her feet and gazed upon him, round-eyed.

"Don't you understand?" said Maxwell, restively. "I want you to marry me. I love you, Miss Leslie. I wanted to tell you, and I snatched a minute when things had slackened up a bit. They're calling me for the 'phone now. Tell 'em to wait a minute, Pitcher. Won't you, Miss Leslie?"

* Complete version in *The Four Million*, by O. Henry, Doubleday, Page & Co.

The stenographer acted very queerly. At first she seemed overcome with amazement; then tears flowed from her wondering eyes; and then she smiled sunnily through them, and one of her arms slid tenderly about the broker's neck.

"I know now," she said softly, "it's this old business that has driven everything else out of your head for the time. I was frightened at first. Don't you remember, Harvey? We were married last evening at eight o'clock in the Little Church Around the Corner."

What is the effect produced by this story? It touched your feelings certainly. There is a laugh in it, a laugh about a definite, single thing. You undoubtedly were also impressed by the nervous drama of the busy office; possibly you sensed the charms of the newly married stenographer; there is a touch of romance in the "surprise ending," and yet none of these impressions is the dominant, single effect. What is it? Amusement, certainly; but amusement about what specifically? Who does the amusing thing? The broker. What are we told about the broker? He's busy. Very well, our single dominant effect is amusement at the fantastic act of a busy broker.

Detailed analyses of effects such as these, let me say again, are not necessary to an enjoyment of the stories; but we are not concerned here with the problems of the reader except in so far as a knowledge of his reactions helps us in our writing. To be able to control his reactions we must, first of all, understand them. If you would gain this certainty, you must have patience with just such nice distinctions as this.

Other Familiar Examples

Now let us examine the single effects of some other notable stories. Among those with which most students are well acquainted is Maupassant's little masterpiece, *The Necklace*. Its single effect surely is ironic pity. Tragic gloom is the dominant impression produced by Poe's *Fall of the House of Usher*, while the same writer's famous puzzle story, *The Gold Bug,* moves the reader to a feeling of mysterious, adventurous thrill. Stevenson's *Markheim* leaves the reader with a dominant impression of tragic awe at the workings of Markheim's conscience. A shock of ironic surprise is the main effect of Irvin Cobb's best-known story, *The Belled Buzzard.*

6. The Length of the Short Story

During the foregoing discussion you have been impatient to tell me, I can well believe, that narrative producing more than one emotional effect *can* be written most effectively because multiple effects can be found in all the great novels and novelettes. Correct. The plot outline, for instance, on page fifty, might be written out in one hundred thousand words instead of in the all-too-brief nine thousand that were suggested. Each of the three conflicts might be *fully* developed, making the whole story most impressive. Since this is so, we have to ask ourselves just what the unity of a novel consists in and when a short story should cease trying to be a short story and blossom forth as a novel or novelette. Let us take the latter of these two problems first.

At the beginning of this chapter I stated that the limit of length of the short story is determined by the length of time a reader can follow a single effect without fatigue. If a reader did *not* get fatigued, there would obviously be no reason why a short story could not be as long as a novel. This, however, it cannot be, and the reason once again lies not in any abitrary literary or editorial rule but in a very interesting and important fact about the human machine. The fact is this: The mind can give continuous attention to one thing for only a limited length of time.

Mobility of Attention

The mind fatigues quickly in any effort at concentration. The most characteristic thing about attention is its mobil-

ity. The mind cannot attend carefully to more than one
thing at a time and it cannot attend to even that one thing
very long unless there are elements of change and variety
that furnish fresh and lasting stimulation. Students of
psychology are familiar with the simple experiment of gazing fixedly at a small group of dots. Every few seconds the
mind, in an effort to induce variety, itself changes the
pattern of the dots.

The thing in story telling which holds the attention of
the reader is the " thread of the narrative," the what-will-
happen-next interest. This " thread " is the emotional interest of the story. The emotional interest of a story, however, contains factors of change and variety in the characters, setting and action. The emotional interest thus
becomes, in the language of psychology, a unit response
to a number of stimuli.

Simple instances of this faculty of the mind are observable in the other arts. In listening to music, for instance,
your ear catches several notes at once, but you do not
concentrate on any one of them: your focus of attention is in the melody or harmony which results from
varying or combining them. The same thing is true in
painting. In gazing at a canvas your eye detects several
colors and shapes, but the thing that fixes your attention is
the total effect of these colors and shapes in agreeable
combination.

Attention Endurance Deciding Factor

Such are the principles by which the story writer also
holds the reader's attention. The narrative " flows,"
changes constantly. In time, however, the reader's mind,
in spite of the most skillful manipulation of the character,
setting and action, becomes fatigued. There is a limit to
the length of time the mind can make a uniform response
to even multiple stimuli! Suppose you are writing a love
story. Your purpose is to arouse in your reader a feeling

of romance. You play for his attention by telling the tribulations of the lovers, how they overcome an irate father, poverty, business troubles. It is possible to string out the account of obstacles met and overcome until they no longer interest the reader. He is " fed up " on these lovers; he feels that it is high time for father's blessing and a conclusive embrace. If you do not end things at or before this juncture the reader will simply yawn and throw your story aside.

Your one means of keeping his interest in your story any further is to cease trying to vary the elements of your single effect, and vary the single effect itself. You can keep him with you, possibly, if you will introduce an extended account of the father's own romance, or of the young man's struggle to keep his job, or the young lady's prowess with a tennis racket; and will tell these things in such a way as to call upon emotional responses differing definitely from the particular romantic effect with which you began. The minute you do this, however, you in a sense begin all over since it is now necessary slowly to build up the new emotional response. This can be done, of course, but when you do it, you have passed from the form of the short story to that of the novelette or novel.

No fixed physical limit can be set for the length of the short story. Trained and sophisticated minds can, of course, follow a single emotional interest for a longer period than untrained minds, and true short stories written for them, like Henry James's *The Turn of The Screw,* or Mrs. Wharton's *Ethan Frome,* run to over forty thousand words. For the average reader the limit has been discovered to be about eight thousand words. For this reason and also others connected with the physical make-up of the magazines, this is the extreme limit for most of them.

To Poe again belongs the credit of first clearly grasping the principle of controlling the length of the short story. His words directly concerned poetry but apply equally well to the short story:

It appears evident, then, that there is a distinct limit, as regards length, to all works of literary art — the limit of a single sitting — and that, although in certain classes of prose composition, such as *Robinson Crusoe* (demanding no unity), this limit may be advantageously overpassed, it can never properly be overpassed in a poem.

If the novel cannot have a single effect but can have an unlimited number of effects, in what does the unity of the novel consist? You will note that Poe in the passage quoted above states that prose narratives of the length of *Robinson Crusoe*, since they are too long to be built around a single effect, have no unity at all. Obviously Poe here confuses "single effect" and "unity." The short story is unified by its single effect; but there are other ways to secure unity, one of which is by organizing the material of the story itself. And it is precisely this that gives the novel its unity. Its unity is in its subject matter.

Novel and Short Story Compared

We can see roughly the difference between the unity of the short story and that of the novel by the following diagram:

THE SHORT STORY FORM

THE NOVEL FORM

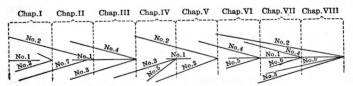

PATTERNS OF SHORT STORY AND NOVEL.

The numbered " factors " represent characters, settings, plot actions. The narrative is viewed as moving from left to right. The focusing of these factors to a point indicates the dramatic development of separate effects. You will note that the short story has only one focal point, the novel several. The short story thus has only one climax; the novel may have many. The factors in the novel, however, are more or less the same throughout the action; this fact is the sole fixed basis of its unity. In many carefully organized novels the focusing of the different emotional effects occurs definitely towards the end of each chapter. In novels published serially the various installments are often organized much like separate short stories. There are also books of short stories related to each other in no way at all except in having the same characters and settings.

Emotional Effects of Novels

In the second diagram you will note that from the beginning to the end of the novel a certain amount of pyramiding or focusing is indicated. This does not mean that smaller short story emotional effects are pyramided in such a way as to produce at the end of the novel an emotional effect whose intensity is equal to the sum of all the smaller effects. The emotional effect felt at the end of a well-written novel may well be, and often is, more powerful than any that could be produced by a short story. This is certainly true of all the great dramatic novels, such as *The Ordeal of Richard Feverel, Tess of the D'Urbervilles,* and *Madame Bovary.* This stronger emotional effect is not, however, produced by a pooling or pyramiding of all the effects in the novel. If it were, it would mean that a single emotional effect had been held through the whole novel and this we have already seen is impossible. It is brought about because at the final scene, the reader, having lived in his imagination with the characters and setting for a longer time and learned much more about them than he could have learned in a short story, is in a better position to appreciate the full tragedy, pathos, or romance of the final scene.

The unity of the novel is dependent more upon its subject matter than upon its emotional effects for its unity. The unity of *Robinson Crusoe* arises from the fact that it concerns itself with the adventures of a single ship-wrecked sailor, occurring on a single island at a particular time; the unity of *The Ordeal of Richard Feverel* derives from its underlying thesis that it does not pay to bring up a youth by the sheltered life, while the novel, *Main Street*, is unified by the fact that its material is a selection of the more sordid and unaesthetic facts about a typical American town. Things, not effects, are unified in these novels.

A novelist may succeed without any unity at all among the various emotional effects he produces, but he must have some unity in his subject matter. The novel, unlike the short story, may deal with any subject and run to any length and be handled in any manner conceivable so long as the writer does not write about too many things or let the relations among the parts be too tenuous or unintelligible. Conversely, the more unity in the subject matter of the novel, and the more closely the subject matter is integrated with the final emotional effect, the more effective will the story be.

Novelettes like Novels

The problem of the unity of the novelette is much the same as that of the novel except that it has fewer episodes and is therefore not quite so long. In general the different principles which apply to the novel apply to it. As a literary form it is not, as many imagine, half way between the short story and the novel. It is, as its name implies, a short novel and not a long short story. It has no single emotional effect. It is unified by its subject matter.

I propose that we work out in practice narrative unity only as it affects the short story. Unity in the novel and novelette is both an easier and a bulkier problem. The mastery of short story writing interests more students than the writing of novels; most (but not quite all) students, in fact, will do well to serve an apprenticeship in the short story before tackling the novel. They can experiment more freely in the shorter form and benefit much from the mental discipline of handling its greater technical difficulties.

Merely understanding what narrative effects are has been our purpose so far in this chapter; some simple exercises in producing them will be given in the assignments at the end of this chapter and further practice with more difficult effects will be given in later chapters.

ASSIGNMENTS: CHAPTER TWO

ASSIGNMENT A

In these exercises on the " single effect " please remember that as already stated, the effect may be anything from a slight *impression* up to a deep emotional reaction. The words " emotional effect " really apply only to the full length story. Considerable length is necessary to produce a powerful effect; the short quotations given here therefore will produce only slight effects, if any. Trained to detect slight effects, you will find the bigger ones easier to handle.

These exercises are not easy, but they are worth struggling with, even though you make many mistakes. I have given answers to the more difficult ones in the Appendix to guide your study. You cannot do too much of this kind of work. More than anything else it will develop your artistic sensibilities.

The questions you are to answer about each of the following are these two:

1. Is a single effect produced and if so what is it? How intense is it?

2. If the effect produced is plural, explain what makes it so.

1. On the table a candle-box was placed, and within it, swathed in staring red flannel, lay the last arrival at Roaring Camp. Beside the candle-box was placed a hat. Its use was soon indicated. " Gentlemen," said Stumpy, with a singular mixture of authority and *ex officio* complacency, — " Gentlemen will please pass in at the front door, round the table and out of the back door. Them as wishes to contribute anything toward the orphan will find a hat handy."

The first man entered with his hat on; he uncovered, however, as he looked about him, and so, unconsciously, set an example to the next. In such communities good and bad actions are catching. As the procession filed in, comments were audible, — criticisms addressed, perhaps, rather to Stumpy, in the character of showman, — " Is that him? " " mighty small specimen "; " hasn't mor'n got the color "; " ain't bigger nor a derringer."

The contributions were characteristic: A silver tobacco-box; a doubloon; a navy revolver, silver mounted; a gold specimen; a very beautifully embroidered lady's handkerchief (from Oakhurst the gambler); a diamond breastpin; a diamond ring (suggested by the pin, with the remark from the giver that he " saw that pin and went two diamonds better "); a slung shot; a Bible (contributor not detected); a golden spur; a silver teaspoon (the initials, I regret to say, were not the giver's); a pair of surgeon's shears; a lancet; a Bank of England note for £5; and about $200 in loose gold and silver coin. During these proceedings Stumpy maintained a silence as impassive as the dead on his left, a gravity as inscrutable as that of the newly born on his right.

Only one incident occurred to break the monotony of the curious procession. As Kentuck bent over the candle-box half curiously, the child turned, and, in a spasm of pain, caught at his groping finger, and held it fast for a moment. Kentuck looked foolish and embarrassed. Something like a blush tried to assert itself in his weather-beaten cheek. "The d——d little cuss!" he said, as he extricated his finger, with, perhaps, more tenderness and care than he might have been deemed capable of showing. He held that finger a little apart from its fellows as he went out, and examined it curiously. The examination provoked the same original remark in regard to the child. In fact, he seemed to enjoy repeating it. "He rastled with my finger," he remarked to Tipton, holding up the member, "the d——d little cuss!" *

(Luck of Roaring Camp, Bret Harte.)

2. His very throat was moral. You saw a good deal of it. You looked over a very low fence of white cravat (whereof no man had ever beheld the tie, for he fastened it below) and there it lay, a valley between two jutting heights of collar, serene and whiskerless before you. It seemed to say, on the part of Mr. Pecksniff, "There is no deception, ladies and gentlemen, all is peace, a holy calm pervades me." So did his hair, just grizzled with an iron gray, which was all brushed off his forehead, and stood bolt upright, or slightly drooped in kindred action with his heavy eyelids. So did his person, which was sleek though free from corpulency. So did his manner, which was soft and oily. In a word, even his plain black suit, and state of widower, and dangling double eye-glass, all tended to the same purpose, and cried aloud, "Behold the moral Pecksniff!" *

3. They would have lynched me had I not been secretly hurried away to the jail at Peoria. And yet I was going peacefully home, carrying my jug, a little drunk, when Logan, the marshal, halted me, called me a drunken hound and shook me. And, when I cursed him for it, struck me with that Prohibition loaded cane — all this before I shot him.

They would have hanged me except for this: My lawyer, Kinsey Keene, was helping to land old Thomas Rhodes for wrecking the bank, and the Judge was a friend of Rhodes and wanted him to escape, and Kinsey offered to quit on Rhodes for fourteen years for me. The bargain was made. I served my time and learned to read and write.*

(Spoon River Anthology, Edgar Lee Masters.)

4. They walked out on the terrace where the moon made soft shadings across the long, even lawn. The breeze which brushed so lightly across his face, he could see stirring, barely, in the branches. Above the faintly winking stars checkered a cloudless sky. He felt

her hand creep snugly into his own. He turned and smelled the freshness of her hair. Her profile outlined itself softly. He saw a swallow dip gracefully in the distance and disappear as silently as it had come into view. They stopped then.

"Damn it," he said, "I'm sick of my job. I sweat and sweat all day long and come home so tired I can't do anything but flop in bed."

"Quit crabbing," she snapped, "you're better off than plenty of others."

"Don't hand me that stuff," he growled. "You never did a day's work in your life. You don't know what you're talking about."

She turned and kicked him in the ankle.

At that, he twisted her arm until she screamed.

"There," he said, "now we're even."

5. Midge Kelly scored his first knockout when he was seventeen. The knockee was his brother Connie, three years his junior and a cripple. The purse was a half dollar given to the younger Kelly by a lady whose electric had just missed bumping his soul from his frail little body.

Connie did not know Midge was in the house, else he never would have risked laying the prize on the arm of the least comfortable chair in the room, the better to observe its shining beauty. As Midge entered from the kitchen, the crippled boy covered the coin with his hand, but the movement lacked the speed requisite to escape his brother's quick eye.

"Whatcha got there?" demanded Midge.

"Nothin'," said Connie.

"You're a one-legged liar!" said Midge.

He strode over to his brother's chair and grasped the hand that concealed the coin.

"Let loose!" he ordered.

Connie began to cry.

"Let loose and shut up your noise," said the elder, and jerked his brother's hand from the chair arm."[1]

6. He was old. He had hair in his ears. Of course, his barber attended to it, and kept his skin pink and clean, and his valet was conscientious about his clothes and his bath. But—he was old. There was the odor of age in his flesh, under the delicate expensive perfumes that he affected. His teeth—he still had several of his own—were yellow and collared with gold fillings. His hands when he touched her were dry, the nails ribbed and thick—no manicuring skill can prevent that after a certain time.

She married him. Not twenty years old she was—sweet to look at as a flower, full of little sensitive flushes of feeling, ready for tears or laughter at the merest hint from those around her. She was drunk when she went up the aisle. The maid of honor was under orders to keep the gin on hand that morning and the bride had a last generous glass just before she started toward the altar on her uncle's arm.

Among the gifts was a complete table service in gold from the

[1] Reprinted by permission from *How to Write Short Stories*, by Ring Lardner, published by Charles Scribner's Sons.

officers of the groom's company. Mr. and Mrs. S. sailed on the Laronia. They plan a leisurely trip around the world.*

7. "There was nothing to forgive," Honesty informed him. "I liked your kissing me. I told you so."

The others had wandered up the beach. . . .

"Well, that's very generous of you," Kit was saying uneasily.

"Not at all," Honesty regarded him with level eyes. "I — you excited me, here." She laid her hand on her alluring breast, and her eyes on his did not falter. It was he who flushed. "I loved it, and you are even better-looking than I believed. I'm crazy about you, and I see no reason why I shouldn't tell you so. I was wondering if you thought it just a physical attraction."

He faltered into speech. "My dear girl — you mustn't — that is — You're kidding!" he said with a forlorn hope.

"No." Her eyes, blue as lupines, were sorrowful. "You're like all the rest," she told him mournfully; "you can't endure hearing the truth."

If there was anything he loathed it was to be classed with the mob. He defended himself angrily.

"I'm not. It's refreshing. I'm exceedingly honored, but —" He sank into silence. She was a witch; her eyes were azure spells. He must be going, he thought, far away. What a girl! He wondered wildly how he could get back to Southampton, to town, to Tibet. . . .

"If," pondered Honesty, "I decide it isn't just a biological trap —" She looked at him suddenly, her gaze clouded. "I'm right in assuming that you felt — the same way about me?"

"If you mean," he asked, lost to all reason, "do I think you are the most damnably seductive and beautiful creature ever put on earth to trouble a man's pulses, you're one hundred percent right."

"That's what I thought," she agreed calmly.[1]

8. The deeds to Sam's land carried the title back to old Indian grants. The place was as much his as his name. The house that he had been born in contained as its central hall the log cabin which had been the first home on the original clearing; the stone in his fences had known the hands of his father and his father's father; the crops that he harvested were the fruit of their labor as well as his.

Then the city people came and told him that they would need his place. Twenty miles south they planned to build a dam to hold a great water supply. The little streams that had watered his acres would help to fill a lake that was to drown the whole valley.

"Nothing doing," said Sam. No price they offered him was enough. But they fought it through the courts, and his daughters helped them, and Sam lost. He went to live with the older daughter.

When excavation was begun on Sam's place, some interesting relics were found — tools and utensils of the Folsom period, and traces of a stone temple of a prehistoric civilization. Before the engineers let the water rise in the new lake, many archaeologists came to take

[1] Reprinted by permission from "Honesty's Policy," by Faith Baldwin, published in *Cosmopolitan* and reprinted in *Short Story Hits, 1932*, Harcourt, Brace & Co.

photographs, make accurate measurements, and to remove all the stone work, which they intended to set up carefully in the city museum. The scientists told newspaper men that no remains of equal importance had ever been found in that region. Sam hadn't known of it; it wasn't in the land record.

No trace of the ancient temple was left by the time the engineers let the water in. Every piece had been labeled and carted away in boxes marked " Fragile." Sam's house and barn had been torn down long before. Sam didn't last long after the dam was built.

9. Dead? It simply wasn't true. She'd been alive — in his arms — two hours ago. On his handkerchief was the red of her rouge that he'd wiped from his lips after he left her! He loved her, — he even loved her lipstick. Automatically, because he had to see her and prove that it was a lie, he started toward her home. The same soft night wind was blowing.

He stood on the steps, where two hours before they had stood together, covered with darkness, but now light poured out from all the windows and from the open door.

He stepped inside. Two men were talking.

" This drug didn't cause the death," said one. " Her mouth and throat are OK, and she ain't been vomitin'."

" A swell looker, all right," said another voice. " I wouldn't mind going on with the oxygen a while longer. A corpse isn't often so restful to the eye."

10. It was all as before, but infinitely more rapid. Never had Mr. Arcularis achieved such phenomenal, such supernatural, speed. In no time at all he was beyond the moon, shot past the North Star as if it were standing still (which perhaps it was?), swooped in a long, bright curve round the Pleiades, shouted his frosty greetings to Betelgeuse, and was off to the little blue star which pointed the way to the unknown. Forward into the untrodden! Courage, old man, and hold on to your umbrella! Have you got your garters on? Mind your hat! In no time at all we'll be back to Clarice with the frozen time-feather, the rime-feather, the snowflake of the Absolute, the Obsolete. If only we don't wake . . . if only we needn't wake . . . if only we don't wake in that — in that — time and space . . . somewhere or nowhere . . . cold and dark . . . *Cavalleria Rusticana* sobbing among the palms; if a lonely . . . if only . . . the coffers of the poor — not coffers, not coffers, not coffers, oh, God, not coffers, but light, delight, supreme white and brightness, and above all whirling lightness, whirling lightness above all — and freezing — freezing — freezing. . . .[1] *

11. She didn't know when she married Lance that he was a gambler. He dressed well, but not too well; he had better manners than any man she knew; people liked him. She didn't know that nobody quite trusted him, and if she had known, perhaps it would not have made any difference. She knew that he loved her. Worship would be a truer word.

[1] Reprinted from " Mr. Arcularis," in *Among the Lost People*, by Conrad Aiken, published by Charles Scribner's Sons.

He adored her innocence of mind — she was intelligent, but dirt, meanness, treachery, she never seemed to see. Somehow she managed to insulate herself from ugliness. This might have annoyed some men; but Lance, living on the edge of danger, keyed up most of the time to the point of excitement, needed her gift for excluding reality. Going to her was like going into a church, full of blue light, with cool gray walls that shut out the world.

About six weeks after he was buried, she arranged to have the body exhumed. He'd been buried in his soup-to-nuts, and a lottery ticket in an inside pocket had been buried with him. She had found that the ticket had won $25,000.

ASSIGNMENT B

We shall now again analyze some famous passages written by noted authors and experiment in reproducing the effects, still with the object of gaining control over the unified impression. The first presents setting; the second and third present setting and character, and the last, setting, character, and a hint of a situation.

1. The first selection is from Dickens' *Little Dorrit*. The writer's purpose is to impress the reader with a certain sensuous quality in the setting of the story. This is a selection from a novel, not a short story — the short story writer seldom has space in which to build so deliberately the impression of setting alone. The passage is useful, because it enables us to single out this one task of the many which the writer must learn to do simultaneously. Observe with how many different words and how many varied details Dickens has reiterated the feeling of heat, in order to make the reader respond to just that selected quality in the scene.

Thirty years ago, Marseilles lay burning in the sun.

A blazing sun upon a fierce August day was no greater rarity in southern France then, than at any other time, before or since. Everything in Marseilles, and about Marseilles, had stared at the fervid sky, and been stared at in return, until a staring habit had become universal there. Strangers were stared out of countenance by staring white houses, staring white walls, staring white streets, staring tracts of arid road, staring hills from which verdure was burnt away. The only things to be seen not fixedly staring and glaring were the vines drooping under their load of grapes. These did occasionally wink a little, as the hot air barely moved their faint leaves.

There was no wind to make a ripple on the foul water within the harbor, or on the beautiful sea without. The line of demarcation between the two colors, black and blue, showed the point which the pure sea would not pass; but it lay as quiet as the abominable pool, with which it never mixed. Boats without awnings were too hot to touch; ships blistered at their moorings; the stones of the quays had not cooled, night or day, for months. Descendants from all the builders of Babel, come to trade at Marseilles, sought the shade alike — taking refuge in any hiding-place from a sea too intensely blue to be looked at, and a sky of purple, set with one great flaming jewel of fire.

The universal stare made the eyes ache. Towards the distant line of Italian coast, indeed, it was a little relieved by light clouds of mist, slowly rising from the evaporation of the sea; but it softened nowhere else. Far away the staring roads, deep in dust, stared from the hillside, stared from the hollow, stared from the interminable plain. Far away the dusty vines overhanging wayside cottages, and the monotonous wayside avenues of parched trees without shade, drooped beneath the stare of earth and sky. So did the horses with drowsy bells, in long files of carts, creeping slowly towards the interior; so did their recumbent drivers, when they were awake, which rarely happened; so did the exhausted laborers in the fields. Everything that lived or grew was oppressed by the glare, except the lizard, passing swiftly over rough stone walls, and the cicala, chirping his dry hot chirp, like a rattle. The very dust was scorched brown, and something quivered in the atmosphere as if the air itself were panting.

Blinds, shutters, curtains, awnings, were all closed and drawn to keep out the stare. Grant it but a chink or keyhole, and it shot in like a white-hot arrow. The churches were the freest from it. To come out of the twilight of pillars and arches — dreamily dotted with winking lamps, dreamily peopled with ugly old shadows piously dozing, spitting, and begging — was to plunge into a fiery river, and swim for life to the nearest strip of shade. So, with people lounging and lying wherever shade was, with but little hum of tongues or barking of dogs, with occasional jangling of discordant church bells, and rattling of vicious drums, Marseilles, a fact to be strongly smelt and tasted, lay broiling in the sun one day.

Study this; analyze it. Now, for the same effect of heat, write a study of some setting that you are familiar with, bringing out the heat with as many different details as you find in this study. Use the large objects in your setting, use the characteristic life of the place, in industry or commerce, use animals, objects, buildings, making each picture sharply the setting, and making each contribute to the single impression.

Try the same setting for an impression of cold, then for an impression of dreary rain. You can vary this assignment indefinitely. With each added study in which you find ways to use a given setting deliberately to produce an impression, you will gain facility in both planning and writing.

2. The next passage for analysis is from *Lorna Doone*. Here Blackmore builds up for us a picture of the countryside, which conveys an impression simultaneously of the farm and the farmer's

affectionate pride in his land. Character interest and setting are combined, to produce a single impression.

Almost everybody knows, in our part of the world at least, how pleasant and soft the fall of the land is round about Plover's Barrows farm. All above it is strong dark mountain, spread with heath, and desolate, but near our house the valleys cove, and open warmth and shelter. Here are trees, and bright green grass, and orchards full of contentment, and a man may scarce espy the brook, although he hears it everywhere. And, indeed, a stout good piece of it comes through our farm-yard, and swells sometimes to a rush of waves, when the clouds are on the hill-tops. But all below, where the valley bends, and the Lynn stream goes along with it, pretty meadows slope their breast, and the sun spreads on the water. And nearly all of this is ours, till you come to Nicholas Snowe's land.

Write a study using a scene with which you are familiar, to picture a setting in such a way as to produce an impression of both the scene and some character connected with it. Picture a farmer who hates his farm; a baker who is proud of his bake shop; a suburbanite who loves his little house and lot. Be sure that each detail contributes to both elements in the effect. Try the exercise first to produce some kind of sympathetic response to the character — pity, admiration, and so on; next try the same exercise with a group of character-scene combinations to provide negative effects, shock, disgust, disapproval, and so on.

3. The passage below is from Mrs. Wharton's *Ethan Frome*. Here three elements are combined: the setting, the response of the man to the setting and the response of the man to the girl. The purpose is to impress the reader with the third predominantly, to make him feel the romance.

It was during their night walks back to the farm that he felt most intensely the sweetness of this communion. He had always been more sensitive than the people about him to the appeal of natural beauty. His unfinished studies had given form to this sensibility and even in his unhappiest moments field and sky spoke to him with a deep and powerful persuasion. But hitherto the emotion had remained in him as a silent ache, veiling with sadness the beauty that evoked it. He did not even know whether any one else in the world felt as he did or whether he was the sole victim of this mournful privilege. Then he learned that one other spirit had trembled with the same touch of wonder: that at his side, living under his roof and eating his bread, was a creature to whom he could say: "That's Orion down yonder; the big fellow to the right is Aldebaran, and the bunch of little ones — like bees swarming — they're the Pleiades . . ." or whom he could hold entranced before a ledge of granite thrusting up through the fern while he unrolled the huge panorama of the ice age and the long dim stretches of succeeding time. The fact that admiration for his learning mingled with Mattie's wonder at what he taught was not the least part of his pleasure. And there were other sensations, less definable but more exquisite, which drew them together with a shock of silent joy: the cold red of sunset behind winter hills, the flight of cloudflocks over slopes of golden stubble, or the intensely blue shadows of hemlocks on sunlit snow. When she said to him once: "It looks just as if it was painted!" it seemed to Ethan that words had at last been found to utter his secret soul . . .

Now select a character, place him in a setting that is closely identified with his hobby, his work, his sport, or whatever you choose, and introduce into that setting a girl he is attracted to. Try to make *each detail* impress the reader with some sensuous quality of the setting, and simultaneously with the man's relation to the setting, and focus the whole predominantly on the love interest. Try this study with three or four different characters — a man who loves the sea, a man who loves horses, a woman who likes good food, a woman who likes flowers, giving each the setting that will be most helpful to you in bringing out this trait, and subordinating setting and trait to the impression of the action which emphasizes the romance.

4. In the following highly wrought passage from *Madame Bovary* by Flaubert you have again an integration (combination into unified effect) of three elements: a setting, a character and a situation. The setting is Paris, as Emma dreams of it; the trait is her longing for romance in that setting; the situation is her being compelled to live in a place that frustrates her dream of romance. The impression is an objective comprehension of the woman's nature.

Paris, more vague than the ocean, glimmered before Emma's eyes in an atmosphere of vermilion. The many lives that stirred amid this tumult were, however, divided into parts, classed in distinct pictures. Emma perceived only two or three that hid from her all the rest, and in themselves represented all humanity. The world of ambassadors moved over polished floors in drawing rooms lined with mirrors, round oval tables covered with velvet and gold-fringed cloths. There were dresses with trains, deep mysteries, anguish hidden beneath smiles. Then came the society of the duchesses; all were pale; all got up at four o'clock; the women, poor angels, wore English point on their petticoats; and the men, unappreciated geniuses under a frivolous outward seeming, rode horses to death at pleasure parties, spent the summer season at Baden, and towards the forties married heiresses. In the private rooms of restaurants, where one sups after midnight by the light of wax candles, laughed the motley crowd of men of letters and actresses. They were prodigal as kings, full of ideal, ambitious, fantastic frenzy. This was an existence outside that of all others, between heaven and earth, in the midst of storms, having something of the sublime. For the rest of the world it was lost, with no particular place, as if non-existent. The nearer things were, more-over, the more her thoughts turned away from them. All her immediate surroundings, the wearisome country, the middle-class imbeciles, the mediocrity of existence, seemed to her exceptional, a peculiar chance that had caught hold of her, while beyond stretched as far as eye could see an immense land of joys and passions. She confused in her desire the sensualities of luxury with the delights of the heart, elegance of manners with delicacy of sentiment. Did not love, like Indian plants, need a special soil, a particular temperature? Sighs by moonlight, long embraces, tears flowing over yielded hands, all the fevers of the flesh and the languors of tenderness could not be sepa-rated from the balconies of great castles full of indolence, from boudoirs with silken curtains and thick carpets, well-filled flower-stands, a bed on a raised dais, nor from the flashing of precious stones and the shoulder-knots of liveries.

For practice on this more difficult type of integration, choose any character who is in a predicament due to a certain setting, and who reacts strongly to that setting. Write a study in which your details will produce an impression of all three elements, for any effect: sympathy, contempt, objective comprehension, amuse-ment, and so on.

ASSIGNMENT C

We shall now answer some questions concerning an interesting bit of fictional raw material. These questions and their answers will bring you close to problems often faced by professional writ-ers in "working up" real-life material into finished plots and stories, and all of them involve mastery of the principle of the single impression or effect.

The selection on page 89 is just about as confused and unor-ganized as most actual experience. We are not yet ready to turn such bits into complete stories but we can learn something about the very important first steps in planning good stories, by answer-ing the following questions:

1. What *effect* in this selection would interest the largest num-ber of readers? *

2. What other general *effect* which runs through the sketch contrasts strongly with the romantic effect? *

3. What third *effect* is present, which in a rather startling and inexplicable manner contrasts sharply with both the general effects just named?

4. Run over the sketch again now carefully and underline or mark those lines which add nothing to any of the three effects which you have singled out. This may not be easy for you, but

keep at it until you identify all those sentences not directly associated with one of the three effects. How about the first sentence, for example? The near-poverty of John and Susan, to be sure, motivates their riding with a corpse, but this particular sentence itself is not related to the romance, or to the gruesome effect, or to the third effect. This sentence *might be* written to harmonize with one or the other of these effects, to be sure, but it is not now so written, and this I want you to see. In the finished story, for example, if the effect is to be young romance, the author may rewrite the sentence thus: " In the four-room flat, where John lived with Susan, the only thing that was new and shining was their happiness." Most of the sentences in our sketch as it stands are *not* so fused with or integrated into any one effect, and this is just the trouble with it.

5. Is the general effect of this sketch single or double? Answer: It is worse than double; it is confused, because the three or more effects are not related intelligibly or fused into an artistic (emotionally unified) whole. Why, for instance, should the reader be asked to contemplate the young honeymooners riding with a corpse if they are totally indifferent to it? Their love-making in the train would be just as interesting with no corpse in the baggage-car. And there is the third effect, which you discovered. This, being unexplained, is unrelated and thus confusing and unsatisfactory.

6. Could the gruesomeness of the corpse and the sympathetic romantic material be fused into a telling single effect? Answer: Most easily. Love and death are the creative writer's richest themes. The travel-hungry young lovers and their lifeless travelling companion are story stuff made-to-order! The one manipulation most needed is some aversion to the corpse on the part of one or both of the youngsters. With this change, dramatic conflict (which we will study later) enters, and the entire sketch is pulled together and begins to take the form of a short story. What would be the effect of their taking the trip while Susan constantly shudders at thought of their fellow passenger? Romantic pathos. What would be the outcome? This question leads us beyond our present purpose but you see how awareness of mixed effects and the concern for a unified impression introduces order into the writer's first attack upon his material.

7. What change might be made in the original sketch to produce a single impression of romantic tragedy? Not straight tragedy, but *romantic* tragedy, which has a far wider appeal, and is more fascinating to work with?

8. What should we do with the incongruous, unexplained material producing the third effect we found above? Answer: Kill it.

John and Susan lived in a four-room apartment. The living-dining room was furnished with the old easy chair and reading lamp that John's mother had lent him from the family home at the time of their marriage a year before, and secondhand chairs and table bought at auction and repainted; the bedroom had orchid rayon bed covers and drapes — dirty (there was no money to have them cleaned). The bathroom was orchid too. John was especially neat in the bathroom; he always rolled his toothpaste and shaving cream tubes evenly.

In the kitchen there were many new bright-painted cannisters, a cookbook for two, a coffee percolator battered in its service to John in his pre-marriage housekeeping. There was a big hole in the ceiling plaster — the people upstairs had left the water running in their washtubs one night. There were creatures called cockroaches on the insect powder can, but always referred to by Susan delicately as water beetles. A big stain on the floor, that looked like blood, Susan had never been able to scrub clean.

They did not own a car. They had never been on a trip anywhere since their marriage. One day the man who owned the funeral parlor next to the shop where John worked came in and asked John if he'd like to take a trip. He had to send a corpse by train for burial to a town about a hundred miles away. You can't send a corpse without a corpse carrier. John could have the trip if he wanted it.

John hurried home to Susan. They could afford a second ticket by scrimping. How would she like to go? They'd call it a honeymoon. John told her he was sorry she'd had to wait so long for it.

"Don't be silly," she told him. "Who's the bozo we're taking along in the express car?"

"I don't know. He won't bother us," and John winked at her, and laughed.

When he'd gone back to work, Susan packed everything she owned in their two shabby suitcases. One John had bought when he went to college. It looked as if birds had nested in it. Hers she had bought when she had an invitation to a house-party the last year she was in high school. The imitation leather was peeling away from the metal corner pieces. She packed her cap and gown, her tennis shoes, a half dozen hoover aprons, her French lingerie, her business dress, and the shabby old flannel bathrobe. Rolled up in a pair of stockings, tucked into her galoshes, she packed a shining, six-inch stiletto. The jewels in its handle were probably worth more than all the furniture in the flat. Susan took it along for safe-keeping.

John came home that night hurrying. She ran into his arms. "Everything is packed," she said with the air of importance that he found her funniest.

"Whose everything?" he asked, and kissed her ear.

They had pot roast, that night, with cabbage, and noodles, and a blueberry pudding. He had two helpings of everything.

They went to bed at ten o'clock, their usual hour, and slept well, but there was a good deal of noise in the street about two in the morning — some policemen were helping a drunk who couldn't remember his house number. John and Susan watched a while. Then the door across the way opened, the drunk went inside, the police went away, and John and Susan went back to bed.

They got up at eight. For breakfast they had stewed prunes, and toast and coffee. The milk was sour so they drank the coffee black. John said it was better in the old days when he made coffee alone, and kept a can of condensed milk on the window sill. Susan said he could do that hereafter; she didn't know of any reason why not.

They were early at the station. John left Susan alone with the suitcases. When he came back he said: "It's all right. The box is on the truck out on the platform."

He sat beside her, waiting for the train. She felt his gaze on her and looked up, a smile of intimate knowledge flickering around her eyes. "I love you," she whispered, and laid her hand softly on his arm.

"Don't look at me like that," he whispered. "I'm liable to kiss you, and how would you like that?"

"I'd love it," she said, lazily.

The train was on time. John helped Susan into a seat, and found places for their luggage. The car was a day coach, upholstered in shabby green velvet. The air was foul with the odor of stale food, sour babies and unwashed adults.

The train moved out of the station. "That was Mary Blake on the platform," said Susan. "I wonder if that tramp brother of hers is coming home at last. She's been expecting him for months."

"Our seat is at the back of this coach," John announced firmly.

"If I had a brother like that . . ." Susan meditated aloud grimly.

"Damn Mary Blake's brother," said John. "Kiss your husband!"

She turned from the window, and lifted willing lips. No one saw. "I've never," said Susan, "been kissed like that in a railroad car."

John kissed her again. "Twice," he said — and "three for luck."

"The Apache's honeymoon," she said, trying to look fierce.

The conductor came through. He collected the three tickets, one for John, one for Susan, and one for the box in the express car.

ASSIGNMENT D

We come now to experiments with romantic effects. The seven selections chosen for study are climax scenes taken from impressive stories by contemporary authors. The problem here differs from that of the preceding assignment chiefly in that it deals not with widely differing effects but with shadings of the same effect. Capturing shades of romance and reproducing them with different materials is more difficult than the same task with effects produced by death (Chapter I, Assignment E), but for most of us it will be more agreeable.

1. Identify the precise flavor of romance made by each of these excerpts, and state this effect in a single sentence.

2. With your own materials, write studies producing the same effects. Give close attention to the characters. Romance is a quality deriving more from people than from settings or even incidents.

The essential of the discipline is to reproduce the effect of the model as nearly as possible with materials differing as widely as possible. If you cannot easily invent scenes using your own materials, use the characters given in the models, but in this case, change the setting and either increase or decrease the intensity of the original impression.

In the first the effect is pity with a flavor of irony at the girl's efforts to hold a man who is slipping. Your sketch might picture an accidental encounter between the two on the street, or in the home of some friend, a day or so later than the scene in the model.

In the second selection, the impression is a slight distaste at drunken love-making. Your new invention might be the scene when the man and his wife first became acquainted; he is mildly drunk.

Additional material for this same sort of practice can be taken from any of the selections offered as models in other chapters, and, of course, from any scene lifted from a published story, from an episode from real life, etc. In such work you will develop your dexterity. Your task as a writer is to develop facility in invention, and facility means that you can take any sort of material that may appeal to you and do things to it to make it fit into a given purpose.

In practice work like this and the exercises for all of Chapter II you have a method for first attack upon any material. You run through a newspaper. A headline stirs you. You analyze this feeling, identifying the character, situation, or idea, to which you are reacting and the nature of your reaction. Then, recognizing this effect, and its cause, you go ahead as in the above assignment, and write a little scene that produces this effect, with some development of other action for the same people. Then, perhaps, you try out some other possible characters, or another setting, to produce this same feeling. And then, possibly, nothing more will happen, in which case, you drop the whole business into your file for further incubation. Or as you work your feeling may intensify, your sense of the characters grow more real, and presently you'll be on your way to a deliberate arrangement of this stuff for a story. The further checks and controls that must come into play at this next stage will be considered in later chapters.

Or the process may start with a bit of free association writing. As you read it back, some bit of action, some memory will have a certain feeling tone. You identify it, and begin to invent other action using the same or other characters, which will reproduce the same feeling.

Don't be discouraged if you work slowly at such exercises. Facility comes only with much practice. And you will not really win your reward until processes like this have become so habitual that you go through them automatically.

1. "That's what's so swell about us," she said eagerly. "We've really got something. I mean I never get sick of going around with you — and everything. We have a swell time, don't we?"

"Sure," he said.

"We've got so many little things between us, too. Like 'Body and Soul' being kind of our tune."

"Listen," he said, "will you excuse me just a minute? There's someone over there I got to speak to."

"Certainly." She laughed the little laugh. "Hurry back."

He got up and went to the other end of the room. The partition of the booth hid him from her sight.

She got out her powder and lipstick and did her face carefully. When she had finished she looked to see if he was coming back. He was not to be seen, so she took the pocket mirror, larger than the one in her compact, from her purse, and surveyed her face by sections, as much as the mirror would show at a time. She licked her finger and with it smoothed her lifted eyebrows. He still wasn't back.

She didn't want him to come back and find her doing nothing, as if she had nothing to do but sit and wait for him, so she took an old letter from her mother from her purse and read it over and over. She kept looking out of the corner of her eye to see if he was coming.

Finally she saw him standing in the door. He was shaking hands and saying good-by to a man and a girl. When he came back to the table she was deep in her mother's letter.

"Oh, hello!" she said. "Did you miss me?"

He sat down and finished off his sandwich.

"Who's your friend?" she asked.

"Man I used to go to college with." He wiped his mouth with a napkin.

"No, I mean the girl."

"That's his sister."

"Do you like her?"

"Sure, she's a damn nice girl."

"Do you like her better than me?"

"Of course not."

"Honestly, don't you?"

"For God's sake, no."

She laughed again.

"Well, you don't have to get mad. I was just fooling."[1]

[1] Reprinted by permission from "Colloque Sentimentale," by Nancy Hale, published in *Scribner's*, August, 1931.

2. They circled around the room solemnly, colliding at intervals with other dancers. At last Liz stumbled and sat down on the floor. She burst out laughing again till the tears came and streaked across her make-up. Her skirt was pulled up above her knees. John picked her up in his arms and carried her unsteadily to the table. His eyes seemed on fire. He sat down and held her in his lap. He kissed her violently and with maudlin passion. He kissed her lips and her cheeks and her nose and her neck and her hair and her ear. Then he licked his lips and put her back in her chair. She was still laughing.

Through the fog of tobacco-smoke John became aware that all the people were looking at him and snickering. He drew himself out of his chair with dignity. He raised his right hand and rocked a little on his toes.

"Ladiesh and gen'lemen. Thish a lil family party whish I hope you'll exshuse. If thish lady here thatsh laughing wasn't my wife, you could laugh all you had a — had mind to. But she ish my wife, my lil wife Liz, the besh lil wife a man ever had." [1]

3. He felt her slowly relaxing against him, unfolding her tight resistance, as a ripened bud opens. Kissing her throat, he felt a glad tremor spread down through her body, like swiftly growing roots. He stood above her, shoulders thrown back. His limbs were molten, planted in black flame. He took her hands, urging her away toward the levee's crown, where the sand beneath the grass still husbanded the warmth of the sun. They stood embraced. On the brink of the moment possessive, Carey stood bereft of utterance, deferring further ecstasy to realize that their woes had merged and their wills had blended. The heat of her response blinded him like a vapor. [2]

4. She came in the bedroom, a cigarette in her hand. With her free hand she took off her hat and ruffled her hair evenly. She leaned close to a mirror and looked at her clenched teeth, then she sat down on the window-seat and smoked, swinging her very pretty legs. "Why are you home? Were you fired?"

He looked up quickly. "Yes. How'd you know?"

"Why else would you be home?" . . .

"Listen, kid. I'm terribly sorry about last night. I really am. I don't blame you for going out with Muddy. I deserved it."

"Deserved it? What on earth are you talking about? Deserved what? Lord God, can't I go to a speakeasy with one of your best friends without your saying you had it coming to you, as though I were punishing you? Have some sense."

He got up and put on his tie and vest and coat. There was complete silence while he dressed. Then she said: "Listen, Buzz, if they fired you they must have given you a couple of weeks' pay, so give me a hundred dollars before you go out and spend it all, will you please? We'll need it."

[1] Reprinted by permission from "Holiday," by Charles Yost, published in *Harper's*, July, 1930.
[2] Reprinted by permission, from "Potent Delta," by E. P. O'Donnell, published in *Harper's*, March, 1933.

He smiled broadly and went to her and kissed her. "Oh, I do love you, kid. You love me, don't you, really?"

"Look out for my cigarette," she said.[1] *

5. "Can't he see if it weren't for this I'd never, I'd rather die than—" His voice gave out. "Nell, Nell, I'm so unhappy . . ."

My love, my little love. She put out her hands and took his, and drew him down beside her. Their hands touching. All at once there was only that. It did not change what they had been saying, it set it apart from them, a world apart. She felt the flesh of his hands against hers. His hands were not too firm or too supple, not too hot or too cold. And all of himself was in them, for he was like that. He was all of a piece, nothing divided, nothing held back. Simple, people called it. Was there no place in the world for men like that?

He sat close beside her and gradually everything yielded to the touch of their clasped hands. And vague there came to her something she had seen in a book — The transitoriness of the universe can take from me nothing that was once truly mine. Take from me! She closed her eyes over her tears.

"Ed, come closer."

Her voice was a whisper and came from far down, painfully deep in her throat. He lay on the bed and his weight on top of the covers pinned them tight over her. Their bodies lay alongside each other's close, the covers between. She felt the flow, profound, of all of her to him, all of him to her. She felt her strength flow to him, her will, her vision that he had to have. The vitalurgic fluid that was herself. And when her strength was gone? When she died out there? Ah, then perhaps Ed would find his own.[2]

6. "Oh, I think you're wonderful!" jeered Candace. "Oh, how strong you are! Oh, what marvellous, big, enormous muscles!"

Meeting the mockery of her black eyes and parted lips, he felt a glow of excitement because her small body was close, and it was warm and silken, and firm and smooth as a young birch tree.

He pulled her nearer and kissed her with tentative gentleness. Her lips clung. She relaxed in his arms, and her soft responsiveness sent an answering flood through his veins. Her mouth was sweet and passionate. He went blind with the dim consciousness that something amazing and wonderful had happened.

When she turned away, Scott found that he was shaking. Her face was flushed; she looked shy and couldn't find any careless words to say. . . .

He could not explain that inner trembling and the fact that Candace now seemed entirely different. The contours of her small face had all at once become a matter of quickening interest; her brown hands were suddenly dear. The way she held her funny square shoulders, the turn of her throat, the smooth skin of her back, the

[1] Reprinted by permission from "Early Afternoon," by John O'Hara, published in *Scribner's*, July, 1933.

[2] Reprinted by permission from "What Was Truly Mine," by Grace Flandrau, published in *Scribner's*, August, 1932.

soft, sulky twist of her lips, even her thin elbows — these had suddenly become curiously vital and disturbing. . . .

"Listen, darling!" Scott began again, but he hadn't the least idea what he wanted to say.

After a moment Candace said: "We can't be like this, Scott. I don't know what happened — what got into us." She had, after all, the feminine urge or necessity to talk all around and over an emotion. "You see we've had an unusual kind of — comradely sort of thing, you know — and working together. And it's really idiotic to get sloppy the very last night you're here."

Her cool voice might have deceived Scott but for the luminous flush just below her eyes, the way her eyes evaded his, struggling not to kindle again.

He took her face between his hands. "You're an adorable fiend. And I'm terribly afraid I've fallen in love with you."

. . . For a while she was perfectly still, looking past him through the window at the moonlight. Then she folded her arms about his head and held it against her breast with the most beguiling tenderness.

"Why are you afraid?" she asked. "I've loved you all summer. Scott! Dear, dear Scott!"

"Dear, dear Candace!"

"And you really do love me then?"

. . . . . .

She ran her fingers through his brown hair. "You have the softest hair. It has a little bit of wave in it. I wish you would go to Chicago instead (of New York)."

"Why?"

"Then you wouldn't be so far away . . . Oh, Scott! I'm wheedling you like the silliest little flapper. I didn't suppose I could ever be sickening like that!"

"What's the good of Chicago when you can go to New York? I like to have you want me close, though."

He kissed her, and the passionate, unreasoning emotion shook him again.

"Candace! You are wearing perfume."

She looked embarrassed. "I know it. It's almost the only idiotic thing I like — except you, of course. I love it. Do you love it?"

"I love you. What kind is it?"

"Chypre."

He laughed. "A girl told me Chypre was supposed to be seductive, esoteric, wanton — "

"I don't care. I wanted you to like me. I read in a book that if you wore a certain kind of perfume, a man would think about you and his senses be stirred and everything."

"My senses are stirred. But I don't need Chypre. Candace, you're a little hussy."

"I don't care. I wish you wouldn't go away." [1]

[1] Reprinted by permission from "Skywriters," by Lois Seyster Montross, published in *Good Housekeeping,* September, 1930.

7. "You *are* a one," she brought out, with dry-lipped coquetry. He moved his hand round her waist. Abruptly her bulk unstiffened, clamped itself against him with clumsy exasperated voluptuousness. As her hand pulled against the back of his neck he observed his ironical intention lose its edge, soften into sensation, and harden suddenly into impulse. He kissed her lips, interested by their roundness and innocence of paint, and went on kissing, fascinated by her genteel scent of violet-talc and mild perspiration, by the animalism and intermittent prudery which made her embrace, in that minute or so, a quintessence of feminine courtship. . . . Speculatively and because she was heavy, he drew her down beside him on the edge of the bed. She reacted as he had foreseen. She banged to her feet and began to tidy her hair. He was relieved; and dimly infuriated. He took out his handkerchief, wiped his mouth, and blew his nose while she was saying that he'd "got a nerve." [1]

Note to Student and Teacher

I wish to add a final word to this chapter to emphasize the importance of the exercises with which it concludes. They cannot be too conscientiously performed if the learning writer is determined to attain the maximum of skill in the minimum of time. Unlike most of the assignments concluding succeeding chapters, these at the end of this chapter involve much writing. Writing long passages of narrative dominated by a consciously held single effect has great disciplinary value. Furthermore, no principle in story writing, as I have stated elsewhere, is held to more consistently by good writers of all grades than this of unified impression. At this stage of the student's progress, every minute spent in the analysis of effects or in the writing of effect studies will be rewarded by a sure increase in power and skill.

[1] Reprinted by permission from "Vacuum Cleaners," by Sylvia Thompson, published in *Harper's*, July, 1932.

PART TWO

THE MATERIALS OF NARRATIVE
A Study of What the Writer Works With

PART TWO

THE MATERIALS OF NARRATIVE

A Study of What the Writer Works With

CHAPTER THREE

KINDS OF STORY INTERESTS

Art is the best way of doing a thing.
— ANONYMOUS

In the preceding chapters we have studied the narrative purpose. We learned that the fiction writer's purpose is to produce certain " effects," and that the length of any story limits the number of effects which it can produce successfully. We shall now learn how these effects are dependent also upon the nature of the material itself. We therefore take the next step in our study of plotting by learning how to analyze our story ideas.

The mastery of literary materials is the narrative writer's most baffling task; baffling because, as explained in our introduction, his materials are far more complex and elusive than those with which any other artist works. His material is human nature itself; but what is human nature? No one knows. Philosophers from Aristotle to Dewey have studied this problem exhaustively and have succeeded only in discovering certain guide posts which help the scientist in his great task of understanding. This we do know: of all the infinite number of human acts only a few combinations are possible and only a small part of these few are harmonious and pleasing enough to be used as literary material.

In our study of material, the narrative purpose itself will give us our best guide. For one thing, it narrows our problem. We know that we need not make any effort to gain complete scientific understanding of our materials; if we know enough about them to be able merely to make an

97

impression, it will suffice. If our story lights up only one little spot of life, presenting it in magnificent isolation, it may not produce understanding at all, but it will succeed in its purpose.

1. Classification of Interests

Our first problem is to reduce the chaos in which story ideas generally occur to us. We must find some order or classification for the phenomena of life itself. One method of classification immediately suggests itself. If our artistic purpose is to produce effects, why not classify all our materials in accordance with the effects they obviously may be made to produce?

The difficulty of doing this is evident. We have already seen that the effects possible to the narrative writer are infinite in number. Of these we might list a thousand or so, and sort all our materials accordingly, placing them under one or another of these thousand emotional effects. In doing so we would have joined together the material and the purpose, and something definite would be gained; also we'd be tottering into our graves with the job unfinished and no writing done!

Prodigious and futile task! No classification of material can obviously be of much practical use to the writer unless the categories are very few. Research into this question has disclosed the fact that all emotional effects can be put under four heads according to the materials from which they derive. These four heads are going to be of the utmost importance to us. Let us examine them. The emotional effect of a story may be produced by —

1. Emphasis on character;
2. Emphasis on an event;
3. Emphasis on setting;
4. Emphasis on a general truth.

All the material that goes into a story may be put into one or more of these classifications. They are, in other words, kinds of materials; they are not story patterns nor even effects. A given effect could conceivably be produced by any or all of these different kinds of material. These four classifications may, in fact, be applied to story material before any use whatever has been made to put it into stories. The stuff of narrative is human conduct and these categories exist in all human conduct; all human activity, in short, is composed, of *people, actions, places* and *ideas* about people, actions and places. The four categories are scientific rather than artistic groupings. They are ultimate divisions.

Faulty Methods of Division

This cannot be said of the many attempts to classify story material on the basis of the patterns in which it can be used or the effects which it can be made to produce. " The story of dramatic incident," " the love story," " the humorous story," " the psychological story," and " character sketches," classifications used in Professor Benjamin A. Heydrick's little collection of *Types of the Short Story,* are based not only on kinds of material (character story) but also on ways they can be used (stories of dramatic incident and the psychological story). Similarly in Mr. J. Berg Essenwein's *Writing the Short-story* we find short story divisions based on "types of humanity," "moral nature," " occupations," " locality," " wonder," " social classes " and " emotion." Here we have fundamental classifications of subject matter mingled with story patterns and effects. This scheme of grouping and that of Professor Heydrick are suggestive guides for readers, but as working bases for a systematic attack on the problems of understanding story material and plotting they are of no value whatever.

A more notable and curious effort to discover ultimate divisions in dramatic materials is Georges Polti's erudite *The Thirty-Six Dramatic Situations.* The very fact that the " situations " are stated to be dramatic indicates that

Polti's divisions apply not to the raw stuff of human conduct but to this stuff after it has been manipulated into given story patterns. Now the variety of patterns into which human activity can be arranged is obviously infinite. Polti's categories as an arbitrary summary of certain patterns of action he has discovered in stage plays, from which he takes practically all his illustrations, are an academic compilation of use only to those interested in — academic compilations! Polti himself expresses doubt about there being only thirty-six dramatic categories. Some of them, such as " Disaster " and " Obtaining," could easily be made to include just about all the others! The list is, as Polti observes, " unaccompanied by any explanation " of its sponsors; no statement of the relations among the different categories has ever been attempted.

There is as much revelation about the essential nature of drama in these cabalistic groupings of Polti's as there would be revealed about the culinary possibilities of a binful of potatoes by arranging them in piles according to the pattern of their nubs. As to Polti's assertion that there are but thirty-six emotions — it can scarcely be taken seriously; how about, for instance, the possible *combinations* of these emotional imperatives? Is it possible that they are not only immutable but also isolated, solitary entities never to be mingled with each other?

No, if you wish only to make a rough grouping of stories for the convenience of the reader, divisions based upon effects and patterns can be made to do; but if you wish to understand literary processes you must begin with a classification of the thing you begin with. Our beginning is " story ideas," observations, knowledge of life. This is our raw material, and therefore we accept from psychology the four convenient divisions mentioned above: *people, actions, places* and *ideas* about people, actions and places.

I hold it to be absolutely necessary that the story writer should know, and hold constantly in mind from the first step with his plot, the kind of material he is working with.

Before we take up the questions of story patterns at all or ways and means to secure given effects with these materials, we must devote our attention to these four fundamental groupings of story material. They form the foundation of all we shall do from now on. They will guide our thinking as we plan our stories and help us focus our emotions as we write them. Let me therefore attempt more detailed explanations.

The Four Patterns Explained

1. *Effects produced by Character:* There can be of course no dramatic situation without human beings. Even in the one apparent exception, the story with an animal hero, a human trait is read into the creature and made to sustain the narrative. Story material which belongs in this category means not a story with a character, but one which interests the reader more by reason of its character development than in any other way. The character, in other words, dominates. The reader is attending to the conduct of an actor rather than to the interests produced by the other three categories. And, above all, his emotions center upon some aspect of the character.

2. *Effects produced by Complications:* The word " complication " in general means the entanglement of persons and circumstances which makes the plot — the rich man's designs against the poor working girl, the old mother who finds that her only son no longer loves her, the passion of two men for the same girl, the struggle for business supremacy which makes men scheme against each other — these are commonplace examples of the limitless congregation of factors which in general are called complications. This word, however, is used in this system of classifications in a somewhat narrower and more technical sense. It means again not merely complicating factors, but material presenting a sharply defined twist of events. The reader's attention, in other words, is held and his emotion roused more by a peculiar or striking event than it is by any of the other three methods.

3. *Effects produced by Atmosphere:* Generally speaking, the place where the plot unfolds is the story setting, and gives it atmosphere; and all the furnishings of the place belong to the setting. The hill top on which the beacon fires are lighted to save the ship at sea; the valley where the conspirators meet at night; the cluttered room with the battered oaken chest which holds the old squire's will — of such stuff, geographical and otherwise, are settings made.

Once again, for the purpose of this category, the word atmosphere has a special technical meaning. It means more than setting; it means that the setting is so important in the plot action that it itself acts as a leading character in the story. The things that happen in the action are directly the result of the quality of the atmosphere, and through this quality the emotional effect is produced in exactly the same way as through a character trait in a character story.

4. *Effects produced by Theme:* The word " theme " is here also used in a special technical sense. The general dictionary meaning is, of course, " a topic, a subject of discourse." For the purpose of this classification, it means not the plot idea but rather the underlying truth about life which the plot action illustrates. The thematic plot, which often produces the finest type of story, is the most difficult type of plot to handle, and few students ever master it. One difficulty is that the technical meaning of the word itself is not understood. In a thematic story the theme is the idea of which the narrative is the dramatic expression. It is to narrative what the *motif* is to a piece of music, what the " lesson " is to a religious picture, what, in fine, as we shall learn in Chapter Seven, the " moral " is to a fable or parable. In the thematic story, the characters, settings, and the action are conceived as means for presenting a truth about life.

The Importance of Four Patterns

Now all this is pretty abstract, and will possibly inspire you to say: " If I have to bother over a lot of definitions such as these to learn literary technique, I'll none of it! " These statements, however, are not useless definitions: they are classifications, and, as you shall see, they are a convenient means to a much-desired end.

You will, for one thing, discover as you continue with your writing that you will tend to use story ideas which belong to one or two of these categories more than to the others. You will, like William Dean Howells, for instance, become especially interested in beginning with character types and working out actions which exemplify their characters, or like Maupassant, you will be most interested in dramatic complications, and will add such characters as will bring out these complications. Like O. Henry and Anton Chekhov you may be most interested in writing stories which express your philosophy of life; or possibly your interest may be that which has so often inspired Conrad's pen — you will wish to portray landscapes, exotic, fateful atmospheres, and show their effects on the human soul.

Examples of Four Story Patterns

Let me now continue to develop the four categories given above with some concrete examples. In considering these examples you will do well to review the more abstract statements above. It is not enough to be able to identify a few instances; you should interest yourself in the principles; and they have been set forth clearly above. Let me take material which was finally used in a published story reprinted at the end of the last chapter of this book, and show you how it could have been manipulated to fit each of the four categories.

First Category — Character

A Russian entomologist whose life passion is his zeal for discovering new species of poisonous insects and spiders, spends several months every year in the heart of a torrid, desolate desert, risking his life with tarantulas and scorpions to further his scientific work. He is warned continually by the natives that he takes his life in his hands. Still he continues his work. On one occasion he was bitten by a tarantula and barely escaped death after weeks of terrible suffering.

Second Category — Complication

The same Russian professor built himself a little stone house in the center of the desert where the insects were most numerous. In this station he kept several glass boxes full of live insects. On one occasion he accidentally upset these boxes so that scores of deadly insects flitted about over the walls. Inasmuch as they were attracted by the odor of human perspiration they clustered especially deep around doors and the two small windows. This made it impossible for him to escape. The spiders began dropping upon him from the ceiling. He smashes the door with an ax and escapes.

Third Category — Atmosphere Material

The same Russian professor struggles desperately against the loneliness and heat of the desert. His zeal for his work makes him scorn the enervating effects of the heat, the blinding glare of the sun, the danger of the continually shifting sand, and the utter desolation. In time the influences of the sand, sun, and heat, and loneliness wear on him, until finally his reason is affected. He has a delusion that fresh lakes bordered by cool grass and trees are not far away. Constantly appearing mirages deceive him. Finally when he can stand it no longer, he strolls away from his little station to find relief at one of these supposed oases. He never returns.

Fourth Category — Theme Material

The Russian professor has a companion. The two men get on each other's nerves. It is impossible for them to escape for a certain period. They must remain together. Their enmity grows. They discuss the origin of the instinct of fighting. They finally reach a morbid state where they agree that they cannot settle their differences in any way except by a duel which will eliminate one of them. They find, however, that if one of them perishes the other will also perish. Two men are needed to erect the shelters against the desert winds and load the camels. This dependence upon each other forces them to delay their murderous plan until they emerge from the desert, when they discover that their enmity has vanished.

The theme demonstrated dramatically by this last episode is this: Men learn to stand together by being forced to do so by some external danger greater than their menace to each other.

I hope you see clearly in what way the above narrative outlines differ most from one another. The *materials*, the ideas themselves, are in each instance substantially the same. The differences among them are variations in the pattern or scheme of organization. We have, as a matter of fact, advanced a step beyond mere classification of our raw materials. We have by manipulation brought out so strongly the inherent differences among the different patterns that we have produced four fairly complete story outlines. The very great possibilities that lie in this process we shall inquire into at length in later chapters.

The first example produces its effect through character. There is *something* of complication and atmosphere and theme in it, but these latter are distinctly subordinate to that of the character interest. The hero is an enthusiastic entomologist. He is absorbed in his work to such an amazing degree that we call him, in literary language, " a character " All the action in the story has but one aim: to illustrate, dramatize, prove this one peculiarity of his nature. The effect is produced through emphasis on character.

The second outline produces its effect through a complication. Search for the scientific zeal mentioned in the first version; it isn't there; nothing is said about it. The man probably *is* interested, but we don't emphasize the fact; it is necessary to give him merely enough interest in his work to bring him into the setting where the story takes place. Our mind is now centered on something else, another effect, a complication, an event rather than a trait of character: the *situation* of the man trapped by the insects.

The third example may be more difficult to understand if, like most people, you have always thought of setting as merely the place where the story action is located. In the vast majority of cases it is just this and no more; but it *may* be more than this. It may actually become as important as a leading character; it may *be* the leading character. Settings — earth, rocks, water, buildings — obviously can't have desires or motives; but they can have mood, temperament, and even movement or conduct. In the third outline above, for instance, there is a conflict between the scientist and the desert. The character trait of scientific zeal is opposed by the " trait " of withering heat. Since the heat conquers, the desert itself has played the predominant role and is therefore the main character or hero. The effect here, then, is produced by emphasis on a quality of the setting.

Still greater difficulty faces us in gaining a clear understanding of the fourth classification. The difficulty is due to an almost inevitable confusion between form and content, between purpose and materials, and to a lack of words which express accurately the necessary distinctions. Clear understanding depends largely upon grasping the technical meaning given the word " theme." The explanation on page 102 should be read carefully and compared with the fourth plot above.

2. Noted Stories Analyzed for Interests *

The four classifications of material which we are studying are not standards, or divisions, to be imposed forcibly

* In addition to the examples given in this chapter, other recent stories illustrating the four classifications will be found in Section H of the Appendix, and in *Short Story Hits, 1932* and *1933*.

on our story ideas; they are not preconceived patterns. They are divisions which *are actually in, and a part of, every conceivable bit of human activity which could be used for a narrative.* We can see this clearly if we take a number of more or less well-known short stories and see how they all illustrate these classifications. The more perfect and powerful the story, in fact, the more exactly and precisely it exemplifies one or more of our classifications.

We will examine a few stories which you have read, or which you can probably secure in your school or town library.

Character Stories

The Piece of String,* by Maupassant: The main character is Hauchecorne, the old peasant, and the whole story concerns his trait of sensitiveness. He is falsely accused of stealing a purse. He denies it with pathetic eagerness. The purse is found. In spite of this proof of his innocence, he is so sensitive that he continues to deny his guilt and keeps this up until he goes crazy and dies still protesting that he did not take it.

What is the single effect of this story? Obviously it is pity for the tragedy of a super-sensitive old peasant. "Pity" expresses the *nature of the effect,* but "a super-sensitive old peasant" indicates *how the effect was secured.* From beginning to end this trait of character is reiterated. As a result you have an effect due to tragic moral sensitiveness, an effect due, that is, to character.

Other character stories which you may read and analyze to profit at this stage are: *The Substitute,* by Coppée; *Uncle Jim and Uncle Billy,* by Bret Harte; *A Cosmopolite in a Cafe* and *The Romance of a Busy Broker,* by O. Henry; *Only a Subaltern* and *Namgay Doola,* by Kipling; *Brooksmith,* by Henry James; and *Once More,* by Galsworthy.

Complication Stories

The Cask of Amontillado, by Poe: The complication idea of this story has been used, and is still being used by many

* In *The Odd Number,* Harpers.

authors — a man being sealed up alive in a wall, to remain there until he dies. In this story the hero lures his enemy into a cellar and manages, by a ruse, to fasten him in a recess in a wine crypt. He then proceeds to seal him up with cement and stones. "For a half of a century no mortal has disturbed the masonry."

The interest here is plainly in the walling-up-to-die business. Interest in character is secondary. Poe himself was so much absorbed with the idea of killing a man in this manner that he did not even tell the reader the motive for the horrible revenge: the perpetrator of the crime had suffered a "thousand injuries" at the hands of his enemy. The author lets it go at that. As for explaining the hero's diabolical cruelty, he merely assumes that the reader "knows the nature of his soul"! The single effect of horror depends entirely upon the manner of the death; there was need therefore merely to narrate it and stop.

*The Gift of the Magi** by O. Henry: In this story the author, who was given to bizarre inventions, used an especially neat and well-defined entanglement. A wife is bent upon making her husband a present of a much-desired watch chain. Being without the necessary cash to purchase it, she has her hair cut off, sells it, and with the money buys the gift. At the same time the husband, equally anxious to please his wife, sells his watch and with the money buys her a comb for her beautiful hair! "Of all who give and receive gifts, such as they are the wisest. Everywhere they are wisest. They are the magi."

No argument is needed to establish the focus of interest in this story. The single effect of sympathetic amusement at the ironic mal-coincidence of the gifts is dependent upon nothing but the event itself. The author, apparently sensing the weakness of the character interest, endeavored to supply the defect in part by appending a final paragraph of commendation of the self-sacrificing devotion of the married lovers, part of which is quoted at the end of the outline above.

Other well-known stories which depend for their effects

* In *The Four Million*, Doubleday, Page & Co.

almost entirely upon complications are: *An Episode under the Terror* and *The Grande Brétêche*, by Balzac (the latter containing the same complication idea as in the *Cask of Amontillado*); *Rappaccini's Daughter*, by Hawthorne; *The Siege of Berlin*, by Daudet; *The Furnished Room*, by O. Henry; *The Sire de Maletroit's Door*, by Stevenson; *On the City Wall* and *The Strange Ride of Marrowbie Jukes*, by Kipling; *The Necklace*, by Maupassant; *The Pit and the Pendulum* and *The Black Cat*, by Poe; *The Lady or the Tiger*, by Frank R. Stockton; *A Sight for the Gods*, by Gouverneur Morris; *What Was It? — a Mystery*, by Fitz James O'Brien; and *The Monkey's Paw*, by W. W. Jacobs.

Atmosphere Stories

The Merry Men, by Stevenson: The main character of this story is the sea about the Isle of Aros on the west coast of Ireland. The sea's "main trait" is its "desolate melancholy" produced by storms, rocks, reefs, and shipwrecks. The influence of these "sad sea feelings" is so great that an old ex-sailor living on the island is driven from superstitious melancholy into a morbid fear of the sea which ends in his rushing into the swirling surf and drowning himself.

This narrative (which is analyzed in detail in Chapter Eight) produces an effect on the reader of awe and horror — an emotion much like the mood of the seascape in the story. The harmony found here between character trait (mood of setting) and effect is impossible with other story types. The technique involved in this type of narrative is dealt with later.

*The Lagoon,** by Conrad: The main character of this story is a Malay country whose mood or trait is thus described by the author: "a shadowy, mysterious country of inhuman strife, of inextinguishable desires and fears, a battle-field of phantoms terrible and charming, august or ignoble, struggling ardently for possession of our helpless hearts." Two lovers hiding from wrathful pursuers in this jungle region are gradually overwhelmed by its baleful influence. The woman dies; the man is left in "the darkness of a world of illusions."

* In *Tales of Unrest*, Doubleday, Page & Co.

The single effect of this atmosphere story is again much the same as the emotional tone of the setting described — a brooding, fatalistic depression.

The number of powerful stories which produce their effects mainly by the development of atmosphere as the main character is small indeed. The student who wishes to examine other narratives of this type will do well to study the stories which depend for their effects only in part on the development of atmosphere. *The Fall of the House of Usher* by Poe is capitally suited to such analysis. Although, as explained in Chapter Eight, it gives equal emphasis to *character, complication,* and *atmosphere,* a careful study of the last element will disclose much of the artistry of this story. O. Henry's story, *A Matter of Mean Elevation,* should be read as a carelessly handled instance of forcing the effects of settings upon human souls to the point of burlesque.

Our purpose here is merely to learn how to identify *atmosphere material* as we proceed. It will be advisable for some time for you to file away all such ideas to use later when you shall have developed greater skill in the use of the simpler story forms.

Thematic Stories

An Unfinished Story,* by O. Henry: In this brief sketch — it is scarcely more than that — Dulcie, a department store sales-girl, is faced with the problem of living on six dollars a week. She is insufficiently fed, poorly clad, and has no pleasures. Her only " company " is Piggy, an immoral wretch, a " connoisseur in starvation." He calls. Dulcie, restrained by the reproachful face of General Kitchener looking down from his gilt frame on the wall, doesn't go out — this time. " The rest of it comes later — sometime when Piggy asks Dulcie again to dine with him, and she is feeling lonelier than usual, and General Kitchener happens to be looking the other way; and then — "

Here we have a clearly marked " thematic story." Its essential material is not character, complication, or atmos-

* In *The Four Million,* Doubleday, Page & Co.

phere, but — an idea! The idea, or theme, is this: " The most heartless villainy in the world is hiring working-girls at starvation wages." The single effect is pity for the tragic fate of Dulcie and abhorrence of the men who make her suffering inevitable. The emotional presentation is accomplished by the story itself which proves the theme. It is emotional because it is dramatic. The story of *one* underpaid shop girl itself grips and holds you; the *idea* of *all* underpaid shop girls also enlarges and intensifies your thoughts about the whole problem dealt with, though you may not be as conscious of your thoughts on the subject as you are of your emotions. The author, indeed, fearing that you might " miss the point " of his little story, begins and ends it with some " irrelevant stuff " which tells you quite definitely what it is all about.

*Old Age,** by Anton Chekhov: An elderly man returns to the small village where he spent his youth and young manhood, only to find that he is practically forgotten. He visits the grave of his wife, now long dead, thinking he will drop a tear of pity and regret; but, though he swallows hard, no lump comes into his throat, and, blink his eyes as he will — there are no tears.

The essential material or underlying idea of this brief story is: " Age wipes out all." The single effect is *melancholy* or *consolation* (depending upon the age of the reader) *at the thought of how old age prepares one for death.* Although utterly different in subject matter and treatment from the thematic story above, it nevertheless secures its chief effect by exactly the same technical means, the dramatic development of an idea about life. Story and theme of both this story and the other just above are analyzed in Chapter Seven. Here we are interested only in identifying thematic materials when we see them.

As explained in Chapter Seven, the plotting of the thematic story presents problems baffling to all except those of a philosophic turn, who by much practice have gained skill in handling literary materials. Beginning a story with

*In *The Horse Stealers,* Huebsch.

a character, a complication, or an atmosphere presents not a fraction of the difficulty in beginning with a theme, an abstract idea about life. The manipulations of character involved in arbitrarily fitting people to themes are often so great as to destroy the life-like spontaneity of these characters. This is a heavy price to pay. Where, as fortunately often happens, a theme lies embedded in the original real life characters and their acts, the problem is much easier; for such opportunities we must be especially watchful; and since they do sometimes occur we shall include the thematic story in our present search for and study of story materials.

Other stories like the two outlined above which attain their effects almost entirely by thematic development are: *The Beggar*, by Maupassant; *The Birthmark*, by Hawthorne; *William Wilson*, by Poe; and *Thrown Away*, by Kipling. Stories in which the effect is produced by one or more of the other three means as well as by use of a theme (such stories are much more numerous than the pure thematic) are: *The Municipal Report* and *The Roads We Take*, by O. Henry; *By the Rod of His Wrath*, by William Allen White; *Ligeia*, by Poe.

3. Importance of Mastering Interest Patterns

We are now ready, I think, to begin putting to practical use this story material. Much practice will be necessary to make the scheme your own; you will not even sense its value until it begins to operate automatically without your being aware of using it. For some time, doubtless, this method of seeing and plotting stories will seem clumsy and mechanical. This is inevitable in the mastery of any new process. For a time at the beginning you must be laboriously conscious of every step, in order that some day you may be unconscious of them; in no other way can you win your artistic freedom. A runner during a critical race does not think of the way his legs are performing; his stride is straight, his toes reach the cinder path before his heel, simply because at the beginning of his training he watched his knees, toes, and heels. " Art," someone has said, " is efficiency of function," and we are now isolating the simplest of the story writer's functions and trying to perfect them.

The particular function we are studying in this chapter is that which solves these problems: Just where *is* the story? How can I tell one when I see it? How shall I begin the plotting of it? All too often the young writer spends long hours in futile and distressing efforts to plan a story simply because, while he may have excellent material, he doesn't know what a story is! He travels furiously — in circles! He palpitates with creative afflatus; he wants to write something mightily, just what he isn't sure. He is unable, in the language of psychology, to fix his attention on the end-result.

4. How to Secure Story Material

Before we begin work on the " raw material " in the assignments for this chapter, I must say a word about this raw material itself. How are we going to get it? What is the technique of securing ideas of things to write about? This problem was touched upon in the Introduction and in Chapter One. A desire to say something must be part of the student's original equipment if he is to attain real success. Some help, however, can be given. Like the man in *Acres of Diamonds* you may be setting out for distant and perilous gold fields, unaware that precious nuggets are imbedded in the stone wall before your cottage!

In the Appendix you will find a memorandum on *How to Secure Story Ideas* which may suggest new sources of material; it will also give you a plan for storing your ideas away systematically. Please read it carefully before going further with this chapter and make a beginning at least of the plan for filing your material. Remember again that even in such mechanical matters as filing literary notes the main objective just now is not the securing of smashing story ideas or writing powerful narratives. Your purpose now is to gain system, method, to eliminate worry over details by mastering them. If you are still in college, or younger than twenty-five, you may be quite sure that practically all your ideas and manuscripts will some day be thrown away for the product of your more mature years. Don't for that reason postpone your beginning at collecting and arranging your observations on life. Don't imitate; be yourself; be sincere; if your ideas are your own it is enough. Quantity, not quality, of ideas is now the important thing.

Characters Real and Imagined

At this point many student writers will ask this question: Shall I write about people I see in real life or should I " make up " my characters? The only advice that can be given is to try both ways and keep to the one which gives the best results. Make experiments. Try yourself out. Study your own psychology. Some writers work after the manner of newspaper reporters: they secure all their effects from actual observation; they are generally good observers, and their writing is realistic in manner. Other writers work after the manner of poets; they are dreamers; they are gifted with creative imagination; and in general they write about their hopes, their desires, their Castles in Spain! To know in which of these two classes of writers you belong — and you may, like many others, belong more or less to both classes — is an important piece of self-knowledge. Expert personal guidance here is of more value than anywhere else, and you should avail yourself of such help if you can secure it.

Two Types of Writers

Most young writers are of the " reporter " type described above. They feel an urge to write about the life that is going on about them. You perhaps belong to this class. You want to tell other people what you see. You complain, however, that there is a sad lack of " human interest" materials in your city, village, or college community. So far as you can see no one around you is enacting a Dickens novel or a *Main Street* best seller or an O. Henry story. You may even be dreaming of that happy day when you can go to Some Other Place where you *know* there is story material because you have read wonderful stories pitched in those climes. Vain delusion! The best places to cull story ideas are precisely where other writers have *not* been. If there are no story ideas where you live now, there are probably none anywhere — for you! Story ideas there are a-plenty wherever there are people.

Many students are helped most in taking hold of this particular problem by being told exactly how it is handled by someone else. Let me therefore give you an account of my own activity in this department of my writing during the last three days before writing this chapter. I happen to be a cliff-dweller of Manhattan. Certainly no one could imagine a less romantic or adventurous setting than this world of endless brick apartments, throbbing automobile traffic, subways, and preoccupied, busy throngs. Here the layman sees thousands of people daily and knows not one of them well enough to speak to. His neighbor living but six inches away in the adjoining cubicle might just as well be living in China for all he knows about the man's personality or life problems.

The Story of Four Plot Ideas

During the last three days before writing this, however, I have without special effort, gathered the following material:

1. I was having my shoes shined in the little repair shop across the street. The newspapers that morning were full of despatches from the Near East about massacres by the Turks. I asked the shoemaker, who was obviously a foreigner, from what country he had come. He was an Armenian. A few inquiries disclosed the fact that during the war he and his family had been driven out with all their village. He saw his mother shot down. One sister had drowned herself. Another sister had disappeared.

2. A silk merchant from a southern town was introduced to me by a friend of mine. This merchant, who had come to place an order for $40,000 worth of silk goods, could neither read nor write, and was convoyed about New York by a twelve-year-old boy. The lad read the subway signs for him!

3. I noticed the shabbily dressed bent figure of an old woman who walked up and down before the subway entrance. This woman, who, I discovered, belongs to a well-to-do family, lost two sons during the war. She was officially informed of their deaths. She has ceased to care about her dress, and spends almost the entire day pacing up and down before the subway entrance, examining each one of the hundreds who come out, hoping that some day among them she will discover her sons.

4. A clerk in a nearby drug store is a Russian Jew. Upon being questioned about his home country he informs me that his brothers and sisters and his mother are still living in the soviet country and writing him constantly their eager desire to leave for America. The aged mother, however, is an invalid and cannot stand the journey. There are no friends or relatives in their village with whom they could leave her. For three years they have waited for her to die. The brothers in their last letter, the clerk told me, had submitted to him a plan by which they would simply lock their mother in the house and start out for America, leaving her to her own fate!

5. The Writer's First Writing

Each of these experiences was briefly jotted down at once as raw material, in the form of notes, in my pocket notebook. Before filing them away, I classified each one and gave it a first manipulation in the direction of a story plot. Let me now explain these two processes.

I wished to do two things: first, definitely classify the material; and, second, write out the " inspirations " that occurred to me as I had the experience or reviewed it afterwards. Let us take them in order:

1. *The Armenian shoemaker:* This story immediately classified as " thematic material." I arrived at this decision simply from the way the experience hit *me.* I had this thought:

Think of the millions of Americans who will see those tragic headlines about the deaths of thousands in the Near East without a tremor of emotion; they will turn over the page, thinking, ' Too far away, doesn't touch me,' and will pore over an account of how the Giants the day before at the ball grounds "slaughtered " the Green Sox! We Americans are no longer justified in our ancient attitude of isolation from the Old World.

The important part of the Old World, her people, has come over in large numbers to our shores; it is living next to us; it is blacking our shoes!

This reflection I entered as the possible theme of a story. The statement of it would, of course, have to be considerably condensed, but that could easily be done later.

So much for the first step. As for the second: I made no effort to develop the idea any further than to enter beneath the thematic statement above this off-hand suggestion for a plot which of course needs further revision:

A native New Yorker is arguing the Washingtonian policy of ' no entangling alliances ' with the Old World with a business associate, a Turkish tobacco merchant, while the latter insists that Americans should tie up with Europe and Asia not out of idealism but out of self-interest. The New Yorker scouts this idea. They enter the shoe-shop where the shoemaker recognizes the Turk as the murderer of his mother and sister and kills him with a trimming knife. The Turk owed the New Yorker a large sum of money and now that he is dead the New Yorker will never be paid.

2. *The illiterate silk merchant:* For the first stage of classification I entered this episode at once as " character material." A man who can make a fortune in our day without being able to read and write is certain to be an unusual personality. If I could learn more about him I

could see what traits might compensate for lack of education in building up a business and could then write a story
to bring out these traits. The result promised to be an
interesting business character story.

For the second stage I merely made a note of the name
and address of the friend who introduced me to the merchant so that I could follow the matter up when time
offered.

3. *The war mother:* This note suggests, of course, a
story of patriotism; but I discarded this thought on the
score that now is not an opportune time for such stories.
I classified it as complication material. My mind is fascinated by several easy possibilities in connection with this
tragically bereaved mother. Suppose her two sons should,
after five years' absence and in spite of the official notifi-
cation of their deaths, some sunny morning walk out of
the subway and into their mother's arms. What would
happen? Suppose two men disguised themselves as her
sons and " returned to her." What then? Suppose the
sons came home, heard their mother was crazy, went out,
looked her over without her knowing it, and slipped away
again without ever letting her know. What then? All of
these suggestions, if carried out, would probably make
strong complications.

For the second step I wrote out a description of how the
woman looks and acts. I did this because I see her often
and have the picture of her well fixed in mind. It therefore requires no time or special effort to get these details
down. When I come to write the story, just that
much less time and energy will be expended on necessary
detail.

4. *The brutal Russian family:* This is the only idea
of the four which occasioned any hesitation as to classification. The horrible idea of the mother being abandoned
helpless in a locked house of course suggested a complication. But how use the Russian setting? And why keep
the people Jews? No use at all. There is nothing pecul-

iarly Russian or Jewish about the idea. I decide therefore
to enter it first simply as a " complication for a horror
story." A moment's further thought as to *why* sons and
daughters could conceivably think of doing such an un-
speakable deed suggests the irresistible desire of each
young generation to live its own life without being held
back by the older one. I therefore enter the idea also as
" thematic " and note down this tentative statement of
the theme:

> We shudder with horror when we read of savage races which
> kill off the old people who are of no further use to the tribe,
> but do we not also in a more subtle way do the same thing?
> Life is lived less for the sake of old people than for the young;
> certainly one feels this is true of New York.

This thematic note I enter in my files under " themes "
and cross-index it to the lengthier entry made under the
complication.

Second step: Of these two suggestions the first interests
me more than the second and I give a few moments'
thought to the technical problems involved in the horror
story possibility. For one thing the idea itself is probably
too horrible to be used in a simple complication story told
in chronological order. The killing of the mother, to be
used at all, would better be told reminiscently. I therefore
make this further entry on the complication card:

> Ghost story. Behavior of midnight spirits about an old
> place are explicable only on the basis of some almost unthinkable
> crime having been committed. Story opens raising question
> of what the crime was. Outcome: Villain hero locked his aged
> mother in cellar twenty years ago.

I do not expect you to have much difficulty in classifying
your story ideas with sufficient accuracy; but for a time
you may have many misgivings as to whether your " second step " notes or " first stage manipulations " are all they
should be. Don't let this disturb you. Write out for your
" second step " all your inspirations in whatever form they

occur to you. If the item is classified as character, take a piece of paper and begin immediately to jot down all the details of that character with which you are acquainted. If it is complication, set down at once all the entanglements.

The Writer Who Doesn't Write

If you can classify you can already see at least the beginning of an emotional effect. Without knowing what the plot is or how it will come out, certain scenes, settings, episodes will flash into your mind. Grab these fragments and *put them down on paper*. Don't wait until the plot is completed; don't wait to discuss it with somebody; don't wait until you " understand " it better; don't wait until you have more time or feel better. Write it down and write it down *now*.

I say this with vehemence because postponement of actually committing ideas to paper is the prize habit of most writers who fail. A literary idea unwritten is an idea not half possessed. After a brief interval of time, it may easily be lost forever. The most pathetic spectacle in the literary world is the writer who doesn't write. He has " grand ideas " — " especially in the morning," as one of them explained to me. He wastes hours, days, planning the use to which he will put a certain idea when he " sees how it should go."

Very few seasoned writers can do this sort of thing; beginners should not. In most cases they cannot know exactly *what* they have in the way of an idea until it *is* written down. The first rough writings are to them what the rough charcoal sketches are to the painter. They help to focus attention on essentials. They give, moreover, a facility that is absolutely invaluable when the time for the big performance arrives.

The First Million Words

The average beginner may well expect to write a million words before he will have noticeable facility in style. Facility means shortening the distance between the idea, or better, the effect, and its execution on paper; or, to change the figure, it means a minimum of friction in the operations of putting effectively on paper a given idea or effect.

The more detailed information I get as to the things successful writers *actually do* (as distinguished from the things that are often written and believed about them) and compare it with the actual deeds of young writers, the more I am convinced that the thing to be envied in the successful writer is not so much his " genius " or even his " personality," as it is his willingness to write for the sake of writing in his years of apprenticeship. The painter spends years at his drawing, the pianist a like amount of time at his scales, but the writer too often thinks he has adopted an art without these laborious preliminaries. Not so. You can no more write good stories without playing literary scales than you can execute a Brahms concerto on the piano without your years at the keyboard.

I remember a story about Francisque Sarcey, famous French dramatic critic, which thrilled me when I was in college. He and his pal, Abel, came down to Paris from the provinces determined to ascend the literary heights. They secured a room together and, as Sarcey's biographer states, they kept the neighborhood supplied with wrapping paper by the volume of pages they scribbled and threw away! Many and many an idea or fancy they committed to paper for sheer joy of the exercise and without having the slightest notion of what they would do with the work when finished.

Literary Scales that Count

If you would succeed, you also must begin the energetic practice of your literary scales. So that you may be quite certain what I mean by them, I have taken at random ten fictional ideas of the briefest sort from the notebook of a college student. I assume that they will be much like the first plot ideas you will wish to store away. After each note, I suggest the two steps, as described above, which you should take with them: first, classifying, second, "first writing," suggested by the idea.

1. A mother, in poverty, faced with the alternative of bringing up her child, deeply loved, in privation or of giving him to her husband's family who despise her but who will give the child the comforts and luxuries that money buys.

    (a) Complication
    (b) Write a scene showing the mother arriving at the wealthy home and turning her passionately loved child over to the wealthy relatives, knowing that she will not see the child again for five years.

2. A hunter is lost in a mountain forest, his only companion a dog. The dog is wounded in a fight with a bear, by which his master's life is saved. The man carries the dog, unable to walk, as he continues his struggle to find his way.

    (a) Character
    (b) Write a sketch showing the man's love of the dog.

3. Professor D. teaches mathematics, in which he appears wholly absorbed, and he lives alone. Women find him very unapproachable. A friend of his told me the other day that Professor D. had been married three times.

    (a) Character
    (b) Write a sketch of Professor D. bringing out his absorption in mathematics as a consequence of his unhappy marriage experiences.

4. A wife, much in love with her husband, is jealous of a first wife's child, whom the husband loves dearly.

    (a) Character and complication
    (b) Write a sketch of the wife, to create sympathy for her.

5. A woman murders her husband and allows her lover to be sent to prison for the crime.

    (*a*) Character and complication
    (*b*) Write a study to give an objective impression of the character.

6. A golden chalice has been stolen from the altar of a church, and two sisters devote themselves to a search for it as a holy pilgrimage.

    (*a*) Characters
    (*b*) Write sketches of the sisters, to bring out their piety.

7. A four-year-old boy, tagged like a piece of luggage, is sent by bus from New York to San Francisco, travelling alone in the care of the bus drivers.

    (*a*) Complication
    (*b*) Write a sketch that will impress the reader with the pathos of such an experience; then do another to create amused sympathy for it as an adventure.

8. A minister's wife, tired of doing for others, is entrusted with a legacy intended for the church. No one else knows the nature of the giver's intention. The minister's wife is extremely poor, has no pretty things for which she has always yearned.

    (*a*) Character and theme
    (*b*) Write a sketch of the sufferings of the wife because of her husband's low salary. Also another sketch of the moment when the temptation comes to spend the money that isn't hers.

9. Rich parents find their young son incorrigible. They try to force a certain responsibility on him, believing it will be good for him, but fail. They lose their money. The boy now takes this responsibility easily.

    (*a*) Complication and theme
    (*b*) Write a scene, using all three characters, showing the rich parents trying to interest the boy in the responsibility.

10. A young lawyer is appointed to defend a man accused of crime. Believing in the prisoner's innocence, he feels that the latter's greatest danger is due to the inexperience of the one who is to defend him.

    (*a*) Complication and character
    (*b*) Write a study of the trait to create sympathy.

11. John T. is a football hero who is poor and has an invalid mother dependent upon him. The only way he can support her and remain in college is to play professional baseball during the summer. He knows he can " get away with it " if he is careful, thus making it possible for him to play as an amateur the next fall at school; but it will be dishonest and some day he feels sure he will be found out.

    (*a*) Character and complication
    (*b*) John plays baseball and receives the money. That night he receives a letter from his mother. Write a sketch showing the effect on John which induces him that night to return the money.

These ten plot ideas offer, as you see, material for five character, three complication, two thematic and no atmosphere stories. That is about the proportion that exists in most finished stories as well as in the raw material from which they are made. Probably four-fifths of all short stories published are either character, or complication, or character-complication stories. The thematic story is found much less often, and very few writers, as stated above, ever even try to produce a story of pure atmosphere.

6. Writing More Important than Plotting

In this chapter we have taken two important steps: one classifying, involving analysis but no writing; and another, the writing of first inspirations, involving thought plus rapid writing. The treatment of the ten plot ideas just above will show you how you may begin at once to do the first writing on your own plot ideas. The first step will increase your comprehension; the second will help establish a valuable habit.

Of these two steps the writing is the more important. I do not say it is an easy step; but I do say unequivocally that it is the surest way to master the technique you are now studying and it is the price almost every writer must pay to win success. Such practice writing you should continue in addition to the exercises appended to this and succeeding chapters. If it is in you to become a writer you will feel, as Stevenson did, that facility in writing is a " proficiency that tempts " you; and you will keep at your practice writing with conquering enthusiasm.

ASSIGNMENTS: CHAPTER THREE

ASSIGNMENT A

Classify the following story ideas as to the most effective material in them for use in stories. Use the four groupings of material developed in this chapter. Each of these story ideas belongs definitely to one or another of the four classifications. Sorting them out should not be difficult.

1. Mr. X is so enthusiastic about golf that he neglects his business to play. Opening the newspaper in the morning, he looks first of all to see the golf news. On the way to work he plays "mental golf" imagining the fine game he will play on the morrow. He pays for lessons with money which should go for clothes for his wife. His wife hates the game but loves to go to the movies. Mr. X., however, plays golf so late that he can never take his wife to the movies.*

2. The wife of a world war soldier, hearing of her husband's death and burying what she thought was his body in the family plot, marries again. One day she receives a telegram from her husband as follows: "Have just landed from Aquitania; will leave immediately for home."

3. A man with the "blues," sour on life because of business failure and discord in his home, goes to the east Florida coast for a vacation and rest. There the bright sunshine, the gorgeous colors, the pure air, the tang of the sea, restore his vigor, re-animate him, make him see life sane again and he starts homeward — an optimist.*

4. Johnny, aged seventeen, is in love, his first offense. Sunday afternoon he spent walking with his adored little Lucy, too terrified, however, to speak of much but the weather. He dreamed fantastically of the rich happiness they would find in life together, but he could not tell Lucy about it. He was tongue-tied, spellbound by her mere presence. The next day he was still living in a dream of rosy-tinted fairyland. He went to the office but could not work. He rested his head on his hand and gazed dreamily out of the window. When his employer called to him to get to work, Johnny murmured: "Yes, dear."

5. The court ordered Mrs. Clarke to wear for thirty days each year the $100,000 pearl necklace of a relative under police guard in order to keep life in the gems through their contact with the human body. Mrs. Clarke has a horror of pearls because they cause her to lose her memory.

6. A woman stayed in hiding in New York several weeks by

registering at a hotel under her own name and eating in the
public dining-room.*

7. A soldier serving abroad for two years is filled with so great
a nostalgia for his home that he deserts and returns. The old
orchard, the mill by the stream, his old friends, the bucolic beauty
of the tilled acres, the healthful toil, all lure him irresistibly to
return.

8. Mary, fourteen years old, attempted to end her life because
she was tired of being "nothing but a drudge as mother was."
Since her mother's death two years before she had taken care of
father and four younger children, doing all the cooking and housekeeping and sewing. Her father was a slave-driver and very
stingy. He gave Mary a little money to buy bread. Instead Mary,
wild with desire to have a little enjoyment, took her little brother
and went to a movie. She was so terrified at thought of the
scolding her father would give her that she decided to end her
life.

9. A sentimental old lady on a bitterly cold winter night leaves
her coachman on his box in front of the theatre while she attends
the play. During the play she weeps with sympathy at the sufferings of the hero. On leaving the theatre to return home, she
finds her coachman dead, frozen to death.*

10. A woman of thirty, unmarried, remains in a house on a
lonely spit of sand jutting out in the sea to nurse her old father
during his last days. Her mother is buried in the graveyard behind
the house. Neither she nor her father can leave the dreary spot
because of the associations with the days when mother was alive
and they were happy. The rolling, naked dunes, the pounding
waves and winds whistling mournfully over the shore line have
turned their minds in on themselves, made them morbid, willess,
unable to tear themselves from sorrow and sadness. They wait
by the graveyard, hoping their own time will come soon.

11. When Diamond Jim Brady decided to sell railroad supplies
instead of being a hotel porter, he put all the money he had into
a one hundred dollar bill, tore the bill in two, and sent one-half
to a great railroad man with this message: "The other half of
this would like to see you."

12. A wife enters her husband's office unannounced and finds
him kissing his pretty stenographer.

Further drill in classifying character and complication story
materials is provided in Assignment A, Chapter Six.

ASSIGNMENT B

The following literary jottings have been taken from "The
Notebook of Anton Chekhov" (Huebsch), the great Russian
short story writer. Classify them as in the previous assignment,

on the basis of character, complication, theme, or atmosphere. If one item seems to have possibilities for development by more than one of these story patterns, note them all down. If no pattern at all is suggested, make note of that fact.

1. Ordinary hypocrites pretend to be doves; political and literary hypocrites pretend to be eagles. But don't be disconcerted by their aquiline appearance. They are not eagles, but rats or dogs.*

2. If the Prince of Monaco has a roulette table, surely convicts may play at cards.*

3. Iv (Chekhov's brother Ivan) could philosophize about love, but he could not love.

4. People are bachelors or old maids because they rouse no interest, not even a physical one.

5. The children growing up talked at meals about religion and laughed at fasts, monks, etc. The old mother at first lost her temper, then, evidently getting used to it only smiled, but at last she told the children that they had convinced her, that she is now of their opinion. The children felt awkward and could not imagine what their old mother would do without her religion.

6. The difference between man and woman: a woman, as she grows old gives herself up more and more to female affairs; a man, as he grows old, withdraws himself more and more from female affairs.

7. A scholar, without talent, a blockhead, worked for twenty-four years and produced nothing good, gave the world only scholars as untalented and as narrow-minded as himself. At night he secretly bound books — that was his true vocation; in that he was an artist and felt the joy of it. There came to him a bookbinder who loved learning and studied secretly at night.*

8. To look for that in a woman which I have not got myself is not love, but worship, since one ought to love one's equals.

9. The so-called pure childlike joy of life is animal joy.

10. A schoolboy treats a lady to dinner in a restaurant. He has only one rouble, twenty kopecks. The bill comes to four roubles thirty kopecks. He has no money and begins to cry. The proprietor boxes his ears. He was talking to the lady about Abyssinia.

11. A man, who, to judge from his appearance, loves nothing but sausages and sauerkraut.

12. His income is twenty-five to fifty thousand, and yet out of poverty he shoots himself.*

13. Terrible poverty, desperate situation. The mother a widow, her daughter a very ugly girl. At last the mother takes courage and advises the daughter to go on the streets. She herself when young went on the streets without her husband's knowledge in order to get money for her dresses; she has some experience. She instructs her daughter. The latter goes out, walks all night, not a single man takes her; she is ugly. A couple of days later three young rascals

on the boulevard take her. She brought home a note which turned
out to be a lottery ticket no longer valid.

14. His character is so undeveloped that one can hardly believe that he has been to the University.

15. Z goes on Sundays to the Sukharevka (a market-place in
Moscow) to look for books; he finds a book, written by his father,
with the inscription, "To darling Nadya from the author."

16. "And now he appeared with all his decorations."

"And what decorations has he got?"

"He has a bronze medal for the census of 1897."

17. A government clerk gave his son a thrashing because he had
only obtained five marks in all his subjects at school. It seemed to
him not good enough. When he was told that he was in the wrong,
that five is the highest mark obtainable, he thrashed his son again
— out of vexation with himself.

18. A serious phlegmatic doctor fell in love with a girl who
danced very well, and, to please her, he started to learn a mazurka.

19. The hen sparrow believes that her cock sparrow is not chirping
but singing beautifully.

20. When one is peacefully at home, life seems ordinary, but
as soon as one walks into the street and begins to observe, to
question women, for instance, then life becomes terrible. The
neighborhood of Patriarshi Prudy (a park and street in Moscow)
looks quiet and peaceful, but in reality life there is hell.

21. The more refined the more unhappy.

22. A large fat barmaid — a cross between a pig and white
sturgeon.

23. Two young officers in stays.

24. My neighbor V. N. S. told me that his uncle, Fet-Shenshin,
the famous poet, when driving through the Mokhavia street, would
invariably let down the window of his carriage and spit at the
University. He would expectorate and spit: Bah! His coachman
got so used to this that every time he drove past the University,
he would stop.

ASSIGNMENT C

In this exercise all your practice will be with character materials. I have grouped these together to make more apparent the
ways in which distinctly character material differs from complication material. It is important for the writer to be very clearly
aware of the nature of his own response to a given bit of story
stuff. If he identifies some incident as character, and begins to
try to plot to bring out character interest, when the most striking
quality in the idea is its odd situation interest, he will be in trouble.

The following are brief character studies suggesting several different phases of each subject. (Sketches like these, by the way,
should go into your files frequently — as often as you encounter or

hear about a character whose life impresses you. You will not always be able to use them at once, but if the sketches are in your file ready to remind you of what you felt, you will find them useful some time.)

1. Joanna fell in love with Dudley when he was in his first year of medical school. Since that time she has supported him during his study, although they did not think it wise to marry until after his graduation. She has worked for a number of years in the complaint office of a large department store, and she writes — and sells — feature articles on " customer " and personnel problems. He has not yet begun to practice, and she is still supporting him while he does some research work in bone diseases of children.

Joanna is a big woman, of peasant build and type. When she talks about Dudley she gets kittenish. She believes that a woman should submit her judgment to her husband's, but she has been independent for years, and is now supplying most of their income, and her attempts to act dependent and docile in the face of the facts, are insincere and look foolish.

Dudley wants her to quit her work, and live on the little he can now earn. She says she can't do it. She loves to entertain, and give presents, and wear good clothes. If she gave up her position, these would be impossible. She is economical, in using scraps of food and making over clothes and hunting bargains, but she can't resist a " bargain " in clothes, even when she does not need it.

Write two studies, one making the reader sympathize with Joanna's habit of independence, and one creating sympathy for her desire to be happy in marriage.

2. Frances was little and colorless, and she got a job in our office because she wanted it so desperately. She wasn't fitted for it, but she learned, not because she had any business talent, but because she was so determined. She arrived before eight, and never left until her boss was gone. She was so afraid of losing her job that she'd break out into perspiration whenever she was called into the office for dictation, and she could hardly answer coherently when she came back. In spite of this her speed was extraordinary, and she never made a mistake in dictation; she was always called for very difficult letters. With her nerves jumping so, such accuracy didn't seem possible.

She wore no make-up, never went anywhere, wore the same dress day after day, although she got a good salary, and lived alone with her two older sisters.

One of the boys asked her to go to a picture show one evening, but she refused. The girls kidded her about it, and she burst out that she didn't want boy friends of any kind; they tied you down too much.

When she had been in the office a year, she asked for an extended vacation. She and her sisters had been preparing a three-sister act for the stage or radio, and were going to New York for try outs and coaching. They were all taking their vacation time for this, now, and the next year they intended to cut all jobs and go to New York to try their act, " sink or swim."

Write two sketches. In one create an impression of the character's absorption in her work; in the second invent at least six bits of behavior around the office which express her desire to succeed as a dancer.

3. Della's family have always been in small town politics. She was born ambitious for the publicity and power of political life. She turned down one or two offers and married Warren who by accident was holding a small office in the town; she foresaw a political career for him. Actually he was rather shy, and reluctant to face people. He had a little money, a fine old farm home, and secretly he had literary ambition. She pushed him politically, entertaining extravagantly, and pulling strings that he didn't know about.

In spite of himself, he advanced. Then, one day, he woke up long enough to realize that there was a child labor bill to be voted on. It just happened that his part of the state didn't like the bill; his neighbors used a lot of child labor — they called it " helping the kids earn a little money this summer."

Well, Warren voted wrong! That finished him politically. Della has never, since then, known what to hitch herself to. She doesn't want to go into politics herself; what she wanted was the society end of it. She wanted to be a great lady, in a drawing room. Now she's nothing except a writing-farmer's wife, and it doesn't give her much satisfaction to queen it over the Sunday School picnic that comes every year to Warren's Grove.

The interest here is in the character of an ambitious woman. The effect would probably be ironic amusement at her ambition; it might be pitying admiration; or the material might even be developed to impress the reader with some theme about politics. For any effect, the emphasis would be on this phase of the woman's character.

Write a scene between Della and Warren soon after she discovers that he is on the wrong side of the bill.

4. He was young, thin, lanky and freckled. He stood on the deck, watching me puttering around with the engine.

" Need any help? " he asked eagerly.

" Nope," I said. Just another kid wanting a ride around the bay. I bent over the engine.

Suddenly he was down beside me.

" Swell engine! " he said.

" Lemme run it! Huh? " He demanded and pleaded.

" Know how? "

"You bet! I can run any boat!"

I nodded. The kid grinned a mile wide. He made a dive for an oil rag on the deck. " I'll clean her up for you."

The interest here is in the boy's love of engines. Go on with the narrative, inventing action in which the boy's character can be brought out, in this setting or other settings. Try to make the reader respond with amused sympathy to this one phase of the boy's character. Don't introduce any situation interest. Get your effect altogether with character.

ASSIGNMENT D

In the following notes, the interest is in an oddity of situation or complication. Each contains some character interest, but the flavor of the idea depends in every case on the peculiar nature of the predicament. The problem in plotting will be to bring out that flavor. A useful method by which to discover the special quality of a story idea is to write an experimental scene. In the assignments below, I have suggested such experimental writing.

1. A young garage man discovers that most of his quarrels and misunderstandings with his fiancee are due to the ideas of masculine strength and importance that she has developed from associating with the big real estate man in whose office she works as stenographer.

Some writers might be struck by the comic possibilities in this material and would begin at once developing it for romantic-comic effect on the reader; others might see its pathos; still others might want to use it to support some moral (theme). But in every case the impression would be produced by the oddity: a man is blocked in his love affair by something quite outside his own range of experience, which is due to his sweetheart's business life. The first experimental writing should emphasize the oddity of this block.

Write a scene, between the young garage man and the girl, in which you show by her action, speech and so on, that she is dissatisfied with him, in ways which might be due to her admiration for her employer's habits. Show that the boy does not understand what the trouble is. Use the garage as the setting.

For instance, you might begin with the young man summoned back to the garage from a near-by motion picture house, where he'd taken the girl. He is bawled out by the chief mechanic, in the girl's presence, and in his embarrassment he makes blunders. The girl's boss doesn't take orders; he gives them; and he is never forgetful or inefficient.

2. A woman who loves a man devotedly, and who is entirely con-genial to him in every way except in his sport, is compelled for some reason — either his wish, or her own, or accident — to share his sport for a time before their marriage.

This is a trite situation. It will do for practice, but if it is to be marketable, some element in the story must be made to freshen the old idea — either the setting or the nature of the sport or the peculiar development of the drama.

Again, the effect will be chosen according to the response of the writer. It might be comic to him, it might be tragic, and accord-ing to his own reaction, his purpose in plotting will be to stir a similar response in a reader. But whatever the impression, the means by which it will be achieved will be an arrangement of this situation.

Write a scene in which the woman tries to charm the man away from his interest in the sport.

3. A mechanic (chauffeur, machine operator, or electrician) knows that the apparatus he runs is defective and that his own life and pos-sibly the lives of others are endangered by it. He knows that the company is covering up these defects to save money, and that if he refuses to work the machine he'll lose his job.

To some writers this will be tragic, to others merely pathetic, to yet others it will point a tragic moral (theme) on the dangers in the profit system. In every case, however, the effect or impres-sion will be achieved by some manipulation and development of the strange predicament of the boy who must work to live while at the same time his job threatens his life.

Write a scene in which for the first time he recognizes the danger in his machine.

4. A young married pair believing that a little mystery will keep love alive, agree on twenty-four hours apart each week, and no ques-tions asked.

This, to most writers, would have comic flavor, and would be developed for comic-romantic effect on the reader. Some might find it thematic.

The essential quality of the idea is due to the oddity of the plan. What indication of the characters do you see in the scheme? What sort of people are these? Where did they pick up such a notion? Why do they stick to it? After this brief preliminary consideration of possible characters, write the scene of their meet-ing after the first twenty-four-hour separation.

5. A young boy is accused of a theft. His fingerprints are found in the place robbed, and he'd been seen nearby with his dog on the

evening of the crime. He is proved innocent, because the dog on the scene of the crime had been heard to bark, and the boy's dog doesn't bark; it has a defect in its throat.

This has a flavor of mystery, blended with pathos. The effect would be produced by emphasis on the odd dependence of the boy on the dog, and on the fact that the dog has a speech defect! One problem in the planning will be to focus sympathy on the boy.

Write a scene with him and his lawyer showing the boy in danger and bringing out his inability to establish an alibi, his affection for his dog, and the fact that the dog had been the first reason for connecting him with the crime. (You'll need a young lawyer! A man of more experience would get at the facts about the dog too soon!)

ASSIGNMENT E

The materials offered below are the sort of notes, clippings, and sketches that will gradually accumulate in your files. Only those to which you respond most intensely will produce effective stories, of course, but all will provide practice work. Dexterity can be developed with deliberate, uninspired practice. The problem is, first, to classify, identifying the kind of material to which you are reacting. Don't be surprised if today you react to the character interest in one of these notes, and to complication interest in the same note a week from today!

The different circumstances under which you attack a batch of notes will affect your response. The important thing is to make some record of your feeling. If you get a flash on a character, or an odd angle on a situation, don't trust it to your memory; make some notation on the sketch, and file it with the bit of material that set you thinking.

If any of these should arouse your interest especially, begin work on it according to the steps suggested in Chapter I, Assignments C and E, and Chapter II, Assignment D. *Classify the material, and identify your feeling toward it, and then develop a sketch, or character study, or scene, that will emphasize that feeling.* Suppose you don't rise to any of these. If you really want some day to succeed with your writing, you will roll up your sleeves, and go at them grimly, setting yourself a certain effect for each whether or not you feel it very intensely yourself. The result may not be great art; but the object of this assignment is not to produce great art. We are attempting now to develop a certain skill, which, one of these days, will enable you to produce the best work that you have in you.

A. The first notes below are like the brief jottings that you will put into your pocket notebook. Bits of gossip, oddities of behavior that you see on the street or in public places, a good line from a conversation, a sudden flash on a character or situation that may come to you in the theater — or in church — all these should go into your never-absent notebook, to be transferred at leisure to your file.

Some of these brief notes are marked " trite." These will present a special problem. The situation or character interest may be good, but because it has been used many times, your chief task in attempting it again will be to find some way to freshen it.

1. Mary B. is trying to persuade her father to divorce her mother.

2. Anne went on a tour to Europe where a fortune-teller had told her she would capture a husband. She made a nuisance of herself to the whole party trying to get into romantic situations. Before she reached home she was engaged to the director of the tour.

3. An eccentric old miser wants to leave his money to someone who will not waste it. He hires a detective to watch his only living relatives, the daughters of a distant cousin, to see whether they deserve his wealth. *Trite.*

4. A man, hard up, leaves his small farm to earn money by selling farm machinery. His daughter must leave college to run the farm.

5. A young chemist, on a low salary, employed by a very conservative old drug firm, does some research work in restoring life after death, which, without his so intending, brings him a great deal of sensational publicity. He is dismissed.

6. A man, in love with his wife's sister, is in an automobile or railroad accident or shipwreck, with both women. He can save one of them. *Trite.*

7. A newsreel picture provides an alibi for a man accused of crime.

8. A weak, unimportant little man, who is ignored by his associates, does something through his weakness or stupidity which imperils the lives or fortunes of them all. For a short time they hate him and he is important. He enjoys it.

9. A woman, about to divorce her husband, is compelled to spend several days in a house associated with her husband's boyhood. She discovers something that makes her understand him better. *Trite.*

10. A young doctor, very poor, but able and conscientious, struggles to establish a practice in a community where the only other physician is strongly opposed to socialized medicine.

11. A business woman marries to have a child, and divorces the man before the baby's birth.

12. A young girl whose mother is beautiful and charming, and socially a great success, is educated very correctly in European convents. She returns after graduation. Before her debut, she disappears. The mother is half insane with anxiety. She fears kidnapping. The girl is found, hiding in a convent.

B. Next follows a group of character sketches, notes like those which you will keep in your general character file:

1. Inventor Spurgess had married an artist wife. The story was told that in his bachelor days he was trapped on a glacier for some time. During this experience he tired of loneliness and married the first woman he met after he returned to civilization. She happened to be a professional painter.

When anything went wrong in Spurgess's laboratory, he would be absolutely silent for hours; then he'd suddenly seem to see his wife for the first time in days, and he'd say, " The trouble is, Susan, you're a darn fool." That would start a furious row.

Sometimes it was Susan who started things, and after a fight that made everybody in their neighborhood miserable, a fight that might last two or three days in intermittent spasms, she'd do one of her finest pictures. It was her way of warming up. It may have worked the same way for him, but no one knew enough about his angle of science to know. He was recognized internationally in his field.

He was so brilliant that many younger men coveted a chance to work under him, but none of them lasted long. He couldn't be suited. Nothing that an assistant did was ever right, and he told them so, insultingly.

He distrusted outsiders. Thought the whole world was in a conspiracy to cheat him. If he caught a tradesman cheating, he'd spend an hour or more battling to get the price down.

He always went to the best restaurants, took taxis instead of street cars, bought the best clothes. He received a great deal of money for some of his processes, but no one knew where it went — he, least of all. He was constantly borrowing from his friends.

2. Mrs. F. patronizes a crystal gazer. About two years ago the crystal gazer told her that Mr. F. should sell his business; that if he delayed it would soon decrease in value. Mrs. F. gave him no peace until he had disposed of it. The new owner is now growing rich with the plant — rich enough to pay very easily the $50 demanded by the crystal gazer for her part in the trick.

Mrs. F. has a strong sense of family. She opposes her daughter's interest in a boy who has no ancestors, and she broke up her son's engagement to a girl who washed dishes to earn her way through college.

During the depression when Mr. F. was in despair over his business troubles, she insisted on contributing to various funds, and hired unemployed workmen to do work around the house that Mr. F. could have done, and that he wanted to do. " No! " said Mrs. F. flatly, " nobody is going to say that we can't take care of ourselves. And what would the neighbors think if they saw you washing windows? "

Mrs. F. keeps her daughter very strictly at home. She tells Mr. F. that it isn't safe to give the girl more freedom; there's too much danger ahead of her. She entertains for the girl in their home. She can't afford help for such parties, and so, to get things ready, repairing, polishing, painting, etc., she gets up and does the work herself before the neighbors awake, so that they'll not know she can't afford help. On one occasion, because the rugs were shabby, she had two sent from a store on approval, and after the party, returned them because she simply didn't like the pattern.

3. J. was a country vet. After six months at a veterinary college he came home with a diploma, and a silk hat, that he wore rain or shine. His office was a shabby old car, with a bag of instruments thrown in the back, and a chest of bottles. So far as the neighborhood could tell, those tools and the silk hat were the only difference after he came back from college; the brutes died the same as they always had.

He never admitted a mistake. Once a race-track man who was shipping some horses, called him to look at a horse that had gone lame in the car. Doc looked at the leg, and after a while dug a rough stone out of the frog in that hoof. This satisfied the horse owner, who went on then with his animals. Afterward Doc admitted to his wife that the pebble was one he'd taken from his pocket to fool the man.

He gave both his sons good educations, but they both hated him. In their boyhood he tortured them and set them at revolting and exhausting tasks. Their mother protected them all that she could, but it was a relief when she could help them get away from home. They would not take his money, but he found a way to lend it to them anonymously.

His wife must have loved him. That was lucky for him. He always did exactly as she told him to, and the money they managed to save was banked because of her planning.

The only person in the world that he confided in was the old hostler down at the livery stable. He'd known the old chap from the time he was a little boy. And the hostler was the only person on earth who knew something that happened to him when he was four years old. He had disobeyed his mother. She snatched him up from his play and plunged him head first into a bucket of rinse water that stood on the kitchen floor. She held him there until he nearly drowned. Then she sat him down hard, dripping, on the floor. Soon after, his father came in, heard what had happened and laughed at him.

It was the old hostler that was with him when he died. Doc's wife had died four or five years before, and the sons wouldn't come near him. He died of pneumonia. It choked him, cut off his wind. The hostler told afterwards that old Doc thought he was a little kid again, strangling in the bucket of rinse water! The last words he spoke were " Ah don't! Don't! Ma, I can't breathe."

NOTE: The interest here is in the character, especially in the scar of a childish experience which appears in adult life. Because there is nothing in the external incidents of great interest, and because of the nature of the terror (a complex) which is at the bottom of the man's conduct, this material suggests possible development as a psychological story, to illuminate the subconscious fear. On the handling of such stories, see Appendix D, page 459. This will be an advanced assignment. If you have not yet studied these mental problems fully enough to be sure of yourself with such materials, you can begin work on one of the more obvious phases of the character, perhaps a study of the relation between father and sons. The father seems to have a sense of inferiority that he's disguising under a domineering attitude.

C. The following notes are newspaper clippings. Any clipping that hits you hard belongs in your file, and with it should go a brief note of your reaction to it at the time of filing. You will generally find that the clippings most useful to you suggest situations that either provoke thought or contain conflict. Characters whom you find in the news are seldom sufficiently revealed in any brief news account to give you much to work with. Your characters will have greater validity if they originate in your own firsthand observations of life.

A good exercise with clippings, obviously, is to try to put into some odd situation from the news a character whom you know, combining the two arbitrarily in a brief sketch focused on any chosen effect. For practice, work, if you must, grimly, deliberately; you can develop right habits in this way, with or without feeling. Feeling is a necessity to the success of the finished story, but it may be a disadvantage in practice, during which the student should be preoccupied not with any specific result, but with ways of working.

1. A desperate struggle in which Rob Winston, Fairview air pilot, knocked out a passenger who attempted to commit suicide, was related today by officials of Hill City airport.

Sam Honan, 19, arranged for a flight yesterday afternoon. At 2,000 feet the pilot noticed Honan was attempting to crawl out and had one foot on the wing. He seized Honan's coat, but the youth pulled free. The pilot put his plane in a glide, removed his fire extinguisher and struck the youth over the head.

For three minutes Winston struggled to return the unconscious Honan to the cockpit. When this was accomplished the plane was only 500 feet up. Honan told police he had brooded over low school grades. Police believe he was despondent over a love affair.

2. Charged with killing a man by giving him deadly germs, three of Calcutta's most prominent doctors were committed to trial in High Court today. It is alleged they obtained plague germs and introduced them to the body of the victim by smearing them on his spectacles. The man became extremely ill, but recovered.

Then, it is charged, the accused physicians obtained from Bombay deadly germs unknown here and injected them into the man's body by a pin prick. The man died.

3. James C. Crane, a hero, whose body was punctured fourteen times when he and two comrades scurried across a lead-infested field on the western front on a lovely May morning in 1918 and induced four Germans to leave their machine-gun nest, is out of the hospital at last. He has no job, four medals, and a limp.

He has lived in hospitals for sixteen years, and the doctors have used their knives on him eleven times.

The government pays him $15 a month, but he has to support his sickened mother, his sister, and his sister's two children, and he does not think he can do this on $15. The government used to give him $100 a month, but last year the government decided to economize. Anyway, he wants a job. He would like to get a newsstand. The only trade he knows is machine-gunning.

4. Over 3000 miles of the Pacific a radio message was relayed today to a hospital here asking for medical advice which might save the life of Sewell Anderson, round-the-world traveler and author.

Anderson, the message said, has been stricken with acute appendicitis aboard his thirty-foot boat in Tagus Cove in the Galapagos Islands, where he was engaged in scientific research.

5. In the autopsy room, Dr. Shipley Sargent, chief medical examiner, glanced at the body on the slab.

Mechanically he unwound the bandages that swathed the head. The last loop of gauze came off, and Dr. Sargent, startled, discovered the body was that of his colleague and assistant.

6. Experts who have studied many thousands of cases of desertion over the last 25 years say that husbands are more inclined to stay with their wives and families during a depression than during an era of prosperity.

7. A $100,000 reward for the bandit is suggested by a Florida sheriff who contributes $25, and suggests the sum be raised by the nation's sheriffs, some of whom, presumably, are tired of being shot by this outlaw.

The Superintendent of Schools in a mid-western state, a student of backward and criminal children, makes an interesting statement:

" If the State of Indiana had spent $50 on this criminal in his boyhood years, the country would have avoided spending hundreds of thousands on him later."

CHAPTER FOUR

THE PRINCIPLES OF DRAMA

THE QUANTITY TEST

Were you to ask me to name the kind of news for which the people yearn, I surely must reply that it is the details of a contest — a fight whether between men or dogs or armies. —
— CHESTER S. LORD, formerly editor *N. Y. Sun.*

We now approach the study of drama, what it is and how to control it. All that we have considered in the two preceding chapters has dealt with the narrative writer's purpose: the effect must be emotional and it must be unified. With the study of drama we are led to a more critical examination of the nature of the material with which we work. We shall confine our attention here to a study of drama as such, isolating it as a problem as much as possible from all others.

While the principles of unity determine the *quality* of an emotional effect, the principles of drama determine its *quantity*. The test of unity answers the question " What emotion? " The test of drama, " How much emotion? " As we have already learned, the ideal of unity is an absolute artistic ideal. All narrative is made more effective by being unified as to its effects. The ideal of strong drama, however, is optional. Some narrative materials call for little or no drama. Our ambition is to be able to handle skillfully those stories which do call for drama and are less effective than they might be without it.

The relation to our new inquiry of what has immediately preceded is made clear by the following diagram:

I. Analytical View of Principles (Theory)

Effective narrative follows principles of

1. *Unity* (*required*)
   In short story, a single emotional effect.
   In longer forms, unified organization of subject matter

2. *Drama* (*optional*)
   Exhibits two ideals:
   (*a*) Emotional conflict
   (*b*) Revelation of character

Covered in first half of this chapter

II. Constructive View of Principles (Practice)

The Material Principles of Unity (quality)	Principles of drama (quantity)	Purpose achieved
	Covered in second half of this chapter	
Character pattern	Dramatic (strong) Non-dramatic (weak)	Emotional effect
Complication pattern	Dramatic (strong) Non-dramatic (weak)	Emotional effect
Atmosphere pattern	Dramatic (strong) Non-dramatic (weak)	Emotional effect
Thematic pattern	Dramatic (strong) Non-dramatic (weak)	Emotional effect

The story idea itself follows

These two diagrams show you at a glance the stage we have reached in our study. The first gives an analytical view of the principles or theory upon which our practice is to be based, and the second presents a picture of the way these principles should appear in your mind in actual use. In actually plotting a story, for instance, you have to have the idea, or material itself, and then, in manipulating it, you provide for unity, drama, and the final effect. At first you will probably find yourself handling these problems in the order given — idea, the pattern of unity, drama, and, lastly, the effect. As your skill increases, however, you will find yourself beginning with the dramatic conflict and the idea simultaneously, deciding next on your final effect, and lastly working out the unifying pattern. At a still later stage of development, when your technical skill has, by much practice, become an unconscious part of your mental processes, you will find yourself, with perhaps the merest suggestion of an idea or indeed none at all, beginning with your final effect and working backwards as you develop your plot.

Our new problem can be seen still more concretely if we once more consider the story material given in the forms of the four different story patterns on page 104. Let me show you what the problems in drama are in each case:

Character pattern:

The Russian professor because of his passion for his study of desert insects remains in the desert until he is finally bitten by one of the insects and dies. This is a clear-cut picture of character, but is it dramatic? Does it give an emotional effect of maximum intensity?

Complication pattern:

The professor finds himself in the small cabin in the desert unable to escape from the poisonous insects which flit over walls, floor and ceiling. Is a situation like this dramatic? We know the chief interest is in the episode itself; but how about the *degree* of the interest? Could it be made stronger than it is? Should we *try* to make it stronger?

Atmosphere Pattern:

In this version the professor was mentally disintegrated by the heat, silence and loneliness of the desert, until he followed a mirage to his destruction. How about the quantity of emotion here? Could it not be made just as great and yet not have required the death of the devoted entomologist? Does not the fact that he succumbed to the terrors of the desert indicate a passive attitude toward it, involving no struggle at all?

Thematic pattern:

The professor and an assistant in the heart of the desert " get on each other's nerves," quarrel and talk of violence. So bitter is their enmity that they are both eager to fight to relieve the tension. Both agree that when hate is as strong as theirs, a fight to the death is absolutely the only way to end it. They do not fight, however, simply because both know that if one of them is removed, the other will certainly die: one man alone cannot care for the camels, erect the canvas shelters against the hot wind, and prepare the food necessary to sustain life. The terrors of such a death force postponement of the fight until they emerge from the desert, when good food, cool weather and plenty of sleep make them friends again.

The action in this case is a narrative proof of the philosophic idea that men are forced to get along with each other by fear of dangers greater than their fear of each other. Although hating each other, the two men dared not fight because neither could live alone in the desert. What part does drama play here? Is drama necessary to every narrative presentation of a theme?

Questions such as these are questions of drama. They are fairly simple here and easily answered because the dramatic struggle in each of the stories outlined above is well marked. Very few ideas, however, are found in as completely evolved forms as these. Most of them, as they first occur to the writer, are vague, fragmentary, fleeting fancies, involving the merest suggestion of dramatic conflict. Often indeed alluring story material is found which contains no drama at all; if it has any dramatic possibilities they are latent and have yet to be discovered. Discovering the drama, developing, perfecting it is comparatively easy for the writer who fully grasps the principles underlying it. If we can get at these principles we will penetrate many of the supposed " mysteries " of fictional technique.

1. The Double Ideal of Drama

First of all, what *is* drama?

We will begin with the following definition: *Drama is conflict involving character.* In this short sentence is contained a law as important to the narrative writer as the laws of perspective to the painter and the laws of vibration to the musical composer. We must now analyze it carefully; a full understanding of " conflict " and " character " as used in this definition will take a writer far in the mastery of fictional art. These two words represent the two ideals of drama.

2. First Ideal: The Conflict

The first ideal of drama: it must involve a conflict. If the main purpose of the writer is to make the reader feel, to stir his emotions, as we have learned in previous chapters, we now face the question of how this is done. It is done by exploiting the reader's sympathetic imagination. If char-- acters in a story experience danger and excitement, the reader will vicariously experience them also if they are realistically portrayed. The reader indeed receives the thrill without the danger! It is important, however, that the emotion of the actor be realistically portrayed. How to do this? What is an emotion?

Emotion results from an interruption to one's behavior. Generally, and in most violent emotions, this interruption is sudden. Sensations which are not localized in a definite sense organ are called *feelings,* as when we say, " I feel warm," or when we feel happy or bitter or when we are up-lifted by the beauty of a sunset or of orchestral music. An *emotion* is more intense than a feeling. It has three characteristics:

1. *A clash:* This results from the " interference with behavior " mentioned in our definition. A woman alone in an apartment suddenly hears someone cry " Fire! " — the desire to escape opposed by the vision of flames might well be the beginning of the ensuing clash. And so with all emotional clashes of varying degrees of complexity.

2. *Action:* The clashing desires discharge into muscles which bring about overt movements. Very violent clashes of impulses sometimes cause an initial jam or deadlock, preventing for an instant any outward action as in the familiar

example of a man unable to move from the middle of the road on suddenly seeing an approaching car. This is known as the *paralytic* response. When a person in a violent emotional state is "too excited to think," he acts in what is called a *chaotic* pattern. In this state we act first and think afterwards. When the clash is such as to allow the actor to think before or while acting we have a third type of emotional state which we call *the clash with a reflective delay*. In this third type, as we shall see later, we find the richest possibilities for the fiction writer.

3. *The physical response:* Every emotional state is accompanied by physical disturbances such as, in terror and fear, the " sinking feeling " in the solar plexus, facial pallor, cold perspiration, staring eyes, rigid muscles. Milder emotions result in blushing, quickened heart beat, irregular speech, loss of appetite, sleeplessness, and so on.

This brief outline of the physiology of emotion makes possible this *rule for depicting emotional states:* (1) explain the cause of the clash, the stimulus, (2) trace out the inner clash of desires, the response, showing how the conflicting impulses and desires fight with each other for existence, and (3) describe the accompanying physical disturbance. Of these three elements, the second, as we shall see, is much the most important. When we say " trace out the inner clash of desires " we are merely expressing in psychological language the mechanics of character analysis. The mechanics of character in action can in fact be reduced to a formula: *Desire A, opposed by Obstacle B, produces Emotion C.* This formula we shall find use for later.

We must note here also an exceedingly simple but useful classification of the stimuli which produce emotional states. These must of course themselves be clashes or conflicts and there are three types: man in a clash with nature, man in conflict with man, and man in conflict with himself. In the last type, the stimulus may be internal. When man opposes man the emotion is experienced by one or other or both of the men. In the first conflict we have the simplest type.

Here we have only one main desire, the desire to survive. The struggle is produced by the opposition offered by the dangers of the woods and rivers.

Now these distinctions may seem to you tediously academic and discouragingly remote from your eager desire to write good stories; but we are now, I assure you, getting at the very heart of one of the most important and fascinating of all problems of fictional technique. More short story manuscripts fail to win success because their authors do not understand the matters we are now discussing than from any other single cause except failure to produce a single effect. We are trying to master drama. One important ideal of good drama, I have said, is that it involves an emotional conflict. It is absolutely necessary for us to understand exactly what emotion is and how it is produced.

Non-emotional Activities

I have said above that there are many human activities which are not conflicts and so do not produce emotion. No emotion is produced because, while there is action, possibly very intense action, the interference or opposition, required by our definition, is not encountered by the desires behind the action. Let me give you a few examples:

The simplest instance is simple play activity. Two boys frolicking like young animals, a girl skipping rope, football practice — such activities involve a certain amount of desire, but *the desire is not opposed*. It is provided with what psychologists call a " simple energy release." Activities such as these are infinite in variety and are often as complicated as life itself. They may be defined as all the things men desire to do and *do without opposition*.

These human activities are of immense importance to us in our study of drama and emotion, since they are often extremely violent and, being violent, deceive us into the belief that they are emotional and therefore dramatic. A boy, for instance, may have so intense a desire to play baseball that he forgets his meals and " cuts " his classes at school; he plunges into his favorite sport in the back lot and plays to exhaustion; if the lad has come through with no " scraps " over the score, we can truthfully say that he has seen the end of a happy day *without conflict.* He has made great *efforts,* but these have not been interfered with.

A business man may have a towering ambition to succeed at his business; no obstacles oppose him but hard work; he works hard, fifteen hours a day: there is no conflict. A mother has a passion for her babies; she expresses her passion in caring for them, — no conflict. A commuter — to use a simple example again — is late for the train. He sees it coming; he runs and catches it just in time: again no conflict. He desires to catch the train; he puts forth energy to do the trick; he succeeds without opposition. He might very well be an athlete, a runner, who had been wishing to run to stretch his legs, but was reluctant to do so from fear of being laughed at; he would then be grateful for the opportunity to take his little sprint.

If, on the other hand, our commuter were naturally indolent, or if he grew tired before he got half way to the station, he would then experience opposition to his desire to run. In the former case the opposition would come from within himself, his laziness; in the latter case, the opposition would be from without, the natural factors of distance and time. In either case his desire would be opposed and a true emotional conflict would result.

Distinction a Practical One

This singling out of these special types of activities which are not emotional may seem to you a straining after merely theoretical distinctions. " No one," you may be thinking, " would be so foolish as to attempt to make stories out of people who are merely playing or perform-

ing their ordinary business duties or doing easily the things
they want to do." No one? Thousands do it, literally!
Legions of the manuscripts sent to editorial offices are
rejected mainly because they are elaborations of just such
unemotional activities. The editor may not sense the real
reason for the lack of an emotional "kick," but he is
unerring in his decision that it is wanting. The heroic
young business man who slaves night and day to provide
for his loved ones and who wins out by some lucky stroke
of fate for which he was not responsible; the young girl
who yearns and yearns for a lover, until, without effort
on her part, he duly appears with good manners and a
shining automobile and asks for her hand; the woodsman
who *without danger to himself* shoots a bear just in time
to save his friend's life — many indeed are the stories
built upon patterns such as these — all pretentious in their
implications of drama, all wanting in true dramatic effect
simply because wanting in the conflict that produces
emotion.

All of which, I hope, makes clear to us one of the ideals
of drama — an emotional conflict. We learned in our first
chapter that the central purpose of narrative writing is to
produce emotion, and in our study of conflict we hit upon
a very important revelation of the mechanics, if you will,
of emotion. The mechanics cannot be fully understood
without much practice in actual writing. That will come
presently. Just here our main purpose is to explain the
principles.

An emotional conflict is only *one* ideal of drama. There
is *another* ideal still more important. An emotional situation alone is not enough. For example, take the commuter
mentioned above who has to run for his train. Suppose
he is, as suggested, physically indolent. He runs until
he begins to suffer from the effort, then suddenly stops
and misses his train. There is a conflict involving a
clash of desires; he wants to catch the train and he
wants to walk and "take it easy." While this conflict

lasts there is some emotion but if he stops running as soon as he begins to be winded, the whole business is not very exciting either to himself or, say, a fellow commuter, watching him. A conflict as brief and weak as this would in another way fall short of effective drama: it would be weak in character revelation. Our definition of drama requires that the conflict "involve character." Anyone watching our commuter might, of course, say that he was " lazy," that he was not a conscientious employee, that he was thoughtless in not providing himself with an accurate watch. His inability to exert himself might not be laziness (he might be convalescing from influenza) and even laziness as we ordinarily use the word is too much a general physical disposition, too negative and vague, to be a genuine trait (see definition of trait below). Our commuter, moreover, might be very conscientious and he might, in the incident given, have an accurate watch and so might not be thoughtless. In other words, the man might or might not be many things; the incident reveals nothing about the man *with any certainty*. How may we report his actions in a way to convince the reader that he is as we say and no other?

3. Second Ideal: Revelation of Character

This question brings before us many problems, all exceedingly fascinating, of the ways of human beings and what writers do with them and what readers feel and think when they read what the writers write. Character may be portrayed in words in more than one way, but this chapter is devoted to an exposition of drama and its appeal and so we will confine our description here to the dramatic exposition of character; in later chapters other patterns into which character can be effectively fitted will be touched upon.

How is character [1] portrayed convincingly in dramatic

[1] I must make a distinction in the use of this word which will occur to students of psychology. " Character " in the psychological sense may be said to include all human attributes. In this sense the

action? [1]   This question we can divide conveniently into two: (1) How is character portrayed at all in dramatic situations; what is the basic pattern of character portrayal by dramatic means?   And (2) How is character portrayed *convincingly* by this same means?   How is character *proven* by drama?

1. *How is character portrayed by drama?*   Let us begin by considering some very simple acts which are undramatic and therefore wanting in character revelation.

a. *Pure thought:* A woman is buying groceries.   How much will she pay the grocer?   By adding up the cost of the different items on her list she learns the answer.   A carpenter wishes to know how much lumber he needs for a given job; he has already measured the door or wall or sides of the house and by calculation learns his answer.   A biologist sits reviewing a large number of scientific data and speculating upon the probable origin of life.   All these activities involve pure thought.   The problems each of these three people face are solved by thinking but not acting.

b. *Unreasoned action:* A child, faced with food at table, eats.   A man thinking of business problems as he starts to cross the street hears an automobile horn and pauses without thinking of the automobile or checking his train of thought.   A friend of mine told me that on being suddenly

---

condition of a man's digestion and blood circulation or the subtlest phenomena of his psychic life are elements of his character.   If revelations of the truth about such matters were admissible in narrative writing, all the proceedings of the psychological and medical societies would be documents of " human interest " !   The word " character " is used here, however, in the narrower or moral sense, comprehending especially those attributes which affect a man's judgments and his conduct in general.   A brilliant study of this aspect of character and its significance in social problems is contained in John Dewey's *Human Nature and Conduct.* (Holt.)

[1] Here again I must explain my special use of a word which occurs frequently in this text.   The word " dramatic " is used here not as it is usually understood in colloquial discourse as anything sudden or shocking or filled with suspense; it is used in the narrower technical sense indicated by the definition on page 142.   The essence of the dramatic as understood here is the clash or conflict of desires.

caught in a street battle in Russia in the days of the revolution and hearing the rapid firing of guns, his first reaction was to turn up his coat collar. All these situations involve action *without thought;* they are what we term impulsive or instinctive acts; they are uncalculated, automatic — " conditioned reflexes " in behavioristic terminology.

The Reflective Delay

Neither of these two classes of response reveals character. The old adage, " As a man thinks so is he," is unsound psychologically. Our thoughts become significant only when they deal with something besides abstractions. Action alone of the impulsive type also is devoid of character interest for the simple reason that it is, as stated, automatic, and while it may be interesting, like the last example cited, and may involve moral consequences, it yet does not reveal character. Dumb animals act always, so far as we know, in this same unreflecting manner and are supposed to have no " character." Character revelation is wanting in both these types of response because the pure thought does not involve action and the pure action does not involve thought. It is no profound feat, then, to conclude that *character-revealing action is action in a situation which provokes thought.*

This definition we must now examine. The woman buying groceries, for example, suddenly discovers that she left her pocketbook at home and remembers that the store sells on cash only. Now she must think as well as act and her responses will tell us something about her. The child at table observes, let us say, that its plate contains only the hated spinach while it craves the fried potatoes which the others are eating. Now whatever happens is certain to tell something about the child even if it promptly hurls the spinach on the floor, for, while this response would be largely an unreasoning impulse, it would not be the end of the response, it would not be a solution; thought *and* act will inevitably be involved.

In this special third type of response we discover the essentials of what is known as " human interest." We have already encountered it in our analysis of emotion; it follows the pattern of the clash with reflective delay; the clash may be slight and so the emotion it produces slight, but a clash it always has. It draws from the reader more than mere attention (students of advertisement writing take notice!) in that attention is a passive, while human interest is an active, response. We *give* attention but we *take* an interest. The interesting thing is that which makes us think. All human interest episodes involve problems; actually they *are* problems. Life itself is a problem-solving business and a man never reveals himself more than when he is making an important decision.

The appeal to the reader of reflective delay activity is, as already stated, that he sympathetically enters into the efforts to solve the problem with the character in the story. The reader's thoughts, that is, as well as the actor's, are provoked by these character-testing, human interest episodes. For the first real understanding of this peculiar, all-important mechanism of *reader response* we are indebted, according to Professor Pitkin, to our pragmatic philosophers. The emotional response of the reader, as we have seen, is due to his viewing and sharing sympathetically the emotional experience of an actor. But how about the *thought* response? Nobody really wants to think! The answer is given us by the philosophers and phrased by Professor Pitkin: *" Thought is provoked by any situation from which our instincts and our established habits do not automatically deliver us."* Mastery of the character-revealing (informative), human interest (appealing) episode is easy to him who can understand how the reader's thought is provoked and so his attention held. The human interest episode is that which compels *the reader* to recognize with the character the alternatives he faces and to think with him. The story actor thinks and worries; the reader merely thinks! In art the spectator always gets the breaks.

2. *How does drama prove character?* The answer to this most important of all problems of dramatic technique is now at hand. *Character revelations are convincing and may be said to be proven when the reflective delay involves an emotional clash of maximum intensity.* None of the various examples of response we have just considered, not even those having human interest, provide convincing pictures of character and for the simple reason that they are not unequivocal pictures. Take the woman in the grocery store who left her purse at home. She decides to go home and get her purse rather than ask the grocer or a neighbor in the store for a favor. From this response we might conclude that she is punctilious in her performance of all her duties. May we be sure that this is an unequivocal character trait? Not at all. It is quite possible that that same evening she might leave her very sick child with a neighbor while she went to a movie, or she might be a very slovenly housekeeper or might even at times fail to pay her bills at the grocery store.

Character is proven in fiction in more than one way, but since we are occupied with drama, we will confine ourselves to the dramatic proof of character. Proof involves logic and we bring logic to our assistance thus: *We provide our character with a clash of desires in the reflective delay of such intensity and in such a situation as will make it absolutely necessary for him to think and act and in acting to choose between alternatives of supreme importance to him.* Before testing this formula and discussing its practical value to creative writers, we must pause for a summary of our exposition to this point.

4. Importance of Two Ideals

We have reviewed the two ideals of drama: the emotional conflict and the character-revealing situation. All actions which exemplify these ideals are dramatic. These ideals are the marks of the species. They will guide us in selecting the right materials for dramatic effects, but they will do more than this. Not every action fulfilling these ideals has the *maximum amount* of drama. Not every story, indeed, as we said at the beginning of this chapter, demands a maximum conflict. Securing the maximum amount of drama is a special problem of manipulation which we shall soon consider. Before doing so let us see once more why it is that neither of these two ideals is *alone* sufficient for the most powerful dramatic effects and why the best effects are secured by their appearing in combination.

Consider the first ideal, an emotional conflict:

A husband returns home unexpectedly and finds his wife in another man's arms. He loves his wife madly and, although he knew she was interested in other men, he never dreamed she was actually unfaithful. He is now fully convinced that she is. Maddened with jealousy, he whips out his revolver and shoots and kills his wife's lover.

Here is conflict and the most intense desire, a desire for revenge, but who would say that the episode gives a real picture of the husband's character? The very fact that he was "maddened" by his passion indicates that the most characteristic thing about his act was that it was *devoid* of any conscious control. He "didn't think," as he would doubtless testify in a court of law; [1] and to the extent that he didn't think, his act fails to reveal character and so falls short of genuine drama. It has no more interest than the usual distressing details of a tabloid "triangle tragedy."

Another instance of violent action which might be devoid of genuine character drama is a prize fight. Some fights are so "built up" that they have character interest, but a pair of unknown sluggers might put on a gory combat which, while completely satisfying the savage instincts of the mob, would leave intelligent beholders with mere dis-

[1] As this is being written, a judge in a murder trial in New Jersey instructs the jury as follows: "The evidence shows that the defendant drove his victim upstairs at the point of a revolver, thus invalidating any plea of self-defense. The only justification for homicide is when a man is aroused to sudden passion by finding his wife in another man's arms."

gust. They might still be interested in it but the quality
of the interest would be similar to that aroused by watching a scrap between two stray dogs on the street.

Examples of Character Appeal Only

So much for emotional conflicts which do not fulfill the
second ideal of good drama. Let us now examine narrative which does fulfill this second ideal for revealing
character but which is weak in emotional conflict. Here
is an example taken from the opening of *Babbitt* by
Sinclair Lewis:

He was forty-six years old now, in April, 1920, and he made
nothing in particular, neither butter nor shoes nor poetry, but
he was nimble in the calling of selling houses for more than
people could afford to pay.

His large head was pink, his brown hair thin and dry. His
face was babyish in slumber, despite his wrinkles and the red
spectacle-dents on the slopes of his nose. He was not fat but
he was exceedingly well fed; his cheeks were pads, and the un-
roughened hand which lay helpless upon the khaki-colored blanket
was slightly puffy. He seemed prosperous, extremely married
and unromantic. . . . Yet Babbitt was again dreaming of the
fairy child, a dream more romantic than scarlet pagodas by a
silver sea. . . .

Babbitt moaned, turned over, struggled back toward his dream.
He could see only her face now, beyond misty waters. . . . As
Babbitt sank blissfully into a dim warm tide, the paper carrier
went by whistling. . . . He roused, his stomach constricted with
alarm. As he relaxed he was pierced by the familiar and irritating rattle of someone cranking a Ford: *snap-ah-ah, snap-ah-ah,
snap-ah-ah!* Himself a pious motorist, Babbitt cranked with
the unseen driver, with him waited through taut hours for the
roar of the starting engine, with him agonized as the roar ceased
and again began the infernal patient *snap-ah-ah!* . . . Not till
the rising voice of the motor told him that the Ford was moving
was he released from the panting tension.

This passage is typical of the manner followed throughout this novel. It is preëminently a work of characterization, and, because of the skill with which it is done, it

displays the appeal of this manner of writing at its best. It also displays its weaknesses. As a record of the daily activities of a type of the genus American it is interesting to readers who like to see themselves as others see them without interpretation or any high lights of emotional struggle. They are the kind of people who would be interested in a motion picture film " shot " by a camera man who set his machine in the corner of any typical American home on the curb of any typical American street and ground his crank with realistic enthusiasm. Such people exist; you and I are probably of their number: but the fact that we are in the minority is sufficiently demonstrated by the fact that the motion pictures which draw the millions to the " movie " houses are precisely the opposite type — they exalt emotional scenes at a sacrifice of truth about character.

Melodrama Weak in Character

We can now see how it is that as between narrative strong in emotional conflict but weak in a revelation of character, and narrative rich in character revelation but weak in conflict, the latter makes the higher or more intellectual appeal while the former wins approbation mainly from immature and unsophisticated minds. Violent conflicts with little regard for character produce the melodramatic literature of the adolescent reader. Character-revealing novels, like *Babbitt*, and sketches like most of the documents in William Allen White's *In Our Town*, and many of the shorter writings of Galsworthy, Chekhov, and Sherwood Anderson find their audiences altogether among people of discriminating intelligence.

The chief difference between these two general types of appeal is that melodrama, being untrue to life, has no significance; and cultivated readers are interested only in those things, even entertainments, which have *some* meaning. As Professor Pitkin states the issue: Melodrama gets somewhere but means nothing, while undramatic character writing gets nowhere but means something.

Dramatic appeal, as I have said before, is not the only appeal possible in fiction; nor is it the only device by which character can be portrayed, but it *is* the most fundamental of all appeals and can be made to incarnate human beings with an impressiveness unequalled by other arrangements. In the greatest of novels such as Tolstoy's *War and Peace,* Butler's *The Way Of All Flesh,* Dostoievsky's *Crime And Punishment,* and of the more recent writers, *Sons And Lovers,* by D. H. Lawrence, *Main Street,* by Sinclair Lewis, *Point Counter Point,* by Aldous Huxley, *Of Human Bondage,* by Somerset Maugham, *The World's Illusion,* by Jacob Wasserman, *The Magic Mountain,* by Thomas Mann, *Farewell To Arms,* by Ernest Hemingway, *Three Soldiers,* by John Dos Passos, *The Unpossessed,* by Tess Slesinger, as well as in the greatest short stories, drama is used as the main device for both moving the reader and impressing him with the reality of the people evoked by the author's imagination. Drama to the artist writer is a means to his greatest effects, to the commercial writer, his most certain. Life is many things, but before all, it is struggle. From great literature and from life itself, then, we have extracted some understanding of emotion, of human interest, and of the two fundamental functions of drama.

5. Actual Use of Principles

We have dipped into the psychology of drama only that we might the more easily and quickly establish sound habits of thinking about, planning and writing dramatic stories. How can these principles be applied in a practical way to our writing? They can be learned most quickly by mastering both theory and practice. The principles should be learned absolutely; individual ways of applying them may be worked out by each student for himself. I merely give you the method *I* use. My own students constantly ask me to do this for them, saying that if they can see how one writer works out the smallest details, they will be helped not only in working out a practical method of their own but in understanding the principles themselves; and I have found that it is really helpful.

Our problem is now one of invention and manipulation of given material to produce the strongest possible dramatic scenes. Naturally, you will not always wish to manipulate every bit of material into the most powerful dramatic scene possible: maximum dramatic strength, as already stated, is not a desideratum for all types of stories; exceptions are character sketches, brief surprise-ending stories, and many stories built around a philosophic theme; but most of your stories will not realize their full value until you have brought out the utmost drama of which they are capable. By learning how to achieve maximum dramatic effects, moreover, you will the more easily be able to handle effectively scenes of all degrees of dramatic strength.

6. Producing Emotional Conflicts

We will build our actual practice upon the principles set forth above. In our two ideals of drama, the emotional conflict and the character-revealing situation, we have already at hand convenient divisions of the problem. Let us first build up maximum emotional conflicts. From our study of the nature of emotion we can formulate the following rule for inventing emotional situations:

First Practical Rule: To secure the maximum intensity of emotional conflict look for the desire or desires present in the given material, give them maximum intensity and set against them maximum opposition. An obvious corollary to this rule is that when there are two or more desires, these desires must be opposed to each other, and that when there is only one desire, this desire should be opposed by some natural (non-human) obstacle. For most writers the easiest conflict to handle is that involving only one main actor and two desires, the resulting conflict in this case being, of course, internal — two desires in the same actor opposing each other. Let us take for purely illustrative purposes the situation given on page 152. We will call it our " story idea " and state it in the way in which, we will say, it first occurs to us:

A man comes home to find his wife gone with another man. His baby is abandoned in its crib and is crying from hunger. The man does not really love his wife, and cares very little what happens to her. The baby is not sick, can be supplied with food in an instant, and could safely be abandoned for an hour or so.

The desires in this case are very weak. The man has a slight wish to go after his wife and bring her back; he also, under the circumstances, has but slight anxiety with regard to the baby. We can now represent this situation graphically as follows:

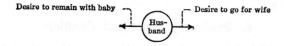

The circle here represents the husband himself; the arrow indicates the direction in which he is being pulled by a particular desire. The desires are pulling in opposite directions, thus producing the conflict. The length of the arrow indicates the strength of the desires. In this case the arrows are quite short. Since the desires are weak, the dramatic conflict itself is weak and the resulting emotion is weak.

Let us strengthen one of the desires and keep the other as it is. Suppose the husband was madly in love with his wife, and never knew that she had fallen in love with another man. His desire, then, on discovering his wife's defection, would be very great indeed. If his baby was not very sick and could be left alone for a time, the desire to remain with the child would not be great. The situation, then, would look like this:

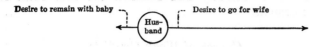

Desire to remain with baby   Hus-band   Desire to go for wife

In this case the husband would follow his desire and pursue his wife, and, since there was no other desire of great intensity opposing him, the conflict itself would be weak, and the resulting emotion would also be weak.

The same result as the above would be obtained if again we say that the husband did not care for his wife and if the baby were in such danger that it might die unless a doctor were secured for it within a very short time. The dramatic situation in this case is as follows:

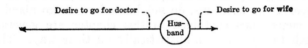

Desire to go for doctor   Hus-band   Desire to go for wife

Again, since there will be no strong desire opposing the husband's desire to get a doctor for his child, he would promptly go for a doctor, and the conflict would be weak, and so would the resulting emotion.

If, lastly, we strengthen *both* desires, making it clear that the man loves his wife very much and is stricken at thought of losing her, and also sees that his child may die unless he secures a doctor at once — in this case, we have a conflict which looks like this:

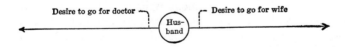

Desire to go for doctor   Hus-band   Desire to go for wife

Here we have strong desires directly opposing each other. A strong clash is produced, the drama is intense and so will be the emotion resulting from an account of the clash. We thus have brought the emotional conflict to maximum intensity and satisfied the first ideal for strong drama.

Causes of Weak Conflicts

Literary invention as simple as this will seem to you quite easy, and you may wonder why I take the trouble to set it forth. It is indeed simple, but it is also true that an amazingly large number of beginning writers fail to perform it in plotting their stories. Probably more than half of all the manuscripts editors reject are found wanting in dramatic strength which could be provided by manipulation as simple as this. Why do the writers not attempt such manipulation? Many, I have discovered by questioning numbers of them, do not see the necessity for it, or, seeing the necessity, do not know how to go about it. The suggestions contained in this chapter are generally enough to set them enthusiastically on their way. They lack only method.

Too often, however, I discover another, quite different and more serious obstacle to strong dramatic invention. It deserves a word here. Some students fail in this department of their plotting not because they don't understand the problem, but simply because they are too timid, too shy or conventional to see the thing through. Such writers often confess candidly: "I suppose I haven't the moral courage deliberately to make my story people face serious difficulties. I'm that way myself. I go around a difficult problem rather than face it squarely." Thus they testify to a solemn fact about writing: Big effects cannot be produced by little people. Character, good or bad, must be robust if it would project itself into robust narrative.

We all of us in our ordinary lives are accustomed to solving problems and avoiding troubles; doing so is a habit, and the habit influences us in our plot-making: at the first hint of difficulty for his characters, the author busies himself to find them a safe way out of their predicament. It should rather be his delight to create worse difficulties for them to surmount. Creative literature is the history of personal troubles. The happy nation, we are told, has no history; let its people remain in this plight long enough and they will be without literature!

Here is a plot typical of this kind of timidity in invention:

A wife finds herself serving as " door mat " and general drudge to her hypochondriac husband. She tells him that she will be one no longer. He decides that she has ceased to love him, and permits her to go. She has the alternative of losing his love, or of returning to be his door mat.

The student solved this by having the wife submit and return — a possible solution, of course, but there are any number of other possible solutions more dramatic and more interesting. Both alternatives imply a kind of capitulation. The wife must lose in either choice, and the story is weak because the author has provided a character of a type which cannot possibly make a strong dramatic conflict. If his purpose is to write strong drama, he has failed; he can do nothing in the writing which will redeem this structural weakness.

Let me counsel you, then, to be bold in your inventions. The stories which probably give you the greatest pleasure to read are those in which the actors endure the greatest distress, suffering and anguish. " True," you may answer; " but those stories are *true;* the authors surely took them from life; my own life is but a placid and uneventful affair; they have lived through all the horrors they depict." Seldom. More of those " horrors " were deliberately piled up in a cunning conspiracy on your emotions than you will ever believe. If you would be wise, if you would be a genuine literary artist and know the great rewards, go and do likewise. Courage! Daring has its rewards in literature as elsewhere.

Importance of Action

Students doing their first exercises in creating drama should be cautioned not to make all their conflicts mental struggles; the first inventions of most beginners present this type of conflict only, doubtless because it is easier to recount memories of past action or speculations as to future action than it is to describe the actions themselves. Here we tend in writing as in all of life, to take the easiest way out. Thoughts, of course, are activities as much as more overt physical conduct, but stories confined to this type of activity — so-called "psychological" stories — are merely analyses of mental processes and thoughts, and are bound to make a limited appeal. Certain types of stories, such as the character story whose climax depends entirely upon the character's reaction to a given situation, as in Stevenson's *Markheim*, are inevitably "psychological" stories. All other types which can best be told by physical action are made less effective and are often spoiled by being handled in any other way.

As an instance of this false use of the psychological manner, let me give you a story ruined by being wrongly handled in this manner: The story concerns a woman, married to a drunken wretch of a husband, whom she decides to kill in order that she may go to her lover. This plot obviously offers opportunity for swift action. The first few pages of the manuscript, however, were handled in the manner of the following:

Lisa hung up the receiver, dazed. She groped her way to a chair; her world had tumbled about her. He had come back — this renegade, this wretch who, legally, was her husband — he had found her; and she was to meet him tonight. "To-night" — the phrase had been upon her lips and in her heart all day. She had been almost singing it. For tonight she was to meet Victor [the lover], who doubtless, did not know how much she loved him; but whose happiness — like her own — would be boundless when he knew.

Her momentary dulness cleared away. She was too young and too self-reliant to be helpless before her difficulties. But, as she was painfully aware, she could not instantly command her strength and recover from the blow; because it was as though she had been stabbed in the side just as she had reached for a kiss. The voice of her husband had forced her back to those days of defenseless dread when she was a bride fleeing from horrors whose disillusionment had overwhelmed her.

Old phantasms passed before her, as her eyes became fixed in a stare, and her hand gripped the table edge. She rapidly lived again some of those moments of two years ago; and she held to the table as though to prevent the influence of her husband from forcing her back into the pit he had once made for her. His brief message over the telephone echoed suave and confident in her ears, as something tightened upon her heart; while all that she had accomplished in the consuming ambitions since her flight, faded and became unreal.

7. Conflicts in Famous Stories

Many of the greatest stories, it is fair to assume, had their inception in "inspirations" containing very little emotional conflict. Suppose now, in continuing our study of the actual building up of maximum conflicts, we take a few well-known stories and build up their conflicts as their authors may well have begun, with the most timid suggestions. Maupassant, for instance, may very well one day have hit upon the following idea:

A very shy man sat in a restaurant with his wife. A gentleman diner near them opened a window causing a draught which brought the wife discomfort. The wife asked her husband to request the man to close the window.

The husband, after one glance at the sour looks of the gentleman, may have been afraid to speak to him.

Internal Conflict

Here we have in very weak form another internal conflict between two desires. We can represent this conflict as follows:

Fear of displeasing } the other man. { opposed by { Fear of { displeasing wife

Here we have practically the same general character trait, timidity, inspired by two different people. To follow our rule, now, and increase the emotional conflict, we have only to intensify this specific character trait. Timidity is of course basically fear; we therefore intensify the fear by altering the factors which inspire it, keeping them in direct opposition. This we do as follows:

The husband sees his wife being annoyed by the leering gaze and audible remarks of an intoxicated diner. The episode is witnessed by other diners at adjoining tables. The husband hesitates to order the man to cease annoying the wife, fearing that he will precipitate a fight and be injured or humiliated. At the same time he is afraid not to face the man, knowing that not only his wife, but the surrounding diners will feel contempt for his timidity.

The conflict of desires has now reached this stage:

Fear of other man $\Big\}$ opposed by $\Big\{$ Fear of contempt of wife and other diners.

This conflict is more intense, but it is not yet at maximum intensity. We now carry it another stage:

Our hero is now dining with a friend and the friend's wife. We give him this time a minor trait of chivalry to women. When the intoxicated man leers at and talks about his friend's wife he impulsively orders the man to cease his offensive conduct. The intoxicated man rises, and in a voice which the whole restaurant hears, challenges the hero to come outside and dispute the matter further with their fists. He is afraid to do so, feeling sure he will be beaten up. He knows too that if he doesn't accept the challenge, his two friends and the other diners in the restaurant will feel contempt for him.

The emotional conflict now is:

Fear of being beaten up $\Big\}$ opposed by $\Big\{$ Fear of the contempt of his friends and the other diners.

Here we have a man in a very serious " pickle " indeed, and many plot-makers would be content to stop at this

point. Surely the hero is tortured sufficiently; let us proceed to write the story. Not so. Courage! Is there not a more intense conflict than this? What more serious fates could he face than public and private contempt or a severe beating? Well, what is the most serious thing that can happen to any man? Death, surely. Very well, let's continue until we kill the gentleman. In doing so we reach the emotional conflict in Maupassant's very remarkable story, *The Coward:*

Count Lasalles, a very chivalrous gentleman, while dining with a friend and his wife, sees that the wife is annoyed by the way another diner *looks* at her. Instantly acting on impulse, he orders the man to cease his offensive attentions. Both men spring to their feet. No words are exchanged; the Count slaps his opponent with his glove; they exchange cards, and a duel is on.

The count is a coward. He fears to fight the duel, feeling sure he will be killed; he is so distraught that he knows he will not be able to defend himself. On the other hand he knows, if he refuses to go to the duel he will be scorned and ostracized by society at large in Paris. Unable either to fight or to endure the desperate consequences of not fighting, he commits suicide.

Man and Man Conflict

The emotional conflict in this famous story can be stated thus:

Fear of being killed in the duel.　　opposed by　　{ Fear of becoming a social outcast.

The emotional conflict in this and the first illustration used are internal. Let us now take a conflict between one man and another, again employing a situation used in a well-known short story. This time we will use the trait of honor, giving it to each of the main characters in a somewhat different form. One of them, a young man, has a definite sense of chivalrous honor touching the opposite sex; the other, a father, is strong on the honor of his family. The beginning stage, or "first inspiration," we will say is as follows:

The father, seeing his only daughter advancing into her twenties without a suitor, tactfully invites the young man to call at his home. It is obvious to the young man that the father desires him to pay court to the daughter. He knows the young woman quite well, and, being certain that she does not like him nor he her, he politely evades accepting the invitation.

Here is merely a suggestion of conflict between the two men but it *is* a suggestion, and upon it we build by following our rule of intensifying the desires given each man. This we can do by making more serious the consequences to each man if they fail to follow their desires:

The young man is deeply in love with the young woman but he knows that she does not love him. His strong sense of honor about women forbids his paying further suit under the circumstances. The father, knowing that the young man is an excellent "catch" and feeling sure that his daughter will learn to love him if she marries him, tells both young people that if they don't marry he will ruin the business of the young man and bring him to poverty.

Once again we have created genuine distress all around; but we must not stop with mere distress. The young man will lose his fortune if he refuses. What more serious disaster might threaten him? Again — death. We are now ready to picture the conflict in Stevenson's *The Sire de Maletroit's Door*:

Sire de Maletroit suddenly detects his fair and only niece in a secret flirtation. His sense of family honor is so outraged that he, being a medieval gentleman, decides to force his niece to marry at once and to trap a young man for the purpose. He therefore constructs an outer door to his house such that it will open at a slight pressure from a passerby, but cannot be opened from within. Anyone who enters will be unable to escape. One night young Dennis de Beaulieu is caught.

The old man faces him, produces his niece, and commands him to agree to marry her within two hours or be killed. Young

Dennis having a strong sense of chivalrous honor about young women, refuses absolutely to marry the girl.

The outcome of this story we will review a little later; just now we are interested in the degree of emotional conflict in the climax of this ingenious story. The young lover will allow himself to be thrown to his death from a castle parapet rather than marry the fairest maiden in the land if the maiden does not love him! This surely is a " supreme test " of chivalrous honor. The father, rather than abandon his plan, however fantastic, to maintain his family honor, will kill a prepossessing young neighbor in cold deliberation — maximum intensity of devotion to an ideal of family honor.

Man and Nature Conflict

Manipulations such as these can as easily be applied to the third type of conflict, that between man and natural obstacles. A man, say, on a cold day is surprised, and possibly alarmed, to notice that one of his fingers has lost its sense of feeling. He hastens to rub it with snow to restore the circulation. The episode might well be the beginning of a powerful story whose essential dramatic features could be worked out by simply intensifying the desire not to succumb to the influence of cold and strengthening the obstacles which prevent the satisfaction of this desire. Keeping the desire, to survive the cold, the same throughout, the natural obstacles might be built up as follows:

1. Man flaps arms to get warm.
2. Man runs and so warms himself.
3. Man lights fire with last match and to keep it from going out, burns the flesh of his hand.
4. Man with no matches left and no fire tries to kill his dog, cut its body open, and warm his fingers by plunging his hands into its body.
5. Man with hands and feet frozen so that no sensation remains might, in last desperate effort to save himself, run and

stagger forward though he felt as if he were floating in the air, suffered exquisite pain, and had already seen that he would freeze to death.

This climactic series of conflicts between the same desire and different natural obstacles is used by Jack London in his powerful story, *To Build a Fire*. The man finally dies, dreaming of the discovery of his body by his friends.

All the above are fairly simple illustrations of conflicts. They are markedly one or the other of the three types, internal, man and man, and man and nature. Many stories, some of them the very greatest, as we shall learn hereafter, employ two or even three of these patterns. Kipling's *Without Benefit of Clergy*, to suggest one illustration, employs all three types. The desire of the hero, Holden, is his passionate love of Ameera and Toto. His shame for his unhallowed love provides an internal conflict; fear of the condemnation of his countrymen provides a conflict between man and man; and the disease germs of India furnish the final obstacles which complete a tragic catastrophe.

8. Producing Character Revelations

How shall we now manipulate our material to carry out the second ideal of good drama, namely, that the action reveal character? Let us take the episode of the man who returns home and finds his wife gone with another man. We developed the internal conflict to a point where the man had a maximum desire to get his wife back and a maximum desire to save his baby's life by going at once for a doctor. We might depict this maximum conflict in action and yet fail to produce the most effective drama if we fail to provide the man a sufficient reflective delay in which to display his character. When he returns home, let us say, his wife tells him about her lover. In spite of his pleas, she heeds the command of her lover to come to him. The husband sees that if he follows her, their baby may die from want of immediate attention. The lover enters suddenly and the husband, maddened to desperation, draws a revolver and shoots and kills the lover.

Why action of this type reveals practically nothing of character we have already seen. The decisive act is one of impulse, a manifestation of primitive instinct; it is distinguished by its *lack* of any display of character. It no more characterizes the man as an individual than does his hunger exhibited in eating. The real actor was his savage ancestors.

The problem of manipulation leading to a genuine picture of character is more complicated than the problem of securing greater emotional intensity; but we have already in our analysis of the reflective delay and the logic of character proof in dramatic situations discovered how it is brought about. We have only to refer to our conclusion reached on page 152 to provide us with an extremely useful second working principle:

Second Practical Rule: *To secure a maximum impression of character we provide our actor with a clash of desires of maximum intensity in the reflective delay and allow him to respond decisively to that one desire, or trait, which is to be proven.* The important elements in this formula are the *clash* and the *logical proof.* For a demonstration of this rule let us return to the woman, used above in our discussion of human interest, who found she had no money to pay for her groceries. We saw that whatever she did to escape from her predicament would reveal *something* about her. If she left her groceries in the store and walked a mile to her home and book again rather than ask credit of the grocer, we might conclude that she is punctilious in money matters. Logic is involved in such a conclusion, thus: she shrank from walking an extra two miles, but she preferred this to asking for credit, ergo, punctiliousness in money matters is stronger than her disinclination to walk two miles — but because the alternatives are slight the strength of the trait is still in doubt. The alternatives, then, must be greatly strengthened. Suppose she leaves her groceries in the store and ventures forth to find the money to pay for them. She hasn't the money at home; she cannot ask for a loan; she knows that a neighbor has money hidden in her house and that if she kills the neighbor she can get the money. *After due deliberation,* she commits the murder, finds the money, returns to the store and pays the grocer.

The complete logical proof in this invention is: We may assume that nothing is worse to this woman than deliberate murder; faced with this murder or not paying her bill, the woman pays the bill; ergo, paying her bills is supreme among her desires. The deed we have given this woman may seem fantastic to you and indeed it is, but it would not be impossible to a woman with a sufficiently morbid compulsion concerning money. I have kept rigidly to the trait in the original episode in order to display the extremity to which the writer is sometimes driven in his inventions *if* he wishes to produce the most powerful impression with a *given* trait. The crucial action could be made much more plausible by changing the trait to a desire to feed a starving family.

Please note that the *supreme* character proof involves the *maximum* emotional clash. In the greatest character drama, then, we find the clearest logic involved with the highest emotion. In such climaxes the logical pattern (reason) and the emotion (excitement) are functions of each other. Rules for depicting an emotion were given on page 144. They concerned the cause of the clash, the clash itself and the feeling-response.

It should be both interesting and profitable now to examine the character-proving patterns to be found in stories of lasting merit. Three of the stories whose emotional clashes were analyzed under Practical Rule One will serve our purpose. Let us try especially to see how these three authors handled the all-important second stage in actual writing just mentioned. The " clash " of this second stage in the emotion is the character-revealing reflective delay. We can see by the analyses which follow that these famous stories not only are emotional but also exhibit a multiplicity of conflicts within one and the same emotional pattern. In the written version of *The Coward* the main alternatives are as follows:

1. So great was the Count's *fear of being killed* in the duel that when he picked up the revolver with which he would fight his hand trembled so that he had to put it down; *fear* of being unable to go to the duel and so *earning the contempt of his friends* forced him to try to calm himself by drinking wine, by going to sleep, by reading.

2. *Fear of the contempt of his friends* made him want to fight, but *fear of being killed or wounded* was so inspired by one look at the "little hole, black and deep, that spits out death." that he knew that he would be unable to retain the strength necessary even to take him to the place of meeting.

3. *Fear of the contempt of his friends* was inspired by thought of the "dishonor, of the whispered comments at the clubs, of the laughter in the salons, of the disdain of the women," while at the same time, when he raised the hammer of the weapon, he saw the "priming glitter beneath it like a little red flame," so that he "experienced a confused, inexplicable joy" at his first thought of suicide, the one way left to end his *fear of being killed*.

A duplication of the emotional clash is also clearly marked in the text of *The Sire de Maletroit's Door*. The main alternatives are:

1. When Dennis learns from the young lady that the uncle intends to force him to marry her, he (impelled by chivalrous honor) faces the uncle and flatly refuses. The uncle (impelled by his family honor) points out of the window to a rope dangling from the side of the castle, saying he will hang the young man there at sunrise unless he consents.

2. Dennis (impelled by his chivalrous honor) offers to fight the uncle with swords. The uncle, being old (and impelled by his family honor), meets the challenge by disclosing in an adjoining room "a dusky passage full of armed men," who are ready to fight for him.

3. Alone with the young lady Dennis convinces her that (his sense of chivalrous honor being so great) he would die for her "blithely" rather than marry her against her will. The uncle remains obdurate during the allotted two hours, indicating that his cruel threat (inspired by his sense of family honor) would have been carried out had the young people not agreed to marry. As it was, they managed to fall in love with each other within the allotted time and, on seeing them in each other's arms, he "wished his nephew a good-morning."

Lastly, in *Without Benefit of Clergy* we have a character-revealing " reflective delay " which deserves the most patient critical analysis on the part of the student. The reason for the power of this story, the wonder and despair of so many writers, is very definitely due to the intensity of the desires involved (first ideal of drama) and the rich variety of alternatives with which the conflict of these desires is presented (second ideal of drama). As we learned above, the main desire of the hero, Holden, is his passionate love of Ameera and his baby, and the satisfaction of this desire is opposed by other desires in himself (internal conflict), by fear of the condemnation of other people of his own race (man and man conflict), and by an epidemic of cholera (man and nature conflict). Let me cite just a few of the emotional clashes in this story:

1. Holden, after the death of his child, hears other parents tell of the achievements of their children and wishes to do the same; his fear of the censure of these people belonging to his own race, however, prevents him. (Internal conflict).

2. In reliving the days before the child's death, he thought over and over of the things which might have been done to save it, knowing all the time that the cholera germs of India had already written the final pages of the baby's life. (Man and nature conflict.)

3. Infinitely appealing is a later phase of the same conflict (man and man) when Holden and the child's mother chide each other for faults at once true and imaginary:

"He was all my heart to me. How can I let the thought go when my arms tell me every night that he is not here? Ahi! Ahi! O Tota, come back to me — come back again, and let us be together as it was before! "

"Peace, peace! For thine own sake, and for mine also, if thou lovest me — rest."

"By this, I know that thou dost not care; and how shouldst thou? The white men have hearts of stone and souls of iron. Oh, that I had married a man of mine own people — though he beat me, and had never eaten the bread of an alien! "

"Am I an alien — mother of my son? "

9. General Formula for Dramatic Intensity

We are now ready, I think, to formulate finally a useful general rule for fulfilling both ideals of strong drama: *The intensity of a dramatic situation varies as the intensity of the conflicting desires, and as the pattern of the conflict is made to reveal character.* Geometric as this sounds it is an abstraction which lies at the very center of all art which portrays the heart-beat of humanity. The greatest story writers, poets, play-wrights, never heard of it — true; but their works show that they actually achieved the double ideal therein set forth; *some* method was inevitably involved: if you can grasp their method and use it, well and good; if you can't, I suggest that you master the method here set forth. You will need practice, and much constancy in your labors. You will do well to drill yourself first in the first ideal of drama, then with the other, then both together, using the assignments at the end of this chapter; after which you will see your writing gain in vision and power and you will know some of the joys of the real artist.

10. Criticism of the Finished Story

The knowledge of drama we have now obtained can be put to use not only in your plot-building but in criticizing your story after it is written. The gift of self-criticism is an asset of great value to any writer and, contrary to the general belief, it is a gift which can in large measure be cultivated. An ultimate verdict on a piece of writing lies, of course, with the audience for which it was intended. Tests of the skill with which an emotional piece of writing has been handled can, however, be made. The principles for such tests are now in hand.

We must focus our attention on the emotional conflict in a reflective delay. If there is no reflective delay and the story is one of impulse only, then the final decisive act alone comes under review. Whether or not it be true is a question of the value of the material itself rather than of its manipulation. In a well-defined reflective delay, however, we face a problem of manipulation which can be examined on the technical side. Since the clash of desires in the reflective delay is the means by which a character expresses himself, we may be sure that a proper handling of the clash will at once satisfy both our ideal of a strong conflict and our ideal of a revelation of character. Analysis of drama in which the *materials* are adequate to the purpose may, therefore, be reduced to a study of the clash itself.

As a general guide in our analysis we will use the formula for emotional conflict which has already been presented: *Desire A opposed by obstacle B produces emotion C.*

Let us take the converse of this formula: If the desires in the conflict are not opposed there will be no resulting emotion. Remove B, in other words, and C disappears also. " Opposition " means actual conflict. The desires and obstacles, that is, must be clearly portrayed in conflict. This is exactly what we fail to find in most pieces of writing weak in drama, and the errors shine forth in two distinct forms:

1. The clashing desires and obstacles are not portrayed. A and B, that is, are not described. There is action but it simply isn't the kind of action which describes the clash: the action is irrelevant, or it involves simple responses which portray no desires at all.

2. The emotion itself is named. This fault is a corollary inevitably resulting from fault number one. The writer, sensing his failure to portray the impulses which produce the emotion, tries to remedy the matter by naming the emotion itself. Either he does not understand the conflict, or, understanding it, he is too indolent to set it forth. In the former case he is asking his reader to do something which he can't do himself, and in the latter instance he is calling upon the reader to perform labor which the reader justifiably expects the writer to do for him. The result

in both cases is failure. Phrases — strung up and down through miles of amateur manuscripts — such as " a terrible fear seized him," " she was filled with indescribable ecstasy," and " he was overwhelmed with an intense passionate longing," are signposts of literary failure; they are confessions of an inability or unwillingness to perform the most fundamental artistic duty to the reader.

Faulty Drama Analyzed

Let us look at an example of a beginner's writing which illustrates for the most part fault number one. We will examine the close of the student love story presented on page ten. Lee Howe, you will remember, because of his love for Rita Rodney, had helped her regain possession of the old family mansion which she had lost. The story ends with Howe's arrival at the mansion to declare his love. Obviously, following our formula, the emotion to be produced, C, is romantic passion. The desires, A, are two in number, the romantic love of each of the lovers. The only obstacle left, B, is the lady's maidenly shyness. Since this is a weak obstacle, the desires, we have a right to expect, will be of an intensity which will rush things to a happy final embrace. Miss Rodney is so modest, the author tells us, that she believed that Lee really saved her house for her uncle's sake and not for her's. The scene continues:

" I would do anything for John Rodney, but I didn't do that for him."

His words were significant.

" My ingratitude hurt and drove you away."

" Yes, but that littleness passed away after hours of thought."

" I not only forgave you long ago, but I believe you did Sarah Jameson a kindness by sending her back to the city where she longed to be, for her spite was making her unhappy, yet through force of habit she could not give up."

" And you yourself? "

" I wanted the place more than I could tell."

" I may come every day? "

" But you are going west this week? "

The author's "his words were significant" are an un‹
conscious confession that she knows that she is not portraying the truth about her scene. She knows Lee's words are
pretty weak. She thought that the reader, by using his
imagination, would get the right idea. This trick is merely
a form of naming the emotion instead of portraying the
clash which produces it.

Rita's next statement that "Lee was hurt and driven
away" might be called a factor opposing Rita's love for
him; it does not have this effect, however, because we do
not yet see that there is *any* love on her part. He was
driven away. What of it?

Next we learn that Lee had spent hours of thought over
Rita's conduct. What took place in these hours of thought?
We do not know. Undoubtedly, the author again intends
us to see that this meditation is a "significant" fact. The
author gives us the task of imagining all the clashes that
took place during this meditation. Since we are reading
for amusement, we refuse to do this and pass on.

Rita's next statement simply dodges the issue. It contains no idea whatever about her desires; it merely says
that "she feels that Lee's conduct has been kind." By
this we merely know that she, Rita, is a "proper" young
lady.

By Lee's "and yourself?" we gain a hint that he is interested in Rita. Since he is a man and she a young
woman, we can guess that his desire may be a romantic
one, but we can only surmise. Rita "wants the place,"
but — how about wanting Lee? She again dodges the issue.
Lee's desire to come every day again is in the right direction. Its weakness is simply that it is a statement of
a weak desire.

Since the whole miserable thing had been settled, she could be
her own self again.

She felt that this would be indefinitely.

The garden was once again in bloom for it was summer,
but the Rodney home was closed, for John Rodney had gone

West months ago, and Rita and Lee Howe were on their honey-moon on their way East.

Error: Not Describing Clash

This conclusion is a masterpiece of unromantic banality. The lady, supposedly in the ecstasy of her tumultuous desires for her lover, surveys their whole past adventures and thinks of them as a " whole miserable thing." She sighs with relief " that she can be her own self again." Being her own self is being without a lover. This suggests a definite desire to get along as best she can without him.

In the next sentence we learn for the first time that the lady " feels." Just what she feels we are not sure. It actually seems to state that she resigns herself with satisfaction to her former state of spinsterhood. It is quite probable, however, that this is a supreme achievement in propriety on the part of the author. The lady will remain in her old home as happy as before; you are to guess that her husband will be with her as a lover, but it is better not to state it so!

In the last sentence, for the first time, we find a word which has any connotation of passionate desire — honey-moon. A fault here is in naming the emotion, though in this case it is one or two stages removed even from naming the emotion. It merely names the state in which emotions are commonly experienced.[1] The idea, however, of a honeymoon for these two young people with no more desire for each other than has yet been portrayed is positively shocking. They are satisfying desires which never existed!

[1] This use of the word emotion in connection with a honeymoon may suggest that here, at least, is a highly emotional state involving *no* conflict — in the honeymoon the conflict is over! The truth, alas, is too often otherwise. Obstacles to honeymoon desires are commonly enough experienced. If there are no obstacles, the ecstasy is one of pure feeling. The end of — how many! — pale love stories is but the beginning of genuinely big drama. Such, we can readily believe, was the fate of Rita Rodney. Why more love stories do not begin rather than end with the honeymoon is a problem that deserves inquiry. French literature presents no such problem.

Error: Naming the Emotion

Fault number two, naming the emotion instead of describing the clash that produces it, is the chief cause of the weakness of another student story, part of which is quoted below. Here a wife, Marion, is the unhappy witness of her husband, Jay, as he makes love to another woman, Roberta.

The tenseness with which Marion leaned over the balcony revealed how *tumultuous were the emotions* within her. It seemed like a hideous dream when she saw her husband hold the other woman close and kiss her *passionately*. For a moment she thought she would faint. Then she heard Jay speaking and could detect the *intensity of desire* in the tone of his voice.

" It is you I want," she heard Jay's *lover-like words*, making her *shudder with hatred* of the woman, " not my wife. If she won't agree to a divorce, you and I will go away, dear. No matter where we are, our *tremendous love* for each other will keep us happy." And again he kissed her with *voluptuous ecstasy*.

Is this an effective love scene? It is not, and for the simple reason that the author in the phrases italicized is telling us what she is trying to do while not doing it. She is naming her effects, not producing them. She has yet to learn that words themselves are not dramatic or emotional and evoke a feeling response in the reader only *when they depict actors undergoing emotion.*

Efforts by students to grasp the full meaning of this important principle involved in the actual writing out of dramatic action frequently result in two confusions: (1) they assume that emotions should *never* be mentioned, and (2) they assume that the actor's feelings should never be described. Both these assumptions are wrongly deduced from my exposition above. Regarding the first: emotions may be mentioned when the author is merely referring to them and not trying to portray them. For example: If the wife in the above episode later in a talk with a woman friend referred to her experience, the writer might say: " Once more hate and the desire for revenge swept over her." Or he might write: " Her emotions exhausted her." Or, in commenting upon the action, the author might write: " Love, rivalry, fear, self-pity, and finally desire for revenge." Words connoting emotion have their uses. As stated above, however, they should not be used *instead of depicting the emotion* or *in addition to depicting the emotion.*

The second confusion arises from not distinguishing the actor's feelings from the general emotional purpose. The three elements necessary to a full account of an emotion have already been outlined.[1] The actor's feeling-response, we learned, as well as his internal clash and his movements, should be indicated in any attempt at complete portrayal of emotion. A distinction then must be made between the actor's and the reader's feelings. In the first sentence of our faulty example we are told that the wife leaned over the balcony (action), that she was tense (feeling) and that the emotions within her were tumultuous (naming the emotion). The action is correct, although it would be more effective if it were the expression of her main trait and so related to the clash which is missing from this sentence and the entire passage. If, for example, she planned revengeful violence against the intruder, the action might be: " If she could but witness the woman's treachery! She leaned over the balcony." The tenseness, a physical response, describes her feelings and so is relevant. The rest of the sentence can be discarded. The sentence, then, would be more effective reading thus: " If she could but witness the woman's treachery! She leaned over the balcony, gripping the rail " In this final phrase I have avoided naming even her feeling, suggesting it rather by what she does. This revision suggests one of the most important principles in the code of modern realism. Successful writers today with few exceptions (the poetically gifted) strive to tell their stories with a technique borrowed from the theater. They write as if their characters moved upon a stage before them and as if they wished

[1] Page 143.

their readers so to behold them also. Where the materials are suitable[1] the device has no equal for swift and concentrated power. In such writings there is a minimum of analysis, a maximum of emotional evocation.

An Example of Good Modern Drama

An excellent and by no means extreme example of such modern dramatic writing is Fred R. Miller's story, *Happy New Year*.[2] Since in objective writing of this type the situation itself must be obvious and of life-and-death importance, we are not surprised to find in this narrative that a family is facing death by starvation. In simple, unaffected, almost colloquial language we are told how a very humble working man's family, husband, wife, and little girl, eat their last meal together. The wife cooks a few potatoes, the last food in the house. The husband insists that his wife and child eat the potatoes, asking for himself only the water in which they have been boiled. The water is set before him in a bowl by his wife who addresses him:

Want some coffee? she asked. We still got a little a that.

No. Save it till tomorra. This'll do me for one meal, jerking a thumb at the bowl of water. Where's the salt shaker? He took a seat at one end of the table and Margy pulled up the wicker armchair he had just left and seated Babe, who was whimpering with eagerness, at her side, while the molly parked itself near Farley's chair and meowed expectantly.

Keeping half a potato for herself, Margy mashed the rest with the fork. She began feeding the baby. Farley went at his bowl of hot water. The warm mealy smell of the potatoes coming across the table got him — gas grumbled in his stomach, his forehead crinkled as if with pain. Babe wriggled, kicking her heels on the seat of the chair, she gobbled her mash happily. Now and then she let out a squeal of satisfaction. The cat, blinking, lifted her nose to sniff, then stretched herself flat for a long wait.

Boy, if I only had a slice a punk to go with this, Farley mum-

[1] See *The Technique of the Point of View,* page 410.
[2] *Short Story Hits, 1933; Blast,* Sept., 1933.

bled. The stuff didn't taste much like the fat broth he had imagined, even with the soup-spoon to help kid himself along. It was just hot salty water. He gave up the spoon and at one gulp drank down what was left of the " potato juice cocktail." Shoving the bowl away from him, he said, The Last Supper. Huh, Margy?

This action is not yet of supreme intensity; this comes later when the husband, driven by his frantic determination to feed himself and his family, goes out on the street bent on violence. In this passage, however, we find a true reflective delay dexterously set in the developing dramatic pattern. Note how the author " lets the story tell itself " by not naming the emotions or commenting on the action. The feelings and sensations of his pathetic little group are sometimes told (the smell of the potatoes) and sometimes artfully suggested (the vision of the meat and the cat " lifting her nose to sniff ") and only once does he enter a character's mind — " the fat broth he imagined." Fully to envision a scene, to understand all the facts involved and to set forth the facts simply and without signposts to the reader in the shape of emotional *words* — this is the formula for success in the highest type of dramatic writing today.[1]

11. Types of Conflict

It now remains to consider more carefully the three patterns of dramatic conflicts mentioned on page 144. Through much of this chapter we have been thinking of dramatic conflicts as either weak or strong, seeking a method of creating the strong conflicts; but there is also another classification based *not* on degree of intensity, but on *differences in kind,* differences in the *ways desires are grouped within the conflicts.* Desires clash in three distinct patterns, as follows:

[1] Other expert handlings of dramatic scenes by noted writers may be found in the stories and novels mentioned on pages 156 and 504. Close study of several of them will amply repay the student.

1. Clash between man and the physical world.
2. Clash between man and man.
3. Clash between two desires in the same man.

This classification, let me repeat, has nothing whatever to do with degrees of intensity of drama; all may be weak, all may be strong. Their importance lies in the fact that they furnish us with *valuable rough classifications of the qualities of dramatic effects.* Each of the three types of conflicts, in other words, makes a different kind of appeal. Understanding these types, we understand something about effects. You must learn to recognize them instantly. You will be able to do so if you study carefully the following distinctions and perform the exercises based on them in Assignment H at the end of this chapter.

Analysis of Types of Conflicts

1. *Conflict between man and nature — the elemental clash:* Into this type fall man's battles for existence when he is opposed not by other men but by the terrors and hardships of inanimate nature herself. Primitive man fighting wild animals in prehistoric jungles; exploring navigators buffetting tempestuous seas; aviators facing the perils of lightning, fog and wind; the farmer drudging a living from the stubborn earth; the automobile driver racing against time for doctor or speed record — all such are of this elemental pattern. Because such struggle reflects man's eons of prehistoric battling with the terrors that fly by night and because it generally is enlivened with much action it appeals to more minds than either of the other types of struggle. Seldom does it produce a subtle story although of course it may; in some atmosphere stories man is arrayed against the dark powers of nature alone. It is the story most certain to interest the lowest intelligence and the immature or adolescent reader. It is found commonly in motion pictures, melo-

dramatic plays, in the fiction of the cheaper grade of magazines, and in adventure books for boys.

2. *Conflict between man and man — the social clash:*
We call this the social clash because in it one always sees man struggling with one or more of his fellows.   Here his

THE " SIEGFRIED " (ELEMENTAL) CONFLICT

desire, his passionate yearnings are opposed, not by fire and wind and flood, but by the desires and passions of other human beings.   As long as society is so organized that all of man's desires cannot be satisfied, there will be struggles among men and a vital interest in seeing them portrayed. The struggle of two classmates to be president of the class; a business man trying to " sell " a client during the depression; a detective capturing a bandit; a difference between a young woman and her parents over a matter of her conduct

— all these instances of opposed desires are phases of man's quarrel with his fellows and so are called social. Their appeal is distinctly higher than that of the elemental clash; the problems they present are more complicated; but since all of us deal with social problems nearly every minute of

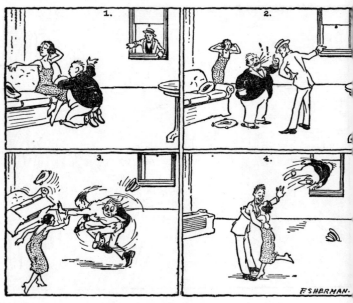

THE "RIVAL LOVERS" (SOCIAL) CONFLICT

our lives, this type of struggle provides the most satisfying kind of appeal to the average, moderately intelligent man and woman.

3. *Conflict between desires in one man — the psychological clash.* The psychological clash can be understood and appreciated only by those who have an interest in some of the subtler processes of their mental machinery. An atmosphere story, for instance, in which a lonely fisherman on a bleak untenanted bit of seashore is driven to sadness and despair

by the mere contemplation of the scenery would call for this type of mental analysis. Most of the action of the story might take place as the man sat before his cabin smoking his pipe. An account of the fleeting, vagrant, yet devastating impulses, images, and terrors which sweep in and out of his mind, clashing, jamming, disintegrating his soul would deal with a *subject matter* with which very few people indeed ever concern themselves. The conflict in this type of plot appeals therefore only to the highest intelligence.

Internal conflicts calling for more overt action have produced some fairly popular story types. The most-used plot pattern of this sort that I can think of is that between the traits of love and honor in one person. It has appeared in dramatic literature from early historic times to the present. It shows up at least once a month in magazine offices from some beginning scribe in the shape of a doctor who discovers he has a rival for his wife's affections. The rival, of course, is soon thereafter suddenly afflicted with a critical disturbance of his appendix, giving the husband, the famous surgeon who must perform the operation, his opportunity to illustrate this very high-class brand of drama. We turn the husband-surgeon into a ball and make him perform as follows:

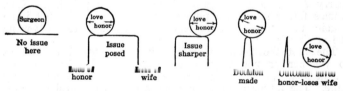

THE "LOVE AND HONOR" (INTERNAL) CONFLICT.

The above illustrations show these various levels in their "pure" state. Often, however, more than one level of conflict will be found in one story. In an adventure story, for instance, in which the hero, the captain, pilots his ship through a storm only to find it necessary to kill an enemy in a hand-to-hand conflict after the storm is over, we have, first, a struggle between man and nature and, secondly, one between man and man.

An instance of a double struggle, first between man and man, and secondly internal, would be that of a lover with a rival for the affections of a given young lady. The hero might face a coming fight with his rival. Besides his love for the girl he might have a strong tendency to cowardice. This would make him hesitate as to whether he would fight with his rival or not if he has a chance — an internal struggle. The young lady appears, and under the inspiration of her charms his courage would be revived, whereupon he fights his rival and defeats him. This second action would be a struggle between man and man.

A Three-Level Plot

Some stories involve all three levels of conflict. Here is a not-too-serious scenario of one:

Mr. X. the hero, is genuinely in love with Jane, who is full of many charms and graces, his ideal of a wife. The hero, however, is a poor man, an artist, and feels that with a wealthy wife he would further his art and win fame. He is madly loved by Anna, whose father is wealthy, and who offers, if he will marry Anna, to send him to Paris to study painting. Now, Anna's father is a stock plunger and the hero feels that if he is going to get any of the father's money he ought to get it while the getting is good.

The first movement, therefore, is X.'s internal conflict as to whether or not he will marry Anna and take a chance on the money, or whether he will give up this chance and marry Jane. The father returns while he is in this dreadful dilemma, announcing that he has lost everything. Immediately the hero, impelled by his strong affection for Jane, drops Anna's lily-white hand, grabs his panama and beats it in the direction of the bungalow on the lakeside where Jane is spending the summer. As he bolts from the house he is called to the telephone where Jane's mother informs him that Jane, hearing of his courtship to Anna, is threatening to commit suicide, and she doubts if she can restrain her.

The hero dashes towards the front door, but is opposed by Anna's father. The father, knowing that his daughter's heart will be broken if she is jilted, tells the treacherous hero that he must marry her. The hero refuses. There is an altercation and a visible conflict between man and man ensues. The hero triumphs, however, and, led by love for Jane, starts out to reach the bungalow, the temple of his desires, before the lovely Jane joins the fishes in the bottom of the lake. Since there are no trains and no motor cars he must find his way through a dreadful forest. He is opposed by trackless wastes, rushing streams and wild animals. In overcoming these obstacles he has a man and nature conflict.

He finally succeeds and reaches Jane in time to provide the reader with a happy clinch.

The three levels of conflict in this plot may be indicated as follows:

A UNIFIED THREE-LEVEL CONFLICT.

12. Special Problems in Drama

An examination of many defective stories shows that certain of them are popular with most beginners. These often-recurring typical faults are incorporated in plots which are analyzed and explained in Section B in the Appendix. Before attempting Assignment I at the end of this chapter the student is requested to study carefully these weak plot patterns. In some of them the dramatic factor is peculiarly difficult to detect.

Because of the importance of drama in practically all narrative writing I have given considerable space to it in this chapter. It must be remembered, however, that drama is itself but one means to a given artistic end. We have not yet learned how to apply it to specific purposes: we have not learned how drama is handled in conjunction with the principles of unity outlined in chapters two and three, nor how it is applied differently in the different special types of stories, such as the surprise-ending, mystery, detective and thematic stories: this will be done in the succeeding chapters. Before beginning with them we must wrestle with the assignments which follow.

ASSIGNMENTS: CHAPTER FOUR

ASSIGNMENT A

Here is a number of simple human activities. Is the individual mentioned by name in each case having an emotional experience or not? The answer is either "Yes" or "No." Write out your answers, adding an explanation where one seems necessary to support your belief.

1. Johnny stood by the window watching the fire-engine race down the street with its siren shrieking, smoke and sparks streaming from its chimney and a crowd following hard after. As soon as it passed out of sight he turned to his mother and said: " Mother, where is that book I was reading? " *

2. Johnny stood by the window watching the same fire-engine with its noise and hubbub and, when it had passed out of sight, turned to his mother and said: " Gee, I wish it would come past again! " *

3. Johnny stood by the window watching the same fire-engine, dancing up and down with excitement, and begging his mother, " Let me go out, mother; let me go out! " *

4. Mr. Brown stood in the midst of a subway crowd trying to read his newspaper. People rushing to and fro bumped into him and knocked the paper from his hands; someone told him to " get out of the way "; and when his car came along he was jammed through the door by a violent push from a guard. Once inside he continued calmly to read his paper.

5. Captain Cartwright stood on the bridge of the great Atlantic liner giving commands for warping her up to her dock. Crowds cheered and a band played on the pier. Handkerchiefs waved from all the decks of the great ship as the Captain gave the signals which moved the forty thousand tons into place.*

6. Miss Hermione stood at the edge of a precipice in the Grand Canyon and murmured: " Ain't nature grand! " *

7. Miss Hermione stood at the edge of a precipice in the Grand Canyon uttering her famous line when her friend seized her by the arm, drew her back, and gasped: " Good heavens, I thought you were going to fall in; you mustn't stand so close to the edge! "

8. Minnie stood at the street car transfer point. Two cars approached. She was uncertain which one to take. If she took the wrong one, she would be too late to get a job for which she had been waiting and working for six months. She had been told that a policeman stationed there would direct her. Sure enough, there

he was standing beside her. She asked him and he told her the right car.

9. The same situation as No. 8 except that the policeman told Minnie to take the wrong car, and she did.

10. Mrs. Jones was cleaning house, pausing from time to time to call out cheerfully to her neighbor across the street.

11. Sam came home drunk, began to scold his wife, and threatened to beat her with a stick. His wife screamed and tried to get away. When Sam had slept off the influence of the liquor, he apologized humbly to his wife.*

12. George and Henry locked in each other's embrace were scuffling and laughing about on the floor.

13. Hiram and Dave sat about the hot stove in the country store smoking their corncob pipes with other male villagers arguing in favor of war. Their arguments were opposed by the other villagers. The discussion lasted until well past midnight when Hiram and Dave treated the bunch to a glass of cider and all went home quietly.*

14. Mrs. White sat by the coffin of her husband sobbing inconsolably.

15. Rastus lay dreaming that he sat at a table on which stood a huge roasted chicken. Every time he reached toward it, it jumped out of reach. He pursued it by running around the table, finally enraged, plunging over the table, coming down with a crash which woke him up. Trembling, perspiring, he sat up, scratching his head, and wondering what he had been dreaming about.*

ASSIGNMENT B

Note: For answers to exercises with asterisks, see page 500 ff.

1. Is the cat in the following episode having an emotional experience?

The passengers on a river steamer crowded to one side of the boat to watch the efforts of a cat to climb on a ledge of a stone support of a bridge. The passengers gasped with pity as they saw it almost lift itself from the water only to be washed off again by a wave.*

2. In the above episode are the passengers having an emotional experience? Explain your answer.

3. Are there any emotional conflicts in the following quotation from O. Henry?

Half a dozen of Macuto's representative social and official caballeros were distributed about the room. Senor Villablanca, the wealthy rubber concessionist, reposed his fat figure on two chairs, with an emollient smile beaming upon his chocolate-colored face. Guilbert, the French mining engineer, leered through his polished nose-glasses. Colonel Mendez, of the regular army, in gold-laced uniform and fatuous grin, was busily extracting corks from champagne bottles. Other patterns of Macutian gallantry pranced and posed. The air was hazy with cigarette smoke. Wine dripped upon the floor. Perched upon a table in the center of the room in an attitude of easy preëminence was Mlle. Giroud. Upon her lap rested a guitar. In her face was complete serenity. She was singing to a lively accompaniment a little song:

> When you see de big, round moon
> Comin' up like a balloon
> Dis nigger skips fur to kiss de lips
> Ob his stylish, black-faced coon.

4. Are any *well-marked* desires exhibited in the following episode?

A section gang was working on a culvert when the through express came along. Old Jake, who was partly blind and deaf, did not hear or see the approaching train. All the other men stepped off the track. The train was almost upon Old Jake when Danny, a young workman, suddenly seeing the old man's danger, gave him a shove which sent him sprawling at the side of the track, thus saving his life.*

5. The following quotation from F. Scott Fitzgerald * produces a definite feeling in the reader. What is it? What is the conflict?

Perry enters Mrs. Nolak's shop in search of a costume for a circus ball.

"Something for you?" she queried pessimistically.

"Want costume of Julius Hur, the charioteer."

Mrs. Nolak was sorry, but every stitch of charioteer had been rented long ago. Was it for the Townsends' circus ball?

It was.

"Sorry," she said, "but I don't think there's anything left that's really circus."

This was an obstacle.

"Hm," said Perry. An idea struck him suddenly. "If you've got a piece of canvas I could go 's a tent."

"Sorry, but we haven't anything like that. A hardware store is where you'd have to go. We have some very nice Confederate soldiers."

"No. No soldiers."

"And I have a very handsome king."

He shook his head.

"Several of the gentlemen," she continued hopefully, "are wearing stovepipe hats and swallow-tail coats and going as ring-

*From *Tales of the Jazz Age,* copyright, 1922, by Charles Scribner's Sons; by permission of the publishers.

masters — but we're all out of tall hats. I can let you have some
crepe hair for a mustache."

" Want somep'n 'stinctive."

" Something — let's see. Well, we have a lion's head, and a
goose, and a camel — "

" Camel? " The idea seized Perry's imagination, gripped it
fiercely.

" Yes, but it needs two people."

" Camel. That's the idea. Lemme see it."

The camel was produced from his resting place on a top shelf.
At first glance he appeared to consist entirely of a very gaunt,
cadaverous head and a sizeable hump, but on being spread out
he was found to possess a dark brown, unwholesome-looking body
made of thick, cottony cloth.

" You see it takes two people," explained Mrs. Nolak, holding
the camel in frank admiration. " If you have a friend he could be
part of it. You see there's sorta pants for two people."

Perry tentatively gathered up the body and legs and wrapped
them about him, tying the hind legs as a girdle round his waist.
The effect on the whole was bad. It was even irreverent —
like one of those mediaeval pictures of a monk changed into a
beast by the ministrations of Satan. At the very best the ensemble
resembled a humpbacked cow sitting on her haunches among
blankets.

" Don't look like anything at all," objected Perry gloomily.

" No," said Mrs. Nolak; " you see you got to have two people."

A solution flashed upon Perry.

" You got a date tonight? "

" Oh, I couldn't possibly — "

" Oh, come on," said Perry encouragingly. " Sure you can!
Here! Be a good sport, and climb into these hind legs."

With difficulty he located them, and extended their yawning
depths ingratiatingly. But Mrs. Nolak seemed loath. She backed
perversely away.

" Oh, no — "

" C'm on! You can be in front if you want to. Or we'll flip
a coin."

" Oh, no — "

" Make it worth your while."

Mrs. Nolak set her lips firmly together.

" Now you just stop! " she said with no coyness implied. " None
of the gentlemen ever acted up this way before. My husband — "

" You got a husband? " demanded Perry. " Where is he? "

6. Is the man in the following episode experiencing any emotion? Explain your answer.

Mr. X. had not been to the dentist's for three years and now
the cleaning he was enduring brought him exquisite pain. His
face twisted with suffering as the dentist scraped the tender spots

with his sharp instruments. Mr. X. however, showed such fortitude that the dentist finally broke out in admiration: "Sir, I don't see how you can control yourself as you do." *

7. Criticize the following story outline on the score of the emotion, if any, which it would produce on the reader when written out:

Burton Andrews, a mining engineer in California, visits the home of his sister in Oakland, hoping to meet some of his sister's girl friends. He is looking for a wife. He is introduced to a number of girls of the flapper type who disgust him: they seem to him to care only for auto rides, theatres, flowers and dancing.

He picks up a magazine and reads an article describing the home established by half a dozen Boston school teachers who have banded together to make themselves happy though unmarried. He admires their ideals and writes a letter to one of them named Emily Peters.

After returning to his mining post he in time receives a letter from Miss Peters. He writes again and their correspondence shows him that she is a hard-working, wholesome, dignified young woman. He finally decides to go East to meet her. Once in Boston they become friends, fall in love, and are married.*

8. Explain why the following brief passage is one of the most passionately moving in the entire Bible:

And He came out, and went, as His custom was, unto the Mount of Olives; and the disciples also followed Him. And when He was at the place, He said unto them, "Pray that ye enter not into temptation." And He was parted from them about a stone's cast; and He kneeled down and prayed saying, "Father, if Thou be willing, remove this cup from me; nevertheless not my will, but Thine be done." And there appeared unto Him an angel from heaven, strengthening Him. And being in an agony, He prayed more earnestly, and His sweat became as it were great drops of blood falling down upon the ground.

9. What are the desires evidenced by Perry and Mrs. Nolak in No. 5 above?

10. Two desires, somewhat related, are expressed by the action of Burton Andrews in No. 7 above. What are they?

ASSIGNMENT C

This assignment will provide some fairly simple writing exercises in emotional conflicts. The purpose here is not, as in the two previous assignments, merely to see if you understand the principles involved in specific cases; it is that, but it is more importantly to give you practice in using them in your writing. An understanding of the problem is, therefore, no reason for not writing it out. The principles we have studied will never be really mastered until you can use them without thinking of them; such facility comes only by much conscious practice.

1. Decide definitely what the desire is in the following action; and write another paragraph of action which expresses the same desire. Desire is the dynamic element in any character trait. The work on this assignment is a direct preparation for your work on the character story. See Chapter V, especially pages 225–228.

David the Freshman began cramming for the history examination immediately after supper and "boned" away until one o'clock that night when he found he could repeat the history syllabus almost by heart. He rose, yawning, and muttered to himself: "I'll bet I show Dad whether or not I'm a failure as a student; I'm going to get at least a ninety-five tomorrow, you watch."

2. Two desires are definitely expressed in the following action, one a desire to play football, the other to keep a date with a girl. Re-write the exercise, making all the action express one desire only. Try to relate *all* the material to the one desire. See Chapter II, Assignment D, No. 4. The easy way to do this exercise is simply to cut out one desire, but if you have done the preceding assignments thoughtfully, you should be able now easily to manipulate all the details in this sketch to support first one of the desires, and then in a second study, the other desire.

Herbert rushed out of class and ran across the campus toward the gymnasium. In the locker-room he called to the other fellows who were already dressed to wait until he was ready before starting the game. "I've got an eighty-yard kick in me today," he told the coach, as he broke a shoe-string in his eagerness.

As soon as the game was over and he had had his shower and was again dressed, he dashed out. He was late. Would she wait for him? He started on a run toward the library. He had so much to tell her! And he wanted to invite her to the next hop. This he had to do today. What if that guy Hinky Dink had found her and taken her off! He could see no one on the library steps. He was too late! He ran around the building, came back to the front, stopped, and began mopping his brow, when he heard a silvery laugh behind one of the stone pillars. His heart was in his mouth, he jumped for the pillar and — there she was, laughing at him.

3. In the action outlined above there is no conflict between the two desires mentioned. Now re-write the action making a conflict between them. Put Herbert between the library which shel-

ters the adored creature and the football field where the boys are getting out for practice and make him do things which picture the conflict. He wants both to see the girl and to play ball. Be careful not to name either desire. Invent overt, external action to express the clash.

4. There are two distinct conflicts in the following action. Rewrite it, to the same length, so that there will be only one conflict:

Henry was hungry and was on his way to the hotel to have dinner with his roommate when suddenly he remembered that his father had warned him that if he spent any more money on hotel dinners he would take him out of college. He sat down on a campus bench to think the problem over when Jimmy, a fraternity brother, appeared and urged him to come over to the College Union to meet a newly pledged classmate. Henry tried to beg off, saying that he was too hungry to do anything but eat. Jimmy upbraided him with lack of loyalty to the fraternity. Henry didn't know what to do, to go to the hotel, to the Union, or to the fraternity house where his board bill was paid by his father.

5. The selection below, from " Romeo and Juliet," is one of the most beautiful dramatic conflicts in all literature. We have all heard the poetic lines, but we do not always remember the life-or-death conflict which underlies the elaborate imagery. Shakespeare depended on skilled actors to convey to his audience, by their action, the intensity of the desires. Romeo's life is at stake, and Juliet is his bride of a night. What then are the desires in this conflict? Re-write the scene, both action and dialogue, omitting the poetic figures and using modern speech appropriate to a moment so intense.

> *Juliet.* Wilt thou be gone? It is not yet near day:
> It was the nightingale, and not the lark,
> That pierc'd the fearful hollow of thine ear;
> Nightly she sings on yon pomegranate-tree.
> Believe me, love, it was the nightingale.
> *Romeo.* It was the lark, the herald of the morn,
> No nightingale: look, love, what envious streaks
> Do lace the severing clouds in yonder east.
> Night's candles are burnt out, and jocund day
> Stands tiptoe on the misty mountain tops,
> I must be gone and live, or stay and die.
> *Juliet.* Yon light is not day-light, I know it, I;
> It is some meteor that the sun exhales,
> To be to thee this night a torch-bearer,
> And light thee on thy way to Mantua:
> Therefore stay yet, thou need'st not to be gone.
> *Romeo.* Let me be ta'en, let me be put to death;
> I am content, so thou wilt have it so.

6. Re-write what you have just written for No. 5, omitting all conflicts but keeping the speakers' love for each other. The scene here assigned might be merely a husband telling his wife good-bye on going to work in the morning.

7. Here are two distinct desires or motives. Give them both to a football player, opposing one to the other in action which takes place the night before a big game.

Desire one: To secure some money quickly so as to be able to pay back some gambling debts.
Desire two: To have the college team win on the following day.

Don't make this an internal conflict. If he wants the money, let him *do something* to get it. If he wants the team to win, let him do something about that. Plan overt action to reveal his desires.

8. Give the first desire above to a player and the second to a girl the player is in love with, and outline a conflict between the player and the girl. Don't make this an internal conflict for either. The boy's desire must be made to oppose the girl's in overt action and speech. Put them in a setting where their action will have most meaning. For example, the office or factory or store where the boy has gone to earn some money would enable you to let him reveal his desire in terms of action as well as talk. Such surroundings will help you in the invention of action to express the boy's desire.

9. A woman has never outgrown her dependence upon her father, whose judgment and opinions she prefers to her husband's. The husband has a business opportunity in a distant city. The wife and her father oppose his going, since it will mean separation of father and daughter. Outline a clash between the husband and the other two. His desire is to control his own home; the desire of the other two is not to be separated.

10. A middle-aged couple receive a small legacy. The husband has had his nose on the grindstone so long that he wants to spend this money for a trip somewhere; the wife wants to save it. Outline a clash that begins in his office or place of business and continues along the street until they reach the bank where she wants to deposit the money. Arrange this setting, both in the office, on the street, and in the bank, to help you bring out in convincing action and speech both desires. Let the husband make his last stand on the steps of the bank. It's now or never!

ASSIGNMENT D

The exercises in this assignment are mainly for practice in analyzing narrative for its revelation of character. Please remember that the word " character " as used here means not the whole nature of any individual but merely *the trait or traits of character which are relevant in a given dramatic situation.* You should search simply for the desires, motives or impulses which impel the character to a given action. *Be especially careful not to confuse violence of action with power of character revelation.*

Write out the answers to these questions: To what extent does the action reveal traits of character in the actors whose names are italicized? Is the revelation powerful, or slight, or wanting entirely? Why? If traits are revealed, name them.

1. The feud between the Duggers and the Mallins had not yet been fought out. *Jim Mallin* and *Jake Dugger* still remained alive. Mallin was the more brutal in temperament, while Jake was the better shot; seldom, in fact, had the mountain folk known a more marvelous shot than Jake Dugger.

The end of the feud came at the little railroad station of Cedar Creek where Jake lived. He was leaning against the little station watching a train pull out when suddenly, as the last car passed him, a shot rang out and he felt a bullet zip past his cheek. Jake wheeled, saw Jim's head at a window of the caboose, jerked his gun from its holster and fired from his hip. His first shot and Jim's second rang out together. Jake lost a finger from his gun hand but Jim disappeared from the window and was taken off at the next station dead.*

2. *Angus* was " buzzarding " Mr. Griswold's peach orchard. Mr. Griswold refused to put any more money into it; Angus could make the best fruit possible with his own efforts, and at the end of the season the two would split on the returns.

All day long he and Dossie, his wife, and their two boys, eight and nine years old, worked to exhaustion on the trees. Angus meant to do his best, and when a man does that, he told Dossie, the Lord is bound to be on his side. His war bonus came just in time to pay for needed spray and fertilizer. Dossie wanted to put the money into a little farm of their own; but Angus said the money coming as it did was a sign from heaven. The Lord was on his side; and later the Lord would make the price right, and they'd be fixed for life.

The crop was big — about eight carloads. Angus had the trucks ready for the hauling. The county agent came. He said there was no use shipping the peaches. All he'd get back would be a freight bill. All the big pack houses were shut down. Cheaper to let 'em rot.

Angus tried to turn the crop into liquor, but revenue officers caught him.

— Katharine Ball Ripley, " What's a Man to Do? " published in *The Atlantic Monthly,* October, 1932, and in *Short Story Hits, 1932.*

3. *Cassandra Lewis* is a young girl who when she was only twelve years old had a childish love affair with Kenneth Ridgely. Now after several years abroad she returns to her home town to visit her girlhood chum, Frances Buckingham, secretly hoping to meet Kenneth.

At the train to meet her is her friend and Kenneth too. Unexpected good fortune! He would certainly remember their childish love affair. It would not be as difficult to make him fall in love with her as her mother had led her to believe. She is subtle, she makes no effort to fascinate him at once — tomorrow perhaps. There is nothing sordid about it; she feels already the wings of the love bird fluttering in her heart. He terrifies her still, but in a breathless, delicious way. Sitting beside him in the car is ecstasy.

In the house her friend strips off her gloves and Cassandra sees that she wears a very fine diamond; it is Kenneth's engagement ring. Cassandra does not over-rate her own charm, but she knows that if she wanted to she could break the affair and marry him herself.

All one night she struggles with the idea; Frances is her friend and hostess; she should not come into her house and steal her betrothed. On the other hand, " all's fair in love and war." Frances didn't need him so much as she did, it wasn't a life and death matter with her. Why not? She finally decides to abandon all her bright hopes and avoid him entirely.

Her visit drags on an ever increasing agony. She loves Kenneth so much that she knows that there will never in this world be any-one to take his place, but she's a good sport; never once by either word or act does she show her feelings.

4. *Sid McCoy* was on a tear. He was on a tear, and he wanted everybody to know it. The day before had been Saturday and pay day, and Sid had invested the major portion of his earnings in the cup that cheers — and also inebriates.

Waking Sunday morning with a splitting head, he found a quart bottle that, through some oversight, he had missed the night before, and proceeded to surround it, on the assumption that the hair of the dog is good for its bite.

Along in the afternoon, the effect of that quart began to wear off, and a raging thirst assailed him. A thorough search of his quarters assured him that there were none but dead soldiers there, so he started out to see if he couldn't acquire some liquid nourish-ment elsewhere.

But the day was Sunday, and the lid was on tight. His only hope lay in a drug store, and the druggist would sell whiskey only on a prescription.

But luck was with him. As he neared the drug store, he saw Dr. Spencer coming out.

" Oh, Doc! " he called. And as the physician reluctantly turned and waited for him to come up, " I want some whiskey, Doc. Gimme a prescription! "

Spencer looked him up and down contemptuously. " You'll get no whiskey from me! " he said, and started to walk away.

McCoy grabbed him by the shoulder and rudely whirled him about. " I won't, eh? " he stormed in quick rage. " You—— "

He got no further. Spencer's fist caught him under the chin and lifted him clean off his feet, landing him on his back a half dozen feet away. Then the Doctor turned and started home.

He didn't get a dozen feet. Lying where he had fallen, McCoy drew his gun, steadied it against his hip and emptied it into the Doctor's back.

5. *Mike* was a bricklayer and was constantly being sworn at by the boss for his carelessness. He bumped into the other workmen carrying hod over dizzy platforms; he left his tools about so that they were lost or stolen; he did his work so badly that at times he was compelled to do it over. One day, while he sat in front of a building, eating his lunch, the boss reminded him that he had left a pile of brick several stories up where they might fall off and hurt someone. Mike expressed indifference and was asserting profanely that the brick couldn't possibly fall when someone unintentionally bumped into them, whereupon they did indeed fall, hit him on the head, and knocked him unconscious.*

6. At three in the afternoon *Geraldine* finished ironing her dress, and went up to her room. She sat for a time by the window watching the children at play in the vacant lot next door. They were noisy and quarrelsome. After a time she heard her mother call to remind her that Robert Wallace was coming to take her out to dinner, and that she must be ready. " I'll be ready," she called back good-naturedly. Her mother wanted her to marry Robert, who was wealthy, but he was fifteen years her senior. Her mother assured her that such a difference in age didn't matter when people really loved each other, but Geraldine thought differently. Of course, it would be nice to have a lot of pretty things and to tell sales girls to deliver rich furs and jewels to Mrs. Robert Wallace at 4 Piedmont Drive, and to see her name in the society columns, but there were other things in life. Geraldine liked books, and ideas; she liked going to concerts, and seeing good plays; she'd written some poetry. None of these things would ever be interesting to Robert. He told her often that she was beautiful, but when he came to see her he spent most of the time telling her about new ideas he was working out to make more money with his store. Some day, she felt, there would be someone with whom she could be happier. " Mother is wrong," she sighed, and picked up a book of poems that lay on her bed table.*

7. To the people in the small hotel in southern France *Mr. Salesby* was " The Englishman." He didn't talk to anyone; his speeches to his wife, who fluttered delicately in her speech and gestures, were monosyllabic. They had come for her health. Doctors had said that two years in a mild climate would make her well, and because she could not bear to come alone, he had accompanied her. The other guests and the servants liked Mrs. Salesby, who enjoyed everything, going into little shivers of excitement over small events like the fragrance of foliage or the arrival of the mail from home. Her husband replied to her briefly; most of his remarks had to do with her health. Was she warm enough? Didn't she need her wrap? And so on. He was not a man, agreed the gossipy old women who watched his formal cool politeness to her, he was an ox. He never left his wife's side unless she insisted that he needed a constitutional, and then he returned at exactly the time appointed.

One afternoon, when at her insistence he had gone for a brief walk, he found her sitting in the garden without her cloak when he returned. When they reached the lift she was coughing. He frowned.

She sat and waited, while he rang and rang, and although she protested, kept his finger on the bell.

The door of the *salon* opened. The guests, disturbed by the noise, began to cry out, what was the matter? A dog belonging to one of the elderly ladies, began to yelp. Someone shouted for the manager, who came running, and who, when he discovered the cause of the disturbance, declared that he himself would take up Mr. and Mrs. Salesby in the lift. After he had ushered them in, he went to the door of the *salon*, and apologized to all the guests for the annoyance of this prolonged bell-ringing. Waiting, Mr. Salesby stood in the elevator, sucking in his cheeks, staring at the ceiling, and turning the signet ring on his little finger.

When they reached their room, he brought his wife her medicine at once. "Sit down," he said. "Drink it. And don't talk."

Later we learn that his furious ringing, which had disturbed the whole place, had broken the bell.

— Katherine Mansfield, *The Man Without a Temperament*.

8. The channel steamer was about to dock at Dover and *Miss Johnson* suddenly discovered that she had lost her passport. In a panic of fear that she might be returned to France she appealed to Mr. Symonds for help. The latter remembered that his wife's picture was on his passport together with his own and, inasmuch as his wife was not travelling with him, he offered to pass Miss Johnson off as his wife. The resemblance was close enough to make the attempt at deception fairly safe.

When the English passport inspector came to Miss Johnson, he looked up and said, " Mrs. Symonds, have you any children? "

" Children! " exclaimed Miss Johnson, " why, I'm not married! "

9. *Betsy,* who was a well-trained cat in her way, was chased around the house during a raging storm by Bowser, a bull pup, owned by a neighbor. Betsy stood at bay and spit and scratched the dog when the latter caught up with her. Soon, however, her strength gave out and again she fled frantically about the bushes in the garden, over the porches, and under the walks. Several times she jumped as if to waken her owners and arouse them to her rescue; but the noise of the winter storm was so great that they heard nothing.

Finally, Betsy leaped to the rear door and jumped at the knob to which was attached a wire. This wire had been put there by her mistress so that she could announce her desire to come into the house. Again and again Betsy leaped at the wire only to fall each time almost into the cruel pup's jaws. Each time she fought him back until again she could jump and effect one more desperate signal to those within who alone could now rescue her.*

10. *Handy Gus,* the robber, softly opened the door and entered the bedroom to find himself suddenly and unexpectedly face to face with a lovely woman. The woman on seeing him gasped, screamed, and ran to a French window to escape.

" Aha, my pretty one," gloated the robber, pocketing his revolver, "this is a treat. I thought I might find your husband, but — no, you can't get out there!" He sprang towards her, seized her roughly by an arm and threw her into a large chair.

"What do you want?" cried the woman, shaking with fear, "who are you? O, go away! If my husband were here . . ."

"So, he's not here, sweetheart," laughed the burglar.

"Go away, go away," screamed the woman; jumping to her feet.

"Shut up, you silly fool!" growled the burglar, as he seized her in his arms and covered her delicate mouth with his rough hand. "You might as well be quiet. I mean business. See, can't you see I'm crazy about you — Lord, Lord, what a beauty!" He tried to kiss her, but she struggled in his grasp and tried feebly to beat him on the head.

"Help! Fire! Police!" screamed the woman, between his clutching fingers.

"Shut up, or I'll kill you," muttered the burglar, as he produced his revolver, and raised it above her head as if to strike her. Maddened by contact with her, the burglar dropped the weapon and continued his efforts to kiss her while she screamed and kicked and writhed in his arms.

A shout heard on the lawn in front of the house brought the burglar to his senses. He dropped the limp form of the woman, snatched his revolver from the floor and, with one bound, leaped out the door the way he had come.*

11. *Sambo* was a victim of the hookworm. He slept most of the time in the barn, out in the orchard on the soft, cool grass, and even sometimes along side the road towards town where the constable would come upon him, kick him away and order him to go on about his business.

But Sambo had no business in particular. He was given his meals by Aunt Sally behind the kitchen and was never driven away because Mr. Fairfield, the owner of the plantation, liked to have him sing the old plantation songs to his children and also — Sambo played a good crap game when he wasn't too tired to shuffle the bones. This noble pastime was Mr. Fairfield's only recreation and with Sambo, out behind the smokehouse on summer eves, he had his game.

Sambo now, however, no longer kept these rendezvous. Instead, he loafed on the street corners in town, hung around the kitchen, or slept endless hours wherever he happened to be. He became a thoroughly "no account nigger" and "as slow as Sambo" became a stock expression on the Fairfield plantation.*

12. The prisoner, *Bill Tucker,* was brought to the laboratory of the famous psychologist, Professor Wright, to undergo a scientific test of his veracity or lack of it. The man in all the grillings he had undergone at the hands of the police insisted doggedly that he had not killed his wife. He had not been able to prove an alibi, and yet the evidence against him was only circumstantial. Over and over he repeated, "I never done it; I never done it."

In despair the police commissioner had exclaimed: "If we only had some way to X-ray a man's heart and see if he is telling the truth." The comment came to the ear of Professor Wright who claimed that he had invented an instrument, based on French experiments, which would detect a lie if the consequences of the detection of the lie were momentous as in this case.

The noted scientist sat his subject in a chair, attached delicate instruments to various parts of the man's body and connected these instruments to automatic recorders on his laboratory table. Then he began talking to the accused. At first he spoke of inconsequential matters, gradually leading up to a detailed description of the horrible condition of his wife when she was found. Suddenly then, he quietly introduced this question: "Why did you do it?"

The prisoner replied in the same calm, even tone in which he had been talking: "I never done it. How often do I have to tell you?"

Ten minutes later Professor Wright faced the assembled detectives and police officials and announced: "My patient, when he answered my last question, told me what he knows is not true."*

13. "My name, *Hortense Robbins,* used to be in the papers daily as having dined somewhere, or traveled somewhere, or rented a house in Paris, where I entertained the nobility. I was forever eating or traveling, or taking the cure at Baden-Baden. Now I am here to do honor to Spoon River, here beside the family whence I sprang. No one cares now where I dined, or lived, or whom I entertained, or how often I took the cure at Baden-Baden!"

MASTERS, *Spoon River Anthology.*

14. A king of olden times decreed that every person accused of crime should be placed in a great amphitheatre, where in the presence of the king and the people, he should open one of two doors, just alike, and side by side. Behind one door was a tiger, and behind the other a beautiful girl, who, if he was lucky enough to open her door, was immediately to become his bride, regardless of any previous ties. Behind which door was the tiger who meant death, and behind which the lovely lady, was a profound secret at each trial.

A young courtier of humble rank won the love of the king's daughter, and the king, learning of the affair was so enraged that he had the youth imprisoned, to be tried in the arena. *The princess* managed to find out behind which door the tiger was to be placed, and behind which the lady. Then she faced a horrible alternative. By some signal she would be able to tell her lover which door to open. Which should it be? If he opened the one door, he would be devoured and lost to her forever. If he opened the other door, he would live, but in the arms of another—the fairest maiden of her court. At last she decided. On the day of the trial, she managed to signal her lover to open the right hand door. He obeyed.

"Which came out of the opened door—the lady, or the tiger?"*

—STOCKTON, *The Lady or the Tiger?*

ASSIGNMENT E

The writing exercises in this assignment are somewhat more difficult than those in Assignment C. You are here asked to apply the first practical rule for intensifying weak dramatic material with the object of strengthening the emotional conflict. The task of invention will be made easier if you will in each case make certain that you understand the desires involved.

1. Manipulate No. 5, Assignment D, to produce an intense emotional conflict between Mike and his boss.

2. Manipulate No. 6, Assignment D, to give Geraldine an intense conflict between love for Robert and some other desire. Introduce into the scene either Robert, or some character identified with the opposing desire. This second character will intensify the clash, and enable you to invent more varied action by which to express it.

3. Manipulate the same material to produce an intense emotional conflict between Geraldine and her mother. Try to work out the clash on all three levels.

4. Manipulate No. 7, Assignment D, to reveal in action the clash between Mr. Salesby's devotion to his wife and his longing to get away from the dullness of the hotel. Introduce another character, if necessary, to externalize the clash.

5. Increase the tension of the clash in No. 7. Make the wife desperately ill. Keep the man's self-control the same even in this greater conflict and invent action similar to the violent ringing of the elevator bell in the story, which will reveal this more intense emotion.

6. Re-write No. 10, Assignment D, making the burglar's chief desire a determination to steal a diamond necklace and the woman's chief desire a determination not to give the necklace up. Make the conflict between the woman and the burglar intense and sharp, but with a minimum amount of character revealed.

7. Write the same episode changing and, if necessary, lengthening it so that a clear picture of the characters of both is given. Present the burglar as a greedy, though cautious criminal, and the woman as a person of resource and presence of mind.

8. Re-write the same episode, reducing the emotional tension, and picturing the burglar as a sentimental and chivalrous man and the woman as shallow-brained, flattery-loving and vain.

9. Louise Darrow, not yet twenty, gives her father many anxious hours. She has no mother, and her father has lost all influence over her. He loves her and he wants to protect her from the dangers that he foresees in her all-night parties, wild auto-

mobile rides with crowds of young people, reckless drinking, and her indifference to the future. He has tried to use argument and then threats. He has told her that the first night when she isn't home by one o'clock she must go to work somewhere where he can keep an eye on her. Write the scene when she returns toward dawn, and finds him waiting for her. The assignment is two developments of the scene: 1, give the clash maximum emotional intensity; 2, give it high emotional tension, and make it also reveal the characters.

10. In the following situation, Dorothy is given a slight desire which in turn is opposed by a slight obstacle. Re-write it so that a very strong desire is opposed by a very stubborn obstacle. Do not write the action out at length; simply write down an act indicating a strong desire and another act showing a strong obstacle.

Dorothy is seated in the waiting room of the hospital waiting the outcome of an operation on one of her mother's fingers which had become infected. She had a fear of hospitals and hoped her mother would not faint or suffer too much. The nurse reassured her that the operation was a simple one, and that her mother would be able to go home with her after a few hours' rest.

11. A newspaper man, given to drink, writes a letter addressed to his son (imaginary — the man has no son!) in which he warns him of the evils of drink and bad companions. In the quotation from his letter given below you will find suggestions for dramatic conflict. The two paragraphs contain a fairly full suggestion of two characters, a boy and his father. Treat the material as if it were a clipping or a sketch from your notebook, intended to stimulate your own imagination.

The assignment is to write out an intense emotional scene that will express in action the desires hinted at in the quotation. Don't plot a debate between the father and son. Show desires, not ideas, and show them in action. You might, for instance, let the boy plan to go with his irresponsible gang to some notorious resort; and let the father discover this plan, and try to oppose it, ending the scene with the father restraining the boy physically. And so on. Choose a setting that will be closely related to one of the desires, and which will be useful in offering opportunity for action. Give both characters desires of maximum intensity.

" It's rather up to you, Bub. In the next few months you will have to decide whether or not you are going to hell. Of course ' The vilest sinner may return ' at any point along the road — but to what? To shattered health; to a mother heart-broken in her grave; to a wife damned to all eternity by your thoughtless brutality; and to children who are always afraid to look up the alley, when they see a group of boys, for fear they may be teasing you — you, drunk and dirty, lying in stable filth! To that you will 'return,' with your strength spent, and your sportive friends gone to the devil before you, and your chance in life frittered away.

"When you are old, the beer you have swilled will choke your throat; the women you have flirted with will hang round your feet and make you stumble. All the nights you have wasted at poker will dim your eyes. The garden of the days that are gone, wherein you should have planted kindness and consideration and thoughtfulness and manly courage to do right, will be grown up to weeds, that will blossom in your patches and in your rags and in your twisted, gnarly face that no one will love."

— William Allen White, *In Our Town.*

12. In Assignment A, No. 15, Chapter I, you find a murder scene. The story from which it was taken pictures a quiet, industrious, unoffending negro laborer, murdered in cold blood by two white men at work on the same job.

Give some thought to this situation. What desires does it suggest in the opposing characters? Write out an emotional scene taking place some time before the crime, in which you show in both action and speech the desires which you think might lead up to such a killing.

13. (a) Please turn to page 8, Chapter I, the quotation from Conrad Aiken's story, *Your Obituary, Well Written.* Observe how this writer has developed his own feeling-response to items that he discovered in the "personal" column of a newspaper. Please consider the romantic development in this paragraph, and then outline and write out a scene in which the person who inserts this first notice is shown in a strong emotional conflict. What is the desire? What blocks it? In what setting can you best reveal the clash? Give this any length.

(b) Go now to your own newspaper. Turn to the personals, and write out quickly brief records of your own feeling-response to any of them. These studies should be similar to the material in Mr. Aiken's first paragraph in his story. Now select those in which you discern a conflict, and analyze these until you are sure that you understand just what desire is being opposed. Develop this conflict in an intense emotional scene. For instance, if you find such an item as this: "Come home, Mother worse, Jennie." — the clash is obvious. A sick mother wants to see her son before she dies, and her daughter, wanting to do one last thing for her mother's happiness, is trying to get in touch with him. You might write the scene in the sick room where the mother is calling for the boy, and the sister watching anxiously for the postman, is trying to make excuses. Or you might write the scene where the boy sees the item in the home paper. He is broke, in a strange city, with no job in sight. Your scene might picture his desperate struggle to get some money to return home before his mother dies.

Practice like this will help you develop the habit of looking for emotional possibilities everywhere. You will detect conflicts more easily and by writing out such scenes, your facility in invention and visualization will increase. Such sketches laid away in your files, may give you the initial stimulus for stories later. Don't consider the practice worthless if you can't see a way to develop a plot at once, and write out a story from a certain suggestion. Work with it, let it grow in your mind and feeling.

14. Turn now to Assignment E, No. 3, Chapter I. In this brief quotation is clearly stated an intense emotional conflict. The elements of the conflict are announced: an Indian mind, a Gringo soul, and a beautiful body. The tragedy of the mixture of race. If you know anything about such problems, analyze the elements in the conflict as you have observed it, and plan and write a scene which will reveal the clash sharply in action. Or you may use some similar clash not involving race. Take, for instance, a boy who is the son of a millionaire who made his money in mechanical work. The boy, like his father, is an extrovert and likes physical activity, but his conventional education has given him no opportunity to develop as he should normally.

The troubles of any misfit are likely to be good story stuff. What misfits do you know? Analyze their conflict, the desire, and the characters or circumstances that block it, and plan an intense emotional scene developing that conflict. Some misfits might be: a farmer who on losing his farm, has to become a salesman; a brilliant laboratory man who has to teach young students; a boy, educated in an orphanage, who is adopted by wealthy, unimaginative people; a young wife, who has to live in a home presented fully furnished as a wedding gift by the husband's parents, who live next door, and who are entirely different from her in temperament, background, and taste; a girl who finds city life most congenial and who must live in a country town; and so on. In all such exercises the problem is first to locate the conflict and then to develop it in an emotional scene of maximum intensity. Don't be afraid of the big effects, and the strong emotions. Read the examples in this book taken from some impressive stories of recent years. These authors took life and death conflicts to work with. No writer can equal their effects who hasn't equal skill in portraying strong emotion. For this reason exercises like the above are valuable.

15. Study the emotional experience given on page 22 for the conflict involved. Can you suggest changes which would intensify it?

16. Take the emotional experience you wrote as suggested just before this one in Chapter I and see if you can intensify the conflict, possibly one of the conflicts, it involves. If you can, then re-write the experience, centering it around the one conflict as altered.

17. Select for study four acquaintances whose lives have involved much struggle. Analyze their main conflicts to discover exactly what desires and what obstacles were involved. Write for each a scene of maximum emotional intensity, developing this conflict, using either real life or invented material.

ASSIGNMENT F

All the exercises in this assignment will give you practice in detecting the three levels of dramatic conflict. The answer in each case is simply internal, man vs. man, or man vs. nature conflicts. In some cases more than one conflict is indicated. Name them all.

1. Two young men in love with the same girl.*

2. A captain struggling to bring his ship through a storm.*

3. A man struggling to give up the drink habit.*

4. A painter who keeps on at his painting after his eyes have weakened so that he can scarcely see.

5. A runner calling upon all his powers in a race to finish ahead of his opponent who keeps close to his side.*

6. Two football players who struggle on the one-yard line until the referee takes the ball from them, when they begin to fight each other.

7. A boy with no money is offered a good job. To take it he must give up his plans for college.

8. A girl who prays ardently for the conversion of a girl friend.

9. A swimmer who is drowning and cries for help.

10. A daughter begging her father for money to buy a new dress.

11. A young man who in spite of the entreaties of the girl he is in love with knocks down his rival in a rage of jealousy.

12. A robber who is shot at by an automobilist he tried to rob attempts to swim across a river and is drowned.

13. A politician who defies the convention which refused to nominate him and bids for election on an independent ticket.*

14. A small boy, knowing that he will be whipped if he is caught going swimming, goes to the creek and, after a three-hour dip, gets into a fight with another boy. He "licks" the other boy who threatens to tell his mother that he has been swimming. Our hero therefore is uncertain whether he should go home and wishes there were other places to go besides homes.

15. After a month's careful investigation the detective discloses the identity of the criminal, and the motive. He states that the guilty man killed his business partner after a bitter fist fight in their office.

16. A mother, after giving her entire life to her three children, sees them one by one leave the home nest never to return. She writes them pleading with them to let her see them, but they refuse. She falls ill, and, after a lonely but courageous struggle against death, she recovers.

17. A young girl falls in love with her foster brother and is heart-broken when the foster brother falls in love with and marries another girl.

18. The exploring party after many vicissitudes reached the treasure mountain and found gold and diamonds hidden in the abandoned cave of the robbers.

19. A youth struggles against ill health and poverty to put himself through college.

20. The father whose child was stolen and held for a ransom, searched the countryside with breaking heart, for many weeks.

21. A young husband hated his mother-in-law intensely and quarreled with his wife who refused to send her mother away. After long and miserable deliberation he decided to tell the mother-in-law himself to leave his home, and did so. The mother-in-law refused to leave, saying that if she did she would take her daughter with her. The daughter stood with her mother. The husband did not want his wife to leave.

22. The missionary for twenty years braved the diseases and hostile tribes of Central Africa in the name of the Cause he served.

23. A husband has lost his love for his wife and is madly in love with another woman, who loves him. His wife will not give him a divorce and he is uncertain whether or not he has a right to abandon her even though he no longer loves her.

24. Romeo fights and kills Tybalt, the cousin of Juliet whom he loves.

25. A sister weeps with grief over her dead brother.

26. A girl from a large city marries a small town doctor and attempts to improve the cultural standards of both her husband and the town in general. Her progress is checked by the stubborn moral and intellectual mediocrity of both her husband and the townsfolk, and also by her own want of resolution and diplomacy. (*Main Street.*)

27. The Virginian falls in love with Molly Wood, a school teacher from Vermont, and woos her faithfully, cowboy fashion, for three years. To Molly the differences in their culture and education seem for a time insurmountable obstacles until she finds him lying wounded in the woods with no succor at hand. She supports him on her horse a distance of five miles to her home. By devoted nursing she saves his life, marries him, and takes him to visit her relatives in the east. The visit is a trying ordeal to The Virginian, but he survives it. (*The Virginian.*)

28. *Drifting Sands*, Adolph Bennauer. (In *Detective Stories.*)
Two men, captured for robbery of the express and murder of the messenger, hide their loot in a crevice in a rock in the sand dunes. They go up for twenty years, and never will reveal where

they put the money. Sentence expired, they go back to the place. They kill a man who they believe is following them. When they are only ten miles from the hiding place, one kills the other, in order to have the full amount. Then he goes on, and when he gets to the rock he finds that the drifting sand in twenty years has buried the rock almost entirely. The money is under fifty feet of sand.

29. *The Diamond Lens,* Fitz James O'Brien.

A scientist, mad about microscopes, invents lenses of higher and higher power. By communicating through a medium with Lee-uwenhoek, the great microscopist, he finds that the greatest lens must be made of a diamond. He gets the diamond by murdering its owner, prepares the lens, and looks at a drop of water. He sees a new world, and in the midst of it floating a beautiful creature with the body of a girl. He falls passionately in love with this Animula, as he calls her, and cannot tear himself away from watching her. Day after day he spends at the lens, until one day she begins to change. He looks at the drop of water, and sees that it has dried up. Through the lens he sees her death agony, and goes mad.

ASSIGNMENT G

This assignment provides some writing exercises in the three levels of conflicts. If it is desired to supplement them, almost any dramatic material elsewhere in this book can be used by simply manipulating it to produce the different levels singly and in combination. The answers may be written very briefly, most of them in a few lines.

1. Rewrite as much of the following action as you can to produce a sharp man and man conflict:

A young music teacher with a down-town studio flirts with a book agent who drops in. Later in the evening, very drunk, the man comes to the studio and demands to be let in. She has locked the door. He threatens to shoot her through the glass panel unless she lets him in. While she is crouching out of the way, a man comes down the fire escape, and the drunk fires. The newcomer falls dead. The drunk manages to avoid a policeman who enters the building. The policeman comes into the teacher's room, finds the gun which the drunk had thrown into the room and finds the girl fainting by the side of the body. He carries her into the other room, and tries to revive her. When she comes to, he goes back into the studio, and sees that the body has disappeared.*

2. Write the above action again so as to produce a sharp man and nature conflict.

3. Write the above action again from the point of view of the woman, keeping constantly to her desire to escape, and carry her through, first, a sharp man and man struggle, then a sharp internal struggle, and, finally, a sharp man and nature struggle.

4. We now have five exercises based on the passages reprinted in Assignment D, Chapter II, pages 90–96. These are climax scenes from stories emphasizing the love interest.

a. In which four of the seven passages do you find man and man conflict, with the lovers themselves the opponents? In which three is there man and man conflict, with no barriers between the lovers? In which one is there strong internal conflict? In which one is there strong man and nature conflict?

b. In No. 1, the girl's love is opposed by the man's interest in another girl. The conflict is weak. Write a new sketch, building up this man and man conflict between the man and the girl to greater intensity.

c. Again in No. 1, you will discover a hint of internal conflict in the clash between the girl's love and her pride. Write a sketch introducing the other girl in such a way as to produce an intense internal conflict in the first girl.

d. In No. 2, there is a hint of external opposition in the behavior of the onlookers. Write a sketch that will develop to greater intensity this man and man conflict.

e. In No. 5, there is a natural obstacle of maximum strength, with a strong social obstacle, the man's successful competitors in the business world. In No. 7, you find the climax of a strong internal conflict, with a fairly strong man and man conflict. Write new sketches, in which you develop only one of these conflicts, eliminating all material related to the second.

5. Take the ambition to be wealthy and indicate action expressing this trait which carries the hero through all three levels of conflict.

6. Take moral courage as a main trait for the hero, and put him through an action having three distinct man and man conflicts, each conflict being with a different person. Keep the trait of moral courage throughout.

ASSIGNMENT H

The exercises in this assignment are designed for students who wish drill in dramatic principles more advanced than that offered in the preceding assignments of this chapter. Before attempting these problems the student should study carefully Section E in the Appendix. There he will find the principles already outlined applied to specific and oft-recurring types of plots weak particularly in their dramatic handling.

With these exercises the student begins his criticizing of complete story plots. He will begin to see, I hope, how very much he is helped to a mastery of narrative material by a sound mastery of the theory and practice of drama presented in this chapter.

All the following plot outlines are defective in their dramatic handling. Some of these plots or others following the same patterns, if written up well, could doubtless be sold; plots like them are indeed often found in published stories. They are nevertheless, like innumerable published stories, weak in drama; and it is our business to know what these weaknesses are.

1. Jud Hawkins, manager of a big colliery company, puts himself at the head of a movement to clear out the ring that has bossed the local politics for years. Immediately he begins to receive anonymous threats, demanding money, and threatening his life and the lives of his wife and daughter. Finally he is told to bring the money to the drawing room in a certain Pullman car on a specified train. He is to knock and enter with his hands up. He does so, and a masked figure promptly feels him over for weapons, then demands the money.

"I suppose I can take my hands down to get it?" he asked the figure. The latter frowned, then nodded. Hawkins lowered his arms deliberately, stretching them and shaking them to restore the circulation, then reached his hand into his inside pocket and brought out a bundle of bills. The masked figure reached forward eagerly for them but even as Hawkins handed them to him with his left hand, fire spurted from the gun in his right and the masked man spun around and fell flat. Hawkins had kept his gun up his sleeve.*

2. Jonathan Absalom, foreman, was a good workman when sober, but he was usually drunk. His wife determined that he should remain sober, and went to the company cashier and demanded that no money from that time be given to her husband. The cashier was afraid of her and followed her orders. Jonathan could draw no money. He could still make purchases at the company store, charging his goods on the payroll. The store sold patent medicines, some of them almost pure alcohol. Jonathan had a friend among the store clerks, who agreed with Jonathan that a dollar was a dollar in value whether you spent it for Hicks's Sure Cure or for socks. Accordingly Jonathan's store bills mounted and his wife became more and more amazed at her husband's need for goods and commodities at the store!

Jonathan thought serenely that he had solved the riddle of existence, until the end of the second month. Mrs. Jonathan had gone over the accounts and had discovered that in the two months he had worn out seventy-three pairs of overalls. She met her lord on his return with blood in her eye, and from that moment there was a total falling off in the demand for Hicks's Sure Cure, charged either as itself or as lanterns, socks, overalls, or gloves.

3. A newspaper editor, pictured as a weak and spineless creature, has by sound judgment and hard work built up a fortune for the owner of the paper. The owner is a skinflint and a business crook; lets the editor work for a mere pittance. The editor's family go in rags, unfed, without doctor's care. Although the editor sees the unfairness of the situation, he has not enough courage to make a stand for his own rights, until one day his family doctor shames him into action by telling him that the fortune of the owner of the paper is due to the editor's efforts, and that he, the editor, can get money out of the owner, unless he is afraid. The editor accepts this as a challenge to his pride, walks into the owner's office, insists on immediate admittance, tells the owner that he lies in his teeth when he, the owner, defends himself, demands a large salary and a large block of stock in the paper and threatens to resign unless he gets his requests. The proprietor capitulates and the editor becomes a happy and successful man.*

4. A learned professor decides to take a vacation. He is going all to pieces, is forgetful, and absent-minded. He thinks a change will do him good, but he takes his young lady secretary along on the vacation to help him with his correspondence and work on his book. His difficulty does not improve.

One day in the fields he finds his secretary who has fallen and hurt her ankle and is lying apparently unconscious. He picks her up to carry her back to the house. He holds her closer and closer, and finally, still believing her unconscious, he kisses her. With the kiss, he realizes what has been the matter all along. He loves her. She comes to, and he tells her what she had known from the first.
                — BARRIE, *The Professor's Love Story.*

5. The vein of a certain gold mine has faulted. Ruin is in sight unless it can be rediscovered. Meanwhile the last of the high grade ore is being amalgamated. Bowles and Cram, on night shift as amalgamators, plan to steal the amalgam. Bowles is caught red handed by the other men on night shift. While they are fighting, Cram who had been posted outside, learns that the vein has been rediscovered. He mixes in the fight and shoots Bowles, hoping to get credit for killing a thief and so escape himself. Bowles, hearing the conversation, through the haze of unconsciousness, knows that his partner has killed him to save himself, and he shoots. The two conspirators die together.

6. Dr. Harrington, interne in a hospital, is on duty alone, when the victim of an automobile accident is brought in. He finds that the man is his rival in love. Examination shows that the man is suffering from cerebral hemorrhage, and that he must be operated on at once. There is no one available to operate except Harrington. He is only an interne, and so theoretically not competent to operate. He could follow medical ethics strictly, and wait for the

other doctor who was in the midst of a serious operation in the other room. Meanwhile the rival would die. As he stands thinking, he sees from the window a leaf hanging by a thread from its branch. Another minute he watches, and the leaf falls.

He turns quickly to the operating table, and begins work. He saves the rival's life.

Just as the rival is being dismissed from the hospital, he tells the doctor that the reason for the accident was not that he was drunk, but that the girl he loved had just thrown him over, and had told him she was going to marry some young doctor. The shock had unnerved him and the accident had resulted.

The doctor thus learns that he had both saved his honor and had won the girl he loved.

7. A man embezzles a large sum, and flees. He spends twenty years, constantly trying to escape his pursuers, never feeling safe. Finally, in desperation, he turns back to give himself up, prison being more endurable than this constant fear. He finds that he had never been pursued. His crime had taken place at a time when the bank was in a bad way. The directors had not made his crime known, for fear of having attention attracted to the condition of the bank.

8. An old jeweler is robbed of some very valuable diamonds, not yet paid for. The robber is not traced, and the jeweler becomes bankrupt. The only person that he knows very well is a friend of his boyhood, who has a room in his house. This friend because of his miserly habits, has the reputation of being very rich. He has a little safe in his room. The old jeweler, on the verge of ruin, finally decides to rob his friend who has never offered to help him, pretending to have nothing. The old jeweler breaks open the little safe and finds his missing diamonds.

9. A sheriff has brought in a young criminal seriously wounded. He wants the reward for the boy alive. Physicians say that the boy's only chance for life is transfusion. The sheriff is ready to give the blood. During the operation his pity is aroused for the helpless lad, and he determines to get him off. He does so by withholding the evidence that he alone has.

10. A man who has been dissolute in his youth, repents in his maturity. He remembers his first victim, a young Italian girl, to whom for a time he had sent money and whom he had long forgotten. He goes abroad to try to find her. He learns that there had been a child. The woman had disappeared with the baby, and he tries to trace her, taking a detour in his wanderings to have a look at Monte Carlo. There he forgets his repentance when he meets a ravishing young demi-mondaine. He pursues her madly. She plays him skillfully, until she has wheedled a goodly sum out of him. Then in her apartment, just as she is about to yield to him, he discovers that she is his daughter.*

11. A boy is under the influence of a clever crook who tries to pin a murder on him by making the boy say threatening things about the future victim and making him take an automatic with

silencer. The crook himself wearing the boy's shoes, which are of a special make, then commits the murder and, after the crime, goes to the boy's father, telling him that the boy is a murderer and must fly. He tells the father that the boy had sent him to get money to get away with. The father insists on going to the boy. He takes police officers along. In the presence of the boy the father, seeing that the crook is still wearing his son's shoes, accuses him of the murder. The crook is arrested and convicted.

12. Slick Fred, just out of Sing Sing, finds that prohibition has closed his familiar haunts of former times and that Billy Boyle, with whom he had left $200 to begin on when he should be let out, is dead. He is driven back to his old game. He goes to one of his old stands, and nabs a purse, in which he finds a powder puff and a nickel. He tries again, and gets a fair haul, but just then he sees a detective, known of old, and he tries to make a get-away through the subway. The nickel is no good, and will not work the new feather-weight gates, and the detective catches him. He searches him informally in a quiet corner, and finds the roll. It is counterfeit money. Fred then has the alternative of imprisonment for the theft, or for passing counterfeit money. The counterfeiting carries the heavier sentence, and he chooses to take two years for picking pockets.

13. A society woman has the habit of dropping linen, napkins, silverwear, and valuable toilet articles into her hand-bag when she visits her wealthy friends. These she " forgets " to return when she discovers them on reaching home. Her friends understand the weakness, and say nothing to her about it. The woman's maid, noticing this conduct of her mistress, begins to do the same thing when she visits her friends. As a result she is caught in the act, a policeman calls, arrests, and jails her. Her mistress, shocked at the suffering her thieving causes, reforms and does no more stealing.

14. A young prize fighter is told by his sweetheart that she will marry him only on condition that he give up his fighting. He continues to train for the prize fight, and is out on the road running with his trainer one day when he sees his sweetheart in the arms of a tramp who has robbed her and is trying to stifle her screams. The hero pounces upon the tramp laying him out on the road only after the tramp has fired a revolver at the hero, wounding him in the shoulder. The girl by this act is convinced of the hero's love of her, and the hero because of the peculiar nature of the wound is unable ever to fight again. They marry and are happy.

15. A wife is abandoned by her husband for another woman. She loves her husband, but her hatred and desire for revenge against him increase as the time of his absence lengthens. Finally she receives from the Bureau of Vital Statistics a marriage certificate showing that her husband had been married to another woman. The certificate was returned to her instead of being kept at the office because the officiating clergyman forgot to sign it.

The wife with this information in her possession is able to wreak her vengeance upon her husband by having him arrested and sent to jail for a long term for bigamy.

16. The following plot outline won a prize in a contest offered by a writers' magazine for the best plot built on a certain problem. The problem was as follows:

Tom Cooper, coach of the Jenks College football team, is preparing his team for the big game of the season with Landor College. He is especially interested in winning, because the coach of the rival team is his rival for the love of Janet Gray. A week before the game, three of his crack men quit, giving no reason, and his team is thus wrecked. Five days before the game, Tom learns that some of his players are betting against their own team.

The prize winning solution of this plot was as follows:

The day of the game the three men who had first quit, and all the other deserters, walked into the dressing room, in their togs, and asked to play, assuring him that they were ready. Tom put them into the game, and defeated Landor. Afterward they told him that their desertion had been planned as a way to make Landor over-confident. They had kept up practice secretly, and had even been betting against Jenks College to make the plan go through.

Tom asked who had thought of the scheme and he found that Janet herself had planned it. Tom marries Janet.

17. A New England woman, unmarried, lives alone in a lonely house. She really suffers from her loneliness, but finds one comfort in watching the lights in a house which she can see several miles off, on the other side of the valley. She feels that she knows the people whose gayety she is able to watch at this great distance, but the only time that she ever comes any nearer to them is on a Sunday, when she learns that the owner of this house had attended church that morning and had occupied a pew somewhere behind her. The woman had gone before the lonely soul learned of her presence. The spinster finally becomes very ill, and on her death bed writes a litte note to the stranger, to tell her how her light had comforted her. The wealthy occupant of the great house is interested, and comes over to the house where the first woman lies dead. Among her papers she finds evidence that the dead woman is her sister, who had left their Southern home years before, in disgrace, and had never been heard of since.

18. A sailor, returning after twenty years, has a sudden recurrence of his former love for his boyhood sweetheart, and makes a pilgrimage to seek her out. In the garden of her old home, he meets her in the full loveliness of her youth, and he is once more enraptured. Just then, as he is about to avow his love, out of the house door comes a dowdy, middle-aged woman, the mother of the lovely girl. Something that the girl says reveals the fact that it is the mother who had been his sweetheart. He leaves without revealing his identity.

19. In the depot of a small town the station agent was drowsing one day, when suddenly he noticed that from one of the trunks left by the last train, a stream of blood was flowing. Afraid to go near the trunk, he called the police. Officers arrived. The owner was a farmer's wife. It was known that an uncle of hers had disappeared from the neighborhood not long before. The police go out to the farm, accuse the woman of the murder, and, without telling her of their discovery, arrest her, bringing her back to town with them to confront her with the trunk. In her presence they tear it open and find at the bottom a mass of currant jelly, the contents of a dozen broken glasses.

20. A young girl is so very much in love with a handsome young man, that her whole happiness depends upon him. He is coming on a certain night, and she knows that he will ask her to be his wife. She awaits him eagerly, but hour after hour passes, and he does not come. Next day she sends him a frigid note, to tell him that she does not care to see him again. She never sees him again, and he marries another girl. Many years later she learns that he had tried to get to her that evening, but had been hurt, and could not get to the house. He had tried to telephone, but the 'phone wasn't working. He had managed to drag himself then to the door, but the bell was out of order, and he had gone away, thinking that there was no one at home.

ASSIGNMENT I

Replot the story outlines in Assignment H, eliminating the weaknesses you have discovered. Don't slight this drill; a careful and thorough performance of this exercise in constructive invention will fully repay you.

By "eliminating the weaknesses" is meant not only omitting the "mistakes," "coincidences," and tricks, but re-arranging what is left to produce an outline of strong dramatic action. In No. 19, just above, for instance, it will be a temptation to write this episode over, merely saying that when the station agent saw the jelly juice he knew it was jelly and not blood. Doing this is identifying the "mistake" but no more. What you are asked to do now is to substitute for the errors inventions that will be genuinely dramatic.

For example, taking No. 19 again: When you say the agent knew the jelly was jelly and not blood, you remove the "obstacle." The main desire here is obviously the determination on the part of the agent and the police to solve the murder. If only jelly juice is involved, there is no murder and no "obstacle." It is necessary, then, to change the jelly to real blood. Now there is an authentic desire and obstacle which can be developed into really dramatic action.

PART THREE

FINISHING THE NARRATIVE PLOT

A Study Of Actual Practice In The Use Of Principles

CHAPTER FIVE

THE CHARACTER STORY

THE STORY THAT PAINTS A PORTRAIT

There are three kinds of audiences: thinkers, who demand characterization; women who demand passion; and the mob who demand action. — VICTOR HUGO.

We now set out to help those writers who, in planning their stories, are " unable to finish the thing." They are the college students who, having faithfully completed courses in rhetoric and composition, attempt stories of the professional grade and fail most of all because of a faulty pattern. They are the struggling free lance writers who produce and sometimes sell " pot boilers " but who cannot see the difference between their management of their plots and the manipulations of those who have really " arrived." They are also the well-known writers agonized at times by the possibilities of a " big idea " whose bigness is too much for them.

1. The Problem of Finishing Plots

The hero, let us say, quarrels with his bride in their honeymoon cabin in the great forest. He can endure her disillusioning temper no longer and wrathfully strides off toward the mountain hotel. Meanwhile his scheming rival comes out of hiding, lopes across the clearing and enters the cabin. Now (thinks the writer) if I can bring the husband back to the cabin there would be something doing! The idea of having the husband get lost and, by going in a circle, return to the clearing, is, of course, the first that suggests itself; but this trick is shop-worn, is altogether too trite to be used again. How to "pull off a new one" in getting the husband back? The writer thinks of twenty ways; none is quite satisfactory: he gives up; the big scene in the cabin which he saw vividly, which perhaps he has already written, is never given to the waiting world. He can't finish the plot.

Another writer, let us say, is thrilling to the revolver shots of a ripping detective story. A wealthy woman is found murdered in her room in a hotel. Investigation shows that the only other person who entered her room was a nun. Evidently the nun's costume was merely a disguise affected by an escaped convict. None of the woman's jewels were taken. These particulars must be kept for the sake of the effect desired; but what was the motive for the crime? The problem proves too deep, and the otherwise good plot is abandoned.

Here is another common enough problem in plotting: A struggling young writer has his seaside tragedy returned to him by an editor who writes: "This story is beautifully handled, but it is too tragic for our use. If you can provide some relief to the tragedy, I think we can use it." His first opportunity for an acceptance! He has no objection to making his story less sordid, but how to do it? What *is* "tragic relief" anyway? He isn't sure, but he tackles the job with enthusiasm. Hope wanes. He spends sleepless nights agonizing over garbled pages. Finally he gives it a ride, hoping he has "hit" it. Riding back it comes with the comment: "Not so well done as the other. Sorry."

Perhaps you are laboring over a romance of the "younger generation." You "see" the whole story except the heroine's conduct in the climax; she simply won't — but why continue? Such problems are endless. The need of help in solving them needs no argument. What we want is better *method* in our thinking. This I shall try to give you in this and succeeding chapters.

Doubtless you are by this time impressed as never before by the many exasperating torments that afflict you in your labors to achieve proficiency as a writer of stories; some of them, however exhausting your efforts, will always be present: but for your comfort let me assure you that finishing your plots *need* not be one of them. There is definitely a limit to the labor necessary to master this part of your work. Given material worth working with, it can be plotted. Every story idea worthy of the name can be plotted. On some days you will perform better than on others, but, with a reasonable apprenticeship behind you, the job can be done.

2. Rewards of Proficiency

Method of the kind I have in mind will, moreover, be found to be of immense help in departments of the art other than plotting. One of these is self-criticism. You write a story from a perfectly sound plot, knowing quite well when you have finished the first draft that you have " gone off the track " somewhere. Where? If the plot at the beginning was merely a " happy inspiration," you will probably be unable to locate your error. The more you wrestle with it, the more " fuzzy " your mind gets. If on the other hand, you had followed sound principles in making the plot in the first place, you would have had no difficulty in determining where your Pegasus plunged from the trail into a valley of confusion.

Sound criticism comes high. The editor might tell you your faults, but doing so is not one of his functions. Your friends will attempt it, but they are too kind, if not too unenlightened. Your instructors cannot remain with you always. With method in your literary kit you can do the thing for yourself. And method can be learned.

The possession of method in plot-making will also enable you to salvage much excellent literary material which you might otherwise have thrown away. One of my students, a talented and energetic lady, whose life has been enlivened by many stirring adventures in the romantic corners of the world, brought as her first manuscript a romance staged in modern Greece. " It's utter drivel," she said, on presenting it. Drivel it was indeed except for a chance remark of one of the characters to the effect that in Greece the father of a fiancée with a " damaged reputation " is expected to increase his daughter's dot in proportion to the seriousness of the damage. Buried in the midst of courtship banalities of a distinctly American flavor was this gem of a story idea. Being unfamiliar with the identifying marks of good story material she overlooked it entirely.

I have discovered that young ladies who were turning in insipid and imitative stories for their class work were at the same time writing home to their folks letters rich with whimsy, gossip and adventure! When asked why they did not make stories of this material, they replied that they did not see how it could be used. They lacked " story sense," a deficiency which was remedied as they acquired a better method. They were in the same case with another gifted student whose life was a dream of romantic luxury in New York society, but whose literary output was a trunkful of half-finished tragedies. A study of method taught her that romance was just as easy to plot as tragedy, and that she herself was her own best heroine; whereupon she began to sell her writings with éclat.

Saddest of all is the poor fanatic who nourishes the picturesque delusion that the more difficulties a given story idea gives him, the greater is his obligation to realize its latent beauties and offer it to the world. His like is to be met with everywhere. If he could get but a gleam of insight into his problems, he would see at once that the rightful destiny of his great idea is written all over it: " The waste basket." Many ideas there are which are not worth working with. In such cases the shortest cut is to abandon them and try others, and this he will not hesitate to do if he has a knowledge of method.

3. Differences Between Plotting and Writing

Perhaps I should repeat here that the method we are here concerned with involves the planning but not the writing of stories. This is an important distinction. Building the story, since it involves preëminently design and logic, is a process of science more than of art, while the actual writing of the story, since it seeks mainly a realization of emotional values, is more an art than a science. The way in which our different faculties are used in the two processes is indicated roughly in the following analysis:

Plot-making (a science)	1. Knowledge of technique	50%
	2. Skill by practice	30%
	3. Knowledge of human nature ..	20%
		100%

Writing the story (an art)	1. Knowledge of human nature ..	70%
	2. Facility in writing	20%
	3. Gift for language	10%
		100%

We shall now deal with only the first and second faculties above. If you have mastered the principles set forth in the earlier parts of this book you already have a good working knowledge of the fundamentally important principles of narrative technique. We must see how these principles are put to work to produce finished plots.

In this and succeeding chapters we shall confine our attention chiefly to the short story instead of to the novel. Method for controlling short stories can be used in plotting novels by holding in mind the distinctions between the two forms set forth in Chapter Two. For those whose main interest is in writing the longer forms of narrative, the drill in method outlined here will most certainly serve as a helpful apprenticeship. The notable differences in method in plotting called for in handling the two different forms of narrative we shall note as we go along, and at the end of each of the succeeding chapters I shall consider briefly technical problems peculiar to the novel.

We begin with the plot of the character short story. We have learned that all short stories secure their single effect by means of emphasis on character, complication, theme or atmosphere, or combinations of these patterns. Probably nine-tenths of all stories published secure their effects by stressing character or a complication or both character and a complication. Since this is so, and since these plot patterns are easier to control than the others, we shall study them at greater length than the others.

4. Definition of Short Story

We have not hitherto attempted to define the short story. We shall now do so. Let us take the crisp definition formulated by Professor Pitkin: " *A short story is a dramatic narrative told with a single effect.*"

Please note that this definition contains no startling novelty which calls for a reconsideration of what has gone before. It is, in fact, but a brief summary of what we have already learned. All it says is that this particular form of narrative which we call the short story is distinguished by two ideals: drama and the single effect. We now know what these ideals mean. Our definition therefore is no formula or rule or academic assumption deriving from any theory about art; it is a logical deduction based upon an exhaustive study of the most impressive stories of all time, down to the present moment of modern writing. Externals of style and treatment vary, but the fundamentals do not change. All good stories actually do create a single impression; all good stories are dramatic. These ideals we shall now follow.

5. What is a Character Trait?

In plotting the character short story we of course make special use of our character material. To make the most

of this material we must now take a somewhat closer look
at it, for it is obvious that within the brief limits of the
short story no complete picture of any character, however
simple, can be presented.   Selection of certain aspects of
a given character must be made.   And right here for the
first time we encounter the problem of securing brevity
or how to make a short story short.   This is also spoken
of as the problem of " compression," of the " art of leaving
out," even Stevenson in a desperate attempt at self-anal-
ysis, writing, " There is but one art — to omit."   Chekhov
once advised young writers to prepare their stories and
before sending them to a publisher, to cut off the beginning
and the end!

Brevity in narrative calls for no such procrustean meas-
ures.   Compression is a false ideal.   If you have so much
material in your hands that it takes " art " to eliminate
some of it, the sensible thing would seem to be not to try
to handle so much in the first place!   The solution of the
problem of brevity in a short story is (to use sculptor's
language) not to set up a wire skeleton for a six-foot figure,
slap on the clay until it is nearly " roughed out " and then
begin hacking at it until it is reduced to a three-foot figure,
but to erect a three-foot frame in the first place.   The art
that is needed is not destruction but *selection*.[1]   Questions
of brevity, in other words, should be settled not during the
writing of a story nor even during the plotting, but when
the material is chosen.

Let us see now how selection of this sort is demanded
in plotting the character short story.   We must at the very
outset decide what particular phase of character we shall
present within the length of the story we wish to write.
This phase we shall call a " trait."   In the previous chapter we learned something about character as a whole as it
is used in narrative; it is the person's entire manner of

---

[1] An important principle of art which achieves economy of
words *without* omitting anything essential is involved in integration.
It is explained in Assignment C, page 386.

responding to his environment. Character is, of course, a functional unity; none of its phases can be entirely isolated, nor could they be completely named or numbered: but for practical purposes we find it necessary to pick out a single pronounced trait, arbitrarily think of it as more or less isolated, and view the whole character in terms of that trait.

There is no word in common usage which expresses exactly the technical sense given here to this word, *trait,* namely, a special manner of responding to certain situations. The words " habits," " tendency," " moral characteristic," all connote something of the meaning we are giving the word trait. It is distinguished from " impulse " in that impulse denotes the energy behind an act while trait is the pattern of that act. This is not the full truth of the matter, but any effort to pursue psychological distinctions [1] further than this would probably do us more harm than good at this stage.

A simple diagram which directly connects the idea of a trait with conduct or action, the thing we actually see, may be helpful here. The narrative writer, it must be understood, is not able to present dramatically *any* and *all* traits of character; he can present forcibly only those traits of character which are pronouncedly developed; in most cases of successful short story characterization the selected trait will be by far the most prominent trait in the subject's character; it will color definitely most of his activity. For this reason, " eccentric " characters are easier to handle effectively than well-balanced characters. People who are " a little off," as we sometimes say uncharitably, are easy to " write up " because practically all their conduct is activity illustrating the controlling trait. You may even take it as a definite principle that the nearer your fictional prototype is to actual insanity without yet really being insane the easier will be your task of selection for short story purposes. The entire conduct of a completely insane

[1] See *Human Nature and Conduct,* by John Dewey, pp. 172–181.

person suffering from a mania is single trait activity, though he is unsuitable for use in narrative on account of his inability to reflect on his conduct, as pointed out in the previous chapter.

Suppose we take three people who have pronounced traits. Our definition of trait, given above, states that it denotes a special manner of reacting to a fixed situation or object. For our illustration, therefore, we need both a fixed object and three people who react to this object in different ways. The object, we will say, is an automobile. Here is what our three people do when they see it:

WANTS CAR   BORED BY CAR   FEARS CAR

THREE CHARACTER TRAITS IN ACTION

The first party is " automobile mad." He feels, has felt for years, that he needs only a " car " to make life perfect bliss. He reads all the automobile advertisements in the magazines; he knows all the makes; he envies his neighbors who possess cars; he is putting a second mortgage on his little home for a " twin-six " that will bankrupt him. This is the way *he* reacts to the idea, " automobile." His main trait is *desire for a car*. The second party is, you will be surprised to learn, a " society lady." She has ridden in automobiles so much that she is sick of them. She would far rather walk, anywhere, always, but she is forced to ride. That's the way *she* reacts to the idea, " automobile." Her main trait is *hatred of motor cars*. The third party is a nervous old gentleman who was once knocked down by an automobile. Although he had a life rule never to run in front of any vehicle when crossing the street, he was caught in a traffic jam and painfully hurt by a careless chauffeur. Now he hates to go downtown so great is his fear of motor cars. When he sees one approach a block away, he runs for his life. This is *his* way of reacting to the idea, " automobile." His main trait is *fear of automobiles*.

In each of these cases we get a definite idea of the way a given person acts when affected by a given stimulus. We have, in other words, the trait pattern. Now a *character trait study* or *character sketch* would be composed of a series of concrete acts showing the character responding to such a stimulus according to his pattern. Notes of activities, centered, for instance, around the first trait, would look something like this:

Main Trait: Desire for car

He stops on the way home to study show cars in the windows.

He reads every word of the automobile section of the Sunday paper instead of going to church or taking his family for a walk.

Every week he figures the amount he could lay aside to buy and support a car, if he had certain raises in salary — although there is no assurance of any raise.

He cultivates the acquaintance of people who have cars, hoping they will take him riding or teach him how to drive.

Although he hates any work about the house, he one day

painted the chicken house, thinking of the time when he would have his car and would make a garage of the chicken house.

Without letting his wife know, he places a second mortgage on his home to secure a hundred dollars extra towards his car. Still he hasn't enough to make a first payment. He then for the first time entertains the thought of trying to steal some money from his employer, etc.

Our process up to this point has been mainly analysis of our story material. As practical mental aids in learning method for finishing plots, we shall here add two other processes:

> *Stating the Problem,* and
> *Manipulation.*

6. The Special Processes of Plotting

All the processes for finishing plots can now be set down as follows:

The Processes of Plotting.

1. *Analyzing the story idea*

Classifying as to $\begin{cases} 1. & \text{Single effect} \\ 2. & \text{Drama} \\ 3. & \text{Editorial value} \end{cases}$

2. *Stating the problem*

Setting down definitely what is missing, given the above and the author's purposes.

3. *Manipulation*

Using invention, imagination, notebooks, discussion, and what-not to get the plot to fulfill the writer's purpose.

We will deal with all the factors except, at times, the one of editorial values. This factor, which, of course, the professional writer generally holds definitely in mind, can for the most part be eliminated while building plots for practice only. Since it involves the practical purpose to which the writer will put his narrative, no criticism of this purpose is here possible. In our examples we can only assume an editorial purpose and work the plot out upon this assumption. Strictly speaking, all editorial problems are problems of the function rather than of the structure of narrative.

The processes set forth above in such detail may seem elaborate and difficult to you; but please do not be distressed: the whole process will soon simplify itself: often enough some of the above processes take place at the same time. The really skilled plot-maker uses them all more or less at once and unconsciously! Just what is meant by these processes we can see by observing how they are used in the building of an actual plot.

7. A Simple Case of Plotting

Let me take as our first illustration in building a character short story plot an actual exercise as it was first performed in a class of beginners. First, the story idea itself. Since we were to plot a character story, I asked the class to " give me a character." A student said: " A man who wants to write successful short stories."

This brought the subject matter close home; the suggestion was accepted. This, then, was the story idea: " A man whose outstanding trait is his desire to write successful short stories." Now the first mental process, according to the above, is

1. *Analysis of the material:* With material as meager as this very little had to be done in the way of analysis. The single effect, it was generally agreed, would be either admiration or tragic dismay, depending upon the manner in which the hero won out with his story writing — it was decided that he *must* win out. It was agreed to set down no editorial standards: the story could be either a comedy or a tragedy. We went at once, therefore, to the second step of

2. *Stating the problem:* What now is missing? We have given little more than a character trait or desire. To create

drama we know we have to invent obstacles for this desire. An internal struggle seemed to be the easiest type of drama to follow here. In this case the obstacles must obviously be other desires. What other desires can be effectively opposed to the desire to succeed at writing? After stating this, our main problem, we were ready for the final process.

3. *Manipulation:* Instantly the obvious suggestions were made: The hero gave up a good job to devote himself to his writing. This created a conflict with his literary desire and his desire to live well and to support his family. His family suggested a stronger conflict. By not having a steady income his family suffered: the rent was not paid and he had to move into cheaper quarters; the children had to be put to work; the mother was reduced to sewing for her neighbors; finally, just as the hero succeeded in a big way, the youngest baby died of improper food and neglect.

These tests for the hero's stern ambition suggested to the students a picture of the hero's writing a thrilling romance of love and happiness as his child lay dying. This was easily a " supreme test."

The plot was obviously finished except for the last touch or outcome. At this point the class began to suggest all manner of " trick " endings and far-fetched freaks of fate which might save the poor wretch this tragic loss or otherwise stun the reader by some clever invention. Their eager imaginations were firmly restrained: the single problem with which the manipulation began was repeated; they were asked to keep their eyes on the hero's character trait; the most effective ending of the story was there or nowhere.

" Bearing in mind the hero's absorption in writing stories," I said, " let us simply watch him and see what he does."

" He enters the room in which his dead child lies. He would doubtlessly be deeply moved by a conflict between his paternal love and his desire to write. What would he do therefore? His paternal desires would lead him to gaze at the baby's dead face. So much for the paternal desire. What would the other, the main desire, make him do?"

"He would say," suggested a member of the class, "'What corking material for a story!'"

This suggestion gave us our final episode and completed the plot. The whole task took less than fifteen minutes. It was one of many handled merely for practice in manipulating story ideas. The dramatic proof of the hero's main trait is, if anything, too strongly developed; not that such insensate ambition is incredible, but that such ruthlessness would forfeit any sympathy most readers might otherwise have for the hero. This, however, is an editorial problem, and, except where we deal with stories actually published, we shall try to simplify our tasks by not considering questions of marketing. Technically the plot is a true character plot. It is so classified because, to repeat language used in Chapter Three, its effect is secured by emphasis on character materials.

Checking plot for ideals

The effect the story makes, or would make if written out, is a rather horrible dismay at the tragic picture of a writer's ambition. The dramatic struggle is, as we noted at our second step of stating the problem of the plot, an internal conflict between his desire to succeed at writing and other various desires. Is it now perfectly clear to you that the plot we have made effectively fulfills both these requirements? I want to be sure that it is. Here are our two ideals of single effect and drama which we have been studying for some time — here they are for the first time incorporated in a simple but complete short story plot. We must be sure that we see *how* they are incorporated. Let us therefore analyze the plot that we have made.

I am going to write the plot out in three different ways. The first version we will call a "bald report"; it will be a condensed scenario of the entire action, the sort of outline

you would have before you were you to sit down to write
the story out full length. The second version will show up
our materials, and reveal why we call it a "character
story," while the third will disclose our dramatic conflict.
First the

Bald Report

Mr. X., in order to have more time to devote to story writing,
leaves his job as bookkeeper in the bank. He spends his days
and his nights at his writing desk at home. His stories do not
sell; soon the rent is overdue. He keeps at his work, however,
hoping against hope that the big story he is working on will
bring him both fame and money.

The expected sale, however, does not come, and, since he
fails to pay the rent, he and his family are evicted. His wife,
in order to keep a roof over their heads, takes over the management of a boarding house. Mr. X., with his children crowded
about him, distressing him, and his wife working herself sick,
labors away at his writing in the corner of the single room they
now occupy.

Since the wants of the family are still being unsatisfied, two
of the three children are forced to leave school and go to work.
The mother, in order to care for her boarders, has to neglect
her baby. The latter, therefore, becomes sick. A doctor is called
and advises the parents to take the child to the country. The
mother pleads with the husband to take up some other work.
He refuses. The baby gets weaker.

The father works on desperately. He has received a letter from
an editor which encourages him. Finally, as the baby lies dying,
the writer makes a sale, receiving a large sum. Fame follows and
reporters come to his door to make him known to the world.
At the same time the undertaker comes for his dead baby.

As the baby lies dead, the father, still dazed, the mania of
his writing still afflicting him, gazes at its face, muttering:
"What corking material for a story!"

The above skeleton of the action sets forth mainly the
logic and chronology of the plot. It is an unemotional
presentation of the "argument" or "meaning" of the
story. To make clear why it is a character story, we must
resort to our second arrangement of the action.

Outline Emphasizing Classification

The hero leaves his job in order to write — significant of his *literary ambition.*

The hero loses his home in order to write — an impressive indication of his *literary ambition.*

The hero sees his wife become a sickly drudge in order that he may write — a distressing picture of *literary ambition.*

The hero lets his baby die in order that he may write — a tragic picture of *literary ambition.*

The hero, seeing his dead baby, makes comments in a way that shows his literary desires — an ironic touch to a tragic picture of *literary ambition.*

Here we see where the emphasis *as to material* is in our story. "Literary ambition" is a character trait; since we use it constantly without inserting other important materials, we conclude that the story as a whole is a character story. Selection alone, that is, largely determines the kind or type of story. Not so the *effect* of the story — the effect or impression the story makes is a matter of the *repetition of a pattern of conflict. The logic, the meaning, the ideas of your story, in other words, are conveyed by being logical and precise; the emotion of the story is conveyed by repeating a conflict pattern over and over.* The emotion-producing pattern repeated in this story is fairly well exhibited in the second version of it above. It is set forth still more sharply in the following:

Outline Emphasizing Emotional Pattern.

1. The hero's desire to write is opposed by his desire to have the money which comes to him regularly from his job in the bank. He cannot do both these things. Since his desire to write is the stronger impulse, he follows it and gives up his job.

2. He next finds that if he keeps on writing and failing to sell, he will have no money to pay the rent. Since he loves his family and his home, he desires to keep his home. He cannot continue to write without a sale and also keep his home — a stronger clash, since he gives up the home.

3. It may not seem so, but the man really does love his wife. He desires to keep her happy and healthy. In order that he may

continue his writing, however, it is necessary for her to work so hard that she becomes a sickly drudge. He cannot keep her happy and healthy and also continue his writing. Since his literary desires are stronger than his love for his wife, he lets his wife become a drudge.

4. Lastly, the hero's dearest wish, aside from his desire to succeed with his writing, is his desire to see his sick baby live. He sees that unless he gives up his writing the baby may die. The clash now is between his desire to see the baby live and his desire to succeed in his writing. Since the latter desire is stronger than the former, it triumphs and the baby dies.

In this outline a series of conflicts is repeated each of which is a crisis involving a reflective delay, and thus testing character.[1] The unity here, clearly, is in the character; if we can be sure that in each crisis the character is impelled by the desire that we wish to emphasize, we can be confident of the unified impression of our plan. To give maximum dramatic force to a climax, often the preceding episodes test and prove the strength of the main obstacle. The logic of this is, of course, that the more powerful the antagonist, the more impressive the triumph of the main trait.

The series of situations testing character need not be climactic. In the modern story the tendency is toward less and less seeming artifice in arrangement, and a climax, deliberately prepared for, seems to have a neatness and completeness that do not satisfy the modern taste for realism. A climax is not necessary, providing the series of situations portrayed gives a clear enough picture of the character to be convincing, and enough drama to hold the reader's interest. Drama, the most useful device of character test and of contact with the reader, is almost always important in giving emphasis to a character whether or not the action be arranged in a climax. In a character story the unity of impression is secured by selecting episodes which test in dramatic conflict, with or without climax, the trait that we want to emphasize.

The two types of character stories which produce their im-

[1] See Chapter IV, pages 148–152, 157–160, 169–170.

pression by logical rather than dramatic proof, I shall discuss at the end of this chapter.

In the preceding outlines, emphasizing first the character
interest and second the emotional pattern of the character
story, the use of dramatic conflict in relation to specific characters, has prepared us for a definition of plot.

What, then, is a plot?

*A plot is a series of events, generally climactic, each one
of which affects and is affected by the characters involved.*

The plot of a character story is a design of action made up
of incidents selected for their logical or dramatic emphasis
of some quality in a given character. The unity of a character story depends upon the sustained emphasis of the trait.
Most successful character stories combine with the character
interest some situation interest. Situation interest obviously enters as soon as a trait is opposed, and becomes important as the obstacle is original or striking. In the student plot just analyzed the situation is too ordinary to be
interesting in itself; success in the writing would depend
upon dramatic emphasis of character.

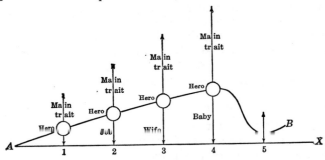

INTEGRATION OF TWO IDEALS.

In the above figure the line $A - B$ represents the emotional effect. The higher it rises from the base line $A - X$,
the greater is its intensity; in other words, the more gripping is the dramatic struggle. The little circles represent

the main character himself in different stages of the story. The vertical lines represent the character traits.

Once more the line representing the main trait is made longer than the opposing line, because it is the desire which triumphs. Since it does triumph in each case, it draws the line representing the emotion higher and higher, until during the fourth episode, it is at its highest pitch. This last episode represents the hero's success, followed by the death of his child. Since the dramatic conflict is now ended, the curve of emotional intensity falls rapidly. The significance of the hero's remark when looking at his dead baby is that it adds a final startling touch of reality to what has been our main interest all along, the man's character. This episode is represented by line 5. It shows that the hero is the same ghastly old sixpence.

Value of discipline

I do not say that every character story can be built in exactly this way. I have given each step in detail mainly in order that you may see what I mean by method and how the principles we studied in earlier chapters can be put to practical use in plotting character stories. Following these manipulations is but another form of mental discipline. We are now, like the pianist, learning scales in order to forget them. Once you are convinced of the value of method, I shall trust you to discover satisfactory initiative and originality in formulating methods of your own. To this end I propose to take another plot worked out with a student and again show graphically how a systematic adherence to the principles of drama and single effect helped her in her task.

8. A More Difficult Plot

The story idea, which again concerns a writer, was taken from the student's note book. It read as follows:

Upon a beautiful stretch of seashore I found a young man living in a picturesque cabin alone. I stopped for a glass of water and discovered that he was spending his time writing. He said he never tried to publish his work, that he was afraid if he did he would try to alter it, commercialize it, and so lose his inspiration. He didn't show me his work. He seemed sane enough and was quite good looking. His only companions, he said, were his Airedale and a little girl of seven years who sometimes visited him and entertained him by playing her flute.

The student who presented this idea had no knowledge of the principles of plotting. She stated that she had worked on it for several days without success. She wished, she said, to make a plot which would give the reader a thrill of admiration, or amazement, at the successful struggle of a literary genius who stuck to his highest ideals through thick and thin. After much labor the best she could do in the way of a finished plot was as follows:

Phillips, the hero, after living a poetic, idyllic life in the pursuit of literary ideals in his cabin on the seashore, is lured to the big city by the letters of a friend who assures him that he, the poet, can sell his poetry just as he has written it for big figures. Phillips, once in the city, makes the rounds of editors, meeting only discouragement. He falls madly in love with a movie woman who breaks his heart, fleeces him of all his money, and deserts him. Disillusioned, penniless, he returns to his lonely cabin stoutly resolved never again to leave it in search of the flesh pots. Editors can come to him after this.

How lack of method confuses

The student, who possessed a good sense of story values, was dissatisfied with this plot because it contained too much material for a short story. Two conflicts, one over his literary ideals, and another over the movie woman, suggested to her that there were really two stories here instead of one. Both conflicts might be used in the form of a novelette, but she didn't want to write a novelette. The hero " travels " too much, she said; she was distressed to know how to handle his activities in the city. She also agreed that there was as yet no clear-cut picture of dramatic struggle; the clash of desires was only vaguely suggested. Lastly, she finally admitted that the " tests " for the hero's character trait of devotion to his idyllic, idealistic literary life were not convincing. Why did he return to his cabin? He wasn't a good salesman; he couldn't write; he allowed himself to be " trimmed " by an actress! Apparently, he returned because he was a dub at everything else. Such activities will scarcely inspire the emotion of admiration which the student wished to give her reader.

The chief reason why the student was not able to make progress with her plot was that she was trying to do too many things at once. Our inquiry into the human powers of attention in Chapter Two showed us how limited is the capacity of our brain in this respect. Even one idea can't be held in mind for more than a few seconds unless it is " jazzed up " by varying it in some way. By introducing variety into them, two — even three ideas, may be held fixedly in the mind for some minutes; but beyond three we soon reach the limit of the human power of attention. Now the student in trying to solve her plot of *The Flute* was trying to grasp some sixteen ideas at once!

By careful inquiry I discovered that she had divided her task up into four general " problems ": the hero himself, the seashore setting, the adventures in the city, and Dolly, the little girl who played the flute. If, now, we set down each of her main ideas, we can see that the chaos of her mind looked something like the sketch opposite.

How method simplifies

Hopeless task! Writers who let their plot problems stagger them in this fashion can hope to succeed only by " sudden and happy inspiration." Such inspirations do indeed sometimes occur; but no amount of living in a romantic garret or smoking a particular brand of tobacco, will bring them when most needed; they do not come so regularly as one's bills; and so — enter, the necessity for system, represented by the three stages of (1) Analysis, (2) Stating the Problem, and (3) Manipulation as given above. Let us now see how the problem was delimited and quickly solved by the use of these three processes. First of all —

THE PLOT THAT CAN'T BE SOLVED

1. *Analyzing the material*. Taking both the original plot idea and the defective plot: the single effect is definitely set forth by the student herself — a thrill of admiration at the picture of the hero's clinging to his literary ideals. Obviously the plot will follow the character story pattern. The story concerns the hero's literary ideals. No well-marked complication is given. The drama will therefore simply be effective tests for this trait, successive

clashes between his desire to stick to his literary ideals and other strong desires. These successive clashes will give us the repetition necessary to work up the reader's emotions.

2. *Stating the problem:* The problem of finishing the plot is obviously, from the above analysis, simply to present the hero in the simplest and quickest manner with tests for his character trait, and to devise an outcome which harmonizes with the single effect.

3. *Manipulation:* Our task of plotting is now comparatively simple. The problem calls for " test of his character trait." Let us proceed to do this, refusing resolutely to be distracted by other interests. First of all, let us turn back to the diagram of the plot as it was in the student's mind, and simplify it.

How about these problems centered about the " visit to the city " ? Is it absolutely necessary to take the hero to the city to have his character tested? It is not. So we eliminate altogether the idea of his going to the city.

How about the various character traits which are suggested as being true of the hero? Well, knowing that we have a character story and that this pattern can develop only one trait and that we have decided that this trait is devotion to his idyllic literary life, we can at once eliminate all traits but this one.

How about the various moods and characteristics suggested for the setting? Our problem, to which we must persistently adhere, is to find tests of character. How can we use the setting to help us with those tests? The struggle is between his desire to remain and his desire to go away to follow another life. Where does the setting fit in here? Obviously the setting is part of the life he loves. The quietness, tranquillity, health and beauty of the wooded shore would be a concrete part of his beloved bucolic paradise. Very well, let us give the setting those qualities and say that it both harmonizes with and inspires the hero's main trait.

We have left only little Dolly. Shall we throw her out

as we eliminated the city? We might, and still make a good plot. Before we discard her, however, let us ask the big question: *Does she help provide tests for the hero's main trait?* The thing he wishes to *do* to express his trait is to remain where he is and continue his work. Would Dolly have anything to do with this desire to remain? If we conceive of her as a wood sprite, a teller of lovely fairy stories, a magic player of the flute — yes, she might very well be a vital part of his desire to remain. This trait of the hero's is a rather ethereal, subtle thing! The *quality* of the girl harmonizes pretty well with it. Let us keep her, then, and say that she is simply part of the landscape.

Now, with these eliminations and interpretations, we may now set forth our conflict thus:

Love of idyllic literary life opposed by lure of the big city.

It is obvious from the above that the emotional conflict is weak. The only desire opposing the main trait is a rather vague feeling of what might be if he should go to the city. The falling in love and getting fleeced have nothing to do so far with opposing the main trait. We must make more precise and intense the opposing desire.

Let us take the most obvious and simple things that occur to us. Why does anyone go to the city to live? To earn more money, certainly. Very well: let us say the hero receives offers of large sums of money to come to the city and write photoplays. This temptation, since he is a hermit soul, will not affect him deeply; but it will make some impression, so that our conflict looks like this:

Love of idyllic literary life opposed by desire for money.

The next question obviously is: What is another test stronger than money? Fame! Yes, fame would undoubtedly appeal to such a man more than money. After all, he has been struggling for fame with his " high brow " writings. He may now be tempted by simply another *kind* of fame. Our struggle now looks like this:

Love of idyllic literary life opposed by desire for fame.

Final integration

Still the opposing desire is not strong enough. It will take a terrific jolt to wake up this temperamental dreamer. What will it be? What will be a convincing " supreme test " of this Horatian proclivity of his? Once more — the obvious things! What are the strongest human desires? Hunger and sex. Hunger we abandon. If we make him live in the woods *starving* we change the trait we are working with: a man who will try to produce Literature living on roots and salt air and flute notes is a maniac and not a rational human being. We are therefore reduced to sex, or let us say, passionate love, or just passion.

Now how are we going to vamp our hero? Since we have decided, in the interest of brevity and simplicity, to have the whole action take place in or about his cabin, we must bring his temptress to him. Whom to bring? We return to the student's original plot outline to see if we cannot save time by using material in hand without having to invent new stuff. She speaks of a movie actress. Suppose this actress comes to his cabin to get him to leave? She might indeed tempt him by her charms. The trouble here, however, is that our hero is not exactly the kind of man to fall for a movie queen vulgar and cheap enough to try a trick of this kind. The idea of the woman coming with the offer is all right, but the woman must be a cultivated person with charm and her appeal must be plausible.

The answer is clear; she is his wife. They had been married, but, being temperamentally incompatible, had separated, he to live in seclusion, she to win fame in motion pictures in the city. Now that his stories begin to be published, she sees in him a source for beautiful scripts for her acting, and she pilgrimages, with softened heart, to his sylvan retreat, and, like Satan of old, presents her three tests: Money, fame, herself!

We now have our " big scene," a conflict that will satisfy any editor; and we can represent it as follows:

Love of idyllic literary life opposed by desire for love.

Everything is provided for but little Dolly and the outcome. The outcome has already been settled for us by our premise as to what the main trait is. *If* his *dominant* trait is his love for his idyllic existence, he will resist all temptations to go away and will remain. If he did anything else, we would have to create another dominant trait. No — he remains. He loves his wife; she offers herself; he refuses, and remains.

What about little Dolly? She, we agreed, is part of the landscape. She is part of the idyllic picture he loves. *How* is she a part of it? Her elfin figure, her pretty fairy tales, the ineffable music of her magic flute. Can we let any of these lures be a deciding factor in the fierce struggle that goes on inside the cabin? It might be awkward to let her appear in person. Our scene is not to be one for children to witness. This eliminates her appearance and her tales; but — how about the music of the flute? Why not let it be wafted to the ears of the literally and figuratively hard-pressed husband at the critical moment? His stout resistance is melting before the soft blandishments and kisses of his wife when lo! faintly yet sweetly and clearly, like the clear voice of the woods itself, comes the quavering flute note through the night air! It is enough to arouse the drugged conscience. The husband springs up and rushes out into the night. His battle is won.

I have outlined the making of this plot in considerable detail in order to show clearly some of the mental shortcuts possible to one who has mastered the principles of short story form. It may seem that the plot was devised to illustrate the principles; but such, I assure you, was not the case: the plot was arrived at exactly as described in the course of routine instruction.

9. Use of Schematic Outline

The process I have outlined for making a character story plot soon becomes, however, more elaborate than necessary in practical use. As soon as the student gains any facility at all he will find himself conducting all of the processes of analysis, stating the problem, and manipulation at the same time. A brief form for presenting a plot is needed. Let me sugggest a form that can be easily confined to one sheet of paper. I shall use the plot that we have just worked out.

SCHEMATIC OUTLINE OF CHARACTER STORY

The Flute

A. Type of story — Character.

B. Effect to be made — Thrill at seeing character win in struggle for his ideals.

C. Conflict — Between desire to live idyllic literary life of high ideals and desire for money, fame and love.

1. *Initial complication:* Talented and imaginative man marries beautiful young girl with talent for acting. They are strongly incompatible, in that he loves the rustic, simple life, and she yearns for the excitement and commercial atmosphere of the large city. She leaves him and goes into the movies. He goes to a sylvan retreat on the seashore to pursue his writing. He finally writes stories which are beautifully adaptable for her acting. She therefore comes for him and pleads for him to return to the city with her. He refuses.

2. *Main character:* Phillip Stanton, the writer.

3. *Main character trait:* Resolute devotion to the bucolic, classical ideal of literary art, a determination to work out his literary destiny by cultivating his best inspirations in solitude.

4. *Crucial situation:* The actress wife first offers her husband a contract to write for her with a salary for him of $25,000 a year. He refuses. She argues the certainty of fame and adulation for him: he will be written up: his name will be on thousands of movie screens: he will be interviewed, consulted, admired by the wit and beauty of the motion picture and theatri‹

cal world. He is tempted but refuses. The presence of the wife arouses his former passion for her. She observes this but refuses his caresses. He wanders out into the woods to think it over. There he encounters a little girl named Dolly, the eight-year-old daughter of a fisherman. To him she is a sprite belonging to the witchery and beauty of the woods and shores. She tells him a story of a poet who once tried to put so much wine in a fragile cup that the cup broke and spilled all the wine. She comforts him by playing her flute. The sweet, wild note soothes and strengthens his resolve to stand by his ideals. He returns to the cabin to find his wife provocatively attired, alluring, tempting. She deliberately vamps her husband. He resists, confesses his desire. She says: "Accept my offer and you can live with me again: refuse and — I go at once." He wavers, melts, succumbs to her kisses and embraces when far off in the distance, along the shadowy shore line he hears the thin, serene, spiritual note of Dolly's flute.

5. With a wild gesture he dashes out into the night. His wife returns to the city without him.

Explanation of terms

Let me now explain the terms used in this schematic outline. The meanings of the first three, A, B, and C, are, in the light of what we have already learned, obvious. You will generally find that the "initial complication" is substantially your original "story idea." In it you express the essence of the emotional conflict. The full dramatic conflict of the story need not be developed in this section, but it should be clearly indicated. It may, and often does, contain matters which happen before the actual story, as you finally write it, begins.

The main character is obviously the one who dominates the story. Sometimes there will be two or even three or more main characters. In each of these cases the decisive trait of each character must be clearly indicated. The main character trait obviously means that peculiarity or tendency in the main character or characters which is exemplified in all the episodes of the story. It is important in an outline of this brevity that this trait be stated as explicitly as possible, since every episode in the story must be examined to see that it illustrates, proves and tests this trait.

In the crucial situation we find the " soul of the story." It is substantially what is often called the " climax." It should give explicitly though briefly a cross-section of the dramatic struggle at its highest pitch, and here we should see exactly what the conflict of desires is. The intensity of the struggle should also be clearly brought out, though it need not be developed. The crucial situation should be carried up to a point where this main struggle is clearly presented, and then should stop.

In the " outcome " should be given merely the close or ending of the story. Most modern short stories are rather finite, and indicate some definite conclusion or wind-up of events.[1] This conclusion should be definitely stated in this last part of the outline. It is important also inasmuch as the modern short story often ends with a surprise or sudden turn in events which gives the story a peculiar emphasis in the last paragraph. This device is often very helpful and striking, and therefore deserves special thought in plotting.

In general in using this outline you will do well not to let it extend beyond one typewritten page, single spaced. The reasons for this are two-fold: first, in order to compress the action into as brief a space as this you will be forced to think clearly; second, the enforced brevity prevents you from attempting to " write up " your material; you thus leave out all attempts at emotional or picturesque writing and keep yourself to the " bare bones " of your narrative — all of which is part of our general plan of separating the planning of the story from the actual writing. The whole process of creative composition is complex — to master it, one must, as in other things, " divide and conquer."

[1] This generalization must now be modified in view of changes in the past few years. There has been a gradual but steady reduction of artificiality in plot constructions even in popular fiction magazines. See note, page 253, at the end of this chapter.

A Maupassant story outlined

All good short stories carrying out the ideals of single effect and drama can be put into the above schematic outline. To illustrate this, let us take one of the most famous stories of Maupassant, *The Piece of String,* which you probably have read. You will remember that in this swift, brief story of three thousand words, we review the tragic end of a simple Norman peasant, Maitre Hauchecorne. He was falsely accused of finding and keeping a pocket-book lost by a fellow farmer. He protested his innocence, the pocket-book was found, and then being mentally upset by the attacks made on his honesty, he continued to protest his innocence. Never could he be reassured that he was no longer suspected. He finally went insane, babbling protests of his innocence. We can present this character story as follows:

The Piece of String

A. Type of story — Character.
B. Effect to be made — Tragic irony.
C. Conflict — Between Hauchecorne's desire to prevent suspicions as to his honesty, opposed by statements first serious and later jocular of the suspicions of his countrymen.
1. *Initial Complication:* Hauchecorne, a sensitive, simple farmer, is seen to pick something up from the street during a country fair. Soon after, another farmer reports the loss of a pocket-book containing money. A harness-maker, an enemy of Hauchecorne, tells of having seen him pick something up, so that he is brought before the mayor and accused of stealing the pocket-book. He protests his innocence but is not believed.
2. *Main character:* Hauchecorne
3. *Main character trait:* Simple, superstitious sensitiveness.
4. *Crucial situation:* The pocket-book is found and official and in general popular suspicion is removed from Hauchecorne. Later, nevertheless, having had his honesty attacked, he continues to protest his innocence. His neighbors, feeling him now to be a ridiculous figure, amuse themselves by continuing to accuse him, with the brutal desire of hearing him protest his innocence. Hauchecorne struggles with the supposed attack on his honesty until he is "struck to the heart" by the injustice

of the suspicion. His mind becomes entirely occupied by the story of the string. He wastes away, his mind grows weak.

5. *Outcome:* Hauchecorne dies and in the delirium of the death agony continues to mumble his protests of innocence.

10. A Two-Character Story Plot

All the plots we have handled so far in this chapter contain internal dramatic struggles. Since there is generally but one main character in this type of story it is easier to elaborate than the story using a man-versus-man conflict. The processes outlined above are, however, just as applicable to the man-versus-man and man-versus-nature types as to that with the internal struggle. To illustrate this and also show how the above processes of plotting can be telescoped or handled simultaneously when skill is acquired, we will work out a student plot involving each of the two other types of conflict.

The first contained a man-versus-man conflict. The original story idea, taken from the notebook of a student who had spent the summer in Wyoming, was as follows:

The cowboy gentry in this part of the country are all spoiled. They let their wives become hard-driven drudges on the farms and ranches, refuse to hire servants, and altogether treat them as if they were squaws. The white man's association, indeed, with the Indian on these plains seems to have been another case of the conquered absorbing the conqueror. There are several times more men than women in the state and one result of this is that white men are still to be found taking squaws for wives. These squaws are willing to work themselves to death, but — woe betide the eastern girl who comes out here a bride, expecting to find her dreams with a Wyoming cattle man!

Taking two steps at once

Here are the processes actually used in making this plot idea into a story which was later published. Analysis and statement of the problem were conducted together. The student was asked, in other words, what part of the original idea suggests a plot. His answer was: " The last few lines about the eastern girl marrying a cowboy suggest a dramatic conflict."

" And that conflict is — " he was asked.

" Her ideals versus his as to what a wife's duties are," was the correct answer. (This gives us our drama.)

" And how does the struggle end? " was the next question. (This raises at once the questions of type of story, the single effect, the editorial factor, and also continues to state the problem.)

" Well," replied the student, " it would be more novel and also more thrilling to see a white woman for once fight for her right to a more civilized treatment from her husband and win out."

" Good, this is acceptable editorially. Now if she takes a stand as heroic as this and, as you say, fights through and wins, what kind of a story have we? "

" Character."

" How many characters? "

" Two, obviously: man and wife, each with different ideals."

We had completed the analysis and answered all problems except details of the crucial situation and outcome, which were easily taken care of after again consulting the student's notebook for further " local color." A schematic outline was then drawn up as follows:

The Clearer View

A. Type of story — Character.
B. Effect to be made — Thrill of witnessing wife's triumph.
C. Conflict — Between eastern and cow country ideals about women's domestic rights, each held by man and wife respectively.

1. *Initial complication:* Jeff Dawson, a young, strong, handsome Wyoming rancher, while on a visit east, marries Edith Sutherland, and brings her home with him. She soon sees that he intends treating her like a squaw as regards the work about the house. He refuses to get her a servant, although he can afford it, and lets her know that he expects her to chop wood, make fires, do the washing, and clean floors and windows. One day Mrs. Dawson tells her husband that she will not live with him if he continues this treatment of her.

2. *Main character:* Mr. Dawson, whose trait is grim determination to make his wife do all the chores. Mrs. Dawson whose trait is grim determination not to be treated like a squaw.

3. *Crucial situation:* In desperation Mrs. Dawson runs away, while her husband is out on the range, and tries to reach the railroad station to return home. Her husband rides after her on his swiftest pony, and sweeps her up on his saddle just as she is about to drop with exhaustion. The husband relents a little and agrees to bring in the wood. He refuses to wash the floors or windows. His wife still insists. She tries to telephone for help, but he cuts the wires. She again tries to run away, but he locks her in the store-room. Later she refuses to notice his presence unless he will wash the dusty, cobwebby windows. He refuses. They fight. She wounds him with a blow by a heavy brush. Exhausted, they sit facing each other through a long night of suffering, the girl unconscious most of the time.

4. *Outcome:* When morning breaks, Mrs. Dawson rouses herself, and is surprised to see the warm, mellow sunshine streaming through the windows. They have been washed clean in the night! She knows he has capitulated and falls upon his breast. Through the clean window, they can now for the first time see the snow-capped purple mountains rising to serene and noble heights, and as they stand together watching them Jeff Dawson murmurs: "It sure does give a clearer view."

11. A Man and Nature Plot

This type of plot presents problems but slightly different from those already studied. The main technical difference is that the obstacle to the main character's efforts is not another trait within himself or the trait of another man, but a stubborn resistance put up by some non-human factor. The plotting of a story of this type, written by a student from the Pan-handle State, had its beginning from this observation in her notebook:

The great drought of a few years ago brought suffering to Texas which the rest of the country has never realized. Cattle died in ghastly numbers. Whole herds, still alive, were abandoned on the parched plains. The owners knew that if rain did come the cows were already too far gone ever to regain their former marketable value. I know of only one herd in our part of the country which was saved. It belonged to my uncle. He simply didn't have the heart to let his animals die, at least not without making a heroic effort to save them. He hasn't quite recovered yet from his terrific ride from San Reos to Priest's Landing.

Here again the drama is clearly marked, and we seize upon it at once, thinking ahead to the finished plot as quickly as possible. The trait is obviously love or pity for the cattle. The crucial situation is the last few miles of the drive to Priest's Landing on a river. The outcome is — the cows were saved. The plot is finished — all but minor details. By these swift jumps we have determined that the story follows the character pattern, that the single effect will be admiration for the pitying cattleman and a thrill at the greatest rigors of his journey, and our editorial conclusion is that the story will sell if the interest is focused on the man and not too much on the cattle! The important problems were solved almost as soon as posed and a schematic outline was drawn up as a check on the unity and dramatic force of the inventions arrived at.

12. The Writing of the Character Story

Solving all these problems of invention and design is no guarantee that the student will be able to write a successful story. The schematic outline is intended, like an accountant's trial balance, to make certain of the plan, but it can do no more than this. Most students will need another outline, simpler, more chronological, perhaps longer, perhaps shorter, to write from. And the writing should be done, fragments of the story at first possibly, *when the mood is upon you,* with or without an outline. Your schematic outline may be of most use in planning a revision!

In order to show how the schematic outline is used to locate defects in planning, I have reproduced on the next page a faulty version of our story, *The Flute,* as it came from the student's typewriter, together with my suggestions for correction.

THE FLUTE *not yet!*

Type of story: character.
Single effect: [thrill] at character's
struggle for ideal.
Conflict: between desire for ideals
and temptations of money, fame, and love.
Initial complication: Talented young
author who loves quietness and solitude of seashore, quarrels with his wife, who leaves him
to enter the "pictures". He removes to a sylvan retreat on the seashore where he writes
stories which are published by the best literary magazines. Hoping to lure him to join her
and write photoplays for her directly his wife
visits him and urges him to come. *not shown*
Main character: Phillip Stanton.
Main trait: [Resolute] devotion to his
classical, non-commercial ideal of literary art.
Crucial situation: The actress wife
first offers her husband a large salary to come
and live with her and write her plays. He refuses. She tempts him with fame. This staggers
him and he wanders into the woods to think it
over. There he encounters a little girl six
years old, named Dolly, a fisherman's daughter,
who plays her flute to amuse him and to win
from him fairy stories. To his horror he finds
her dead body on the sand; she has been drowned.
He returns to his cabin to face his wife who has
adorned herself bewitchingly. <u>She announces that
she has decided to spend a week's vacation with
him</u> and persuade him that he should come with
her and commercialize his talents. He welcomes
her eagerly but insists stoutly that she'll never
dissuade him from his determination to live where
he is and write what pleases him.
Outcome: The week's vacation is over
and Stanton still refuses to leave with his wife.
She returns without him.

(right margin, handwritten) False note violates simple effect as part of his idyl? — not keep Dolly — Why not keep Dolly as a final temptation.

(bottom, handwritten) This shows consideration for your hero but how about your reader? You promise him a "thrill" — you say your hero is resolute — show it then by making his wife offer herself as a final temptation.

Supplementary Notes to Chapter V

(*Third Edition, 1934*)

The most appealing of all methods of revealing character, and the most powerful, is by subjecting it to the supreme dramatic test as outlined in this chapter and the one preceding. In two other ways character may be effectively revealed in narrative: one by the "uniquely characteristic act" and the other by an act which is a consistent violation of some law or custom which society has ordained for its preservation. Neither of these devices is an invention by modern writers; both have been used by writers of all time: in our age, however, the ironic spirit, the glee with which the sophisticated puncture the superstitions and hypocrisies of the conventional have made these devices newly impressive.

The Uniquely Characteristic Act

Nothing is truer of human beings than that they are not what they seem. Speech seems to be used more to conceal than to reveal the real motives of our acts. Seldom indeed do a man's acts sharply and unequivocally betray him for what he is. Every force in society that makes for politeness and conventional propriety works constantly to prevent frank, revealing behavior. Occasionally, however, a man is caught off-guard, is faced with an unfamiliar crisis in which he may say or do just that one thing which is uniquely and sharply revealing of one of the deeper springs of his life.

Of such acts in their humorous aspects most of the stories of O. Henry were compounded. In Katharine Brush's *Night Club* [1] we find a coat-room woman who, surrounded with the wild melodrama of city night life, seeks excitement in reading a cheap magazine. In *Rest Cure* by Kay Boyle, the main character, who seems to have only vindictive scorn for his father's memory, reveals at the end his terrified

[1] For further information on stories cited, see page 504.

longing for that father's protection. In *Consecrated Coal Scuttle,* by Dorothy Thomas, an old man revered for his godliness and piety is revealed as a witless automaton — a senile imbecile.

While this type of character story reveals character, it is not dramatic revelation; the reader is impressed not so much by sharing the character's experience, as he does in the dramatic story, as by the surprising truth of the revelation and by the humorous or ironic incongruities involved.

The Consistent Act of Violation

The impressiveness of this second character revelation lies not in the surprise but in the shock deriving from another pattern of incongruity. The character acts in violation not of what he was thought to be but of some law or custom whose observance is deeply imbedded in the consciousness and habits of the masses of his fellow citizens, among them the reader. The classical example of this type of story is Merimée's famous story, *Mateo Falcone,* which recounts the killing of a son by his father for disobeying the Corsican law of hospitality. To readers who do not share the father's devotion to this custom but regard the protective love of a father for a son as a foundation of society itself, the act is appalling. In this shock, this contrast, lies the power of such acts of consistent violation.

Of recent stories following this pattern are: George Milburn's " Sugar, Be Sweet " (in *No More Trumpets*) ; Vardis Fisher's " The Mother " (*Short Story Hits, 1933*) ; and Erskine Caldwell's " August Afternoon " (in *We Are The Living*). In the first, a man buys sugar with trading stamps which he asks for when he buys his daughter's coffin (violating our ideas of paternal sentiment) ; in the second a man kills his babies (violating the universal instinct of paternal love) ; and in the third, a man who knows that his wife is being seduced by a stranger makes no resistance (violating the jealous possessive instinct of the male for his mate).

ASSIGNMENTS: CHAPTER FIVE

The following exercises are a continuation of our study of character, especially in its dramatic and emotional aspects. If some of the steps or processes outlined in this chapter have seemed to you difficult to understand, you will find them easier to follow after performing the tasks given here. The first ones are merely the simplest possible instances of the creative processes already outlined; later ones involve the making of complete plots.

ASSIGNMENT A

Each of the following simple acts reveals a single definite trait of character. Write down in each case this trait. To secure the correct answer you have only to ask yourself: " What kind of a person would do such a thing? "

1. Joe often shoves his work aside, lolls back in his office chair, clumps his feet on a table, and, yawning from time to time, watches the hands of the clock go round.*

2. Louise has sent a photograph of herself to Mary Pickford's studio, thus entering herself in a beauty contest in filmdom. Without waiting to hear the result she has packed her trunk and has even bought her ticket to Hollywood.

3. Little Willie was given an apple which he was to share with his little sister after school. It was cut in two. After school he found he had lost one of the halves; he proceeded to eat the one remaining, telling his sister it was hers that was lost.

4. When George meets a lady he doffs his derby holding it at such an angle that he can see his own reflection in the small mirror he has fitted inside. After the lady is past, George, continuing to look into the mirror, raises his fingers to his sparse hair and busies himself with the parting.

5. Frank went to a baseball game instead of to the office where he was employed. When he was asked why he had failed to report for work, he admitted where he had been and consequently found himself without a position.*

6. One day a stranger walked past Mrs. Lawton's house and rapped at the door of her nearest neighbor. Not finding anyone at home he wrote something on a slip of paper and put it in the mail box. As soon as he had turned the corner and disappeared from sight, Mrs. Lawton, settling her glasses more firmly on her nose, went over to her neighbor's and, fishing the slip of paper from the depths of the post-box, eagerly scanned its contents.

7. Much against his will John Hopkins was induced to take his small nephew to the final game between the Yanks and the

White Sox. Straw hats were thrown to the skies and the heavens split with a million voices as John Hopkins sat in the grandstand reading, with all concentration, *The Yale Review.*

8. One evening Henry Davis, a wealthy young man, invited a girl to go to a dance with him. When Henry heard that it was to be a formal party, involving flowers and taxies, he sent the girl three carnations and borrowed a friend's flivver to go after her.

9. One morning upon leaving home for the office, John thrust his arm into a rip in the lining of his overcoat. Swearing violently, John stamped on the coat, tearing it from top to bottom.

10. Mrs. Alexander never speaks to her maid on the city streets.*

11. For hours Mr. Crawford worked in the country mud, trying to drive his car through. Off would come his chains, and out would go Mr. Crawford, whistling blithely, and on would go the chains for another trial.

12. Sally and her sister, Anna, were both interested in Jim. Jim rather favored Anna. Sally forbade her sister to go out with Jim. One day Sally, seeing Anna and Jim walking together arm in arm, walked up to Anna and struck her with her parasol.

13. While the other boys go to ball games and parties Howard sticks to his studies working nearly every night until bed-time.

14. Mrs. Devoe cries at the theatre, gives a dollar to every beggar that appeals to her and refers to dogs and cats as " darlings."

15. Ethel vows one week she will marry one boy, the next week another, the third week a third.

ASSIGNMENT B

This assignment will give you the simplest possible practice in dramatizing character. It is the reverse of Assignment A. The following list of character traits are to be presented briefly (25 to 100 words) in action. The thing you write out, that is, will look much like the bits of action you have just analyzed above. The action need not be complete dramatic proof. It may merely *indicate* the trait of character you have in mind.

1. Parsimonious
2. Extravagant
3. Pious
4. Craving luxury
5. Romantic love
6. Fastidious
7. Envious
8. Jealous
9. Superstitious
10. Tolerant
11. Mother love
12. Professional ambition
13. Family pride
14. Hypochondriac
15. Voluptuous

ASSIGNMENT C

The following exercises in analysis of character are much like those in Assignment A except that they are somewhat more difficult. In each case, unless otherwise directed, you are to write out as precisely as possible the trait of character exhibited by *the person whose name is italicized.* Do not hesitate to use several words if you can thereby make your answer more exact.

1. In Daudet's sketch, "Old Folks," the narrator, who has agreed to pay a visit to the grandparents of his friend, Maurice, tells of his arrival at the quaint little home, thus:

" Good day, good people! I am Maurice's friend."
Oh, if you had seen *the poor old man* then; if you had seen him come towards me with outstretched arms, embrace me, shake my hands, and run wildly about the room, exclaiming:
" Mon Dieu! Mon Dieu! "
Every wrinkle in his face laughed. His cheeks flushed, and he stammered:
" Ah! monsieur; ah! monsieur."
Then he hurried towards the end of the room, calling:
" Mamette! Mamette! " . . .
When she came in, *Mamette* began by making me a low reverence, but the old man cut it in two by a word:
" This is Maurice's friend."
Instantly she began to tremble and weep, she lost her handkerchief, turned red, red as a peony, even redder than he. Those old people had but a single drop of blood in their veins, and at the slightest emotion it rushed to their faces. . . .
" How is he? What is he doing? Why doesn't he come to see us? Is he happy? " and *patati!* and *patata!* that sort of thing for hours.*

2. Here is Daudet's presentation of the character of one of the old popes of Avignon. His chief character trait is almost stated, but not quite. What is it?

There was one . . . whom they called Boniface. Ah! how many tears were shed in Avignon when he died! He laughed so heartily from the back of his mule! And when you passed him — though you were simply a poor little digger of madder, or the provost of the city — he would give you his blessing so courteously!

Every Sunday, after vespers the excellent man went to pay court to his vineyard, a tiny vineyard which he had planted himself; and when he was there, seated in the warm sun, with his mule by his side and his cardinals lying at the foot of the stumps all about, then he would order a bottle of native wine opened . . . and he would drink it in little sips, looking at his vineyard with a tender expression. And when on his return to the city, he rode over Avignon Bridge, and his mule, stirred by the music, fell into a little skipping amble, he himself marked the time of the dance with his cap, which scandalized the cardinals terribly, but caused the people to say: " Ah! the kind prince! Ah! the dear old Pope! *

3. A rather common human characteristic is definitely hinted at in the following quotation from the *Saturday Evening Post:*

Breck Field was growling to his wife one day because he is a slave to the tobacco habit. He smokes an old pipe a good deal, but is always trying to smoke less. If he gets a drop of nicotine on his clothing he is compelled to throw the suit away. An old pipe is an offensive thing, and Breck hates himself for using one.

His wife said she had seen a pipe advertised somewhere that was self-cleaning; a pipe so constructed that the accumulation of nicotine was impossible.

"This," Breck replied wearily, looking at his offensive pipe, "is one of them."

4. The dominant characteristic of the husband in the following quotation, again from the *Saturday Evening Post,* is very clearly suggested. What is it?

Mrs. Dave Grant takes in sewing, but says her husband doesn't know it. Her efforts to keep it from him amuse everybody. She is always begging her customers to say nothing to their husbands of her efforts to help in paying the family expenses.

"I don't know what *Dave* would do," she says, "if he found out; the Grants were always such aristocrats."

But the general opinion is that Dave knows it; surely he can't think that the women who call at his house so regularly are attracted by his wife's popularity socially, since she has a tired look, and her dress is always full of pins.

Dave probably knows it, all right, but pretends that he doesn't to keep his reputation as a one hundred per cent American unsullied.*

5. *Ethel* attended art school every evening after her day's work in the hope of becoming an artist. Ted was in love with her and wanted to marry her, but he did not want his wife to follow a profession. Ethel loved Ted but she could not give up her art. A home-loving girl became interested in Ted. He asked Ethel once more to be his wife, on his condition that she give up her plan of a profession. Ethel realized that this was final, but after a struggle with herself said no. Ted married the other girl and Ethel painted a picture of home life which secured her a place among recognized artists.

6. *Joel Withers* and Michael Dade had been lifelong friends. Joel had few friends as he put his own interest above everything. Michael understood him, however, and a more or less genuine friendship existed between them. Michael's affairs became involved and he was about to lose all he had, including his home. He asked a loan of Joel, which would have saved the situation, but Joel refused, giving excuses. Later Joel bought Michael's property at auction for a song, thus losing the only friend he had.

7. Jane and *Mary* were both popular girls in the same set, but Jane in her desire for leadership endeavored to injure Mary by

innuendoes. Mary knew this but her popularity did not suffer on account of it. Jane, baffled, became indiscreet in her remarks about Mary and incurred the disapproval of the young people. Mary, realizing that Jane at heart was all right, and that her folly was largely due to vanity, made a point of being seen with her often and so helped to restore her in favor and to a better understanding of herself.

8. *John Williams* was a rising young man. He chose carefully his friends both professionally and socially with an eye to their financial standing. He allowed himself to fall in love with a fair visitor who was apparently wealthy. Later he learned that the girl had nothing, but was helped by rich relatives. As he had not yet committed himself he withdrew in favor of a rival and a business opponent on the tacit understanding that a certain deal would be thrown his way if he gave up his obvious advantages with the girl. The rival won the girl and John Williams made a million.

9. *Mrs. X.* was forever giving benefits for relief near and far and giving of herself and her stores for the less fortunate at home. Mr. X. would say jestingly that he never knew whether he would find a change of clothing on his return home, as it always depended upon how many others needed the clothing first. This fear was realized when Mr. X., preparing to dress for a banquet which his wife had long looked forward to, learned that she had loaned his dress-suit to a poor but ambitious protegé who had been asked to his first formal function. Mr. X. was glad to get out of going to the banquet, but Mrs. X. wept a few quiet tears. She cheerfully put her disappointment aside, however, and planned a little party somewhere just with her husband.

10. *Mrs. Jones* coveted the excellent servants of Mrs. Brown, who had been a neighbor and good friend for a number of years. Mrs. Jones had much more money than Mrs. Brown. She persuaded Mrs. Brown's man to work for her on extra time at very high wages. She made excuses for interviews with the cook on various matters. Throughout her stratagems she spoke to Mrs. Brown slightingly of these same servants. When she finally made them a definite offer, they declined.

11 Here is a bit of the action in Bret Harte's *Tennessee's Partner* which pictures sharply a trait of the Partner's character. What is it?

Tennessee, after holding up a man, has been captured by some indignant citizens, who are giving him a form of trial although they intend to hang him. *Tennessee's Partner* appears at the trial. This is his version of the case. He had known Tennessee four years, "in luck and out o' luck." Tennessee's ways were not always the ways of his Partner, but his Partner knew everything that he'd been up to. Tennessee had wanted money and had taken it from a stranger not liking to ask it of his Partner. The citizens had caught him and were holding him for taking that money. "And now, what's the fair thing? Some would say more; some would say less. Here's seventeen hundred dollars in coarse gold and a watch — it's about all my pile — and call it square!"

He poured the contents of the bag he carried out on the table. The men trying Tennessee were enraged at this attempt to condone the offense by money, and they finally convinced Tennessee's Partner that his money was of no use. "His face took a more serious and sanguinary hue, and those who were nearest him noticed that his rough hand trembled slightly on the table."

12. Here is an interesting crucial situation from Coppée. What does it tell about the character of Miraz? The scene takes place at his burial.

Dr. Arnould whispered in my ear, "You know that Miraz killed himself?"

I looked at him with astonishment. But he pointed to Madame Miraz and her daughter, who were sobbing under their long veils . . . and he added:

"For them. Yes, for six months he threw all his medicines in the fire, and designedly committed all sorts of imprudences. He confessed it to me before his death. I had not understood it at all — I, who had expected to prolong his life at least three years by creosote. At last the other night, when it was freezing cold, he left his window open, as if by forgetfulness, and was taken with bleeding at the lungs. Yes, that he might leave bread for those two women. The curé does not dream that he is blessing a suicide."

13. How would you characterize the acts of the husbandmen in the following parable:

There was a man that was a householder, who planted a vineyard and set a hedge about it, and digged a wine-press in it, and built a tower and let it out to husbandmen and went into another country. And when the seasons of the fruits drew near, he sent his servants to the husbandmen, to receive his fruits. And the husbandmen took his servants and beat one, and killed another, and stoned another. Again, he sent other servants more than the first, and they did unto them in like manner. But afterward he sent unto them his son, saying, They will reverence my son. But the husbandmen, when they saw the son, said among themselves, This is the heir; come, let us kill him, and take his inheritance. And they took him, and cast him forth out of the vineyard, and killed him. When therefore the lord of the vineyard shall come, what will he do unto those husbandmen? They say unto him, He will miserably destroy those miserable men and will let out the vineyard unto other husbandmen, who shall render him the fruits in their seasons.

14. Read carefully the Parable of The Prodigal Son, St. Luke, Chapter 15, verses 11–32. Which is more fully developed, the prodigality of the son or the forgiving, tolerant nature of the father? Is the parable rightly named

15. Here is a bit of characterization from Turgeniev. Two traits are indicated. What are they?

Pavel was a regular Russian soul — upright, honorable, simple, but, unhappily, somewhat languid, without tenacity or inward ardor. Youth did not bubble up in him like a spring; it flowed like a tranquil stream. He was a victim of the Slavonic curse of laxity. When he dreamed of work, he soared like an eagle; it seemed as though he could move earth from its place, but in the execution, he immediately grew slack and weary. So he was content to dream and plan and resolve and do nothing.

Once in love, Pavel felt a strange weight on his heart — a deadly burden, an irritation which he found incomprehensible, a torment that rent him asunder. He lay down on the grass and idled away whole hours. He made youthful speeches, now fervid, now thoughtful, now rapturous, but almost always they were obscure and meaningless. A secret restlessness ate at his heart. A tremulous animation surrounded him. Nothing refreshed him. His mood was not that of an all-embracing happiness when the soul widens out, reverberates, when it seems to understand everything and love everything. No! The thirst for happiness was kindled and nothing, it seemed, could ever satisfy it.*

16. What is the *chief impression* you get of the character of the Delorme sisters in the following news item?

Classroom questions were put to a number of witnesses called today at the opening of the trial of Abelard Delorme, ex-priest, charged with murder of his half-brother, Raoul, Ottawa University student, in this city last January, for insurance money.

Gustave Monette, counsel for the accused, who, at the morning session introduced records of insanity in the Delorme family, propounded the questions when certain relatives of the defendant were called to the stand. Some touched on arithmetic, others on scripture. One was:

"Noah had three sons: Shem, Ham, and Japhet. What was the name of their father?"

"I do not recall that by heart," replied one witness, Florence Delorme, who said she was related to the accused.

Miss Lillie Delorme, half-sister of the defendant, also was unable to tell the name of the father of Noah's sons.

17. What trait of character is displayed by the Commandant Hilier in the following episode?

Commandant Hilier has invited me to lunch. He is installed in an abandoned abbey, the ancient and venerable walls of which have been riddled, cracked, ravaged by the enemy guns. The chapter-room alone remains intact. It is there the table is laid. . . . The meal is simple. There are only three of us: the Commandant, his aide, Abel, and I. The major speaks to us of the destinies of our country.

Suddenly a deafening uproar makes the walls tremble. The cook, with the helmet of an English soldier on his head, dashes into the room.

" My commandant," he cries, " two great shells have fallen beside my kitchen and the stove with the fritters has vanished. . . ."

Commandant Hilier makes no sign. Calmly, gravely, slowly, he says:

" Well! Why do you wait to bring in the cheese? "

And he apologizes for offering me so frugal a luncheon.

18. In plain language what is the nature of the character depicted by O. Henry in the following?

Piggy needs but a word. When the girls named him, an undeserved stigma was cast upon the noble family of swine. The words-of-three-letters lesson in the old blue spelling book begins with Piggy's biography. He was fat; he had the soul of a rat, the habits of a bat, and the magnanimity of a cat. . . .

He wore expensive clothes; and was a connoisseur of starvation. He could look at a shop-girl and tell you to an hour how long it had been since she had eaten anything more nourishing than marshmallows and tea. He hung about the shopping districts, and prowled around in department stores with his invitations to dinner. Men who escort dogs upon the streets at the end of a string look down upon him. He is a type; I can dwell upon him no longer; my pen is not the kind intended for him; I am no carpenter.

19. In Chapter II, Assignment A, No. 5, what trait is suggested? In No. 7? In No. 8?

20. In Chapter II, Assignment D, which selections have most character interest? Is there any character revelation in No. 2?

21. What is the main trait of Johnny, in Chapter III, Assignment A, No. 4?

22. In Chapter III, Assignment E, what traits are suggested in A–1? In A–8? In A–11? In A–12?

23. In Chapter III, Assignment E, B–1, what impulse apparently starts Professor Spurgess's quarrel with his wife? Under what circumstances would he probably dismiss an assistant?

24. In Chapter III, Assignment E, B–2, what is Mrs. F.'s trait? If Mrs. F. were offered $2,000 to buy either a cottage in a region

not yet discovered by summer people, or an automobile, which would she probably take?

25. In Chapter III, Assignment E, B–3, what motive accounts for most of the action?

26. Below are a number of episodes, briefly outlined. Name the trait for each, or explain why no trait is revealed. Where you find traits, is the revelation strong, or weak?

1. A woman leaves her husband, in anger, and tries to make her way alone, but she is unsuccessful in business, can't find another man, and finally returns to him.

2. The hobby of a prominent dentist is collecting cloisonné.

3. A landlubber buys a small coast freighter as an investment, and to save money for train fare, travels on it whenever his errands and the destination of a given cargo make it convenient. During a terrific storm he is found in the cabin figuring his probable loss.

4. A farm wife, childless, works long hours in her flower garden. The little money that she can lay hands on, she spends for seeds. She once sent to Switzerland for a very fine variety of pansy seed.

5. A man who is a fair golfer, only a little better than average, can play phenomenally well when he has a lot of money on the match.

6. A girl, of simple farm background, goes to a large city. To her new acquaintances she pictures her family as distinguished.

7. Thomas Byers, middle-aged and successful, returns to the home of his boyhood. There he advertises in the local paper: " An invitation to dinner at the Eagle Hotel is extended to all in this community who can remember Thomas Byers."

8. A city engineer refuses to approve a type of iron pipe in which a member of the city council is interested.

9. A man wounded in a fight near his frontier home, drags himself back, bleeding, to his cabin, to die in his wife's arms.

ASSIGNMENT D

This assignment is much like Assignment B above except that it asks for a more extended development of a character trait. Select from the list of fifteen character traits in Assignment B five which can be more or less applied to people you know. Without naming the people (or better, giving them fictitious names) write out in from 500 to 1,000 words things you have seen them do which illustrate these traits. *Be sure not to name the trait itself in the sketch; keep strictly to their acts, what they do.*

ASSIGNMENT E

This assignment will give you a start in handling real life people as you know them with all their outstanding traits, the process being that already described in Chapter Three, page 116. Your first sketch, in other words, will be the kind of note you will put into your notebook for future use; your second sketch will be the same material worked over for the purpose of singling out a single trait for use in a short story.

1. The following four sketches are in the first stage. They present four people from real life without any attempt at developing a single trait. Read each one carefully, then —

(a) Write out the main trait, or the trait that most interests you, expressing it, if possible, in one or two words.

(b) Then rewrite the entire sketch to about its present length, inventing new episodes, if necessary, but making all the action display the one trait.

(a.) Mrs. X. is an exceptionally good linguist and took high honors in college in languages and literature. She still reads voraciously. She adores her husband, her life being so centered on him that she jumps to meet his every want, anticipating them when she can. "What did you say, dear?" she calls from another room when at times he has said nothing. When she is not thinking of her husband she is worrying about her baby. Having only one child and being something of a specialist in children's diseases, she has a more than normal fear that some mishap will occur to her son. At the slightest sign of indisposition in the child, she rushes to a doctor.

(b.) Mr. Y. is an official of one of the biggest corporations in the country. He says that he won his post of great trust because of his absolute honesty and his life-long practice of doing more than he was paid to do. When a conductor forgets to take his fare, he always offers it. He worked himself into invalidism at the age of fifty, then took up golf. Now he is as enthusiastic about golf as about his business. When he was fifty-five he played one hundred holes in a single day, ending in a drenching rain. Normally he is undemonstrative and talks but little, until you begin talking about golf. Then he brightens, his memories are aroused, and he becomes a happy conversationalist, full of genial witticisms and anecdotes.

(c.) Mr. Z. rose at the last minute each morning, ignoring his wife's admonitions to rise, until it was absolutely necessary to move in order to reach the office in time. He dressed in irritation, scolding his children, complaining to his wife about the maid, and expressing impatience lest his car be not at the curb when he went out. He drank his coffee standing, and with the last of his toast in his fingers, grabbed his hat, and, kissing his wife absent-mindedly, fled down the porch step. Arrived at the office he spoke a friendly good-morning to each of the stenographers as he passed them, and soon was plunged deep in his work. He smiled pleasantly at his secretary when she appeared with his mail, the letters of commendation and praise for his work on top of the pile.

(*d.*) Desplein was a French sculptor deemed eccentric by his confreres. At times he would attire himself in stately splendor and at others he would appear in careless habiliments, like a Bohemian. Sometimes he rode in a carriage, sometimes he strolled along on foot. In the ordinary routine of his life he was close-fisted, a reflection from the days of his poverty as a student; after dinner, however, or when in the company of friends, he would display a kindly interest in the careers of struggling artists and beg them to accept the accommodation of a few hundred francs as long as they needed it, and without interest. He liked to have people think him religious, and when at court he would let a prayer-book be seen protruding from a pocket, but his comrades knew well that he was a confirmed atheist. This habit, it was believed, was merely a manoeuver to further his chief ambition which was to receive a decoration. He appeared to scorn the talents of men in other walks of life and often declared, in his hatred of politicians, that had he chosen, he could have won as great esteem as a statesman as he had won as a sculptor.

2. Write out four sketches of your own like the above, using people you know, presenting them as you know them, without effort at selecting any one trait. Afterwards rewrite these sketches, developing a selected trait as you have done with the sketches given.

ASSIGNMENT F

Here are a few somewhat more difficult exercises in character analysis. Each of the following outlines of action is taken from a student character story which was defective in its handling of character. Study each one carefully. In each case the specific trait of character which the student was trying to prove dramatically is given, and in each case there was an error in the *logic of the proof.* In the first case, for instance, the trait is given as *love of social activities.* You have only to ask yourself: " Would a man with this trait do as he did? " The question, remember, is not: Is his conduct consistent or possible? It may well be. When the story is to be a character story, and the trait is given, the trait must be followed consistently through out. The trait sets the pattern which must not vary. The outlines might or might not make good stories as they stand; that is not our concern here: we are interested in drill in trait development. The trait here is everything; stick to it. In each case *write out* the error as briefly as possible.

1. Trait: *Love of social activities.*

Charles Van Vrancken, a well known club man of independent means, was for many years well known in social circles. He was a favorite "hostess's friend" and was the "beau" at all débutante parties. Finally old age began to show its ravages: he became gouty, grew weary easily, his jokes lost their flavor, and the "younger generation" began to treat him with veneration rather than warm friendliness. In vain he took courses of health-building and exercise to keep the appearance of youth. Realizing at last that he is now fit company only for doddering old men with whom he can never be happy, he takes passage on an ocean liner saying he is going on a trip around the world. Late one night he slips over the side of the liner and is never heard of again.

2. Trait: *Physical cowardice.*

Tommy Dodd, the son of a western sheriff, is tied to his mother's apron strings. To the disgust of his father, who is the nerviest man and the quickest shooter in the state, Tommy shows no interest in becoming the next sheriff. He spends his time at home digging in the little garden, and going to school for what his father calls "useless book larnin'." As the boy grows of age and his father's strength is waning, a noted criminal escapes from the town jail. The father tries to get his son to help him pursue and capture the bandit. The son refuses. He loves his father, but not his calling. The father pursues the criminal into the woods alone. When the sheriff does not return, his son, alarmed, goes after him. After roaming the woods all night, he comes, as dawn is breaking, upon his father face to face with the bandit. Sheriff and bandit shoot at each other and the sheriff is wounded. As the bandit leaps towards the sheriff to finish the job, Tommy shoots and misses. Tommy then leaps upon the bandit and clubs him to death with the butt of his rifle.

3. Trait: *Unscrupulous love of another man's wife.*

Henry Clegg, a man of moderate means, is in love with Martha Sanders, wife of John Sanders. Clegg, desperate at his failure to persuade Mrs. Sanders to leave her husband, lures her husband into risking all his money in a wildcat oil speculation. The oil enterprise fails and Sanders loses all his money. Meanwhile Clegg, who has been lame all his life, learns of a surgeon who can perform an operation which will cure him. The operation necessitates a long stay in Europe, and will be exceedingly expensive. As he is about to leave, feeling sure Mrs. Sanders will follow him, Mrs. Sanders comes to his home and pleads with him to give her husband a loan which will put him on his feet again. She asks him to do it "on account of his love for her," and, after a bitter struggle with himself, he lends Mr. Sanders the money he had intended to spend on his operation, and remains home, still lame, still without the woman he loves.

4. Trait: *Spineless timidity.*

Harold Lane was afraid of his companions while at school, afraid of failing in his lessons, afraid to call his soul his own. He fell in love with Fanny Willets but she would never have discovered it had she not done the proposing herself. They were married and a friend of Harold's secured him a job in a bank. His salary was not enough to support his family which in time included two babies. His wife was certain he would get a raise if he would only ask for it, but he was afraid he'd get "thrown out" if he tried it. A quarrel arose over the issue, until one day Harold's mother-in-law arrived and persuaded her daughter to leave her husband unless he at least asked for a raise. After considering the matter for three days, Harold walked into the office of the president of the bank and told him "to go to the devil." The president was so impressed by Harold's "backbone" that he immediately gave him a substantial raise.

5. Trait: *Love for a young woman.*

Donald was in love with Lucy and wanted to marry her. Lucy's papa, who was a bit quixotic, hated to lose his daughter of whom he was very fond. One evening when Donald arrived in his motor at the big house where his lady fair lived, he was given a note from papa saying that he had driven off for their mountain shooting lodge with Lucy. If Donald could overtake them, he wrote, he could marry Lucy: if he didn't, he couldn't have her. Donald stepped on the gas and sped for the mountains. Before he had driven ten miles he overtook papa and daughter. Papa capitulated, adding: "One of my cylinders isn't working."

6. Trait: *A woman's honor.*

Miss Atherton, a struggling young actress, falls in love with a very wealthy man, only to discover that he is already married. Resolved to hold fast to her ideals of womanly honor she refuses to have anything more to do with him. He then sends her a check for $25,000 with a note saying: "As long as I am married, you will never hear from me again. I appreciate your stand; you are right. As a friend, however, let me help you in your fine struggle for success in your art. I do and shall love you always." She cashes the check, invests the money in needed gowns and dramatic lessons, and wins success. Once a year she dines with her benefactor and lets him kiss her once as he says good-bye.

7. Trait: *Vanity.*

In a negro literary club a dispute arose between Susie, the belle of the colored district, and Mandy Hanks, the school teacher. Susie was very vain of her "good looks" which were indeed no better than those possessed by several of the colored ladies, but Susie "wore the clothes"—and dresses whose color could be seen for miles. Mandy criticized Susie's taste in dress. Susie accused Mandy of flirting with the negro parson. The disputants approached each other, gesticulating, talking at the same time, and were about to substitute blows for arguments, when the door opened and a policeman thrust his head in, saying: "Hey, what's goin' on here?" Silence fell over the meeting which was finally broken by the president's voice: "Now, ladies, as you wuz sayin' about this here Shakespeare pusson—"

8. Trait: *Wife's devotion to husband.*

Louise, a girl brought up in the city and unused to the hardships of farm life, marries John, a farmer, and goes to live with him on his farm. She finds the farm life too hard for her and persuades John to leave his old father to take care of the farm, and go to the city with her to live. After a year or so in the city John learns that his old father is weakening rapidly. He is conscience-stricken, feels that his duty is to return to the farm, and he goes, leaving Louise to struggle between a desire to remain in the city where she can live with her parents and be comfortable, or return with her husband to the hardships of the farm. Soon after reaching the farm, John sells out his interest in the town dairy, and with the proceeds outfits his farm with modern electrical equipment and comforts which will make his wife's tasks much easier. Louise joins him.

9. Trait: *Unselfish devotion to a teacher.*

Frank and Edith in their last year at college are both ardent admirers of Professor Mallin of the history department. Frank loves Edith deeply and wants her to marry him, but *Edith does not love Frank and Frank knows it.* Professor Mallin loves Edith and she reciprocates his love. Professor Mallin proposes marriage but Edith cannot accept because she had already promised to marry Frank. She asks Frank to release her. Frank, because of his unselfish devotion to Professor Mallin, relinquishes claim on Edith, who marries Professor Mallin.

10. Trait: *Woman's determination to get what she wants.*

Elizabeth Delancy loved Eton Hall but married Bion Pike, a shrewd farmer, and remained a dutiful wife to him. Hall, being a timid man, never proposed. His home and farm in time became mortgaged to Bion Pike. Bion Pike dies and Hall comes timidly to the Pike home to entreat Mrs. Pike to give him an extension on his mortgage as he is struggling hard to make a living. He still loves Mrs. Pike, but knows he is too timid to tell her. To his surprise Mrs. Pike hands him a deed to his

farm and home made out to him for one dollar and " other considerations." Hall is too obtuse to see the point. He asks what the " other considerations " are. Mrs. Pike says that she herself is one of the other considerations. Hall accepts and they are married.

ASSIGNMENT G.

We will at this point make certain that our analysis of the defects in the plot outlines of Assignment F were accurate by using them in replotting. You are to rewrite each of the above ten plots so that each contains a dramatic " supreme proof " of the trait given. This will tax your inventiveness and your sense of logic. Take, for example, Van Vrancken, the superannuated dance party mascot in No. 1: If his trait is love of social activities, he will not demonstrate his desire for such things by killing himself. A man, no matter how old, who kills himself *wants to die,* not to dance with fancy young ladies. If he wants to dance, he dances, or tries to. Such is the logic of the case. Now what *should* he do? Well, if he wishes to dance, let him dance and keep it up, *keep it up* (sticking to the trait), until — if he must die — he drops dead. There is nothing especially remarkable or thrilling about such an ending, but it *is* true to trait, *is* a supreme proof of the trait, and, as such, is all that is required here. Such manipulations develop skill in dramatic invention.

ASSIGNMENT H.

Most students find it easier to " think up things " in building character stories than in testing the validity of these things for the plot in hand. They are, in other words, better at invention than at reasoning. This is not to be wondered at. The difficulty in reasoning results not because of weak intellects but because of the unfamiliar and elusive nature of the materials handled. Also the student often exalts " truth to life " (meaning truth as *he* has *happened* to see it in a particular instance) above dramatic strength. The best remedy for these tendencies is for the student to study the relentless logic of character development in the stories of the greatest masters and to practice much with this type of reasoning, using as far as possible materials of his own. We will try to do this now in this and the succeeding assignment.

This assignment presents a number of crucial situations taken from short stories by writers acknowledged to be masters of the craft. Enough of the action is given to display clearly the trait of character involved and the dramatic proof with which it is presented. There may be, of course, two or more main characters. Please study these outlines carefully for the logic of the character delineation. Your interest in the task will be increased if you will read the full text of such of the stories as are available in your library, though this is not absolutely necessary. In each instance write out briefly the logic of the character development. The first example, for instance, can be worked out in this way:

What is the main character trait? Miraz's love for his wife and daughter. What is the final action? He deliberately hastens his own death. How does this "test" his trait? Thus: Miraz in the crucial situation can do one of two things, either use up his savings for a trip to southern France and so prolong his life but bring his family to destitution, or hasten his death and so leave his family enough to live on comfortably. He chooses to die quickly. This proves (here is your syllogism) that he cares more for the comfort of his loved ones than for his own life; there is nothing more precious than life for him *to* give up; therefore (Q. E. D.) his love of his family is supreme.

1. *A Voluntary Death,* by Francois Coppée, in *Ten Tales* by Francois Coppée, Harper's.

Miraz, a writer, after several years of bitter struggle, succeeds in saving enough money to give him an income sufficient to support his family the rest of their lives, when he contracts an incurable, lingering disease which makes it impossible for him to work. His wife can do nothing to increase the family's resources. Doctor's fees begin to eat into the little capital with alarming rapidity. He is told by the doctor that if he removes to sunny southern France his life will be prolonged. He knows that if he does this he will deplete his savings, and, at his death, leave his family destitute. He therefore commits rash imprudences which bring his death speedily.

2. *Brooksmith* by Henry James, in *The Lesson of the Master and Other Stories,* Scribner's.

Brooksmith, as the butler of Mr. Oliver Offord, had intellectual opportunities. The conversation of Mr. Offord's salon was brilliant. Brooksmith, unusually sensitive to the social atmosphere, basked in the witty talk. On Mr. Offord's death, he received a very small sum — not enough to set him up in any business, and he was obliged to find another situation. He found a place finally with a very common-place, banal, well-fed household, but he left very soon. After a time of drifting about from one house to another, he became one of the servants who "go out," having no permanent employment. At last, unable to endure the vulgarity and lack of intellectual society, he "disappeared."

3. *He Who Wore a Husk,* by Anton Chekhov, in *The Steppe,* Stokes.

Bielikov was a teacher of Greek. His peculiarity was that he wanted everything wrapped up, his feet in goloshes, his carriage curtains closed tight when he rode, his ideas safely wrapped up with authority. He was comfortable only in a situation graced by the approval of antiquity. A girl, the sister of one of his colleagues, came to the town to live. He liked her, and people began to talk of their marriage. One day, however, he saw her and her brother start off on their bicycles. He was horrified, and later in the day went to the brother to protest at such unseemly behavior, saying as he was about to leave after the interview that he would have to report the outrage to the authorities. The brother threw him downstairs, and just as he was tumbling down, the girl came in, saw his predicament, and laughed aloud. He went home without a word to her. He had been made ridiculous. The whole town would hear of it. He took to his bed, and in a month he was dead.

4. *The Captain's Vices,* by Francois Coppée, in *Ten Tales,* Harpers.

Captain Mercadier, retired on a small pension, betook himself to a little town, where after he secured lodgings, his first concern was to find a convenient café where he might enjoy his favorite vices, tobacco, absinthe and cards. There he became a fixture, until one day, driven from his favorite haunt by the market-day crowds, he saw a little goose girl, with a wooden leg, driving her geese past his lodgings. There was nothing paternal in his bachelor heart, but that pathetic little wooden leg touched the soldier. He found that she was an orphan, in service to his landlady. He decided that he needed a servant, and hired her. The little girl proved her gratitude by her zeal, and she managed to make his bare room seem homelike. To humor her requests for things to use about the house he gradually, in turn, gave up his absinthe, his cigars; he finally reduced his betting at écarté to the stingiest limits. He was often tempted, but Pierette got what she wanted.

5. *On the Stairs,* by Arthur Morrison, in *Tales of Mean Streets.*

Bob Curtis is very ill. His mother, discussing funerals with a neighbor who is famous in the neighborhood for having given her husband a "'ansome funeral" with plumes and mutes, confesses that she would like mutes, but doubts whether she can afford it unless she gives up the plumes. As they talk on the stairs outside the sick boy's room, the doctor's young assistant comes to see the sick man. After a quick look, he comes from the room, and orders a stimulant. The man is sinking, a little port wine will make all the difference. If he can be pulled through the day with a stimulant, he may live. When the old mother mumbles at the expense, he gives her the money — not knowing that his principal had done the same thing the day before. The young doctor goes. The mother does not get the wine. The boy dies. Next morning, Mrs. Curtis tells her neighbor that she will have both mutes and plumes. She can " do it repectable, thank Gawd! "

6. *Once More,* by John Galsworthy, in *A Motley,* Scribner's.

A little flower seller, whose husband, also a flower seller, has left her for the third time, has just seen him on an omnibus with his arm around another woman. The little wife was in rags — she had pawned her suit three weeks before to renew his stock of flowers — and the other woman was plump and attractive. All the next day she rages with jealousy and the desire for revenge. She watches the omnibuses for the pair, and she vaguely plans an affair with some other man just to show him. At midnight, when she is sleeping restlessly, the boy husband comes in, and slumps down before the fire, shivering with cold. She watches him, hating him for making himself so at home, wanting to kill him. He had come back frozen and starved as on the other times when he had gone away. He turned his head, and his asking eyes were like the eyes of her baby. He made an attempt to speak, but he was shivering so that he made only an inarticulate sound — like the sounds the baby made. She pulled his head down on her breast, and with all her strength clutched him to her, trying to warm him with the warmth of her little body.

7. *Uncle Jim and Uncle Billy,* by Bret Harte, in *Stories in Light and Shadow.*

Uncle Jim and Uncle Billy had been partners for six years, working the mine named for them, The Fall and Foster. At the end of the time the mine was still promising no more than at first, their sluice-boxes were falling in decay, and Uncle Jim, having managed to lose to his partner in a game of cards his share of the claim, dug out. Uncle Billy left alone was disconsolate, and to cover his hurt, he made up tales of Uncle Jim's prosperity in San Francisco. Some time later Uncle Billy struck gold. He did not stay to work it, but sold out, and with twenty thousand dollars in his pocket, went to Frisco to find Uncle Jim. He finally located him in a shanty. He had been working as a crossing sweeper, and was very proud of the amount that he had saved from wages and tips. He was rather condescending to Uncle Billy, who after hinting and indirect questioning, learned that Uncle Jim would have cleared out for foreign parts, had Uncle Billy by any chance come with more wealth than he had. That night Uncle Billy gambled away the whole of his twenty thousand except the few hundred to equal Uncle Jim's pile, and next day the two started out equal partners in a wheat ranch.

8. *Moonlight,* by Guy de Maupassant in *The Odd Number,* Harper's.

The Abbé Marignan was a priest, who felt that he understood the purposes of God very thoroughly. He was never satisfied in any situation until he had related it to some divine purpose. He hated women, whose purpose, he was sure, was simply to test the hearts of men in temptation. His young niece was to be a nun. One day to his horror he learned through his housekeeper that the girl was meeting a lover. That evening he determined to spy upon their tryst, his rage at the situation being so intense that as he was going out he broke the back of a chair with his heavy stick. On the threshold he paused. The world was clothed in ineffable beauty. He viewed the familiar scene under the glory of the moonlight. An unwonted feeling of tenderness and doubt assailed him. Why had God made all this? There was no answer in the Abbe's system of thought. Then he saw the lovers, the man's arm around the waist of the girl, his head bowed to kiss her, and the moonlight seemed created simply to frame them. The priest thought of the great love stories, Ruth and Boaz, the Song of Songs, and the answer to his question came to him: "Perhaps God made nights such as this in order to cast the veil of the ideal over the loves of men." If God did not permit love, why did he visibly encompass it with glory such as this? The priest went softly back to the house, leaving the lovers together.

ASSIGNMENT I

Let us try to produce crucial situations of our own which are just as conclusive in the logic of their character development as are those which we have analyzed in Assignment H. We have the logic of the character pattern well in mind. The task is to keep this same pattern and work it out as far as possible with people you know. You may be able to use some of the characters you developed in Assignment D and in No. 2 of Assignment E, above. Let me show you how you might use the pattern of the first story by Coppée:

You may be acquainted with a man, say, who is an invalid like Miraz of this story. He may, however, have an independent income, or his wife may be supporting him, and he may have no children. No matter. Manipulate the facts freely. Make his disease more serious; make his wife an invalid who can't work; and give him a daughter. Let's suppose he is exiled in Arizona for his health. Their income is so small that they can't afford to live apart; his wife and daughter are with him. We must be unrelenting. The wife is homesick for her own home up north and suffers from the Arizona heat. The daughter is too young to work, and, moreover, gives promise of becoming, with proper training, a great musician. His doctor's fees would pay for her education. If, now, the father is supremely devoted to the happiness of his wife and daughter, he can show it dramatically **by** doing something which hastens his death.

Continue carefully with each of the plots in Assignment H **in** the same way.

ASSIGNMENT J

Let us complete and prepare for writing each of the plot developments you have worked out for Assignment I. With the character trait given and the crucial situation worked out, the remaining tasks should not be difficult. Prepare each finished plot in schematic outline as shown on page 244, then test it out carefully to see that it is consistent and convincing. If there are any weaknesses they will be immediately visible. Examine again the defective schematic outlines on pages 253 and 254.

ASSIGNMENT K

The finished plots prepared for Assignment J may now be used for writing up full-length stories. Select the two or three which most interest you and write them out, letting them run as long as you feel necessary to produce the greatest possible emotional effect. Before beginning the writing prepare a "bald report" of the action like that given on page 232. This will be easier to follow than the schematic outline.

ASSIGNMENT L

To plot and write character stories which are entirely your own and which may be submitted for publication, you have only to follow the processes outlined in the assignments for this chapter. These processes are:

(a) Write out in about 500 words character sketches of ten people you know who interest you most as literary material.

(b) Select from these the three which lend themselves best to development of a single, dominant character trait.

(c) Plot these three, giving each trait a supreme proof. Prepare schematic outlines of each one.

(d) Prepare bald reports of each one.

(e) Write them out full length one by one.

CHAPTER SIX

THE COMPLICATION STORY

THE STORY THAT FEATURES PREDICAMENTS

The normal reader is in a receptive mood. He is prepared, without consciousness of the fact, to have his emotions stirred by intelligent exaggeration. — HARTLEY DAVIS.

Plotting the complication story is a more difficult and at the same time a more fascinating task, than plotting a character story. It is more difficult because it often necessitates inventing backwards. With most character stories the writer has his character in mind, and builds his events up in chronological order, starting at the beginning of the story. With most complication story plots, on the other hand, it is necessary to begin with the end of the plot and work backwards to the beginning. In this chapter we shall consider this method of plotting. Again we shall begin with the short story.

1. Definition of Complication Story

Our first concern is to be sure that we understand what a complication story is, especially how it differs in form from the character story which we have just studied. Complication interest, we learned in Chapter Three, is the basis of one of the four fundamental patterns into which all short story material can be classified. Complication interest simply means that the reader would be more interested in some unique or striking event or twist of fate than in development of character, atmosphere, or theme.

*The complication story, then, is a narrative whose single
effect results mainly from the dramatic presentation of
some striking event.*

You will remember how we defined the short story in
Chapter Five — *a dramatic narrative with a single effect.*
From the definition of the complication story in the preceding paragraph you can see how it satisfies both ideals
of the short story.   The central complication, when presented dramatically and with emotional unity, produces
the single effect.   The matter will be clearer if we compare
character and complication stories thus:

	Character story	*Complication story*
Single effect produced by	emphasis on char- acter development;	emphasis on a unique event.
Drama produced by	character trait op- posed by obstacles	no fixed pattern.

Differences between complication and character

The meaning of this little analysis will be made much
clearer by taking concrete material.   Let us once more use
the Russian story material mentioned on page 104.   The
character story, you will remember, depended upon a development of the Russian professor's main trait which was
his zeal for scientific work.   The crucial situation was his
facing the alternative of either remaining amid the dangers
of the desert to pursue his work, or leaving his work and
returning to safety.   He remained in the desert, thus " proving " his character trait.   This same material we used to
illustrate a complication, by having the professor in his
cabin, overturn boxes containing poisonous insects which
escape and threaten his life.   The crucial situation was that
the professor faced death if he remained, and also if he
tried to get out.   The outcome, we will say, is that he
fights his way safely out of the cabin.   Let us now
restate the differences between single effect and drama in
the cases of the character and complication stories.

	Character story	*Complication story*
Single effect produced by	emphasizing trait of zeal for scientific work	emphasizing peculiar predicament resulting from loosing insects
Drama produced by	conflict between scientific zeal and dangers of desert	conflict between professor's desire to escape and the insects that opposed his escape.

Two important revelations stand out from these diagrams. One concerns the single effect: In the character story the single effect is produced by emphasis on character; in the complication story the single effect is produced by emphasis on some unique event. Secondly, drama is produced in the character story by the obstacle which opposes the chief trait of the character and in the complication story the dramatic clash varies greatly, depending upon the nature of the crucial situation. (While in some stories drama may seem wanting, the clash, actual or implied, is always present in any impressive narrative, long or short.)

Once again let us illustrate these differences by using the material in one of the most famous of all complication short stories, *The Necklace*, by Maupassant. The main trait of Madame Loisel, the chief actor, is honesty or a sense of honor which makes her work ten years to pay back the money she had to borrow to replace a necklace she had borrowed to attend an official ball. In a character story this trait of honor would be developed in successive conflicts which test and prove the trait, ending in a final episode which would serve *mainly* as a supreme proof of this trait. This pattern of events, we will say, represents *The Necklace* replotted as a character story.

In the real story of *The Necklace* Madame Loisel, you will remember, after drudging ten years to pay back the money borrowed to restore the necklace, discovers that whereas she restored a diamond necklace, the one she lost was of paste and was worth only a few cents! Now this episode of *discovering the facts* not only does not furnish a supreme proof of the trait of honesty; it has no *necessary* connection with it. Madame Loisel might have been *dishonest* but endowed at the same time with a sensitive conscience. The latter trait might have caused her distress greater even than that depicted in the real story of physical drudgery and frustration of life aims; she might have lived in luxury but with gnawing remorse. The shock of discovering the real nature of the lost necklace would be equal to that in the real story. In this way we could produce much the same effect of the final episode with a different trait. From this it is surely clear that the interest in the story is in the *twist of events* rather than in character.

Analysis of " The Necklace "

Observe, secondly, how drama is handled by the two versions of *The Necklace*. In the character story the conflict is simply Desire A (main character trait of honesty) opposed by Obstacle B (other desires, say; her health, her husband) resulting in the effect of admiration for her heroic moral standards. In the real story the conflict is again Desire A (honesty) opposed by Obstacle B (love of refinement and luxury) and at the end of the story the surprising discovery that the struggle itself was unnecessary produces an effect of tragic irony. The question of whether drama terminated by an " accident " of this nature can be sound is answered later on page 290. Enough here to see that in the character story the drama is used to intensify the picture of a character, and in the complication is used to intensify the picture of a peculiar event.

We can now compare these two ways of using the material in this story as follows:

	Character story	*Complication story*
Single effect produced by	emphasis on trait of honesty	emphasis on ironic turn as a conclusion of character's struggle
Drama produced by	conflict between honesty and other traits	conflict between honesty and other traits

The differences between character and complication stories are not always sharply marked. The development of a character type is so well marked in some complication stories and the crucial situation in some character stories in itself so interesting that each tends to secure its effects by equal emphasis on both character and complication; and there is no reason why they should not do so. Where character and complication *are* equally emphasized we have, of course, a character-complication, or two-phase story. This and other multi-phase story types we shall study in the next chapter. In the interest of discovering method in plotting we shall here confine our attention to pure complication stories.

The pure complication story

The above examples of complication stories presented fairly strong developments of character. There is a much purer type of complication story which is almost devoid of character interest. Such a story type is bound to be weak in reflective delay; in most cases indeed it has no reflective delay at all. It is in reality but an expanded anecdote. A notable example published in France some years ago effected a reform in church practice. Here is an outline of the story:

A certain Bishop was one of the leading figures in a provincial French town. He was much loved by everybody. On the occasion of the thirtieth anniversary of his taking office he gave a public celebration to all the townspeople.

His guests gathered amid bright lights, decorations and much hilarity and good feeling, in his large reception hall. The Bishop rose on a platform, and, beaming upon his friends, welcomed them with a brief speech. He began by saying that his career among them had been most fascinating and full of interesting events, adding that the very first man who appeared before him in the confessional, pleaded guilty of three adulteries and a murder.

The instant after he made this statement, a Mr. A., the leading merchant and banker of the town, entered, having been detained at his office. Mr. A. was also a very much respected citizen, standing high in the community, a pillar of the church of which the Bishop was the head. Mr. A. and the Bishop were fast friends, and smiled at each other with friendly good-will.

The Bishop asked Mr. A. to step to the platform. As Mr. A. shook hands warmly with the Bishop, he announced so all could hear: " Do you know, Bishop, I have a special interest in this anniversary, inasmuch as I was the first to come to your confessional."

Here we see a minimum of character interest and a pronounced complication interest. Obviously the Bishop could be almost any kind of a churchman and Mr. A. need be only a man highly respected in the community to keep the maximum effect of the story. The only drama in the story takes place after it ends, thus making the surprise-ending story's characteristically strong appeal to the imagination.

An interesting experiment was conducted a few years ago by *Life* magazine to determine how short a narrative could be and still qualify as a short story. Practically all the stories published featured pure complications. The close relation between them and the anecdote was evident. Here, for instance, is one of them which, like the story of the Bishop and the merchant, is, because of its low character interest, more an anecdote than a short story:

WHAT THE VANDALS LEAVE

By HERBERT RILEY HOWE, from *Short Stories from Life.*

The war was over and he was back in his native city that had been retaken from the Vandals. He was walking rapidly through a dimly lit quarter. A woman touched his arm and accosted him with fuddled accents.

" Where are you going, M'sieu? With me? hein? "

He laughed.

" No, not with you, old girl. I'm going to find my sweetheart."

He looked down at her. They were near a street lamp. She screamed. He seized her by the shoulders and dragged her closer to the light. His fingers dug her flesh, and his eyes gleamed.

" Joan! " he gasped.

The prize-winning story in this collection was not achieved with any such brevity. It combined both strong character and complication interest. A summary of the plot of this story follows:

A boy is called upon to give his blood in a transfusion operation to save the life of his sister. He is obviously terrified but finally consents. Pale and weak, after the ordeal, he looks up at the surgeon and asks: "Say, Doc, how soon do I croak?" It was then revealed that the lad during the entire operation had supposed that he was giving his life. Assistants in their haste had forgotten to explain the nature of the operation!

2. Varieties of Complication Stories

The complications usable in the complication type of story are of course of infinite variety. They may produce detective stories, such as the Sherlock Holmes series, or mystery stories like Poe's *Gold Bug,* in which the reader is fascinated by the peculiar *ways* in which the treasure is hidden in the sand and finally found. They may produce horror stories such as the famous plot idea, used by Balzac, Poe, and many other writers, of sealing an enemy alive in the wall of a house and allowing him to remain there until he dies. A variation of this type of horror complication is found in Maupassant's story, *La Mere Sauvage,* wherein a mother who has lost her son in the war, lures several soldiers on the enemy's side to her home, locks them in, sets fire to the house, and burns them alive.

The use of sharp complications as a means of producing light comedy effects is found in most of the stories of O. Henry. A characteristic example is the prank of fate recorded in his *The Gifts of the Magi.* The complication in this case is that a husband and wife each give the other a gift bought by sacrificing the one thing needed to make the gift of the other usable. The wife cuts off her hair to give her husband a watch chain, while her husband sells his watch to buy his wife some hair combs! To achieve a complication as sharp and startling as this it was inevitable that character values be sacrificed; no postulation of character traits, in other words, would give the above action even a glimmer of inevitability. Having thus lost character values, the author, at the end of the story, attempted in vain to restore them by the following final lines:

And here I have lamely related to you the uneventful chronicle of two foolish children in a flat who most unwisely sacrificed for each other the greatest treasures of their house. But in a last word to the wise of these days let it be said that of all who give gifts these two were the wisest. Of all who give and receive gifts, such as they are wisest. Everywhere they are wisest. They are the magi.

I hope I have made clear now the distinctions between the character and the complication story. Unless you see clearly upon what the single effect and the drama of the complication story depend, you will scarcely grasp the method of finishing complication story plots which I shall now set forth.

3. Plotting the Complication Story

Once again let us fall back upon actual experience for our first illustration of method. Let me trace through the various stages through which I passed one of my own story ideas up to the writing of the published story. I do this merely in order that you may know what I mean by method. I shall begin at the very beginning.

Talking one day with a friend during the first year of the great war I was interested to hear him say that a friend of his had bought a hat which fitted him nicely at first, but which after a few days proved to be much too large. It turned out that the man had received a bump where the hat band touched. When the bump receded, the hat no longer fitted him.

This scrap promptly went into my plot notebook. A few days later an editor, knowing that I had been in

Russia, asked me to do him a Russian story. I went over my notes and hit upon this complication. It seemed unusual enough to be worth a try.

In this way I got my story idea. Then I began the actual plotting. This followed rather unconsciously the three general steps which we used in plotting the character story. We shall use them again here. Thus:

> 1. *Analyzing the idea for*
>   a. single effect
>   b. drama
>   c. editorial considerations.
> 2. *Stating the problem*
> 3. *Manipulation.*

In plotting this first complication story I shall include the handling of the editorial problem since it was quite specific.

The first step

I. *Analysis:* What is the nature of our story idea? It obviously suggests a complication more than it suggests character or theme or atmosphere. I thus decided at once that my single effect would strongly stress a complication. There is no indication of dramatic struggle: it is just a strange and bizarre idea. I found that I could not decide what the exact emotion of my single effect would be until I had found some way to harmonize the story idea with what I knew about life in Russia, and with what the editor would probably like. The idea itself, in other words, would not be acceptable until I could see more to it than what my friend told me. I therefore played with the idea as a queer complication.

Soon I hit upon the idea of a bump on a man's head making him taller than he actually was. What significance might this additional height have? Since the hectic days of mobilization in Europe were just over, the idea of a man's being drafted because of the slight additional height struck me. Immediately I thought of the terror which military life had for the Russian peasant under the old régime. During my stay in Russia I had seen and heard a good deal of this aversion and the reasons for it. Since we were not yet in the war ourselves, the chances of selling an anti-militaristic story were good. This preliminary manipulation made me think more of my idea and I decided to continue with it.

Our analysis calls first for speculation as to a single effect. I had already decided that I could give a picture of a Russian peasant being drafted in spite of himself. The effect here obviously would be tragic. In order to picture the inevitableness of military service in Russia, I saw at once that tragic irony would be more effective than pure tragedy. The idea of being drafted in spite of every effort to avoid the draft was in itself a sufficiently ironic thought. My single effect therefore was tragic irony. My editorial factor was also settled. I was satisfied that an ironic picture of a Russian being forcibly drafted would be acceptable to the editor.

The second step

The second point in my analysis, the dramatic struggle, I was still uncertain about. I found this problem could not be immediately solved. Knowing, however, that dramatic struggle is generally less important in a complication than in a character story, I decided to let this factor decide itself after I had launched into my final manipulation. With these things done, I was now ready to:

II. *State the problem:* Our known and unknown factors now are:

> *Single effect:* ironic tragedy of hero's being drafted by reason of a bump on his head;
>
> *Drama:* unknown.
>
> *Editorial:* Single effect, as above, deemed adequate to purpose.

Our chief problem obviously is to invent the dramatic action. We are also as yet without any idea of the main character, how the extraordinary bump came to be administered, or how the whole disaster ended. Because of the nature of this problem we are going to find it necessary to plot backwards. Just why this is necessary you can see from the following diagram:

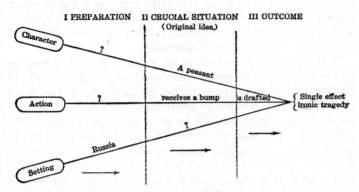

PLOTTING BACKWARD: THE MISSING LINKS.

This diagram divides the development of the story into three parts: preparation, crucial situation, and outcome. The stream of the narrative is conceived as flowing from left to right. The width between the lines at the opening represents the want of close relationship among character, action and setting. As the story progresses this relationship becomes closer and closer until the climax is reached. Since our climax is the inflicting of the bump, we know that this falls at the end of the crucial situation. Our plotting problem, then, is to begin with the second and third parts, which are given, and work out the first. This brings us to our third task:

The final step

3. *Manipulation:* Filling in the gaps is merely a matter of a little invention conducted under rather rigid logical control. Fortunately there is nothing mysterious about logic; it is merely the mechanics of clear reasoning. By way of premise we must hold firmly in mind what we already know: The main character receives a bump which causes him to be drafted; the circumstance must produce a single effect of ironic tragedy. This we know and must remember. Now for our character:

If the peasant is mobilized by a bump in such a way as to produce ironic tragedy, what *must* be his character? If he is depicted as a sympathetic, likable person, the effect of having him suddenly condemned to years of terrible servitude in the army will be pure tragedy, tragedy without relief. We wish the relief of irony; there must be, in other words, something amusing about the fate that befalls this peasant; he must get what he deserves. *If* he met a cruel fate and *deserved* it he was inescapably a cruel man himself. Logic. We put this down: the main character is cruel or obnoxious in some way.

Leaving the first line for a moment we take the second one, the line of action. Here we begin with the fact of the bump being received. To fill in part one of this line we must obviously decide *how the bump was received.* Once again we hold before us our single effect as the most important premise: ironic tragedy. We also know that he is an obnoxious person. How can the bump be brought about in a way to give the reader ironic amusement? The bump can't be a *pure* accident as that would be undramatic. We have as yet no other character to whom we might give the rôle of delivering the needed blow.

We return to our main character again: suppose he were *himself* to cause the bump? How? Look at his trait — cruelty. *What* is the cruelest thing he could do before the drafting? Surely, torture his comrades, who knew that they would be taken, by taunts, threats, defiance. Could not the bump be received *as a more or less direct result* of taunts of this sort? Why not? He actually, in his delirious triumph, strikes them with his fists and in one of his wild lunges slips, falls, and strikes his head on the stove, thus producing the bump.

This provides us with preparatory action which satisfies the single effect and it also gives us a more exact idea of the character of our peasant. To make action such as the above credible we shall have to make him a bully, a cruel, obnoxious bully, and we accordingly modify the first part of the first line.

The third line concerns the setting and is easily handled. The question with settings always is: Can they be so used that they will serve a greater utility than merely being a place where the action occurs; can they, in other words, be integrated with and so intensify either the character or action or both? [1]

An intimate knowledge of a setting is always required to solve this problem realistically. In this case I found in my travel notebooks data about the " enervating life-lessness of the air, the languor of clouds and water which accord with the sad faces, measured speech and heavy gestures of the peasants — all reflecting the helpless fatalism of the lives of these people." I decided to use this material in my opening to sound the fatalistic mood of the story and to give the " feel " of the characters of the people. The setting in the crucial situation would be the crudely decorated, hot interior of a cabin where the fight took place and a flag-bedecked riverside where the young men were rounded up for the training camps.

[1] For a thorough exposition of the principles and practice of intensification through integration see pages 92 to 216, in *The Art and Business of Story Writing*, by Walter B. Pitkin. (Macmillan).

Complete plot analyzed

We are now ready to fill in the vacant spaces in our diagram as follows:

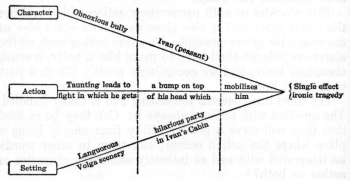

I PREPARATION II CRUCIAL SITUATION III OUTCOME

"MOBILIZING IVAN": FINISHED PLOT.

With this outline before us we can express the whole plot in the form of a schematic outline such as was used in Chapter Five. We therefore write it out again as follows:

Schematic Outline

A. *Type of story:* Complication
B. *Effect to be produced:* Ironic tragedy
C. *Complication idea:* Bump on head increases height enough to mobilize a man.

1. *Initial Complication:* Ivan, a Russian peasant, expecting to be freed from the draft on account of his short stature, makes life miserable for everybody else by reason of his vindictive rejoicing.
2. *Main Character:* Ivan Kuldoon
3. *Main Character Trait:* Cruel, obnoxious bluster.
4. *Crucial Situation:* Ivan, in the course of his spiteful and cruel celebration of his triumph on the eve of the draft, works himself into such a pitch that he slips and falls in his own house, striking himself on the top of the head, and so creating a bump.

5. Outcome: Ivan, when dragged before the recruiting officers, is dumbfounded to find that he will be forced to serve his eight years along with the other " cattle."

This schematic outline shows us that the plot " hangs together." All its essential factors are there. Note that C has become " complication idea " instead of " conflict " as with the character story. Before actually writing out our first full-length draft we can profit much by having a more definite idea of just where the story will begin, and how the events will follow one after the other. We therefore write out the following:

Bald Report

MOBILIZING IVAN

The Russian peasant under the old régime found the hated years of military service inevitable. He could not escape it in spite of all his tragic efforts at self-mutilation. Fate itself seemed to play into the hands of the military authorities. An instance of this occurred in the Province of Kostroma.

A young peasant named Ivan Kuldoon, learning that he was a half inch too short to be drafted, bullied and tormented his fellows because of their approaching sufferings. An easy life lay before him. The prettiest girl in the village, who had intended to marry Yakov, was given to Ivan by the village matchmaker. Food, leisure, romance, everything was coming his way.

Ivan finally gave a celebration, and during his hilarious rejoicing he sang, drank, danced, and fought, until finally, aiming a blow at Yakov, he slipped on the beer-splashed edge of a table and struck his head on the corner of a stone oven.

The next morning when the young men were dragged into the recruiting shed, Ivan, to his amazement and terror, was among them. In spite of his hysterical protestations, he was measured and it was discovered that his height was just sufficient to send him into the Czar's army for eight years' hard and ruthless service.

This bald report was used as a writing outline and lay before me on one sheet of paper when the first draft of the story was written. Brief as it is it contains all the story except its " soul." This latter can never be in any outline; the full length writing alone can evoke it.

Outcome legitimate coincidence

The student will perhaps detect a weak link in the chain of logic in the above plot outline, namely, the accidental nature of the bump itself. Ivan's fighting was, let us say, inevitable enough once given his character trait of bullying; but it was not equally inevitable that he would be injured in that particular part of his anatomy. Here we hit upon a distinctive feature of the pronounced complication story.

As explained in Section B of the Appendix, the character story alone calls for explicit connection between character and action; he is rash who would demand inevitability in all types of stories. It is true that any story whose difficulties are solved by accidents is, as explained in the same section, weak in drama; but *there are types of stories which make little or no use of drama for their effects.* The surprise-ending complication story is of this class. In its solution Fate often plays a leading rôle; and this is precisely its purpose, to portray a weird prank of fate.

Fate is, of course, a lady — three ladies, in fact — whose purposes are sealed to us; but we have nevertheless certain beliefs or emotions about her and her ways and these beliefs bolster the credibility of an ironic surprise-ending story. The mood in which I tried to write the story of the Russian peasant was that of impending fate hanging over his head. The opening sentence was: " ' One may sometimes cheat a Jew,' say the peasants of Kostroma, ' but one can never escape being a soldier.' " The sardonic grin of Fate which pursued the Bishop in the French story is one which we have all seen or imagined in our own social experiences. The Fate in Maupassant's story of the necklace is the cruel monster which many of us feel lurks among us, ready to fall upon the most unoffending with devastating effect. From this interpretation of the prank-of-Fate story we might indeed argue that it features the character of Fate herself and that thus these accidental endings are " in character."

Here is another way to look at the same problem: The literary artist's purpose, as we have already learned, is not so much to record the "truth about life" as it is to give *impressive pictures* of life. These pictures must be composed of action showing the interaction between character and events. Now in the character story the impressive thing was the manner in which the moral qualities of certain individuals worked themselves out logically and rather inevitably through definitely related events to either a triumphant (happy ending) or a disastrous (tragic) close.

In the ironic complication story, like the one we have just plotted, character and events, as far as the climax is concerned, are not logically or inevitably related; we jump to the opposite extreme; the events are a striking frustration or *negation* of the character's trait. Such frustrations are, quite possibly, "true to life," but they are more than this; they also fulfill our artistic ideal. They are *impressive pictures*. So far as logic of character is concerned there are two artistic handlings: one, where the character works itself out logically, and another where the character is strikingly frustrated.

The one plot pattern that is *not* impressive is that where no relation between character and events, actual or imagined, can be discovered; such happenings we call " coincidences " or " accidents "; they are invariably undramatic, never ironic, and are always to be avoided. They are fully illustrated and explained in Section E of the Appendix, under the headings " The Mistake Plot " and " Stories Solved by Coincidence," and the " True to Life " Fallacy.

4. Plotting Irvin Cobb's " The Belled Buzzard "

With very few exceptions, the plotting of a complication story begins with the complication idea, even as the plot-

ting of the character story generally begins with a fairly
definite idea of character. As a test of this fact I have
selected Mr. Irvin S. Cobb's *The Belled Buzzard,* which
is probably the best known pure complication story that
has appeared in an American magazine in recent years.
Printed originally in *The Saturday Evening Post,* it can
also be found in the collection of Mr. Cobb's stories published under the title, *The Escape of Mr. Trimm.* Mr.
Cobb has kindly furnished me with a statement of the
origin of this story. He says:

"It will not require many words for me to give you the genesis of my story: *The Belled Buzzard.*

"One morning I was returning in a motor-boat to my father-
in-law's summer cottage on Tybee Island, Georgia, after a fishing
trip to the mouth of the Savannah River. On a sand-pit a
flock of buzzards fed on a dead shark. The sight of them, with
their ungainly, flopping movements, their naked heads and their
unwholesome contours, set me to thinking. My mind went
back to the stories I had heard in a country newspaper-office in
Kentucky of that hardy annual of rural correspondents, the
belled buzzard. To myself I said that here a man might find
material for a short story.

"That same day I got the notion for my beginning and picked
on a name and a personality for my principal character. The
following day, I think it was, my climax came to me, all in a
flash.

"I was busied for the moment with other work but when I
returned North, a fortnight later, and went up to the Adiron-
dacks, I sat down and wrote the yarn in about four days of
fairly steady grinding. The *Post* printed it and it became perhaps the best known of all my serious stories."

I am going to trust to Mr. Cobb's good nature in permitting me to expand his brief outline into a more detailed
account of the technical principles which might possibly
have been followed by a writer less skilled, who could not,
like him, telescope the preliminaries, but must work out
the same process with more conscious deliberation.

Analysis of plot idea

From the above statement we see that the initial inspiration of the story was again essentially a complication idea, which took shape in the author's mind somewhat as follows:

> Buzzards hover about and devour dead bodies. Strange, grue-some habit. They locate carrion. That old story about the buzzard with the cowbell tied around his neck. Suppose that old bird should go clanking over the body of a murdered man and somehow identify the criminal?

Applying the tests previously employed, what have we here? First our analysis. The type of story is obvious — it has a strong complication interest. The single effect — obviously it will be the effect of seeing a guilty man trying to conceal his guilt but finally frustrated by the queer habit and the inexorable tonking of the bell in the sky — something tragic about that, something ironic. The effect then will be tragic irony. (There were, undoubtedly, other emotions aroused by the spectacle of the carrion birds, before this complication was arrived at, but they were soon fused into the striking effect promised by this happy inspiration.) As for the drama: that also is defi-nitely hinted at; the guilty man will naturally struggle to avoid detection; the conflict will thus be between his desire to escape detection and the fateful proclamation of the ominous bird.

Stating the problem

With the above data in hand it is easy to state the remaining problems for finishing the plot. They are as follows: What must be the character and special status of the murderer? What is the outcome of the story, the exact manner in which the criminal is to be discovered? The crucial situation evidently will be the finding of the

body. The first problem then is to plot backwards, deciding what kind of a man the murderer must be in order
to act consistently in this crucial situation. The second
calls for plotting forwards to the end of the story. From
Mr. Cobb's statement we see that he plotted backwards
first, deciding upon the " personality " of his hero soon
after hitting upon the crucial situation. The outcome, or
" climax," as he calls it, the finest inspiration in *The Belled
Buzzard*, and the supreme ironic stroke, required further
meditation and " arrived " only on the day following.

By what steps, already suggested in this chapter, might
a writer have dealt with this problem?

Final manipulation

First the character trait of the hero: in our analysis
we stated that the dramatic struggle would be produced
by the murderer's " desire to escape detection." This desire determines in general his main trait. Can we say
anything more specifically about it, having in mind our
single effect of tragic irony? The ending will be more
ironic certainly if, following our interpretation of character in complication stories, we make the frustration of
his desires as *striking* as possible. It would *not* be especially striking if we accept the obvious use of the belled
buzzard and have him by his clanking appendage lead
the police to the dead body after which we detect the
guilty man by some ordinary story-book sleuthing. If we
did this, we would have used the belled buzzard as a generating circumstance only; but we want to get him into
the climax.

Obviously the belled buzzard must run down the guilty
man as well as his victim. The thing that draws the evil
bird to the dead man is that he is — dead. The murderer
isn't dead — yet! Since, then, the buzzard has no special
interest in the hero, we must give the hero a special interest in, or susceptibility to, the buzzard and his bell. What

should this be? We are trying to make the frustration of his desire as striking as possible. Suppose we say that the murderer was superstitious; the sound of the bell recalled his crime to him; it aroused his conscience — there, we have it! He killed his man, thinking he could do it deliberately as a necessary thing, and proceed to forget it; then the sight of the buzzards hovering over the swamp where the dead body lay, and later the accusing clangor of the "belled and feathered junkman of the sky" would rouse fears of a supernatural judgment on his deed. His character trait, then, is *morbidly superstitious fear of punishment for murder.*

Then for the outcome: We begin here with the data just arrived at. Our hero struggles in vain against the winged accuser. This is, very sharply now, the dramatic conflict. All that remains is to hold this conflict resolutely in mind, and push it to its most emotional and striking conclusion. The bell must pursue and overwhelm the murderer in some extraordinary fashion. His desire is to escape detection. The most complete frustration of that desire will be to let his superstitious fear of the belled nemesis finally bring him of his own accord to confess the crime.

Right here we face a difficulty in a hard fact of nature: there is a limit to the "pursuing" which the buzzard can do; we must not "nature fake" to make a plot. It is plausible enough that the buzzard would sail about over the guilty man's house, but further than that we can't go. Right away, therefore, we see that, first, we may have to use the *sound* of the bell only in the end, discarding the buzzard, and, secondly, we must at once begin to put the murderer in positions where he would be peculiarly susceptible to the sound of the bell.

Beginning with the second suggestion, we consider possible situations into which we can put him, where the sound of the accusing bell would especially flay his soul. Suppose, for instance, he were brought before the body of the man he killed, and *then* the bell approached — this feels

like an impressive and calamitous end — how can we bring
it about? Well, the body would be found (following the
actions of the buzzards) and there would naturally be an
inquest. Our hero would, perhaps, have to attend. In
what capacity? What would make his suffering most
impressive? Could he not be a justice of the peace, who
in the absence of the coroner, might have to preside at
the meeting?

The hero, then, while presiding over the inquest, collapses and confesses. This, we already know, is the ending. We haven't yet, however, carried out our dramatic
pattern of having his final disintegration occur as a direct
result of the fateful pursuit of the accusing bell. The
bell (keeping rigidly to the conflict) must ring in his ears
as he hears testimony at the inquest. We can say that
the buzzard pursues the justice as he rides to the house
where the inquest is held; we can conceivably say that
the bird sails low over the house once the justice has arrived, but we cannot have it perch on the chimney and
ring the bell down the flue! Yet the bell must ring in his
tortured ears!

We must act on the suggestion arrived at above of using
the sound of the bell, simply, and discarding the buzzard.
The question then is reduced to this: How can we most
easily ring a clangorous cowbell at the inquest? If the
inquest is held at a farmhouse, which is easily possible,
there would most certainly be an old cowbell about the
premises. Granted this, how bring the bell, ringing, into
the house? Who would do such a thing? No sensible
adult person, certainly. A child, though — yes, that is
quite possible — since the story is to be pitched in the
southland, a pickaninny, let us say, has found our old
cowbell, and is using it as a plaything. While the inquest
proceeds, the agonized justice hears the old bell ringing
outside the house; it comes nearer; it enters the hall; it
approaches the door — the guilty man shrieks his confession to rid himself of this pursuing demon and then

The door swung open. In the doorway stood a negro child, barefooted, and naked except for a single garment, eyeing them with serious, rolling eyes — and with all the strength of his two puny arms, proudly but solemnly tolling a small rusty cowbell he had found in the cow yard.

Complete plot analyzed

With our finished plot we can now show by our diagrammatic form how character, action and setting are focused together around the single effect of the complication:

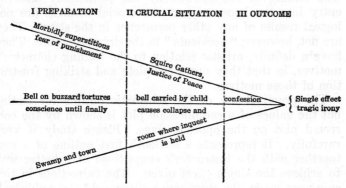

I PREPARATION   II CRUCIAL SITUATION   III OUTCOME

Morbidly superstitious fear of punishment

Squire Gathers, Justice of Peace

Bell on buzzard tortures conscience until finally

bell carried by child causes collapse and

confession

{ Single effect tragic irony

room where inquest is held

Swamp and town

PLOT OF "THE BELLED BUZZARD."

This story we can now present in schematic outline as follows:

THE BELLED BUZZARD

Type of story. Complication.
Single effect: Tragic irony.
Complication idea: A belled buzzard might be used to bring a murderer to justice, by awakening his conscience and superstitious fears.

Initial complication: Squire Gathers kills his wife's lover in a swamp and leaves the body there, thinking it will not be found. Soon afterwards he is disturbed to see buzzards circling over the spot where the body lies.

Main character: Squire Gathers.

Main trait: Fear of some supernatural punishment.

Crucial situation: After an apparently successful effort to escape the avenging tonk-tonk of the buzzard's bell, the Squire, while presiding at the inquest over the dead body, is horrified by hearing the bell entering the house and coming up the corridor towards him.

Outcome: The Squire collapses and confesses his guilt, just as a pickaninny opens the door, and stands watching the men, ringing the while a cowbell which he has found.

Here again we find a want of inevitability in this story. The finding of the cowbell by the pickaninny and his entry into the house at just the crucial moment are not logical results of any other occurrence in the story. They are not, however, " accidents " in the dramatic sense. They have a definite, artistic relation to the leading character's motives, in that they are a complete and striking frustration of those motives.

The practical use of the schematic outline for testing out the values of a complication plot is shown by the corrected plot on the opposite page. Please study it very carefully. It represents a student's first outline of a plot together with the instructor's suggestions of a better way to achieve the single effect given. The corrections in this case were made, the story was written, sold and published.

5. The Surprise Ending Story

This type of story is commonly called the Surprise-ending Story. We can profitably define it here since it always has a strong complication interest. *The Surprise-ending Story is a narrative whose primary interest centers upon a sudden change in some fact of the story at or near the end.* Like the detective and mystery stories it uses artificial suspense; unlike them it uses the surprise for the sake of the surprise. Detective and mystery stories often end with surprises but the interest in the unexpected revelation is incidental: the chief interest is in the nature of the

THE WOLF

Type of story: complication.
Single effect: tragic irony.
Complication idea: man is lured out
of his cabin by cry of wolves, thinking cry
comes from a visitor who often jokingly imi-
tates the cry of wolves.

Initial complication: Jake Mitchel
marries Sally Dorcas and takes her off to live
with him on an island in the Missouri River,
miles from the nearest village. He is middle-
aged, eccentric, and harbors a fear that some
young man will take his young bride away from
him. David Dorcas, Sally's ~~brother~~ *former sweetheart*, is the
only other man ~~he will allow~~ to visit his lit-
tle farm and fishing post on the island. David has the ability to make a cry like the
wolves in mid-winter when they swoop across
the ice of the river and kill the cattle shi- *who comes*
vering in their pens and stalls. When David's
boat is still a quarter of a mile away his
shrill wolf cry can be heard on the island. *Jake drives him away.*

Main character: Jake Mitchel.
Main trait: ~~fear he will lose his wife.~~ *intensify trait to mad jealousy.*

Crucial situation: Winter comes.
David according to a long-standing promise is
expected to visit the island farm on New Year's
Day. Darkness falls with a blinding snowstorm
in the middle of the afternoon, but still David
has not come. Jake and Sally decide he is not
coming. A ranger passing by a few days since
said a wolf pack was on the rampage up the river. Suddenly, however, in the dead of night,
the wolf cry is heard in the little cabin.
Jake, thinking it is David, rushes out into the
night, to meet him. *deaf to his wife's warnings.*
Outcome: Jake is surrounded and overwhelmed by a starving pack of wolves.

*Not an ironic outcome unless
above changes are made. Jake's
error here is stark tragedy. If David
is a lover whom Jake hates — then the
frustration of that hate will be ironic.*

complication, and the suspense and drama with which the search to solve the crime or mystery is conducted.

The surprise-ending story is of two kinds:

A. Complication surprise: this type has a " blind " reflective delay; the real nature of the main complication itself, that is, is not clear until the surprise is sprung; and

B. Character surprise: the revelation at the end of this type of story reinterprets the character.

The complication surprise

A notable example of the first type is the story we have already studied, Maupassant's *The Necklace.*

In this story we have a real reflective delay in Madame Loisel's determination to pay back the borrowed diamond necklace and her ten-year struggle to do so. The fact that at the end of the ten years she learns that the necklace was paste reinterprets the whole nature of this reflective delay. The chief interest of the narrative is not in the drama but in the irony of the uselessness of the struggle.

This first type of surprise-ending plot was favored by O. Henry in many of his whimsical narratives. Such are *A Service of Love,* and *The Romance of a Busy Broker.* In the first of these a husband and wife, each without the other's knowing it, abandon artistic strivings for menial labor, in order to make a living while the other woos a fickle muse. In the second an hysterically busy broker struggles for time to propose to his stenographer only to discover finally that, because of being so busy, he had forgotten that he had married her the night before! In each case the interest is not in the character-revealing struggles but in the comedy of *the way in which* the truth about the struggle was discovered.

The character surprise

The second type of surprise-ending story again flowers at its best among the literary pranks of the same author. Examples are *The Cosmopolite* and *The Proof of the Pudding*. In the former the main character boasts that no man really has any affection for the town of his birth. When a man, suddenly appearing, insults his home town, the main character knocks him down. In the second story two men discuss the actions proper to a husband who suddenly learns that his wife has left him. When suddenly they learn that their wives have decamped, the one who had been protesting that he would speak in commonplace language, burst into a melodramatic cry of protest, while the other, who had been arguing that the situation would normally induce a passionate outburst, merely said, "Say, ain't that a hell of a note?"

These latter stories have a very definite human interest appeal and yet they seem to defy our accepted pattern of character development. Instead of a series of acts exhibiting a given desire ending in an act which is a supreme exhibition of the desire we have apparently a final act which is the exact opposite of what the preceding development would lead us to expect. I say "apparently" for the truth is the author would have us believe that men who show by their crucial acts that they have certain desires or traits, *characteristically in their conversation* profess exactly opposite ones. In this sense the early development of their characters is entirely consistent with what follows. The real trait is their gift for professing to be the opposite of what they really are. The *apparent inconsistency* of their characters is precisely the chief interest of the stories. It is a character interest.

The *dramatic* weakness of this second type of surprise-ending story is obvious: it is weak in not having a character-revealing reflective delay. The actor, faced suddenly with the real situation, acts suddenly, purely on impulse.

The story is a story of impulse and nothing else. The final act may be entirely consistent and true, but, for reasons which we have already reviewed, we may thereby learn nothing at all about the real character of the actor. Who knows what the *Cosmopolite* would do when given an opportunity calmly to face the possible consequences of assault and battery merely because of a chance remark about the town where he was born? And the two men who lost their wives — after they got home and thought things over, have we any means of guessing whether they conducted themselves in accordance with the way they talked before they learned the news, or the way they acted afterwards?

Status of surprise-ending story

All of which brings home to us this fact: all such types of " trick stories," however mordant their irony or convulsing their comedy, can never aspire to the lofty place of honor held by narratives truly and powerfully dramatic. At their best they present a point of view of life by highly artificial means and at their worst they are but jokes made tolerable as stories only by the sheer hilarity with which they are expanded. Because of this fact we witness the vanishing of the vogue of most of O. Henry's writings. Just before his death, be it said to his credit, he was at work on longer and more genuinely dramatic stories.

I hope it is clear that the complication as well as the character story can be plotted effectively by a methodical application of the two general principles of the single effect and drama. Plotting the complication story makes special demands on the writer, such as the cultivation of skill in inventing backwards, which has already been demonstrated. Other special problems arise and we can now touch on the more important of them here.

6. Special Problems of Complication Story

First of all, the writer who wishes to succeed with stories beginning with complications, must make certain that he has on hand a good stock of — complications! He must keep notebooks and carefully store away every idea that comes to him in the nature of a complication. If he does not do this he will find himself some day in need of a good idea and desperate at being unable to hit upon one. Some of the very greatest writers have been guilty of lack of system of this sort — and O. Henry was one of them — and they paid terribly for their unwillingness to go to this trouble. More detailed advice on this topic is given in Section F of the Appendix.

An abundance of story material in interesting episodes of all kinds, is useful in two ways. First, all the material itself produces some suggestions for full plots. Secondly, when once a plot is under way, and the writer strikes a " snag," often it is absolutely impossible, as we have seen, for him to depend on sheer invention or imagination any longer. It is absolutely necessary to turn either to his files or someone else for " inspiration " and a well stocked file in such cases is much more reliable and trustworthy than any person.

Another point: the complication story, though it subordinates character interest, often requires greater knowledge of life in the plotting and writing than does the character story. In most complication stories, the character will have to be invented to fit the action, instead of the action being invented to fit the character. Now it is much easier to invent action than character. If the writer beginning with a character idea, runs out of material, he can, if he is using a prototype from real life, actually go to the character, look him over, perhaps talk with him and get the needed information. Not so with the writer of the complication story. His complication calls for a very specific type of person; he must generally use this type and

no other. The chances are he will not have among his acquaintances any such person. He will therefore be compelled to imagine such a person and do the best he can.

Again: Try to avoid all the old literary plot " chestnuts "
such as a girl who is undecided whether she will marry
the noble but poor lover, or the rich, but wicked suitor;
the young girl who learns to love the hero because he
plunges into a fire and saves his great aunt and her pet
cat; the surgeon tortured by uncertainty whether to save
his rival's life by an operation or let him die and so solve a
triangle; and the wife who refuses to have babies until
unexpectedly left in charge of a nursery!

Another thing: If you are convinced that your idea
itself is a good one, do not despair if the plot is not easily
finished. Any writer will at times run into difficulties
which cannot be solved in a hurry. You must give the
thing time, be willing to sleep over it a few nights. If
after several attempts it does not work out, put it in a
special file labeled " Waiting for Inspiration," and occasionally take these out and try them again. You will
often find that on second encounter they will go with a
bang. In any case, do not expect magic results: he who
does would do better to take up gambling.

Advisedly in speaking of plotting, I have generally used
the word " invention," instead of " imagination." Mental
processes implied by these two words overlap and yet there
resides in the words a distinction important to the story
writer. The process of completing a plot involves more
invention than imagination, while imagination more than
invention is used in the actual writing of the story. Facility in invention can be cultivated, while imagination is an
inherited attribute not easily affected by educational
training.

Invention is changing or rearranging facts to give them
new significance. Imagination gives the facts themselves
new meanings. Thought of a man sitting on the head of
a horse is a manipulation of well-known facts, and involves

invention. Combining a horse and a man in thought into one, thus creating a centaur, involves imagination. You are inventing when you decide which, among all the settings you are acquainted with, you will give two lovers for their courtship. You are using your imagination, however, when you liken the lady's hand to the " frosted blossom of a May night."

7. The Use of Complications in the Novel

In the difference between the use of complications in the short story and their use in the novel we again can see clearly where these two narrative forms part company. The short story can have only one main complication; the novel may have any number. Any book which developes one main dramatic scene, centering all character, setting and action on it, is a short story, no matter how long it is. The limitations put upon such length we have studied in Chapter Two.

The greatest novels, like the greatest short stories, are strongly dramatic; and, being dramatic, they have well-marked complications. Many of the most powerful novels end with a dramatic complication which is much more intense than any other complication in the story, as in *Tess of the D'Urbervilles*, *The Ordeal of Richard Feverel*, *The Return of the Native*, and *The House of Mirth*. The emotion evoked by the final dramatic conflicts in these stories is greater than any short story could possibly produce. The reason for this is that the situations themselves are bigger and the preparation for them has been more thorough than could be the case in a short story.

The difference in the nature of this " preparation " marks off the difference between the complication short story and the novel ending with a powerful complication. In the former case the preparation must bear *directly* on the complication, so closely that the mood or tone of the final action is felt or sounded as the preparatory action is detailed. In the case of the novel, however, the preparation may be *indirect;* it must have some relation to the final event, and this is all that can be said. It need not produce the same emotion at all. It may, in fact, produce an entirely opposite emotion. The emotion produced, for instance, by the final episode of *Tess* is stark tragedy. In the body of the novel, however, are to be found happy rustic scenes which sound the various moods of bucolic joys.

So indefinite and plastic is the novel as a literary form that all we can say of its use of complications is that it employs them when it needs them; they are merely one of the devices novelists use to gain their ends. The complication to the short story writer, on the other hand, is often *the* story. A study of this one complication will reveal the best means of plotting the narrative with beauty and power.

ASSIGNMENTS: CHAPTER SIX

Plotting from " complications " is, as stated at the beginning of this chapter, more difficult than plotting from characters. Complications are harder to " see " than characters; they are also harder to get; and the plotting must often work backwards as well as forwards from the " complication." In the character story, moreover, the character is generally given to begin with and the events are altered to suit the exigencies of the effect to be produced, while in the complication story the chief or crucial event is generally given to begin with and the characters must be altered to suit. Most students, having youth's faith in the dominance of desire over destiny, find it easier to alter events than character. These obstacles to success with the complication story we must attempt to deal with by the discipline in the following assignments.

First of all, we must learn to know a complication when we see it. Extremely important is it to be able instantly to tell the difference between a sharp " character idea " and a " complication idea." The word, " complication," let me remind you, is used here in a very technical and rather narrow sense. It does *not* mean the " initial complication " nor a " generating circumstance," nor indeed the main complexity of events or problem of a story generally. While the pure character story, such as we studied in the last chapter, has a complication in its crucial situation, it does not have a complication in the sense in which this word is used in the complication story. To prevent confusion, therefore, we will refer to the complication in the complication story as the " complication idea." The word " idea " will keep before us the fact that the distinguishing peculiarity of the complication story is that it springs from and is an expansion of the idea of a complication rather than the idea of a character.

A complication idea, then, is distinguished from a character idea in two important ways:

a. It arouses interest in some event or predicament rather than in character.

b. It is immediately recognizable as unusual, unique or striking in some way.

Take for example, the following:

Character idea: A young man who loves his wife so much that he gladly sells his most prized possession to buy her something she wants.

Complication idea: A young husband and young wife love each other so much that at Christmas time, being poor, he sells his much prized watch to give her some combs which she coveted for her hair, while she at the same time has her beautiful long hair cut and sold to buy her husband a chain for his precious watch!

This complication idea, taken from O. Henry's *The Gift of The Magi* and already studied, arouses interest, as demanded above, in a predicament rather than in a character and, secondly, it is instantly recognized as a unique or unusual predicament. Not all complication ideas are as well developed or as striking as this one; some, as we shall see, are mere suggestions; but always they express or suggest a twist of events that is odd or peculiar.

ASSIGNMENT A

For our first assignment we will attempt to do nothing more than distinguish between character ideas and complication ideas. All the examples given are definitely one or the other and the complication ideas are more than mere suggestions; they are clearly outlined. Your task is merely to write down which is which.

1. Danny's devotion to his former playmate and old friend, Jack, was the most touching thing in his life.*

2. When Danny and Jack both fell madly in love with Dorothy, Danny knew that it was equally impossible for him to give up Dorothy and to deprive Jack of happiness by marrying her himself.

3. Jarvis was passionately fond of flowers and, although he lived in the midst of the squalor and grime of a factory town, he kept his cottage covered with vines and surrounded with gardens which in summer made his little home seem like a fragrant bouquet.

4. Jarvis's little cottage in the midst of the squalor and grime of a factory town was covered with vines and surrounded by a garden which in summer made his little place seem like a fragrant bouquet. None of the factory people living about him had any flowers. Jarvis was insane.

5. Allen, on his way west to take a coveted job, stopped in St. Louis to propose to his girl. The proposal took longer than he had expected, causing him to miss his train. On arriving at San Francisco he found that because of his being late, he had lost the job.*

6. A woman living in a cabin on the prairie is bitten by a poisonous snake while her husband is absent in a distant town. Her only chance for securing help is to send her five-year-old son on horseback to notify her husband.

7. Bitter business rivalry arose between two publishing houses whose whole business was printing and selling Bibles.

8. A traveler in the South Seas became so lonely for people of his own race that once on shipboard bound for home he proposed to the first white woman he saw.

9. A traveler in the South Seas grew to long so for people of his own race that once arrived on shipboard bound for home, he proposed to the first woman he saw, the only one on board. She seemed to him marvellously fair, but on arriving in San Francisco, he found that in comparison with other women, her skin was a deep olive. She then made him think of the detested "black skins" of Oceanica.*

10. During the war an English Colonel, being strong on social caste, warned a lieutenant not to be seen associating so much with a certain private. "The trouble is," replied the lieutenant, "the man is my brother."

11. A dog finding a carved horn, containing several diamond rings, and thinking it a bone carries it out into the garden and buries it.

12. The winner of the motion picture beauty contest, Nancy Belford, was found to be not only extremely lovely in face and figure, but of a dainty, modest and winsome personality.*

13. The winner of the motion picture beauty contest was found to be so stupid and clumsy-mannered that the newspaper reporters dubbed her "The Cheese Belt Beauty."*

14. Old Scroggins was so afraid that the prohibition agents would get his beloved wines that he concealed them in the walls of his cellar, cementing the hiding places so that no one would ever suspect his trick.

15. Poor Fortunato having incurred the wrath of the old Italian wine connoisseur, was lured to the latter's wine cellar, chained against the wall of a crypt, walled in and sealed up where he remained until he died.

16. Jones on this sweltering summer night was unable to sleep in the stuffy hotel room. The one window was jammed; he couldn't open it; he was too tired to call for help. After an hour's tossing about, he rose, and without turning on the light, again tried to open the window. Enraged, he struck it with his cane, smashing it. Lying down, he felt cooler with the breeze blowing over him, and slept peacefully. In the morning he discovered that he had smashed a mirror and that the window was still stuck fast.

17. A husband seeing that he is falling in love with his stenographer dismisses the stenographer and puts his wife in her place.

18. A jealous husband.

19. Horace, a Freshman, becomes so lonely during the first three months at college that he packs up and goes home.

20. Horace, the Freshman, becomes so lonely that in order to increase his popularity with his dormitory mates, he stands under his window at night and calls out his own name: "Horace, O Horace!"

21. A man extremely sick has been living for weeks on the strictest, simplest regimen of food, when suddenly one day a tray, loaded with all the delicacies he has been craving, is brought to him. He knows that this means that he has been given up to die.

22. A spinster lady who is sentimentally fond of her ancestral home.

23. A student working alone in a chemical laboratory leaves his gold watch on his work table while he goes to secure a new beaker from the stock room. When he returns in a few seconds the watch is gone.

24. Charles falls madly in love with a woman five years his senior.

25. Charles falls in love with his father's second wife, who is only five years his senior.

ASSIGNMENT B

In the previous assignment we gained practice in "seeing" complication ideas. Our next problem, as stated above, is — how to get them. Here I must again urge the very great importance of the literary notebook. As stated in the body of this chapter, very little can be done with the complication story without a plentiful supply of complication ideas; and these ideas cannot be "pulled out of thin air." The practice of "waiting for an inspiration," as explained in Section F of the Appendix, is an amateurish affectation; it may be picturesque but it doesn't get results. Successful writers don't depend upon it; nor should you. In Section F of the Appendix you will find practical hints on securing story ideas which will be especially useful in this connection. In this assignment we will try to learn something about collecting complication ideas.

The most important principle of practice for the note-taker to remember is this: Do not wait until you chance upon a complication so strong that it knocks you down before you put it into your notebook. You will be fortunate if you find one complication idea a year which, as it first occurs to you, is developed fully enough to be put as it stands into the crucial situation of a story. Most of your complication ideas will, in the form in which they first occur to you, be exceedingly slight. Practically all will need some elaborating before being used. You must train yourself to "spot" them in this slight and undeveloped form. We learned in Chapter Four how two stories powerfully dramatic, Maupassant's *The Coward* and Stevenson's *The Sire de Maletroit's Door*, might have had their inception in very slight complication ideas.

Below are eleven complication ideas in the "first observation" form in which they might occur to a student literary observer. Each one is capable of being manipulated into a powerful crucial situation; they were, in fact, taken from the crucial situations of stories by well-known authors. These eleven ideas display the form and nature of the entries with which you should fill your notebooks, if you wish to succeed with the complication story. In making such entries, however, you should always endeavor to append to each, if only in a word or two, some manipulation which will suggest its possible use or intensify it in some way. Your task now is to manipulate each of these eleven ideas.

Illustration: The first note states that the man tried in vain to get the dog to drop the stick. If it stated that he threw the stick into the pond and the dog brought it to him, the action would be so commonplace that it could scarcely qualify as a "complication idea"; but the will of the man on land being defied by the action of an animal in the water suggests a peculiar situation and invites manipulation. Without any concern about the final effect of the story, we simply note down quickly any and every change in the original note which will intensify it. There are three elements: the man, the dog, the stick in the dog's mouth. Taking each in turn, we note the following:

Change the man to a lady wearing a gown which will be ruined if the dog shakes himself near her or a child which is terrified by the dog. (No good.)

Change the playful, friendly dog to a wild dog (in Alaska, say); the man on the shore keeps the animal off by throwing sticks into the water; soon all the sticks on the shore are exhausted. (Better; but not satisfactory.)

Change the stick in the dog's mouth to something dangerous — what? What's the most dangerous small, *stick-like thing* — dynamite! (This is satisfactory; a man fishes by blowing up the muddy depths of a pond with a dangerous stick of explosive; his dog sees him throw it, fetches it, pursues the man, who runs for his life and is caught just as the dynamite explodes — the plot idea of a Jack London story.)

In writing out your suggestions for manipulation you need not write out all your attempted changes, as above; just copy off the original idea and note beneath it briefly your most successful idea for a change. After the first idea, for instance, it would be enough to write: "The dog might fetch from the water instead of a harmless stick something extremely dangerous."

1. A man amusing himself by throwing sticks in a pond for a dog to fetch, tried in vain to get the dog to drop a stick while swimming and go for a second which he had just thrown into the water.

2. A husband enters a room much frequented by his wife. His wife has died only a short time before. He seems to feel her presence in the room.

3. A citizen of a conquered city will not allow himself to go to the window to watch the entry of the conquering troops; he cannot endure the disgrace.

4. A poor but romantic young man who has adorned himself for a special occasion, tells a young girl that he is extremely wealthy and she believes him.

5. "The old story tellers had it on us," complained the writer; "they could give their characters three wishes and by some hocuspocus of magic, let them get their desires. If nowadays we could only — "

"We can," replied the editor; "why not? Good complication for a mystery story. Do it half way decent and I'll buy it."

6. The payment of a marriage portion by the bride's father, a custom still followed in the older Jewish communities, might be made very embarrassing for the young lovers.

7. The idea of a medieval monk hoeing cabbages in the monastery garden for the glory of God has both its comic and pathetic aspects. Suppose an acrobat became a monk?

8. The ship's papers revealed the fear of the whole crew for the Chinese cook. Several times, while far out at sea, attempts to kill him had been made, but each time a yellow cat which haunted the cook's galley crossed the would-be murderer's path and frightened him off.

9. The records of the regiment contain the strange story of a deserter named Bendell. He took the disguise of a farmer when he fled. On his first night in a rural inn he shared a room with a thief who finally confessed that he too was attempting to escape.

10. He was so romantic that you had only to describe a pretty girl to him and he'd promptly fall in love with her.

11. A beautiful girl, of a savage people, falls in love with a white traveler, who promises to return and marry her.

ASSIGNMENT C

The purpose of this assignment is to provide further drill in "seeing" the complication idea of a complication story. This time we have brief outlines of eleven stories containing strong complications: the eleven "first observations" of Assignment B were taken from them. The task now is to read each outline carefully and then write out in *one sentence* the complication idea of the story. Do not rewrite the whole plot; do not comment on the effect the story might make; simply write out crisply the central twist of events in the plot. Your answers, if correct, will show you something of the maximum possibilities in the slight complication suggestions you manipulated in Assignment B.

1. *Moonface,* by Jack London.

The narrator of the story hates his neighbor, John Claverhouse, for no reason at all except the other's " moon face " and his irritating smile. The man was harmless, and friendly enough, but he could not endure him. The narrator does everything he can to injure " Moonface," burns his buildings, lets his cattle stray, poisons his dog, and still the other remains calm. At last the narrator buys a dog which he proceeds to train very carefully, especially to retrieve sticks thrown into water. The dog is trained always to bring the object back directly to the one who threw it. When the animal is trained, the narrator gives it to Claverhouse, who is much surprised at this first evidence of friendliness. Soon afterward, Claverhouse goes fishing, accompanied by the dog. He had a queer method of fishing by dynamiting the trout pools. This day he lights the short fuse on a small stick of "giant," and flings it into the stream. The dog at once retrieves it, and in spite of the man's commands and efforts, brings the thing back toward him. Claverhouse runs, the dog close upon him. The narrator, watching them from some distance, sees the finish of his intolerable neighbor. It was skillfully done, a purely " accidental death."

2. *A Ghost,* by Maupassant.

A man is asked by his friend to go to the friend's country house and secure some papers from his bed-room. The friend's wife has just died very suddenly, and he himself cannot bear to return to the place where they had been so happy. The man carries out the request. He finds the house deserted except for an old gardener. The place looks as if it had not been inhabited for years. In the room where he is to look for the papers there is wild confusion; the things had evidently not been touched since the woman's death. The shutters are rusted so that he cannot open them, and in the semi-darkness he begins hunting for the papers. Suddenly he hears a sigh at his shoulder, and turns to see his friend's wife standing beside him. She begs him to comb her long black hair. Benumbed with horror, he does as she asks, and after he has plaited the long, cold locks, she disappears. He returns to the city, sends the papers to the friend, being too much unnerved to see him at once. In a day or so he goes to the man's apartment, only to find that he has left. No trace of him was ever found. He begins to believe that it was all an illusion, when he notices that the buttons of the coat he had worn to the country place, are wound around with long black hair.*

3. *The Siege of Berlin,* by Alphonse Daudet.

Colonel Jouve, a proud, patriotic ex-soldier of France, had weakened to the point of invalidism when Paris was besieged by the Germans in the Franco-Prussian War. His granddaughter, intrusted with his care, denied herself needed food in order that the Colonel might have the comforts to which he was accustomed, and especially in order that he might not know that Paris was invested by German troops and was doomed to capitulate. To keep up his spirits, she and the doctor told him that the French troops were about to take Berlin, and she read fictitious letters from his son, really a prisoner in Germany, that the deception might be more complete. Finally, when Paris fell and the conquering German troops poured into Paris, the truth could no longer be kept from him. The shock of it killed him.

4. *Lost on Dress Parade,* by O. Henry.

Mr. Towers Chandler, a New York architect's clerk, once every ten weeks went forth in the evening to enjoy himself and to spend the ten dollars which he saved up during this time. On one such occasion he encountered and became acquainted with a girl who had slipped on the ice and hurt her ankle. Although she looked like a shop girl of the better type he asked her to dine with him, and she accepted. Since he was parading as a man of wealth and leisure, he boasted to the girl of his clubs, golf, kennels, trips abroad, until he convinced her that he was a rich waster. He liked her very much, and afterward rather regretted his silly brag. The girl, who had not given her name, returned to her home on upper Fifth Avenue, where she told her sister of her dinner with this stranger. She said that she hoped to marry a man with some ambition, some work to do, no matter how poor he might be. She described her dinner companion in a way that indicated that it would be easy for her to have loved him if only he had not lived an idle life between society and his clubs.

5. *The Monkey's Paw,* by W. W. Jacobs, in *The Lady of the Barge.*

Sergeant-Major Morris, returned from India, brought with him the 'mummied paw of a monkey, which a fakir, he said, had endowed with the power to grant three wishes to the owner. He wanted to get rid of it, but no one would buy it. His host, Mr. White, paid him a small sum for it, and after he had left, talked with his wife and son about what he should wish for. He finally decided to wish for 200 pounds to lift the debt from their house. He was horrified to feel, as he made the wish, that the monkey's paw moved in his hand. Next day his son Herbert was killed in the factory where he worked, and the firm sent a representative out immediately with compensation money which the firm felt should be paid the young man's family — the sum of 200 pounds. About two weeks after the funeral, the mother in a paroxysm of grief, demanded the monkey's paw. Holding it in her hands she wished her son back again. About half an hour later — the cemetery was at some distance — there came a terrible knocking at the lower door. The mother rushed down the stairs with a glad cry — her son had come back to her — but the old father felt something horrible in that knocking that filled the house. He hunted about in terror until he found the monkey's paw, and, while the thunder of the knocking still echoed through the house, made the third wish, that his son — or the thing that knocked — would return peacefully to the grave. The sound ceased. He rushed down stairs, found the door open, his wife weeping with disappointment, and the street outside utterly empty.

6. *A Rose of the Ghetto,* by Israel Zangwill.

Leibel, a young Jew, decided to get married, and put his case in the hands of Sugarman the matchmaker. Sugarman was not able to find anyone to his liking, chiefly because Leibel was in love with Rose, the daughter of his employer. Rose helped Leibel find out what was the trouble, and their troth was plighted, much to the distress of the matchmaker. A match managed this way meant a small marriage portion from the father, he told Leibel, and naturally a small commission for himself. At length the father was persuaded to promise a settlement that Sugarman would accept, and the marriage was celebrated. Leibel and Rose were one of many couples that day. Gradually all the other couples were married off, and still Leibel and Rose did not appear. All sorts of rumors were circulated among the crowd, but finally the truth came out: Leibel was waiting for the father to come across with the sum he had promised. Time passed. The minister went to the two men and said that they had to settle things, or he'd close the place in ten minutes anyway. At last Rose herself went to her lover, at the ninth minute. Laying her hand softly on his arm, she said: " Do not give in, Leibel. Do not let them persuade thee! " Eliphaz, the father, surrendered, produced the money. The marriage was performed.

7. *The Juggler of Notre Dame,* by Anatole France.

Barnaby was a juggler in the time of King Louis. He made a meager living, following the fairs, and doing his little act for the crowds. He was not a mountebank, but a simple, God-fearing soul, and finally on the persuasion of a monk whom he encountered in his travels, became a monk himself. In the monastery he found that each monk was worshipping God with whatever skill God had given him, writing, illuminating manuscripts, carving holy images in stone. Poor Barnaby was discouraged, until he heard a story about a monk who had been blessed with a miracle, although he was unable to do anything except say the Ave Maria. From that time Barnaby began to disappear at the time when the other monks were engaged in their special labors. The brothers noticing this, watched him and found that he went to the chapel; and the prior and one of the brothers determined to spy upon him. They saw Barnaby before the altar of the Blessed Virgin, head downwards, and he was juggling with his six balls of copper and a dozen knives. The two old monks were horrified and were about to interrupt the sacrilege, when they saw the Holy Virgin descend the steps of the altar, and with the hem of her robe, wipe the beads of sweat from Barnaby's head. The old brothers fell cn their faces, saying: "Blessed are the simple-hearted, for they shall see God."

8. *The Yellow Cat*, by Wilbur Daniel Steele.

The Abbie Rose was picked up at sea, running loose, under little sail, without a soul of her crew to be found. There was no sign of violence aboard and everything was in perfect order. McCord, an officer of the ship which found the Abbie Rose, was put aboard her with one sailor to bring her into port. He reached port a nervous wreck. The sailor, he said, had fallen overboard. To a friend who visited him in the cabin of the ship as it lay in the harbor, he told this story: He had found, in his first search of the ship, a personal record of the Captain, who told in detail of his own fear of the Chinese cook, and how the whole crew were coming to share this fear. They tried to kill him, but found that their guns had disappeared. There the record ended. All that McCord found on the ship was a yellow cat, which he was ready to believe, was the soul of the Chinaman. One night soon after they took the ship, the sailor had asked if he might put on more sail. McCord gave permission, and the next morning when he wakened, the sailor was gone. Next night, hearing a sound that he thought was made by the cat prowling around the galley, he looked at a patch of moonlight outside his cabin door, and saw the shadow of a human head with a queue. He shot at the shadow, and then went over the ship again, finding only the cat calmly washing her face. In the midst of McCord's story the cat appeared, and the two men followed her. She climbed up to where a sail was bundled against the cross trees. McCord followed her, and there in the bulge of the sail he found the answer to the mystery. The Chinaman had been hidden in the sail all the time. He had escaped to the shore while they had been talking.

9. *Incident in the Life of Mr. George Crookhill*, by Thomas Hardy, in *A Few Crusted Characters*.

Georgy Crookhill, returning from the fair, a little uneasy lest someone follow him for a certain shady transaction which he had pulled off, caught up with a young farmer, riding a very good horse. They became friendly, and when dark fell, decided to put up at an inn together. In the night, Georgy, remembering the episode at the fair, rose stealthily while the other slept, put on the latter's clothes, went down and paid the bill, and started off with the other man's horse. During the morning he was seized as a deserter. He told the police about the change of clothing, and appealed to the young farmer who came riding up just then, to corroborate his story of the joke. The farmer refused to recognize him, and rode away in the other direction. As soon as Georgy and his captors reached town, soldiers of the deserter's company released him. He was not the man wanted, they assured the police officers. The real deserter, aided by this double change of clothing, got away and was never traced.

10. *Marjorie Daw*, by Thomas Bailey Aldrich.

A young man, John Fleming, who has broken his leg, is so melancholy and irascible an invalid, that the doctor appeals to Fleming's best friend to do something to give the invalid an interest in life. The friend, who is spending a vacation in the mountains, begins a whimsical correspondence with Fleming, mostly details about the girl who lives across the way from the inn where the friend is staying. His reports of how he meets her and tells her about Fleming to her evident interest, appeal very much to Fleming. The friend tells this Marjorie Daw so much about Fleming — so he writes — that the girl seems actually to be falling in love with him, whom she has never seen, and this when she is about to be married by her father to a man for whom she cares very little. Fleming is by no means well, but he cannot endure the thought of the girl compelled to marry against her will, and with his man servant he starts off for the mountain resort from which his friend had written. Arrived there, he finds that his friend had departed leaving a letter. The letter explains that the whole correspondence had been a part of the treatment of the broken leg. The friend was fleeing because — there was no Marjorie Daw.

11. *Lispeth*, by Rudyard Kipling, in *Plain Tales.*

Lispeth, a beautiful hill girl, had been practically adopted by the chaplain of the district and his wife. She became a Christian, and absorbed rapidly many of the interests of the family where she lived as a kind of companion and playmate for the children. On one of her walks, she found a man, an English scientist who had been deserted by his bearers, after being seriously hurt in a fall. She brought him in, nursed him, and declared that she was going to marry him. The chaplain and his wife decided that it would be better to humor her, that she could not understand the situation. The man, who had a sweetheart in England, and had no idea whatever of marrying a native woman, enjoyed Lispeth's adoration during his convalescence, and when he went away, at the suggestion of the chaplain and his wife, he told Lispeth that he would return. She waited, always hoping, until finally the chaplain's wife told her how they had deceived her, thinking that they could not make her understand that the man would never marry her. On discovering that the chaplain and his wife had lied to her, Lispeth promptly reverted to all the habits of her hill forebears, becoming worse if anything than they. She married a man who beat her, and made her old in a few years. Sometimes when she was very drunk, she would tell the story of her love.

ASSIGNMENT D

In all the ideas below there is added to the complication interest fairly strong character interest. The problem of this assignment is to recognize the complication interest, and the character interest, and to develop them first separately, then together. You are to put each of the ten ideas below through five stages. The fifth stage offers important practice in integration. To make your task clear, I will indicate these five stages in the manipulation of the following story idea:

A man, discovering his wife a suicide, makes her death appear a murder in order to keep his name longer in the news.

1. Identify the complication, and state it without indicating the character interest.

In our example the complication would be: A suicide is made to appear a murder.

2. Identify the trait, and state it without the complication.

In our example the trait would be: Desire for publicity.

3. Write a scene developing the complication. About 600 words.

In the case of our example, this might be the scene where the police arrive and the man tells his fake story.

4. Write a study of the trait. About 300 words.

For our example, this would be a sketch giving five or six varied situations in which the man would show in action his desire for publicity. (See Chapter V, Assignment D.)

5. Revise the scene written for No. 3, above, introducing details of overt action which will express or suggest the trait.

In the example given, the scene with the police would be rewritten, with added details to show the man's pleasure in the attention he is getting.

Continue as above with the ten story ideas which follow.

1. A man who is very unhappy with his wife, but too much afraid of her to divorce her, finally runs away, and to prevent her locating

him, undergoes some plastic surgery. In consequence he is mistaken for a notorious escaped criminal.

2. When a great private yacht is driven ashore on a lonely coast in a terrific storm, the few natives are too preoccupied with stripping the wreck to observe that there is still life in one of the bodies on board.

3. Longing for romance with her fascinating middle-aged employer, a little office girl is disillusioned when after a lavish dinner, the prelude to what she hopes will be the romance, she sees him take his digestive tablets.

4. After his son has been deeply injured by an enemy, a man prays for a chance for revenge through the enemy's son, but when the opportunity comes, confronted with the boy's youth and helplessness, he spares him.

5. After her return from a holiday abroad, during which she has become engaged to a writer of international reputation, a girl discovers in her fiancé's latest novel, her own conduct during their courtship, portrayed without change.

6. An elderly woman, on discovering that her niece to whom she is devoted is being somehow influenced or intimidated by a man with a known criminal record, kills the man.

7. A youthful executive, believing in young blood, surrounds himself with young workmen and assistants, but he has only moderate success until he introduces into the group some older men.

8. A young boy on a sinking ship takes several rolls of snapshots of the scene.

9. Sometime after her divorced husband's marriage to a woman who makes him very happy, the first wife returns, sick and penniless, and the second wife insists on taking her into the home.

10. A husband, who has let his wife divorce him in order that she may be happy with her lover, sees her two years later with a third man.

ASSIGNMENT E

As our first exercise in actually plotting complication stories let us first of all be sure we understand and can analyze the complete plot outlines given in Assignment C above. Before attempting to plot entirely original complication stories we will, as with the character story, use story patterns already worked out. This we will do in the *next assignment*. For *this* assignment turn back to Assignment C and write out both the *single effect* and the *drama*, if any, of each of the stories there outlined. The answer should be confined to a single phrase or sentence in each case.

ASSIGNMENT F

Your analysis in Assignment C and Assignment E has now given you the *complication idea,* the *single effect,* and the *drama*

of the eleven stories in Assignment C. Using the same complication idea and single effect and, as far as possible, the same
dramatic struggle, plot these stories over again, using now, as far
as you can, people and settings with which you are familiar.
Bring the story home, in other words. Your plotting should
follow this general order:

 a Reproduce the complication, making sure you have kept to a
sharp complication and have not merely developed character.
 b Work out the single effect.
 c Work out the drama.

A very definite check on your finished plot can be made by
reducing it and the original plot in Assignment C to a schematic
outline as shown on page 288. The original plots will fall neatly
and accurately into the schematic outline. Yours, if it be handled
skillfully, will do the same. Whatever weaknesses there are will
show by checking over as shown on page 299.

ASSIGNMENT G

Go back now over the various complication ideas and first
manipulations of Assignments A, B and D, and select ten ideas or
manipulations that have especially interested you or that seem
to be best adapted to your life experiences and plot them as you
plotted the stories in Assignment F. These plots when finished
will be yours in every respect but the initial inspiration; such
inspirations, like newspaper headlines, have no copyright; your
inventions will make them sufficiently yours to warrant your
writing out full length those which most appeal to you. The
resulting manuscripts will be yours to do with as you choose.

ASSIGNMENT H

As soon as your notebook contains a sufficient assortment of
complication ideas, go over it carefully, select the most promising
fifteen, say, and submit them to a first tentative manipulation,
giving each about half an hour. This done, go over the manipulations again, select the three most promising, plot them carefully, put them first in schematic outline, then in the form of a
bald report, and write them out at length. The resulting three
manuscripts will be original in all respects. If you have handled
the various *processes* with certainty you may feel sure you have
finished your apprenticeship with the complication story and
may henceforth concern yourself entirely with securing better
ideas and with increasing your facility and power in actual
writing.

CHAPTER SEVEN

THE THEMATIC STORY

The Story That Says Something

> Fables in sooth are not what they appear,
> Our moralists are mice, and such small deer,
> We yawn at sermons, but we gladly turn
> To moral tales, and so amused we learn.
>
> — La Fontaine.

Of the four fundamental types of short story which we are studying the thematic story generally fascinates the student most. It is the story that "says something." When he learns that this type of story not only entertains his reader but also influences his conduct and his ideas about life, he exclaims: "That's what I want to do with my writing. Books have inspired me — if I can only inspire others! I'm going to write thematic stories." Excellent ambition!

1. An Exalted Form of Narrative

Here is a form of writing in which the greatest literary artists have gloried. From their experiences, their matured philosophy of life they evolve great truths and by sheer art they force multitudes of people to understand and accept them. These truths, because they force people to abandon their cherished villainies, perhaps are unpalatable; people do not welcome such interference with their lives. How, then, to get the message "across"? Put it in narrative form. Sugar-coat it. Entertain the evil soul while uplifting it! Thus they compel the world's attention. They triumph both as reformers and artists.

321

By these very means Molière poked the finger of scorn at the degenerate affectations of the court life of his time and became the greatest of French dramatists. By these means Ibsen, the leading dramatist of the last century, fashioned his play called " The Doll's House " in which he helped shock the western world into a recognition of the rights of women. In this way Upton Sinclair by his novel, *The Jungle,* effected a reform of the packing industry in this country, Winston Churchill by his novel, *The Inside of the Cup,* energized the socialization of the church in America, and O. Henry, to name but a single example in the field of the short story, by his fantasy, *A Municipal Report,* awakened the tired business soul of America to an appreciation of the glowing romance in its towns and cities. All these writings were " thematic " in the sense understood in this chapter.

2. Most Difficult to Plot

The management of thematic materials, however, presents the most difficult of all plotting problems. While the atmosphere story is the most difficult to write, the thematic story is the most baffling to plot. We consider it before the atmosphere story because it occurs much oftener than the latter type of story.

Our study of this form of plot we must regard as advanced technique. Because of its complexity, we cannot hope to expound it fully, either in principle or practice; but some consideration of the thematic story plot is necessary even for the elementary student, if for no other reason than to enable him to avoid it! Even the beginner, for instance, should know when a " theme " has crept into his plot; he should know whether, in considering story material, he is undergoing a moral or an emotional reaction: if he knows only this much he will often save himself much unnecessary effort. He will not attempt a task beyond his present powers.

Why is the thematic story so difficult to handle? It is

difficult simply because the writer sets out to make the reader *think* as well as *feel*. To the general dramatic pattern which we have been considering so far is added a special problem of reasoning. New difficulties arise, you see, not only from the necessity of fusing these two patterns, but also from the fact that the qualities necessary to a firm grasp of both these patterns are seldom found in one and the same writer! The deepest, keenest student of life, the philosopher, is little likely to burst forth in an emotional rhapsody. And the person of " artistic temperament," the dreamer, the purely creative, emotional type — we are satisfied if he exhibit the most ordinary gifts of ratiocination. Yet both these opposite qualities are precisely what are needed for the great performance in thematic narrative.

Where shall we ever find such a combination in one person? You will not find it very often, and when you do you will have found one type of " genius." Genius in this sense is the ability to plan work with the precise reasoning of a professor of philosophy and write it with the fervor of an emotional actress. Our concern here as elsewhere is the reasoning. Happily for us it is the easier of the two gifts to acquire.

Another difficulty with the thematic story is that it is a story with an idea and — not all writers have ideas! Most writers, indeed, see life as pictures and not as problems. Their reactions, in other words, are emotional and not philosophic, and a certain philosophic turn of mind is indispensable for consistent success with this type of story. The thematic writer must have some convictions. If he has not already come to some conclusions, however tentative, on such problems as war and peace, party government, capitalism, bolshevism, prohibition, education, divorce, he will search his mind in vain for usable themes, and if they are given him he will be little better off: it is generally impossible to write effectively unless your subject rouses in you sympathy, if not belief.

3. How to Get Themes

" Where can I get a theme? " The answer to this question, asked often by beginners, is indicated above: From your own meditations on life. Those students who have themes in their systems but have not recognized them, will be helped by the expository portions of this chapter, and by the section on " How to Get Story Ideas," in the Appendix. Others — well, there is no formula that will serve them. Growing older alone will help. Characters in general are taken or adapted from those people a writer knows best, those who live close to him; themes come from viewing these few people *as units of society*. Even the younger student, if he will but look sharply at the thrilling spectacle of the world we live in, cannot fail to find much to meditate about. He must become philosopher as well as psychologist. He must make up his mind about things. In the broad sense he must be a reformer, an agitator. Contented never; curiosity — his watchword.

Writes William Allen White:

" Twenty thousand people committed suicide last year in the United States, which fact seems to be a reflection upon our well-ordered life. It would seem that the great panorama which history is unfolding before us day by day, forever beckoning with its tomorrows and luring us with big events just around the corner from today — it would seem that that gripping panorama ought to hold us all in our seats upon this planet. We may be forsaken, we may be cold, sick, unlovely, and unloved, and yet it would seem that the daily story of life about us, the great tragic events that are looming before us in Europe and in Asia and the great comedy that should cramp our sides with anguished laughter here in America, should hold us tightly upon the planet. Yet, 20,000 of us have voluntarily got up and walked out, left the show cold and flat — and for what? Perhaps they are going to the big show, perhaps they are only going to bed. But they are missing a mighty good thing nevertheless. The spinning world never before has held so much to charm the eye and engross the soul as it holds today."

As in the two previous chapters we will consider first the principles involved in plotting the thematic story and afterwards see how these principles are applied in practice.

4. Principles of Thematic Plot

Let us begin with this definition: *A thematic story is a narrative in which the reader's interest centers more upon an underlying truth about life than upon character or events.* In the case of the short story, which form we shall consider mainly here, the ideal of the single effect will be found always, and the ideal of drama generally. A story may, as we have already learned, depend for its effect equally upon theme *and* one or even two of the other three kinds of story interest, but in this chapter, in the interest of simplicity, we shall consider the thematic story in its " pure " or one-phase form.

What is a theme?

There is no word in our language which exactly expresses the sense in which " theme " is used in the above definition. We are again compelled to take a word and re-define it for our own special purposes. " Theme " in the dictionary sense, as explained in Chapter Three, means " a subject or topic of discourse." In our technical sense *theme means a positive declaration of some truth about life,* such as, " Honesty is the best policy " or " Look not upon the wine when it is red."

Narrative in our technical sense is action; theme is thought about such action. Narrative is concrete; a theme is abstract. The narrative action is the body of the story, the theme, its soul. The theme is never merely a part of the narrative; it is rather something expressed by the narrative. The theme is never merely a subject or topic, such as, " The Splendor of Life " or " The Value of Advertising "; the true themes would be: " Life is splendid " and " It pays to advertise."

Non-thematic (*emphatic*) *narratives*

A few of the simplest possible examples will perhaps help us here. Let us take first some examples of narrative which have nothing to do with a theme. Such narratives, since their purpose is to *emphasize* an effect rather than prove anything, we will call *emphatic stories*. The simplest possible example of narrative told solely for its effect on the reader's *feelings* or *emotions* is the anecdote. Here is a typical conversational anecdote which is told about a one-time famous Wall Street " character " who stuttered. We will call him Puffer.

Puffer one day was walking along Wall Street toward Broadway with a friend who was trying to sell Puffer a small bulldog, which he was leading by a string. The friend argued the dog's fighting qualities. Puffer was about to pay over his money when he spied a small boy with a box one side of which was covered with wire mesh.

" Whacha g-g-ot there, b-b-boy? " asked Puffer.

" A rat," replied the boy; " going down to the river to drown him."

Seized with an inspiration, Puffer said: " W-w-ait a m-m-m-in-ute, boy." He took the bulldog from his friend, dropped it inside the box, closed the lid, stood back, and said: " N-n-now we'll see if he c-c-c-an f-f-fight."

The two men and the boy were amazed to see the rat spring at the dog with such ferocity that the latter cowered, whimper-ing, in a corner. Whereupon Puffer turned to the boy and said: " Wh-wh-what will you t-t-t-take for the r-r-r-rat? "

The *emphasis* or *effect* of this anecdote is humorous; we smile or laugh, showing that our feelings have been reached. Has it affected us in any other way? Can we relate it to life in general? Does it arouse a meditative mood, inducing us to think about a problem and so affect our reasoned convictions? It does not. No reflection of any consequence could be based on so trivial a human document.

This same absence of content which touches the more

universal issues of life is true of the many delightful little narratives which are too much wanting in drama to be called short stories, but which are of the emphatic rather than thematic type. Many of Daudet's prose poems, such as *The Death of the Dauphin, The Sous-prefet Afield* and *The Lighthouse of the Sanguinaires,* are of this nature. The last of these is merely a colorful little picture of quiet happy days spent by the author on the Bay of Ajaccio, Corsica, with his friends, the lighthouse-keepers. Many of the shorter sketches of Chekhov are also of this emphatic type. In one of them, for instance, he tells how two men watched over a dead body in the woods. A third man came along, begged for a few coppers, received them, and went on to the city. That was all. Simple *emphatic* narrative, inspiring no particular reflection at all about life.

In the field of the short story and novel we have as examples of non-thematic or emphatic narratives practically all the stories and novels we have considered in the previous chapters. We were occupied in securing emphasis on character or complication in the stories we worked out. Their appeal lay altogether in such emphasis. If the particular action of each story was true and consistent — that was enough; the implication about life *in general* did not at all concern us. The same is true of character novels like *Vanity Fair,* and *The Egoist,* or character-complication novels like *David Copperfield* and *The Return of the Native.* The story's the thing in all such emphatic writings. Thematic interest is wanting.

Thematic narratives

Let us take the simplest possible type of narrative in which a theme appears. Our materials, we will say, are as follows:

Narrative: A horse is seen by several men to step on a coin
Theme: The Scotch people are thrifty.

A thematic anecdote can now be produced by manipulating and combining these two factors as follows:

In Aberdeen, Scotland, a horse stepped on a penny and it took
four men to lift his hoof.

What is the *source of the interest* in this simple statement? It is not certainly in the mere act of the horse
and the four men. The interest is in the *implication of
the episode*, namely, that the Scotch people are so thrifty
that even their horses can't be made to part easily with
pennies " found " ! The *effect* is *amusement in the revelation of a general truth about a race through the conduct
of a dumb horse*. Further proof that the interest here
is in the underlying generalization about life and not
in events or character may be seen from the fact that
the same effect can be produced with different story
materials. Note:

A Hebrew, journeying to Edinburgh with the intention of
setting up business in that city, came upon a Scotchman who
had paused with his horse and wagon for the noon-day meal.
The traveler saw the Scotchman finish his meager repast, and
then remove the bag of oats from his horse's nose. He next
saw the Scotchman look into the bag, walk to the rear of his
wagon, remove a hen from a crate, thrust it in the bag and wait
patiently until the hen had gobbled the remains of the horse's
meal. Whereupon the Hebrew faced about and returned whence
he had come.

Note also the effect of this:

A group of Scotch boys were waiting for a train in a station.
Suddenly they missed Sandy, one of their number. After searching for a long time they finally found him lying, dead, in front
of a penny-in-the-slot lung tester, a "See-how-much-you-can-
blow" contrivance. They were puzzled as to the cause of
Sandy's demise until they saw the notice on the dial of the
machine: "If you blow one thousand you get your penny back."

Here we have practically the same effect produced by
three different episodes. They are alike only in their
themes. They are thematic anecdotes.

To this class of joke belong all the quips about the Ford automobile. A man meets another standing in the middle of the road gazing up into a tree with a crank in his hand. " What's the matter? " asks the first man. " Oh, it flew out of my hand." The effect here, as in the other Ford jokes, is amusement at a striking revelation of some inferiority of this particular make of automobile. All the jokes about wives, mothers-in-law, and spinsters which express cynical beliefs about the *institution* of marriage and the *fact of love* are also truly thematic.

The fable

Another type of brief narrative which differs from the thematic anecdotes in that it is generally longer, seldom is humorous, and usually has animals or inanimate objects for its characters is the fable. The animals and objects personify moral qualities and the action is generally improbable. Familiar examples are the fables of *The Tortoise and the Hare*, and *The Boy and the Wolf*, in the latter of which the boy guarding the sheep was eaten by the wolves because, having twice given a false alarm, no help arrived when the wolves finally did come. The underlying themes here are respectively, " Persistence wins," and " Practical jokes can be carried too far." Evidence that La Fontaine, the great fable writer, understood and consciously employed the " thematic " principle is found in the very knowing quatrain quoted at the head of this chapter.

The modern fables of George Ade are thematic in the same fashion as those of La Fontaine. Certain short stories, like Kipling's *The Walking Delegate* in which horses personify the issues in a social problem, belong to the same classification. So also do most of Mark Twain's shorter satires.

The parable

Another form of thematic narrative is the parable. The moral or theme here is not quite so apparent as in the case of the fable, and there is generally more action. Real people are involved, and the events themselves are probable. The Biblical parables of "The Prodigal Son" and "The Sower" come instantly to mind. The themes expressed through these narratives are explained by Christ himself. Of "The Prodigal Son" He said: "There is joy in the presence of the angels of God over one sinner that repenteth"; or stated philosophically, "The greater the offense, the greater need to applaud repentance." The explanation of "The Parable of the Sower," that the seed is the word of God, which cannot bear fruit in hearts too much absorbed in the pleasures of this world, can be briefly stated: "Virtue to be possessed, must be practiced."

The parable is a form occasionally used today for social criticism, when the subject is sufficiently simple to be expressed clearly through symbolic, but obvious human conduct. An example is "Saul Among the Prophets," by Moe Bragin (*Short Story Hits, 1933*), which conveys a proletarian social theme by means of the action of farm laborers, struggling to get some hay into a barn before a storm.

One of the most original and charming parables of the past few years is "Martin Forgot," [1] by Ellis Parker Butler. The story dramatized this theme: The misadventures of life on earth are laughable to the man who can remember at all times that he is an immortal spirit. In the narrative action, an immortal prince of the planet Betelgeuse had chosen, in an experimental mood, to be born an inhabitant of earth. Grown old and sullen with his hardships, one day he suddenly remembered that he was still a prince, and that he had deliberately chosen this period of earth life for the adventure

[1] *Delineator*, July, 1922.

of it. All his life he had complained and groaned over his lot, but when the memory at last returned to him, he nearly laughed his ancient body off of his chair.

The allegory is another and still lengthier example of thematic narrative. It generally takes a poetic form. Like the fable, its actors personify moral qualities. The most famous allegory in our language is, of course, Bunyan's *Pilgrim's Progress*. Its theme is the desirability of adhering to Christian virtues. Swift's *Tale of a Tub* is a pungent and exuberant prose satire whose underlying theme is a criticism of the warring religious sects of that day. Spenser's *Faerie Queene*, a metrical romance in allegorical form, argues the splendor of the six virtues of knighthood. In our day we have, in novel form, the allegorical writings of Cabell, and in play form, the Bohemian drama, *The World We Live In*, in which the players act the rôles of insects which in turn personify moral qualities. The underlying theme of this grim play is: " Human life is no better than the life of ants and beetles," or, more briefly, " What's the use? "

5. Thematic Narratives Didactic and Dramatic

We have now, I hope, a clearer idea of the difference between emphatic and thematic interest. Before plotting thematic short stories, however, I must set forth another important distinction. Thematic narratives do not all give the underlying theme the *same* degree of stress. Emphatic interest and thematic interest are sometimes combined so that the thematic appeal is scarcely detectable by the reader. This fact, however, does not invalidate our distinctions: the writer may always understand them if he take the trouble. His effects are what he chooses to make them. Where, however, a definite theme *is* found in a narrative, it may be handled in two different ways, in the *didactic manner* or the *dramatic manner*. *A thematic narrative is written in the didactic manner when the reader is impressed mainly by the theme and secondarily by any feeling or emotion aroused by the events themselves. A thematic narrative is written in the dramatic manner when the reader is impressed by the feeling or emotion aroused by the events and only secondarily by the theme.* Here again didactic and dramatic manner sometimes shade off into each other, but they can generally be definitely identified. The distinction is exceedingly important to the student of literary technique. It can be shown as follows:

The Dramatic and Didactic Thematic Story

The emphatic story
    (Purpose: to make an
    emotional effect)

The thematic story
    (Purpose: to point to a
    truth about life)

combine to produce

Story in dramatic manner (Emphasizing drama).

Story in didactic manner (Emphasizing theme).

The fable, parable and allegory affect the reader's mind more than his emotions; they are thus didactic. The dramatic thematic story which we are more interested in and which we shall presently study, affects the reader's feelings more than his convictions; it is handled in the dramatic manner. The action in a didactic story is generally merely an illustration or instance of the truth of the theme; the action of a thematic story written in the dramatic manner is a definite proof of the truth of the theme. This proof can be as clean-cut as the propositions of Euclid.

Notable thematic dramatic stories

Let us examine some well-known thematic stories in which the emotional dominates the thematic effect. An example is O. Henry's *Unfinished Story*, a beautifully simple and effective piece of dramatic thematic writing. You will remember that the author encloses his little story of the temptations of Dulcie, the shopgirl, in a frame which marks off the beginning and the end of the story. This frame sets down quite boldly the underlying theme: the most brutal villainy is hiring shopgirls at less than a living wage. This is the soul of the story and for a time at the beginning of the story you may say that you are impressed more by the author's moralizing than you are by the story. But — read the story and you shall see! So sympathetically and touchingly vivid is each little characteristic action of Dulcie, that you are more interested in her personal sufferings than you are in the tragic significance of her fate. The story becomes, in other words, a true " human interest " story. The underlying theme glorifies the narrative, giving it deep and reverberating overtones.

The same interpretation in general applies to another story by O. Henry, which is by many people considered his best, *The Municipal Report.* Its chief interest is in its dramatic presentation of this theme: " Romance has no geography." Here again, although O. Henry with fantastic directness hints boldly at his underlying thought, he makes his events so vivid that the story itself wins more interest than the underlying theme. Story and theme being thus beautifully interwoven, with the story rising above the theme in importance, we have a narrative of extraordinary power and beauty.

Many of the short narratives of Chekhov, the most famous of Russian short story writers, produce lasting effects not because of their strong drama, but because of their underlying philosophy, developed in the non dramatic manner. A typical one is called *Old Age.* It recounts the return of an elderly man to the home of his childhood and early youth. Nobody recognizes him except an old waiter who was once his lawyer and who divorced him from his wife. The old man visits the wife's grave hoping to indulge his sorrow. He swallows hard, hoping to raise a lump in his throat — which is not there. He blinks his eyes to make the tears come — his eyes are dry. Here, by the simplest possible touches, a theme of powerful import is suggested, namely, "Age wipes out all."

The general idea of the unwisdom of bringing up a child under the theory of the "sheltered life" has been used as a theme for both a powerful short story and a notable novel. Kipling used it in his tragic short story, *Thrown Away*. The narrative here is that of a youth who is sent to India before he had been hardened to withstand the shocks and blows of frontier life. He finally commits suicide.

A notable thematic dramatic novel

Meredith's best known novel, *The Ordeal of Richard Feverel*, presents an elaboration of the same theme in true dramatic form, by recounting the entire youth of the sheltered son of a titled English family. Although the theme of the novel is definitely and constantly reiterated in the shape of questions from a book being written by the hero's father, it is nevertheless not so prominent as the action. To bring this about in spite of frequent didactic philosophizings, the author was forced to pen a closing scene which Stevenson declared was the most powerful dramatic passage in English prose.

The distinction between the didactic and the dramatic story may be still clearer to you if we speak of the theme as being presented by a preacher, and the plot as something presented by an actor. The preacher affects us by straight argument. He appeals directly to our mind. His instrument is logic. The actor appeals directly to our senses. He wishes to make us feel; he appeals to our emotions. His instrument is drama. Now the difference between the didactic story such as the fable, parable and the allegory, and the thematic dramatic narratives which we have reviewed just above, is that in the former the preacher is more successful in his efforts than the actor; while in the latter, the truly dramatic narratives, the actor

is more successful than the preacher. The highest performances of narrative art in this form are those in which
the preacher and actor both perform simultaneously, with
the actor standing in front of the preacher and out-por-
traying him. Perhaps I can show this best by the diagrammatic picture on the following page.

Didactic thematic stories are those written from the
point of view of the moralist, or preacher, in this
diagram, while dramatic thematic stories are those written
from the point of view of the artist. The former looks
straight at his moral and talks about it directly; the latter
sees it only indirectly, behind his actor, and all that he
has to say about it is *implied* from the way his actor per-
forms and what happens to him.

6. Actual Plotting of Thematic Stories.

In actually plotting a thematic story, where are we to
begin? Very few published thematic stories have been
plotted by beginning with the theme itself; most of them
were either thematic without the writer's knowing it or,
if he did know it, the material with which he began contained both story and theme in fairly complete form, thus
requiring only the finishing touches. The difficulty in
beginning with the theme is patently that the action and,
what is worse, the characters have to be chosen or invented
to fit the theme and none but the most experienced writer
can hope to do this with much success. It is easier to
invent action and themes than character.

7. Beginning With Theme Only

It is the *writing* of a thematic story that is made difficult
by beginning with the theme, not the plotting. For the
sake of examining the entire process of plotting the thematic story, however, we will make our first plot by beginning with a theme. Let us deliberately select a familiar

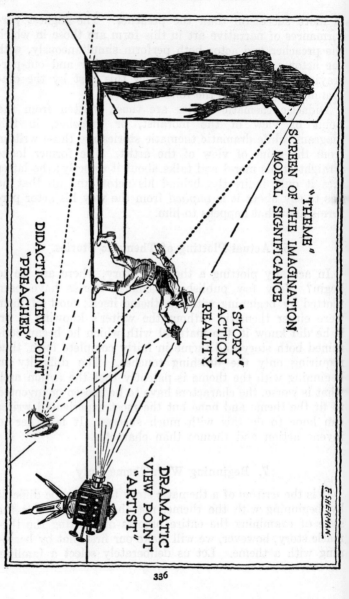

THE DIDACTIC AND DRAMATIC POINTS OF VIEW

"THEME"
SCREEN OF THE IMAGINATION
MORAL SIGNIFICANCE

"STORY"
ACTION
REALITY

DIDACTIC VIEW POINT
"PREACHER"

DRAMATIC VIEW POINT
"ARTIST"

F. SHERMAN.

336

and simple theme: " It is better to have loved and lost than never to have loved at all."

In plotting our story let us bear in mind that proving the theme is a matter of logic. We must think clearly, invent shrewdly. The argument of the plot must be irrefutable.

The above theme was submitted to a class of students and one of them presented the following plot:

Poor blind girl is wooed by young man in the dark on summer hotel porch. Should she allow him to do this, knowing that when he knows of her condition, he will leave her? Her life is lonely and loveless and will doubtless always be so.

She allows him to make love madly. He in time learns her condition and never comes again. Meanwhile the girl has recovered her sight as the result of the disappearance of a nervous disorder which her happiness over his wooing had removed.

The young man goes as an aviator to war and is killed, leaving the girl a large sum of money. She builds a memorial to him, never marries, and dwells upon his virtues throughout the rest of her life.

Faulty logic

This plot does not prove our theme for two reasons:

1. What a blind girl with no opportunities for romance will do is certainly no criterion for a girl who is normal, happy and fully occupied with sport, friends and work. The blind girl, in other words, is a special case. A girl who had *other* means for happiness would be less willing to enter upon a hopeless love affair.

2. Accompanied with the loss of the loved one in this case is a definite improvement in fortunes in other respects: blindness cured, an end of poverty. Her happiness at having loved and lost therefore would be no criterion for a girl who gained no special advantages by having loved, who, for instance, was crushed, in despair, brought to the verge of suicide with everything lost.

The theme which this student plot expresses is this: " To love and lose, when attended by special advantages, is better than never to have loved when life is without joy or color." Or, this: " To love and lose is sometimes better than never to love."

Let us submit the above plot to the severest tests of logic and get a plot which *is* a proof. To do this our first step is to examine very narrowly the original theme and see exactly what it means, and rewrite it so as to bring out the full meaning. If it means anything at all it obviously means this: " It is *always* better to have loved and lost than never to have loved at all." A somewhat abstract form of this theme which gives us a definite hint of what our problem in plotting is, is this: " The worst case of loving and losing is always better than the best case of never having loved."

Correct logic

If we rewrite the situations plotted above, in order to satisfy the demands of the theme as restated, we have the following:

A young girl, healthy, happy, provided with all the boons of life except love, suddenly falls madly in love with a young man who later meets and agrees to marry another girl. The heroine is jilted. She is heartbroken; the joy goes out of her life; her health is undermined; she thinks of suicide and is an invalid for the rest of her days. She never regrets her violent and ill-fated love affair. Late in her life, where the story would begin, a young girl, say her niece, comes to her for advice. The niece says a man she likes does not love her, and she is afraid that if she allows herself to love him he may jilt her, and so break her heart. What shall she do? The old lady tells her story as above, finally advising her niece that " real love, in any form, is the greatest thing in the world; do not be afraid of it."

In this plot we have, let us say, a " worst possible case of loving and losing "; we also have the best case of never having loved; and lastly, we make it very clear by the action that the former state was better than the latter. The demands of logic are thus taken care of and drama and theme are harmonized.

It is obvious that the chief object of the above manipulations was to get the plot to "match" the theme. The theme, in other words, may be considered one part of an equation, the plot being the other. This being so, we can set down plot and theme and check one off against the other, phrase by phrase. The two plots just given for instance, furnish the following equations:

Defective Plot

Theme	Plot
Worst case of loving and losing,	Girl refuses to marry. She builds a monument to a dead soldier, whose love restored her sight and who left her a fortune.
is always better than	out of gratitude at being removed from
best case of never having loved.	her former condition of blindness, poverty and want of love.

Correct Plot

Worst case of loving and losing	An elderly woman whose life has been ruined by a lover who jilted her in her youth
is always better than	advises a beloved niece to take the same risk she did in loving a man of the same type
best case of never having loved.	even though the niece, like herself in her youth, has health, happiness, and all the boons of life.

It is clear from these analyses that the second plot proves the theme better than the first because its action more completely fulfills the demands of the theme. A woman's refusal to marry and her building a monument to a former lover do not necessarily prove that she now prefers her present sad memories to her loveless condition before she met the man. If a woman, on the other hand, suffers unspeakably from an ill-starred love affair and afterwards calmly advises the person dearest in life to her to risk having the same thing happen to her, we can be pretty sure that " it is better to have loved and lost than never to have loved at all."

If you quarrel with the action and say that it couldn't happen, I must reply that it is as true as the theme and remind you that our concern now is not whether the theme is true or false; we have assumed that it would make an effective story if plotted properly; if we have done this, we have achieved our purpose. The question of whether a given theme is itself suitable for use in narrative is a special problem which is considered at the end of this chapter.

8. Beginning With Material and Theme

The great majority of thematic stories, as already explained, sprout not from a theme alone but from some actual happening which itself suggests a theme. Plotting such material involves less invention of new material, the main task being manipulation that makes certain that the story itself is both sufficiently dramatic and also a logical proof of the theme. Let us now plot a thematic story in this manner, using actual notebook material about the scientists in the desert which has served for illustrative purposes in previous chapters. Suppose in searching through a travel journal one day, for a " story idea," I come upon the following entry:

Vladimir and I have had enough of each other. We wrangle constantly. Over our tea this evening we fell into another dispute over our political philosophy. He continued to defend czaristic bureaucracy, maintaining that the peasants are all brainless animals and that nothing but a mailed fist can keep them in order. I argued the good old Lincolnian idea of democracy, though I later regretted it. Vladimir gets personal in such discussions; tonight he pounded the table and swore. The heat is "getting" him. Strangely enough, however, when he saw a tarantula on the wall behind me and warned me, there was positive tenderness in his voice.

On reading this note I pause and consider. It has a different "feel" from most of my notes. It strikes me in a peculiar manner and I am immediately curious to analyze this reaction. What causes it? I must determine the kind of interest here. Obviously it isn't character interest, nor atmosphere interest, nor even complication interest — there is nothing unique about the poisonous spider's presence during a tea-table conversation for we were in the desert to collect those insects and saw them constantly. The interest therefore *must* be in its thematic implications.

Discovering the theme

What is the theme implied here? I reason the thing out: My companion hates me in argument, then, on seeing me in danger, suddenly becomes gently considerate. Why? If he *really* hated me, wouldn't he enjoy seeing me in danger? Not necessarily. If *his* safety depended largely upon my being kept in able-bodied condition, he would be much concerned over any danger to me. This was the actual case when this note was made. Vladimir could not have finished his work without me. We were quite alone.

What does all this prove about life in general? I am struck by my companion's being *forced* to be considerate in spite of his "boiling up" inside. Do not all men do the same thing? If a man's *safety*, his life, depends upon his being kind to others, he will be kind to others. This is sound sociology and I now write my theme down as follows: "Men learn to stand together and conquer their primitive combative instincts when they are forced to do so by some external danger greater than their menace to each other." This theme, I decide, is sufficiently true and striking to hold to and I now proceed to manipulate the actual occurrence so that it will prove it more dramatically.

Disclosing weaknesses in material

We can at once make an equation of theme and plot material in condensed form and so discover the weakness of the latter:

Theme	Plot
Men learn to stand together and conquer their primitive combative instincts	A. and B. in the midst of a desert quarrel over different political beliefs, when suddenly A. shows concern for the safety of B.
by being forced to do so by	
some external danger greater than their menace to each other.	who he sees, is in danger from a tarantula crawling up the wall behind him.

The want of parallelism and sound logical relation between theme and plot here is evident. Since the theme is a statement true of mankind in general it means that *all* men in whatever case will learn to stand together when menaced. However, in the plot as it now stands, the two men are engaging only in a mild dispute. Proving that men thus disputing with each other will cease their quarrel when faced by a greater external menace proves nothing about what men who are mortal enemies will do in the same circumstances. In other words, to prove that all enmities can be forgotten, we must make the enmity in our plot as extreme as possible. Let us say therefore that both A. and B. hate each other so that they are ready to kill each other at a moment's notice.

Eliminating weaknesses

Secondly, our plot states that the spider was merely " crawling up the wall " behind B. The theme, however, states that enemies cease their attacks when faced by a danger " greater than their menace to each other." The menace to each other we have now intensified to a determination to kill. Our external danger must therefore *exceed this menace.* Can we use the insects to produce such a menace? Yes, if we place the men so that if one of them is bitten the other not only will be unable to finish his work, as first stated, but will lose his life in some horrible manner. With these manipulations we can now restate theme and plot correctly as follows:

Theme	*Plot*
Men always learn to stand together and conquer their primitive combative instincts	A. and B. exploring desert wastes together quarrel until each is ready to kill the other and would do so
by being forced to do so by	were it not for the fact that
some external danger greater than their menace to each other.	if A. kills B., A. will be unable to get out of the desert alive.

This plot " checks " with our theme. It proves the theme, whereas the actual happening with which we began is only a *suggestive illustration.* This plot, even though reduced as it is to the barest skeleton, suggests enough conflict to make the story genuinely dramatic. It is quite easy by using other notebook material, to outline briefly the story which, you will recall, has already been used as an example of the pure thematic story in Chapter Three:

Professor Petrov, noted entomologist, penetrates the unknown desert wastes with an assistant, Anton. Their task is to study and collect specimens of the poisonous tarantula and scorpion. Professor Petrov has taken an assistant because it is impossible for him to erect the canvas shelter against the desert winds or load the camels, or handle the wireless set effectively without help.

Differences of political beliefs arouse animosities which, under the blazing torture of the heat and wind, increase to hatreds. Both men nourish murder in their hearts, but each time knife or revolver is drawn, the tragic warning comes that if the other fellow is incapacitated, both will die, and the one left alone will meet the more horrible death of the two.

The poisonous insects also constantly menace their safety. Each, in spite of his murderous hatred, watches the other with the greatest solicitude. Finally when one is bitten, the other eagerly sucks the poison from the wound, thus saving his life. By the time they near the end of their journey their bitterness has worn away and when they reach sight of flower-dotted prairies and cozy villages, and regale themselves with hot baths, sumptuous meals, and long, cool drinks, they find they are fast friends for life.

Here are analyses of two other thematic stories:

9. Analysis of Notable Thematic Stories

The Unfinished Story

By O. Henry

Theme	Plot
Working girls forced to accept starvation wages are	Because the $6.00 which the department store manager pays Dulcie as her weekly wage is not enough for her to live on
victims of the most heartless villainy.	she, in spite of her innate sense of decency and honor, is driven by hunger into the arms of a human pig who despoils her forever.

Old Age

By Anton Chekhov

Theme	Plot
Age]	An elderly man, too old to be remembered by the people of his home village when he returns after many years' absence
wipes out]	finds to his surprise that because of his age he no longer is interested in the townsfolk, that the memories of his adventurous youth no longer stir him, that
all.]	he is even unable to drop a tear at his wife's grave or feel even a pang of regret.

In these two stories by writers given to frequent use of "the story that says something," we have pronounced emphasis on the theme. In the O. Henry story, as already pointed out, the theme is stated so boldly in the frame of the story as to make it verge on the didactic; whatever it has of drama is implied and not expressed. The Chekhov story is practically devoid of conflict, the whole effect depending upon the startling, tragic nature of the theme itself.

10. Analysis of a Thematic Novel

The problem of plotting a thematic novel is the same in principle as that of plotting the shorter narrative form we have been considering. The difference in practice is merely the greater length and complexity of the novel plot and the larger scope of its theme. Although space in which to analyze completely the plot of a thematic novel is wanting, we can exhibit the problem in its essentials by examining " equations " of the short story and novel using related material, mentioned on page eight.

Thrown Away.

(Short story)

By Rudyard Kipling.

Theme	Plot
" To rear a boy under what parents call the ' sheltered life system ' is	The Boy, after being spoiled by his parents, pampered in military school, and kept " unspotted from the world " in a depot battalion
if the boy must go into the world and fend for himself	goes to India to carve a career
not wise, and he may come to extreme grief."	and there is so stricken by what he felt was the " criminal folly" of gambling and extravagance, and by a military reprimand, that he shoots himself in despair.

By greatly condensing the plot of the novel we have the following:

The Ordeal of Richard Feverel.

(Novel)

By George Meredith.

Theme	Plot
A parent who grimly insists on his son's living in accordance with any pre-conceived system of perfect conduct will,	Sir Austin Feverel brings his son Richard up under " a system of education " whose general purpose was to protect him from a knowledge of evil, even to the point of refusing to allow him, when ready for love, to meet and fall in love with girls of his own class. The boy meanwhile encounters, falls madly in love with, and secretly marries Lucy, a farmer's niece.

if he continues to try to bend the boy's life to this theory after it encounters the boy's mature natural desires,

Sir Austin's opposition to the marriage on the score of the girl's being too young, of a lower social class, and of a different religion, forces young Richard to abandon his wife.

bring disaster.

Exiled from both wife and father, the boy, unprepared for life's temptations, falls into a scheming woman's wiles, and is led into a duel in which he is wounded. The young wife, now with a baby at her breast, goes mad and dies from the shock, thus blasting the boy's whole life.

The theme of Kipling's story is quoted from the opening words of the narrative. It is obviously narrower in scope than the theme of the novel. The former concerns merely the "sheltered life"; the latter embraces a whole "preconceived system" of conduct ruthlessly applied to a boy's life. Regarding the things which make up the sheltered life we are all fairly agreed, and Kipling summarizes them convincingly in a few lines. An explanation of Sir Austin's carefully elaborated philosophy of education, of which the "sheltered life" is merely a part, demands the spacious limits of a novel.

The main difference in the *plots* is that the short story gets its drama from the single specific struggle of The Boy with his hostile environment, while the drama of the novel is the struggle between the elaborate controls of the father's "system" and the developing maturity of his son. In the short story, moreover, there is no character change: The Boy was already spoiled by the sheltered life theory before the conflict in which "the theory killed him dead." In the novel, however, young Richard passes through several character changes under stress, the most notable of which are, of course, his romance before his marriage and his amour afterwards with the seductive Mrs. Mount.

Our study of the use of themes in current fiction we shall take up with the assignments at the end of this chapter. In working out answers to the problems there presented and comparing them with the answers in the Appendix you will gain some idea of why the writers of today are succeeding and failing in handling this difficult type of story.

11. What Are Acceptable Themes?

Another important problem always present in connection with the thematic story is that of determining whether or not the theme itself is a good one. There are no rules by which this can easily be done. Difficulty arises from the fact that in deciding upon the acceptability of a theme you face both a technical and an editorial issue. These issues are:

Technical: Can the theme be presented by a given narrative form?

Editorial: Will the theme thus presented appeal to the audience for which the story is to be written?

It is not the function of this book, as previously explained, to expound editorial problems; experience alone will give the writer the needed wisdom here as practice and the gifts of philosophy and logic will solve the technical problem. Some guidance will, however, be of immediate use and I offer the following:

Observations on Narrative Themes.[1]

1. *A theme for either short story or novel should not be too obvious.* This is the most common error exhibited

[1] For a discussion of the question as to whether the writer should understand or believe in his theme, see pp. 58–62, *Art and Business of Story Writing*, Pitkin.

by the themes of beginners. " Love is the greatest thing in the world," is of this class. This theme, as far as technique is concerned, might be proved in either short story or novel, but an editorial objection arises. For the youthful mind that devised it and for readers whose minds are equally youthful, the theme might have sufficient novelty and importance to enable it to become the main interest in a story embodying it; but for the mature reader proof of such an axiom would have much the same effect as proof of " It's better to do right than wrong! " The *story* itself might be very interesting to the mature reader, but, if so, the interest would be emphatic and not thematic. It would not be a " story which says something."

Every action of course proves *something*. The simplest kind of love story might be said to prove that when young people well mated and sympathetic with each other meet, they will fall in love and, other things being equal, will marry. An adventure story like *Robinson Crusoe* might be said to prove that a man as adventurous as Crusoe will struggle to survive when cast upon a desert island; but such statements of themes are so close to the action itself that they are indeed more plots than themes. *As themes* they are too obvious to be interesting.

2. *A theme must not be too large or universal.* This presents a purely technical problem. There are some truths or generalizations which are too big for a short story and some too comprehensive even for a novel. " America is God's country," for instance, might be, and probably has been proved in a novel, but it is too big for a short story. " God's in His heaven " and " It would be a great world if it weren't for the people in it," are too big for demonstration in any form of narrative.

3. *A good theme must be striking or unique in some way.* This, as in the case of observation number one, is largely an editorial problem. Examples of themes acceptable from this standpoint are: " Women are human be-

ings before wives or mothers "; " Notoriety is scandal **if** you are poor, advertising if you are rich "; and " Temptation has no geography."

4. *A theme must be something a reasonable number of people will believe.* The theme need not express only things which people already know; they may not know them until they are told; but if they recognize them and are impressed by them when they are told, the theme has been skillfully chosen. Here are examples, good and bad:

American village life is mentally, morally and physically sordid and ugly.

The great majority of the American people did not believe this before Mr. Lewis's novel, *Main Street*, appeared; the majority of them do not believe it yet. When told in this story, however, they saw enough truth in it to add to their pleasure in reading the book.

Practically all human nervous disorders have their origin in some sex mal-adjustment.

This is true, but it is not suitable for use in narrative for general reading simply because the vast majority of people not only don't believe it but are so prejudiced against believing it that they will get no pleasure in having the facts rammed home, no matter how painlessly the ramming is managed.

Mothers who, without absolute need, wear themselves out caring for their children so that when their children leave home they collapse from want of occupation, are victims of their own blind self-indulgence.

This theme probably stands on the border line. Its wise use is purely an editorial problem. For a publication read by really intelligent people it might provide an interesting shock, but the idea of motherhood held by the great uncultivated mass of readers is so colored by sentiment about mothers that any attempt to persuade them to a philosophic view of it would be hopeless.

5. *A theme should not be too controversial.* This is also purely an editorial consideration. It applies only when the writer's purpose is specifically commercial as well as artistic, when he wishes to sell his manuscript to the highest bidder. When this is his purpose, he will do well to avoid themes which involve the deeper faiths, life-long convictions, and personal tastes of large masses of people. Examples are questions of race superiority or inferiority, religious disputes, political party allegiances, and social questions such as prohibition, socialism, and divorce.

A thematic story outline presented as suggested in this chapter and having the instructor's corrections is given on the next page.

AMERICAN BEAUTY

Type of story: thematic.
Single effect: sympathy for old man
who is misunderstood. *and appreciation of theme*
Theme: No man who creates beauty in
American towns can be called crazy.
Initial complication: "Queer" old
chap lives on ugly outskirts of town. His
hobby is flowers. He spends hours working a-
mong vines and plants he keeps blooming around
his little home. It makes a lovely picture in
a drab community. A young gambler from the
town disappears. He had a large sum of money
in his possession. Had been drinking. Was
last seen talking to old man. They were in
heated argument because young man had trampled
some plants under foot. Old man is suspected
of murder.
Main character: Dave Bender, old man
called "queer".
Main trait: Love of flowers.
Crucial situation: When mob comes to
old man's place and accuses him of murder.
They trample and destroy all his beautiful
flowers. Dig up newly-made flower bed, but
find it contains only rare bulbs. Old man protests. Officers come to quell riot. Decide
old chap is crazy, and lock him up. He is given hearing. The judge before whom it is held
is a famous legal light visiting his home town,
taking the place of a sick friend. He allows
old man to return home. Says he is only sane
one in crowd. He creates beauty. Others don't
even/see it!
Outcome: Old man is released.

Make clear that mob hates him because it doesn't understand him.

This point must be established to make proof of your theme complete. Why not have judge produce proof that the missing man committed suicide because of the general ugliness of the town?!

ASSIGNMENTS: CHAPTER SEVEN

Some of the first of these assignments may seem too easy to be worth doing, but I assure you again that a mere general comprehension of the principles involved in these exercises is not enough: the exercises, especially those which require writing, must be *done* if you are to train your abilities as a creative writer. We learn by doing, not by mere thinking. Facility in *actually handling* such problems as are presented here will help you, moreover in departments of writing other than plotting thematic stories. *Remember, too, that it is not necessary that the action of a fable or parable prove a theme; it is enough if it is an illustration of it.*

ASSIGNMENT A

The first two assignments present fairly simple practice in determining the differences between didactic and dramatic writing. The first calls for analysis, the second for writing.
1. Is the following quotation didactic or dramatic?

He that is slow to anger is better than the mighty; and he that ruleth his spirit, than he that taketh a city.

2. Is the following improvisation didactic or dramatic?

Dallin's hobby was collecting birds' eggs. For ten years he had gathered, mounted and labeled specimens from all over his state. For several days now he had been thrilling with the knowledge that one of the leading ornithologists in the country was coming to his home to view his collection. The day the noted scientist was due, Dallin went home early to arrange his collection. On reaching home he found that his four-year-old son had pulled out the boxes containing the delicate specimens, upset them on the floor, and stepped on and smashed most of them. Time and again the father had told the little fellow not to touch the egg boxes. The house was no small and there were so many that he could not secrete them from the boy's reach. The boy knew he had done wrong, for he ran at his father's approach. His father, seeing the wreckage, ran after his son, seized him in one hand and a heavy walking stick in the other and was about to beat the lad when he paused, trembled, threw the stick in a corner, released the boy, and, with tears of disappointment and dismay streaming down his cheeks, staggered toward the telephone in the next room.*

3. Which in the following is given greater emphasis, *ideas or story action?*

Dallin was a man who believed that the greatest virtue is self-control. Moral courage, he said, was of a much higher quality than physical courage, and control of temper displayed the finest type of moral strength. His beliefs were severely tested one day when he returned home and found that his four-year-old son had, in his mother's absence from the house, got into a fine collection of birds' eggs and smashed most of them. As soon as Dallin saw the wreckage of several years' patient labor, he felt an instinctive impulse to punish his little son severely, and seized a heavy stick for the purpose. Immediately, however, he remembered his creed about self-control. "I must pause and consider," he said to himself. "If I punish the lad, it must be because it will do him good, and not because it will be an exhaust to my own terrific emotions." So reasoning, he finally decided not to punish the boy. He was too young, he felt, to be judged responsible.*

4. Is the following close of O. Henry's story, *The Gift of the Magi,* didactic or dramatic?

And here I have lamely related to you the uneventful chronicle of two foolish children in a flat who most unwisely sacrificed for each other the greatest treasures of their house. But in a last word to the wise of these days let it be said that of all who give gifts, these two were the wisest. Everywhere they are wisest. They are the magi.*

5. Is the opening of this same story didactic or dramatic?

One dollar and eighty-seven cents. That was all. And sixty cents of it was in pennies. Pennies saved one and two at a time by bulldozing the grocer and the vegetable man and the butcher until one's cheeks burned with the silent imputation of parsimony that such close dealing implied. Three times Della counted it. One dollar and eighty-seven cents. And the next day would be Christmas.

6. The following opening of Kipling's story, *Miss Youghal's Sais,* contains both didactic and dramatic material. Note down which is which and where one ends and the other begins:

Some people say that there is no romance in India. Those people are wrong. Our lives hold quite as much romance as is good for us. Sometimes more. Strickland was in the Police, and people did not understand him; so they said he was a doubtful sort of man and passed by on the other side. Strickland had himself to thank for this.

7. Here is a more difficult test. In the midst of his story, *Sisters of the Golden Circle,* O. Henry, in referring to the wedding trip of his heroine, inserts the following bit of whimsicality. Is it didactic or dramatic?

Dear, kind fairy, please cut out those orders for money, and 40 H.P. touring cars and fame and a new growth of hair, and the presidency of the boat club. Instead of any of them turn backward — ah, turn backward and give us just a teeny-weeny bit of our wedding trip over again. Just an hour, dear fairy, so we can remember how the grass and the poplar trees looked, and the bow of those bonnet strings beneath her chin — even if it was the hat pins that did the work. Can't do it? Very well; hurry up with that touring car and the oil stock, then.

8. Is the emphasis of the story of George Washington and the cherry tree, ending, " Father, I cannot tell a lie; I did it with my little hatchet," more on the *idea* of truthfulness or on the *picture* of someone acting in a truthful manner?

9. Which of the following two versions of the same fable is the more didactic?

a. A fox saw a crow in a tree holding a piece of cheese in her beak. " My, what a fine-looking bird you are! " the fox said to the crow. " If your voice is as lovely as your looks, you are indeed the queen of birds." The crow, hearing this speech, tipped her head one way, then the other, shook a foot, dropped the cheese and began cawing raucously. The fox picked up the cheese and made off with it.

b. A sly fox one day saw a stupid crow sitting in a tree with a piece of cheese in its beak. The fox, having sharpened his wits by much trickery, spoke flatteringly to the crow of her beauty, adding, " If your voice is as fine as your looks, you are indeed the queen of birds." Hearing this, the silly crow dropped the cheese and began to crow raucously. " My dear madame," said the wily fox, " I would remind you that the flatterer lives at the expense of those who listen to him. This advice is worth more to you than the cheese." So saying, he picked up the cheese, and made off with it.

ASSIGNMENT B

1. Write a brief episode like No. 2 in the previous assignment, making it an illustration of a man carrying out in his conduct the moral precept set forth in No. 1 above.

2. Do the same with the following proverb: " Better is a dinner of herbs where love is, than a stalled ox and hatred therewith."

3. Write out an instance of a boy's discovering that " Honesty is the best policy," using two boys working in an office. One of the boys is tempted to steal from his employer.

4. Write the same episode again, this time making it as purely dramatic as possible.

5. Rewrite the following version of a fable, eliminating all didactic elements and making your account as dramatic as possible:

An instance of the evil of vanity is to be found in the story of the frog who tried to be as big as a cow. This vain little animal, accompanied by a sister green-back, one day found himself confronting a cow, lying down in a pasture, quietly chewing her cud.

Immediately the vain little frog began to strut and boast: "See, am I not as big and fine as the cow?"

"You are not," said his companion, who scorned his presumptuous egotism. She was wiser than her friend, too, for observe now how the vain little frog came to grief because of his silly vanity.

"Watch me!" cried the vain frog, and he began to inflate nimself. "See, am I not now as big as the cow?"

"Never!" answered the truthful companion.

"Well, watch, just watch!" cried the vain little frog, who continued to swell and swell until he burst.

6. Write out from memory the fable of *The Tortoise and the Hare,* omitting all didactic comment.

7. The moral of the fable of *The Tortoise and the Hare is* "Persistence wins." Rewrite it, bringing out this thought: "The steady plodder wins but the fickle wanderer has a better time on the way."

8. Write a brief parable by using the moral in the fable of *The Frog and the Cow* ("Vanity is its own destruction,"), and substituting people and actions appropriate to them.

9. Write another parable in the same way using the moral of the original fable of *The Tortoise and the Hare:* "Persistence wins."

10. Rewrite *The Tortoise and the Hare,* giving the tortoise a head-start on the hare and handling it in such a way that the story is purely dramatic and has no moral or thematic significance at all.

11. Rewrite the parable asked for in No. 8 above, changing the action freely in the same way (as directed in No. 10).

12. Rewrite the parable asked for in No. 9 above in the same way (as directed in No. 10).

ASSIGNMENT C

The following are brief outlines of published short stories which clearly and effectively express a theme in the dramatic manner. The task here is to determine what the theme is in each case and write it down in a single, declarative sentence. Reason the matter out carefully.

1. A Belgian soldier after the armistice returned one evening to his own village which had been ravaged by the destructive fury of the double lines of battle. He scarcely recognized the muddy clutter of ruined cottages, gaping churches, and shell-torn streets along which a few pitiful refugees were returning to the remains of their former homes. The soldier was, however, used to such scenes and his mind dwelt upon the young and lovely sweetheart whom he had left behind. Where was she now? His meditations were interrupted by a ragged, worn woman who touched him on the arm and said in fuddled accents: " Where are you going, M'sieu? With me, hein? "

The soldier laughed. " Not with you, old girl,' he answered. " I'm going to find my sweetheart."

He looked down at her. An improvised street lamp lit up her face.

She screamed. He seized her by the shoulders and dragged her closer to the light. His fingers dug into her flesh and his eyes gleamed. He recognized her as her whom he sought. " Joan! " he gasped.*

(*What the Vandals Leave,* see page 280.)

2. Wilbur Haskett, naturally timid and afraid of his own opinions, has tried in vain to follow his father's advice and take responsibility. He is fired from three jobs. Then he gets one where he stays happily in the background, taking no responsibility. His refusal to decide on a new sales manager, putting the decision up to the salesmen instead, wins the approval of the head of the firm. He is promoted time after time, always as the result of having shifted responsibility or divided it. He gradually sees that all the other successful men are doing the same thing. Finally even in his proposal to the girl he loves he puts responsibility on the other party.

(*The Buck-passer,* Hugh McNair Kahler.)

3. A poor beggar, because of a crippled body and defective mind, is unable to earn a living. He limps about the countryside on a pair of crutches, beseeching food of the farmers and sleeping in fence corners and haystacks. An untrue rumor that he is vicious is spread about. Thefts of eggs and chickens are finally unjustly laid to his account. As a result no one feeds him. He begins to starve. Maddened by the pangs of hunger he throws a stone at a chicken, kills it and is preparing to eat it when he is caught. He is immediately taken to jail as a desperate villain and locked in a cell. The next morning, to the surprise of the jailer, he is found dead.

(*The Beggar,* Maupassant.)

4. The Sunset Express twenty miles west of Tucson, Arizona, was held up and robbed by three bandits. The leader, " Shark " Dodson, aided by Bob Tidball and an Indian named John Big Dog, blew open the safe in the express car, removed $30,000 and

fled in the locomotive which they detached from the coaches. The Indian was killed by a bullet from the rifle of the express messenger. The other two robbers left the locomotive with their booty, and plunged into the forest.

Three horses were tethered there awaiting them. That belonging to the Indian they untied and set free. Mounted on the other two they rode through the forest and up a lonely gorge. There Tidball's horse slipped and broke a foreleg and had to be shot.

A discussion then arose as to how the two men could continue their flight. Tidball wished to "ride double." Dodson, however, was afraid that his exhausted mount, which he called Bolivar, could not possibly carry them both to safety. In answer to Tidball's honest flattery of Dodson's skill as a desperado, Dodson explains that he came from New York State and that his coming west was merely an accident.

He was walking, with his clothes in a bundle, towards New York City, he declared, when he came to a fork in the road. He didn't know which fork to take. He finally decided on the left-hand fork which took him west. "I've often wondered," he said, "if I wouldn't have turned out different if I'd took the other road."

"Oh, I reckon you'd have ended up about the same," said Bob Tidball, cheerfully philosophical.

The discussion about the lone horse continued. "There ain't any chance for but one of us," said "Shark" Dodson, pointing his revolver at his companion, "Bolivar cannot carry double." In spite of Tidball's pleadings, Dodson shot him in cold blood, mounted his horse and galloped off.

As he galloped away, however, the woods seemed to fade from his view; the revolver in his right hand turned to the curved arm of a mahogany chair; his saddle was strangely upholstered, and he opened his eyes and saw that he, Dodson, of the firm of Dodson and Decker, Wall Street brokers, was being spoken to by his confidential clerk. "I must have fallen asleep," he yawned, blinking, and asked the clerk what he wanted.

The clerk stated that a client named Williams had come to pay for stock purchased of Dodson. The stock had risen in value so that if Williams paid at the market price as agreed his business would be bankrupted and he would lose his home besides.

"What is the present market price?" asked Dodson.

"One eighty-five, sir."

"Williams will settle at one eighty-five," said Dodson. "Bolivar cannot carry double."

(*The Roads We Take*, O. Henry.)

5. An old man visits the office of a prosperous manufacturer, who is obviously much pleased with recent improvements in his office furnishings. During the conversation the old man mentions that his daughters have just returned from visiting their brother's grave in France, and had seen the grave of the manufacturer's

son. The old man is apparently more interested in the exorbitant prices which the girls had to pay at restaurants, and in the upkeep of the cemetery than in the fact of the boy's death, now six years past.

After the old man's departure, the manufacturer shuts himself up, but he finds no tears. He thinks about his wild grief when he first knew of his son's death, and when he had felt that he could never live it down. The business which he had built up for the boy had seemed at once purposeless. Now six years have passed. He is enjoying recent improvements in his plant, and he has no tears.

While he is meditating, a fly gets into the ink. He helps it out, and watches it dry its wings. When it is just able to crawl, he drops a big drop on it. The fly begins again. Just as it is again able to crawl, he drops on it another drop. It tries again more feebly. He drops another drop, and that is the end. He flings it into the waste basket. He has forgotten what he was thinking about before the fly episode.

(*The Fly,* by Katherine Mansfield.)

6. Nell, sick of the endless routine of mothering four children and tending a house, rebels. She arranges a vacation in the city visiting a friend, and all the rest of the family go off for ten days to do the things that they want most to do, the father fishing, the daughter visiting a friend in the city, the grandma entertaining a friend of her youth, the baby farmed out, the two boys on the uncle's farm. In the city Nell finds herself envying her friend's freedom and mental emancipation.

She decides to leave her husband and go it alone. That night she is called by long distance, but before she hears a word the connection is broken by the storm. She feels sure that no one would have called her unless in some dire emergency. She suddenly realizes that she loves her family, and does not want a career.

She hurries home by the first train, and finds everyone well. They had all come back sooner than they had intended, after finding their vacation plans in one way or another disappointing. The telephone call had been from her husband who had tried to let her know that they were all back, and hoped that she would come too.

(*Nell Custom Lets Her Family Shift for Itself,* Bess Streeter Aldrich.)

ASSIGNMENT D

In this assignment we shall attempt some fairly simple problems in plotting stories in the dramatic manner. In Assignment B the narratives we wrote in the dramatic manner were intended to be only instances or illustrations of certain themes; now we go further and make our narratives prove as conclusively as possible the validity of their given themes. We shall here find use for the theme-plot equation explained in the body of Chapter Seven.

1. Build a plot in the dramatic manner around the theme in Assignment B, No. 3, above: "Honesty is the best policy." The two boys suggested in this other exercise are, say, Jack and David. Jack pilfers from his employer, spends the money and has a good time, while honest David, having only his meager wage, is denied such pleasures. On this showing, *dishonesty* would seem to be the best policy; but we believe in our theme and must deliberately manipulate the story to prove the theme *is* true and true in *all* cases. The logic of the matter is obviously this: If it *always* pays to be honest, it pays even when the dishonest man, let us say, gets away with a lot of money, and when the honest man is left in more or less poverty. The fate of the unluckiest honest man, in other words, is better than the fate of the luckiest dishonest man. Decide what such fates might be and write out your plot.

2. Rewrite the above plot now so as to prove the opposite of the above theme, namely: "Dishonesty is the best policy."

3. The theme of the following published story purports to be this: "A rich girl has no right to compete in work with poor girls." Study it carefully, matching theme against plot. The plot because of a serious logical weakness fails to prove the theme. Exactly what is this weakness?

Gerda Breck, the daughter of very wealthy parents, goes to a college which specializes in fitting women for useful work. She refuses to live on her parents' wealth, after graduation, and gets a position as stenographer, and will not listen to the entreaties of Bram, her lover. She makes good and gets a raise. Bram pleads with her to quit and marry him, but she refuses him flatly.

Soon after, when a number of the girls are fired, she is promoted for her good work, and is given the position of secretary to a member of the firm, over the head of a woman who had long been in line for the place, but who was getting old.

The next day the papers have the news of this older woman's suicide. She had been the sole support of an invalid sister and her two small children, and she had killed herself in order that they might have her insurance to live on.

Gerda, horrified at the revelation of the terrible competition in the business world, sends in her resignation. She will no longer keep a job away from a girl to whom it may be a matter of life and death. She marries Bram.

4. Let us see if we can turn the fable of *The Tortoise and the Hare* into a thematic story in the dramatic manner. David, let us say, will represent the tortoise, Jack, the Hare. The theme is: "Persistence wins." Both boys are members of the

college track team; the crucial situation is a mile race. Outline the story.

5. Here is a student plot which was designed to prove dramatically this theme: "Efficient business girls are not efficient candidates for love and marriage." Read it carefully.

Dorothy Hollis, an attractive and efficient secretary, fell madly in love with her employer, John Carew. On her part she had ample opportunity to admire Carew's good looks, honesty, and ability and to sympathize with his ambitions. Knowing that he was heart free she allowed herself to become more and more absorbed in his every slightest word and gesture. Because she was efficient as a business woman she dressed inconspicuously, kept her feelings to herself, and conducted herself as if she were a piece of well-oiled office machinery.

Mr. Carew, on his part, appreciated Miss Hollis's secretarial abilities and paid her generously, but he never fell in love with her. Dorothy therefore went unloved and unwed.

This plot almost, but not entirely, proves the theme. The plot as it stands is only an illustration of the idea of the theme. If Dorothy with all her natural charm could not win her man because of her office handicaps, no girl could — so that is taken care of. But how about the employer? The theme expanded out of its epigrammatic form into an exact statement of what it obviously means is this: "No efficient office girl has a chance for love and happiness with any average, normal sort of employer." This suggests the weakness of the plot. Rewrite it now, completing the proof.

ASSIGNMENT E

Here are a few brief suggestions for more advanced technical drill with thematic material. They are intended mainly to suggest to instructors and advanced students ways of elaborating exercises which will bring them close to professional plotting of stories for publication.

1. Take any of the Poor Richard maxims like "Honesty is the best policy," "God helps them that help themselves," or "Never leave till tomorrow that which you can do today," or "It is hard for an empty bag to stand upright," and write, first fables, using animals, then parables, using human characters, illustrating these themes in the didactic manner.

2. Take the same themes and plot narrative proofs of them in the dramatic manner, making the emotional presentation in each case first pleasant, then tragic.

3. In order to secure familiar material as well as themes with which to plot thematic stories do a bit of philosophizing about the activities of the people with whom you are best acquainted. You have heard people say, referring to some occurrence, " Well, serves him right," or " He practices what he preaches." Can you say such things about the people you know? If you can, what were the principles involved in the action in question? Formulate the principles in the shape of a positive theme, and, *using as far as possible the same people and events which inspired the reflection,* plot your story. The result should be original and interesting.

4. For a still more advanced test of thematic plotting, write a brief but very frank and specific statement about your deepest convictions about life: the moral principles upon which you are trying to conduct your own life, your own explanation of the evil and crime in the world, your own idea of what should be done about it. From such a statement you should be able to cull themes which you can plot, using as far as possible people with whom you are acquainted. Since these themes are quite your own you will be able to throw into the writing of stories expressing them all the sincerity and fervor you possess.

CHAPTER EIGHT

THE ATMOSPHERE STORY

THE STORY THAT MAKES PLACES LIVE

There is a fitness in events and places. One place suggests work, another idleness, a third early rising and long rambles in the dew. The effect of night, of any flowing water, of lighted cities, of the peep of day, of ships, of the open ocean, calls up in the mind an army of anonymous desires and pleasures. . . . Some places speak distinctly. Certain dank gardens cry aloud for a murder; certain old houses demand to be haunted; certain coasts are set apart for shipwreck.

— STEVENSON.

With the atmosphere story we enter a field of literature attempted by but few writers. Only the greatest have shown anything like complete mastery of it. Given the material, it is not difficult to plot; but it is the most baffling of all forms of prose narrative to write. Since it is more mood than action and indulges in subtle effects, it appeals to but few readers. For all of these reasons, probably not more than one story among a thousand published is a true atmosphere story.

This tone poem of narrative, however, can be made to produce a magic beauty, a beauty that to many readers seems sadly lacking in these days of the canonization of brute fact and swift action that has no time to set a stage or dress the actors! Fiction cannot long remain disembodied. The rich exploitation of setting in the best work of Joseph Hergesheimer, Wilbur Daniel Steele, Evelyn Scott, Thomas Wolfe, E. P. O'Donnell, and, in less degree, Sinclair Lewis, is sufficient proof that the highest achievements in fiction will always have a habitation and a home. The partisans of *Anthony Adverse* praise immoderately Hervey Allen's poetic emphasis on setting. " He has brought mood back to the American novel." The genius of Thomas Hardy — is it not shown mainly in his majestic management of a brooding and tyrannical destiny which is but the atmosphere of a single locality, his native Egdon Heath? Hawthorne was an atmospherist. Conrad's looseness of form and ponderous deliberation are forgiven because of his exotic, colorful " style," which is again his atmosphere. Kipling in his *An Habitation Enforced, The Brushwood Boy,* and *They,* shows how greatly he was fascinated by the possibilities in effects in literary atmosphere. The influence of atmosphere on the human soul, meditated O. Henry in *A Matter of Mean Elevation,* " reaches as far back as time itself. There is an unnamable kinship of man to nature, a queer fraternity that causes stones and trees and salt water and clouds to play upon our emotions." And, to cite but one of a number of brilliant French masters of the lighter, gayer effects of this type — Daudet: you have read his *The Sous-Prefet Afield?* As you see that pathetically lovable official in his cocked hat, succumb to the warm, spring-time sun, the birds, violets and tender grass by " the little wood of green oaks," you witness the lovely, poetic triumph of a Provençal atmosphere!

This, then, is the story that makes landscape live, and we must learn something, if only a little, about it. You should write at least one good atmosphere story before you end your career! You can begin now. You can learn what your materials must be; and, even if you decide that the feat is forever beyond your powers, you will have in an understanding of the principles of atmosphere an asset for all other writing you may do. How this is so, you will soon see.

First of all, why is the atmosphere story so difficult? How is it distinguished as a plot pattern from the other forms we have studied? It is within our purpose here to attempt only brief answers to these questions.[1] Let us

[1] The student who wishes to go further into the problem of the psychology of atmosphere than is attempted here is referred to *The Art and Business of Short Story Writing,* by Professor Pitkin, pp. 193–216.

first of all examine two important facts about the structure of the atmosphere story.

1. Structure of the Atmosphere Story

The main character in an atmosphere story is the atmosphere itself. The atmosphere is the mood of the setting. Many students think that setting, that any description of an environment is atmosphere and they try to produce atmosphere by elaborating details of scenery. Real atmosphere can be produced only by handling settings *in a special way*. It is necessary to make a strong *impression* about the quality of the atmosphere just as, in handling the character story, it is necessary to make a powerful impression of human character. No mere description of a scene will suffice. The single effect of an atmosphere story harmonizes with the mood of the atmosphere, but it must be more than a mood or feeling; it must be a deep and powerful emotion; this emotion is produced by a conflict — the atmosphere dramatized.

Description by effect

Since atmosphere is composed only of things, and so cannot act, human characters have to be chosen to act for it. How did we secure an impression of character in the character story? In each case the character exemplified his trait by his conduct, by action. In one case, you remember, the main character displayed his savage determination to write successful short stories by neglecting his wife and baby until the former starved and the latter died. In another case, a lover braved the dangers of forest and flood to come to his beloved before she killed herself. Proof in each of these cases is dramatic proof. Says the popular proverb: "Tell me what you do and I'll tell you what you are." Proof of this sort can be made conclusive.

Nature cannot act as these characters acted. Nature does

not move, it simply *is*. You *can* depict human characters
in mere description without action by simply naming the
person's qualities; and in the same way you can give the
mood of a setting by description without action. The ob-
jections to such descriptions are, however, two in number:
First, they are not intense, and, second, having no movement and little variety they are monotonous, and could
not hold a reader's attention more than a few minutes. To
secure the needed intensity and variety there must be
action and drama; and therefore human beings must be
introduced.

2. Psychology of Atmosphere

How can human beings be used to represent or dramatize
the "character" qualities of a given setting? In the answer to this question lies all the peculiar subtlety of the
atmosphere story. We can most easily understand *the use
of human characters* in atmosphere stories if we think of
the problem for the moment as one of description. You
have learned in your study of rhetoric that *description by
effect* is the best of all ways to give a strong impression
of a person or place. This gives us our clue.

*Human characters in atmosphere stories are used mainly
to depict atmosphere by showing its effect on these characters.* This is the only way to achieve drama for a
"character" which has no conduct. The essence of this
method might be expressed by altering the popular proverb
above: "Tell me how you affect your friends; and I will
tell you what you are." The essential problem in plotting
the atmosphere story, therefore, is to show the effect of
the atmosphere on given characters. The resistance of
these characters to the influence of the atmosphere produces the story's dramatic conflict. Obviously, then, the
effect on the human character chosen must not be merely
casual or temporary. It must be decisive if not overwhelming. The greater the effect on the human character,

the greater the drama and the more powerful the impression on the reader. We must simply choose the *kind* of person who *will* and *can* be so affected.

This is not easy. Indeed, this necessity of matching, as it were, character and atmosphere is *the* difficulty of the atmosphere story which we set out to discover. From what has already been stated it might seem that atmosphere stories could be plotted by simply choosing any interesting landscape mood, selecting almost any person we might know well, and making this person react strongly to this atmosphere. It can't be done — not so easily, at any rate!

This difficulty of matching characters and atmosphere effects is not, as many believe, a " mystery," but it does involve some fairly abstruse problems of psychology and esthetics. It is not our purpose to go deeply into them here. For our practical needs it will be enough if I state as clearly as possible the two facts about atmosphere which bear most directly upon this problem and ask you, if you do not understand them, to take my word for their truth.

1. *The emotional qualities of places or settings have a much narrower range than the emotional qualities of human conduct.* All settings, that is, are much nearer alike as to their effect on the beholders than human beings are.[1] As regards emotional qualities, the gloomiest scene is more like the sunniest and brightest than the most brutal act of murder is like the most tenderly sympathetic act of a devoted mother. There is less shock, in other words, in turning from the contemplation of a *melancholy* autumn day to a *sparkling* spring day than there is in turning from the *tragically mournful* funeral of a friend to the *rough jests* of a circus clown.

2. *Atmosphere produces a greater variety of emotional effects in the beholder than does human conduct.* This is

[1] In speaking of the qualities of human beings I have in mind, of course, character qualities only, and specifically the moral qualities which we agreed in Chapter Four were of most interest to the narrative writer.

not so obvious as the first statement. Atmosphere with its narrow range produces more different effects than conduct with its much greater range. In all natural scenes there are some emotional qualities in common. Poets there are who find a certain "melancholy beauty" in all phases of nature, in a volcanic eruption or a thunderous storm at sea, as well as a pastoral woodland view. All natural scenes, in other words, differ from each other in their emotional qualities more in *degree* than in kind.

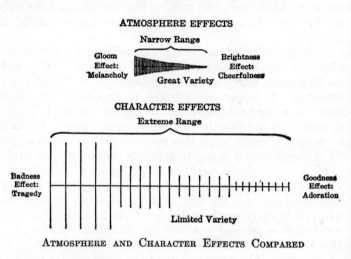

ATMOSPHERE EFFECTS

Narrow Range

Gloom Effect: Melancholy   Great Variety   Brightness Effect: Cheerfulness

CHARACTER EFFECTS

Extreme Range

Badness Effect: Tragedy   Limited Variety   Goodness Effect: Adoration

ATMOSPHERE AND CHARACTER EFFECTS COMPARED

Human conduct, on the other hand, as regards its emotional qualities differs in *kind* as well as in degree. Not only are some acts, that is, more sorrowful than others, thus differing in degree, but all acts inspiring pure sorrow are as unlike acts arousing sheer, clownish hilarity as diamonds are unlike potato bugs. Now things alike in kind can shade off into each other with infinite variety. By simply changing the light that falls upon a given scene one can almost run the entire gamut of atmosphere effects. Not so with things distinctly different in kind. They don't shade off at all. Many acts of conduct do, of course, blend with others in a way to produce a compound emotional effect, such, for instance, as tragedy and irony; but by and large, human acts seem to fall into great groups which as regards their emotional qualities are as far apart as the planets. Since there is this limit to the extent to which they can be blended, there is a limit to their variety.

These distinctions will perhaps be made clearer by the diagram on the opposite page.

3. Limitations of the Form

Remember that the structure of the atmosphere story requires that the author find a character who will react strongly to its influence and you see at once wherein the chief difficulty in managing the atmosphere story arises. Human conduct is too limited in variety, and atmosphere in range. Only in certain ways can the two be combined in the vital intimacy of dramatic action. Some examples will make this clear:

An altogether charming and lovely young woman, let us say, is picking early violets in a sunny, April meadow. Would it be difficult to discover a human being who would react strongly to the sight of the maiden? It would not.

Describing a young man who would fall madly in love and, on being repulsed by her, would do some noble deed or commit some desperate crime to attain her love is a task performed a hundred times a day by the newspaper reporters and novelists of America. But now remove the young lady. Let the April setting be the only dynamic force to work upon the hero, and you see at once the greater difficulty. Where is the man whose life will be saved, who will desert home and business, who will perhaps kill someone because of the influence of that April setting? It is not impossible to find him, but it is exceedingly difficult. And the difficulty is that the quality of human conduct is, as explained, comparatively limited in variety.

As an instance of the handicap placed upon this task of matching atmosphere and characters by the extreme range of human qualities, take this: A coldly calculating, keen, diabolically clever man, resolved upon winning great wealth by crushing every obstacle in his path — let him be the character. Now where is the atmosphere which will powerfully affect such a person? He might be drowned in the ocean, frozen in the north winds, or burned in a forest fire, but, if so, such influences on him would not be *atmosphere* influences: water, ice and fire are not qualities; they are things, and the predicaments they cause are ordinary complications. An atmosphere which would affect a man of this type probably cannot be found; the very nature of the brute is that such influences don't touch him. The difficulty here is that this person for dramatic purposes is *outside the range of all atmosphere.*

4. Action Must be Dramatic

These are fairly subtle matters, but you must not let them appall you. If they do not seem clear to you on the first reading, they will later, especially if you perform the assignments appended to this chapter. You are quite possibly wondering why it is so difficult to find characters who will respond to certain atmospheres and atmospheres which will affect certain people. " All people," you may be saying, " are affected more or less by all atmospheres; where is the difficulty? " True; but you mistake the problem; you have omitted the dramatic factor; you forget that we are just now dealing with the short story and that one of the ideals of this form of narrative is a dramatic struggle, and that in general the more spirited this struggle, the better the story. This being so the problem is not merely to discover people who *are influenced;* our task is to find people who are *overwhelmingly influenced.*

5. Psychology of " The Fall of the House of Usher "

This dramatic necessity as well as the peculiar limitation imposed by the subleties of atmosphere is strikingly
illustrated by Poe's *The Fall of the House of Usher*. The
quality of the atmosphere in this story is a " mysterious "
and " insufferable " gloom. The apparatus with which the
author produces this gloom is vacant and eye-like windows, dank walls covered with fungi, trees which think,
bed-rooms built over burial vaults, cataleptic living skel-
etons, funeral music and muffled screams in the dark.
What would you and I or any ordinary human being do
in a house offering such entertainment? We'd say, " This
place gives me the jimmies," and depart, promptly. But
while the character foil for an atmosphere may *also* be
terrified, *he must be lured, fascinated, because if he isn't,
he also will depart and, character and atmosphere being
parted, the story will come to a premature end.* He must
be the kind of person who both sticks around such places
and is overwhelmingly affected by them.

Whom did Poe choose for this purpose in *The Fall of
the House of Usher?* Roderick Usher. And here is what
Poe says of him:

The character of his face had been at all times remarkable.
A cadaverousness of complexion; an eye large, liquid and luminous beyond comparison; lips somewhat thin and very pallid,
but of a surpassingly beautiful curve . . . these features, with
an inordinate expansion above the regions of the temple, made
up altogether a countenance not easily to be forgotten. And
now in the mere exaggeration of the prevailing character of
these features, and of the expression they were wont to convey,
lay so much of change that I doubted to whom I spoke. The
now ghastly pallor of the skin, and the now miraculous lustre
of the eye, above all things startled and even awed me. . . .
The silken hair, too, had been suffered to grow all unheeded, and
as, in its wild gossamer texture, it floated rather than fell about
the face, I could not even with effort, connect its arabesque
expression with any idea of simple humanity. . . . .

What sort of a " bird " is this? Did you ever meet such a person — outside a madhouse? Probably not. All of which means that Poe felt that the atmosphere's the thing, and, since there was no real human being who would respond as powerfully as he wished to the particular atmosphere he wished to write about (because of the comparatively small variety of moral character patterns), he would take a character from the fantastic, irresponsible world of his own imaginings. He lets the insufferable gloom work upon Usher until, with other closely integrated tragic events, it brings him to his death.

6. Pattern of the Atmosphere Story

The relation among atmosphere, character, and action in this story of Poe's, and indeed in all pure atmosphere stories is indicated by the sketch on the opposite page.

In this drawing the narrative is conceived as moving from left to right with the progress of the little figure. The atmosphere itself is indicated by the shaded portion. The shading is practically the same depth throughout for the reason that the intensity of the actual quality of the atmosphere remains practically constant throughout the story. The thing that increases in intensity is the impression made on the reader by the conduct of the chief human actor.

The irregular line traces the action of the chief human actor. Since during the story he is constantly under the pressure of the atmosphere, he is pictured as never at any moment escaping from the limits of the atmosphere. His efforts to escape, however, are indicated by his movements up and down toward the limits of the field of the atmosphere. The increasing intensity of the whole dramatic situation is indicated by the tapering of the lines towards the climax of the story. The nearer the actor reaches the climax the less space he has to move about; that is, the less chance has he of escaping from the influence of the

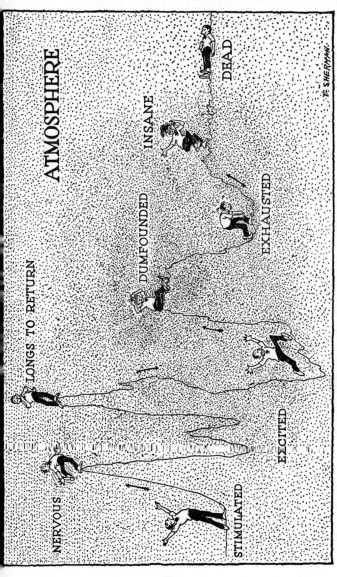

THE PATTERN OF THE ATMOSPHERE STORY

atmosphere. When finally he has reached the apex itself, no further movement at all is possible, and he is either dead, in the case of a tragedy, or he is completely transformed, in the case of a happy-ending atmosphere story.

7. Atmosphere Both Tragic and Comic

Most atmosphere stories written by the greatest writers, Stevenson, Conrad, and Hardy, make the atmosphere the villain as does Poe in *The Fall of the House of Usher*. The atmosphere story, however, need not be a tragedy. The atmosphere " character " might very well in a real atmosphere story serve as an admirable and beneficent hero or leading lady, in the case of a melancholy man, say, who suffering from overwork and disillusionment went to the coast of Florida meditating suicide. The influence of the seashore, the magic of the sunshine, luxuriant foliage, flamboyant colors and choruses of exotic birds might very well effect permanent cure. The influence here would of course have to be kept strictly to the mental effect of a mood. The awe and majesty of the mountains might also be used as an environment which might in the same way permanently change the life of some cynical or dyspeptic unbeliever. In *A Matter of Mean Elevation*, (O. Henry), the atmosphere is a practical joke!

In handling happy-ending stories of this type, however, the writer could not avoid the same subtle difficulties of matching character and atmosphere as are presented in the more tragic form. Our greatest atmospherists, Poe, Conrad, and Hardy, generally make the atmosphere the villain mainly because the tragic form is capable of more powerful effect. The spectacle of fear, disintegrating gloom, will-destroying heat, bringing a man to his death is far more momentous than the picture of his being cured of illness, however serious, by the sunny seashore, majestic mountains or wind-swept prairies.

8. Story with Atmosphere

A sharp distinction must be made here between the *atmosphere story proper* and the *story with atmosphere*. There are, in fact, many more of the latter type than of the former. *Any story whose setting affects any of the characters may, strictly speaking, be called a story with atmosphere,* although *the story with atmosphere, as a technical term, refers to the story which makes considerable use of setting (without being a story of setting exclusively).*

Atmosphere in both these types of stories is depicted at its best in exactly the same way — description by effect. Right here we see where the study of the atmosphere story proper increases one's skill in handling all other types of story. Master atmosphere and you master setting. Examples of stories with atmosphere and exercises based on them are contained in the assignments at the end of this chapter.

Some stories with atmosphere make so much of their settings that they approach a borderline between two types. Stevenson's *Will o' the Mill*, for instance, begins by showing the elevating influence of a rustic environment on a character, but the exaltation is carried on by the agency of a lovely maiden with whom the hero falls in love — an atmosphere story turned into a romance! Hawthorne, in seeking uplift qualities in atmosphere often gave his settings a spiritual influence, identifying them with the moral law. Such is *The Great Stone Face*. While the hero of this story was actually composed of rock on the hillside, nevertheless this rock is substantially the personification of a god. The story is a parable.

9. Actual Plotting of Atmosphere

So much for a brief outline of the main principles underlying the structure of the atmosphere story. In approaching now the problem of actually plotting this type of story we shall gain most, I think, if we make a brief analysis of a notably successful story of this type, Stevenson's *The Merry Men*. This story, although the illusion in places is weakened by what now seem to us labored affectations of style, is well-nigh faultless in structure and beautifully illustrates all the important practical principles for plotting this type of narrative.

These practical principles we can now state as follows:

Five Principles of Plotting.

I. *Determine your atmosphere and master every detail of it.*

II. *Select a character or characters which will be impressively influenced by it. Be sure you understand the psychology of this influence.*

III. *Plot the action of the selected character in such a way as to prepare for the climax of the story and at the same time show how the atmosphere is affecting him. This process is called integration.*[1]

IV. *The climax or " crucial situation," as we termed it in the other plot patterns, must be conclusive and if possible remarkable or unique in some way.*

V. *Tell the story, if possible, from the point of view of a looker-on or a minor participating actor. If this is impossible, use the point of view of the chief person on whom the atmosphere acts.*

---

[1] The principles of integration as applied to plotting and writing narrative belong properly to advanced technique. It is impossible not to mention here the important part this principle plays in the management of the atmosphere story, and some practice with it is given in the assignments at the end of this chapter. Integration is the only means of securing compression without the sacrifice of essential values. There is no reason why a short story writer should think any more about eliminating material or " cutting out details " than a novelist, but he will find a close integration of character, action and setting to be a technical necessity more urgent upon him than it is upon the novelist. If given story material, in spite of skillful integration, proves to be still too lengthy for short story treatment, the right remedy is not to proceed to mutilate the material but to write a novel or — get other and less unwieldy material!

Analysis of " The Merry Men " *

Stevenson himself referred to this story as " my favorite work . . . a fantastic sonata about the sea and wrecks. . . . It is really a story of wrecks as they appear to the dweller on the coast. It is a view of the sea . . . passion, romance, the picturesque, involved: startling, simple, horrid, a sea pink in sea froth! " Thus did the redoubtable R. L. S. himself grope for words to depict the mood of his atmosphere. Herein we see at once the very great importance of Principle One above — determining exactly what the atmosphere *is*.

That Principle Two is also sound we are assured by the author's deciding to describe his atmosphere by showing how it affected the uncle of the narrator. " Yet my uncle himself," he adds, " is not the story as I see it. Only the leading episode of that story."

Let us examine a passage of the story with just enough comment to bring out further the significance of these and the remaining principles mentioned.

The setting of the story is the Isle of Aros on the west coast of Ireland. The story is told from the point of view of a minor participating actor, as recommended in Principle Five. I shall refer to this character as the narrator. The narrator first presents his uncle, the chief foil of the atmosphere, in straight description in the second paragraph of the story as

a man whom ill-fortune had pursued; he feared, cumbered as he was with the young child (his daughter), to make a fresh adventure upon life; and remained in Aros, biting his nails at destiny. Years passed over his head in that isolation and brought neither help nor contentment.

Early in the story the Isle itself is presented to the reader in straight description. This passage shows with what industrious and deliberate intention the author de-

* By permission of Charles Scribner's Sons.

termined upon the nature of his atmosphere (Principle One). Does not the following sound as if it were taken directly from a well-filled notebook?

The Ross, as we call it, is a promontory neither wide nor high, but as rough as God made it to this day; the deep sea on either hand of it, full of rugged isles and reefs most perilous to seamen — all overlooked from the eastward by some very high cliffs and the great peak of Ben Kyaw. . . . Off the south-west end of Aros these blocks are very many, and much greater in size. Indeed they must grow monstrously bigger out to sea, for there must be ten sea miles of open water sown with them as thick as a country place with houses, some standing thirty feet above the tides, some covered, but all perilous to ships, so that on a clear, westerly blowing day, I have counted from the top of Aros, the great rollers breaking white and heavy over as many as six-and-forty buried reefs.

But it is nearer in shore that the danger is worst; for the tide, here running like a mill race, makes a long belt of broken water — a Roost we call it — at the tail of the land. I have often been out there in a dead calm at the slack of the tide, and a strange place it is, with the sea swirling and combing up and boiling like the caldrons of a linn, and now and again a little dancing mutter of sound as though the Roost were talking to itself. But when the tide begins to run again, and above all in heavy weather, there is no man could take a boat within half a mile of it, nor a ship afloat that could either steer or live in such a place. You can hear the roaring of it six miles away. At the seaward end there comes the strongest of the bubble; and it's here that these big breakers dance together — the dance of death, it may be called — that have got the name, in these parts, of the Merry Men.

The above is not the atmosphere; it is the material out of which it is made. The atmosphere is a mood and a real beginning in developing it is not made until the writer *shows its effect on various* people (Principle Two) thus:

The country people had many a story about Aros as I used to hear from my uncle's man, Rorie, an old servant of the Macleans, who had transferred his services without afterthought on the occasion of the marriage. There was some tale of an unlucky creature, a sea kelpie, that dwelt and did business in some fearful manner of his own among the boiling breakers of the Roost. A mermaid had once met a piper on Sandag Beach and there sang to him a long, bright midsummer's night, so that in the morning he was found stricken crazy, and from thenceforward till the day he died, said only one form of words; what they were in the original Gaelic I cannot tell, but they were thus translated: "Ah, the sweet singing out of the sea."

Following this is a direct description of his uncle as a "rough, cold, gloomy man" who "never laughed." He shows next how his uncle's religious, superstitious sentiments are all closely interwoven with a morbid fear of the sea *which also fascinated him.* The disasters he had witnessed during long service as a seaman had convinced him, for instance, that the vasty deep was full of sea monsters, and he was wont to cry out, "O, sirs, the horror, the horror of the sea!"

The reader is now told that some time before a foreign ship had been wrecked off the coast of the island, and only one sailor safely reached the land. The narrator discovers a solitary grave near the scene of the wreck, and harbors gruesome suspicions as to his uncle's having been the murderer of the lonely seaman. Details such as this neatly accomplish the needed integration of character and action suggested in Principle Three above. By such episodes out of the uncle's past the reader's impression of the effect of the setting on the uncle's character (atmosphere) is intensified, while at the same time his mind is prepared for another wreck which is to form the climax of the story. This particular scene, where the climax takes place, is called Sandag Bay, and is described as

a pretty large piece of water compared with the size of the isle; well sheltered from all but the prevailing wind; sandy and shoal and bounded by low sand-hills to the west, but to the eastward lying several fathoms deep along a ledge of rocks.

A considerable section of the story here describes certain explorations of the narrator about this gruesome bit of water. Here again we see the effect of the setting on a

human being; but by choosing the narrator himself rather
than the uncle we discover one place where the author fell
short of perfection in managing his difficult materials.
It is more than probable that the writer unconsciously
shrank from attempting to probe too deeply into the actual
mental processes of the scarcely human uncle. Nowhere
in the story does he get inside the uncle's mind, and in
this middle portion of the story he contented himself with
showing the effect of the most important part of his setting
on the narrator himself.

The narrator is pictured as roaming about this region
whelmed in melancholy scruples, searching for some relics
of the ill-fated ship. " Sad sea feelings," he states, " scraps
of my uncle's superstitions, thoughts of the dead, of the
grave, of the old broken ships, drifted through my mind."
The discovery of a rusted iron shoe buckle filled him with
" desolate melancholy." Finally the narrator describes an
investigation beneath the water itself, made by removing
his clothes and plunging into the bay.

I was about ready to leave go, when something happened
that sent me to the surface with my heart in my mouth. I
had already stayed somewhat late over my explorations; the
current was freshening with the change of the tide, and Sandag Bay was no longer a safe place for a single swimmer.
Well, just at the last moment there came a sudden flush of
current, dredging through the tangles like a wave. I lost one
hold, was flung sprawling on my side, and, instinctively grasping for a fresh support, my fingers closed on something hard
and cold. I think I knew at that moment what it was. At
least I instantly left hold of the tangle, leaped for the surface,
and clambered out next moment on the friendly rocks, with
the bone of a man's leg in my grasp.

Immediately after this scene a gale blows up. The
whole world was shadowed over; rain began to fall in
great drops, the sea rose with every moment, a band of
white encircled Aros, and on his way home the narrator
became aware that a large, heavily sparred, handsome
schooner lay struggling in the waves off the coast of the

Isle. This marks the beginning of the crucial situation. A forecast of the fate of the ship is sounded by our being told that she was hitting for the Merry Men. " Upon so wild a coast, the coming gale was not unlikely to bring death upon its wings."

When the uncle was told of the impending shipwreck we get our first intimation of the swiftly enacted final disintegration of the uncle's soul (Principle Three). The narrator tells his uncle what he has seen, then:

I had no time to go further; indeed, I not only forgot my words, but even my weariness, so strange was the effect on Uncle Gordon. He dropped his pipe and fell back against the end of the house with his jaw fallen, his eyes staring, and his long face as white as paper. We must have looked at one another silently for a quarter of a minute, before he made answer in this extraordinary fashion: " Had he a hair kep on? "

The narrator speculates that the sailor buried on the coast must have worn a hairy cap, that he did come ashore alive, and that his uncle was indeed his murderer. The memory of the dead stirs fiendish desires in the old seaman's heart. He speaks exultingly:

" Eh, man," he continued, touching me on the sleeve, " it's a braw nicht for a shipwreck! Twa in ae twalmonth! Eh, but the Merry Men'll dance bonny! "

He insists on going out to view the last struggles of the doomed ship and shows by his exclamations that his mind is full of the previous wreck (Principle Three).

" I maun see the hail thing, man, Cherlie," he explained; and then as the schooner went about a second time, " Eh, but they han'le her bonny! " he cried. " The Christ-Anna was naething to this."

Already the men on board the schooner must have begun to realize some part, but not yet the twentieth, of the dangers that environed their doomed ship. I tell you, they had to stand to their tackle: there was no idle man aboard that ship, God knows. It was upon the progress of a scene so horrible to any human-hearted man that my misguided uncle now pored and gloated like a connoisseur.

The uncle remained outdoors, " lying on his belly on the summit with his hands stretched forth and clutching heather all night." In the morning the narrator " beneath the flying horror of the sky and facing a wind which blew the breath out a man's nostrils," joined his uncle at his look-out. Together they watched for the final catastrophe out among the reefs:

And yet the spectacle was rather maddening in its levity than impressive by its force. Thought was beaten down by the confounding uproar; a gleeful vacancy possessed the brains of men, a state akin to madness; and I found myself at times following the dance of the Merry Men as it were a tune upon a jigging instrument.

The uncle's unholy glee reaches such a pitch that the narrator is now quite certain that his uncle had killed the seaman who came ashore from the previous wreck. The uncle continues his mad exultation:

" Eh, Charlie, man, it's grand! " he cried. " See to them! " he continued, dragging me to the edge of the abyss from whence arose that deafening clamor and those clouds of spray; " See to them dancin', man! Is that no wicked? "

The narrator describes the end of the ship:

The whole sight we had of her passed swifter than lightning; the very wave that disclosed her fell, burying her forever; the mingled cry of many voices at the point of death rose and was quenched in the roaring of the Merry Men. And with that the tragedy was at an end.

Again the uncle refuses to return home. " Tremulous and weak in mind and body, and with the eagerness of a child," the uncle examined the shores of the island searching for remains of the wreck. The nature of the horror eating at the uncle's soul is skillfully suggested by a description of his efforts to " draw his pitiful discoveries beyond the reach of the returning wave." " Once when his foot slipped and he plunged into a pool of water the shriek that came up out of his soul was like the cry of death." (Principle Three).

Soon it is discovered that once again a seaman, this time a negro, has been left ashore from the wrecked vessel. It is discovered that he was one of a party which had rowed to shore on the previous day, he for some strange reason, being abandoned. When the uncle, now an incurable and dismal lunatic, beheld the abandoned seaman, the horrible memory of his previous crime finished his moral disintegration. Now, he no longer permitted his nephew, the narrator, to approach him. He fled like a wild man over the moor. He remained out all night. Food left for him was next morning found scattered about, uneaten, among the heather.

The final act and " unique " climax (as demanded by Principle Four), was a chase on the part of the nephew, the black seaman and the servant to capture and restrain the mad uncle. His madness lent new vigor to his bounds; he sprang from rock to rock, over the widest gullies; he scoured like the wind along the hilltops, silent like a beast.

Finally the uncle was cornered. Retreat back over the island was impossible; his last means of escape was in the direction " of the wreck and the sea in Sandag Bay ":

My Uncle Gordon saw in what direction, horrible to him, the chase was driving him. He doubled, darting to the right and left; but high as the fever ran in his veins, the black was still the swifter. Turn where he would, he was still forestalled, still driven toward the scene of his crime. . . . My kinsman did not pause, but dashed straight into the surf; and the black, now almost within reach, still followed swiftly behind him, Rorie and I both stopped, for the thing was now beyond the hands of men, and these were the decrees of God that came to pass before our eyes. There was never a sharper ending. On that steep beach they were beyond their depth at a bound; neither could swim; the black rose once for a moment with a throttling cry; but the current had them, racing seaward; and if ever they came up again, which God alone can tell, it would be ten minutes after, at the far end of Aros Roost, where the seabirds hover fishing.

ASSIGNMENTS: CHAPTER EIGHT

With the exception of the last assignment, the exercises set forth here are designed not so much to prepare you to write the atmosphere story, as to help you grasp its essential principles. Such knowledge will be of use in handling the other less difficult types of stories. Our main subject here, in other words, is *settings* rather than atmosphere. In the earlier parts of this course we have concentrated much on character study and the management of action; here we center our attention on the third important element of narrative — the setting.[1]

ASSIGNMENT A

1. Here is the opening paragraph of Maupassant's story, *Two Friends*. It is an effective bit of setting. Why is it effective? Give an explicit answer.

Paris was blockaded, famished, at the last gasp. Sparrows were scarce on the roofs, and the sewers were depleted of their rats. Every mortal thing was being eaten.

2. Here is another handling of the same scene which is less effective. What is the chief difference in technical handling between this one and that in No. 1 ?

Paris was blockaded. The streets were full of soldiers; civilian life seemed to have stopped. The windows of the stores were boarded up, the doors barred. No smoke rose from the city's chimney pots. The faces of the citizens betrayed hunger and terror.

3. Analyze carefully the use of description by effect in the passage from Daudet's *Lighthouse of the Sanguinaires*, quoted on page 55.

4. Examine carefully the passage from *Little Dorrit*, in Chapter II, Assignment B. In this an atmosphere impression of heat is presented by details of its effect upon both people and things. Study the passage especially for the effect on things.

5. Read carefully the passage quoted from Daudet on page 32, No. 1. Here an event is described by its effect on a setting. Note, however, that the setting is affected only through the intermediation of people. The passage, thus, is essentially an account of effects on people.

[1] Other exercises on use of setting, Chapter II, Assignment B, page 83.

ASSIGNMENT B

The exercises below are planned to give you further facility in handling setting in combination with character or situation; they will continue the practice begun in Chapter II, Assignment B.

1. In "The Fire in the Flint," by George Bradshaw (*Short Story Hits, 1933*, reprinted from *The Saturday Evening Post*, May 27, 1933) the setting is the complication idea. The point of the story is that the main character who finds Greek ruins beautiful when with one girl, and dull when he is with another, thus learns which he really loves. Here he is with the right girl:

> The Acropolis is a very good-looking place, especially about sunset or when there is a full moon; although I will always regret the fact that I did not see it in the fifteenth century, when the Parthenon was a mosque and had a large dome. That must have been something. But even now it is the most pleasing historic monument I know of.

Now he sees the same scene with the other girl:

> The Acropolis, I am sorry to say, didn't look so well that morning. It reminded me of a bunch of tumble-down buildings that were waiting for a house wrecker to take them away. Everything looked bare, there seemed to be an unnecessary lot of stones lying around, the marines were disagreeable, the photographers indifferent.

Assignment: Write two studies of a scene as it appears to a character in the company of two very different people in turn.

2. Make a series of studies of a setting that you can watch closely and continuously. Do a detailed picture of it first on a summer day of medium temperature. Be sure that you have catalogued everything! Forms, masses, shadows, colors, sounds, odors — all possible sense impressions. Record also the routine, typical behavior of the people who may occupy that setting. Later, on a day of rain, do a new study, including detail that will show how this change altered previously observed material. In such studies you develop habits of seeing and writing with your mind focused on the sense impression.

3. Such full descriptions never have a place in the short story, and seldom in the novel. When you are ready to use this material, your problem will be to select from the mass of detail, the few sense impressions that are most saturated with the effect you want. For practice in such selection, take up these sketches from time to time, and try to revise to suggest with one or two — instead of a dozen — details, the quality of a rainy day, or snow,

or the first warmth of spring. The problem is to choose details so expressive that they imply all the rest.

4. In "Silent Snow, Secret Snow," by Conrad Aiken, setting is used with notable literary skill. The problem of the story was to convey the age and character of a boy of twelve, while at the same time suggesting that he is in an abnormal mental condition. Study the passage to discover by what means this is accomplished. We accompany the boy on his walk home from school:

There were many kinds of brick in the sidewalks, and laid in many kinds of pattern. The garden walls too were various, some of wooden palings, some of plaster, some of stone. Twigs of bushes leaned over the walls. . . . Dirty sparrows huddled in the bushes, as dull in color as dead fruit left in leafless trees. A single starling creaked on a weather vane. In the gutter, beside a drain, was a scrap of torn and dirty newspaper, caught in a little delta of filth: the word ECZEMA appeared in large capitals, and below it was a letter from Mrs. Amelia D. Cravath, 2100 Pine Street, Fort Worth, Texas, to the effect that after being a sufferer for years she had been cured by Caley's Ointment. In the little delta, beside the fan-shaped and deeply runnelled continent of brown mud, were lost twigs, descended from their parent trees, dead matches, a rusty horse-chestnut burr, a small concentration of sparkling gravel on the lip of the sewer, a fragment of eggshell, a streak of yellow sawdust which had been wet and now was dry and congealed, a brown pebble, and a broken feather. Further on was a cement sidewalk, ruled into geometrical parallelograms, with a brass inlay at one end commemorating the contractors who had laid it, and halfway across, an irregular and random series of dog-tracks, immortalized in synthetic stone. He knew these well, and always stepped on them.[1]

Assignment: Use some setting for which you have made one of your detailed catalogue studies for Assignment B, No. 2, above. Picture this scene from the angle of several characters successively, a child, an elderly man, a woman who is afraid. Select your details to picture the setting, of course, but primarily to reveal the character and his state of mind at the moment.

ASSIGNMENT C

This assignment concerns mainly the principle of integration as applied to settings and atmosphere. A footnote on the importance of integration will be found at the bottom of page 287. *Integration in narrative is a process of attaining both*

[1] Reprinted by permission from "Silent Snow, Secret Snow," by Conrad Aiken, in *Short Story Hits, 1932,* reprinted from *Virginia Quarterly Review,* Winter, 1932, and included in *Among the Lost People,* published by Charles Scribner's Sons.

greater brevity and vigor by advancing more than one element in a story in one and the same passage. In a passage, for instance, wherein a person " acts in character " we have a simultaneous development of both character and action. The passage is thus integrated. If its action also shows the person's reaction to a setting, integration is carried still further: character, action, and setting are being advanced at one and the same time. The following exercises will provide you some practice with double integration, particularly as it affects the handling of settings.

1. First let us analyze a simple example of " double integration." Integration is " double " when of the three elements of narrative, character, action, and setting, two are advanced in one and the same passage. Here is a quotation from the opening of *Main Street,* page 33, which advances both character and setting. There is no action since the first paragraph tells us that Carol had *finished her walk* and now stood still and looked about her. We have therefore only the record of *how the setting affected her.*

When Carol had walked for thirty-two minutes she had completely covered the town, east and west, north and south; and she stood at the corner of Main Street and Washington Avenue and despaired.

Main Street with its two-story brick shops, its story-and-a-half wooden residences, its muddy expanse from concrete walk to walk, its huddle of Fords and lumber-wagons was too small to absorb her. The broad, straight, unenticing gashes of the streets let in the grasping prairie on every side. She realized the vastness and the emptiness of the land. The skeleton iron windmill on the farm a few blocks away, at the north end of Main Street, was like the ribs of a dead cow. She thought of the coming of the Northern winter, when the unprotected houses would crouch together in terror of storms galloping out of that wild waste. They were so small and weak, the little brown houses. They were shelters for sparrows, not homes for warm laughing people.

She told herself that down the street the leaves were a splendor. The maples were orange; the oaks a solid tint of raspberry. And the lawns had been nursed with love. But the thought would not hold. At best the trees resembled a thinned woodlot. There was no park to rest the eyes. And since not Gopher Prairie but Wakamin was the county-seat, there was no court-house with its grounds.

Let us rewrite this passage, separating the character from the setting. First, write out the setting objectively, omitting all mention of Carol. Your first sentence will read something like this: " Main Street presented the usual succession of two-story brick shops, of story-and-a-half wooden residences, muddy expanse from concrete walk to walk, and huddle of Fords and lumber-wagons."

Second, write out the revelation of character in the original text, omitting all reference to the setting. You can deduce, for instance, from the first sentence of the second paragraph, the following: " Carol was not wont to interest herself in the close-at-hand sordid realities of life." Continue in this manner.

2. As a slightly more difficult task in analysis of double integration take the opening paragraph of Chekhov's story, *Grief*, quoted on page 66. Here again both character and setting are advanced. Note how the horse is used to help present both story elements. Write out again the setting minus character and the character minus setting.

3. As a still more difficult task in analysis of double integration of character and setting take once more the passage from Daudet referred to in No. 4 of Assignment A above and quoted on page 55. Here is a rather subtle mingling of these two elements. Write out again a statement of the observer's character and another of the things he observed.

4. Let us write a first piece of double integration and at the same time see how very much character and setting are dependent upon each other for their best effects. In the original passage from *Main Street* quoted above the character was used for the sake of presenting the setting, the setting of Main Street being the important thing. Let us use exactly the same setting *for the sake of presenting a character*. The character is, let us say, a plump, jovial broker with a sentimental streak for Gopher Prairie, his home town. After a number of busy, homesick years in New York he returns on a summer day to Gopher Prairie, and stands at the corner of Main Street and Washington Avenue. Tender, romantic scenes of boyhood stir his memory. Rewrite the passage with humorous sympathy integrating these memories with the details of setting given in the original passage.

5. In this and some of the succeeding assignments I am going to try to show you something of the practical, or, if you wish, artistic advantages of integrated narrative. To begin with take the opening paragraph of the Chekhov story, *Grief*, referred to in No. 3 of this assignment, and quoted on page 66. Although something of the effect of the snow and cold on Iona is given, the passage is written in the objective manner; only later in the story does the author penetrate the cabby's mind and tell the reader what he thinks and feels. Would the opening be improved if it, too, were told strictly from the point of view of Iona, the main character? Rewrite the passage very care-

fully and compare your version with the original. Let your opening be something like this: "Iona Potapov, the cab driver, turned to a white phantom by the snow, sat bent double on his box. If a whole snow drift fell on him, he would not move; he was thinking of his son." Continue.

6. I do not think we can improve the passage from Daudet analyzed in No. 3 above, but try rewriting it using a character trait only *slightly different* from that in the original and endeavor to integrate it and the setting as closely as in the original. The trait in the original seems to be a physical languor coupled with a wistful, dreamy abstraction. Say you are the spectator, a painter, and that your character trait is a passionate desire to create the beauty of marine views. Or try a boy's desire to go to sea or a girl's yearning for travel and adventure.

7. Another opportunity for practical experiment with double integration of character and setting is offered in the opening paragraph of Irvin Cobb's *The Belled Buzzard* mentioned in No. 9 of Assignment B above. If you are not acquainted with this story please read the outline of it on page 297. The opening paragraph, you will note, presents only setting with no hint of either character or action. Not until the story has progressed some twelve hundred words do we see any integration between setting and character. By this time the murderer, Squire Gathers, has left the swamp and is nearly home. Bearing in mind, now, that the trait is a *beginning fear of detection* rewrite this opening, telling all that is told there from the point of view of the Squire and integrating his trait. Compare your version with the original.

8. A similar experiment may be made with the opening of Maupassant's story, *The Piece of String.* You will find the story in the collection called *The Odd Number (Harpers).* Read it, if you haven't already done so, and note that no mention is made of character or action in the opening. Setting alone is presented. No action of the story furthermore takes place on the road with which the story opens. The chief generating circumstance of the story, the finding of the piece of string, takes place in the town in front of M. Malandain's shop. Rewrite the opening, keeping the picturesque procession but describing it from the point of view of M. Hauchecorne who is in the procession; show the procession passing before M. Malandain's shop. Compare your opening with the original.

9. Some settings are effective because they are integrated in harmony with the character and some because they form a contrast to the character. An instance of contrast with character is contained in Maupassant's *Moonlight,* also to be found

in the collection mentioned in the preceding exercise. The subtle beauty of the moonlight here contrasts with the hard, uncompromising asceticism of the Abbé. Rewrite the moonlight passages, now, from the point of view of the young lovers, closely integrating the moonlight atmosphere with their love for each other. This will harmonize character and setting.

10. An example of double integration which advances character and action without setting follows. It is the opening of *The Preliminaries* by Cornelia A. P. Comer, in *Atlantic Narratives*, First Series.

Young Oliver Pickersgill was in love with Peter Lannithorne's daughter. Peter Lannithorne was serving a six-year term for embezzlement.

It seemed to Ollie that there was only one right-minded way of looking at these basal facts of his situation. But this simple view of the matter was destined to receive several shocks in the course of his negotiations for Ruth Lannithorne's hand. I say negotiations advisedly. Most young men in love have only to secure the consent of the girl and find enough money to go to housekeeping. It is quite otherwise when you wish to marry into a royal family, or to ally yourself with a criminal's daughter. The preliminaries are more complicated.

Ollie thought a man ought to marry the girl he loves, and prejudices be hanged! In the deeps of his soul, he probably knew this to be the magnanimous, manly attitude, but certainly there was no condescension in his outward bearing when he asked Ruth Lannithorne to be his wife. Yet she turned on him fiercely, bristling with pride and tense with over-wrought nerves..

"I will never marry anyone," she declared, "who doesn't respect my father as I do!"

In integration of this kind it is impossible to write action without telling something about character; but character *can* be suggested without action. A rather definite idea of Oliver's character is given here. What is it?

Rewrite the passage, pitching the scene in the young lady's parlor, and integrating character and setting only.

11. Here is another quotation integrating only action and character. It is the opening of *Possessing Prudence* by Amy Wentworth Stone, also to be found in *Atlantic Narratives,* First Series.

"A lie's an abomination unto the Lord a hundred and twenty-four, a lie's an abomination unto the Lord a hundred and twenty-five, a lie's an abomination unto the Lord a hundred and twenty-six," recited Prudence Jane, and paused.

"Go on," said Aunt Annie, looking up from her sewing and fixing her eyes severely on the small blue back across the room.

Prudence Jane, with the heels of her little ankle-ties together and her hands clasped tightly behind her, was standing in the corner, saying what was known in the family as her punish-sentence. Whenever she had been unusually naughty she had to say one four hundred times up in Aunt Annie's room. It was, no doubt, a silly sort of punishment, but it was one that Prudence Jane strongly objected to — and that, after all, is the essence of a punishment.

What is the character indicated here?

ASSIGNMENT D

The exercises in this assignment all deal with triple integration, the closely knit form of narrative, that is, which advances character, action, and setting at the same time. There is no limit to the number and fascinating variety of effects possible with this potent principle of literary technique. I give only enough to point the way to further study. None of them are easy; all are problems of advanced technique: but students with patience enough to master them will be gratified at the power they will gain.

1. First let us take a simple case of analysis. A striking passage of triple integration is contained in O. Henry's story, *The Furnished Room*, in *The Four Million*. In this story, you remember, a young lover seeks his lost sweetheart in the boarding houses of New York's West Side. He finally engages a room " third floor back; " the land-lady leaves, and he looks about him. He gazes at the " sophistical comfort which came in reflected gleams from the decayed furniture."

Then, suddenly, as he rested there, the room was filled with the strong, sweet odor of mignonette. It came as upon a single buffet of wind with such sureness and fragrance and emphasis that it almost seemed a living visitant. And the man cried aloud: " What, dear? " as if he had been called, and sprang up and faced about. The rich odour clung to him and wrapped him around. He reached out his arms for it, all his senses for the time confused and commingled. How could one be peremptorily called by an odour? Surely it must have been a sound. But was it not the sound that had touched, that had caressed him?

" She has been in this room," he cried, and he sprang to wrest from it a token, for he knew he would recognize the smallest thing that had belonged to her or that she had touched. This enveloping scent of mignonette, the odour that she had loved and made her own — whence came it?

What character trait is developed here? What is the action? What is the development in atmosphere?

2. From each of the passages listed below select a trait suggested by the incidents outlined, choose a setting that will affect this trait, and write a scene to portray both the trait in action and the setting: Chapter I, Assignment D; Chapter II, Assignment C; Chapter III, Assignment C, Nos. 2 and 3; Assignment E–A, Nos. 9 and 12; Chapter IV, Assignment C, Nos. 7, 8, 9 and 10; Assignment E, Nos. 2 and 3, and 13 a and b.

3. The following verses definitely suggest character, setting and complication. Expand the suggestion in several prose paragraphs integrating the three elements as closely as possible. You might write your first draft in the romantic manner of the verses, and then a second in realistic vein.

> And because I, too, am a lover,
>   And my love is far from me,
> I hated the two on the sands there,
>   And the moon, and the sands, and the sea.

4. The exercises in Assignment B, preceding this one, can be used for further drill with triple integration, thus:

To the character and setting of No. 4 add action by having the sentimental broker walk up and down Main Street seeking in vain someone of his old friends who would recognize him.

In No. 5 have the old cabby bent over not so much by the weight of the snow as by the weight of his grief over his dead son.

In No. 7 open with the actual shooting of the Italian, following immediately with the effects of the sights and sounds of the swamp on the awakening fear in the heart of the murderer.

In No. 8 try integrating the finding of the piece of string with the old peasant's sensitiveness and the local color data given in the opening of the original.

In No. 10 try to add setting to character and action by having the scene take place in the young lady's parlor. An interesting triply integrated opening might also be pitched in the jail itself.

In No. 11 add setting to character and action by having Prudence look slyly out of the window at the children playing in the yard, and yearn to escape.

5. Still more advanced drill with integration can be secured by taking settings, characters, and plot ideas from your notebooks and working them out, fusing first two, then three together.

ASSIGNMENT E

This assignment merely comprehends a few suggestions for those more advanced students who wish to pursue their study of the real atmosphere story. This work is not recommended to any but those who have a sincere feeling for places and something of a gift for portraying it. Intimate associations with the sea, the prairies, mountains or forests is an invaluable asset for the atmosphere story of adventure. Such an asset when genuine has brought more than one writer to his first successes.

1. An interesting pure atmosphere story handled with unusual brevity and skill is *The Lagoon* by Conrad in the volume of short stories called *Tales of Unrest* (Doubleday, Page). It is worth careful study after the manner of my analysis of *The Merry Men* in this chapter. The main character of this story, let me suggest, is a region on a nameless river in some Malay country. It is described as "a shadowy country of inhuman strife, a battlefield of phantoms terrible and charming, august or ignoble, struggling ardently for possession of our helpless hearts; an unquiet and mysterious country of inextinguishable desires and fears."

On what characters does this atmosphere work?
List some of the specific disintegrating influences.
What is the outcome? Is it overwhelming or not?
What is the point of view?

2. For a writing exercise rewrite Stevenson's story, *Will O' the Mill* which is almost a happy-ending atmosphere story and make it a happy-ending pure atmosphere story.

3. A study of atmosphere in the fantastic vein is presented in O. Henry's story, *A Matter of Mean Elevation,* in the volume called *Whirligigs*. The author's interest in a spirited complication all but ruined the piece as an atmosphere story and marks of the struggle are to be found in the text. A narrative of atmosphere it is, nevertheless. The author himself declares that his purpose is to "express the unnamable kinship of man to nature, that queer fraternity that causes stones and trees and salt water and clouds to play upon our emotions."

Is the handling of atmosphere here convincing?
Has the story a single effect?
See if you can improve the story by replotting and rewriting it.

CHAPTER NINE

THE MULTI–PHASE STORY

THE STORY THAT PRODUCES THE BIGGEST EFFECTS

"The later facility comes, the better tools you'll graduate with."
— BOOTH TARKINGTON.

In the previous chapters we have been studying pure, or single-phase, story patterns. Such stories secure their effect by an emphasis on any one of the four kinds of story interest: character, complication, theme, or atmosphere. Some stories, we have seen, shade from one pattern into another; others follow very definitely one pattern and partially develop others; and, of course, some stories give strong and equal emphasis to two, or even three, of the four plot patterns. These latter are called two- and three-phase stories; generically they are known as the multi-phase story.

Plotting the multi-phase story is distinctly a task in advanced literary technique. For this reason I shall treat it but cursorily here, confident that if you have faithfully performed the tasks set up to this point you will have but little need for further formal discipline. No assignments are appended to this chapter. You will need only a brief introductory survey of the two- and three-phase patterns in order that you may realize how closely connected they are to our previous study and how varied and inviting are their possibilities.

There are altogether fourteen possible combinations of the fundamental plot patterns, as follows:

One-phase.

1. Character
2. Complication
3. Theme
4. Atmosphere

Two-phase

5. Character-Complication
6. Character-Theme
7. Character-Atmosphere
8. Complication-Theme
9. Complication-Atmosphere
10. Theme-Atmosphere

Three-phase

11. Character-Complication-Theme
12. Character-Complication-Atmosphere
13. Complication-Theme-Atmosphere
14. Theme-Atmosphere-Character

There are undoubtedly published stories representing all these types, although some of them, such as numbers ten, thirteen and fourteen, are very rare indeed. Patterns one, two and five alone, with shadings into each other, have been followed by probably eighty per cent of all published short stories. They are the staple art forms in all narrative, since dominant emphasis on theme and atmosphere is as rare in novels as in short stories. As a general rule a two-phase story with its opportunity for double emphasis is more effective than a one-phase, and a three-phase story is the most effective of all.

1. The Supreme Story Types

Seldom do any but the greatest literary artists attempt the three-phase story. Not all the most notable short stories follow this pattern, but of the famous stories a very large percentage are three-phase. The narrative generally considered the most famous short story written in America, for instance, Poe's *The Fall of the House of Usher,* is a character-complication-atmosphere story. So also is the most notable of all British short stories, Stevenson's *Markheim. Ligeia,* another well-known story by Poe, follows the character-complication-theme pattern, as does also Mrs. Wharton's remarkable story, *Ethan Frome.* The most distinctly original, if not the best, of O. Henry's stories is his *A Municipal Report,* a character-complication-thematic story. His most poignant tragedy, *The Furnished Room,* is a character-complication-atmosphere story. The best of Maupassant's short stories is probably his *La Boule de Suife,* a character-complication-thematic story. As for Kipling — *Without Benefit of Clergy,* probably his best-known story, is very definitely character-complication with strong shadings of both atmosphere and theme. His *The Man Who Would Be King* is strongly character-complication, again bordering on both theme and atmosphere.

A four-phase story is not an impossibility, although I have never discovered one. Any effort to integrate into a single short story striking and equally definite emphasis on character, complication, theme and atmosphere is almost certain to produce an artificiality of structure whose obtrusiveness no artistry can quite conceal. None of the magazine stories in which it has been attempted have been successful.

2. Control of Multi-Phase Story

In actually plotting multi-phase stories the number and nature of the phases is, with most writers, a matter of accident. Either the original "story idea" itself definitely suggests strong emphasis on more than one pattern of emphasis or these other patterns evolve naturally during replotting or rewriting. Many writers with long experience in plotting constantly increase the significance and multiply the emotional overtones of their stories by adding character emphasis to complication interest and thematic interest to that, and so on — without being able to explain just how or why. Most of those, however, who work thus by haphazard deplore the fact that they were not taught early in their careers some deliberate method of controlling their plotting.

Sufficient knowledge of narrative technique to enable you to recognize possibilities in your material for the high-powered multi-phase story is one of the main objects of all the previous instruction of this book. If you have made the previous chapters yours, the handling of these compounded effects will not be difficult. To include anything like an extended exposition of their magic possibilities would lead us into discussions beyond the scope of this book.

3. Plotting a Two-Phase Story

It will be enough, if we glance briefly at the making of three plots which will show clearly how the different phases may be multiplied with deliberate design and artistic control. First, let us take an example of actual plotting in which a complication story *of itself* evolved into a character-complication story.

By " of itself," I mean that there was no intention at the beginning of producing a two-phase story: during work with a one-phase idea, a second phase appeared, was seized upon and developed deliberately. Here, then, was the original story idea, a jotting which had been waiting attention in my notebook for some six years:

Suppose a man addicted to sleepwalking should disclose some important secret while asleep and on waking not remember what he had done in his sleep!

Now very briefly:

Analyzing the idea: This idea is obviously as it stands pure complication. It is a *circumstance* and it is *odd* — or might easily be odd. The *single effect* will be amazement at the queer turn of fate — tragic irony if the hero fails utterly to remember the secret, and ironic amusement if he succeeds. The *drama,* while nebulous as yet, will obviously be the hero's struggle to remember something he has forgotten. The *editorial* problem — the story will appeal to a wider audience and so the more easily find a publisher if the ending is comic rather than tragic.

Stating the problem: Our original idea, happily, is so explicit that our plot is not far away. What is mainly missing? Three things:

The character of the sleepwalker.
The thing hidden.
The manner of finding it.

Manipulation: The compulsion of sleepwalking is, of course, not a character trait; it is merely a physical disability beyond conscious control. We need a genuine character trait. What will it be? Well, unless the loss is due to the hero himself, is *characteristic* of him, the fact of the loss will be an accident; the story will open with a coincidence. This is not impossible, but it isn't necessary. The thing was lost because — *that's the kind of man he is.* He's always losing things. Now if he loses things because he doesn't care where they are or whether they are ever found, we'll run into difficulties with our complication: it calls, as we found, for a struggle *to find something.* All right: our hero hides his possessions *to ensure them against loss* and, in this instance, hides this particular thing so well that he can't find it!

Now what have we? What kind of a man is this? He's no ordinary mortal; he's an interesting oddity, a freak, a sort of human magpie, a " character," in other words; everybody has seen his like at some time or other. With his appearance we face a task of character development as vital as the task of plotting the complication. Thus a two-phase story is born.

Since the hidden object must be both small and extremely valuable we choose diamonds, decide that our hero is a gem connoisseur, and consult our files for data about jewels and furniture with which to complete the very important interior setting. A doll's house is chosen as a satisfactory place to have the diamonds hidden. This done we can write out an analysis of the complete plot as follows:

Type of story: character-complication.
Effect to be made: mystery ending in amazement at peculiar manner of discovery of the jewels.
Conflict: between desire to find jewels and inability to remember place of hiding.
Complication: Finds missing jewels in sleep but can't remember dream on waking.
Character: Magpie-like habit of hiding things.
Initial complication: Missing jewels are not really his; they belong to his daughter; daughter's life plans dependent upon finding jewels; father loves daughter.
Crucial situation: Hero is driven to struggle with his dreams because every night the place of hiding seems to come nearer and nearer. As thoughts of suicide come, the presence of his constantly solicitous daughter gives him an idea for subconscious association. He finds the jewels that night in his sleep without waking.
Outcome: Unaware of his success on waking, he tries to kill himself and is prevented by his daughter's discovering the diamonds — carefully hidden, even in his sleep!

Before beginning to write the story we need our bald report or working scenario, thus:

The Dream That Told [1]

Nothing is more exasperating than the inability to remember when we wish to and cannot. Henry McEldon over a number of years had hidden his jewels away in odd crannies and corners about the house. One day, while his daughter was in Europe, the most precious jewels of all, a pair of diamond earrings, were hidden so well that he could not find them on his daughter's return. Since the daughter's husband was in desperate need of money to save his business, the loss was serious.

McEldon, being a sleepwalker and finding that the where-
[1] Munsey's Magazine, May, 1923.

abouts of the jewels occurred to him in his sleep, set forth to cultivate the dream until his memory was complete. This struggle he kept up until he shattered his nerves. One day, having his mind fixed on his daughter's childhood, his subconscious thoughts started in a new direction. That night in his sleep he walked to the store-room and removed the jewels from the blue-tiled floor of a small Dutch doll house, which secret cavity he had made many years before.

He immediately returned to bed without waking. The next morning, being unaware that the jewels were in his library table drawer, he seizes his revolver and starts to shoot himself. His daughter at this instant opens the drawer, discovers the jewels, and stops him just in time.

4. A Character-Complication-Atmosphere Plot

Let us take an actual case of plotting which in a similarly typical manner developed a three-phase story. In this instance also the additional patterns evolved of themselves. This plot differs from the preceding not only in having one more phase but also in the fact that the story began with a single effect only. An editor is asked what kind of a story he needs most. "A mystery story with a grim touch," he replies. With this hint only we begin.

The single effect is *gruesome mystery*. Let us hold it in mind now while we look for material. The editor, manifestly from the nature of his request, frankly wants a "detective thriller." Interpretations of life, keen character analysis, literary style — these things are of less interest to him than novelty of idea, swift, startling action, and, above all, gripping suspense artfully sustained.

We have, let us say, recently visited the American Museum of Natural History. "There are a lot of queer things in there," we meditate, and pause to consider. We recall the stuffed apes. The idea sticks. Horrible things. *Gruesome mystery!* Immediately we look for a scene with the apes that will arouse horror and mystery. "Never mind how and why," we reason; "if we can get the scene, the rest will be easy."

Mystery: that means a man is killed and no one knows how or why. All right — a man who works on the apes (stuffs them) — is one morning found dead in his workroom. His skull is crushed. His temple bears the imprint of the teeth of a gorilla. Beside the body lies a huge female gorilla, its mouth open, and one long hairy arm stretched across the man's chest. The animal's teeth match the marks on the man's temple. This, we decided, is gruesome enough to satisfy any editor! For good measure we imagined a chest of bones in a corner which, upon examination, was found to contain mingled with monkey bones, the entire skeleton of a young woman!

To intensify the mystery we assume that the windows and doors were all firmly locked, indicating that no one had entered. There were no fingerprints. The man had no known enemies. There had been no robbery. The man had recently returned from a long exploration in Africa. He was a lonely, unobtrusive soul, unmarried, devoted to his science, and, so far as known, there was no " woman in the case."

Our inventions cease at this point. We have enough, very likely too much, mystery to work on; we may have to simplify the problem itself somewhat before we can solve it; we have, however, made progress; we have single effect and material. The rest is pure ratiocination coupled possibly with a little research.

Right and Wrong Attack

The problem of finishing the plot from this point was submitted to a beginning class in plotting. The students were asked to answer two questions: How was the unfortunate man killed? What was the motive? The students were much more interested in the first question than the second. A collection of the most ingenious and elaborate *means,* mostly mechanical, by which the explorer could have met his gruesome end, was produced. Steel springs in the female ape's jaw, flame shooting through an open window, mysterious poison — every imaginable trick for killing the poor fellow was suggested. There was little speculation as to motive. Almost no interest was evinced in the *character* of the unhappy victim.

We then solved the mystery and made our plot, simply by adhering quite rigidly to the principles governing *kinds of interest, single effect* and *drama* as developed in this book. The whole process, although it took only a comparatively short time, involved a sifting of ideas too numerous to be set forth here completely. A summary of the successive steps, with emphasis on the technical principles used and the successive appearances of the different three phases, follows:

Analysis of material: Death scene and *single effect,* as above, given. Now the first question always is, of course; *What kind of a story* is this? *A mystery story?* No; that's part of the *effect* and does not help us in our problem of *construction;* an effect of mystery could be produced by *any* of the fundamental plot patterns. Which of these latter is it: character, complication, theme, or atmosphere?

Answer: We don't know; we can only select one *as a working hypothesis.* From our technical study we have learned that the biggest and most universal appeal is *always* produced by stories featuring character. The character pattern is, furthermore, the easiest to follow. We therefore adopt it as a working hypothesis with which to begin.

Stating the problem: Given: the death scene, as above, the *single effect,* and our tentative pattern of character story. Wanted: *character trait, complication* causing murder, motive for murder, outcome.

Manipulation: If we have a character story we *know* that the crucial situation, the actual murder, cannot be caused by any mechanical contrivance, or melodramatically terrible device; *it must come out of character.* What is the character, the main trait? Our *single effect* gives a clue: something "gruesome," grim. Fear is the first of the elemental instincts to suggest itself and harmonizes most with the given effect. The man was killed by his fear. His death, in other words, resulted from his bringing home from the jungle not a mechanical contraption or diabolical enemy, but — a character trait of fear! We thus have our first phase definitely established.

Developing Second Phase

How did he get his fear? Here progress is impossible without more facts, and a student was assigned to some research on African jungles and gorilla hunters. He discovered the diary of a scientist who had a "close call" with some apes one night in the Congo jungle. We quickly intensified this episode, making the terror so great that the explorer's hair was whitened, his nerves were shattered, and ever after he suffered from hallucinations of his jungle experience. As to the nature of the terrors of the fateful night, it is important here to mention only two:

He heard the continuous screams of the enraged beasts, which were like the screams of a terrified woman, and once or twice the hairy brutes actually brushed against him.

Now our crucial situation. *If* we have a *character story* and the *trait* is fear, the crucial situation must be a supreme act of fear. What act? The easiest thing is to say: "The same act as in the jungle." The stuffed effigies of the apes are about him in the workroom just as in the jungle. If the lights should go out and he were having one of his nervous attacks, he would think he was again in the jungle. This idea we accept. In doing so we admit that our explorer was really a victim of the terror of the jungle; the *jungle* thus becomes our *real* hero and leading character; and therefore our second phase enters — atmosphere!

Developing Third Phase.

To fulfill the *atmosphere pattern* we must reproduce in the work-room as near as possible the night of terror in the jungle. The lights go out. A stuffed ape falls against the scientist. A woman screams. These things would be enough to recreate all the terror of the jungle to a man whose *character trait* is an obsessive fear. And if he meets his death — somebody, some human being, *must* kill him. Any other theory is too difficult. We keep to the obvious: someone enters. Who? In our original material we have a woman's scream; let's accept the idea of a woman.

What woman? Why not simply an employee, perhaps a young girl stenographer? Keeping rigidly to our final episode, his death, and postponing the problem of why she happened to be in the museum, we pose the question of *how* she killed him. We must return to the *character trait, fear.* She screams; she knocks the apes against him in the dark; if all this arouses an hysteria of fear, if he thinks she is an ape, he will try to kill her. What would she do? Defend herself. He, then, attacks her; she strikes back in self-defence and — kills him. Death at the hand of a New York stenographer whose victim thinks she is a gorilla — here is a predicament remarkable enough to be called a genuine *complication;* and thus the *third phase* of our story appears.

Filling Final Gaps

With our three phases outlined and the single effect satisfied, there remains only the invention of causes for results we have assumed. These steps, since they involve only the most obvious and commonplace explanations, are comparatively easy. After a little further research into the methods of stuffing apes and an inquiry by telephone at a bacteriological laboratory, the plot is finished thus:

The bones of the white woman in the chest are thrown

out altogether; we have all our effects without them. In this way only do we find it necessary to simplify the original problem. The stenographer left the employ of the museum a few weeks before because of her fear of the explorer. Being lonely, he had often walked home with her, even tried to philander a little with her, but his frequent sudden starts at passing shadows, his constant talk of jungle horrors, his fits of wild abstraction gave her, as she said, " the horrors." She left, keeping her key to the employee's entrance, and secured another job in an antique shop.

The girl's trait was vanity and she was none too honest. She saw a big fur coat she wanted. Unable to wait for her savings to enable her to purchase it, she took money from her employer's till, intending to replace it before an accounting should be made. An accounting was unexpectedly called for. The coat was bought; the money had to be replaced immediately. She knew of no one to whom she could go but her former eccentric employer. Wearing the fur coat, she goes to the museum on the fatal night.

Shamed by the theft, embarrassed by her mission, and terrified at the thought of facing the " jungle man " at night puts her nerves on edge when she slips through the dark corridors. It is raining; a storm is up; and she wears rubbers which silence her footsteps. The lightning causes the power house to turn off the current for a momentary test. The sudden darkness causes her to scream just as she enters the work-room. Her former employer leaps backward and collides with her. Her fur coat, brushing against him, completes the hallucination of live apes in the jungle, and he begins to lay about him with a long sharp knife with which he had been working.

The lights flash on. The girl sees her danger, snatches from the table an ape skull to which is fixed a brass rod for mounting, and, in fear of her life, strikes him on the temple. The teeth in the skull which strike him are the originals from which the composition teeth in the stuffed ape's head have been fashioned. A moment's reflection arouses fear of leaving anything she has handled, so she tucks the skull under her fur coat, leaves the building, walks to the river and throws it into the water.

The next day she pawns the fur coat and secures enough money to return the sum she had taken from the till.

Although the detective working on the case suspected her on character grounds, from the first, he could not force her to admit her part in the ghastly affair until he discovered the coat. Examination of it discovered a minute blood spot. He then fakes a blood analysis certificate which identifies the dried blood (which of course couldn't be done) with that of the dead man, and with this frightens the girl into confession.

This story, since its effect is largely dependent upon suspense, would of course be told from the point of view of the investigation into the cause of the crime, and in this respect it would follow the conventional pattern of the usual detective story. The building up of the atmosphere of the jungle by a study of the explorer's hitherto unread notebooks and reports would be a feature of the writing of the story.

5. Character-Complication-Thematic Plot

Let me, finally, merely outline the making of probably the most difficult of all plots, the character-complication-thematic. In this case, furthermore, the writer's task was made still more difficult by beginning with the theme. I had just finished my technical studies. The possibilities of the three-phase story containing a theme entranced my student mind. "If that type of story," I enthusiastically and ungrammatically vowed, "sounds the big drum, go to — that's me!" There are frailties in my design and its execution, but since my attack on the plotting problem was systematic and since the material of this story has already been presented in various forms for purposes of illustration, we will now examine a very con- densed chronicle of the making of the plot.

Having decided at the very start what my three phases were to be, I quite deliberately filled them out in their first stage as follows:

1. *The theme:* The war had just begun. The topic of most absorbing interest was peace. Very well, something must be said about peace; my message would itself largely determine my all-important *single effect.* I reviewed my notes of Professor Franklin H. Giddings' lectures on *The Theory of a Progressive Society.* Society, it seemed, "progresses" functionally because families became tribes, tribes became peoples, peoples became nations. Fighting and wars meanwhile ceased between the smaller units. After meditation on these facts a theme was framed thus: "Men no matter how great their natural enmity, always stand together when menaced by a danger greater than their danger to each other."

2. *The complication:* My thought here was a purely technical consideration — out of the complication must come the drama, and the dramatic conflict, if the story is to sound the big drum, must be the ultimate in human ferocity. This was obviously two men locked in mortal combat, each trying to kill the other.

3. *The characters:* What men? The characters must integrate with the theme and the complication *and* they must be people the writer understands. I ceased specu- lating and plunged into my notebooks. There came to light a detailed record of adventures two summers pre- vious in the vast Kara-Kum Desert of Turkestan.

Here was some first class *atmosphere!* Could a fourth phase be added? A first story with four phases — that would be a real achievement!

I thrilled, covered sheets of paper, spent sleepless nights, calmed down, and decided then what I still believe to be true — a genuine four-phase story is a practical impossi-

bility. A three-phase story *with atmosphere* was, however, an easy possibility with a desert like the Kara-Kum
to play with, and I adopted the plan. Desert atmosphere
must help produce the drama.

Plot controlled by theme

I continued searching my notes for characters. Soon I
came upon observations about the tarantulas and scorpions which my partner, a Russian scientist, was collecting; also photographs of the little cabin in which we lived.
The idea of the live insects being loosed inside the cabin
and escape being shut off flashed into mind. A capital
complication! I abandoned for the moment the search
for characters, and began immediately to fit this complication to my theme which, of course, was to control my
single effect.

Obviously the danger of the insects supplied the " danger greater than their danger to each other." The two
men are fighting when suddenly the insect box is overturned. This new horror forces them to cease their
fighting. They help each other fight the insects. This is
the end of the story.

The characters manifestly need have only those traits
which will make them quarrel and fight, provided also that
they will be traits peculiar and pronounced enough to
make their development one of the three patterns which
integrate to produce the final effect. I kept my Russian
partner much as he was in real life and turned myself into
a German. I made both of them intransigeant nationalists.
Their quarrel arose over the chief issues of the great war
and was intensified by the galling heat and desolation of
the desert. Thus entered atmosphere in the needed minor
rôle.

With these data in hand it was not difficult to write
out my schematic outline:

The Crucible of Peace

Type of Story: Character-complication-thematic, with atmosphere.

Effect of Story: A thrill of horror at a fight against insects, with the exultant satisfaction at seeing an heroic fulfillment of a deep truth about life.

Conflict: Between man and man on account of the traits given below, and between the two men and nature in the shape of the insects.

Theme: Men, no matter how great their enmity to each other, will stand together always and help each other when they are faced by a danger greater than their menace to one another.

Characters: Professor Petroff, a Russian whose trait is his hatred of his companion for being a member of a "brutal race," and also for his timidity about his insects.

Dr. Zelheim, a German, his main trait being his hatred of the Russian's vindictive use of his spiders and tarantulas.

Initial complication: The two scientists, while endeavoring to work together peaceably, are so affected by the heat and desolation of their surroundings and by the traits given above, that they fly at each other's throats in the small room in their isolated cabin.

Crucial situation: When the fight is at its height and the Russian is about to kill the German with an ax, a glass case of live, poisonous insects is overturned. The insects race about the room. Both scientists, aghast at the horrible danger facing them, jump to the door to escape. The insects gather, however, about the door handle and the windows, attracted by the perspiration left on the door knob and window sills. The men are unable to escape without active coöperation.

Outcome: The German, having the greater terror, collapses. The Russian lifts him on his back, seizes the ax, smashes open the door, and carries his companion safely outside. The Russian discovers that he has been mortally bitten by a scorpion. The German, in gratitude for having his life saved, saves the Russian's life by applying his mouth to the wound, and drawing out the poison.

With this analysis before me I drew up a "bald report" in about one thousand words. This was my "writing outline." The story itself was written seven times and later appeared in *The Saturday Evening Post*.

CHAPTER TEN

POINT OF VIEW IN NARRATION

Selecting the right (artistic) point of view for a story or novel is not the most important of literary technical issues — clarity and unity are more important — but it at times is extremely troublesome. The best point of view for any given story or novel can be arrived at with certainty only by considering the plot and the effect to be produced. Students thoroughly familiar with the principles previously developed in this book should have no difficulty deciding most questions of viewpoint. Occasionally, however, a viewpoint conundrum stubbornly resists solution. I heard once of a dispute between two noted authors over a question of viewpoint which lasted nearly all one night; it turned out that they were not really talking about the same thing. Lack of definitions lay at the bottom of their differences — as it does with most differences. This suggests that we ourselves might well begin with a few definitions.

1. Definition of Viewpoint

Point of view expresses an arrangement of story material to make conspicuous some quality of the latter which the artist desires to emphasize.[1] The point of view means to the writer the same thing that " perspective " means to the painter. The latter, standing before the landscape he is to paint, sees in it some quality of light or shadow, color or form, which he wishes to dominate his painting. With his

[1] *The Art and Business of Short Story Writing*, by Walter B. Pitkin, page 176.

410

predetermined *effect* in mind, he walks about, pausing now
under a tree, now atop a hillock, now perched on a stone
fence, seeking the best spot to set up his easel. As he does
this, he is selecting his point of view. In the same way the
motion picture director's "camera angles" are his viewpoint.

Point of view, then, concerns the controlling vision a
writer has of his material; it expresses the relation of his
story to himself; it is, in a word, literary perspective.

Professor Walter B. Pitkin, in his writings twenty years
ago on the fundamentals of fictional technique, made a distinction between angle and viewpoint; but I think it may be
abandoned. In Professor Pitkin's terminology, "angle"
meant perspective and the artist's attitude was made synonymous with "viewpoint." Artist's attitude, said Professor
Pitkin, expressed "the artist's sensitivity, wish or belief toward a subject," the philosophy or coloring of opinion which
pervaded the writer's pages. This philosophy Professor
Pitkin called "viewpoint." Viewpoint, he said, was in part
what the writer wished to say, and angle, the perspective
chosen to express it. This terminology is clear enough; the
trouble with it is simply that in the literary dialect viewpoint and angle are used interchangeably. Professor Pitkin
so uses them in his writings. It seems common sense to admit this popular use in our definitions.

In the terminology used in this chapter, then, angle and
viewpoint are one and the same. When we wish to refer to
the artist's attitude or philosophy of life we will try to refer
to them as such, and not call them "viewpoints."

Subjective and Objective

Now a confusion involving two other words important to
literary technical shop talk must be dissipated. I refer to
"objectivity" and "subjectivity." Confusion in the use of
these two words results when writers and critics apply them

loosely to both the writer and his characters. Professor
Pitkin, for instance, describes one angle of narration as the
" pure objective." A story becomes objective, he argues,[1]
when a writer refrains from entering the minds of his characters. He assumes that when a writer attempts to portray
the thoughts and feelings of a character he must also portray his own thoughts and feelings; subjective characters,
in other words, need subjective authors. This does not
necessarily follow. An impersonal objective treatment of a
character's feelings and moods as well as his actions is
certainly possible. A supreme example is James Joyce's
Ulysses. *Madame Bovary,* still one of the great novels,
was so written. This method also characterizes the novels
of Thomas Hardy and Theodore Dreiser. These writers,
in other words, are *themselves* objective but the picture we
get of their *characters* is internal as well as external.

In the interest of clarity it would seem that the words
objective and subjective should in the technical dialect refer
only to the writer. Other terms are at hand to explain and
distinguish the treatment of the characters. " Physical
realism " accurately describes the external picture of character, and " psychological realism," the internal; or, more
briefly, we may refer to the two treatments of character as
external or internal.

The Grammatical Form

A third and last source of confusion frequently results
from efforts to solve this perennial question: Shall I tell my
story in the first or third person? Generally the writer
knows which person he can handle most easily and naturally; if he does know this, he should be content to settle
the issue on this basis: he should simply use the person he
likes and consider nothing else. Difficulties arise when,
however, he begins asking himself, what person will best

[1] *The Art and Business of Story Writing,* page 176.

bring out what he wants to say? which person will make the story seem most convincing?

Now the truth is that grammatical form cannot settle the issues raised by these questions. It is useless to speculate as to whether first or third person will " bring out " such and such effects; the same effects can be produced by the use of either: there is no significant relation between the perspective of a story and the use of " I " or " he." This, I think, is made quite apparent by the remaining discussion of viewpoint in this chapter. The problem of grammatical form lies between you and your story, not between your story and your reader. " He downed twenty slugs of whiskey, bumped off four men and yawned " means, to the reader, precisely the same as " I downed twenty slugs of whiskey, bumped off four men and yawned."

Use the grammatical form with which you feel most " at home." The only precaution necessary here, perhaps, is to be careful not to remain at home *too* long! If in writing stories you become so accustomed to the first person that you cannot use the third, you may handicap yourself later in the writing of novels since most novelists use the omniscient angle and that, as we shall see in a moment, requires the third person.

2. Viewpoint at a Glance

The three drawings below represent the three basic viewpoints used in fiction. A thorough understanding of the distinctions made by them and the accompanying text will, I think, enable you to decide upon the most artistic angle to use for all familiar short story patterns.

Each sketch depicts the climax of the most common of all " triangle " plot situations, i.e., the husband's arrival home, gun in hand, to discover his wife in his rival's arms. The figure at the left is, obviously, the author. The solid, heavy lines suggest the bounds of the story. In the second and third sketches the story is fully enclosed because the story, being told *entirely* from the vision of a character, has definite bounds. In the first sketch, however, the solid line is not joined about the story because the author's omniscience deprives the story of finite boundaries.

The light solid lines in the third sketch indicate the bounds of the story as seen from the viewpoint of a minor character in the story. The stout lady, who, let us say, is the wife's mother, is seated to symbolize her inactive or minor role. She sees and may talk about anything within the enclosed frame, including herself, but her chief business as viewpoint character is to spotlight the actors in the triangle who are included within the light solid lines.

My graphic device, it seems to me, fails of completeness only in the second sketch. Here, as in the third sketch, the story action is witnessed by a character in that action, but this time he's in the midst of it! Strictly speaking, the sketch needs light lines from him to represent his view of his own story. My ingenuity fails here.

The dotted lines in the second and third sketches indicate the connection between the author and his partner in the story. He is, of course, aware of all the characters, but we are discussing viewpoint and in these two cases he sees with his viewpoint actor who sees the story. Since the author in the first sketch sees and knows everything, I give him no dotted lines; dotted lines pin the author to the human limitations of one person. The solid black lines in the first sketch merely suggest the author's focus on the story in general.

Please remember now that the definitions or generalizations I shall attempt are not my arbitrary formulations nor are they ideals I set up for authors to observe at their risk. Enduring works of fiction furnish us examples of the most effective use of all the different viewpoints; we have but to try to understand their practice and cautiously attempt formulations of value to others trying to clear their own pathway to fame. Theory to be of value must follow practice.

I. — THE OMNISCIENT VIEWPOINT

(*The Novelist's Angle*)

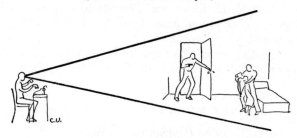

This is the " god-like " angle, the author being outside the story and not committed exclusively to one or more characters. No restrictions are placed upon what he may see, know, feel or comment upon. The third person only is possible with this viewpoint unless indeed the author sets himself up as a god. The writer using this angle can enter the minds of his characters and indulge in comment on the action as much as he wishes, but if he carries either of these possibilities beyond a certain point, one of the other two angles may be found more appropriate. Because of the omniscience of this angle, the variety of uses to which it can be put is very wide; one thing alone it cannot do: it cannot produce the suspense which depends upon withholding from a character information of importance to that character in the story. The reader, to share the suspense, must share the ignorance, but if the writer is omniscient, he cannot consistently withhold any important information. This angle is most naturally and, therefore, artistically employed with all narrative which is obvious, swift, and more or less chronological. Where interpretation of a broad, philosophical nature is necessary in a novel, this viewpoint is flawless. It is also often used in modern objective [1] narratives.

More great works of fiction have used this angle than all

[1] See page 411 for meaning of " objective."

the variations of the two other angles combined. It is *the* angle of the novelist as just stated. It is hardly necessary to cite, as examples, the best works of Meredith, H. G. Wells, Galsworthy, D. H. Lawrence, Thomas Mann, Arnold Bennett, Booth Tarkington, Anne Parrish, Sinclair Lewis, Ellen Glasgow and many others.

Short stories using this angle to be found in *Short Story Hits, 1933* are: " The Catalogues " and " Happy New Year."

II. — THE MAJOR CHARACTER VIEWPOINT

(*The Psychological Angle*)

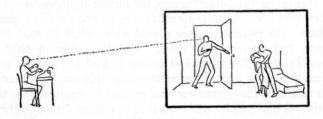

The author by the use of this angle is identified with the main character and may use either the first or third person. This angle is most suitable for stories featuring inner conflicts, psychological analyses, and character studies generally. It is effective also in mystery stories wherein the purpose is to stress the emotions of fear and terror felt by the person most under stress. It is serviceable also in humorous stories wherein the main character is acting without a proper understanding of some fact.

Notable novels using the major character angle are *Way of All Flesh* (third person) by Samuel Butler, *Dodsworth* (third person) by Sinclair Lewis, *Farewell to Arms* (first person) by Ernest Hemingway, *Company K* by William March (with one hundred and thirteen major first person authors), and *David Copperfield* (first person) by Dickens.

Stories in *Short Story Hits, 1933* using this angle are: "Charity Ball," "Cocktail Party," and "The Fire in the Flint."

Three especially interesting examples of psychological analysis using this viewpoint are to be found in *Short Story Hits, 1932:* "A Little Walk" by Alvah Bessie, "The Departure" by Selma Robinson and "Silent Snow, Secret Snow" by Conrad Aiken, the first of these dealing with a normal, the other two, with morbid characters.

III. — THE MINOR CHARACTER VIEWPOINT

(*The Suspense Angle*)

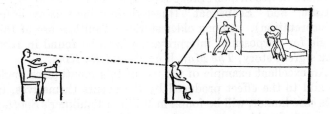

By this angle the author tells the story as it is seen by a minor character; it may be used in either the first or third person. This angle is in a sense more artificial than the other two although it is used successfully at times in the interest of realism. When the author, for example, doesn't know enough about a person or event to make an omniscient story, he may yet dodge the labor of filling out his information by telling the story from the viewpoint of a character who doesn't, or couldn't, know more than he, the author. The perspective furnished the writer by this angle is neither that of the god who knows everything (first angle) nor of the person who experiences everything in the story (second angle) but rather of the person in the story whose knowledge is limited and who experiences only a part of the story. Its most popular use is in the old-fashioned deductive type of detective story where suspense is the story's main appeal. This angle is peculiarly useful also when interpretive or didactic comment is necessary or an expert or eye-witness "slant" is to be used; a character in the story can often furnish these perspectives more naturally than the author.

The most consistent use of this angle in book-length fiction will be found in detective stories. It is highly favored in the popular detective books of S. S. Van Dine, who uses the secretary of the detective as the first person narrator. In *The Door* by Mary Roberts Rinehart you find the story told in the first person by the maiden aunt of the main character who gets the big scare.

Short stories in *Short Story Hits, 1933* are: "The Mother," "Kate," and "Scapegoat" (these three using this angle for interpretation). Among older stories a faultless use of this angle for purposes of interpretation is to be found in Kipling's great story, *The Man Who Would Be King*.

An excellent example of the use of this mouthpiece angle to add to the effect produced by the events themselves, in this case humor, will be found in William Faulkner's *Spotted Horses*.[1] In this story a sewing-machine salesman boarding in the town recounts the confusion resulting from the escape over the countryside of a bunch of wild horses.

As for the use of this angle in producing atmosphere effect: examples will be found cited in Chapter Eight.

Special Uses of Minor Character Angle

Unquestionably this third angle is *the* "tricky" angle of narrative. Four of its most important variations we shall now examine. These are: for atmosphere portrayal, for dramatic suspense, for interpretation, and for conversational coloring.

a. *Atmosphere portrayal:* The use of this angle in atmos-

[1] *Scribner's,* June, 1931.

phere stories is discussed in Chapter Eight.[1] Since any setting is most effective when its effect on a character is given, either the second or third angle is necessary for the most effective portrayal of atmosphere. When the main character in the end goes insane or meets his death, as a result of his struggle with the atmosphere, it is obvious that only the third angle *can* be used: the reader shares the effect of the atmosphere on the minor character and follows his observance of an even greater effect on the major character.

b. *Dramatic suspense:* The principle governing the use of this angle for suspense is: If the suspense depends upon certain facts being withheld from the reader, let the story be told from the viewpoint of a person who also is anxious to know those same facts. In most cases the third will be more appropriate for this purpose than the second or major angle. Why? Why are the Van Dine mystery stories told from the viewpoint of the detective's secretary, and the more famous Sherlock Holmes stories from the angle of Doctor Watson, friend of the immortal sleuth, instead of from the angle of Holmes himself? Because in real life most "mysteries" when tackled by people of any resourcefulness or even common sense are quickly solved — solved or ignored! If we got the story as the detective sees it, we'd know too much too soon. Your story detective is more than ordinarily perspicacious; he's generally glorified by a touch of the superhuman. To increase the reader's awe, the detective at work must be seen by someone in the story who is also in awe!

Manifestly this type of suspense is frankly artificial. The differences between this type and "natural suspense" are outlined below.

c. *For interpretation:* Any one of the three angles may be used for interpretation. The right one can be discovered only by considering the materials and the effect to be produced. The omniscient is used in some of the world's greatest philosophic novels, such as Tolstoy's *War and Peace,*

[1] Pages 365–6, 376.

Meredith's *Richard Feverel,* Dreiser's *American Tragedy*
and Butler's *Way of All Flesh,* and by story writers with
convictions such as O. Henry and Kipling (American story
writers no longer have convictions!). Novels of the philosophic type *using the major character* angle are not numerous; E. E. Cummings' *The Enormous Room,* in the first
person, will serve as an example; interpreted short stories
using this angle are also relatively rare. The reason for
this rarity is obviously that interpretation is essentially an
objective performance, even when it is furnished by the actor
himself; the latter must " get out of himself " to see himself, and this is neither easy nor always convincing in the
telling. A main character cannot be a wholly impartial
commentator on his own actions. As a simple example,
consider a soldier whose war experience unfitted him for the
society to which he returned after being demobilized. Securing a job in a store, he droops about, hardly aware of his
surroundings, totally without ambition. To a stranger he
might seem merely lazy. If the soldier were telling his own
story to the stranger, he might talk for hours about his war
experiences and their terrible effect upon his nerves and yet,
if he told no more, the stranger might well doubt him, might
conclude that the poor fellow was merely alibi-ing his real
laziness with the war story. If, however, the proprietor
of the store says to the stranger, " You see that man there;
when he went to war, he was managing this store and two
others," you would be convinced that the soldier was suffering from more than laziness. This last testimony, given
by a minor actor, is impartial; the latter sees the soldier's
story with more completeness than does the soldier and so is
both more impressive and more trustworthy.

All three angles, I have stated, *may* be used for interpretation. The difficulties of the second I have mentioned. It
remains to indicate the principles governing the differences
between the use of the first and the third. Where the canvas
is spacious and large generalizations about life are to be set
forth, the omniscient angle has been found most appro-

priate; this is, in other words, the novelist's interpretative angle. In the short story, however, the minor character angle is less likely to become monotonous and, since the opinions expressed must be pinned down to a finite character, it is suitable where narrower, more specialized testimony is needed. The minor character's viewpoint may indeed be called the expert's angle.

A sharp example of the expert's angle would be a medical story which represents facts only a physician would be likely to know. Such a story should of course be told from the physician's angle in first or third person. The story would not be truer or more authoritative for being told from a doctor's angle but it would be simpler and would enable the writer to economize his words.[1]

The stories, " The Mother," " Kate," and " Scapegoat," cited above, illustrate more general uses of the expert angle. In " The Mother " the horror of the main event is simply too ghastly to be told as seen by a main character; in " Kate," the author, a master at thematic writing in dramatic form, introduces a minor character narrator to make possible a neat comparison between American and French wives; and in " Scapegoat " the author attains sympathy for an exceedingly weak mother by letting the reader see her forgiven by her daughter who would be least likely to forgive her; by some the daughter would be considered a main character.

d. *For conversational flavor* (always the first person). In this use the viewpoint character tells the story without actually being in that story; the author tells a story that somebody else tells. An example is that childhood classic, *Uncle Remus* by Joel Chandler Harris. Uncle Remus is not one of the animal characters whose adventures he unrolls and in this sense he is not a minor character, but in a technical sense he is a minor character. Harris's chief creation is Uncle Remus; he is more important and more interesting than even elusive Br'er Rabbit. The subject of Harris's narrative is the legendary adventures of the ani-

[1] See comment on conversational flavor, following.

mals within the frame of the old negro and his audience, the little boy. The perspective is that of the negro narrator, the mouthpiece character, and the gain is not in credibility or persuasiveness, but in the flavor of the negro's personality and dialect.

It is difficult for the student to believe that a story gains nothing in credibility from being told by an alleged eye-witness and this sometimes leads to an error in planning. The Uncle Remus tales are more humorous and charming, but not more convincing, because the old negro tells them. Fiction is fiction and can be given no increase in authenticity by any pretense. The case is otherwise when dealing with facts. Eye-witnesses are quoted by newspaper reporters covering a crime or a fire because of their closer association with the facts. If, on the other hand, the eye-witness and the reporter both wrote fictional stories based on the crime or the fire, would the words of one be more persuasive than the other? The principle to remember is that the minor character angle should be used to add some quality other than mere persuasiveness.

Excellent modern examples of the skillful use of this angle for conversational flavor are William Faulkner's " Spotted Horses " [1] and Erskine Caldwell's "Country Full of Swedes." [2] The humor of these narratives depends in large measure on the limited intelligence of the sewing-machine salesman in the former and the hired hand in the latter. These stories told with equal fidelity in observation by the authors in matter-of-fact English would be as convincing as they are in their present versions, but the humor might very well be missing.

These two exceptionally effective stories indicate also the modern tendency of evading the once common " story within a story." Where the frame of the story is itself interestingly related to the narrative proper, as in the case of the Uncle

[1] *Scribner's,* June, 1931.
[2] *Yale Review,* December, 1933.

Remus legends, the device is still indispensable, but otherwise the simpler and more direct method of letting the
narrator-character launch into his entertainment without introduction is much more acceptable as these two stories, just
mentioned, reveal.

3. Viewpoint of the Modern Objective Narrative

(In trying to answer this question we must bear in mind
that in these discussions the word objective applies to the
writer and the words internal and external to the characters.) The viewpoint problems of the objective novelist
differ somewhat from those of the story writer. Photographic realism (external views only of the characters)
which is possible in the short form cannot be adopted in the
long form without serious risk of monotony. When both internal and external treatments are used, the omniscient angle
is obviously the most convenient and since this angle can be
used only in the third person, we find that practically all
notable objective novels use the omniscient angle in the third
person. The works of Dreiser, Sinclair Lewis, Arnold Ben-
net and some of Hemingway's longer works, such as *The Sun
Also Rises*, furnish good examples.

In the short story we may expect to find more examples of
objective-external technique. I haven't been able to find
one which attains complete photographic realism, i.e., where
the camera (seeing) but not the sound apparatus (hearing)
is employed by the writer. It is surprising that amid so
flourishing a school of objectivists as we have in this country
no experiments should have been made with this exceedingly
narrow but nevertheless fascinating technique. Omitting
the talk of characters can obviously be accomplished in several ways: they are deaf or mute or both, or are seen from a
distance or through a window. Such a story would read like
the scenario for a silent movie, and *some* scenarios are interesting! The nearest approach to it in my files is Lowrie

C. Wimberly's " Censored." [1] In this short account of a crucial few moments in a woman's life, using the angle just mentioned, we are given no report of talk except in two places, once where the woman talks briefly to another person and once where, in spite of being strongly religious, she finds it necessary to swear! This latter impulse of the pastor's pious assistant was too much for complete objectivity!

Sight-*and-sound* (i.e., action, appearance, *and talk*) objectivity, omniscient angle, without " psychologizing " or " entering minds," is much more commonly found in current stories. *The Killers* by Hemingway uses it most impressively; Ring Lardner used it with his story *The Champion*, as did Katharine Brush with her equally successful *Night Club*, and Dorothy Parker clings to it in her clipped, biting little dialogues. With suitable themes the device is very effective but complete devotion to it would cramp any writer's style.

The greatest short stories have been objective in mood but they have given internal as well as external views of the characters. The writer has freely exercised his privilege of peering into the secrets of men's souls. Take down the old books from the shelf and study once more the masterly exploitation of this angle — omniscient, external and internal treatment — in the great stories of the past, as for example the two greatest favorites of the generation past: *The Necklace* by Maupassant and *Without Benefit of Clergy* by Kipling. Don't overlook either the writings of Katherine Mansfield, and, to choose a more recent woman objectivist, the excellent work of Stella Benson.

4. Common Errors in Viewpoint

A. *False Suspense:* A characteristic mistake of beginners is what I have called false suspense. The writer (generally imitating older writers) strives for an effect of surprise or

[1] *Short Story Hits, 1933,* page 246.

suspense, but he chooses for his story the angle of a character
who knows all the facts, and who in the course of the events
would naturally report them. These facts can be kept from
the reader, therefore, only by a distortion of the truth about
the angle character. Such artificiality is never necessary.
This mistake is more and more objectionable in these days
of realism. It is essentially a trick on the reader. It assumes many forms, is sometimes perpetrated by the best
writers, and is always questionable. An example is to be
seen in a published story written by one of our leading
authors of literary stories:

A sailor tells the story of how a former engineer on a private
yacht, during convalescence from a serious injury in an accident
due to his own carelessness, for weeks sits despondent in a steamer
chair on the deck of the yacht in the harbor, refusing to rise.
The sailor, who is pictured as entirely simple and frank in his
narrative, recounts in detail how all efforts to get the man to rise
were ineffective. He tells how finally a woman, with whom the
engineer was in love, fell into the sea in an effort to get the
engineer to come out of his lethargy, and plunge in to rescue her.
Still the engineer refuses to budge. At last, the woman, not
loving him, but concerned about his apparent dullness and lassi-
tude, stands in front of him, holding out her hands, and saying
that he can have her if he will walk to her. The sailor tells
how the engineer gets down to the deck and begins to crawl to
the woman — he had no legs. The accident *which the sailor had
witnessed* had crushed the engineer's legs and the sailor now tells
us about it for the first time!

Here, you see, the person who is telling the story knows
all the facts about the engineer, who is the main character.
The narrator is also, of course, in a sense a character of the
story, and he is pictured as entirely frank; he is given none
of the ingenuity or artistry which would account for any
skill in holding back the main fact about the engineer. He
saw the engineer after the accident, and every day while the
man was completing his convalescence, he carried him below
to his bunk. Since the facts are withheld solely for the purpose of maintaining the suspense, we have a want of natural-

ness and so a want of art. Especially is this true when this defect could have been so easily avoided in several ways.

Here is a detective story displaying this same type of artificial suspense:

The narrator, accompanied by two detectives, sets out to force a prisoner accused of the murder of a woman to confess his crime. The three men conduct the prisoner to the morgue where the murdered woman is laid out. *The narrator tells us* that on the way the accused man pleaded his innocence, describing the pathetic plight of his wife and babies if he were condemned. We are told by the narrator that on sight of the dead body, the accused man sobbed out his guilt, drew a knife and raised it to kill himself. At this the narrator tells us that he caught the distracted man's arm and exclaimed: " Never mind; I did it." The narrator was the murderer!

Here again we have false suspense in that the outcome is withheld from the reader not only by the nature of the events, but also because the author gives a false impression of the character of the man who is telling the story. Why, if he should tell the story at all, should not the narrator confess at the start that he is the guilty man? His character is warped for the sake of suspense, which is thus artificial.

The error in both this case and that of the injured sailor is obviously in choosing the wrong point of view for telling the story. If in the first case an onlooker who did not know the engineer, or indeed the woman herself, told the story, and, in the second case, if one of the detectives were the narrator, the outcome in both instances would be logical and satisfying.

There are two general rules for employing suspense correctly. One is involved in narrative following the " natural order " of events and the other in narrative following the " artificial order." We can state them thus:

Natural order: Under this head fall all stories which follow a purely chronological sequence. The story is told as it actually happened or might have happened. The only rule for suspense in stories of this type is that they have none other than the uncertainty that lies in all life itself. We cannot tell what will happen until it has happened.

We have a wrong use of suspense in narratives of this type when any part of the action is "held up," any details of character obscured, or any explanation of events falsified for purposes of suspense. Such attempts are often made by beginners to bolster up a weak plot, and invariably they merely make a bad matter worse. The novice is often impatient with natural suspense; unless the reader is tearing his hair out in a frenzy of uncertainty as to what is coming next, he feels he has failed. He over-values suspense. A safe general rule for the ordinary straight dramatic story is to give no thought at all to suspense.

Artificial order: Of this type are all stories which are more effective when told in some sequence other than chronological. Either the events are told out of chronological order, or from the point of view of someone who would not understand all the action as it occurred; or both these artifices are used. The proper use of the angle of a minor character for contrived suspense is discussed above.[1]

The wrong uses of suspense in detective and mystery stories deserve a word. Knowledge possessed by the investigator must not be withheld, as in the case of the two plot outlines given above; and unexplained episodes which are not involved in the final solution must not be included. Of the latter class would be a detective story at the beginning of which the actual murderer is so characterized that he could not conceivably have committed the crime and, at the end, we are told that he did commit the crime. Another case would be a plot in which the detective fails to solve the problem of a crime because of his lack of facts which the reader knows are right before him as plain as his nose, but which the writer withholds from him for purposes of suspense only! You have a form of false suspense in a mystery of a haunted house if the reader is given a shiver at the be-

---

[1] Page 417.

ginning of the story by being told that horses were heard galloping past the house at night and at the end is informed that the chief disturber of the peace was a wounded dog at the bottom of a well under the house whose yelps in no way cleared up the sound of the horses.

B. *Inconsistent use of angles:* This error results when the writer begins with one angle, sustains it for most of the story, and then abruptly adopts another, or begins with one 'angle in the opening and follows another through the remainder of the story. An example of the latter error may be found in a French short story known to all English-speaking students of short fiction, Maupassant's immortal *The Piece of String.* This all-but-perfect little work of art begins in the omniscient angle with a description of peasants going to market along a country road, but as the action continues, the author becomes absorbed, and rightly, in the psychology of his main character and thereafter keeps to this character's angle. Greater consistency and, I think, more unity of effect would have been attained by sustaining the major character angle throughout. By simply integrating the opening scene with the main character's own journey to market, this could easily have been accomplished.

Different angles may be used in the same story but only where the effect and materials require it. Where no special need for such a shift arises, simplicity and unity are promoted by keeping to one angle.

Two departures from consistency in viewpoint have appeared in the work of modern objectivists in their use of the third angle. One appears in their use of this angle in the first person and the other in the third. I submit a word on each of them.

The objective story with third angle, first person: Objectivity (which, remember, by our definition now refers to the author, not his characters) often tends to an external picture only of the characters; the author, that is, refrains as much as possible from " going into the mind " of his characters. Now if the angle of a minor character is so used *in the first person,* this character can't with any naturalness be as objective as the author. The author can approximate complete detachment by using the omniscient angle, but a character in the story can hardly be omniscient also. The viewpoint character must be individualized in order to be a character and if he is an individual, he can't be omniscient! A story which hardly escapes this error is William Faulkner's *Spotted Horses.*[1] I do not mean to imply that objectivity is impossible with the third angle in the first person; a story may very well be told without comment by someone who is supposed to have seen it, but to do so *consistently* he must be the kind of person who would so control his discourse. If such a narrator were a gossipy, sanctimonious housewife, this angle would seem to be inconsistent if not impossible; if he were a psychoanalyst submitting a report on a patient in narrative form for someone else, let us say, to analyze, this angle would be most appropriate and consistent.

The objective story with third angle, third person: Here again this device may very well provide the needed perspective, but if the viewpoint character is reduced too much to a mere device, i.e., a man who moves and talks but doesn't think or feel, we conclude that this objective device has been used inconsistently. A most interesting example of this is Hemingway's famous story, *The Killers,* one of the most impressive of the objective, hard-boiled gangster stories flowering during the prohibition era. Here are admirable restraint, swiftness and melodramatic power, but the author tells of the delayed killing from the angle of a man in the restaurant without telling the reader anything that that man thinks about the terrific things he witnesses until the end of the story when he allows this man one revealing remark. The minor angle character, in other words, is treated with almost the same externality as the major characters. He isn't quite a character; he's a viewpoint! This viewpoint was needed to sustain the story's suspense and to enable the

[1] Cited on page 422.

author to carry the reader from the restaurant to the victim's room and back again. But the artificiality I describe could have been avoided by giving the reader a more consistent report of how the angle character's tremendous experience affected him; this could most certainly be done without in any way affecting the other very real values of the story.

We deduce from our study of these inconsistencies that complete objectivity is impossible with the use of the minor character angle. Such a character is a character not an author! A man cannot be objective about himself. A minor character may be minor and be needed only as an angle, but he's a human being just the same and must be so handled.

C. *Use of objective angle for subjective story:* The analysis of the inconsistent use of angles in objective narrative, just concluded, brings us face to face with an even more serious indictment of some of the practices of writers of modern objective stories and novels. In their straining for objectivity, to " keep themselves out of the story," they sometimes, apparently without knowing it, attempt to use in subjective narratives the objective angles they find in the great modern objective writings they admire.[1] The result is not merely lack of consistency, which possibly only a pedant would cavil at, but actual absurdities.

Behind all modern strivings for objectivity in fiction are two convictions, one sound, the other unsound. The sound

---

[1] The more the crudities and distortions of our younger, modern objectivists disclose themselves, the more do they seem to me to stem from *Ulysses* and its imitators! The crudities in the work of some of the imitators of Joyce's methods are associated intimately with these efforts at adaptation; they will not be found in fiction written before Joyce's influence was felt. Not Joyce's poetry nor his new language nor his probings of the subconscious have most impressed our younger writers, but rather his detachment. That they themselves do not understand much of *Ulysses* and that several volumes have appeared which try to explain the obscurities resulting from this detachment have given our developing younger writers no pause. *Ulysses,* being without sermons, is without " blah "; conclusion (remarkable!): omit the sermons *at whatever cost.* I criticize not the objectivists but their extravagances.

slogan of objectivism is that Victorian authors, since they insisted upon heavy sentimental moralizing in most of their work, were stuffed shirts and that one can avoid becoming a literary stuffed shirt by omitting the sentimental moralizing. (One is tempted to suggest even here that a modern writer might include moralizing if only it were not sentimental; but I realize the futility of offering any such suggestion. " All moralizing," argue the objectivists, " — out with it! Let us have the story; no story has a meaning, life itself has no meaning: don't be so tedious.")

Their second, unsound slogan is that the ways of objectivity are the only ways of realism. I have at hand the written creeds of some successful objective writers. " I cannot interpret my stories," writes one of them. " Since I am writing realism I cannot let my narrator explain things; my action must speak for itself." The fact that the action in one of this author's stories *didn't* speak for itself did not disturb him in the least. Instead of simply explaining what was obscure, which he could have done easily, he tinkered patiently with his observations. He seemed to me like a detective trying to solve the mystery of a crime by continuing to take photographs of the scene of the murder instead of sorting out the testimony of the people who had witnessed it. Things are what they seem, he believed, and I could not shake him. " If you have told what happened, you have done all," is the controlling dogma of this creed of photography.

Nothing less true was ever uttered. If this were true, all art itself would vanish. Stories with rare exceptions do not tell themselves. Realism is not synonymous with objectivity. And the greatest creative literary achievements are not " transcripts of life "; they are interpreted selections from life. How a man eats is not so important or interesting as why and you won't learn why by photographing.

Why all the " hard-boiled " crook and gangster fiction of the past decade? Since brutal, stupid characters have no subtleties, since all their acts are simple and obvious, their deeds are effectively set forth in objective narrative. Writers specializing in such materials invent violence instead of laboring over the subtleties of more sophisticated characters or exhausting themselves to acquire a philosophy of life. Objective crook fiction, in a word, is easy. I do not think that modern tough guy stories and novels have anything to do with the influence of the war nor with any relaxing of morals nor with any upward evolution of literary technique. They are merely the output of a school of objectivists who begin, as many good writers have begun, with melodrama which is none the less melodrama for following a current mode.

Suppose an objectivist faces the problem of picturing the swift moral degeneracy of a crook in such a way as to reveal the close connection between greed, lust and brutality. Appropriate angles here would be the omniscient or the major character (who degenerates) angle handled internally as well as externally. The author could be either objective or subjective. In a novel of this type, *The Postman Always Rings Twice*, by James M. Cain, we find the major character angle used objectively *with external treatment only!* Here is objectivity forced upon a subjective theme and a subjective angle. Here is the modern straining after detachment of which I speak. The author not only keeps himself out of his story, which I have indicated is possible enough, but keeps his narrator main character out, too! The murderer main character is, to be sure, an inarticulate customer and could hardly introspect and interpret, yet he thinks and feels. His thoughts and feelings here, however, are omitted. Through all the soul-destroying horrors of sex and murder in this book (a psychological story if ever there was one) the main character calmly moves as if he were talking of somebody else! The force of the moral close of the book is lost because the reader has seen nothing of the inner conflicts which moral outcomes involve. The unquestionable grim, melodramatic power of this book is qualified only by this inconsistency in the angle of narration.

This same straining after detachment by modern writers has produced what is called the " collective story." The device of telling a story involving several people by letting each one of them tell his own story without any attempt by the author to anneal these separate narratives is no new thing in fiction but the use of this device *in the interest of realism* is new. The theory on which this new use is predicated seems to have evolved from a realization on the part of the objectivists that there are *some* stories which cannot be clearly presented from the uninterpreted angle of any one character. One of two things is inevitable: either the writer must keep to the angle of one character and interpret as he proceeds (which is subjective omniscience) or keep to the uninterpreted angle but tell enough separate stories or sections of the story to make the whole clear. The former solution has been used by the great novelists of the past; the latter method produces the " collective " story and is used by our intransigeant younger objectivists. " If many important characters are involved," they argue, " we'll let each character tell his own story; that ought to make it clear. Even if it isn't entirely clear, it will be the truth. And we'll have a new literary technique."

Well, it will not be new and it will not be any truer than if it were handled subjectively, and it will always run the risk of not being clear. An excellent illustration is at hand in that vigorous, bold novel, *Company K,* by William March.[1] It recounts the adventures of a company in the great war.

War and Peace by Tolstoy and *Sergeant Grischa* by Zweig use the omniscient angle in the third person; *All Quiet on the Western Front* by Remarque and *Farewell to Arms* by Hemingway use the major character angle, the former in the third person, the latter in the first. *Company K* also uses the major character angle but it has one hundred thirteen major characters! The " collective " technique of letting each character tell his own story without comment from the author is followed here. The author seems to have shrunk from contaminating his characters' stories even to the extent of giving his chapters and the book itself names

[1] Published in 1933.

instead of titles. The book has the name of the company and each chapter the name of the soldier who tells the story. Even the preface of the book is entitled " Private Joseph Delancy "!

The events as narrated seem brutally true; the effect of the book is cumulative horror, and pity is wrung from the reader as he peruses these terrible pages. Note this, however: *the merits of the book have nothing to do with the oddity of the objective multiple narrators*. No novel can have so many narrators and escape some confusion, some want of coherence. The reader striving to grasp the connection of one story with another at times ceases to be absorbed and is irritated. In escaping from what the author seems to have believed were the artificialities of other war novels, he creates even greater ones for himself.

In this instance we can be in no doubt that the author's purpose was to emphasize the social significance of war by his stories for in his preface he writes: " I want it to be the record of every company in every army." He meditates this idea and adds: " I wish there were some way to take these stories and pin them to a huge wheel, each story hung on a different peg until the circle was completed. Then I would like to spin the wheel faster and faster until the things of which I have written took life and were recreated, and became part of the wheel, flowing toward each other, and into each other; blurring, and then blending together into a composite whole, an unending circle of pain. . . . That would be the picture of war."

The wheel which Mr. March seeks lies ready to his hand in any angle of narration handled subjectively.[1] Fusing a war novel through any of these angles, however, entails vastly more labor than spinning a wheel.

D. *Unrealistic use of stream of consciousness:* A mis-

---

[1] The terrific power of that first of all sensational anti-war novels, " Ground Arms! " was, I recall, due in large part to the subjective treatment with the minor character angle, the narrator being a woman who describes her war sufferings and that of her family and other families.

take more frequent among experienced writers is to attempt
the omniscient-internal treatment with stream-of-consciousness development for characters in whom introspection is not
convincing. Faulkner's group of invertebrates in *As I Lay
Dying* do not seem to me to lend themselves to this treatment although he has attempted it; the angle of narration weakens the effect. Caldwell's objective-omniscient-
external treatment is more effective for the same types.

5. What Is the Best of all Viewpoints?

Obviously there is no " best "; different angles are " best "
as they serve to emphasize the effect the author seeks. The
nature of the character, event, theme or setting as well as
the effect — these general factors must always determine in
the last analysis the proper viewpoint. The length of a narrative, as we have seen from our discussion, is an important
factor in viewpoint. In the short story form — especially
the modern " *short* short " types — a writer will always experience difficulty with the omniscient angle, particularly if
he attempts the internal as well as external treatments. In
the novel, on the other hand, the consistent use of a character
angle may easily become monotonous. *In general,* then, the
best angle for the novel is the omniscient and for the short
story, one of the circumscribing character angles. The tendency with modern short story realists is towards the major
character angle.

The point of view which, it seems to me, enables the
writer to spread the widest possible canvas in fiction with
the most profound effect is the omniscient in the psychological manner; necessarily this means the third person and implies the longer form of the novel since spaciousness and pro-
fundity are impossible in the story. Whether these grand
qualities are created better by the objective or subjective
treatment is a matter of the author's temperament and the
reader's taste. By the former, the events tell the story, while
by the latter, the events are helped along by comment from

the wings by the author. If you share the modernist feeling that any author comment by forfeiting objectivity forfeits realism, you have a very famous and very perfect model to emulate: Flaubert's *Madame Bovary*. Here the author is absent but he gives us both external and internal views of his people. In order that we may see just what this type of writing — worshipped by who knows how many writers to-day? — is like I shall quote a short passage. I have italicized the phrases which take the reader from the external to the internal stage of action.

Flaubert's hero, Leon, has come to the cathedral of the provincial town to meet his mistress, Mrs. Bovary. While he is impatiently waiting, a flower seller offers him a bloom.

The young man took one. It was the first time that he had bought flowers for a woman, and his breast, as he smelt them, *swelled with pride,* as if this homage that he meant for another had recoiled upon himself.
But he was afraid of being seen; he resolutely entered the church. The beadle, who was just then standing on the threshold in the middle of the left doorway, under the " Dancing Marianne," with feather cap, and rapier dangling against the calves, came in, more majestic than a cardinal, and as shining as a saint on a holy pyx.
He came towards Leon, and, with that smile of wheedling benignity assumed by ecclesiastics when they question children: " The gentleman no doubt does not belong to these parts? The gentleman would like to see the curiosities of the church? "
" No! " said the other.
And he first went around the lower aisles. Then he went out to look at the square. Emma was not coming yet. He went up again to the choir.

The novelists who have mastered not only the arts of observation and writing but the sciences of life — psychology, biology, philosophy — will inevitably employ the omniscient angle, external and internal, *subjectively.* Such a novelist is Aldous Huxley. In his *Point Counter Point* he not only anatomizes his characters' actions and feelings with a scalpel exceeding Flaubert's in sharpness and versatility, but he steps forth himself occasionally and explains — I almost said lectures on — what it is all about. An example of such comment is this interpretation of the love relation between Walter and Lucy:

Sensuality and sentiment, desire and tenderness are as often friends as they are enemies. There are some people who no sooner enjoy but they despise what they have enjoyed. But there are others in whom the enjoyment is associated with kindliness and affection. Walter's desire to justify — etc.

In this novel the author sees everything, knows everything, and very nearly tells everything about everybody! Truly the viewpoint of a god, and it leads the author to make a god's mistakes; he makes things move but sometimes without much coherence.

MOTTOES FOR RAINY DAYS

He is a poor master whose achievement surpasses his criticism: he only moves towards the perfection of his art whose criticism surpasses his achievement.
— *Leonardo da Vinci.*

Much more would be done if people believed less was impossible.
— *Malesherbes.*

There are no details in the execution of a work.
— *Paul Valery.*

How much art to enter into nature: how much time, and rules, attention, and labor we devote to dance with the same freedom and grace with which we walk, and to sing as we speak, and speak and express ourselves as we think.
— *Montaigne.*

Great minds have purposes, others have wishes. Little minds are tamed and subdued by misfortune; but great minds rise above them.
— *Washington Irving.*

Only those who have the patience to do simple things perfectly ever acquire skill to do difficult things easily.
— *Schiller.*

Woe to the productions of an art, all the beauty of which is discernible but by artists.
— *D'Alembert.*

You understand that in a literary campaign like mine society is impossible. Therefore I have openly renounced it. I go nowhere, I answer no letter and no invitation. I only allow myself the Italian opera *once* a fortnight.
— *Balzac.*

APPENDIX

SECTION A

THE TECHNIQUE OF WRITING THE NARRATIVE

We are here to consider writing rather than plotting your story or novel. The previous pages have been devoted almost altogether to the tasks of arrangement and design; if those tasks have been performed and the writing of the fully embodied narrative faces you, you have quite possibly come to a full halt — or if not a halt, perhaps you find the writing of full drafts of any sort an exceedingly slow and even painful business. You may have expected — you very likely did expect without realizing it — that your study of technique would lessen the difficulties of actual writing and you are greatly surprised that it doesn't. What should you do about it?

I have before me a letter from an exceedingly intelligent young man who has conscientiously performed the tasks set forth in this book. He writes well, understands people and is in tune with his age but — no stories come from his writing desk! One ambitious effort he managed to finish after literally weeks of effort and revision and then — no more manuscripts for the waiting public! If he fails, it seems to me, no one can succeed and so I have asked him his trouble. His answer is echoed by so many learning writers that I feel impelled to quote him.

"It seems to me," he writes, "that there is in your book one small gap which could be bridged for the student's benefit. You urge us to write whenever we are moved, whenever some experience touches us deeply, and to file away this material for later use in stories, but you do not show us specifically how to make use of this raw stuff. It seems to me that if you could print in your book samples of such copy and then show concretely how it is used and shaped up into a complete draft of a story ready to send the editor, you would be doing all of us a genuine service.

"All my life," continues this young man, "I have written fragments of things simply for pleasure, usually turning these impressions into letters to my friends. When at school, writing letters was one of my chief recreations. I would carry a letter in my head for some time, working over and improving it, finally writing it out. My trouble now is that I stick at that stage. I can still write letters but not full drafts of stories. What's the matter with me?"

The answer to this important question cannot be given with any completeness in a few paragraphs, and such a discussion has no proper place in a volume on literary technique. The problems of expression, of literary temperaments, I shall discuss more at length elsewhere.[1] Throughout this book there has been an assumption that the student using it has something to say and that, when the time comes to try his newly developed skill of planning, he will tap these sources and let them flow forth. If he is so endowed and is reasonably expressive in temperament and not too low in nervous energy, the difficulties mentioned in the above letter can be overcome without a textbook to fill a gap in his understanding. The gap is not in his understanding so much as in his practice.

There *is* a technique of writing as well as of plotting, of course; the single effect, the dramatic conflict, the suspense called for in the design must be held to in the writing. Skill in this matter, for those who have thoroughly mastered the contents of this book, will come with practice. If, for example, you have in your notes sketches of three different elderly people and your plot outline calls for an effect of young romance, you are in need of no textbook guidance to tell you that your sketches are not suitable and that you must seek others. Technical problems far more difficult than this are encountered in actual writing but if the student has mastered his theory and has been able to demonstrate his understanding of it in the practice exercises in this book, I do not believe he will be long in doubt about the matters mentioned in the letter quoted, if he merely persists in his experiments.

In most cases, if you are seized by the vision of a story, I would not delay long in writing it whether all the technical problems it raises are solved or not. Too much worry over such problems while writing may check your expressiveness. After a day or so of " cooling," you may test your work as analytically as you will. If it is lifeless, discard it and do another; if it displays signs of life, but needs doctoring, be you then its physician. Creation, like life itself, moves by feeling and energy, not by thought.

All the stalled literary motors I have examined have been defective in one or another of four ways. These defects I have space here only to mention with a very brief comment on each. Thus:

---

[1] *Fiction Writing as a Career,* now in preparation, will contain talks on *The Price of Facility, The Energy Factor* and on the various artistic temperaments and complexes as well as an analysis of the story and novel markets of today.

1. The student either has nothing to say, or, what is more often true, is struggling to be eloquent about the wrong things. In the latter case he is probably writing about things that interest him most and, nine times in ten, such things are new to him. Seldom are people most interested in things they best understand. One of the hardest tasks I know of is to convince most writers from small towns that they should write about life in small towns. My advice here is to ask yourself quite searchingly what people and human problems you have spent your life with. Unless you are a very imaginative, very poetically gifted person, you will do well to make stories and novels of such people and problems whether they " interest " you or not. They *do* interest you actually, far more deeply than remote affairs whose only appeal to you may be novelty.

2. The student can't sort out his ideas and notes and decide what comes first and second in the actual writing because he hasn't really learned his literary technique. It can be learned by studying this book.

3. The writer has a neurosis. Its name is " the perfectionist's complex." The more I learn about the secret pains and labors of writers at work, the more I am convinced of the prevalence of this dread malady. I suppose none of us is entirely free of it. It begins its literary embodiment (its origin is of course in infancy and childhood) with huge doses of great literature during years spent at school and college. In this way are literary ideals formed in all writers. Let these ideals become entangled with certain other less esthetic concerns of life and there's simply no preventing the victim from trying in every paragraph he writes to equal the pages of the great geniuses of literature. " I'll be another Shakespeare or else — ! "

The menace to be conquered first by such sufferers is their zeal for perfection. Escape your fixation if you can. Break it by lowering your ideals. Try for a time to produce bad manuscripts. No writer can learn to write well who has not first been willing to write badly. If your struggle seems to be of this type, if it is actual paralysis and no amount of practice or self-examination brings you release, you may be sure that you face more than a mere literary difficulty; the advice of a competent psychologist is then indicated.

The endless excuses writers with this fixation make for not manfully putting themselves to work are nine-tenths rationalizations or, plainly, alibis. The need felt for another textbook to explain how to write may be one of them. Stalling until enlightenment shall arise is a much fancier excuse than to admit sheer terror of failure. Suppose this search for perfection through the study of theory and principles should continue, paralyzing permanently the nerves and muscles of creation. What will happen? As a fair warning I quote from a letter written by a young man who for several years did stick to this conviction. He wrote me: "I am so damned serious about becoming a writer that I have never felt myself prepared to launch out. I have no wish to join myself to the already-too-large army of writers who can't write and will never be able to write, although they get their stuff printed. That I might be equal to the great adventure myself I have gone through three grammars again and again; I have torn up three rhetorics so that I should never be tempted to go back over them. I have ripped two Wooley's Handbooks from cover to cover after doing each exercise, after looking up each word. The whole business has brought me infinite agony." Here is accomplished suppression, not the expression from which art must always flow.

4. The last diagnosis is just ordinary, delightfully human laziness. "Aren't we all?" These comrades may have taken up literature because, as someone has said, the pen doesn't weigh much. They find when the job of actual writing begins in earnest, that it isn't the pen or even the typewriter that taxes them, but thinking, and who wants to think if he can avoid it? Let my young friend who finds letters to his acquaintances easy but manuscripts to the editor difficult remember that the letters in the main rambled from topic to topic and pretended to no emotional effect. Narrative, on the other hand, is writing under the severest of controls and with a double responsibility — to keep to the subject and to keep to the effect! Such writing demands for sound work a highly integrated nervous response which may not be smoothed out in a fortnight.

These sufferers from the inertness of the natural man deserve, I suppose, most sympathy. Of one superstition they must be disabused: that they alone are singled out by fate for this malign attention. How they groan with envy of other and better writers who, they think, "dash off" many graceful pages before noon to knock off for golf and rounds of cocktail parties and the soft adulation of innumerable fans. Let them learn the truth!

Before me is the testimony of Heywood Broun. "Within the next three or four weeks," he writes, "I must write a novel. I'm not exactly sizzling with eagerness and ideas, but 'way back in the early spring of 1932 I drew an advance from a publisher. According to the contract, it was to be delivered on the first of July." And then he continues with a merry account of his postponements. He had radio engagements; he was starting a musical show; he had many other things to do "first." "It seems to me," he confesses, "that I have been not writing that novel all my life. It takes time to write a book, but nothing like as much as it does to keep avoiding it."

Homer Croy, the humorist novelist, once gave the literary world an essay on *Finding an Easy Way to Write*. He declared that he heard that Tarkington used a certain kind of pencil and he tried that and still writing was work; he tried Balzac's method of drinking pots of coffee, he tried smoking a corncob pipe, he tried everything, even finally psychoanalysis, and nothing lessened the effort necessary for the production of full-length drafts. The last-named method, he explains, required that he lie down and let his subconscious do the work — " it was the best vacation I ever had." In the end, he returned to slugging out the pages as at the beginning and concluded that no easy way to write can be found.

The theme of the writer trying to get himself on paper brought forth from the Sage of Baltimore one of the most humorous and pungently true of Menckenian Prejudices. " But it is essential to their craft," we read of writers in *Birth Pangs*, " that they perform its tedious and vexatious operations *a capella,* and so the horrors of loneliness are added to its other unpleasantnesses. An author at work is continuously and inescapably in the presence of himself. There is nothing to divert and soothe him. . . . The moment the door bangs he begins a depressing, losing struggle with his body and his mind."

And so has it always been. Five hundred years ago Dante, writing of the awful moments of beginning his *Divine Comedy,* confessed: " It seemed to me that I had taken a theme much too lofty, so that I dared not begin; and I remained during several days in the desire of speaking and the fear of beginning." Take comfort; your malady is no new thing. Others have envisioned all the terrors you are envisioning and many more besides and yet have managed to turn off some pretty fair pages. Up and at it!

No one can write a textbook of any value upon the art of turning raw material into finished manuscripts. How many difficulties to terrify him who would undertake it! Creative writing comprehends a vision, a mood — above all, a mood — in the performer, and how can any instruction induce that mood? Suppose, too, that such a textbook did succeed in organizing your writing habits for success, what assurance is there that they will be suitable for another? The creative effort, moreover, involves style, and literary style is of all earthly things personal, intimate, and in adults, unalterable. Grammar, rhetoric, the formalities of style — these things may be taught and you should have learned them long before you undertook the study of technique and labors of literary composition.

One last word. How to learn skillfully to fuse notes, sketches of people and places, into a full-length draft following a previously sketched outline of a plot? This is your practical question. The practical answer is: Don't indulge your curiosity about theory at this point; don't formulate, plan, or hypothesize; set your plot outline before you and write your first rough draft hell-bent. I don't think I'd even pause to consult these precious sketches and fragments. If your rough draft, on being read over the following day, shows any symptoms of life, study your notes carefully and write the story *again*, this time incorporating the best of the notes. If still further drafts seem necessary, they may be written more slowly and, in the end, you should not re-write at all but merely proof-read and edit.

Above all, remember this: If any draft of your story, on being read, seems to you chronically ailing, stuffed with words, urgently needing surgical attention in vital organs, take it promptly to the nearest ash can and drop it therein without a tear. Don't clutter your desk and your room with sickly writings, but don't hesitate to write them! Learning means experiment, means cultivating fluency from practice, means a patiently built up dexterity in co-ordinating many nervous controls as you write. Write! Make your mistakes and make them fast. Use the wastebasket and a severe critic if you can find one, but write first and worry afterwards. Don't worry before writing. And don't ask me or anybody else to write a book on how to make writing easy!

SECTION B

HOW TO ATTAIN PUBLICATION

Practical Considerations for Impatient Writers

Most beginning writers want to succeed in a hurry. It is human to want to begin at the top, and the top in creative writing, for reasons peculiar to our art alone, seems conveniently within reach. For most of us, also, it isn't so easily attained; a long apprenticeship is necessary almost always and this book, as explained in the Preface, is designed to shorten that apprenticeship. A quick and easy success for an artist in any medium, however, has its dangers; it tends greatly to limit the range of subject matter he may use in all his succeeding work. Quick success generally results from luck in using very timely or novel material and the author, fearing failure in using any other material, continues in the same vein until he is lost attempting to handle any other. I realize, of course, that my saying this will not deter very many writers from scanning this book with the rather desperate hope of finding in it a few "practical tips" or "secrets of success" which will enable them to throw together a story that will cause a flurry in editorial headquarters and lift the author's financial, if not spiritual, depression. "With a first sale to encourage me," say these writers — and I can understand, though not always approve, their desire — " and a little money for the grocer, doctor and tax gatherer, I shall feel free to settle down and study in earnest."

Sometimes it works! Sometimes a writer, in tune with his age, naturally expressive and with an instinctive sense of form, can sit down and with little or no previous literary experience, write a story that will find publication. To writers who can do this — and especially if they can sustain success — I naturally have no advice to offer. Such a writer is one in a thousand or more. He enjoys not only natural ingenuity and resourcefulness that may enable him to elaborate a technique sufficient for his needs, but a degree of luck. These favorites of fortune need no prescription. If he has, however, one or two initial successes but finds himself, in spite of patient effort, unable to repeat, I may be of assistance.

I cannot hope that the suggestions offered in this section will be of value to beginners who have as yet written nothing. Preceding the habits of skilled performance comes the habit of work, of organizing one's time and energies for regular sessions at a typewriter. For those who haven't this habit the only needed injunction is: Begin! Specific guidance in shaping stories and novels for publication can be appreciated only by those who have tried, perhaps tried repeatedly, and failed. Such writers face concrete problems. To them I offer advice which has been a factor in the initial successes of very many struggling writers.

1. *Marketing:* If you have unsold manuscripts on hand and you believe in them, try to sell them. Such obvious advice would seem to be unnecessary, but it isn't. With rare exceptions writers are not good salesmen even in this age of salesmanship and ballyhoo. Nine writers out of ten at least, after receiving a few rejections of a story, will, though they may continue to believe in it, wistfully lay it aside. Stories *in which you believe* should be tried from ten to twenty times before you abandon hope.

If you can't send out your stories yourself, use a literary agent. A reputable agent is experienced, numbers established authors among his regular clients, and has proved the soundness of his literary judgments. The only fee he charges is a ten per cent commission on all manuscript rights he manages to sell. Except in special cases he offers no criticism of manuscripts. Any writer who honestly believes his work will sell *as it stands* should not

submit it to a teacher or critic, but should send it himself directly
to editor or agent.[1]

A literary agent, remember, functions as a clearing-house for
all editors and acts largely as an editor would act except that
when he rejects your work, the effect is equivalent to a rejection
by all editors. If a literary agent rejects your work, there is
probably nothing for it but to try again. Even this is not the
whole story, however. Literary agents derive their earnings very
largely from the more or less steady sale of the work of established
writers and not from the sale of unknown authors. Unknown authors are welcomed by them not so much for the sake of a possible
sale as with the hope that the client may in time win a reputation
that will create a market for his work with enhanced fees. Agents
seek not single manuscripts but careers. If, then, your work is
rejected by an agent he may have decided that it would not sell
for a figure large enough to interest him or he may not believe you
will develop as a writer.

In either of these cases you will, if you still believe in your work,
have to market it yourself. A few sales achieved are the best
possible introduction to a literary agent. If you live not too far
from New York City, you will do well to make your first sales
yourself. This is especially true if your beginnings are with the
" pulp " or lower grade general circulation popular story, for the
lower your aim, the less the agent, because of the low fee, will be
interested. If you live at some distance from New York City,
have good reason to feel that you can attain professional success
with fiction and can afford it, you should come East, as do students
of music and painting, to remain until you have at least made
profitable publishing connections.

2. *Self-criticism:* If you have on hand a number of manuscripts
which do not satisfy you or which have been rejected without
explanation, and you want to know what their defects are, with a
view possibly of revising them and again sending them out, I offer
here some suggestions for self-criticism. Don't trust the opinion
of a friendly layman critic! I have never yet found the advice
of a layman of any value in the solution of the kind of problems
we now face.

Stories are rejected by fiction editors chiefly because of errors
which I shall discuss in the order of their frequency and seriousness; they may be tabulated as follows:

A. *Inexpressive style:* no charm, color, force or individuality in
the writing itself.

[1] A list of literary agents will be found in the Classified New
York Telephone Directory and any editor or established writer will
make recommendations from this list.

B. *Trite or out-of-date ideas:* story idea or plot quite possibly excellent ten, twenty, fifty years ago.

C. *Defects in the management of the plot and structure of the story generally:* these are the problems strictly of technique.

Let us consider each of these three groups of errors.

A. *Inexpressive style:* No help in solving this weakness can be secured from a textbook on technique. Competent criticism and advice is here of greatest value. If you are in college, ask your instructor for his opinion. Is your style dead or alive? Have you a creative literary personality or haven't you? Are you writing about things that really interest you or aren't you? Truthful answers to these questions may indicate that the trail to the success you dream of may be too steep for you. If you have a dead style and no amount of experimenting with different subjects and manners of writing can bring some life into it, your instructor is justified in doing his best to discourage you and to direct you to other and easier ambitions.[1]

B. *Trite, shop-worn ideas:* This defect, also, if it exists, cannot be eliminated by any study of technique, except insofar as a writer's message or ideas are themselves a problem in technique. Here again you should seek professional advice if it is at hand. Unless your college instructor is himself a fiction writer or has been an editor, it is possible that he will not attempt to advise you in this matter, but will direct you to a close study of the magazine or group of magazines for which you are writing. Any writer, vendor or editor of fiction should be able to tell you upon hearing a brief digest of your plot, whether it has " market value " today.

Lacking these opportunities for help on your ideas, you have two courses open to you: one, to write what interests you in your own way, clinging stoutly to truth and sincerity, and to keep sending your stories to the literary publications until they " discover " you; the other, to learn how to analyze magazines yourself for current literary fashions in plot ideas! This research seems easier to the novice than it really is. Inevitably he finds the popular magazines full of trite, shop-worn ideas and concludes (falsely) that his way of salvation is to imitate these same old plots. His mistake is in not seeing that there is *something* original in nearly every one of these trite stories! The trick is to see the new twists the skillful popular writer gives the old basic plot patterns. Here is a task in analysis which most writers shrink from, either because of the labor involved or because it seems beneath what they feel to be their dignity as artists (some day). If their

---

[1] The weaknesses in style I have in mind here cannot be corrected by study of grammar and rhetoric; a living style results from having something to say and vitality and expressiveness in saying it.

objectives are the magazines that buy many stories and pay well for them, my advice is that they forget their dignity and settle down to work at this job they can't escape.

In examining your work for its basic " idea " or story germ, you face a task that may be peculiarly difficult without experienced assistance. It can be performed, however, if you have patience and thoroughness. The very first step — and most amateurs take it with strange reluctance — is resolutely to aim at a specific market or a small group of magazines using more or less the same type of story. Most beginners are surprised to learn that there are as many grades of short stories as of shoes, houses or automobiles. They shoot first and aim afterwards. If you have not yet sold, you should take time to study the different reader groupings as represented by current publications and decide to which general group you are to devote your energies.

In order to help you in this study I submit a table giving the important characteristics of the four major groups into which practically all our short fiction may be collected. Examine it carefully. Select *one* group for your first attack, analyze the magazines composing that group and *stick to that group* until you " arrive " in it as one of its regular contributors.

THE FOUR MAJOR GROUPS OF SHORT STORIES

	VALUES	READERS	LITERARY STANDARD
I. Experimental Literary Stories	Literary Trends	Students	Portraying life realistically with originality in form or substance
II. Literary Stories	Art Enjoyment	Cultivated	Portraying life with maximum appeal to mind and emotions
III. Popular Stories	Mass appeal	Average	Reflecting life with maximum, generally sentimental, appeal to emotions
IV. Pulp Stories	Sub-mass appeal	Literate (Anyone who can read)	Also maximum appeal to emotions but with greater violence of action, more stereotyped characters and the most direct appeal to the primitive instincts.

C. *Technical Errors:* Here *Narrative Technique* should be a valuable assistant. To systematize somewhat your search for wisdom in revising your manuscripts, I shall group the technical errors you are to look for under three heads — (a) Beginners' Mistakes in Invention, (b) Dramatic Weakness and (c) Want of Unity of Effect. These three general errors by no means cover all the mistakes to be found in beginners' work, but the chances are easily nine in ten that, if there are serious *technical* defects in your rejected work, such defects will be classifiable under one or another of these three heads. Under each head *Narrative Technique* will help you to criticize your manuscripts constructively.

(a) *Beginners' Mistakes in Invention:* If you have this difficulty, read carefully Section E in the Appendix on "Beginners' Mistakes." If you find that your work exhibits in a major way any of the extremely common errors in design described in this section, the discussion of that weakness in the text will in all probability be a fairly good criticism of your story. If you discover a serious case of either error number 1, 3, 4, 5 or 6, the chances are that the best disposition of that story is the wastebasket. A revision of stories with such defects may not be impossible, but it will be exceedingly difficult for anyone without much experience and, besides, dropping manuscripts into the wastebasket is an excellent habit for most developing writers to cultivate. If " wastebasket " is written on your manuscript, drop it there promptly — without a sigh. Don't clutter your mind or desk with refuse.

(b) *Dramatic Weakness:* If your story plan survives the test for beginners' mistakes in plotting, analyze it for dramatic intensity. If it isn't a dramatic story, it should be. Begin by a thoughtful reading of Chapter Four. Observe especially the first rule for intensification on page 157 and the section on Criticism of The Finished Story, page 173 following. Study now the classification of your story, making sure that it *is* either a character-action or melodramatic-action story. If its emphasis, for example, is not on drama, but on a sharp complication or on a theme, the tests I suggest here will naturally not apply.

Analyze the clash of your story, reducing it to terms of " Desire A " and " Obstacle B " and ask yourself: *Do these two obstacles actually clash* and, if so, is the clash of maximum intensity? If you are inexperienced as yet, and your story is weak dramatically, you will very likely shrink from doing anything about it from fear of being untrue to life or of being too melodramatic. If your objective is a popular magazine, you needn't worry overmuch about either of these fears, especially the latter. If the clash is weak, intensify it ruthlessly as suggested in Chapter Four, page 157, and re write, sustaining this new intensity in every line and paragraph.

(c) *Unity of Effect:* If these two tests for weaknesses in your story fail to reveal much, test it for unity of emotional effect. This test will be more difficult than the others because if the story lacks unity you will with difficulty be brought to agree that this is a defect! Read Chapters Two, Five and Six, especially Five. You can test for unity of impression in any dramatic character story by literally counting the number of sentences or lines devoted to the dramatic development of the trait of character of the main actor.

Read carefully and thoughtfully page 233 and the next several pages. If you can quickly grasp the principles which control the unity of the simpler and commoner types of stories and will resolutely endeavor to experiment with them in revising your own stories, it is just possible, if you are also blessed with expressiveness, that you may whip a refractory tale into such shape as will appeal to an exacting editor. Remember that the short story, like the play, and unlike the novel, is inheritor of conventions that cannot be easily ignored. At its best, now as ever in the past, it is a triumph of intelligent selection and exaggeration. What selection? What exaggeration? The principle of single effect determines the selection and that of dramatic intensity the allowable exaggeration. Believe in these principles. Apply them to your own work. If you must give preference to one of them, stick most closely to the means suggested in this book for attaining unity of effect. Even the most radical, fantastically experimental, so-called " modern " stories seldom depart from observance of the principle of unity.

What is the character trait being exploited? What sharply and specifically (in one sentence) is your complication? Get these things *clearly* in mind; don't guess at them; write them out, and then revise, sticking to them. Don't give up, saying as many beginners have, " If I keep to this one subject much longer, the reader will throw the magazine at me! " He won't. Run over Chapter Two again; note again the bottom of page 4 in the first chapter. Learn to analyze your material, to reduce it to its emotional essence, and then to make your entire writing spring from this central, glowing essence.

These suggestions for short-cutting the processes of learning to be a good fiction writer apply to writers of literary as well as commercial stories. They fail to apply only to the writer who is interested solely in producing what he might call " transcripts from life," the wholly realistic reporting of un-high-lighted human experience; he should not be writing stories anyway; his best field is probably the novel.

Needless to say, the manuscripts sent editors and agents should be typewritten on one side the page only, should be double-spaced, the first page beginning half way down, with the writer's name and address at the top left and the number of words at the top right, of the first page. A stamped, self-addressed envelope should accompany your script. A brief letter giving the editor some idea of the nature of the manuscript may be included. Don't make your letter too long or too interesting. I have known editors to reject manuscripts and accept accompanying letters!

SECTION C

A NOTABLE SHORT STORY ANALYZED

To what extent do the stories of successful authors who have never studied *Narrative Technique* exemplify the ideals set forth in the latter? This question, asked by all earnest students, I propose to answer in concrete form in this section. We will take a current literary story by an established story writer and novelist and run through it noting in the margin wherein it illustrates, disproves or ignores the principles we have been studying. I do this believing it important for the student to understand that all truly sound ideals of art are not arbitrary or merely theoretical dogmas elaborated by fastidious teachers or critics and set before reluctant performers for their observance. Sound theory evolves from successful practice. Mr. Callaghan's beautiful story is but one of many thousands which have been analyzed and studied for what they may reveal of value to the writer still absorbed in his search for effective ways and means.

" A Sick Call " was first published in *The Atlantic Monthly* for September, 1932. My belief is that if all the quality stories published in magazines in that year and the next were voted upon by literary readers, this affecting little adventure of a sick-room would appear at the top of most lists. It was reprinted in *Short Story Hits, 1932* with this comment:

D. H. Lawrence, who, many of us believe, was the greatest literary artist of our age because he so fully understood and expressed it, used to say over and over: " What the world needs is tenderness! " His belief in human love to this end was infinite. Today one searches the world of short fiction almost in vain for pages written without disgust, bitterness, or disturbing self-revelation. A writer who possesses this rare quality of tenderness is Morley Callaghan. In *A Sick Call* he touches the same theme Maupassant handled forty years ago in his famous *Moonlight*. The great French story teller was hard, ironic; Mr. Callaghan's pages are gently comprehending and flooded with life.

Mr. Callaghan's story classifies as character-complication with slight emphasis on this theme: Human love is as important as divine.

The single effect is sympathy and pity for the three characters who in spite of noble, generous impulses are forced to suffer.

The dramatic conflict is chiefly man-and-man, i.e., the priest and the husband; less emphatic but important to the theme is the internal struggle within the priest himself.

A SICK CALL [1]

by Morley Callaghan

FROM "THE ATLANTIC MONTHLY"

Sometimes Father Macdowell mumbled out loud and took a deep wheezy breath as he walked up and down the room and read his office. He was a huge old priest, white-headed except for a shiny baby-pink bald spot on the top of his head, and he was a bit deaf in one ear. His florid face had many fine red interlacing vein lines. For hours he had been hearing confessions and he was tired, for he always had to hear more confessions than any other priest at the cathedral; young girls who were in trouble, and wild but at times repentant young men, always wanted to tell their confessions to Father Macdowell, because nothing seemed to shock or excite him, or make him really angry, and he was even tender with those who thought they were most guilty.

While he was mumbling and reading and trying to keep his glasses on his nose, the house girl knocked on the door and said, "There's a young lady here to see you, Father. I think it's about a sick call."

"Did she ask for me especially?" he said in a deep but slightly cracked voice.

"Indeed she did, Father. She wanted Father Macdowell and nobody else."

So he went out to the waiting room, where a girl about thirty years of age, with fine brown eyes, fine cheek bones, and rather square shoulders, was sitting daubing her eyes with a handkerchief. She was wearing a dark coat with a gray wolf collar. "Good evening, Father," she said. "My sister is sick. I wanted you to come and see her. We think she's dying."

"Be easy, child; what's the matter with her? Speak louder. I can hardly hear you."

"My sister's had pneumonia. The doctor's coming back to see her in an hour. I wanted you to anoint her, Father."

"I see, I see. But she's not lost yet. I'll

[1] Copyright, 1932, by *The Atlantic Monthly Company*, Boston, Mass.

452

[Handwritten marginal annotations:]

SE = Single effect
A = main trait
B = Obstacle to main trait

Appearance

Opening paragraph makes for sympathy (SE) and "A" prepares for the final conflict and outcome and logic of theme

A

Action begins

Sympathy (SE)

A, i.e., desire to perform his religious office.

not give her extreme unction now. That may
not be necessary. I'll go with you and hear
her confession."

"Father, I ought to let you know, maybe.
Her husband won't want to let you see her.
He's not a Catholic, and my sister hasn't been
to church in a long time."

"Oh, don't mind that. He'll let me see her,"
Father Macdowell said, and he left the room
to put on his hat and coat.

II

When he returned, the girl explained that
her name was Jane Stanhope, and her sister
lived only a few blocks away. "We'll walk and
you tell me about your sister," he said. He
put his black hat square on the top of his head,
and pieces of white hair stuck out awkwardly
at the sides. They went to the avenue together.

The night was mild and clear. Miss Stanhope began to walk slowly, because Father
Macdowell's rolling gait didn't get him along
the street very quickly. He walked as if his
feet hurt him, though he wore a pair of large,
soft, specially constructed shapeless shoes.
"Now, my child, you go ahead and tell me
about your sister," he said, breathing with difficulty, yet giving the impression that nothing
could have happened to the sister which would
make him feel indignant.

There wasn't much to say, Miss Stanhope replied. Her sister had married John Williams
two years ago, and he was a good, hard-working
fellow, only he was very bigoted and hated all
church people. "My family wouldn't have
anything to do with Elsa after she married
him, though I kept going to see her," she said.
She was talking in a loud voice to Father Macdowell so he could hear her.

"Is she happy with her husband?"

"She's been very happy, Father. I must
say that."

"Where is he now?"

"He was sitting beside her bed. I ran out
because I thought he was going to cry. He
said if I brought a priest near the place he'd
break the priest's head."

"My goodness. Never mind, though. Does
your sister want to see me?"

453

[Marginalia:] B enters and main conflict hinted at — this announcement also introduces the complication

[Marginalia:] A shown again and sympathy (SE) created.

[Marginalia:] main conflict (A against B) developed here. this advances the theme — the priest must know they have human happiness. hint of reflective delay

"She asked me to go and get a priest, but she doesn't want John to know she did it."

III

Turning into a side street, they stopped at the first apartment house, and the old priest followed Miss Stanhope up the stairs. His breath came with great difficulty. "Oh, dear, I'm not getting any younger, not one day younger. It's a caution how a man's legs go back on him," he said. As Miss Stanhope rapped on the door, she looked pleadingly at the old priest, trying to ask him not to be offended at anything that might happen, but he was smiling and looking huge in the narrow hallway. He wiped his head with his handkerchief.

The door was opened by a young man in a white shirt with no collar, with a head of thick black wavy hair. At first he looked dazed, then his eyes got bright with excitement when he saw the priest, as though he were glad to see some one he could destroy with pent-up energy. "What do you mean, Jane?" he said. "I told you not to bring a priest around here. My wife doesn't want to see a priest."

"What's that you're saying, young man?"

"No one wants you here."

"Speak up. Don't be afraid. I'm a bit hard of hearing." Father Macdowell smiled rosily. John Williams was confused by the unexpected deafness in the priest, but he stood there, blocking the door with sullen resolution as if waiting for the priest to try to launch a curse at him.

"Speak to him, Father," Miss Stanhope said, but the priest didn't seem to hear her; he was still smiling as he pushed past the young man, saying, "I'll go in and sit down, if you don't mind, son. I'm here on God's errand, but I don't mind saying I'm all out of breath from climbing those stairs."

John was dreadfully uneasy to see he had been brushed aside, and he followed the priest into the apartment and said loudly, "I don't want you here."

Father Macdowell said, "Eh, eh?" Then he smiled sadly. "Don't be angry with me, son," he said. "I'm too old to try and be fierce and threatening." Looking around, he said,

454

"Where's your wife?" and he started to walk along the hall, looking for the bedroom.

John followed him and took hold of his arm. "There's no sense in your wasting your time talking to my wife, do you hear?" he said angrily.

Miss Stanhope called out suddenly, "Don't be rude, John."

"It's he that's being rude. You mind your business," John said.

"For the love of God let me sit down a moment with her, anyway. I'm tired," the priest said.

"What do you want to say to her? Say it to me, why don't you?"

IV

Then they both heard some one moan softly in the adjoining room, as if the sick woman had heard them. Father Macdowell, forgetting that the young man had hold of his arm, said, "I'll go in and see her for a moment, if you don't mind," and he began to open the door.

"You're not going to be alone with her, that's all," John said, following him into the bedroom.

Lying on the bed was a white-faced, fair girl, whose skin was so delicate that her cheek bones stood out sharply. She was feverish, but her eyes rolled toward the door, and she watched them coming in. Father Macdowell took off his coat, and as he mumbled to himself he looked around the room at the mauve-silk bed light and the light wallpaper with the tiny birds in flight. It looked like a little girl's room. "Good evening, Father," Mrs. Williams whispered. She looked scared. She didn't glance at her husband. The notion of dying had made her afraid. She loved her husband and wanted to die loving him, but she was afraid, and she looked up at the priest.

"You're going to get well, child," Father Macdowell said, smiling and patting her hand gently.

John, who was standing stiffly by the door, suddenly moved around the big priest, and he bent down over the bed and took his wife's hand and began to caress her forehead.

"Now, if you don't mind, my son, I'll hear your wife's confession," the priest said.

"No, you won't," John said abruptly. "Her people didn't want her, and they left us together, and they're not going to separate us now. She's satisfied with me." He kept looking down at her face as if he could not bear to turn away.

Father Macdowell nodded his head up and down and sighed. "Poor boy," he said. "God bless you." Then he looked at Mrs. Williams, who had closed her eyes, and he saw a faint tear on her cheek. "Be sensible, my boy," he said. "You'll have to let me hear your wife's confession. Leave us alone awhile."

"I'm going to stay right here," John said, and he sat down on the end of the bed. He was working himself up and staring savagely at the priest. All of a sudden he noticed the tears on his wife's cheeks, and he muttered as though bewildered, "What's the matter, Elsa? What's the matter, darling? Are we bothering you? Just open your eyes and we'll go out of the room and leave you alone till the doctor comes." Then he turned and said to the priest, "I'm not going to leave you here with her, can't you see that? Why don't you go?"

"I could revile you, my son. I could threaten you; but I ask you, for the peace of your wife's soul, leave us alone." Father Macdowell spoke with patient tenderness. He looked very big and solid and immovable as he stood by the bed. "I liked your face as soon as I saw you," he said to John. "You're a good fellow."

John still held his wife's wrist, but he rubbed one hand through his thick hair and said angrily, "You don't get the point, sir. My wife and I were always left alone, and we merely want to be left alone now. Nothing is going to separate us. She's been content with me. I'm sorry, sir; you'll have to speak to her with me here, or you'll have to go."

"No; you'll have to go for a while," the priest said patiently.

▼

Then Mrs. Williams moved her head on the pillow and said jerkily, "Pray for me, Father." So the old priest knelt down by the bed, and

456

with a sweet unruffled expression on his florid face he began to pray. At times his breath came with a whistling noise as though a rumbling were inside him, and at other times he sighed and was full of sorrow. He was praying that young Mrs. Williams might get better, and while he prayed he knew that her husband was more afraid of losing her to the Church than losing her to death.

All the time Father Macdowell was on his knees, with his heavy prayer book in his two hands, John kept staring at him. John couldn't understand the old priest's patience and tolerance. He wanted to quarrel with him, but he kept on watching the light from overhead shining on the one baby-pink bald spot on the smooth white head, and at last he burst out, "You don't understand, sir! We've been very happy together. Neither you nor her people came near her when she was in good health, so why should you bother her now? I don't want anything to separate us now; neither does she. She came with me. You see you'd be separating us, don't you?" He was trying to talk like a reasonable man who had no prejudices.

Father Macdowell got up clumsily. His knees hurt him, for the floor was hard. He said to Mrs. Williams in quite a loud voice, "Did you really intend to give up everything for this young fellow?" and he bent down close to her so he could hear.

"Yes, Father," she whispered.

"In Heaven's name, child, you couldn't have known what you were doing."

"We loved each other, Father. We've been very happy."

"All right. Supposing you were. What now? What about all eternity, child?"

"Oh, Father, I'm very sick and I'm afraid." She looked up to try to show him how scared she was, and how much she wanted him to give her peace.

He sighed and seemed distressed, and at last he said to John, "Were you married in the church?"

"No, we weren't. Look here, we're talking pretty loud and it upsets her."

"Ah, it's a crime that I'm hard of hearing, I know. Never mind, I'll go." Picking up his coat, he put it over his arm; then he sighed

457

as if he were very tired, and he said, "I wonder if you'd just fetch me a glass of water. I'd thank you for it."

John hesitated, glancing at the tired old priest, who looked so pink and white and almost cherubic in his utter lack of guile.

"What's the matter?" Father Macdowell said.

John was ashamed of himself for appearing so sullen, so he said hastily, "Nothing's the matter. Just a moment. I won't be a moment." He hurried out of the room.

VI

The old priest looked down at the floor and shook his head; and then, sighing and feeling uneasy, he bent over Mrs. Williams, with his good ear down to her, and he said, "I'll just ask you a few questions in a hurry, my child. You answer them quickly and I'll give you absolution." He made the sign of the cross over her and asked if she repented for having strayed from the Church, and if she had often been angry, and whether she had always been faithful, and if she had ever lied or stolen — all so casually and quickly as if it hadn't occurred to him that such a young woman could have serious sins. In the same breath he muttered, "Say a good act of contrition to yourself and that will be all, my dear." He had hardly taken a minute.

When John returned to the room with the glass of water in his hand, he saw the old priest making the sign of the cross. Father Macdowell went on praying without even looking up at John. When he had finished, he turned and said, "Oh, there you are. Thanks for the water. I needed it. Well, my boy, I'm sorry if I worried you."

John hardly said anything. He looked at his wife, who had closed her eyes, and he sat down on the end of the bed. He was too disappointed to speak.

Father Macdowell, who was expecting trouble, said, "Don't be harsh, lad."

"I'm not harsh," he said mildly, looking up at the priest. "But you weren't quite fair. And it's as though she turned away from me at the last moment. I didn't think she needed you."

458

"God bless you, bless the both of you. She'll get better," Father Macdowell said. But he felt ill at ease as he put on his coat, and he couldn't look directly at John.

VII

Going along the hall, he spoke to Miss Stanhope, who wanted to apologize for her brother-in-law's attitude. "I'm sorry if it was unpleasant for you, Father," she said.

"It wasn't unpleasant," he said. "I was glad to meet John. He's a fine fellow. It's a great pity he isn't a Catholic. I don't know as I played fair with him."

As he went down the stairs, puffing and sighing, he pondered the question of whether he had played fair with the young man. But by the time he had reached the street he was rejoicing amiably to think he had so successfully ministered to one who had strayed from the faith and had called out to him at the last moment. Walking along with the rolling motion as if his feet hurt him, he muttered, "Of course they were happy as they were ... in a worldly way. I wonder if I did come between them?"

He shuffled along, feeling very tired, but he couldn't help thinking, "What beauty there was to his staunch love for her!" Then he added quickly, "But it was just a pagan beauty, of course."

As he began to wonder about the nature of this beauty, for some reason he felt inexpressibly sad.

SECTION D

THE TECHNIQUE OF THE STREAM-OF-CONSCIOUSNESS STORY

Since the appearance of the second edition of *Narrative Technique* questions have come more and more frequently as to the "new type of story," the stream-of-consciousness story, to which, the questioners say, the technical principles set forth in this book do not apply. This section of the Appendix is an effort to answer them, to show that nothing in these new methods invalidates any of the fundamental principles of fictional appeal, and, so far as possible, in this brief space, to show ways of using the new materials. The stream-of-consciousness story is strikingly different in some externals, but when successful, is subject to the same structural laws which have always governed the story-teller's art.

One of the great difficulties every younger writer will experience in attempting to use the materials of the new psychology is that these materials cannot be easily understood. Few, very few, have understood them well enough to produce with them writing of any solid value. The essentials of Freudian psychology were announced to the world over a generation ago; psychologists understood these essentials within another ten years and I suppose all cultivated people possessed an equivalent understanding by 1920. Today most people who can read are familiar with the terms "complex" and "suppressed desires" and "wish fulfillments," although the popular understanding is almost always inaccurate. You hear people express impatience with "these queer stories" which "get nowhere" or "go off the deep end" in trying to analyze mental states and rejoice that the "craze" for this type of writing is about over and that writers will therefore return to sanity. How little they know! The craze has only begun! These new materials have not yet passed beyond the stage of being a sheer novelty even to the average intelligent reader. They "see" only the novelty, not the story!

And this is precisely why younger writers have difficulty in using these new materials. Both they and their readers take the new fiction which probes mental activity as — a probing, and nothing else! So *they* probe and the process is seldom clear or absorbing. The only people who can either write or read psychological literature with any real comprehension are those to whom the new psychology is a commonplace. These people are professional psychologists, patients who have been psychoanalyzed, thorough amateur students of psychology or possibly college students who have "majored" in psychology and worked hard at it and learned something. "Learning something" in this field means *grasping the relation to the problems of character of these new discoveries about mental life*. Many young writers at work today who are experimenting with the "new psychology" — new only to them — haven't yet lived long enough to understand it even if they had used every opportunity to try to do so.

I have talked to several writers who have attained occasionally brilliant effects with free association material and I discovered that every one of them has been psychoanalyzed! This means that they underwent the equivalent of a very thorough scientific training in the new understanding of the relation between morals and the unconscious mind. The purpose of an analysis is to adjust lives, to alter sharply some deep-seated life habits, literally to change character. Months of concentrated effort to attain this result by examining their dreams and free associations were an invaluable discipline in the new materials.

Today older writers of long experience who are interested in character and its moral patterns are incapable of adapting the psychoanalytic technique to their purposes because their prejudices are against it: Freud to them is still anathema because to accept his interpretations of life is to lose many precious sense-gratifying illusions and they prefer to fight for their illusions. Younger writers alone seem to have a chance with the new materials. To them, then, I address the following remarks.

The two ways in which the stream-of-consciousness story differs from the conventional story of the past are: (1) A picture of the subconscious life of the character is added to the picture of his conscious behavior and (2) The portions of the narrative in which this subconscious life is conveyed are written in the free-association manner.

These two contributions to narrative art, coming from the psychological clinics of Charcot, Freud, Breuer, Binet, Janet, Jung, and their disciples, are the developments which, more than changes in vocabulary and narrative style, have annihilated for mature readers so much of the work of the past and made savorless the work of present writers which clings too closely to past tradition. A great many character novels written before 1900 now seem antiquated because in their portraits the writers did not include what is now known about the unacknowledged or unconscious emotional life; the few writers of the past fifty years who seem most likely to survive are those who, by the closeness of their observation, approached the psychological truth as we now know it. Hardy, in *Jude, the Obscure*, and Butler, in *The Way of All Flesh*, are examples; both touch on subconscious problems, and both include behavior which is now recognized as important in revealing the subconscious aspects of personality. (Butler had to wait for Freud to get his audience ready for him, and the response to *Jude* was equally belated; Hardy's pastoral novels went better with the pre-psychological audience.)

The old novels now seem sentimental, even when their writers were trying hard to be serious. *Richard Feverel*, which I have used for illustrative purposes, in Chapter Seven (whatever its now evident lack in character portrayal, its thematic technique is still worth studying) is of this number; the book today seems sentimental and inaccurate because it handles a Freudian situation — a father's interference with his son's normal love life — in pre-

Freudian style. We are allowed to see the ways in which the boy's normal search for love was opposed, but the real nature of the father's disastrous subconscious, psychic interference is not portrayed. Many character works of older literature, notably Dickens' famous portraits, while not inaccurate, now seem narrow, conventionalized and artificial, with their emphasis on single traits, and their omission of subconscious elements.

Even the popular new literature of today is producing its effects by an emphasis on the subconscious. The success of *Anthony Adverse* is due in large measure to the skill with which Hervey Allen has fitted a modern handling of the inner life of his character, revealed according to what we now know of psychology, into one of the oldest adventure patterns. The success of *The Unpossessed* by Tess Slesinger can in part be similarly accounted for. In a word, some of the strikingly successful books of today incorporate the new scientific knowledge of our mental and emotional make-up.

The psychological principle at the bottom of all this new character work is this: from babyhood, as we adjust to the requirements of civilized society, certain primitive impulses and desires are repressed. Forbidden by society, they do not die — as we think — or disappear; they simply retreat into the subconscious. In the conscious mind, however, remain the fears that accompanied the submersion, with their associations, and these often dominate the personality, either continuously (in which case the subconscious material has character interest) or in some more or less important crisis (in which case the subconscious has situation interest). The effect upon Anthony Adverse of the subconscious memory of the lost twin statue when he encounters it in the Spanish courtyard, is such a crisis. These never-realized desires, and never completely recognized memories plus conscious response to varied external stimuli, are the material in stream-of-consciousness writing when realistically handled. The subconscious (forbidden) material can appear only when the conscious, civilized mind is off guard, in dreams, in delirium, in drunkenness, under anaesthetic, or hypnosis, or now and then, less fully in a day dream. Fragmentarily it may appear in the conscious thought-stream without our knowing it, unless we've learned some of the psychoanalyst's tricks for translating it.

The psychologists' purpose in their experiments was therapeutic not literary, but writers who could sense in their own lives the truth of the new discoveries were the first to seize upon them. Among these were D. H. Lawrence and May Sinclair. Lawrence in *Sons and Lovers* and Miss Sinclair in *The Life and Death of Harriet Frean* first impressively dramatized this big news. Outwardly narrative remained the same; the conventional outward behavior was given a new feeling tone by reverberations from subconscious memory and association.

After the war, during which amazing advances in the new science were made, two important new psychoanalytic novels appeared. In Aldous Huxley's *Point Counter Point,* the Freudian view of character was dramatized in the action of a group of young people, and analyzed and commented upon by the more philosophical of them. The plot action here was conventional enough but the author had seized upon philosophic implications of the new clinical material.

At about the same time *Ulysses* appeared, printed in 1922, in Dijon, France — because no British publisher would touch it! This omnibus of modern literary experiment announced explicitly the parallelism between conscious and unconscious life, and the peculiar and revealing incoherent thought-stream was made to function in the exposition of character. Joyce used the new theory of character, and he also used the technique of the psychoanalyst, both the free association record and the dream, in his amazing pages.

Ulysses had a mild vogue with laymen, and a great vogue with writers; its astounding recent success in the United States, due in part of course to its naughty reputation, indicates how much the ten-year interval has prepared the public to understand the Freudian interpretation of character. Psychoanalysis has become almost a commonplace since Floyd Dell startled the literary world by reporting the connection between his experience in being psychoanalyzed and the writing of his novels. More and more the average reader is learning to see the significance in personality of the subconscious life, and also the order underlying the seeming chaos of free-association, which many now accept as part of the novelist's technique. This growth in knowledge accounts for Conrad Aiken, much of William Faulkner, Alvah Bessie, Nancy Hale, and, most recently, Tess Slesinger.

Now, how do the above psychological truths affect the form of the modern story? Their influence can be discovered in three different types of writing.

(1) The writer accepts the classical form, records mostly the conscious life of his characters, and uses the subconscious material for its value in re-interpreting the announced, or rationalized, motives of his people.

(2) The writer abandons classical form, and lets the new analytical principle determine the arrangement of his story, which features the subconscious for its own sake.

(3) The writer ignores character, ignores form, uses the sub-

conscious as his source of inspiration, lets its chaos ride free, and attempts an appeal directly to the subconscious of the reader.

Let us consider these in order.

1. *The story of classical form: character is reinterpreted:* Here you will find the work of most of the notably successful writers who, in the past twelve years, have exploited the new interpretation of mental life. Among them, besides Lawrence, May Sinclair and Aldous Huxley, already cited, are Anne Parrish, William Faulkner, Nancy Hale, and Scott Fitzgerald. The main drama is developed in the external action. The subconscious aspects of the character are suggested in figurative summary (Huxley, Anne Parrish, Virginia Woolf, Scott Fitzgerald) or in modified, highly selective stream-of-consciousness passages (Faulkner and Nancy Hale).

This first method is beautifully and rather simply revealed in one of the most impressive of post-war short narratives, " No One My Grief Can Tell," by Nancy Hale.[1] In this story we find a minimum of plot and external action but a wealth of originality in character interpretation. The scene is a sea beach. A mother is watching her baby play in the sand. Her conflict is internal, being a clash between her love for her baby and her conviction that she should curb her love in the baby's and her own interest (". . . your thoughts about him will kill him.") The author knows that the life-long grip children have on their mothers is instinctive and, being instinctive, is largely subconscious. The mother's intelligence disapproves of her fanatical intensity of concern over her child and tries to conquer it. This is the drama of the story. Quite simply it is a struggle between a conscious, rationalizing mind and an unconscious, irrational and all-powerful impulse. In the passage from this story which I quote we have a stream of consciousness, a passionate sort of day-dream, in which the mother's intelligence tries to subdue her maternal instinct. The " stream " begins with an effort of the conscious mind to seize upon images as far removed as possible from the instinct-stirring stimulus of the baby playing before her:

And the beaches. The yellow sands of the New World, and the chalk cliffs of Dover, the pink beaches of the far Bermudas, the dark and sinister dunes where up climbed the pirates carrying hooped chests under the tropical sun that gave them fever. Where stood Miranda all alone, staring out to sea — come unto these yellow sands. The marooned and the exiled. (My child? Don't look, you must try to become whole, that he can become whole. Don't look, think your own thoughts about yourself, or your thoughts about him will kill him.) Drake in the Pacific, Westward Ho, Salvation Yeo. He

[1] *Short Story Hits, 1932.*

said Sail On, Sail On! Sir Richard Grenville lay. In Flores in the Azores. While the hollow oak our fortress is, our heritage the sea. We — something, something, balked the eternal sea. To hell with it! She had to stand up to see where her child was. . . .

The subconscious wins this round! As she watches him, she grapples with the predicament he has put her in.

Part of me, she thought vaguely, playing with sea-shells. The loosened cell growing to be itself. The sun bakes him to a dry coral baby, dry and clean and well; the sun dries him from the pervading dampness of his beginning. He is being dried and cleaned and healed from the wet wound of me, and lightened from the deep darkness of me, and he is becoming his wound-healed and complete self. As I am healed of him. O loop cut from my skein and once an undifferentiated strand within my skein, flap of my flesh cut away and healed again! He has no rawness where the knife once was, he is round and finished and without seam. And I am healed, but there is scar-tissue that will not whiten, and a seam that is wrinkled and pursed. I cannot forget that something was a bubble of me that now is round and seamless and floats alone.

Here the rationalizing seems to collapse.

She pushed herself up on her elbow and held one hand flat shelved above her eyes and called:
"Baby! Are your feet wet?"
The yellow jersey hummock caved in slowly and reluctantly; the baby stood up scowling furiously.
"Unh-*unh.*" He stared at her with infant resentment for a minute and then jerked himself around, expressively, back to the log and again addressed himself with ferocity to his sea-shells.

Now the conscious mind again takes control.

Let him alone. Let him swell and bubble. Let the sun dry away the primordial dampness and make him coral. What in the world did I call him for? How would his feet possibly get wet? The old scar itches, the flesh presses uselessly against that which once it owned, pressing and pressing, but they are two flesh. You are of me, but I am not of you. . . .

Modified to greater or less degree this method appears in the work of many writers. Faulkner (*As I Lay Dying*) comes closer to a literal transcription of the stream of consciousness with less figurative summary of introspection. James T. Farrell in *Young Lonigan* and *Gas House McGinty* summarizes the thought-stream which he makes incoherent only in its outward, rhetorical aspects. Meridel LeSueur in " Fable of a Man and Pigeons " [1] also depends upon a poetic, figurative suggestion of the subconscious picture of

[1] *Short Story Hits, 1933.*

her character, by which to account for his overt action. Tess Slesinger's *The Unpossessed* uses the conventional plot form with a psychoanalytic interpretation of her characters. Stream-of-consciousness narrative is used to reveal the inner, repressed motives of her characters. In this novel the outward story *might* be said to be less important than the inner.

The main interests of the writers of this first class of narratives are social problems, character appraisals, retelling of old stories. They write with their readers before them and they try to keep the audience from walking out.

From what I have said above, the application of narrative principles to this first type of the stream-of-consciousness story should be evident. Stream-of-consciousness passages are used to suggest the drift of thought, impulse, sensation, and so on which accompanies the observable, overt action of the characters and so motivates it. The main action conforms to the usual story requirements. An unconscious desire is no less a trait than a conscious desire. Most of the successful psychological stories of today involve strong dramatic conflict; the stream-of-consciousness passages merely supplement the reflective delay.

I have referred to those stories which portray character without drama by a sudden flash from the stream of consciousness. *Rest Cure*, by Kay Boyle, is a good example. This is but a variation of the sharply revealing act described in Chapter Five. In the development of the scene the main character is shown tyrannical, quarrelsome, irritable, and so contemptuous of his father's memory that he recognizes the father's likeness in the face of a lobster which his wife has brought from market; but in the final flash from the subconcious, we see that actually, like a frightened child, he longs for his father whom he wants to protect him from the death that threatens.

2. *The story in case-history form: the character is analyzed:* In this second type of psychoanalytic story the inner revelations definitely transcend overt action in importance and both inner and outer are given. Often such books are organized on the plan of a case history. Conrad Aiken's *Blue Voyage,* and his *Great Circle* are in this category, and the greater part of James Joyce's *Ulysses.* The author takes for story material a certain complex, or some phase of it. He arranges the narrative not in a progression of incidents toward a climax, but according to any plan that will put into revealing juxtaposition the conscious behavior and the subconscious life that parallels it and motivates much of it. Some passages from *Blue Voyage* will illustrate this method.

Demarest, the central character, is interesting because of his inferiority complex. The nature of this complex, its origins, and its effects upon the man's daily life, are shown in action that takes place during a transatlantic voyage. Demarest travels second class, the woman he worships first class; thus, even the external circumstances of the novel duplicate the inferiority pattern which is repeated in the character's conscious associations in day dream, in actual dream, and in his behavior with his fellow voyagers.

In addition, Demarest is himself aware of his complex, so that without loss of truth, he can speculate upon it. The whole is drawn together in poetic final interpretation, when at last, after every aspect of Demarest's trouble has been displayed, the miserable wretch writes to Cynthia, the adored one, a letter which shows clearly that he did not love her, but desired her as a child desires his mother.

In the first passage quoted [1] the complex is revealed in a dream. Here we face in symbols the actual buried conflict itself:

It was manifest to Demarest that he had got into the wrong place. It was totally unfamiliar. He walked quietly along the side of the grape-arbor and then, cautiously, passed under a fragrant trellis overgrown with roses. He emerged upon a wide lawn enclosed with trees and flowers, where a garden party was in progress. A score of glitteringly-dressed men and women stood talking, sauntered here and there, or set cups down on flower-decked tables. How horrible! He felt out of place, furtive and shabby, an intruder. But how was he to escape? He couldn't recall where he had got in. Was it over a wall? . . . He turned back through the trellis, hearing behind him a mild laughter. He looked down, and saw that his shoes were covered with mud and that his trousers were torn. Passing this time to the left of the grape-arbor, he hurried along the narrow path of deep soft turf, and was horrified to encounter a group of ladies coming in. They looked at him with hard eyes. Perhaps they thought he was some kind of gardener? . . . This, then, might be the way out? . . . Etc.

He wakens, and his conscious mind speculates on the dream:

That curious dream! It was just a new version, nevertheless, of the familiar theme, — his absurd " inferiority complex." Good God! Was he destined never to escape it? Why was it that he never could be at his ease with those who were socially his equals — only at ease with his inferiors?

The following passages show how the complex is brought out in reverie:

[1] Reprinted by permission from *Blue Voyage,* by Conrad Aiken, published by Charles Scribner's Sons.

Misery. Ashes to ashes and dust to dust. Would you like to kiss your father? No. The others were lifted up and kissed the dead face, surprised. Why did I refuse? Shyness and horror. Etc.

And later a continuation of the same half-asleep dream:

My father whistled Lorelei to the cat — he had a theory that the Lorelei, whistled slowly, was infuriating to cats. But the cat seemed to be delighted. He would now be — let me see. He was thirty-seven. From nought is eight. Fifty-five. What would he think of me, I wonder? Would I be afraid of him still? I am taller than you are. I am more intelligent than you are. Freer from fetiches than you are. . . . Look! You see that scar? You gave that to me, holding my hand in the gas-jet. . . . You see these plays? They come from the deep wound you inflicted on my soul. . . . This is what you did to me by depriving me of my mother. . . . I suppose I liked him when I was very small, before the other kids were born — before I can remember. He must then have fascinated me and drawn me out powerfully and skillfully. Yes, I can feel that he did. There was something angelic about him — later it became diabolic. . . .

Later, in another dream, the meaning of the complex is shown in relation to the woman, a former acquaintance, whom Demarest happens to encounter on the first-class deck:

The bell-note fell down from aloft, a golden ingot of sound, and Cynthia was standing under the tall tree as announced; like a charade for purity and resignation; clad in white samite; and clasping a tall lily with unimaginable delicacy. . . . At the second bell-note,— Cynthia lifted her meltingly beautiful eyes, and the fine blue seraphim, treading the night air above her, began softly, benignly to sing. This was very affecting. . . . At the words "resting place" the five seraphs disbanded, two deploying to starboard, two to port, and the fifth catapulting straight up toward the zenith. At this moment Demarest experienced acutely a remarkable temptation. He desired to rush forward, kneel, bury his face passionately in the white samite, and cry out γύναι, ἰδέ ὁ υἱός σου. Before he could do more than visualize this action, however, the third stroke of the bell was given. The whole night had become a Cathedral. And above Demarest, faintly luminous in the cold starlight that came from beyond, was a tall Gothic window, where motionless, in frozen sentimentalities of pink, white, and blue, Cynthia was turned to glass.

The book ends with a series of letters which Demarest composes to Cynthia, each expressing the impulse from the subconscious which is struggling to the surface: the little boy search for the mother, not the mate. His intelligence is enough in control to hold the subconscious in check; he can't help writing the letters, but he doesn't send them!

Short stories using this technique cannot, obviously, display the whole of a complex; they can present only some one phase of it. Alvah Bessie's " A Little Walk," [1] is of this type. The truth about Blake, the central figure, is easily evident to everyone familiar with psychology. The man had not desired his marriage greatly; subconsciously he wants to be free of his wife. While he is waiting for her return from a walk, this subconscious wish finds a devious entrance into his conscious thought, disguised as fear that she may die, and these fears, narrated quite simply, make the half hour while he is alone, a period of melodramatic violence.

He fears — he wishes that she may die. The subconscious wish-fear emerges in his conscious mind first in a horrifying vision of her lying dead, where she has fallen, hitting her head on a pointed rock; next he pictures her crushed under a fallen tree. Still she does not return! He hears a distant gun shot, and now he thinks of the possibility that some hunter may have shot her, mistaking her for a deer; and finally when an automobile rattles past, he fancies that she has not returned because she has been struck and killed by a car.

From this summary of the inventions in this striking story, it should be evident that the writer who knows how to use such psychological material, has at his command a new method of character portrayal by which he can achieve realistically effects of wild fantasy or melodrama. No other device would enable a writer to kill a woman five times in one story without loss of truth to life!

The effects produced by these stories which focus on the complex or the subconscious for its own peculiar interest are effects of intellectual adventure. Some of the details may stir sympathetic or ironic vibrations or even have tragic, or romantic, or comic quality, but the chief impression is the thrill of exploring the new psychic world.

Above we have considered the two uses of the subconscious which are most likely to be of value to the average writer.

In the case-history type of story, as in the first type, stream-of-consciousness passages give the mental accompaniment of the external action. At times no strong drama is present in the external action. The drama is in the subconscious itself and is often of melodramatic intensity. A complex is a conflict. The stream of consciousness is neither realistic nor interesting if it does not convey to the reader some indication of the forces in that conflict. The drama is in the complex itself; the conscious intelligence is opposed by the subconscious impulses.

A conflict is no less a conflict because it is unconscious, and these

[1] Reprinted in *Short Story Hits, 1932.*

unconscious conflicts serve the writer precisely as do those in the conscious mind — as devices for moving the reader and for giving his characters the utmost validity.

3. *Writing to affect the subconscious of the reader: plot ignored:* This third use of recent psychological revelations is no novelty. Since the war a number of writers have been experimenting with it; you can find some of their work in nearly every issue of *transition*. It is based upon the theory that all " effects " of every sort, whether induced by real stimuli, or by art, are strong just in proportion to the disturbance set up in the unconscious. Our real-life angers and excitements always include intensifying emanations from the subconscious. A literature, then, that could make a direct attack on the subconscious of the reader should — say these theorists — produce the most intense effects. This, the theory of the surrealists, underlies some of the obscurities of *Ulysses*.

The writer is still after effects; he wants to impress the reader. To do so, however, he abandons all portrayal of character, and tries to summon the scenes, the literary allusions, the words, the sense experiences of sound and color, and so on, which will be most likely to agitate the subconscious of his reader. Some of the experiments are fascinating, but the theorists have yet to solve a fundamental difficulty. Writers write for readers; their art is a communication — and the subconscious is by its nature not directly communicable. Anyone can write the stream of his own free associations, or his dreams, but how is he to know that the words, sounds and symbols through which his own, personal subconscious life expresses itself will have either meaning or emotional color for his reader?

Here is a specimen, from *transition*, 1932:

> Alt! — raspcontinu-socialty,brackDissilusion, Charcoal of REED-Instruments, refine-whisper-velvet, FRANCE, BLUEBLACK.
> ehyeh! — U.S. pioneer-diphthontrenches in T.B.M. —

It remains now only to ask if this third type of psychoanalytic literature is a further illustration of the principles of narrative presented in this book. It isn't. *Narrative Technique* is devoted to a study of writing that appeals to, holds the interest of, the reader: its very essence is communication. Writers of this third group address only those initiate in the symbols and patterns of the subconscious. The laws that underly the seeming incoherence of their work may be studied in the critical volumes on James Joyce; the practical value of these principles to most artists has not yet been demonstrated. Such writing seems to ignore communication. The writers no doubt are exhilarated as they produce these works, but pleasure for the average reader is not a necessary consequence of the writer's creative enjoyment.

SECTION E

BEGINNERS' MISTAKES

Mastery of the principles set forth in this book will enable a writer to identify most errors in planning a narrative, including the mistakes singled out for a special word in this section. Since few students really finish their study of these principles and since most of them wish to write for publication during their study, defective narratives are inevitable. Certain of these defects seem common to all beginners.

Risk of inaccuracy is always incurred in condemning specific plot patterns and subject matters; the only postulates about fiction that are wholly true concern principles and ideals and the only absolute errors are violations of these principles and ideals. To say that certain specific arrangements of characters and events are wrong is to court exceptions which may prove one's words false, for, whatever one may say about technical principles, one cannot say that anything is impossible with either people or their doings. Exceptions there are to the plot patterns and effects condemned here and I have tried to indicate them.

The most stubborn trouble experienced by literary novices is not their failure to please editors with everything they write, but their failure to please themselves; they know themselves that their work is weak yet without always knowing why; they attempt one effect and produce another! This is peculiarly the experience (I must emphasize this) of the beginner not the experienced writer. His most typical errors result as much from his misconception of life itself as from his literary inexperience, so that my analyses deal in part with his understanding of life. These notes, then, are addressed specifically to beginners.

It goes without saying that the weaknesses described here will be more apparent if they are considered in connection with the chapters of this book, especially the first four. Most of the errors result from a failure to appreciate the psychology and logic of character as it is exploited in dramatic action. For this reason a reading of Chapter Four especially will make clearer the comments which follow.

1. " Low Cunning "

A wife discovers that her husband is falling in love with another woman. She decides to win her husband back by making the other woman ridiculous. Knowing that the other woman is uncultivated and not used to polite society, she stages an elaborate and formal dinner. The other woman by the crudity of her conduct is made ridiculous to the husband, who is cured of his infatuation, and returns to his wife.

This plot is typical of a great many made by beginners. Its weakness is in the motive of the main character, the wife. It does not give the wife a good opportunity for a genuine display of character. Why?

There are two ways in which a man may solve a difficulty interestingly. One is by a genuine trait of character, such as honesty, moral courage, cowardice, boastfulness, avarice. The other is by what we shall call " low cunning," namely, by " putting over a slick one " on somebody. Now, low cunning may be possessed by anybody regardless of his character. The saint and the sinner alike may be cunning; the babe and the sage, the knave, and everybody save the fool. *Hence it is that low cunning never reveals character in the deeper sense.*

Psychologically, low cunning is an animal trait. The cat, the fox, and the 'possum possess it. The buzzard circling overhead waiting for his prey to die; the tiger hiding beside the water-hole for the helpless deer to appear; the fox running through the stream of water to cover its trail from pursuing hounds — such are animal activities of low cunning. They are interesting as story material for immature minds, and for this reason we find *Aesop's Fables,* the *Uncle Remus Tales,* and many of the thrilling adventures of folk heroes based on them. For this reason again we find that the more trite and crude the fiction in a given magazine, the more low cunning plots you will find in it.

Compare the animal tricks mentioned above with the cunning of a mother who hides behind the door with a switch under her apron, waiting for the return of her recalcitrant son! Equally exalted is the conduct of a wife who takes money from her husband's pocket, cutting a hole in the pocket to make him think he lost the money. Of the same *dramatic pattern* is the act in the plot given above of the wife who wins back her husband by playing a trick on her rival. True, there is a difference between her act and that of the mother with the switch and the wife with the scissors: her *purpose* is more laudable; she feels impelled to use cunning because she loves her husband.

It is, we may say, cunning without being "low." Where the characters have some intelligence it is always possible to eliminate the cunning entirely from a story and give it more genuine character appeal.

We can improve the appeal by improving the character itself. Granted the wife is determined not to give her husband up to the other woman. As the plot now stands, she seems to be the type of woman who will stoop to anything to get her husband back; she is willing to forfeit her own dignity and possibly the respect of her husband. Why not, then, let her hate of the other woman reach such intensity that it becomes an hysterical desire to eliminate her? No woman, if hysterical, can be cunning; her acts are driven by the blind force of her desires and this is just what they should be in strong dramatic — in this case, possibly melodramatic — action.

This replotting produces a tragedy. A happy outcome can be fashioned by precisely the same adherence to the integrity of character and by boldness in invention. Why not give the wife for a trait not murderous hatred but a simple, unquestioning love for her husband? She sees her husband leave her and go to the other woman but she never blames her husband or doubts his devotion to her; she suffers terribly but never complains; her need for her husband, her pride in him, fill her life with a deep affection which seems to flow outward and encompass the world. She even forgives the other woman and receives her and her husband into her home, while her heart breaks. Her attitude affords so great a contrast with the other woman's capacity for deception and essential cruelty that her husband is profoundly impressed and he returns to her. In the melodramatic form of this plot the wife, I suppose, would save the life of the other woman.

There are two types of plot in which low cunning may be used with very good effect. One of them is illustrated in the following plot outline:

The wife of a playwright, at her husband's insistence, deceives another man into believing she is unmarried in order that he will make love to her, and so give her a chance to gather notes on character for her husband to use in a play he is writing. The husband, after waiting a long time for his wife to return, becomes alarmed and goes after her. He discovers her in the arms of the other man, accepting his kisses with an eagerness which indicates that she is enjoying her assignment very much indeed. He faces the guilty pair, and is threatening to beat up his wife's lover when suddenly it occurs to him that the scene is better than anything in the play he is trying to write, and he is so thrilled by its possibilities that he asks the others to remember their speeches and hurry home with him so that he can write them down.

Here is a character farce involving low cunning in which the cunning is part of the initial complication only and is not present in the crucial situation at all; such use is entirely legitimate, and may be made effective.

A second sound use of the low cunning pattern is in a situation where the deceit, used with good motive, is the *only* way out of a difficulty. A doctor, for instance, to ease his patient's suffering might tell the patient that she will live, when he knows very well that she has almost no chance. The chief point of this story, however, is that deceit here is justifiable; it begins to have a thematic interest. The drama could be intensified by making the suffering woman a very religious person, whose closest friend was her beloved pastor. If the pastor were persuaded also to add his word of comforting assurance to that of the doctor, although the doctor confides to the pastor that the woman cannot possibly live, the story will not be one of low cunning if the woman, because of this combined assurance, picks up her courage and lives. The story might be a dramatic proof of the theme that " some lies are justifiable." Another story of this type is Morley Callaghan's " A Sick Call," reprinted in this book.

After having examined many hundreds of low cunning plots by writers who wish their narratives to be the best of which they are capable, I am driven to the unhappy conclusion that the appearance of cunning in story inventions is no accident! It appears in the author's stories because it is used in his life. Deception is a concomitant of low energy and sentimentality. I tested this belief once with two women. Mrs. A., a robust, driving, almost masculine type, was hardly intelligent enough to be considered really cultivated; she was the type known as " breezy," very affable, humorous, strongly maternal. Mrs. B. was a college graduate, was frail physically, soft-spoken, cool and yet earnest and determined to gain her ends. I asked Mrs. B. what she would do if she were suspicious of her husband and his pretty secretary and learned that he had bought a necklace for a hundred dollars but had not given it to her and one day while in her husband's office, she found it draped about the secretary's neck. Mrs. B. said she would say nothing then but would ask her husband that evening for a full account of how he had spent his salary during the past month. Mrs. A., when asked what she would do, said with a show of violence: " I'd snatch it off the hussy's neck! "

It is profoundly certain that strong people alone can invent and write strong stories. It could be argued that the strength referred to here is actually physical, bulk power, with exceptions familiar to us all; certain I am, in any case, that the strength needed is courage, boldness, the physical courage to walk right up to those who oppose one's desires and have it out with them and the moral courage which, without evasion, self-pity, or infantile rational-izations, enables one to face one's own weaknesses and temptations for what they are in lonely vigil with one's own soul and fight it out. Writers need spiritual power to rise above commercial mediocrity, and I know of no better way of defining this power than to say it is that attribute of personality which gets results without resorting to cunning and tricks in either art or life.

2. " Come to Realize "

Next in the order of frequency with which it appears in be-ginners' manuscripts comes the plot type which, for want of a better name, I call the " come to realize " plot. The reason for this name can be seen from a criticism of the following plot action:

A young girl plans to elope with a handsome deceiver. The girl's mother knows that the man is a waster and that he will never make a good husband, and that her daughter is attracted to him only because of his flashy and superficial charms. The mother, in order to protect her daughter, confesses in an emo-tional scene, that she, the mother, in her youth, ran away with such a man, came to grief, and has suffered from it ever since. The daughter, witnessing her mother's emotion, decides that she will not run away with the handsome deceiver.

Judged from one standard this plot is just about as bad as a plot can be and from another it is faultless. It is the perfect pat-tern of the sentimental, escape, " heart interest," commercial, woman's magazine story and is an especially popular version of this type. Both younger and older women can identify themselves in the two sympathetic women characters and " escape " from real life by enacting these two heroic and highly moral roles. Bring it up to date in matters of physical, obvious realism and it will do a cash business for you every time! As a literary story, how-ever, " Nellie's Narrow Escape " is a flop. It is a flop not because it is not true or couldn't happen in real life, but because it simply isn't dramatic.

Consider: Nellie is the main character here and her problem is our chief interest. She is tempted by the gay deceiver and rushes home to get her toothbrush and depart with him. What happens? She has a talk with her mother! Mother says, "You'll regret it if you do." "O.K.," says Nellie, "I'll remain single a while longer." What is Nellie's main trait here? It started out as a desire to collect a big thrill with the handsome deceiver but in the end it seems to be a desire to be good though unhappy, or possibly a desire to avoid her mother's sad fate (my guess is mother had been holding in her "big scene" with difficulty for some time!) or possibly her mother's revelations simply dampened her romantic fever and once she saw she didn't desire to leave, she made the best of the moment and, clinging tearfully to her mother, sobbed: "Mother, I want to be like you." We can't know, in other words, Nellie's character or trait from this plot. At first she is determined to run away with Hulbert but she "comes to realize" she hadn't better, and doesn't.

The plot fulfills neither of the two ideals of good drama: it is not intense and it gives no unequivocal picture of character. It would be intense, and melodramatic, if Nellie's mama, instead of putting on an act about the early days of the republic, barred her daughter's way to the car waiting in the moonlight and daughter tried to push her aside and instead was seized and spanked or shot while the car slunk away in the shadows. It would be more intense and more character-revealing if Nellie met Hulbert long after mama has told her pioneer story and then fell for him hard, knowing herself, without any further coaching, that the "flashy" clothes and the light blue roadster and Florida seaside home were all bought with the illegal sale of bogus mining stock and that he was sought by federal detectives — it would be drama worthy the name if Nellie, passionately loving Hulbert, pleaded with him to "come clean" by returning the money to his poor investors and taking a five year sentence. If Nellie struggles with him all the way to the Florida home and he stubbornly refuses to listen to her and she, in her moral revulsion, begins to heave the furniture through the imported glass of the French windows, crying, "Thief! Thief! Thief!" until he clasps her in his arms and hushes her cries with his kisses and . . . enough — my reflective delay, rich in character-revealing action, is plunging into another melodramatic climax, so I desist. My diagnosis of the weakness in the original plot is, I think, now clear enough.

Please note that I do not say that the original plot is untrue to life or without value. That a girl might be led to abandon a plan to elope with a well-tailored bounder by her mother's account of her own experience no one will question. An excellent popular story, as I have indicated, might be shaped up from such an incident. It would, nevertheless, be a story weak in drama, and these words are addressed to the many writers who wish earnestly not to ape standardized tales for the unintelligent mass, but to illuminate Nellie's life with a flood of light or to say something original or important about eloping maidens and gay deceivers — to say, perchance, that there are no more elopements or gay deceivers or innocent maidens!

The beginner, faced with this more serious and fascinating task, tends promptly to fall into a confusion as to the meaning of " character." This confusion has been mentioned before in Chapter Four; [1] in the interest of many *beginners* it should be mentioned frequently. It results from using the word " character " in the moral rather than the psychological sense. Such beginners, a thousand times more familiar with moral than with literary problems, when the word " character " first appears in their study of fiction, conclude that if they are to give a man character they must give him morals! " He is a man of character " to them means that the man has certain solid virtues. And so they " solve plots " by giving their main actors virtue before the fade-out. How do they do this? How do they see it done in life? In their own lives? Someone, a parent, a teacher, a policeman, warns them in time and they obey — well, they try to obey! They " come to realize." In this same way they plot their first stories.

To this Sunday School training for life are due the many, many stories perfectly suitable for Sunday School pupils and their grandparents. The son about to steal realizes that his father would not do such a thing and refrains; a husband about to abandon his wife feels the mute but tender appeal in their baby's eyes and decides to stick on the job; a bachelor by being forced to contemplate the spiritual loneliness of an old man — a bum on a park bench in the pre-war story — decides to marry; a pilot about to collapse from the struggle of finding his way with a defective plane at night in a fog hears his girl friend's sweet voice over the radio and is immediately fired with courage that leads on to victory — these are a few of the most obvious and least meritorious of plot ideas inspired by the make-the-hero-amount-to-something school.

No one can read Chapter Four in this book without seeing the weaknesses in " come to realize " inventions. The purpose of good fiction is not to parallel the infantile habits of feeble-minded adults who have to be scared or led gently by the hand into ways of righteousness; its purpose, as explained in Chapter One, is to give impressive pictures of life. The most impressive pictures of character are made by subjecting it to life-and-death tests. Characters are what they do — under pressure; and the degree of impressiveness has no relation whatever to the actor's goodness or badness.

[1] Pages 148–151.

One more misconception of beginners which experienced writers have usually outgrown is found in those writers who *wish* to espouse the moral story, who plan *deliberately* to show in their stories how people are weak and inspire them to be strong. Has this not been done in some of the world's greatest literature? And what way better than to show a weak man becoming strong under a good influence?

The purpose here is worthy but the method false. The difference between the didactic ("preachy") narrative and the truly dramatic has been explained in Chapter Seven. The most powerful sermon in fiction is the story of a man exposed to evil influences who succumbs to them and is finally sunk by them. (*Macbeth, Anna Karenina, Madame Bovary, American Tragedy,* and others.) A less powerful moral lesson in fictionized form is the narrative of the true hero who, driven by constructive impulses, overcomes all obstacles in the end. Less powerful I call this pattern because it is less convincing. The most transcendent nobility ever known on earth brought its possessor to death by torture on a cross.

In really dramatic plots no surprising "come to realize" reforms are experienced by the actors. Traits deeply imbedded in their natures are singled out for exploitation and they don't "give" under strain; these traits hold the actors to a uniformity of response to the same stimuli with an almost mechanical rigidity. The writer who has not yet observed this same rigidity of response among his friends and acquaintances has yet before him the most important lesson in the understanding of character.

3. "Coincidence"

The most familiar of all faults in plotting is the "long arm of coincidence." Story-telling novices of all ages have, as the time to end the story arrived, used accidental happenings to bring comfort to the hero, confusion to the villain and a sigh of contentment (if he doesn't know any better!) to the reader. The chief reason for taking coincidences seriously is not that they are always bad and should always be avoided, but that some coincidences are good, some bad, and the trick is to know which is which. Anything like a complete account of the strong and weak uses of coincidence is not possible in a brief note; some understanding, however, of the most common practices, good and bad, is exceedingly important to the student of literary technique. We will consider them in two pairs, each containing a good and bad form.

A. *Coincidences at beginning and end of story:* The principle here is: *A coincidence which is part of the generating circumstances of a story is allowable, but one which solves the plot in a story intended to emphasize character is not allowable.* The reason for this principle can be most easily grasped by examining a plot in which the same coincidence appears at the beginning and the end of the story. Thus:

A mother, Mrs. A., passionately devoted to her son, is stricken to see him ruining his life gambling. She greatly fears for him when his step-father turns him out of the house as a disobedient, worthless young man. She learns that John, the son, has given his I.O.U.'s for gambling debts incurred in one night of heavy losses in amounts far exceeding the comparatively small sums his mother is able to send him. Threatened with violence unless he pays, he rushes to his mother and pleads with her to save him. Desperate, the mother pawns her jewels and gives him the money. This is not reported to the husband and Mrs. A. lives in constant dread lest he ask her where her jewels are. Before long he does ask her. He accepts no evasions. Mrs. A. is about to collapse with fear of her husband when the son arrives and slips her jewels into her hands without the move being seen by his step-father. Later Mrs. A. learns that her son had taken another risky plunge, had recouped all his losses and had thus recovered the jewels.

While there is nothing original about this invention, it yet might be turned by good writing into a usable popular story in spite of the faulty use of coincidence in the ending. As a story about gambling, featuring the pranks of chance, it would have more value than as a story of a mother's blind devotion to her son, but the wording of the plot outline makes it obviously the latter. The *interest* in this case is in the mother and her blind devotion. What does the story say about this devotion? It shows the mother apparently risking everything in the climax and then, suddenly, she is " saved " by her son's luck. At the most critical moment the character interest is ended and so also, for critical readers, would be the interest in the story.

The first big loss at gambling, on the other hand, instead of frustrating the mother's love, sets it into operation. In this sense the first coincidence is a generating circumstance and so is rightly used.

This plot might be saved as a character story of the mother in several ways. An easy method would be not to let the son arrive with the jewels, thus permitting husband and wife to " have it out " without interference.

The number of situations in narratives of character made dramatically weak because of this error of solving them by accidents is legion. The first manuscripts of young writers struggling without guidance are full of them. The noble young heroine is about to see her mother die in a remote spot and has given up in despair when a famous surgeon arrives by airplane — just in time! In another story the remarkable young hero would most certainly have failed to win the heart of his adored (by all the laws of logic and common sense) if only it were not for the lady's being thrown from her horse right at his feet and — you know the rest. The astoundingly fortuitous solutions which close the "thrillers" for boys, the galloping horses, bugle calls and cheers of United States troopers that once, by saving the pioneers from a terrible death by the Indians, electrified our youthful nerves in the old western melodramas; and today in the movies and on the air the endless processions of charging cavalry, the speeding motor cars carrying succor, the Red Cross motor-boats, the suddenly aroused consciences, the fabulous successes in business, the miraculous recoveries of sight and hearing, the cloud bursts, the tidal waves — everything and anything except truth to life and character — frequently, let us admit, we thrill to them — still! My point is not that melodrama featuring sheer lucky "breaks" in the solutions is uninteresting, but that *such solutions do not develop character*. When you are trying to do *that*, you should avoid coincidences in your solutions.

B. *Coincidences in solutions which do and do not have ironic value.* Here we discover that not all coincidences used in solving plots are faulty! In the character-surprise-ending stories, for example, discussed on pages 301 and 302, we find coincidence used to reveal character by suddenly precipitating a response which enables a man's true character to shine forth. All responses of this type, which are generally used for humorous effects and are not as popular as they once were, are "uniquely characteristic acts!"[1]

A much more common plot-solving coincidence of value to the story teller is that which possesses more or less of that heady literary quality we call "ironic." What is irony? A rough definition was attempted in Chapter Six.[2] To clarify further this problem of good and bad accidental endings we must now have patience with more orderly exposition:

An accident is any unexpected happening.

A coincidence is an accident in which an element of fate enters.

Fate is a personification of that influence upon human events which seems to have attributes of intelligence (or lack of intelligence!) and so gives those events design.

Irony is present in some degree in every coincidence and to the

[1] See page 253.
[2] Pages 286 and 290.

extent of the importance of the role played by Fate. Some coincidences are thus more ironic than others. *The maximum of irony results from a coincidence which is both logically related to the character action and produces a result appropriate to that action.*

A few examples will serve us here.

A man on his way to work stumbles and hurts himself. (A mere accident.)

A man threatened with loss of his job if he is late, stumbles and hurts himself on his way to work so that he arrives late. (A coincidence with a slight suggestion of irony.)

A man in very urgent need of a doctor hurries out to summon the nearest physician a mile away. Just before he enters a deep woods through which he must walk, he stumbles and hurts himself so that he cannot proceed. Soon the doctor is seen passing and the man hails him. The doctor reaches the man's home in time to save the life of a member of his family. (A more pronounced influence of Fate here greatly enhances the irony.)

This last invention attains the degree of irony found in the great bulk of stories which attempt to feature coincidence; since the outcome is agreeable, it has some merit but it falls far short of that fine flavor of irony in which Fate plays a more impressive role. It falls short of this impressiveness because the outcome is appropriate only to our sympathies but not yet to the motives or character action of the main actor. Such appropriateness would be more evident if we change the man in our illustration to a small boy, alone with his mother who is sick; he alone can go for the doctor. The boy is frail and afraid of strangers. His mother cautions him not to run for fear he will fall and injure himself and so be unable to continue. The boy promises but *his eagerness to help his mother* urges him to run in spite of her warning. When, *now*, he falls and is injured and, as a result of the injury, *forgets his fear* and calls out to a passing stranger, who proves to be the doctor whom he would otherwise miss, we find Fate standing forth more emphatically as the leading character of the story.

Fate or ironic stories at their best are impossible without heroes and villains and this is perhaps the reason why modern uncompromising realists shun this type of story and look with disdain upon the joyous pranks O. Henry played with life in nearly all his stories. The highly ironic story is *the* preeminent complication story and it is regrettable that the entertainment it affords is now so seldom provided. As an indication of what this entertainment may be and as neat illustrations of the two widely different types of ironic invention I offer two plots. In the first, the plot of a short " silent " picture, we see Fate in a grim mood dealing with a villain and in the second, taken from a short story by Harry Leon Wilson, we find Fate handling a hero in a manner to suit our most fastidious sense of the appropriate.

STUNG!

(Ironic frustration)

A murderous gangster with his stolen money hires a corrupt underworld lawyer to defend him for killing an innocent victim. The lawyer, seeing the evidence against his brutal client, decides that he can hope only to save the latter from the chair. Accordingly he reaches a simple, corrupt member of the jury and bribes him heavily to stand out for manslaughter instead of murder in the first degree. This juror, after the evidence is heard and the twelve men are closeted for their deliberations, is seen stubbornly refusing to agree with the other jurors. After desperate efforts it is evident that he has won his way with them. The jury renders its verdict of manslaughter and the gangster is given a twenty year sentence. Later the lawyer sees the corrupt juror privately, pays the money offered, and asks him what happened in the jury room. The juror, who is dumb as well as venal, boasts of his stubbornness in sticking to the manslaughter verdict through several hours even though the other jurors all tried to induce him to agree to a verdict of complete innocence!

MR. WILSON'S STORY

(Ironic realization)

The story concerns two business men friends in the East who played golf week-ends until one retired and went to California where he could play golf the year around. He became a climate hound, wrote persistently to his friend entreating him to retire also and come out and live in God's golfing country where they would play with each other daily. The friend in the East at last agreed to come to California, play one game in its well-advertised climate and let the result of the game determine whether he would also go West. If he should win, he would return East; if his friend won, he also would settle in California. The two men were evenly matched and had always played with keen rivalry. The game, as in all good golf stories, was closely contested. When they reached the last green the California player had to sink a long putt to win. The ball rolled to the very lip of the cup and stopped. The Easterner, in triumph, exclaimed: "Is that the best your California climate can do?" when suddenly the earth shook in a slight earthquake and toppled the ball into the cup!

4. "Mistaken Characters"

The error in plotting described here is a peculiar form of solution by coincidence. The weakness is not a consequence of the surprise sprung on the reader at the end; we have found in analyzing coincidences in the previous discussion that the reader may in certain ways be surprised to his own amazement and delight. The fault lies in the hoax element in the coincidence, in the writer's leading the reader to believe that certain facts are as he represents them only to reveal at the end — ha ha!! — that they are otherwise. Here is an example:

The story begins with the description of the horror of a man who has just murdered his friend. The thing was done after a quarrel. The man is horrified. Will he be executed? He thinks he will be unless he conceals the body. After great torment lasting through most of the night, he wraps the body up, carries it outside and buries it in a remote place in the woods. He returns to his room and is still suffering from the agony of fear, and is about to collapse, when suddenly he opens his eyes and finds himself looking into the sympathetic face of a trained nurse. It is then explained that he and his friend, both of whom were chemists, were experimenting with a special form of anaesthetic. The hero went under without expecting to. The story is what he dreamed.

Another form of this plot pattern possibly more commonly found among beginners is the following:

A woman left alone by her husband is very much afraid of attack by burglars. Finally she thinks she hears one trying to get into the house. She locks the doors and windows; still the marauder tries the doors and windows. Finally he forces one of the doors, and she comes into conflict with him in the hall. Being terrified into a display of unusual energy, she struggles with the man, until, when she is about to be desperately injured, she discovers that the man is her husband who was trying to get in without waking her. He did not call out to her because he thought if she was his wife she would have let him in. He supposed that she was the new cook turned thief.

I do not say that plot patterns of this type are devoid of all interest. Like plots built on low cunning, they appeal only to readers of low intelligence. For this reason, very few editors indeed buy stories built around such episodes unless there is a great deal more to the narrative than the mistake. The trouble with the mistake plot is that it cheats your reader quite as much as the victim in the story.

When I read a story I want to enter into the spirit of the events. If it be adventure, I want to feel that I too am being pursued by cannibals, along with the hero, or am clinging to a derelict in a howling typhoon. If it is a character story I want to see and hear the men and women, laugh with them, cry over their troubles, and help them struggle through crisis after crisis. Now if you, the author, suddenly show me at the end that all the excitement is a put-up job, you rob me of the thrill I got. And it is just for this thrill that I read your story.

As with low cunning, a mistake may legitimately be employed when the big interest of your story turns on the *subsequent dramatic consequences* of it. In such case, you describe the mistake in the beginning of your narrative and let the reader know it for what it is. You then show the strange complication or character development that grows out of the mistake. In this case, the reader is not cheated of his illusions or his interests.

In the first plot outline above, for instance, the chemist's strange dream might inspire him to try the same experiment again with the object of trying to remember a lost secret or find a lost loved one while anaesthetized. The account of the further experiments would be the real story. The fight between husband and wife, in the other instance, might be made the beginning of an interesting quarrel or reconciliation. In each case the mistake would be a complicating factor and not *the* complication.

5. " True to Life "

The beginners' mistake here described again deals with a special form of coincidence. It raises the old, much-disputed problem of probability. The literary novice misconstrues the nature of truth in narrative; he, properly zealous to take life as his model, copies life too faithfully; he hasn't yet fully comprehended the wisdom in the time-worn adage that truth is stranger than fiction. This leads him sometimes to enter in his notebook for use unchanged in his stories, actual events that are simply too improbable to be believed. Here are a few examples taken from student notebooks, all actual occurrences:

A mother and son living together but separated one evening were both taken suddenly ill that same evening and rushed to the same hospital where they died within a few hours. Not more than five minutes separated their deaths and neither knew that the other was ill or was taken to a hospital.

A woman while shopping for gloves lost her diamond ring. After visiting the three shops in which she tried on gloves in a vain search for the ring, she, a year later, tried on a pair of gloves in one of the three shops, finding her ring in one of the gloves.

These two occurrences are excellent examples of the possible which, however, are not usable because they are not probable. "Fiction dealt first with the impossible," Professor Brander Matthews used to say, "then with the improbable, next the probable, and now at last with the inevitable." Inevitability is undoubtedly an ideal in motivation striven for by modern realists, but it is and always will be merely an ideal, for manifestly it is unattainable in any account of human conduct. You will not find it realized in the greatest of creative literary works. *Probable,* a story or novel, however, must be if it aspires to acceptance by the critical.

Coincidences like the two cited have their literary uses which have been indicated in the discussion of coincidence under Mistake No. 3, page 478.

6. "Private Spite"

This type of plot often appears among the manuscripts of beginners who have not yet fully grasped the fundamental purpose of fiction. They confuse strong hate with strong drama. Here is a young woman writer, for instance, who, when asked what people she is interested in, declares that a Miss A. is very much in her mind, that she wants to write a story about her. Miss A., explains the writer, is a terrible gossip and scandal-monger; she has open ears for all the evil she can pick up about her friends, which evil she spreads about, creating consternation and distress. The writer herself came in for cruel treatment at the hands of Miss A. She therefore resolves to write a story in which Miss A. "will get what is coming to her."

In the story one of the traduced friends of Miss A. suddenly discovers a theft or indiscreet love affair in the past life of Miss A. When Miss A. is boasting of her engagement to a very excellent young man and rejoicing over her coming happiness, her victim lets loose her choice bit of scandal in all its harrowing details. Miss A. is crushed. She loses her fiancé and penitently begs forgiveness.

Now this is a "spite" plot. The chief reason for writing it is not to amuse or inspire the reader, but to indulge a private desire for revenge. The writer cannot "get back" on Miss A. in real life so she does it in her fiction. The resulting story is not interesting to the general reader for the simple reason that the reader, not sharing the writer's hatred of Miss A., does not get the same satisfaction as the writer; likewise the story is weak in drama; merely making Miss A. suffer is not dramatic, because the blow that Miss A. receives is overwhelming; she has no opportunity to meet or resist it. There may be something to say for a spite plot's complication interest with an ironic turn at the end, but most such plots fail to achieve this effect because of their utter triteness. Moral indignation has its literary uses but not if the writer loses sight of his readers, not if he merely wants to " take a crack at " someone.

Here is another student spite plot:

Joe Brooks is stingy. His father is rich but stingy. His mother is stingy. He has been brought up to value money, to save for a rainy day, even if he suffers. His motto is: " Any fool can spend money. It takes a wise man to keep it."

He dresses neatly and eats fairly well but he counts his pennies before spending them. When he buys clothes, he looks about in several stores to see where he can get the most for his money. When he eats out, he looks about for a cheap restaurant. He would rather walk than ride, and thinks a taxi extravagant. He prefers the trolley or subway.

At a summer resort he meets a girl he admires. He later falls in love with her. He knows he ought to spend money on her, but he hates to do it, so he tells her that any fool can spend money. He is always talking about the wisdom of saving money for a rainy day. He invites her out for a day's outing and he buys fruit and sandwiches which he carries in a bag to avoid eating at restaurants.

When they come to the city, he takes her to the theater securing seats in the balcony, telling her that the seats in the orchestra were sold out when he got there. He could, of course, have bought seats in the first balcony, but so long as they had to sit upstairs, one more flight did not matter.

He tells her he wants to get her a birthday present and asks what she needs. She tells him she has everything she needs but would like a luxury such as opera glasses. He buys her an umbrella. Finally she gets angry and tells him what she thinks of him: he is stingy. He is deeply hurt but he decides he'd better look for a girl who is stingy also. The next girl he meets is unscrupulous and pretends she is stingy in order to win him for a husband. After they are married, he finds she is worse than the first one, being very extravagant.

The student who invented this plot had on her hands a problem in the shape of a parsimonious lover. Too weak in real life either to reform the lover or give him up she turned to her writing and poured out her spite in a story. Doing so probably did her some good since it provided a harmless exhaust for her rage, but, once again, in doing so she lost sight of her reader. She was interested only in herself.

Otherwise impressive works of fiction sometimes go hopelessly wrong because of this confusion of spiteful impulse with artistic purpose. A novelist, for instance, with an intense hatred of lynching and a profound determination to write a novel that would stir the country and awaken its conscience as to the rights of the blacks came to grief because she permitted her heart to run away with her head; her emotions got the better of her reason. In her story a white man who instigated and approved the lynching of a negro was himself later mobbed by negroes, strung up to a tree, shot and burned to death. When asked why she did this, she replied with blazing eyes: " I want to show these white men how it feels to be tortured in this manner! They don't stop to think! They imagine negroes are not human! They ——" and so forth.

When asked if any white man had ever been so treated, she said no, not to her knowledge; she even confessed that she thought the action rather impossible. Inasmuch as the publishers did not share her passionately single-idea-ed hatred of lynching mobs, but did see the problem as extremely complicated and controversial and, finally, in any treatment of it wished the episodes to be recognizably true, the novel was not accepted. The author found imaginative satisfaction for her spite but accomplished absolutely nothing as a writer or as a practical reformer. She refused to consider her audience. She had neither the purpose nor the conscience of an artist.

SECTION F

HOW TO GET STORY IDEAS

At the very outset of your writing efforts you will most certainly run short of ideas. Even professional writers who earn a living with their typewriters frequently encounter this difficulty. More literary careers come to an end at this moment than at any other time. " Here I am a writer — with nothing to write! " says the hapless writer to himself; the irony, or the humor, of the situation is too much for him and he gives up in disgust.

Perhaps he should give up. If it is literally true that, with all the willingness in the world to perform, no recognizable thoughts about his own life and environment pass through his mind, then he is indeed barking up the wrong tree: he can never possibly succeed at the craft of fiction; he will do better to apply for work as street-car conductor, soda fountain clerk, or "mother's helper," though I suspect he'll have his difficulties in these vocations also.

If he has no thoughts at all on life — but that is impossible! Obviously the difficulty is not here. The truth is much simpler and more disagreeable: good story ideas fail him mainly because he refuses to do the *work* necessary to turn them up! He wants not ideas, but moral muscle. Let me explain: The problem for you, the *student*, is not how to get great or astonishingly original ideas, but rather how to get a steady flow of ideas good enough to work with. Ideas of matured wisdom come only from matured, experienced people; but if the writer waited until he was mature and experienced he might, in middle age, have ideas but no art to express them with! In your student days, your craft, your habit of expression is everything!

Getting story ideas at any age is a matter of method and energy, especially energy. From discussing the problem with many young writers with empty literary larders, I have learned that their trouble arises from certain fundamental misconceptions of their tasks. Here are three of them, all immensely important:

A. *They wait for inspirations:* The young writer, being also a lover of good literature, often has the notion that writing is a sort of sacerdotal function, a divine art, in pursuing which great ideas descend upon the chosen like radio waves broadcast from heaven. Actual writing requires effort; to get words on paper one must put words on paper — there's no escaping that; but ideas! how can work help one get an idea? You either have one or you haven't, and that's all there is to it.

That is *not* all there is to it. Getting story ideas is a department of your work that needs organization and system and energetic and enthusiastic attention just as does the writing of manuscripts or selling them. If you wait for an inspiration, you're just as apt to forget a good idea as to remember one. (It is, indeed, easier for the mind to forget than to remember; if this were not so our brains would be so cluttered with thoughts that they could not function.) The way to get story ideas is to do something about it: put down in notebooks, journals, or on scrap paper, thoughts, observations, records of all kinds; get the habit; keep it up. Don't censor your stuff too severely at first; let it come; later you can go over it, take the best and throw the rest away. Most great writers kept notebooks continuously during their productive years; you cannot afford to do less. It will pay you to study some of these professional notebooks; those of Hawthorne, Ibsen, Chekhov, Samuel Butler, and a number of others are available in published form.

B. *They don't believe in themselves.* With the young student, the chief impulse to write comes from his love of reading. The great works of literary art stir him profoundly, arouse in him burning desires of emulation, and eventually launch him forth, without his quite knowing it, on a deliberate, rash enterprise of writing equally well and that rather soon too! Worthy ambition! The trouble with it, however, is that a young writer's first scribblings in comparison with these majestic performances just about floor him; the contrast is too great. His own ideas — how utterly trite, banal, childish! Often, all too often, he abandons his own ideas and tries themes like those of his great masters. Again, they are too much for him; and he comes to grief.

The young writer seldom remembers that these masterpieces which he adores are never typical of the work of their performers. They are the careful selections from the output of an entire life time. The *great bulk* of the writings of many authors beloved of the literary student is distinctly indifferent in quality and the early work of most of them is mere drivel. How unfair to yourself, then, to shrink from the bold expression of your own thoughts because they are not so exalted and passion-hued as those to be found in the few greatest writings of the greatest masters! The latter had their beginnings; you must have yours. Give yourself time. Don't try to imitate anyone's style. Believe in yourself. The first output is nothing; the habit, everything.

C. *They are not really interested in life:* Ask nine out of ten beginning students of writing what they want to write *about,* and their answers will have little to do with a deep, abiding interest in human beings and their doings. This fact, with concrete illustration, was covered in our study of literary purpose in Chapter One. Even as you read this, you may be saying to yourself, " Oh yes, I'm interested in people, I am sure of that," and yet in the sense in which you must be interested to succeed at writing you may not be at all.

Here is the distinction: You like to be with people; you have many friends; you are a discriminating gossiper; you like to read about " characters " — no, it isn't enough; you can be and do all these things and yet not be genuinely interested in an analytical, probing, literary sense at all. You may, for instance, be so dynamic, so aggressive yourself that you have no patience with people wanting these same virtues. Their weaknesses irritate you. You may be a stern idealist, religious or moral, and the vices of people distress and appall you. Admirable is such concern, but if you think *only* of their goodness or badness, you will not be really interested in a genuine literary sense. A writer's task is more to portray than to judge. Literature is the record of human frailties; you must be sympathetically interested in these frailties, and your curiosity must endure until you have gone to the very bottom of them.

Special Suggestions

In order to help you apply the above general advice in a practical way to your efforts to secure story ideas, please consider the following suggestions which have been used successfully by many beginning writers:

1. *Getting started:* Let us assume that you have a typewriter oiled up or a pen well filled and are ready to " get " story ideas but find yourself absolutely unable to write a single word. Don't be shocked or panic-stricken. Your trouble is not that you haven't any ideas, but that *you haven't a habit of writing them down.* Give over absolutely, therefore, to begin with, any attempt to set down anything of any value whatever of itself. The very first thing is to cure yourself of " typewriter panic " or a rusty elbow joint! Write *anything.* If you can imagine nothing, write up your own life. If your past flies out of the window, write what you have done since you got up this morning. If *this* expedient fails you, set down the names of the objects in the room in front of you! And if you can't do this, well, you'd better call the doctor or simply marry her at once!

Begin by cultivating a habit of writing, of setting words on paper; the quality of the copy will surely improve if you persist. At first write for quantity only. Get started. When you have trained yourself to set down with fair rapidity (say one thousand words an hour) the interesting events of the day, you may conclude that you have broken yourself in and are ready to begin to try to improve the quality of these notes, cull them, and start storing away your best ideas with definite system.

2. *Notebooks and files:* Every professional writer carries some kind of pocket notebook for jotting down brief memoranda at any time of the day or night, and has in his study some means of sorting and storing away longer studies, sketches and plots. Some practical-minded students immediately exaggerate the above advice into a guarantee that a crowded and orderly file will produce good stories; the mystics, on the other hand, are inclined to resent any such business-like organization of their work, on the theory, I assume, that since the subconscious source of their ideas is chaotic, so also should their desks be! They declare that they cannot write spontaneously in an atmosphere of card indexes. To any such other-worldly beginners, I would say that if you can never feel a strong emotional response to an idea that you have taken out of a file, that in itself is the best of good reasons for having a file. Why hug to yourself a compulsion that will certainly be a disadvantage to your artistic growth?

Keep your materials in any way that makes them conveniently

accessible. Boxes will do; envelopes will do; a regular commercial
file, with folders and guides, is best, if you can afford it.

Use the file divisions that mean most to you, of course. In general, an index corresponding to the divisions in this book should be
helpful, with further sub-heads as material accumulates. You
might begin with the following scheme:

1. Characters.
   a. Men.   b. Women.   c. Children.   d. Abnormal.
2. Complications.
   a. Romantic.   b. Domestic.   c. Business.
3. Settings.
   a. City   b. Country.   c. Seaside.   d. Mountain.
4. Themes.
   a. Social.   b. Domestic.   c. Political.
5. Free writing notes, to be classified later, and filed appropriately.
6. Emotional sketches, to be classified, and filed appropriately.
7. Business.
   Here would go letters from editors, notes on needs of various
   magazines, lists of magazines where each finished story has
   been submitted.

A file, thus organized, is a useful tool, and only a tool. I've
known writers who felt a greater responsibility to the order of their
files than to their writing! Any writer who becomes a slave to any
of his tools is lost. If you find that you cannot write until you
have cleared your desk, if your typewriter must be absolutely clean
before you can compose a sentence, something is wrong. Your best
energy should go into your writing. This should be obvious.

In the above file divisions, two perhaps should be explained,
" Emotional sketches " and " Free writing notes."

Under " Emotional sketches " should be filed studies of emotional experiences, either your own, or those you have observed
closely, rough quick studies of your emotional response to some
happening observed on the street, some situation at home, an episode in a play, and so on. The first object of such writing is practice and the development of facility in the portrayal of emotion.
Such studies may also, of course, be a source of story material.

Under " Free writing notes " should be filed such pages as are
described above under " Getting Started." By " free writing," I
mean what the psychologists call free-association writing. The
idea is to reproduce on paper the flow of your thoughts, your ideas,
impulses, mental images, and so on, without censorship or deliberation. The trick is so simple that it is a good way to warm up, if
some morning you find the writing urge a bit reluctant. This device for opening up the subconscious may be for the writer both
good practice and emotional release. Write so rapidly you can't

think! Write exactly what drifts through your mind, and file the pages for later consideration and possible development. If you find yourself stiffening up toward a certain piece of work, if you are self-conscious about it, or suddenly become painfully conscientious about style, this is an excellent prescription.

For many writers that is all that such writing need ever be — something to prime the pump! From the piles of incoherent manuscript no story ideas may ever come, but no one should, for that reason, question the value of occasional hours spent in this way. The benefits are often indirect and invisible, but no less important for being so.

Occasionally a writer asks me what he should do to make stories out of such ramblings. It may be that there's no real story stuff in them. Some writers, however, seem able to develop impressive fragments from such notes, following the same method which has been indicated in the chapters of *Narrative Technique.* If in one of your " free " pages there is a feeling about a character, develop and expand it in some experimental sketches that will produce the same effect. Treat these free-writing notes as you would treat any other materials. Try to identify the feeling that you have recorded. Single out and name and classify the material that is producing that effect. Write some experimental studies which will produce the same effect, using the same material, with shifts in setting perhaps, with more drama, or less. If, in this process, your feeling grows more intense, and your vision of character and situation sharper, continue with such development, until you have what looks like a story. Then check it with a schematic outline, to make sure that it hangs together, producing the mood of the original sketch, with equal or greater intensity; and from this point continue revision until the narrative satisfies you.

If, on the other hand, your first experimental studies seem to lead nowhere, and to have no stimulation in them, you will be wise to abandon the effort. There may be other sources for your stories.

One final word about the usefulness of your file. It should be something more than a place to keep things until they are wanted. It is — or may be — a device for inspiration in the most practical sense of the word. Every writer needs to find new connections between himself and life, fresh stimuli around which his own personal memories and associations can be assembled with new meanings. Sometimes he gets his impulse direct from life, when by lucky chance an incident observed, a conversation overheard, a bit of rumor or gossip, an experience of his own, stirs him up, and sends him to his typewriter. Just as often, life leaves him cold. At such times, there is always the possibility that if he runs through his file, some character study will connect with a recent personal experience, or a clipping or a note on a situation will give a flash on another note or sketch, pulled out of the file for consideration a few nights before, and remembered — and the process of making a story begins!

The writer is not always a self-starting mechanism; but every professional writer develops schemes like the above for putting the machinery in motion.

3. *Your reading:* A writer's reading is a special problem. Most people read altogether for relaxation and amusement and hardly at all, unfortunately, for information. Writers (when they are mature and hard at work writing) should read almost altogether for information and very little for relaxation and amusement. There are good reasons against a writer's reading for amusement: he should seek relaxation further removed from his business than reading and he should be among people, and if he enjoys his reading too much he is in danger of imitating, perhaps unconsciously.

A writer these days, it seems to me, should read rather voluminously and, for the most part, rapidly and chiefly for information; if he also enjoys this type of reading so much the better, but his selections should be made with his needs for information chiefly in mind. If he is young he needs to read to complete his education about the world in which he lives; if he is older and, let us hope, wiser, he must read to keep his ideas furbished and up-to-date. Writers generally should read for the following purposes, in the order of importance:

1. For understanding of character: chiefly scientific books, psychologies, etc. Occasionally articles in literary magazines.

2. For news of the world, social developments, what people are thinking about, and so on. Chiefly newspapers, news weeklies, and magazines like *Harper's, Forum, Current History,* and so on. This should be supplemented occasionally by a book suggested by current reviews.

3. For information as to literary fashions, and so on: chiefly the best novels and stories, literary reviews like *The Saturday Review of Literature,* and an occasional volume of criticism.

Warning! Many, very many learning writers read fiction as a stimulus to their own writing. Some do this and turn out good work, but the practice is pernicious nevertheless. The stimulus should come from life not books. If it takes a book to get you going, your qualifications may be questioned. This is true of all writers, young or old.

Below I have listed a few recent books of the sort most likely to prove of value to the writer. No effort at a complete bibliography here would be worth while; obviously any writer following his own interests can extend the list indefinitely. In offering these titles I am simply trying to answer the question that comes to me frequently: What reading will help my writing?

On problems of psychology and character:

1. *Human Nature and Conduct,* John Dewey, Holt, 1922.

2. *Contemporary Schools of Psychology,* Robert S. Woodworth, Ronald Press, 1931. Excellent survey of just what title indicates. Important for anyone who wants to know what has been done in recent years in psychological clinics and laboratories. Bibliography.

3. *An Historical Introduction to Modern Psychology,* Gardner Murphy, Harcourt, Brace & Co., 1932. Detailed. For the student not the casual reader.

4. *Adjustment and Mastery,* R. S. Woodworth, Century of Progress Series, Century Co., 1933. Brief, rather popular, but stimulating in its sections on motives, maladjustments, and differences.

5. *The Organism of the Mind,* Gustav Richard Heyer, M.D., Harcourt, Brace & Co., 1934. This book is clinical, but it is full of important suggestive material for the writer interested in the development of character. Emphasizes the inter-relation of physical and mental activity. A valuable and discerning appreciation of Freud, with clear presentation of developments since his first work.

6. *Outline of Abnormal Psychology,* William McDougall, Chas. Scribner's Sons, 1926. Studies of exaggerated mental states that are helpful in understanding the normal.

7. *The Psychology of Achievement,* Walter B. Pitkin, Simon and Schuster, 1930. Lively, stimulating popular account of some facts about personality.

8. *The Psychology of Happiness,* Walter B. Pitkin, Simon and Schuster, 1929. Suggestive, stimulating presentation of some major problems of adjustment.

9. *Habits,* Knight Dunlap, Liveright, 1932. Very readable. Good bibliography.

On the biological background of character: All the books listed are interesting to the lay reader.

1. *The Physical Basis of Personality,* C. Stockard, Norton, 1930.

2. *The Biological Basis of Human Nature,* H. S. Jennings, Norton, 1930.

3. *The Glands Regulating Personality,* Louis Berman, Macmillan, 1922.

4. *Hows and Whys of Human Behavior,* George A. Dorsey, Harper & Bros., 1929.

5. *Heredity and Environment,* E. G. Conklin, Princeton University Press, 1922.

The historic background:

1. *The Story of Man's Early Progress,* Willis Mason West, Allyn & Bacon, 1931. Full bibliography.

2. *Man's Great Adventure,* Edwin H. Pahlow, Ginn & Co., 1932.
3. *Outlines of European History,* James Harvey Robinson and Charles A. Beard, Ginn & Co., 1927.

All these are textbooks, but the material is presented in readable fashion.

The adjustment of character to society:

1. *The March of Democracy,* James Truslow Adams, Chas. Scribner's Sons, 1933. Indispensable to any writer who wishes to understand our present American life. Two volumes. Through 1932. Delightfully illustrated with contemporary drawings, cartoons, handbills, maps, etc. Sports, clothes, arts and so on related to the stream of history interpretatively.
2. *Rise of American Civilization,* 2 vols., Chas. A. and Mary R. Beard, Macmillan, 1927. Stimulating. History with emphasis on social development.
3. *America's Social Morality,* James Hayden Tufts, Holt, 1933. A realistic, readable, general statement of the meaning in social terms of much conduct in business, recreation, sport, and so on, that we see every day without any thought of its significance.
4. *The Human Problems of an Industrial Civilization,* Elton Mayo, Macmillan, 1933. An "analysis and interpretation of the human situations that exist in factory and workshop."
5. *Middletown,* R. S. and H. M. Lynd, Harcourt, Brace & Co., 1929. A study of an " average " American town, its people and their life.
6. *Man's Own Show, Civilization,* George A. Dorsey, Harper & Bros., 1931.
7. *Anthropology and Modern Life,* Franz Boas, Norton, 1932.

For the writer who wants to bring himself up to date:

1. *Guide to Modern Thought,* C. E. M. Joad, Frederick A. Stokes Co., 1933.
2. *Farewell to Reform,* John Chamberlain, Liveright, 1932. An appraisal of the social reform efforts of the period since 1900.
3. *Riddles of Science,* Sir J. Arthur Thompson, Liveright, 1932. Fascinating, popular account of problems the scientists are still trying to solve.

For the writer who wants to understand himself:

1. *Art As Experience,* John Dewey, Minton, 1934.
2. *The Process of Literature,* Agnes Mure Mackenzie, Harper & Bros., 1929. Delightfully witty and penetrating study of how the writer works.
3. *The Road to Xanadu,* John Livingston Lowes, Houghton,

1930. An elaborate and illuminating study of the processes of composition in Coleridge.

4. *The Organism of the Mind,* Gustav Richard Heyer, M.D., Harcourt, Brace & Co., 1934. Studies of subconscious origins of some designs and fantasies are suggestive.

5. *The Art of Learning,* Walter B. Pitkin, Whittlesey House, 1931.

4. The *romantic complex:* This term I give to those beginning writers who simply cannot be made to believe that their own life and environment is interesting. Being young and full of hopes and dreams, they naturally cling to the delusion that real romance, real adventure flourishes best among strange and distant people, in distant climes, or in remote periods of time. They love *Castles in Spain* because they haven't seen them — or is it because the edifices haven't steam heat? Perhaps they are simply bored by their surroundings, and wish (for some possibly very sensible reason) to get away. All well and good, *but* this does not change the fact that *the amount of literary material in any region is exactly proportionate to the number of people who dwell therein.* Because *you* can't see the drama and human interest of your own life is no reason why someone else might not weep with pity or be convulsed with laughter, could he but see what you see, know what you know.

" I'm going to Europe to find material for my stories," said a young woman with the " romantic complex."

" Why so far? " I asked her.

" Oh, I just love ruins! " she replied. Her own story, being lived right here in New York City, is one of the most poignant and appealing I have heard in months. O. Henry might have immortalized her. Here is her one big chance for originality. Instead of writing it, she wishes to write over again themes and places which the greatest masters of the language have done their best to exhaust. She was seeking material with binoculars; she really needed a microscope. And that leads to my next suggestion:

5. *Writing up yourself:* Professor Copeland, I remember, in his famous *English Twelve* at Harvard, used to complain in his inimitable manner of the triteness and insipidity of our student writings. " You young men," he growled, " write of everything under heaven but yourselves, the only topic you understand or, I dare say, are interested in." Fiction writing is the most intimate of all arts and any follower of it who hopes to charm the popular ear by keeping his uniquely precious and sacred emotions locked forever in his jealous bosom had better try something else. Modest youth! Be certain that your best writing will be that which is most *you.* Would you sell your fiction? you must then sell yourself.

What are your dreams, your ambitions? Write them up. What were the main turning points or mile stones in your own life? Examine these turning points carefully. What factors were involved? What happened? What is the significance of each experience? Try to imagine stories around these crises. Put other people into them, if you wish, but keep the same issues, the same emotions.

If you are an imaginative type of writer, you will do best to write up your dreams and aspirations; if you are a realistic or " reporter " type, one who can handle effectively only that which he has actually seen, you will do best to write up your past. Seek facts about life by working from yourself out. It is the artistic attack. Be honest with yourself about yourself. Don't fear your audience. Don't fear the truth.

6. *Your home a laboratory:* Most students can profit by a concentrated study of the human interest problems being worked out in their own homes. Your home surroundings may be tranquil and their events, so far as you can see, quite commonplace. Don't deceive yourself. The chances are that the issues being faced in your own home or among your own friends suggest very definite story ideas which by imaginative manipulation may be made highly dramatic.

For example: A younger brother or sister is under your observation. Watch him with your imagination at work. What do you see? What does he do? What are the problems that absorb him? Who is his hero? How is he working out his worship of that hero in his own activities? Suppose he were to learn in some way that his hero had done some peculiarly ignoble thing? What effect might it have on him? What situations especially rouse his wrath? What is he planning to be? What is there in him that will make him succeed in that career? Has he any qualities that he will have to fight in order to succeed?

Or perhaps a mother and a baby are under your direct daily observation. The mother of course gives devoted attention to the baby's needs. Watch every phase of her care of it. Is she more solicitous about the child than the average mother, or less? What does her conduct suggest of the problem of the over-cultivated, super-sensitive mother? Is she a better mother than a peasant woman who brings up a big brood without worrying greatly about any of them? What reaction upon herself may there be from this intense devotion?

Besides your intensive study of individuals close around you, you will do well to get in touch with some special phase of life; become intimate with a particular social problem, preferably one which you will be able to observe at first hand. Study this problem, seeking especially to discover the emotional quality of every phase of it. Have patience with this work. Take plenty of time for it. If you choose the problem of education, or divorce, or city politics, or the youthful generation, or business morals, decide whether you will center your attention on the comic aspect, the grim tragedy, or the high adventure of your topic. And, as in the character work, don't imagine that you can master it by any mystic process of " thinking it over." Write!

7. *Writing reveals life secrets:* In all your observations, reason back from the facts to their larger significance. Remember that the big human problems don't jump out and bark to let you know that they are there. The most important thing to bear in mind is the fact that you cannot begin to understand a human situation in its larger aspects until you have attempted to express it. You can accomplish little by mulling over your vague thoughts about people. Don't be a " writer who doesn't write." You must record in full detail the character's behavior on innumerable occasions. Presently you will begin to see relations between these various details which you missed in your first formless records. The writing itself brings out the significances.

You cannot *think* your way through to your big idea; at the beginning you can't guess what a thing will sound like written, you must write it down and look at it. Remember it is not mere words that you are handling; it is *ideas. The striking observations come only when you have written everything you have seen and can think of, and — proceed to see and think and write some more!* It is then that the happy revelations begin to appear. By this process, and at first by no other, does one master the art of characterization. " Be sure you know the full truth about a given matter," wrote Mark Twain, " then you may manipulate it as much as you choose."

8. *Learn from great writers:* With many writers characters really do not begin to perform until words about them are put on paper. Turgeniev wrote long, rambling character studies before he began a line of his story proper. Chekhov wrote beginnings and threw them away. Nearly every beginner postpones too long the hour of beginning. He hopes for the beautifully finished plot, the perfect word, the high aspiration. The greatest writers, I repeat, cannot afford to do this. The beginner must not do it. In those moments when it seems your mind literally will not formulate ideas good enough for a plot, you cannot do better than to write what you *do* know. Put away what you have written. The day of inspiration will come. Bear in mind the confession on this point by Thackeray:

"My Pegasus won't fly, so as to let me survey the field below me. He has no wings, he is blind of one eye certainly; he is restive, stubborn, slow; crops a hedge when he ought to be galloping; or gallops when he ought to be quiet. He never will show off when I want him. Sometimes he goes at a pace which surprises me. Sometimes, when I most wish him to make the running, the brute turns restive, and I am obliged to let him take his own time. I wonder do other novel-writers experience this fatalism? They *must* go a certain way, in spite of themselves."

SECTION G

ANSWERS TO ASSIGNMENTS

CHAPTER ONE

Assignment A

1. Pathos.
2. Slight humor of character.
3. Thrill of mystery and adventure.
4. Appeals to mind. Not narrative.
8. Statistics arranged for ironic effect. Not narrative.
14. Shock of horror.

Assignment E

1. Death handled objectively for an effect of suspense. Effect produced by situation, a life-and-death struggle between a man and natural dangers. In writing to reproduce the effect, show the danger clearly at the start, but without focussing any sympathy on the character.

3. The effect here is tragic pathos, produced by the violent death of a character pictured sympathetically. For your own sketch, select an appealing character, and develop the appeal through appearance, conduct of other characters, and the action of the subject character. Use either a scene just before death, as in the model, or a scene during a life-and-death struggle.

CHAPTER TWO

Assignment A

1. Character comedy mingled with pathos.
2. A single, definite, but, of course, slight impression: amusement at the character trait of ostentatious morality.

3. Single effect of ironic amusement at the way the character benefits through political corruption.

6. Double effects here. An impression of disapproval of a marriage of convenience, with one sentence on the girl which produces an effect of tender sympathy, and the last two paragraphs in the manner of a casual news account.

10. Single effect. An impression of the fantastic misery of a dream. This is the thought-stream of a character dying under ether in a hospital operating room.

Assignment C

1. Romantic sympathy for married lovers.
2. Revulsion from the gruesome fact of the corpse.

Assignment D

4. Objective handling of situation to test the character and impress the reader with the quality of the woman's love.

CHAPTER THREE

Assignment A

1. Character.
3. In this, and in No. 7, same assignment, you have material that might be developed as atmosphere, if you made the character respond to some *mood* in the setting. As the action is outlined, the character in No. 3 seems to be responding to the physical qualities rather than to the mood of the setting, and in No. 7 the trait seems to be homesickness. With the right emphasis, both could be atmosphere.
6. Thematic.
9. Complication, conceivably thematic.

Assignment B

1. Thematic.
2. Thematic.
7. Thematic and character.
12. Character, complication, theme, all possible.

CHAPTER FOUR

Assignment A

1. No.
2. Yes, slight.
3. Fairly strong.

5. No. Routine action, without opposition.

6. No, merely feeling.

11. No, although the threats suggest a subconscious conflict and hence some emotion. Emotion in the apology.

13. No, amicable debate is not a conflict.

15. Yes, although it was unconscious and is of value only as a comic complication.

Assignment B

1. We know only the external behavior of animals. Whether this experience means the same thing to the cat that it would to a human being, no one can say.

4. No. See page 148 ff. and 169 ff.

6. No. Here we have an obstacle to the patient's desire to avoid pain, but no obstacle to his main desire, which is to have sound teeth. He is simply suffering patiently — pure feeling.

7. It would produce absolutely no emotion. See page 143 ff.

Assignment D

1. Revelation of character almost entirely lacking. We know that these men are engaged in a feud, that they have deliberately planned to kill, but we know nothing of motives, and in the action portrayed the only thing tested is their quickness and accuracy of aim.

5. There is a fairly definite revelation of character in the details of his conduct at the opening of this note, but the episode of the falling brick apparently was not at all a character revealing happening. Although Mike was careless in placing them where he did, his being hurt by their falling tells nothing about his character.

6. This is merely a pseudo-love scene. It seems to picture a conflict, bringing out a strong trait of love, but it doesn't; what is the matter?

9. This episode raises the whole question of the appeal of animal stories. Here is an animal heroine, the cat. As a matter of fact, we know nothing about the character of the cat on the basis of this striking crucial situation; her " traits " might very well be pure instinct and nothing else. Her *actions*, however, so resemble human actions in similar predicaments that it is very easy sympathetically to endow the cat with imagined characteristics. In this sense the cat's character is being revealed by this episode. This is the psychology of all animal stories.

10. Melodrama! Revelation slight; no reflective delay.

11. Sambo raises an important point. His conduct is that of a lazy man and yet it cannot be said to make *him* out as a

lazy man. The reason for this is that it is definitely suggested that his inertia is caused by a disease. How do we know but that if he was cured of this disease — a fairly easy medical problem — he would be as energetic as the next one? He acts lazily, yes, but we cannot say that it is dramatic proof of his essential character; rather it is proof of the presence of — hook worm!

12. Here is proof of character, the trait of lying, but it is scientific and not dramatic proof. As such it is of no interest to us unless it be used as a complication idea or some other development of character come out of it.

14. Here we have the famous " lady or tiger " story of Frank R. Stockton. It is simply an unsolved crucial situation and nothing else. The interest in it lies in the nice balance in the two traits of love and jealousy given the princess, and the novelty of not knowing the ending. As a revelation of any single definite trait of character in the princess the story is a failure. The two traits mentioned above are suggested but not developed. The main appeal of the story is intellectual.

Assignment F

  1. Man and man.
  2. Man and nature.
  3. Internal.
  5. Internal and man and man.
  7. Internal.
  13. Man and man.

Assignment G

  1. Man flirts with teacher, teacher resists. Man returns in evening to continue flirting and demands to be let in; teacher locks door and cries out for him to go away. He remains, threatens to shoot if she doesn't open the door. She tries to find a place to hide; is terrified; he finally shoots through the door; she lets him in. A man comes down the fire-escape and tries to save the teacher from the drunk's attacks; the drunk struggles with the teacher to free his gun to shoot the new-comer. He finally does shoot the newcomer. The teacher then calls for a policeman; the drunk tries to prevent her shouts, etc., etc.

Assignment H

  1. Low cunning.
  2. " Come to realize " plot.
  10. Coincidence.

CHAPTER FIVE

Assignment A

 1. Lazy.
 5. Honest, but he risks his job to see a baseball game.
 10. Snobbish.

Assignment C

 1. Love of Maurice.
 4. False family pride.
 15. Both traits are clearly named in the sketch itself; a languorous laxity and " in love."

CHAPTER SIX

Assignment A

 1. Character.
 5. Complication.
 9. Complication.
 12. Character.
 13. Complication.

Assignment C

 2. Hair caught on a button proves that an experience with a ghost was not a dream but a genuine supernatural encounter.

CHAPTER SEVEN

Assignment A

 2. Dramatic.
 3. Ideas.
 4. Didactic.

Assignment C

 1. War is hell.

SECTION H

CURRENT FICTION LIST [1]

This list of stories is intended to supplement the citations in Chapter Three, especially on pages 107, 109, 110, 112. The classification according to emphasis on different materials, outlined in

[1] Other stories accompanied by full analytical and critical notes, will be found in *Short Story Hits, 1932* and *1933*.

Chapter Three, is continued here. All the stories in this list are contemporary and of definite merit.

Character Stories

1. Character portrayed with minimum drama:

> Conrad Aiken, " Your Obituary, Well Written," *Scribner's,* Nov., 1927, and in *Costumes by Eros.*
> Katharine Brush, " Big Girl," *Saturday Evening Post,* July 16, 1932, and in *Short Story Hits, 1932.*
> Edna Ferber, " Glamour," in *They Brought Their Women.*
> George Milburn, " A Visit to Uncle Jake's," *Scribner's,* July, 1932, and in *No More Trumpets.*
> Marjorie Kinnan Rawlings, " Bennie and the Bird Dogs," *Scribner's,* Oct., 1933, and in *Short Story Hits, 1933.*

2. Character portrayed with strong drama:

> Mary Hastings Bradley, " Five Minute Girl," *Saturday Evening Post,* Jan. 10, 1931, and in *O. Henry,* 1931.[1]
> Kyle Crichton, " The Orchard," *Scribner's,* March, 1933.
> F. Scott Fitzgerald, " Crazy Sunday," *American Mercury,* Oct., 1932, and in *O'Brien,* 1933.[2]
> Grace Flandrau, " She Was Old," *Scribner's,* Sept., 1932, and in *Short Story Hits, 1932.*
> Dorothy Parker, " Big Blonde," *Bookman,* Feb., 1929, and in *O. Henry,* 1929.
> Evelyn Scott, " Turnstile," *Scribner's,* Feb., 1933.

3. Character proof by violation of law.

> Katharine Brush, " Football Girl," in *O. Henry,* 1932.
> Erskine Caldwell, " August Afternoon," in *We Are the Living.*
> William Faulkner, " Turn About," *Saturday Evening Post,* March 5, 1932, and in *O. Henry,* 1932.
> John Held, Jr., " A Man of the World," *Scribner's,* Dec., 1929, and in *O. Henry,* 1930.

4. Character portrayed by uniquely characteristic act:

> Kay Boyle, " Rest Cure," in *O'Brien,* 1931.
> Kay Boyle, " Kroy Wen," in *The First Lover.*

---

[1] O. Henry, refers to the *O. Henry Memorial Award Prize Stories* for the given year.

[2] O'Brien, refers to Edward J. O'Brien's *Best Short Stories* for the given year.

Katharine Brush, " Night Club," *Harper's,* Sept., 1927.
Katherine Mansfield, " The Man Without a Temperament," in *Bliss.*
Dorothy Thomas, " The Consecrated Coal Scuttle," *Harper's,* May, 1933, and in *O. Henry,* 1933.

5. Character emphasis with strong drama and some complication interest:

William Faulkner, " Death Drag," *Scribner's,* Jan., 1932.
Nancy Hale, " To the Invader," *O. Henry,* 1933.
Ernest Hemingway, " Fifty Grand," *Atlantic,* July, 1927, and in *Men Without Women.*
Ernest Hemingway, " The Undefeated," in *Men Without Women.*

Complication Stories

1. Pure complication:

Erskine Caldwell, " We Are Looking at You Agnes," in *We Are the Living.*
Erskine Caldwell, " Dorothy," *Scribner's,* April, 1931, and in *O'Brien,* 1931.
William Faulkner, " That Evening Sun Go Down," *American Mercury,* Mar., 1931, and in *O'Brien,* 1931.
Edwin Granberry, " A Trip to Czardis," *Forum,* April, 1932, and in *O. Henry,* 1932.
Albert Halper, " Going To Market," *Harper's,* Oct., 1932, and in *O'Brien,* 1933.
George Milburn, " The Fight at Hendryx's," *American Mercury,* Feb., 1932, and in *No More Trumpets.*
George Milburn, " Heel, Toe, and a 1, 2, 3, 4," *American Mercury,* April, 1932, and in *No More Trumpets.*
Dorothy Parker, " Here We Are," in *O'Brien,* 1931, and in *After Such Pleasures.*

2. Complication with character interest:

Conrad Aiken, " Mr. Arcularis," *Harper's,* March, 1931, and " Impulse," both in *Among the Lost People.*
Stephen Vincent Benet, " An End to Dreams," *Pictorial Review,* Feb., 1932, and in *O. Henry,* 1932.
Kay Boyle, " To the Pure," *Scribner's,* June, 1932, and in *Short Story Hits, 1932.*
Robert Cantwell, " The Land of Plenty," *New Republic,* Oct. 12, 1932, and in *O'Brien,* 1933.
James Gould Cozzens, " Farewell to Cuba," *Scribner's,* Nov., 1931, and in *O. Henry,* 1932.

F. Scott Fitzgerald, "Babylon Revisited," *Saturday Evening Post*, Feb. 21, 1931, and in *O'Brien*, 1931.

Thematic Stories

1. Stories emphasizing theme with complication interest:

   Jack Conroy, "Pipe Line," *American Mercury*, Sept., 1932.
   Langston Hughes, "Slave on the Block," *Scribner's*, Sept., 1933.
   William March, "Nine Prisoners," *Forum*, Dec., 1931, and in *O. Henry*, 1932.
   George Milburn, "The Catalogues," *Harper's*, Aug., 1933, and in *Short Story Hits, 1933*.

2. Stories emphasizing theme with character interest:

   Pearl Buck, "The Frill," *Woman's Home Companion*, March, 1933, and in *O. Henry*, 1933.
   Paul Green, "The Wagon," *Harper's*, March, 1934.
   Laurence Stallings, "Gentleman in Blue," *Saturday Evening Post*, Feb. 20, 1932, and in *O'Brien*, 1932.
   Katharine Ball Ripley, "What's a Man to Do?," *Atlantic*, Oct., 1932, and in *Short Story Hits, 1932*.

Stories with emphasis on setting

1. Setting plus character:

   Wanda Burnett, "Sand," in *O'Brien*, 1932.
   Ethel Hepburn, "Bitter Apples," *Scribner's*, June, 1933.
   Edward Harris Heth, "Primer for Maine," *Scribner's*, July, 1934.

2. Setting plus character and complication:

   David Cornel DeJong, "So Tall the Corn," *Scribner's*, April, 1932, and in *O'Brien*, 1932.
   Wilbur Daniel Steele, "Conjuh," *Pictorial Review*, Oct., 1929, and in *O. Henry*, 1930.

3. Setting plus character, and complication, with suggestion of theme:

   John August, "The Bulfinch House," *Harper's*, July, 1934.
   E. P. O'Donnell, "Potent Delta," *Harper's*, March, 1933.

NOTE: Many other impressive stories of these various types have been printed in both the literary and the popular magazines during the past five years. I have included in my list, however, only those which are available not only in the files of magazines, but in collections, hoping thus to make sure that every student using this book may have at his command in city and college libraries an abundance of illustrative material.

SECTION I

SUGGESTIONS TO TEACHERS

Although in working out the plans of study offered below, I have consulted college instructors, I realize that I cannot hope to meet every need. I submit these programs in the belief that with a few suggestions about ways to use *Narrative Technique,* the instructor will modify the assignments to suit his particular group of students.

Let me begin with suggestions for a one-semester course in the short story, suitable for immature beginners. In gauging the amount of work for each week, I have had in mind a first-year college class. Freshman English in most colleges is necessarily still planned around rhetoric and themes, but teachers now are discovering the stimulating possibilities in narrative study for this age level. These experimental-minded instructors should find my suggested program well suited to develop in their students habits of sound self-discipline with a stimulus to creative expression. My belief is that the demand for attention to correctness in the formalities of style, grammar, punctuation, rhetoric, should be relaxed during the study of literary technique and in first rough drafts should be entirely ignored.

My scheme accords with my discovery that all students of every age must be persuaded to the value of technique. *In general the student is to discover in his own writing the need for some knowledge of technical principles.* In revising he should apply his new technical knowledge. Usually a manuscript written as a first assignment can be so greatly improved merely by revising it for greater emphasis that, seeing this improvement, the student is ready to believe that there may be something after all in this business of technique.

For most groups of beginners of this age, or slightly older, it is better to plan to cover in one semester only the first four chapters of *Narrative Technique.* To attempt more may confuse. Unless the student can see clearly step by step how his work gains in effectiveness as he applies the principles successively learned, he is likely to lose interest.

The plan for the sixteen sessions follows:

1st week: FIRST LONG THEME: write an account of some adventure or other interesting personal first-hand experience. Make it interesting!

When this story is completed, read through quickly Chapters I through IV of *Narrative Technique.*

Write out in about 150 words the most important conflict in the story just handed in.

2nd week: Revise the first theme to bring out in detail this conflict, omitting all material that does not relate to the conflict.

Study Chapter I.

Do Assignments A and B.

3rd week: Read Appendix, How to Get Story Ideas, and begin to collect and file ideas.

Continue study of Chapter I.

Do Assignments C and D.

4th week: Submit several story ideas in brief — about 100 words each. Study the suggestions for reading in Section F, pages 494–495, and choose two books for thorough study during the term. No critical review of these books will be required, but at least two story ideas suggested by each book are to be submitted before the end of the term, each accompanied by a note to show where the student got the idea and what kind of a story he'd like to develop from it.

5th week: SECOND LONG THEME: a rough draft of one of the ideas submitted the 4th week.

Study Chapter II.

Do Assignments A and B.

Hand in a brief self-criticism on *second theme* just completed and submitted, pointing out any breaks in unity of effect.

6th week: Continue study of Chapter II.

Do Assignment C.

Read Chapter X on viewpoint.

Submit brief self-criticism on *second theme,* as to viewpoint selected.

7th week: Continue study of Chapter II.

Do Assignment D.

Revise *second theme,* correcting matters of viewpoint, unity of effect, integration of setting and action.

8th week: Submit six ideas for next story, outlined in about 100 words each.

Read Chapter III.

Write two of the sketches suggested on pages 122–123.

9th week: Outline two of the ideas submitted in 8th week, suggesting classification, indicating viewpoint, and a possible setting.

Continue study of Chapter III.

Write any one development from Assignments C and D.

10th week: On Chapter III, Assignment E, write out any two sketches.

Read Chapter IV.

11th week: THIRD LONG THEME: a rough draft of a new story on one of the outlines submitted in 9th week.
Continue study of Chapter IV.
Do Assignments A and B.

12th week: Continue study of Chapter IV.
Do Assignments C and D.
Submit a brief self-criticism of handling of character in *third theme,* bearing in mind principle studied in Assignment D.

13th week: Continue study of Chapter IV.
Do Assignment E, any five.
Report on ideas from reading.
Submit three new story ideas not taken from reading, these to be classified, with effect noted, and suggestions as to character interest and drama.

14th week: Chapter IV.
Do Assignment F and two of G.
Submit self-criticism of *second theme,* submitted during 5th week. Criticism should include single effect, drama, viewpoint, and integration of character with situation and setting.

15th week: Revise *third theme,* submitted in 11th week.

16th week: Chapter IV.
Do Assignments H and I.

In this program, the amount of writing can be varied. The number of full-length drafts of stories can be reduced or increased. For each book assignment the class can be asked to do only one study, or the whole series. In assignments like E in Chapter One and C and D in Chapter Two, which require analysis, classification, and then writing, the analysis can be assigned for one week, and the writing the next.

The self-criticism assignments are intended to accomplish two ends: 1, they provide a check on the student's gain in ability to apply what he has learned to his own work; and 2, they reveal the most important facts about the student's progress, without requiring the instructor to go through a great amount of copy. In a technical course, a student's growth in ability to recognize and correct faults of structure and plan is of first importance; the literary finish in his studies is almost certain to improve with his better understanding of the principles of structure.

A Plan for More Advanced Students

The above program, modified to include more writing of full drafts and a larger number of the writing assignments, should keep a group of older students moving. For these, Chapters Five and Six should be added to the plan.

Another plan of work, suitable if the group is small and aggressively interested in writing, focuses all the work on stories. The textbook would be used, in such a case, for criticism and reference, and no definite assignments would be given in it except possibly a few chosen as test exercises to check on the student's self-study of principles. The assumption in this plan is that with students who have close to a professional attitude toward their work, the instructor need not take the initiative in assigning technical practice. I find that if a writer is genuinely interested in making his work better, he will be on the alert for every possible device promising improvement, and will search the pages of a textbook for all the help it can give him.

To test such a group, and make sure that they understand the principles and are using them correctly in their own self-criticism, the following assignments should be most useful:

Chapter I, Assignments D–3 and E.
Chapter II, Assignments B and C.
Chapter III, any three of E.
Chapter IV, any five of E and all of D, H, and I.

ACKNOWLEDGMENTS

I wish here to express my thanks to the following writers and publishers for their permission to reprint the new illustrative selections used in this edition:

Conrad Aiken, *Costumes by Eros* and *Blue Voyage*, Charles Scribner's Sons; Faith Baldwin, "Honesty's Policy," *Cosmopolitan;* A. Thornton Bishop, *Composition and Rendering*, John Wiley & Sons; George Bradshaw, "The Fire in the Flint," *Saturday Evening Post;* James M. Cain, "Baby in the Icebox," *American Mercury;* Morley Callaghan, "A Sick Call," *Atlantic;* Joseph Conrad, *Typhoon*, Doubleday, Doran & Co.; Grace Flandrau, "What Was Truly Mine," *Scribner's;* Nancy Hale, "Colloque Sentimentale," *Scribner's*, "No One My Grief Can Tell," *American Mercury;* Albert Halper, "Going to Market," *Harper's;* Douglas Haskell, "From Automobile to Roadplane," *Harper's;* MacKinlay Kantor, "Something Like Salmon," *Detective Fiction Weekly;* Ring Lardner, *How to Write Short Stories*, Charles Scribner's Sons; William March, *Company K*, Smith & Haas; George Milburn, *No More Trumpets*, Harcourt, Brace & Co.; Lois Montross, *Skywriters, Good Housekeeping;* E. P. O'Donnell, "Potent Delta," *Harper's;* John O'Hara, "Early Afternoon," *Scribner's;* Alicia O'Reardon Overbeck, "Encarnacion," *Harper's;* Dorothy Parker, *Laments for the Living*, Viking; Louis Zara Rosenfeld, "Travail," *American Mercury;* Ellis St. Joseph, "Introduction to Eric," *Harper's;* Sir J. Arthur Thompson, *Riddles of Science*, Liveright; Sylvia Thompson, "Vacuum Cleaners," *Harper's;* John Barker Waite, "If Judges Wrote Detective Stories," *Scribner's;* P. G. Wodehouse, *Heavy Weather*, Little, Brown & Co.; Charles Yost, "Holiday," *Scribner's*.

T. H. U.

INDEX

513

Chekhov, Anton: analysis of effect of " Grief," 66; analysis of material of " Old Age," 345; notes from *Notebook*, 127

Climax, in dramatic character story, 234; in non-dramatic character story, 253; in complication story, 285

Cobb, Irvin S.: " The Belled Buzzard," genesis of idea of, 292; plotting of, 291–298; schematic outline of, 297

Coincidence, in complication story, 278, 290; weak use of, 478. See also *Irony*

" Collective " story, 433

" Come to realize " plot, 475

COMPLICATION: Chapter VI, 275; how to identify complication materials, 101–112, 276–278; character in the complication story, 278, 284–286, 294–295, 301–303; drama in the complication story, 142–144, 152–160, 162, 276–277, 280, 290–291

Plotting the complication story: first steps, 103–105, 116–117, 140–141, 283, 293; finishing the plot, 284–289, 294–298; use of schematic outline, 285, 288

Examples emphasizing complication interest: 7; 8; 9; 32, Nos. 1, 3; 33, No. 5; 34, Nos. 9, 10; 36, No. 14; 40, Nos. 1, 2; 41, Nos. 3, 4; 42, No. 5; 78, No. 1; 79, No. 3; 82, No. 10; 92, Nos. 1, 2, 6, 279; 280

Stories emphasizing complication listed, 109, 505

Surprise-ending complication story, 298–300

Exercises on complication materials

Conflict. See Drama

Conrad, Joseph, analysis of material of " The Lagoon," 109
on writing, 6
selection from *Typhoon*, 8–9

Criticism, self, 446

Daudet, Alphonse, selection from " The Death of the Dauphin," 32, No. 1

Dewey, John, on technique and the artist, xv

Dickens, Charles, selection from *Little Dorrit*, 83
selection from *Martin Chuzzlewit*, 79

DRAMA
Chapter IV, 139
character revealed by, 148–153
definition, 142, 149
in good story ideas, 145–147
intensification of, 157–160, 169–170, 173
tests for dramatic weakness, 449
unity in dramatic conflict, 171
See also Character, Complication, and Beginners' Mistakes

EFFECTS
how to identify, 25–31
how to state, 26, 28, 31
length of story determined by, 44, 71
tests for unity of effect, 449
unity of story determined by, 44
mixed effects illustrated, 38, 47, 61